HELLENOSEMITICA

HELLENOSEMITICA

AN ETHNIC AND CULTURAL STUDY
IN WEST SEMITIC IMPACT
ON MYCENAEAN GREECE

BY

MICHAEL C. ASTOUR

WITH A FOREWORD BY CYRUS H. GORDON

TWO FOLDING MAPS

LEIDEN
E. J. BRILL
1965

This book was printed with financial assistance
of Brandeis University

PRINTED IN THE NETHERLANDS

A mon cher Maître
Monsieur Charles Virolleaud
Membre de l'Institut
en hommage de respect et de profonde gratitude

TABLE OF CONTENTS

FOREWORD

Western civilization owes much to its Hellenic and Semitic factors. Both peoples met around the shores of the East Mediterranean during the second millennium B.C. and their interaction at that early period constituted the foundation of much that we claim as our own culture.

Bold spirits, such as Victor Bérard, have in the past dared to maintain the Phoenician antecedents of Greek history. Bérard's valuable contributions, however, were marred by his sketchy knowledge of Semitic languages, and by his unawareness of so much of the pre-Phoenician material including even the Gilgamesh Epic.

The steady increase in our ancient sources have changed the picture considerably. In addition to the traditions embodied in Hebrew, Greek and Latin texts, we now have extensive textual and archeological discoveries from Mesopotamia, Egypt, Palestine, Syria, Anatolia and the Aegean. The Ugaritic and the Linear A and B documents are of particular relevance to the problem.

A major contribution to ancient history (such as the book before us) could only be made by a mature scholar, who would work through the classical sources as well as the secondary literatures in various modern European languages, and bring to bear the evidence of the newly discovered texts and monuments from all over the cradles of Western Civilization. To make the work sound and meaningful, the scholar would have to exercise exceptional critical capacity to separate the wheat from the chaff while devising a cogent methodology.

Dr. Michael Astour is one of the few scholars with the knowledge, ability and vision to execute a comprehensive analysis of early Helleno-Semitic relations. Hellenosemitica *is a deep and many-sided study destined to affect the rising generation's concept of ancient history. The reader may feel confident that Dr. Astour's conclusions rest on a control of the original sources as well as on a grasp of the whole field with all of its far-flung ramifications.*

Cyrus H. Gordon

PREFACE

Greek myths placed in the beginning of the Heroic Age in Greece such characters as the Phoenician Cadmos in Thebes, the Phoenician Europa in Crete, the Egyptian Danaos in Argos. Herodotos reported on ancient Phoenician colonies in Boeotia and on the Aegean islands of Cythera, Thera, and Thasos. Thucidides wrote about Phoenician settlements in the Aegean isles. Rhodian historians ascribed the foundation of some of their cities and shrines to Phoenicians. Was there any historical reality behind these reports?

Up to the second half of the XIXth century, this question was usually answered in the positive. Several attempts have been made to find cultic, mythological, and onomastic parallels between Greece and the Semitic East. But the data for achieving this purpose were inadequate. Too little was known of Semitic philology, and still less of Semitic literature, religion, and mythology at the time. Many assumptions were gratuitous, and even guesses which now seem reasonable could not be substantiated by anything more solid than superficial resemblances. A reaction in the Classicist circles put an end to the comparative study of Greek and Oriental cultures. Started in Germany in the eighteen nineties, this trend was led by Julius BELOCH who published in 1894 a short article [1] in which he asserted, with unusual sharpness but with very weak arguments, that all reports on Phoenicians in Greece were absolutely baseless. The reaction went so far that not only Cadmos but even Adonis were declared non-Semitic, and were said to have been purely Greek names and characters.[2] This tendency spread to England and France. The polemic against admitting any Semitic influence upon Greece was conducted with so much passion that its motivation seemed to be derived from external considerations.[3] In any case, there was an undeniable partiality. Eastern influences were excluded a priory, but there was a great predilection for seeking northern (or Nordic) influences on Greek religion and culture.[4]

Almost the only scholar to oppose this trend was Victor BÉRARD

[1] LVI.
[3] E.g., in the famous *Realencyclopädie* by Pauly-Wissowa (CDXI).
[3] Cf. LXV, I, 17; LXIII, 69 s.
[4] Cf. CDLXXVIIIa, 70 s.

(1864-1931), the distinguished investigator of the *Odyssey*. But his books devoted to Phoenician influence upon Greece [1] were intentionally ignored; practically no scholar in the Greek field dared mention them. It is true that they had serious defects. In particular, BÉRARD's central idea—that Odysseus' travels reflect knowledge of real West Mediterranean localities and were based upon detailed Phoenician sea-circuits (*periploi*)—was undoubtedly mistaken. But following this wrong path, he discovered scores of other Semitic elements in Greek mythology and toponymics, and some of his suggestions are there to remain.[2] The works of Gabriel GERMAIN [3] and T. B. L. WEBSTER,[4] published, respectively, twenty-three and twenty-seven years after BÉRARD's death, revealed several basic Near Eastern elements in the Homeric poems. *Mutatis mutandis*, this is a posthumous vindication of BÉRARD's cause.

The situation was different in the nineteen thirties. When, as a student of the Sorbonne, I came to the opening lecture of Professor Pierre ROUSSEL's course on Greek colonization, I was somewhat perplexed by this scholar's statement *ex cathedra*: "Greek historians reported on former Phoenician settlements in several parts of the Aegean. For a long time these reports were considered true. But now it is definitely proven that nothing of the sort ever had place." He did not even deign to elaborate this axiomatic conclusion. The general attitude toward Victor BÉRARD, who had died a few years earlier, was such as to preclude me from opening any of his works, and I became acquainted with them only twenty years later. This nothwithstanding, I soon began to doubt the infallibility of the then absolutely dominant doctrine of Julius BELOCH. The study of the Ugaritic texts that had been unearthed shortly before, and to which I had the privilege of having been introduced by their decipherer and first publisher, Professor Charles VIROLLEAUD, evoked more and more associations not only with Hebrew but with Greek mythology as well. I recall especially well how Professor VIROLLEAUD's casual rapprochement of a character in the Ugaritic epic of Danel with Semele, daughter of Cadmos,[5] opened my eyes

[1] LXII (1894); LXV + LXIV (first edition 1902-03, second expanded edition 1927-29); LXIII (1931, short summary of LXIV).

[2] Many of BÉRARD's suggestions will be cited on subsequent pages. A general evaluation of his conception must be postponed till later.

[3] CXCIII (1954).

[4] DXXXVII (1958).

[5] Cf. p. 170 below.

to the possibility that the myth of Cadmos the Phoenician might, after all, really contain some Phoenician elements. Simultaneously, a deeper acquaintance with Greek religion and ritual (in particular, with the Eleusinian cycle), for which I am greatly indebted to Professor Charles PICARD, frequently brought to my mind Semitic parallels and analogies. However, the way by which Semitic influence reached Greece, remained historically unproven.

Then came the fatal year 1939 which opened for me a decade of detention in Soviet political prisons and labor camps. In 1950, after having exchanged full imprisonment for comparative personal freedom in a city of the Asiatic part of the USSR, I found in *Vestnik Drevnej Istorii* an informative article [1] on the discovery of the bilingual from Karatepe, and its complete Phoenician text. The revelation of the Danunian tribe in East Cilicia provided me with the missing link in my search for ancient Greco-Semitic ties. It became clear to me that the Danunians were a West Semitic tribe and that the Greek Danaans were a branch of that tribe which had migrated to the West. This conclusion became the corner-stone of my subsequent work in this field. I was able to collect a small library of basically important books and dictionaries and to regularly borrow French, British, and American books and periodicals from the Lenin Library in Moscow. I could thus devote most of my free time to study and research, though I had absolutely no hope of completing and publishing their results in the USSR. My notes gradually grew and formed several notebooks, one of which I entitled *Hellenosemitica*. This loose collection of preliminary notes and short drafts became the embryo of the present study.

In November, 1956, I succeeded, at last, in leaving the Soviet Union. For three years that followed I lived in Warsaw and Paris where I was able to return to research and publication. The bulk of my work was then devoted to problems of West Semitic history; I did not, however, forget *Hellenosemitica*, either. Old prejudices still were (and are) strong, but something has imperceptibly changed in the scholarly atmosphere after Michael VENTRIS' epoch-making decipherment of Linear B. The existence of a marked Oriental influence upon the Mycenaean civilization became a recognized fact. Then came the first articles by Professor Cyrus H. GORDON on his identification of the Cretan Linear A tablets as

[1] DVIII.

written in a Semitic language.[1] It was in Warsaw, on November 10, 1957, that I learned about this discovery. I soon found that GORDON's interpretation was very convincing. Although *Hellenosemitica* was based on a different kind of evidence which had its own intrinsic value, the revelation that IId millennium B.C. Cretan inscriptions were Semitic was an outstanding confirmation of its approach. It also seemed that the material I collected on the scope and diversity of Semitic presence in the Aegean of the IId millennium B.C. might show that the Semitism of the Cretan inscriptions was not an isolated, and therefore questionable, phenomenon, but agreed with the historical and cultural context of those place and time. I began to think about developing my preliminary notes into a comprehensive book. The opportunity to devote myself to this work came after my immigration to the United States, where I was amicably received by Professor Cyrus H. GORDON, head of the Department of Mediterranean Studies in Brandeis University.

The systematic work on the present study began in fall, 1960. A very important part of the material collected on subsequent pages first arose in the process of the work. It grew so considerably and achieved such dimensions that after two years of research and writing I decided to make a temporary stop. Rather than give a concise general survey of the entire problem, I preferred to limit this part of my work to the three first and most voluminous chapters, devoted respectively to the three larger cycles, and to provide them with adequate detailed documentation. To these three chapters I added a fourth one which, in the complete scheme of *Hellenosemitica*, was intended to conclude the whole entity. I hope that the remaining part of the work, divided in six chapters, will follow some time later.

The object and the methods of this investigation are expounded in its text, and there is no need to repeat them here. It may perhaps be recalled that while most authors who wrote (both *pro* and *contra*) on Oriental influence on Greece were Hellenists,[2] the author

[1] CCXIX; CCVII. C. H. GORDON's interest to the problem of Greco-Semitic cultural connections dates from at least 1952 (CCXXI); he gave a detailed exposition of his views in 1955, (CCXV), in which, however, the main accent was on Aegean influence upon the West Semites rather than the other way around.

[2] Such as V. BÉRARD, J. BELOCH, O. GRUPPE, F. DORNSEIFF, Rhys CARPEN-

of the present study is primarily a Semitist, which enables him to see the problem under a somewhat different angle. Then, while most of his predecessors have concentrated their comparative study mainly on Homer, the evidence presented in this study is largely extra-Homeric. Finally, lest the author's intentions be perceived in an exaggerated form and in a one-sided light, let it be said that in his opinion West Semitic influence was only one, though important, factor in the formation of Mycenaean civilization, and that Mycenaean survivals (including their Semitic components) were only one, though important, factor in the formation of classical Greek culture. This book, owing to its topic, necessarily limits itself to specifically this aspect of the problem, but it does not exclude nor ignore the existence and importance of other aspects.

Along with points which seem to me more or less substantiated, I included (mostly in footnotes) several assumptions of a more hypothetical character. I was guided thereby by a double consideration: first, some of what seems now to be mere guesswork, may some time in the future obtain a more serious basis; second, even erroneous guesses may lead other investigators to correct conclusions precisely by giving them the opportunity of critical examination.

The bibliography cited in this study does not, of course, cover (even in the essential) all of the corresponding literature—which would anyway be impossible in view of the colossal number of works published on topics connected with its theme. The list of quoted books and articles already became quite long. My references to them have only these exclusive goals: 1) to justify my statements by showing their sources; 2) to note the priorities of the cited views which I share; 3) to indicate the publications the views of which I contest. The reader will easily find further bibliography by consulting some of the works I am referring to. Wherever this was possible without detriment to the reliability of the reference, I tried to quote Oriental texts from books that are accessible to a non-cuneiformist. If, however, my understanding of a text depended on my own translation, I supplied the original version with the necessary justifications of linguistic nature.

Completing this part of my work, I would like to express my sincere gratitude, first of all, to the Faculté des Lettres de l'Université de Paris, which gave me the basic academic training and whose

TER, G. GERMAIN, T. B. L. WEBSTER, Chester STARR. Notable exceptions: Cyrus H. GORDON and H. G. GÜTERBOCK.

impact was not erased by seventeen years of hardships and isolation. I regret that I am unable to express my thankfullness to the Professors Raymond WEILL, Adolphe LODS, and many others whom I did not find alive when I returned to the free world. But I am happy that I can, with all my heart, thank my best teacher, Professor Charles VIROLLEAUD, not only for the knowledge he gave me, but also for his warm interest and friendly help in the scholarly sphere and in practical life he showed me, both in my remote student years and in my mature manhood. I also thank Professor André DUPONT-SOMMER and Professor Édouard DHORME who encouraged and helped my research work in Paris, and Dr. Pierre OFFERLÉ, of the École des Hautes Études, who introduced me to Akkadian cuneiforms.

Here, in my new American home, where I found freedom and peace of mind after many years of worries and travels, I thank, most of all, Professor Cyrus H. GORDON, to whom I am indebted for the opportunity to complete this work. I am sincerely grateful to him for his active interest in it, for his stimulating and encouraging comments, and for his revision of my manuscript and many valuable philologic corrections. He is, however, not responsible for all of the views expounded in this book and for the mistakes it may contain.

Finally, I express my gratitude to Brandeis University for the financial contribution toward the publication of this book.

December 21, 1963 MICHAEL C. ASTOUR

Brandeis University
Waltham, Massachusetts

TECHNICAL REMARKS

1. *Abbreviations used in text:*

AT — Alalaḫ tablets.
EA — Tell el-Amarna tablets.
H-H — Hittite Hieroglyphic.
HT — Hagia Triada tablets.
LXX— Septuagint.
RŠ — Ras Shamra tablets (except those covered by UM).
UM — Ras Shamra tablets in Ugaritic alphabetic script, numbered according to their order in C. H. Gordon, *Ugaritic Manual.* For the epic poems, the symbols introduced by Virolleaud (AB, BH, D, K, NK, Rp., SS) are also indicated.
UM, followed by §, refers to § of grammar or vocabulary in *Ugaritic Manual.*
W-S — West Semitic.

2. *Dates:*

All dates are B.C., unless stated otherwise or obviously referring to modern times.

3. *Translitetation:*

By technical reasons, all occurring words and names in Greek, Hebrew, Aramaic, Arabic and Russian are transliterated in Roman characters. Following particular rules are observed:

a) Greek: spiritus rudus = *h*; η = *ê*; ου = *u*; υ alone = *y*; υ in diphthongs = *au, eu, êu, ôu*; χ = *ch*; ω = *ô*; ϝ = *w*. Accents are disregarded.

b) Hebrew: ח is transliterated either by *ḥ* or by *ḫ*, according to the evidence of comparative Semitic linguistics; spirantization of ב, ג, ד, כ, ת is disregarded; spirantized פ = *ph*; šᵉwa mobile = ᵉ; other semi-vowels = *ă, ĕ, ŏ*; segol = *e*.

c) Ugaritic: as in the chart *UM* § 3.3. except for the signs:
No. 7: *ž* instead of *d*;
No. 23: *ġ* instead of *ǵ*;
No. 30: *ṡ* instead of *ṯ*.

4. *Bibliography*:

Editions of classical authors are not included in the bibliographical list. Only book and articles directly referred to are included. They are indicated in the footnotes by the numbers (in small capital Roman figures) assigned to them in the alphabetical bibliographical list. *Ibid., op. cit.* or *loc. cit.* refer only to works mentioned immediately before, in the same or preceding footnote.

CHAPTER ONE

THE DANAANS-DANUNIANS

Eastern and Western Danunians

In 1945-1947, in the neighborhood of Karatepe on the Ceyhan River (classical Pyramos), in the easternmost part of Cilicia, near its border with classical Syria, a long bilingual inscription in Phoenician and Hittite-Hieroglyphic was found.[1] This represents the solemn declaration by Azitawadd,[2] King of the Danunians, on the founding of a new city at Karatepe named after the founder.[3] It contained an enumeration of the king's merits to his people and country, and an invocation to the gods. The time of the inscription has been variously determined; for some time it was attributed to the end of the IXth century,[4] but now the dating of a century later—end of the VIIIth century—prevails.[5] To us, however, the exact date of Azitawadd's reign presents at the moment less interest than the basic fact of geographical and onomastical character—namely, that in Eastern Cilicia, directly to the West of the already well-known North Syrian states of the same epoch, Gurgum and Śam'al, there existed a people of the Danunians who had created a rather important state on the scale of Syria of those times. Even if the Karatepe inscription pertains to the period about 725, the existence of the Danunian kingdom in the same area is nevertheless attested, a century earlier, in an inscription of the neigh-

[1] Or, rather, three almost identical versions of the same inscription. The H-H text has been published only in part (LXXIV). For the Phoenician text, see bibliography in CDXXXIV, 499. Several publications and studies of the inscription will be referred to in the course of the subsequent discussion.

[2] Phoen. *'ztwd*, H-H *Asitawa(n)das*.

[3] Phoen. *'ztwdy*, H-H *Asitawa(n)dawa*.

[4] The expansion of the Danunian kingdom, boasted of by Azitwadd, was equated with the victory of the king of the Danunians over Kilamuwa, king of Śam'al, mentioned in the latter's inscription (second half of the IXth century). For the IXth century date of Azitawadd's inscription, cf. CCCLIX, 197; CCIX, 109, 112; DVIII, 92; CDXXXIV, 499.

[5] Reasons: epigraphic features, CXXXII, 185; style of Azitawadd's reliefs, IV, 140 s., CDVIII, 351; identification of *'wrk* (H-H *Awarakus*) with *Urikki*, king of Quê under Tiglathpileser III (about 740-730), XXX, 121-124; CCCLIII, 116; CXXXII, 185; CCXXV, 209. CCCXXVIII, 105 ss., lowered the date even to 680.

boring king Kilamuwa of Śam'al.[1] Like many states of North Syria (to which it belonged geopolitically), Azitawadd's kingdom had more than one name.[2] Azitawadd himself called the people of his state Danunians (*Dnnym*—the same name used by Kilamuwa), and the country, Plain of Adana (*ʿmq ʾdn*), after the old city of Adana [3] which still exists under the same name. As his royal residence he mentions *Pʿr*—a city known to the Assyrian king Shalmaneser III (858-824) as *Paḫri*, a royal city of the kingdom Qauâ [4] (since the VIIIth century the Assyrians called it Quê),[5] which lay precisely in Eastern Cilicia, beyond Mount Amanus, and is thus identical with the state of the Plain of Adana.[6] BOSSERT identified *Pʿr-Paḫri* with the modern town of Misis, Mopsuhestia of Hellenistic times, lower down on the Ceyhan, and connected by the Greeks with a hero of their mythology, the seer Mopsos. Azitawadd mentions three times in his inscription "the house of *Mpš*" (*Bt-Mpš*),[7] apparently in the sense of the royal dynasty to which he belonged.[8] We will have to discuss more in detail these and some other ethno-geographical names and terms and the historical informations that can be extracted from them. Meanwhile, in order to define, at least roughly, the geographical framework of the Danunian kingdom, let it be added that its frontiers in the West

[1] *wʾdr ly mlk dn[n]ym*, cf. DVIII, 92; CCCXCVI, 184; CDXXXIV, 500. The expedition of the king of Assyria against the Danunians to aid Kilamuwa is certainly the one of Shalmaneser III's twentieth year, i.e. 839 (CCCXLV, I, § 577, and more in detail in the new text from Assur, CDXXXVIII, col. IV: 22-34).

[2] See below, p. 13.

[3] Mentioned as *Adanat* in an Alalaḫ tablet of the XVIIth century, and several times in Boğazköy texts in cuneiform Hittite and Akkadian, as *Adaniya* or *Ataniya*, to which we shall return further in this chapter.

[4] In the inscription published CCCLXVI, II, 8, col. III: 6-7: ^{m}*Ka-ti* ^{awil} *nakru*^{MEŠ} ^{al}*Pa-aḫ-ri āl šarru-ti-šú e-sir-šú* "Katê, the enemy, in Paḫri, his royal city, I enclosed."—For identification Paḫri = *Pʿr*, cf. CCIX, 113; CCCLIII, 118; LXXIV, III, 294; CXXXII, 185.

[5] Appears as *Qwh* in I Kings 10: 28 (first recognized by Hugo WINCKLER, cf. CCCLXII, 626) and in the inscription of Zakir, king of Hamath (early VIIIth century), cf. CCCXXXV, III, 1 ss.; CDXXXIV, 501 s.

[6] The identity of the names *ʾwrk* (cited as a ruler of the Danunians by Azitawadd) and *Urikki*, king of Quê according to Tiglathpileser III (CCCXLV, I, §§ 772, 801; CCCXCIX, 282 s.) adds to the identity of Quê with the Plain of Adana.

[7] I: 16; II: 15; III: 11.

[8] Cf. in the Bible *Bêt-Šāʾûl, Bêt-Dāwîd, Bêt-ʿOmrî*. The Assyrians often called Syrian states by the name of their dynastic founders: *Bît-Ḫumria* (Israel), *Bît-Gabbar* (Śamʾal), etc.

included in the IXth century the famous city of Tarsus (Assyrian *Tarzi*, second millenium Hittite *Tarša*).[1] There exists a supposition that the divine name *Bʿl-Krntryš* which is mentioned in the Karatepe inscription with special attention, as if it has been a tribal or dynastic deity, also contains this city name.[2] The western frontier of the Plain of Adana kingdom ran, thus, somewhere west of Tarsus, and probably coincided with the natural border of Lowland Cilicia which was in all respects different from western or Rocky Cilicia.[3]

The discovery of the Karatepe inscription has considerably enriched historical science in many respects: 1) the history and ethnology of the ancient Near East gained information about one more state that had been all but unknown until then; 2) light was thrown upon its social, political and religious life, which also elucidated a great deal in the general context of the whole geopolitical complex of Syria on the eve of its conquest by Assyria; 3) the Karatepe inscription turned out to be the largest Phoenician written document discovered to this day. It helped to broaden knowledge of the Phoenician language; 4) because of the close correspondence between the Phoenician and the H-H versions of the inscription, the known vocabulary of the H-H language has grown both in volume and in accuracy. However, for the subject of the present investigation, this inscription is important in another respect: it can shed light on the origin of one of the oldest Greek tribes—the Danaans—and help raise the curtain over the ancient ethnic connections between Mycenaean Greece and the Semitic East, connections that earlier could only be conjectured on the basis of controversial data from several Greek myths. The present chapter will be dedicated solely to this question, though its analysis, because of the nature of the problem, will be complex, and will necessarily touch upon several quite varied details that are connected with the main object.

[1] Tarsus was conquered by Shalmaneser III at the final stage of his fourth campaign against Qauê (Quê), in his 26th year of reign or 833 (CCCXLV, I, § 583; CCCXCVI, 125).

[2] CCLIX, 54; CXXXII, 173 (tentatively). This divine name will be discussed later.

[3] In Assyrian time, Western Cilicia was known as *Ḫilakku* (= *Ḫlk* in the Aramaic of the Persian period; recognized in Ezech. 27: 11 by HALÉVY, cf. CCCLXII, 623, 626). In the neo-Babylonian time, the western border of the Babylonian province of *Ḫumê* (= Quê) was formed by the river Lamos (DLIII, 39-41). About 539, Ḫumê was conquered by Western Cilicia (then known as *Pirindu*), and the name *Ḫilakku* (whence Greek *Kilikia*) became the name of the new unified kingdom (DLIII, 42); but even after, both halves of Cilicia remained basically different in their ethnic and cultural aspects.

Though the location of the Danunian country was only established with the find of the Karatepe inscription, historical science had at the end of the XIXth century already had at its disposal much earlier evidences of a land and a people of the same name which had previously been linked with the Greek Danaans, and who are now compared with the Danunians of Karatepe, though the problem of their interrelationship still remains disputable. Both these evidences were found in Egypt. The earlier of the two was discovered in a letter from the Amarna archives (EA 151),[1] written to the Pharaoh Amenhotep IV by one of his vassals, the king of the Phoenician city of Tyre, Abimilki. This letter (composed, as were all other letters of the Syro-Palestinian vassals of Egypt, in Akkadian, the international language of the epoch) was written about 1365.[2] It mentions the country of Danuna (^{māt} *Da-nu-na*) in line 52. Some scholars supposed at first that Abimilki meant the country of the Greek Danaans, and that the letter was indicative of contact between Phoenician ships and Greece.[3] That such contact existed indeed seems to be (as we shall try to show subsequently) more than probable, but in this case the context of Abimilki's letter does not allow us to make such a conclusion. The relevant passage of Abimilki's letter runs as follows:

> (49) *šarru be-li-ia iš-ta-par a-na ia-*[*ši*] (50) *šá ta-áš-me iš-tu* ^{māt}*Ki-na-aḫ-na* (51) *ù šú-pur a-na ia-ši* (52) *šàr* ^{māt}*Da-nu-na mît* (53) *ù ša-ar-ra aḫu-šú* (54) *a-na arki-šú ù pa-áš-ḫa-at* (55) *mātu-šú ù qár šarri* ^{āl}*U-ga-ri-it*^{KI} (56) *i-ku-ul i-šá-tum mi-ši-i*[*l-*]*šu* (57) *i-kúl ù mi-ši-šu ia-nu* (58) *ù amêlût umman* ^{māt}*Ḫa-at-ti ia-nu* (59) ^{m}*E-ta-ga-ma pa-wa-ri* (60) ^{āl}*Ki-id-ši ù* (61) ^{m}*A-zi-ra nu-kur-tum* (62) *it-ti* ^{m}*Bir*$_5$*-ia-wa-zi*[4] (63)

[1] The numeration of the Amarna letters is that of the classical edition by Knudtzon, followed (with additions) in the English edition (ccclx). Quotations are mainly made from the latter edition, with necessary corrections on the basis of autographed text and recent studies.

[2] The destruction of Ugarit stated by the letter is the one caused by the great earthquake which occurred precisely in the Amarna Age and was dated 1365 by the director of the excavations at Ras Shamra, Claude F.-A. Schaeffer (cf. cdl, 13). It is interesting to note that Kitchen, in his recent year-by-year chronological arrangement of the Amarna Age events, arrived exactly to the date 1365 ("high chronology," corresponding to latest comparative data, cf. cdxxxv) for the letter EA 151 (cclxxxviia, 45).

[3] E.g., ccclxiii, II, 1, 224 and n. 2.

[4] Previously read *Nam-ia-wa-zi* or (elsewhere) *Nam-ia-wa-za*. Corrected after cdlxxxvii, 171.

nu-kur-tum (64) *a-ta-mur ḫa-ba-li* (65) *ᵐZi-im-ri-da* (66) *e-nu-ma ip-ḫu-ur* (67) *ⁱˢelippê ṣâbê iš-tu alâni ᵐA-zi-r[a]* (68) *a-na muḫḫiḫi -ia*

"(49) The king, my lord, has written to m[e]: (50) 'What thou hearest from Kinaḫna (51) write to me.' (52) The king of Danuna is dead, (53) and his brother has become king (54) in his stead, and his land (55) is quiet. And fire has consumed (56) Ugarit, the city (*bît?*) of the king; half of it (57) it has consumed, and its (other) half is not, (58) and the people of the army of Ḫatti are not (there). (59) Etagama, lord of (60) Kidši, and (61) Azira have begun (62) hostilities (63) against Biriawazi. (64) I have seen the destruction (65) on the part of Zimrida, (66) that he has collected (67) ships (and) men from the cities of Azira (68) against me."

This indicates, first of all, that Abimilki included the land of Danuna in the limits of Canaan. The geographical denomination of Canaan, which in the narrow sense of the word designated the Phoenician coast, [1] in a wider sense applied in the XIVth century to the totality of the Egyptian dominions in Asia [2] and to the entire Syro-Palestinian region in general. [3] Furthermore, in his enumeration of the particular Syrian localities, Abimilki strictly follows the direction from north to south: the possessions of Aziru, Etagama and Biriawaza in Middle Syria are mentioned after the North Syrian Ugarit, and the South Phoenician Sidon and Tyre are named last. Danuna, named first, must have been situated to the north of Ugarit, and so is indeed situated the East Cilician country of the Danunians, revealed by the Karatepe inscription. [4] Therefore, there is no doubt that Abimilki understood by Danuna the very same country where Azitawadd was to reign many centuries later, and this, in turn, proves that the Danunians had occupied their country at least since early in the XIVth century.

The name Danuna appears for the second time in Egyptian documents of about 170 years later. Soon after 1200,[5] a mighty

[1] Understood thus in the inscription of Idri-mi, king of Alalaḫ, where the Middle Phoenician city of Ammia is said to be situated in Canaan (*ma-at Ki-in-a-nim*KI), CDLXVIII, 14-15, ll. 16-20; 73.

[2] Thus in EA 30 : 1-2 (passport of a foreign, probably Hittite, ambasador): "To the kings of *Kinaḫ[ḫi]*, vassals of my brother" (i.e., the Pharaoh).

[3] More or less confounded with Amurru; "it is hard to find a satisfactory criterion for use of these names," XI, 13.

[4] That Danuna must be located in the north of Syria, was already presumed prior to the find of Karatepe; cf. CCCLX, II, 496.

[5] The most recent developments in Egyptian chronology refuted the ultra-low dates for the beginning of the XXth Dynasty (CDXXXVI; DIV; XXV, 170) and re-established the year 1200 (CDXXXV; CCXLIX).

wave of north-western peoples came to Egypt. By this time, they had already succeeded in overthrowing the Hittite Empire in Asia Minor, seizing Cyprus, devastating Cilicia, Syria up to the Euphrates, and Palestine, destroying most of the larger cities of this whole wide area and, according to an outstanding specialist in comparative archaeology, in putting an end to the Bronze Age civilization in Western Asia.[1] This grandiose cataclysm is known in history as the Invasion of the Peoples of the Sea, after the name given to them by the Egyptians. The first, relatively weak forerunner of this invasion was the raid repulsed by the Pharaoh Merneptah in 1230. Five peoples participated in it: [2] *'A-qi-ya-wa-ša* (Achaeans),[3] *Tu-ru-ša* or *Tu-ur-ša* (Tyrrhenes or Tyrsenes, then probably still in the Aegean—in Lemnos and Lydia), *Ru-ku* (to be read *Lu-ku*, Lycians, *Lu-uk-ki* of EA 38 : 10 and of Hittite documents), *Ša-ar-da-na* or *Ša-ar-di-na* (Sardinians),[4] and *Šak(a)ruša*—a people identified by some with the Siculi of Sicily,[5] by others with the inhabitants of the city of Sagalassos in Pisidia.[6] Three of these five peoples (Achaeans, Lycians, and probably Tyrrhenes) were from the Aegean, the other two apparently came from still more western parts of the Mediterranean. Let us keep this in mind for a clearer view of what

[1] CDL, *passim.*

[2] The Egyptian names of the Sea Peoples are given as vocalized by ALBRIGHT (XXV, 166-171) according to his principles of reading the Egyptian group-writing, as established in his XXVII. The transliterations of HELCK, following his own system of group-writing (CCL, 240-244), are very close to ALBRIGHT'S.

[3] One is somewhat puzzled by the *chi* of *Achaioi* being rendered by *q* in the Egyptian form of the name. Cf., though, *Bît-Ar-ḫa* EA 79: 21; 83: 29, and (same town) *Bît-Ar-qa* EA 91 : 9; *Quê* (for *Quwê*), later *Ḫumê* (for *Ḫuwê*), cf. n. 16 above. The answer is probably that the Greek *chi* (an aspired *k* rather then a velar fricative *ḫ*) was perceived by the Orientals as sounding closer to the Semitic *ġ* than to *ḫ*. In cuneiform this made no graphic difference, since it has no other means of transcribing *ġ* than by *ḫ*, but the Egyptians rendered the Semitic *ġ* by their own *g* (as in *Nu-g(a)-śa* = Ugar. *Nġš* = cuneif. *Nuḫašše*) or *q* (as in *Qa-ḏa-ta* = Arab. *Ġazzē* = Greek *Gaza* = cuneif. *Ḫazati*). Therefore we have *Aḫḫiyawā* in cuneiform Hittite, but *'Aqiyawaša* (with the common Asianic gentilic *-ša*) in Egyptian.

[4] Not the inhabitants of Sardeis in Lydia, for the native name of that city was *Sfard* (Persian *Saparda*, Heb. *Sephārad*); on the other hand, statuettes of warriors in the same peculiar helmets as those worn by the Šardana on Egyptian representations have been discovered in Sardinia. Cf. XXV, 167, n. 18.

[5] LXXVIII, 467; DCXLIX, 262, n. 3.

[6] CCCLVI, V, 255, n. 1. In spite of the similarity of names, this seems to be too remote toward the east and too continental a homeland for a People of the Sea. Besides, Pisidia belonged at this time to the Arzawa Lands.

the Egyptian understood by the Peoples of the Sea, and the origins of their invasions.

The second, much more enormous invasion of the Peoples of the Sea which broke down at the very gates of Egypt, occurred about 30 years after the first one. There were again five peoples that participated in it (six if we reckon the Šardina who are added in some versions), but with the exception of the *Šak(a)ruša* who already took part in the first raid, their names are different: *Per(a)sata* (Philistines), *Ṯikara, Danuna,* and *Wašaša.* But these names, too, as much as they can be identified, point to an Aegean origin. The same is shown by the external aspect and the armament of the Peoples of the Sea on Egyptian pictorial monuments, which bear no resemblance to the Syrians and Hittites already familiar to the Egyptians, but are very like figurations in Minoan and Mycenaean art.[1] Hebrews, who after the invasion became the closest neighbors of the Philistines, have preserved a tradition of the Philistines' descent from Kaphtor, i.e. Crete,[2] and it is very tempting to identify them, as has been proposed many times, with the pre-Greek people of the Pelasgians who, among other regions, allegedly also inhabited Crete, together with Achaeans, Dorians, Eteocretans, and Cydonians (*Odyss.* XIX: 175-178).[3] The attempts to identify the people of the Ṯikara meet phonetic difficulties because of the ambiguous character of the first and third consonants of the Egyptian transcription.[4] Thence the proposals to identify them with the Siculi (Greek: Sikeliots),[5] the Teucrians from Troad,[6] the inhabitants of Zacro in Crete,[7] or with the Carians [8]

[1] Especially interesting is the head in the typical Philistine feathered helmet, used as a hieroglyphic sign in the famous Phaistos disc of Middle Minoan III—even if it had been imported to Crete from south-western Asia Minor, as supposed CDXIII, 170.

[2] For the most recent and detailed discussion of the question of Kaphtor-Keftiu, see DVI.

[3] Favorably viewed XXV, 171, n. 34, though declared uncertain because of the phonetic difference of the last consonants still not satisfactory explained. Without pretending to suggest such an explanation, we would remark that *g* sometimes shifted to *d* in Greek. According to ancient interpretations, *Dêmêtêr* stands for *Gê-mêtêr* "Mother Earth"; Euripides used *da* for *ga* "earth"; cf. also *Ariadnê* from *Ari-agnê* "the very pure." See CCCXLIV, s.v. *Demeter*; *Theseus*; CDXXXIII, s.v. *Ariadne*.

[4] The Egyptian *r* could as well stand for *l*. The Egyptian *ṯ* could correspond to Semitic *z, s, ṣ*; moreover, under the New Kingdom it became more and more confounded with *t*, and could transcribe the Semitic *d* and *t* as well.

[5] LXXVIII, 477.

[6] CCCLVI, V, 303, n. 1; DXLIX, 26, n. 5.

[7] PETRIE, quoted CCXLIV, 283, n. 1; CDXIII, 260, n. 4.

[8] CDLXXXII, 16-17.

—but anyway with a north-western people from beyond the Mediterranean Sea.[1] It is difficult to form an exact idea as to the origin of the Wašaša (their name has been compared to that of a Cretan [2] or a Carian [3] city), but the very form of the name points to Asia Minor or the Aegean basin, and the statement of Ramses III about all five of the invading nations as islanders [4] is clear enough.

The above applies also to the Danuna—they are even separately characterized as islanders by Ramses III [5]—and therefore, in the general context of the Peoples' of the Sea invasion, everybody believed prior to the discovery of the Karatepe inscription (and many continue to do so even after it) that the Danuna of Ramses III were the Greek Danaans who arrived at the borders of Egypt from Greece.[6] They were in all probability either identical or closely related to the 'Aqiyawaša-Achaeans of the raid under Merneptah. Homer uses the appellations Achaeans, Argeans, and Danaans, indiscriminately to designate the whole of the Greek tribes.[7] To

[1] This tribe had settled, after the unsuccesful assault on Egypt, in the Palestinian city of Dor, where the Egyptian Wen-Amon found it about 1090. In the Xth century Dor became a possession of Israel (I Kings 4 : 11). Unfortunately, the Bible has not preserved the slightest memory of that tribe, and the lack of a Hebrew transliteration of its name prevents us from determining more precisely its phonetic structure.

[2] XXV, 171 rejects without justification the connection of *Wašaša* with *Oaxos* in the western part of middle Crete, spelled *Waxos* in its own inscriptions and known also as *Asos* (which points to an original **Wasos*). **Wasos* and even *Waxos* present a fairly satisfactory resemblance with *Wašaša* (cf. Greek *Maxyes* = Egypt. *Mašawaša*, a Lybian tribe, CDLIV, 164).

[3] *Ouassos* of the inscriptions, otherwise known as Iassos, on the shore of south-western Caria. Suggested many times, e.g. CCC, 230, n. 3.

[4] "The foreign countries made a *conspiracy* in their islands," Medinet Habu inscription, photogr. plate 46, transl. CLVII, 43; DXLIX, 262. See more in detail below, p. 10 s.

[5] Papyrus Harris, LXXVII, IV, § 403; DXLIX, 262: "I slew the Denyen (= Danuna, M. A.) in their islands, while the Tjeker (= Ṯikara) and the Philistines were made ashes. The Sherden (= Šardana) and the Weshesh (= Wašaša) of the Sea were made nonexistent."

[6] Since MASPERO and DE ROUGÉ. "The Denyen (cuneiform Danuna) might be the Danaoi," DXLIX, 262, n. 3.

[7] A. DELLA SETTA, "Achaioi, Argeioi, Danaoi," 133 ss., 136 (quoted CCCII, 30), made the following summary:

	Achaioi	Argeioi	Danaoi
Iliad	605	176	146
Odyssey	118	30	13

CDXL, 344, is of the opinion that in the Homeric poems the term "Danaans" is a more narrow notion that Achaeans, and signifies approximately the military estate. But this does not follow in any way from the Homeric text.

believe Pausanias, who usually acted as a conscientious registrar of facts and historical traditions, the name of the Achaeans was in the pre-Dorian epoch borne *par excellence* by the inhabitants of the two East Peloponnesian realms, Laconia and Argolis, and the people of the latter were, in addition, called Danaans.[1] With Argos are also connected the myths about the heroes-eponyms of the Danaans—King Danaos, his daughters the Danaides, and Princess Danaë.[2]

The data of Abimilki [3] and Ramses III, confronted with the inscriptions of Azitawadd and Kilamuwa on the one hand, and with the Homeric epics and Greek myths on the other, lead to the conclusion that at about 1200 there existed in the coastlands of the Mediterranean *two* tribes with the same name of Danunians: one in the East, where Eastern Cilicia touches North Syria, having lived there at least from early in the XIVth century until late in the VIIIth century; the other in the West, in the Aegean basin, most probably in Peloponnese.[4]

COULD THE SEA PEOPLE OF DANUNA HAVE COME FROM CILICIA?

But the discovery of the Karatepe inscription, and particularly the study of its H-H version, induced certain specialists in Hittite-Anatolian archaeology and linguistics to reject categorically the possibility of the existence of *two* Danuna countries in the IId millennium, and of any connection, in either direction, between the Cilician Danunites and Greece. Thus SETON LLOYD [5] remarked, "One of

[1] Paus. VII: 1:6-7.

[2] CDIII, s.v. *Danaoi*: "properly the subjects of Danaos, then particularly the inhabitants of Argos"; CDXCII, 33.

[3] Other evidence of the Amarna Age will be discussed below, p. 32 ss.

[4] Here is the place to say a few words about another Egyptian evidence which at one time was considered to be a mention of the Aegean Danaans as early as in the first half of the XVth century. Among foreign countries listed in the victory-hymn of Thutmose III on a Karnak stele (translations: LXXVII, II, §§ 655-662; CDLXXIX, 68-71; DXLIX, 373-375, with bibliography), the name *iww wṯntyw* (DVI, 8-12) "the Islands of *Wṯntyw*" figures. Their identification with "Islands of the Danaans" (references CCCLVI, V, 101) is materially impossible. However, if the hieroglyph V-13 (*ṯ*) stands here for *t*, the word may be an Egyptian transliteration (with the Egyptian plural ending) of the Semitic word which is *waṭan* in Arabic, *waṭnâti* or *wadnâti* (plur.) in Akkadian, meaning in the latter "dwellings, nations." If this interpretation is correct, the "Islands of *Waṭnâti*" would then be the oldest known occurrence of the Biblical *'Îyyê hag-gôyîm*, "Isles of the Nations," as the islands of the Aegean are called Gen. 10:5.

[5] CCCXXXIX, 179.

the first important inferences made from the inscription of Karatepe was that the Danuna could only be the Dananians listed among the 'Peoples of the Sea,' who invaded Egypt in the twelfth century B.C. Since they are described at Karatepe as 'People of the City of Adana,' they may now also be identified as true Anatolians."

E. LAROCHE [1] went still further in this direction. His point of departure was the observation that in the H-H text of the Karatepe inscription *Adanawa* corresponds to the Phoenician name of the city of Adana (*'dn*), and *Adanawana* (the H-H ethnic of *Adanawa*) corresponds to the Phoenician ethnic *Dnnym*. Consequently, according to his opinion, the *Dnnym* were the inhabitants of Adana and nothing more. *Adanawana*, as he considers it, became *Adanūna*, and the "vulgar and late Phoenician" often dropped the aleph in the beginning of polysyllabic words, and thus *'Adanūniyim* was shortened to *Danuniyim*. Not only the *Danuna* of El-Amarna, but the *Dnn* (as he spells it) of the Egyptian sources as well were none other than the inhabitants of the Cilician Adana, without any connection with Greece. The "islands" where Ramses III situated the Danuna were tiny islets and capes of the Cilician coast. LAROCHE eliminated the complicated question of the relation of the Danunian *Bt-Mpš* dynasty to the Greek hero Mopsos (which is subject to a detailed examination on the further pages of this chapter) by simply assuming an accidental consonance which led to the identification of the two names.

Similar views had been expressed earlier, soon after the discovery of the Karatepe inscription.[2] W. F. ALBRIGHT did not share them,[3] but in his article on the Peoples of the Sea he did nothing to substantiate his objections. It is, however, necessary to elucidate this important issue before going further. We believe that the standpoint of LLOYD, LAROCHE and scholars of the same opinion cannot be accepted because of the following historical and linguistic considerations.

Ramses III described with perfect clarity the start and the course of the invasion: [4]

> ... The foreign countries made a 'conspiracy' in their islands. 'Removed' and scattered in the fray were the lands at one time. No land

[1] CCCXX, 263; CCCXVIII, 142 s.

[2] LXXIV, III, 283 s.

[3] "There is no solid basis for the idea that the *Dnnym* ... are the people of Adana," XXV, 163.

[4] CLVII, 43; with slight stylistic changes, DXLIX, 262.

> could stand before their arms from Ḫatti, Kode (*Qdy*), Carchemish, Arzawa (*ỉrṯ*), and Alashia (*ỉrs*) on, (but they were) cut off *at* [*one* time]. A camp [was set up] in one place in Amor. They desolated its people, and its land was like that which has never come into being. They were coming, while the flame was prepared before them, forward toward Egypt. Their confederation was the Philistines, Tjeker, Shekelesh, Denye(n), and Weshesh lands united. They laid their hands upon the lands to the (very) circuit of the earth, their hearts confident and trusting: 'Our plans will succeed!'

It follows with absolute certitude from this that the confederation of the five Peoples of the Sea originated on *islands* and included the Danuna since the very beginning, and that Cilicia (Qode [1]) not only did not belong to the confederation, but was crushed and devastated by the invasion of the Peoples of the Sea along with other neighboring countries. This is entirely confirmed by archaeological data. The excavations of the ancient mounds at Mersin and Tarsus gave evidence that the invaders of about 1200 had destroyed the Cilician cities and stayed only for a short time on their ruins.[2] Besides, Ramses III (in the Harris papyrus) explicitly speaks of "the Danuna in their islands." [3] By islands where entire nations dwelt, the Egyptians could have understood only real sizable islands—Crete, Rhodes, the Aegean islands,[4] Sardinia (whence the Šardina originated), possibly also Sicily, if the Šakruša or the Ṯikar actually came from there, and the Peloponnese, which, strictly speaking, is a peninsula, but so isolated that the Greeks themselves called and considered it an island.[5] But the microscopic islets or rather skerries off the shore of Cilicia can by no means be taken into account when looking for the islands of the Danuna; it would be equal to declare the Frenchmen an island nation since there are several small islands along the Atlantic coast of France. Qode (Cilicia) and Arzawa (the western part of the southern coast of Asia Minor) were perceived by the Egyptians as continental

[1] Identification of *Qdy* (Qode; CCL, *passim*: *Qa-di*) with the Cilician lowland already CCCLXII, 476; more about it see below, p. 28 ss.

[2] CDL, 274; CCXLV, 140.

[3] See p. 8, n. 5.

[4] On Lemnos, one of them, an inscription was discovered written in a language closely cognate to that of the Italian Etruscans (Tyrrhenes), and it is known the *Turša* took part in the first raid of the Peoples of the Sea (p. 6 above). The Greek historians remembered that Lemnos was once inhabited by Tyrrhenian Pelasgians. Cf. CDXI, XII, 2, 1929.

[5] *Peloponnêsos* = "island of Pelops." In the Roman times, the Peloponnese was included, along with Cyprus, Rhodes, Crete, Sicily, Sardinia, and Corsica, in the number of the seven largest islands of the Mediterranean.

lands; in the texts of Ramses III they are in contraposition to the islands where the invaders came from, and one shall not forget that the land road from Egypt to Ḫatti [1] crossed the famous Cilician Gates to the north of Tarsus. But, quite apart from other considerations, the land of the Danunians lay in *Eastern*, Lowland Cilicia, whereas the islets suggested by LAROCHE lay off the shore of *Western*, Rocky Cilicia.

As to the assertion that the ethnic name of the Danunians derived from the city of Adana and has lost its initial aleph by virtue of phenomena of "late and vulgar Phoenician," let it be said, first of all, that already Abimilki of Tyre, as early as the first half of the XIVth century, wrote *Danuna*, and his native Phoenician language was neither late nor vulgar. The city of Adana (H-H *Adanawa*) is named *'dn* in the Phoenician text of Karatepe; if the appellation of the people had derived from this city, it would have been in Phoenician simply *'dnym* (*'Adanîm*), as in other Phoenician inscriptions we have the plural ethnicon *Ṣdnm* [2] from *Ṣdn* "Sidon",[3] *'ytnm* from the Cretan city of Itanos,[4] or in Hebrew, e.g., *Gib^{ec}ônîm* from *Gib^{ec}ôn* (epigraphical *Gb^{c}n* [5]). We see indeed that the Hittite possessive suffix *-awa* in the H-H name of ancient Karatepe, *Asitawandawa*, is consistently replaced by the Semitic suffix *-y* in the Phoenician form of the same name, *'ztwdy*. *Adanawa* is by no means the primitive form as compared with *'dn*: the ending *-awa* is a possessive suffix, and *Adanawa* signifies "(the city) of Adan(as)," [6] just as, let us add, in another Indo-European group of languages, the Slavic, such a form as *Ivanovo* signifies "(the city) of Ivan." As was noticed by BOSSERT, later on *Adanos* was actually considered the eponymous founder of Adana. According to Stephanos of Byzantium, Adanos, the mythical founder of Adana, was a

[1] On which a vivid traffic between the two countries was going on. Cf. Papyrus Anastasi II (transl. DXLIX, 470): the king of Ḫatti, preparing to personally visit Ramses II, invites the king of Qode to accompany him.

[2] Thus in the inscription of Ešmunazar (CCCXXXVI, 417); but elsewhere *Ṣdnym* (*ibid.*, 425).

[3] The plural ending *-m* instead of *-ym* as in *Dnnym* is only a question of orthography. The scribe of Azitawadd kept unchanged the gentilic ending *-y* before the plural ending *-m*; the Phoenician scribes usually dropped it because of the assimilation of the half-consonant *y* with the cognate vowel *i* of the ending *-îm*.

[4] CXLIII, 394; cf. p. 141 below.

[5] CDXXI, 45.

[6] LXXIV, III, 284.

son of Uranos and Gaia.[1] We will show subsequently that in the person of Adanos we have the W-S divine title *ʾadân* (S. Phoen. and Hebr. *ʾādôn*). It is precisely *ʾdn* that was the original form, and the Phoenician-speaking population of the Plain of Adana felt it as a word of their own language, otherwise they would have written **ʾdnw*, just as in the contemporary and neighboring Śamʾal the non-Semitic royal names Kilamuwa, Pannamuwa were transliterated *Klmw, Pnmw*. Thus, the Phoenician-speaking inhabitants of Azitawadd's kingdom did not need to proceed from the complex H-H formation *Adana-wa-na* in order to form the ethnicon out of the name of their city.

From the fact that the H-H version has *Adanawa* (people of Adana) instead of the Danunians of the Phoenician version does not at all follow that both denominations are etymologically identical. The same states and peoples are very often called differently in different languages,[2] and it was quite normal in the times of Azitawadd that Syrian states had several names each—one name after the capital, one after the country, and very frequently a third one after the prevalent tribe or the ruling dynasty. We have seen that the Assyrians, Hamathians and Israelites called the state of the Plain of Adana by the completely dissimilar name of Ḳuê. A kingdom contiguous to it was called in its own records both *Śmʾl* and *Yʾdy*, and in Assyrian documents Samʾal, Yaudi,[3] and Bît-Gabbar; another neighboring kingdom was known to the Assyrians as Gurgum (name of the country), Marqas (name of the capital), and Bît-Paʾalla (tribal or dynastic name). Let us also quote the cases of Kammanu/Milid, Ḫatti/Gargamiš, Ḫattina/Unqu, Luḫuti/Ḫatarikka, Aram/Damascus/Ša-Imêrišu, Israel (Ass. gentilic *Sirʾilaya*)/Bît-Ḫumria/Ephraim (prophetic literature). Now let us remember that in the cuneiform Hittite the usual form of a country appellation was *māt* ^{āl}*X*,[4] and this custom was apparently preserved in H-H. Therefore the duality of the two versions is quite common:

[1] CDXXXIII, I, 66, s.v. *Adanos*.

[2] E.g. in our time: Holland/Nederland/Dutch (ethnic in English); Deutschland/Allemagne/Germany/Niemcy; Magyarorszag/Hungary; and so on. In antiquity: Hellas/Graecia/Achaia; Iberia/Hispania; Kemet/Miṣri/Aigyptos, etc. etc.

[3] On *Yaudi* = *Yʾdy* see CCXXV, 219, 228, and our XXXVII, 14-20, with further references.

[4] "It is known that city and city-state play such a rôle in the Hittite time, that not only countries, but peoples as well are named after them . . . (even) KUR^{ALU}*Mizri* 'Egypt,' KUR^{ALU}*Arzaṷa* 'Land of Arzawa,' "CCCIII, 77, n. 3.

the Semitic-speaking population called itself by its tribal name of Danunians, and the Hittite-speaking one, according to its custom, called not only the country, but its population as well, by the name of the capital. We will soon see that—in spite of their common language—the names *ʾdn* and *dnnym* go back to different roots.

Could the Cilician Danunians have come from Greece?

Thus, given the presence of *two* separate homonymous peoples of Danuna—the western in Greece and the eastern in Cilicia—as an unshaken fact (one from which we must proceed in our subsequent research), what can be said of their interrelations? Is the identity of their names just a fortuitous coincidence,[1] or were the western and eastern Danunians two branches of an earlier single people? Many years before the discovery of the Karatepe inscription, when the only known mention of the Danunians was that of the Kilamuwa text, A.T. Olmstead remarked that they "unconsciously call to mind the contemporary Greek Danians." [2] Although E. Laroche categorically denied every connection between the Danunians and Greece, W. F. Albright, in his important article (quoted above),[3] was in favor of identifying the Danunians with the Danaans. Unfortunately, he did not elaborate this question. According to his opinion, which will be examined in more detail later, *Danuna* (*Danōna*) was a Canaanite modification of the original *Danāna*,[4] where **Dănă* is the base and *-na* the Hittite gentilic ending.

> *Danā-na* can thus be perfectly well identified with the Homeric *Dănă-oi* . . . Whether **Dănă* referred originally to a Hellenic or non-Hellenic group will scarcely ever be known, nor does it have any special importance for our present study.[5] But there can be no reasonable doubt that in the first centuries of the Iron Age *Danāna* or *Danōna* did refer to tribes of Greek affiliation, since it appears in Phoenician inscriptions of the 9th and 8th centuries as the name of the people of

[1] Such things happened not unfrequently, cf. *Kûš* in the Bible: 1) Ethiopia, 2) North-West Arabia, 3) land of the Cassites, or the classical *Iberia*: 1) Spain, 2) Caucasian Georgia.

[2] cccxcvi, 184. Of course, the "Danians" (Danaans) were "contemporary" with Kilamuwa (late IXth century) only insofar as they figure, as an archaic term, in the Homeric poems, but no tribe with such a name actually existed in Greece or her colonies at that time.

[3] xxv.

[4] Which he finds, following Luckenbill, in the Assyrian name of Cyprus, *Iad(a)nana*. See pp. 48 s. below.

[5] But it is of primary importance for *our* study, and we shall try to elucidate this question.

Cilicia, ruled by the 'Dynasty of Mopsus' . . . In view of the close relation between the settlement in both countries, it is quite futile to separate the *Dnn* of Cilicia from the *Dnāna* of Cyprus.[1]

It seems to follow from this that the Cilician Danunians were the descendants of the Homeric Danaans, who (apparently, during the great invasion of the Peoples of the Sea in which the Danuna-Danaans took part) had occupied Cilicia and established there the Greek Dynasty of Mopsos. This is stated more clearly by G. M. A. HANFMANN to whom ALBRIGHT refers in the quoted section of his article: "The case history of the Philistines, who settled in Palestine, and of the Danauna who apparently formed a state at Karatepe . . . indicate that various invading tribes settled along the invaders' route after their repulse."[2] But both ALBRIGHT and HANFMANN did not take into consideration, or have deliberately by-passed a difficulty which cannot be harmonized with their construction; the presence in this very same spot, two centuries before the migration of the Peoples of the Sea, of a country with the very same name of Danuna, clearly attested in the Amarna letter of Abimilki.

Vl. GEORGIEV,[3] who also defended the hypothesis of the foundation of the Cilician Danuna-Adanawa by the Aegean Danaans early in the XIIth century, attempted to by-pass this difficulty with the reservation that the Danaans and other Aegean tribes allegedly had, even before the great migration, established settlements on the southeastern coast of Asia Minor. But historical and archaeological facts speak against the posibility of Aegean or Greek settlements in Cilicia before the catastrophe of 1200—as is particulary exposed with utmost clarity by HANFMANN himself.

We shall examine later the positive data from the excavations in Cilicia for the reconstruction of the ethnic and cultural relations of its Bronze Age population. In the context of the present section, we will limit ourselves to their negative data, which eliminate the possibility of an Aegean or Greek penetration into that country. Prior to 1375 (according to GARSTANG[4]) or 1365 (according to

[1] XXV, 172.

[2] CCXLV, 140 s.

[3] CXCII, 64-67. But he believed the Danaans to be a *pre*-Greek tribe of Greece. He also postulated that other states of Asia Minor had been established by pre-Greek tribes of the Aegean: Arzawa—by the Argeians ($g > z$), Kizzuwatna or Kizwadna—by the Cretan Cydonians (**Kydwodnes*?). All this is as substantial as the same scholar's ill-fated attempt to decipher the Mycenaean script.

[4] CLXXXIII, 271 (summary of excavations described in CLXXXII).

SCHAEFFER [1]), there were no Mycenaean ceramics at all in the excavated Cilician cities at Mersin (in the West of the Cilician plain) and Tarsus (in its middle part). Then Mycenaean ceramics appear, but only in scarce quantities that cannot be compared with the overflow in contemporary Syria and Palestine of imported Mycenaean ware. The actual finds must be considered as casual imports from Cyprus. Simultaneously, the country which had formerly belonged to the Syrian sphere (from the archaeological point of view), passed under Hittite domination; it became increasingly connected with the Anatolian plateau, and was covered with fortresses of the Hittite type intended to protect it from Mycenaean seamen.[2] Westward from Mersin, and almost up to Rhodes itself, no Mycenaean ware was discovered.[3] HANFMANN supposes, very plausibly, that the merchant sea route from the Aegean followed along the islands up to Rhodes, then to the good harbor of Telmessos, from there straight across the sea to Cyprus, and from Cyprus to the rich cities of Syria, Phoenicia and Palestine. The rocky shores of Pamphylia and Western Cilicia did not attract the Mycenaean merchants, and the fertile Cilician plain was vigilantly guarded by the Hittite vassal states.[4] We do not belong to the fetishists of ceramic data, but here the picture is absolutely clear: from the entire complex of the East Mediterranean countries, it is precisely Lowland Cilicia, the land of the Danunians, that was least of all touched by Mycenaean influence—a thing which would be impossible if there were a Mycenaean base in that area.[5] Until 1375/1365 there were no wares of Mycenaean export at all in Cilicia; yet it was exactly at the same time that Abimilki's information about the land of Danuna was written, and it shows that this kingdom had already existed for some time (it tells of a normal throne change), and was not a recent formation. In one of the next sections of this chapter we will introduce evidence that the letter of

[1] CDL, 274.
[2] CDLI, 34, n. 3; CCXLV, 138; CLXXXIII, 271.
[3] CCXLV, 139; cf. the map, CCLXVIII, 3.
[4] CCXLV, 140.
[5] It is easy to distinguish a native city importing foreign ceramics from an outpost of foreign settlers. Thus, the German excavations of Miletus in 1938 showed that "rather than an Asiatic city importing Mycenaean wares, this was indeed an actual Mycenaean settlement. They could even infer from it that Miletus was first founded by settlers from Crete" (CCCXXXIX, 152 s.). And indeed we know from the Hittite archives that *Millawanda* or *Millawata* (Miletus) belonged to the *Aḫḫiyawā* (CLXXXIV, chapter on Arzawa).

Abimilki is not the only source that proves the existence of the Danuna state in the XIVth century.

It is thus impossible to explain the common name (as well as the similarity of some other elements) of the western and the eastern Danunians by supposing that the Cilician Danuna was a colony or a possession of the Greek Danaans: it already existed under this name in the Bronze Age when there was no trace of any Greek or Aegean penetration—armed or peaceful—into Cilicia.[1]

Were the Danunians true Anatolians?

The scholars who have rejected the Greco-Danaan origin of the Cilician Danunians, as Seton Lloyd, E. Laroche, the Soviet Academician A. I. Tjumenev, have without hesitation proclaimed them "true Anatolians" (Seton Lloyd),[2] "a Hittite tribe speaking the H-H language" (Tjumenev).[3] Whence this certitude? The only extant inscription left by this tribe is written in *two* languages—not only in H-H but in Phoenician as well. This means that the population was at least bilingual, or included two ethnic elements with different languages. Now if one accepts that the basic mass of the population spoke H-H, how did Phoenician penetrate into the land of the Danunians and how did it win an equal position? Was it the language of the ruling class? But the king who left the inscription bore a non-Semitic name of a purely Hittite type—Asitawandas.[4] It is known that H-H inscriptions are spread widely all over North Syria, and are a heritage of the many neo-Hittite principalities which survived there after the destruction of the Hittite Empire in Anatolia. But before the Hittite conquest of the XIVth century [5]

[1] In the light of modern archaeological evidence, it is hardly necessary to add anything to Albright's judgment of a theory which was quite popular about 25-30 years ago: "Sommer's (cdlxix-M.A.) unhappy localization of the *Aḫḫiyawa* in Cilicia is absolutely impossible" (xxv, 167, n. 15). Nor is *Aḫḫiyawā*'s location in Pamphylia any better justified. The prevailing opinion nowadays looks for the great Achaean kingdom which the Hittites admitted as equal to theirs, where it naturally belongs: in Greece, with outposts on the eastern coast of the Aegean (cf. cdxli, 365-370)—as it was correctly felt by Forrer in the early twenties.

[2] See above, p. 9 and n. 5.

[3] cdxcii, 24, 32, 33, n. 4.

[4] Cf. such Hittite royal names as Arnuwandaš, Zidantaš. Those who deny the nasalized pronunciation of the H-H name compare Madduwattaš and the Lydian Alyattes, Sadyattes.

[5] Or, perhaps, before the invasion of the Peoples of the Sea, when some ousted populations of the outlying districts of Anatolia might have resettled in North Syria, as supposed ccxxxvii, 40, 130.

this whole region was predominantly Semitic, with an admixture of Hurrians in the North. Even afterwards, the Hittite element in it was limited to a relatively narrow circle of the upper, ruling estate. It is significant that the Aramaic language has not inherited a single word from the Syrian Hittites (while it borrowed a great number of Akkadian and, through Akkadian, even of Sumerian words). This excludes the possibility of any wide diffusion of the H-H language among the Syrian populations. The Semitism of the region of Hamath in Central Syria, the very heart of the ancient land of Amurru, cannot be doubted; nevertheless its ruler Urḫilina, a contemporary of Shalmaneser III,[1] left inscriptions in the same H-H language as Asitawandas of the Plain of Adana, without even a parallel Canaanite or Aramaic text.[2]

The basic population of the kingdom of Śam'al (Ya'udi), which was contiguous to the Plain of Adana, was also undoubtedly Semitic. It spoke its own W-S dialect, somewhat different from the classical Phoenician and called "Ja'udisch" by J. FRIEDRICH.[3] As we tried to show elsewhere,[4] both names for the state, Śam'al and Yaudi, are old W-S tribal names; the capital of Śam'al, with the same name, is attested as early as the first half of the XVth century.[5] And yet, there too, Hittite hieroglyphics were used in the IXth century for royal inscriptions along with "Ya'udian." [6] The distance from the capital of Śam'al, the modern Zincirli, to the city of Asitawandas, Karatepe, is only 25 miles—surely too insignificant a distance for us to presume a sharp boundary between a Semitic and a Hittite-Anatolian population.[7] Since the king of

[1] Who called him Irḫuleni, CCCXLV, I, § 610.

[2] CCXLV, 134 s.

[3] CLXXX, 154-162. He sees in the pre-Aramaic language of Ya'udi a dialect with special features cognate to Ugaritic. This shows that it was spoken in the country of Ya'udi since far back into the second millennium.

[4] XXXVII, 16 s.

[5] Listed in the North Syrian list of Thutmose III in Karnak, CDLXIII, list I, No. 314: *Ś-m-ỉ-r-w* (to be read *Śa-m-'a-la-wa*, *-wa* being a Hurrian suffix). It was first recognized by W. Max MÜLLER in 1893, accepted CCCXCVI, 124; XXVII, III: A: 22; cf. XXXIX, No. 110. Despite the disregard of this equation in CDLXIII, CCLXXXIII and DXLIX, 342 s. and the negation of its geographical identity with Śam'al-Zincirli by CCL, 147, there can be no reasonable doubt as to it.

[6] CCCXXXIX, 22.

[7] Of course, Karatepe is separated from Zincirli by Mount Amanus; but this frontier is so far from being impenetrable, that B. LANDSBERGER, CCCXII (1948, but written prior to the publication of the Karatepe inscriptions) attributed Karatepe to Śam'al.

the Danunians had composed his record not only in H-H, the traditional, and probably by that time, already dead language of the ruling dynasties of the whole of North Syria (including his own), but in Phoenician as well, this can only signify that Phoenician was spoken by the predominant population of the country.

And indeed, even a first acquaintance with the Phoenician text of the inscription shows clearly that this is not a translation into an alien language. The language, the style, the phrases, the comparisons reveal an organic medium of Canaanite culture which was, according to its principal features, a single whole from Taurus and Amanus in the North to the Red Sea in the South. This was the impression of many highly competent semitologists who had carefully studied the text.[1] DUPONT-SOMMER was from the very beginning more and more inclined to consider the Phoenician text the basic,[2] which was accepted by DUSSAUD.[3] The text is written in a pure Phoenician, according to C. H. GORDON, HONEYMAN, MARCUS and GELB.[4] The masterly translation by DUPONT-SOMER points up the correctness of his characterisation of the Phoenician text: "A thorough literary work . . . a remarkable care for composition. Neither prose, nor poetry . . . a poetical prose, strongly rhythmicized and even the most frequently with parallelism." [5] All these are features which were completely strange to Hittite style; even poetry, adopted from Semitic peoples, was transposed by the Hittite writers into plain prose.[6] The pantheon and the epithets of the gods [7] are also purely Canaanite, with very close parallels in Phoenician, Ugaritic, and Hebrew texts, and the only case—a very normal one—

[1] ALBRIGHT remained practically alone with his assertion that "the Phoenician was translated from hieroglyphic Hittite as shown by its clumsy literalness and awkward syntax," *BASOR* No. 114 (1949), p. 15.

[2] CXXXIV, III, 305.

[3] CL, 186.

[4] CCXXV, 209: "international literary language." CCCLIV, 197: "the purest known Phoenician." CCLIX, 56: no "solecisms or barbarisms of expression; . . . we must consider Azitawadda as accustomed to the use of Phoenician for lapidary purpose" (but modified view in CCLVIII, 37).

[5] CXXXII, 183. "Pure Phoenician," *ibid.*, 182.

[6] CD, 145, speaking of Canaanite myth translated into Hittite (see below, p. 207), remarks that the traditional Canaanite parallelism of members is missing in the Hittite version. The same is true for all Hittite myths and legends, whether borrowed from the Canaanites and Hurrians, or original.

[7] *Bʿl* (Baal), *ʾl qn ʾrṣ* ("El, creator of the earth"), *Ršp ṣprm* ("Rešeph of the bucks"), *Šmš ʿlm* ("Eternal Sun"), *kl dr bn ʾl* ("all the generation of the gods"), *Bʿl šmm* ("Lord of the Heavens").

of a non-Semitic element is the appellation of Baal (or a Baal) by the name of *Krntryš*; this was apparently the special patron deity of the dynasty to which Azitawadd (a Luwian by his name) belonged.[1]

This predominant linguistic, cultural and religious Semitism of the Danunians in the IXth and VIIIth century was not a result of a recent penetration of Phoenician influence, but was rather one of the whole previous history of Eastern Cilicia, a history troubled, but not interrupted, by invasions or conquests by stronger tribes and states. The data of archaeology and of written sources are in agreement, they complement each other, and present a coherent picture of the historical destinies of the country.

During the Middle Bronze Age [2] the Cilician plain was turned entirely towards neighboring Syria, and not towards Anatolia, from which it was tightly separated by the Taurus mountain range. In Tarsus "the archaeological finds, including the monochromous red, brown or black glazed pottery, the painted ceramics and the bronzes, resemble very faithfully the corresponding finds of Middle Ugarit 3 (1750-1600), 2 (1900-1750), and 1 (2100-1900). During this period, Tarsus was very clearly connected with the civilization of Middle Bronze, so brilliant in Syria; the finds present few ties with Central Anatolia . . . and still less with Troy." [3] The same follows from the find of bronzes in Soli-Pompeiopolis which belong, according to Schaeffer, to the period 2200-1900: "Defenitively, the most decisive rapprochements that can be established join the bronzes of Soli to the types which were current at the end of Early Bronze and at the beginning of Middle Bronze in North Syria with Ras Shamra as geographical center and Palestine (Gaza . . . Beisan . . . etc.) as southern limit." [4] The Middle Bronze Age at Mersin "is distinguished by the rarity of connecting links with the plateau of Anatolia. On the other side, points of contact with Syria

[1] Goetze pointed to the fact that *Azitawadd(a)* is the only Luwian name among the East Cilician royal names of the neo-Assyrian epoch; his predecessor *'wrk* (Ass. *Urikki*, whether this is the same person or not), and the IXth century kings *Katê*, *Kirrî* and *Tulli* (so Goetze instead of *Tulka*) bear purely Hurrian names (CXCIX, 53).

[2] Earlier periods are beyond the scope of this study.

[3] CDL, 273 s.

[4] CDL, 276-278. Schaeffer adds that similar bronzes were found in Tarsus, Lycia, Pisidia, and Mysia, i.e. along the old trade route following the coast of Asia Minor, whether on land or on sea; but no bronzes of the type peculiar for Soli were discovered in Central Anatolia.

were obvious, but signs of relations with Cyprus were surprisingly few." [1] Then, after an interruption which is characteristic for the entire Near East, and was apparently caused by great migrations (Hyksos, Cassites, Hurrians, Hittites, Indo-Aryans), since approximately 1500, Late Bronze begins at Tarsus and Mersin, with a distinctive turning-point around 1375-1365. At Tarsus, up to that time, the material remnants retain a chiefly Syro-Palestinian character, analogous to the contemporary strata of Ugarit, Byblos, Hamath, Beit Mirsim, Megiddo, Tell el-Ḥesi, but with a growing influence from Central Anatolia—especially in weapons.[2] At Mersin, before 1375, the pottery had "definite Syrian affinities;" afterwards it "becomes largely monotone, as in the Hittite wares." A fortress of the Hittite type was also built there.[3] At Tarsus many "bullae" —clay labels—appeared with Hittite hieroglyphics, including one with the name of Putuḫepa, wife of the Hittite king Hattušiliš III. Cilicia passed under the rule of the Hittites at the same time as Aleppo, Carchemish and the whole North Syria. A new, Anatolian, population was superimposed over the basic one which had belonged to the Syrian cultural sphere.[4] The invasion of the Peoples of the Sea which destroyed the Hittite Empire, also put an end to the political dependence both of North Syria and of Cilicia on Anatolia, but it did not prevent the Anatolian ruling class (the "Hieroglyphic Hittites") from retaining power for another half millennium. This domination, however, had influenced the primordial language, culture and religion of the native majority hardly more than the former rule of dynasties with Mitannian (Hurrian and Indian) names. Aleppo, a most important cultic center of Adad under the Amorite kingdom of Yamḫad, retained its prominence under the Hittites and the neo-Assyrian kings; [5] at Hamath, under Zakir,

[1] CLXXXIII, 271.

[2] CDL, 274.

[3] CLXXXIII, 271.

[4] Our main source of Cilician onomastica in the second millennium is the names and patronymics of merchants from the port of Ura preserved in documents of early XIIIth century found at Ras Shamra (CCCXCI, 103 ss., 182 ss., 190, 202 s.). The maritime location of Ura, denied CXCIX, 48, n. 7, is established by the Hittite royal letter RŠ 20.212, CCCLXXXVII, 165, cf. already XXIII, 400. Though Ura lay in Western Cilicia, more than half of the 22 extant names are clearly Hurrian, one is Indo-Aryan (*Mi-it-ra*), one is W-S (*Ia-qar-mi*, RŠ 18.20: 4, omitted in CXCIX, 48-50, though his son *Ku-um-ia*-LÚ is included), the other are Luwian or incertain ("a slight Hurrian admixture," CXCIX, 50, is an understatement).

[5] CXXIII, 108; CC, 205; DXLIX, 201; CCCXCIX, 278 s.

the successor of Urḫilina's Hittite dynasty, the ancient specifically Amorite god Iluwer (Ilu-Mer) continued to be worshipped; [1] at Śam'al even kings with non-Semitic names revered Baal-Ḥamman, Hadad, Rekubel and the god of Ḫarran; [2] and in the Danunian country, as we have seen, the pantheon was not different from the common Canaanite. The cataclysms and invasions of Late Bronze and Early Iron have enriched and complicated the culture of North Syria (particularly in the field of art), but they have not caused any essential ruptures in the evolution of the primordial West Semitic civilization of that region.

The Country of Adana and Kizzuwatna

However, a different opinion regarding the ethnic and political conditions of Eastern Cilicia in the Late Bronze Age is widespread in the literature. Since Sidney Smith [3] proved that the kingdom of Kizzuwatna [4] was situated not to the Northeast of the Hittite metropoly, on the Black Sea coast, but to the Southeast, between Central Anatolia and Syria, this large kingdom of the Hittite geo-political complex was located precisely in the region we are pre-occupied with—in Eastern Cilicia. Sidney Smith identified it with the coast of the Gulf of Issus, known in Egyptian sources as Qode, and he still adhered to this opinion in 1949.[5] He was followed by Olmstead,[6] Goetze,[7] Contenau,[8] Gurney,[9] Garstang.[10] If this location is correct, then evidently it is no longer possible for a separate state of Danuna to exist simultaneously in the very same spot.—But is such a location correct? [11]

[1] CDXXXIV, 501; CXXV, 153-158 (cf. pp. 298 s. below).

[2] CDLVI, 98-100; CCCXII, 42, n. 98; CDXXXIV, 500 s.; CXXXI, 24 ss., 30; CCCXXXVI, 440-444.

[3] CDLXVI (1922); CDLXV (1924).

[4] We shall keep, with Goetze, this spelling of the name.

[5] CDLXVIII, map.

[6] CCCXLVII, 223-234.

[7] CCII, map (with extension of Kizzuwatna up to the upper flow of Saros and Pyramos); CCI, map and text.

[8] CIII, 94.

[9] CCXXXVII, 25.

[10] CLXXXIV, x, map 1; 53.

[11] Albright (1948) considered that "Kizzuwadna is Cataonia, not Eastern Cilicia, except in so far as the kings of Cataonia-Kizzuwadna extended their power southward," XXV, 168, n. 19. He did not elaborate, probably because of shortage of space. But in 1961 he "accept(ed) Goetze's definition of Kizzuwatna as roughly including eastern Cilicia and Cataonia," XXIII, 400, though there hardly was a real need for it.

In his monograph on Kizzuwatna, GOETZE proved with the utmost cogency that Kizzuwatna lay to the east of the Antitaurus; its central sanctuary was the city of Kummanni, the classical Comana Cappadociae, which the Hittites also called ^{URU}*Kizzuwatna*. Another important city of Kizzuwatna, Lawazantiya, is localized by GOETZE between Kummanni and the Euphrates.[1] According to his interpretation of a Hittite text,[2] a few of the cities situated beyond the Euphrates which had formerly belonged to the Hurrian kingdom, were bestowed upon Kizzuwatna. Thus, the eastern frontier of Kizzuwatna ran close to or along the upper course of the Euphrates.[3] But then GOETZE, contrary to his previous analysis, tries to prove that the identity of ^{URU}*Kizzuwatna* with ^{URU}*Kummanni* does not necessarily compel us to consider Kummanni the capital of Kizzuwatna, and that the real center of the country could, consequently, have been situated quite a great distance away from that city, in Cilicia. However, all that we know of Hittite practice indicates that whenever they called a country by the name of a city, or vice versa, such a city would invariably be the country's capital. Moreover, it is extremely probable that the very name of Kizzuwatna has been preserved in the *Cataonia* of Hellenistic times—a geographical term covering precisely the southeast of Cappadocia, between the Antitaurus and the upper Euphrates.[4]

In order to prove that Adana and Tarsus were basic age-old cities of Kizzuwatna, and Tarsus even possibly her capital, GOETZE refers to the find at Tarsus of a clay lump ("bulla") with a seal

[1] Because it is in this city that the Hittite royal headquarters during the siege of Uršu were established, and Uršu was situated very close to the upper Euphrates. More about it see p. 31 below.

[2] Treaty between Šuppiluliuma, king of Ḫatti, and Šunaššura, king of Kizzuwatna, to which we shall return many times in our exposition. The relevant sections are reproduced in transliteration and translation in CCI, 36-59.

[3] CCI, 7 ss.

[4] CDXI, X, 2, 2478 s., s.v. *Kataonia*. Derivation of Cataonia from Kizzuwatna: XXV, 168, n. 19; CCLXIV, 160, 187, 190, 312 and especially 276 (without taking into account his etymological speculations). CCI, 81 and n. 338, following HOMMEL and HERZFELD, believes that the name of Kizzuwatna —with a change of suffix—survived in another classical name of an Asianic region: Cappadocia. We can guess that GOETZE saw the evolution approximately thus: *Kizzuwat-na* > *Kizzuwat-uḫa* > *Kidd(u)watu-ḫa* > Persian *Katpatuka* (Iranian shift *w* > *p*) > Gr. *Kappadokia*. If GOETZE is right, this would prove once more that Kizzuwatna was *not* situated in Cilicia, but in a part of Cappadocia.

impression of [m]*Išputaḫšu* LUGAL GAL DUMU *Pariyawâtri*,[1] who is, on the other hand, known as a king of Kizzuwatna and a contemporary of the Hittite king Telepinuš (about 1460 [2]). However, as GOETZE himself explains, "lumps of clay like that bearing the impression of Išputaḫšuš have been excavated in large numbers in Boğazköy, many of which show the impressions of royal seals. It seems that these bullae had been attached to some merchandise and carefully saved after the merchandise had been unpacked. Perhaps they served as evidence to the effect that taxes and fees had been duly delivered." [3] In this case, however, the bullae were kept not by the state, but by the person paying the duty, whoever he was. The merchandise which had been sealed by the bulla of Išputaḫšuš had certainly crossed the territory of Kizzuwatna on its way to Tarsus, and custom-duties must have been payed for its transit—but whether Tarsus, the destination of the merchandise, belonged to Kizzuwatna does not follow from the above with any greater certainty than does Crete's belonging to the Hyksos kingdom necessarily follow from the find at Cnossus of a vase with the name of the Hyksos Pharaoh Ḫiyan.[4]

On the contrary, we have convincing proof that under Telepinuš (and, consequently, under Išputaḫšuš, too) the region of Adana did not belong to Kizzuwatna, but was an independent state. In a text of Telepinuš [5] are listed cities and countries which left Hittite suzerainty: [URU]*Ar-x-ag-ga-aš* [URU]*x-ti-la-aš* [URU]*Gal-ni-ia-aš* KUR[URU]*A-da-ni-ia* KUR[URU]*Ar-za-wi-ya* [URU]*Šal-la-pa-aš* [URU]*Pár-du-wa-ta-aš* [URU]*Aḫ-ḫu-la-aš-ša*. Six of these eight names merely have the determinative "city," and only Adaniya and Arzawiya are called KUR "land." This means that Adaniya was not just a city, but a state, on an equal level with such an important kingdom as Arzawa. Under the same name *māt* [āl]*A-ta-ni-ia*[KI]

[1] CCI, 73.—CCCXXXIX, 154, qualifies this find "the first shred of tangible archaeological evidence to confirm the philological hypothesis that the Cilician plain was included in the territory of that state. No other has since been found, and upon this single object still rests the responsibility and justification for identifying certain anonymous products of Cilician excavations with historical Kizzuwatna."

[2] We follow for the earlier Hittite kings the chronology of CCCLXII, based on the date of 1530 for the capture of Babylon by Muršiliš I (chronology of ALBRIGHT-CORNELIUS).

[3] CCI, 73 s.

[4] Cf. CDLIV, 112, about this and a similar find: "Today such proofs have no efficiency any more."

[5] The tablets from which this document was collated, are listed CCI, 57.

the land of Adana figures—more than a hundred years after Telepinuš—in the treaty of Šuppiluliuma, king of Ḫatti, with Šunaššura, king of Kizzuwatna; no other city mentioned in the treaty is qualified *māt* "land." [1]

According to the demarcation clauses of this treaty, "the land of Ataniya" had to belong to Šunaššura. The foregoing treaty, far from indicating that the region of Adana had always been a part of Kizzuwatna (much less a central one), points instead to the partitioning of newly-annexed territory between contracting parties. We have seen from Abimilki's letter that at about 1365, Danuna, i.e. the region of Adana, was still a separate state and apparently belonged to the Egyptian sphere of influence—if under "Canaan" is to be understood, as in EA 30, this zone of Egyptian suzerainty. Another Amarna letter (EA 53, on which we will dwell at length in the next section of this chapter), states that at the time of Šuppiluliuma's offensive against Syria, Danuna was seeking Egyptian protection along with other North Syrian states which had lost the support of Mitanni. After his victories, Šuppiluliuma made several dynastic and territorial changes in Syria, appointed two of his sons kings of Carchemish and Aleppo, and succeeded at last in persuading Kizzuwatna, which had long been an ally of Mitanni, to conclude peace with Ḫatti "almost on a basis of equality." [2] We have already mentioned that Kizzuwatna received on this occasion a few Hurrian cities of Upper Mesopotamia. The section of the treaty dedicated to Cilicia is to be understood in exactly the same way: Šuppiluliuma kept for himself the western and northwestern parts of Lowland Cilicia, including the strategically important Cilician Gates, while ceding her eastern part to his new ally Šunaššura.[3] The treaty constantly stresses (though GOETZE did not pay attention to it) that the territory is being partitioned and delimited anew:

[1] KBo I: 5, col. IV: 11: 40-66, transliteration and translation CCI, 50 s.—It is hardly necessary to mention that *Ataniya* and *Adaniya* are absolutely the same name, as the Hittites did not distinguish in writing between voiced and voiceless consonants (CLXXVIII, § 21).

[2] CCXXXVII, 30 s. GURNEY's date for the treaty is 1340; since Šuppiluliuma's death is astronomically fixed at 1346 (CIX, 306 s.), this date is at least ten years too low.

[3] On the other hand, Šuppiluliuma concurrently cut off a corridor towards Carchemish through the territory of Kizzuwatna (CLXXXIV, 58) and took away Kummanni (*ibid.*, 57; CCI, 70). It was therefore important to compensate Kizzuwatna in another direction.

"Toward the sea Lamiya belongs to the Sun, Pitura [1] belongs to Šunaššura; they will measure out the territory together and divide it," [2] and this formula is repeated all the time: the areas between Aruna and Pitura, between Šaliya, Zinziluwa and Erimma, between Anamušta and Mount Zabarašna have to be measured out together and divided. In line 52 the demarcation reaches the old frontier (*la-bar-ma-an-na pāṭū ša ki-il-la-li-šu-nu um-ma*); even if Sidney SMITH's [3] translation, "that old boundary, which they have abolished" is not accepted, and one understands, with GOETZE, "since ancient times the boundary between the two (had been) as follows," the sequel, "whatever (is) on the side of the country Ataniya let Šunaššura keep," where *Ataniya* is countervailed by *Ḫatti* (l. 56), still shows that Adana was considered a separate land and that the "old boundary" was that between the Hittite possessions and the land of Adana. Here the boundary follows the river Šamri (it is not known how far), identified with Saros-Seyhan.

Another proof that under the predecessors of Šuppiluliuma Eastern Cilicia did not belong to Kizzuwatna is the description of the military operations of Idri-mi, king of Alalaḫ and southeastern neighbor of Cilicia, against the Hittites during Mitanni's offensive on Anatolia.[4] Kizzuwatna then sided with Mitanni and changed this orientation only after Mitanni's definitive defeat by Šuppilu-

[1] CCI, 58 identifies *Lamiya* with Gr. *Lamos*, city and river on the western border of Lowland Cilicia (mod. Lamas-su), and believes that the treaty thus left all of the Cilician plain to Šunaššura. We equate *Lamiya* with *Lamena(š)* in Quê under Shalmaneser III (CCCXLV, I, § 583), which lay east of Tarsus, since Shalmaneser III, proceeding from the east, conquered Lamena before reaching Tarzi (Tarsus). Thus the frontier established by Šuppiluliuma started at the seashore at some point east of Tarsus, remounted northward to the Cilician gates, and divided the Cilician plain in two roughly equal halves. By the same token, the often repeated equation of Pitura, on the Kizzuwatna side of the border opposite Lamiya, with the site of Mersin west of Tarsus (CLXXXIII, 271; CLXXXIV, 60) is excluded. Besides, the fortress of Mersin was built in pure Hittite style resembling that of the Boğazköy fortifications—so it was the Hittites, not the Kizzuwatnaeans who had constructed it.

[2] KBo I: 5, IV: 40-42 (CCI, 51 s.).

[3] CDLXVI, 45.

[4] The date of Idri-mi is controversial. Sidney SMITH, CDLXVIII, 58-69, located his reign c. from 1414 to 1385; he was followed by XCIV, 43 s.; LXXIV, III, 290; DLV, 119-126. On the other hand, ALBRIGHT, XXIV, 15-20, assigned to Idri-mi a much earlier reign—1480-1450. DIV, 69 and DLII, 5-8 agree with him. By motives stated in XXXIX, we admit for Idri-mi approximately 1510-1480.

liuma.[1] But the cities of the East Cilician coast, captured by Idri-mi on the instructions of his suzerain, the king of Mitanni, are attributed in his inscription to the "land Ḫatte" (l.64 ss.)—this means that they were occupied at that time by the Hittites, and did not belong to friendly pro-Mitannian Kizzuwatna.

Nor can it be deduced from mentioning two well-known Cilician cities, Adana and Tarsus, in one context with Kummanni [2] that Cilicia belonged to Kizzuwatna. The document deals with sacrifices from the cities of Kummanni, Zunnaḫara, Adaniya, Tarša and [Kikk] i-ip-ra (the location of Zunnaḫara and Kikkipra is unknown). Since the text is a Hittite one, it had been composed not only after the passage of a part of Eastern Cilicia to Kizzuwatna, but even after the latter's total absorption by Ḫatti. Moreover, the sequel to the text, in which still other cities of different parts of the Hittite Empire may have been mentioned, is broken off.

Then in a tablet from Alalaḫ,[3] Niqmepa, king of this city, brings a case to the Mitannian king Šaušŝatar against Šunaššura [4] over the town of Alawari. Šunaššura, the namesake of Šuppilluliuma's contemporary, may well have been the latter's ancestor and precursor on the throne of Kizzuwatna, although this is not stated in the tablet. Niqmepa's predecessor Idri-mi concluded a treaty with Pillia of Kizzuwatna about the extradition of runaway slaves.[5] Nevertheless, neither document proves that Kizzuwatna lay in Eastern Cilicia. Treaties about the extradition of fugitives do not necessarily presuppose that the contracting states are contiguous.[6] Then, if it were true for Mukiš and Kizzuwatna, there is ample reason to admit that the territory of Mukiš touched that of Kizzuwatna not in the north-east, but straight in the north, approximately in the neighborhood of Śam'al. The disputed town of Alawari is

[1] ccxxxvii, 30 s.; ciii, 94. Stated in the treaty between Šuppiluliuma and Šunaššura, cf. cci, 36-39.

[2] KUB: xx: 52 (description of some feast), in cci, 54 s. See p. 387 below.

[3] AT 14.

[4] Written: *Sunaššura* and *Saušsatar*.

[5] AT 3 and dlii, 5.

[6] The clause about extradition of fugitives is standard in all Hittite international treaties, i.a. with Ugarit (RŠ 17. 238, text and translation lxxv, 122 s.; cccxci, 107 s.); Amurru (e.g. the one translated cc, 204, § 15**); Egypt (dxlix, 201 and cc, 203). The Hittite royal domain had no common frontier either with Ugarit, or with Amurru, even less so with Egypt; but in the treaty with Duppi-Teššub of Amurru it is explicitly stated that the clause applies to the fugitives that pass the Amurru territory by transit.

to be equated with the classical Aliaria, in the North Syrian region of Cyrrhestica.[1] Besides, we find in another tablet from Alalaḫ of Niqmepa's time [2] an indirect indication that at the end of the XVth century East Cilicia was ruled by a particular prince. In a dispute between Niqmepa and a certain *Ú-ut-ti*,[3] their common overlord, the king of Mitanni, orders the latter not to take toll from the asses belonging to the former until the arrival of the royal arbitrator Artašumara. The name and the chronological position of *Ú-ut-ti* [4] make it very probable that he was the same person as the *Ú-ut-ti* named in a Hittite document [5] as a great landowner in Eastern Cilicia whose estates were confirmed by Talzuš, king of Kizzuwatna, then by Šunaššura and finally by a Hittite king who had replaced the Kizzuwatnaean rulers. The right to raise customs from caravans implies a territorial sovereignty, while the rôle played by Talzuš shows that Eastern Cilicia recognized by that time the control not only of the remote Mitanni, but of the neighboring stronger state of Kizzuwatna as well.

Now the Egyptian sources of the time of the New Kingdom exclude any possibility of identifying Kizzuwatna with Cilicia. The latter, as recognized by Egyptologists, was known to the Egyptians by the name of *Q-d-y* (Qode or Qadi).[6] However, in the

[1] Cf. xxxix, No. 131, and our map I.

[2] AT 108.

[3] This name, normalized by Wiseman as *Utti*, can as well, as the same scholar remarks, be read *Ú-par-ti*. Both forms are found at Nuzu (*Ú-ba-ri-ia*, var. *Ú-pa-ri-ia*, cxci, 165; *Ú-ut-ti-*[*i*]*a*, var. *Ú-te-ia, Ú-ti-ia, ibid.*, 169). *Ú-ba/pa-ri-ia* is probably formed out of the Akkadian loan-word *ubâru* "client, sojourner."

[4] He was a contemporary of Artašumara, successor of Šuttarna on the Mitannian throne. Since Artašumara was not yet king according to this tablet, it must have been written in the reign of Šuttarna in Mitanni, when Tudhaliyaš III, Šuppiluliuma's precursor, reigned in Hatti, and Talzuš, presumably Šunaššura's predecessor, was king of Kizzuwatna.

[5] Bo 4889, transliteration and translation cci, 61-67. In the translation, *Ú-ut-ti* is rendered in the Anatolian style, *Wuttiš*.

[6] According to the Egyptologist H. R. Hall, quoted cdlxvi, 46 s., this word could have an Egyptian etymology, from a root signifying "going round," so that Qode could have meant "the land where one goes round," i.e. the coast of the Gulf of Issus. dxlix, 235, n. 19, explains Qode as "coast of North Syria and of Cilicia," and *ibid.*, 470, n. 6 even as "north Phoenician coast, carrying into Cilicia." But the Egyptian sources knew Qode as a defined region, with even a king of its own; whereas along the coast of North Syria, not to speak of Phoenicia, there lay two more states well known to Egypt: Ugarit and Alalaḫ. Ugarit, as we shall see, is mentioned in one text with Qode, and so are Qode and Alalaḫ in the Annals of Thutmose III

list of the participants of the Hittite coalition with whom Ramses II fought under Qadeš, Kizzuwatna and Qode are mentioned apart from each other and in different parts of the list. The allies and subjects of the Hittite king are clearly subdivided in two groups.[1] First come the Anatolian peoples: *Ḫt* Hittites, *Na-ha-ri-na* Mitanni (not quite in its geographical place, but accorded second place because of its importance and renown of a former great power), *ʾA-ru-ṯa-wi* Arzawa, *Da-ar-d-an-ya* Dardanians, *Ma-śa* Hitt. *Masa*—Mysians or Maeones, *K-š-k-š*[2] Gasgaeans, *Qa-r(a)-qi-ša* Hitt. *Kar(a)kiša* Carians ?, *Ru-ka* Hitt. *Lukka* Lycians, and *Qi-ḏu-wa-d-na* Kizzuwatna. Then the Syrian allies follow: *Ka-r-ka-mu-ša* Carchemish, *ʾA-ku-ri-ta* Ugarit, *Qadi* (Qode) Eastern Cilicia, *Nu-ga-śa* Nuḫašše, *Mu-šu-na-ta* (a city in North Syria[3]), and *Qdš* Qadeš on the Orontes. In another variant of the list,[4] Kizzuwatna and most of the Anatolian allies are omitted, but Qode figures after Carchemish and before Qadeš and Ugarit—again in the complex of Syrian territories. Qode belonged to this complex even under Thutmose III, about 1480: this Pharaoh states in his annals that the king of Qadeš on the Orontes called to his aid the former vassals of the Pharaoh, and also the people of Naharina, Ḫurru, Qode.[5] We have here the same geopolitical situation that recurred much later, in the IXth century, when Eastern Cilicia (Quê) took part in coalitions headed by Damascus.

According to the data of Ramses II, to which the papyrus of Anastasi III should be added with its poetical description of the Hittite king's visit to the residence of Ramses II, Qode (i.e., Eastern

(LXXVII, II, § 512). Neither of them is identified with or included in Qode, and thus nothing but Cilicia remains to fill the notion of Qode in the Egyptian texts.

[1] The Egyptian names are quoted after LXXVII, III, § 309 (the most complete enumeration, cf. the two shorter ones §§ 306 and 312), but vocalized conforming to the rules of ALBRIGHT (some names are quoted XXV, 168 s.), with some modifications due to HELCK (CCL, 205 s.), and with equations as established or suggested by recent research.

[2] Known in Ugarit as *Kškym* (UM 166: 2).—Instead of *Ma-śa* and *K-š-k-š*, the hieroglyphic versions have *Pi-da-śa*, Hitt. *Pidasa*, and *ʾAr-wan-na*, Hitt. *Arawanna*, two Anatolian peoples of disputed location.

[3] Appears as *Mu-šu-ni* in the Alalaḫ Tablets and as *Mu-šu-wa* in the list of Thutmose III (No. 282); probably became a separate principality after the Hittite conquest and dismemberment of the territorial complex under the rule of Alalaḫ; cf. XXXIX, No. 94.

[4] LXXVII, III, § 306.

[5] LXXVII, II, § 420; DXLIX, 235.

Cilicia, the land of Danuna) was still in the XIIIth century a particular state with its own king. This can mean either that after the annexation of Kizzuwatna by the successors of Šuppiluliuma the autonomy of Eastern Cilicia was restored (perhaps with a Hittite henchman on her head), or that even the treaty of Šuppiluliuma with Šunaššura did not grant to Kizzuwatna the full absorption of the land of Adana, but only the overlordship of it (which she might have exercized to some degree even earlier).

Finally, at the end of our discussion of the problem of Kizzuwatna's location, we come to a piece of evidence that seems completely to disprove our objections against the identification of Kizzuwatna with Eastern Cilicia. This is the fourth edition of the annals of Shalmaneser III, found in Aššur and published by Fuad SAFAR.[1] This king's first expedition to Eastern Cilicia (Qauâ, Qauê) in his twentieth year of reign is described there with more detail than in any of the previously known versions of the annals. He declares that after crossing Mount Amanus along with the contingents of subject North Syrian kings, he conquered the cities of Kate, king of Qauâ: ^āl^*Lu-sa-an-da,* ^āl^*A-bar-na-ni* and ^āl^*Ki-su-at-ni* (IV, 22-34, esp. 26-27). Julius LEWY immediately[2] identified one of these three names with the well-known city of *La-wa-za-an-ti-ia* in Kizzuwatna, and another one with Kizzuwatna itself. No wonder that he found in this text a strong support for his own geographical theories, as well as for the more widely shared location of Kizzuwatna on the shore of Eastern Cilicia.

There can be no doubt that *Lusanda* and *Kisuatni* actually derive from *Lawazantiya* and *Kizzuwatna*. But the documentary evidence cited above, and considerations which will be revealed now do not allow us to accept the extreme conclusions brought out from the new Shalmaneser III text. The ^URU^*Kizzuwatna* of the Hittite epoch could not possibly be situated in Quê, just beyond the Amanus, since that city was clearly identical with Kummanni (Comana Cappadocica), far outside the boundaries of Quê, from which it was separated in neo-Assyrian times by the wide domains of Tabal.[3] The site of Lawazantiya, on the other hand, cannot be detached from that of Uršu with which Hittite texts put it together geographically.[4] Of course, Julius LEWY remains faithful to the identi-

[1] CDXXXVIII, esp. 12, 19 (col. IV: 22-34).
[2] CCCXXXIII, 290 ss. [3] Cf. CCCLXXIX, map.
[4] KBo I: 11. Cf. CCXXXVII, 178 s. Lawazantiya is identical with Luḫuzan-

fication of Uršu with ancient Rhosos, modern ʿArsûz on the Gulf of Issos.[1] But all data available speak against it. In the treaty with Šunaššura, Uršu (Urušša) is connected with Ḫurri, in another treaty—with Waššukani (the capital of Mitanni) and Išmirik.[2] In the story of the siege of Uršu, that city "has contacts with the Hurrian State, the city of Aleppo, and the town of Zaruar, while the forces of Carchemish are keeping watch on a mountain overlooking Uršu". [3] The most precise data on the situation of Uršu are given by the letters of Mari.[4] They prove that Uršu lay to the north of Carchemish, northwest from the Euphrates, in the southern part of Melitene.[5] This region in neo-Assyrian times did not belong to Quê, either, but was a part of Kummuḫu, and the two states of Śamʾal and Gurgum were in between.[6] But the third city of Quê cited by Shalmaneser III, Abarnani, must indeed have been lying close to the Syro-Cilician border: we identify it with *i-b-r-n-n*, already listed by Thutmose III in his great Karnak list together with many localities which we know as having belonged to Alalaḫ.[7]

All these facts cannot be harmonized, and the only way out is to presume that Kisuatni and Lusanda of neo-Assyrian times were not the same cities as their name-sakes in Hittite imperial time. Cases of homonymy and transfer of city names are not uncommon in Asia Minor.[8] It is known that in addition to Comana Cappadocica, a

tiya (CCI, 72) which was the headquarters of the Hittite king during the siege of Uršu (middle of the XVIth century).

[1] DXVIII, 9; CXC, 84; other references CCI, 43, n. 170.

[2] KBo I: 5, IV: 5-10 (CCI, 41 s.); KUB XXIII: 68 (CCI, 43 ss.); Išmirik is located by CCI, 46 ss. to the north-west of Ḫarran, perhaps in modern Severek.

[3] CLXXXIV, 55 s.

[4] Especially XXXV, II, No. 131; I, No. 1. Cf. CLXXXIV, 55 s.; CCCX, 252 s.

[5] LXVIII, 25 s., followed by CCIV, 70, and CCCV, 253.

[6] CCCLXXIX, map.

[7] CDLXIII, list I: 287; XXXIX, No. 98. There also existed a city mentioned as *Abarnium* in the Cappadocian tablets (CXC, 66 s.) and as *Abrania* in the Annals of Tiglathpileser III (CLXVII, 86), and identified by both authors with the Byzantine Abarne, modern Cermük, near the uppermost flow of the Euphrates; but it lay out of reach of Thutmose III.

[8] GOETZE, instead of using the new Assyrian text for strengthening his equation of Kizzuwatna with Eastern Cilicia, concluded about the location of Lusanda, Abarnani and Kisuatni: "I would assume that the mentioned places are on the road that leads from Marʿash northward to Kayseri" (CXCIX, 51, n. 19). A glance on the map shows that Kisuatni would then fall together with the ^{URU}*Kizzuwatna* of the Hittite age, i.e. with Kummanni. This would have been an excellent solution, eliminating the necessity to assume a homonymy, and it would only require to postulate that the territory

famous shrine in the Greco-Roman times, there was another sacral city of the same cult, also called Comana, but situated far away, in Pontus; and the Ancients knew that Comana Pontica was founded by migrants from Comana Cappadocica.[1] Both Kummanni (Comana) and Lawazantiya were important cultic centers in the IId millennium. Is it not possible to suppose that the rulers or the sacerdocy of those two cities had founded subsidiary shrines in two cities of Eastern Cilicia as well, and transferred to them the traditional venerable names of the original sacral centers? This could have happened either in the period of the Kizzuwatna rule in the eastern part of the land of Adana (second half of the XIVth century), or after the invasion of the Peoples of the Sea, when considerable masses of inhabitants of Kizzuwatna and southeastern Anatolia were ousted from their homes and took refuge in North Syria.[2] Those Cilician cities, rebaptized by the newcomers, could very well have kept their old names among the native population and thus be identical with some others of the attested Cilician localities.

Dunanat-Dunanapa and Danuna

We have seen that in the XVth-XIVth centuries the Hittites called Eastern Cilicia "land of Adaniya," the Phoenicians (Abimilki) called it Danuna (just like in Azitawadd's bilingual inscription, seven or eight centuries later), and the Egyptians had their own name for it—Qode (in the new-Assyrian epoch, too, the country was known in more remote regions as Quê). Up to now the name of Danuna appeared only in one place—in the letter of Abimilki, king of Tyre. Now we shall discuss two other references, contemporary with that of Abimilki, to a country with a very similar name, which, as can be presumed, applied to the same land.

In the Amarna letter EA 53, written to the Pharaoh by Akkizzi, king of Qaṭna in Middle Syria, the author complains of the pressure of the Hittite king who requires his surrender, and of the Hittite

of Quê in the IXth century extended to the upper flow of Saros and Pyramos. But topographically it is very difficult to be accepted. Shalmaneser III started by crossing Mount Amanus (IV: 24)—but this ridge does not bar the road from Marʿash (Marqas) northward; he conquered, in a campaign which Goetze himself recognizes as a short one, just three cities and reached the sea (IV: 32-33); this shows that the direction of his march was from the Amanus Gates toward the south. [Lusanda-Lawazantiya appears as *Lwsnd* in RŠ 18.40 (*PRU* V, No. 63): 10.]

[1] CCI, 17.

[2] Cf. p. 17, n. 5 above.

supporter Aiṭugama of Kinza (Qadeš on the Orontes), requests military support from Egypt and declares: "O my lord, even as I bear love unto the king my lord, so also do the king of Nuḫašši, the king of Nii, the king of Zinzar and the king of Tunanat. Verily all these kings belong to the party of my lord, are vassals of thine" (ll.40-44). The location of Tunanat is unknown, but MERCER (*ad loc.*) has suggested in passing, that the ^{māt} *Tu-na-na-at*, named in l. 43, might be identical with ^{māt} *Da-nu-na* of EA 151 : 52. The similarity becomes still more striking if the cuneiform sign No. 58 be read not as *tu*, as did KNUDTZON, followed by MERCER, but *dú*, as this sign could be read in Amarna letters and the contemporary Boğazköy documents.[1] The ending *-at* does not present any difficulty. It is frequently met in the second millennium in personal and geographical names of both Hurrian and Semitic origin which can also be observed without it.[2] The most striking example for our topic is $^{\bar{a}l}$*A-da-na-at*^{KI}, as the capital of the Danuna country (or some namesake of it) is named in an Alalaḫ tablet.[3]

Hesitations in pronouncing vowels in personal and geographical names are a general phenomenon in the Amarna Age, with frequent tendency to change the vocalic pattern of the *qaṭala* or *qaṭula* type into the *quṭala* pattern, and in general to introduce *u* in the place of other vowels.[4] In particular, the vocalic pattern *quṭala/u* (*u-a-a/u*) is characteristic for Ugarit; there, in as far as the presence of the vocalized aleph or of an Akkadian transcription allows us to judge, the vowel *u* often stood in first place, where Hebrew has *a*.[5] Names of the vocalic pattern *u-a-a/u* which sometimes had parallel forms of a different model were also very frequent.[6]

[1] CCCVII, No. 58.

[2] CCCXXXIII, 418: "*Eluḫu/at* and other Hurrian toponyms, anthroponyms and divine names terminating in *-t* alternated with by-forms not provided with the *-t* affix," and more examples *ibid.*, 395. For Semitic toponyms in *-at*, cf. *Ma-aṣ-bat* EA 69: 21 (so corrected by ALBRIGHT instead of the former reading *Ku-aṣ-bat*, cf. CCLX, 78), and the Ugaritic towns: *Ba-aq-at* (*Bqʿt*), *Înu-qáp-at* (*ʿnqpat*), *Ma-ṣi-bat*, *Mrat*.

[3] AT 8: 35, according to DLII, index (the number of the tablet must be wrong, for nothing similar is found in the corresponding line of the autography).

[4] In the Amarna tablets the following vocalic variants of geographical names occur: *Gadašuna/Guddašuna*; *Tušulti/Tušalti*; *Dimašqa/Dumašqa*; of personal names: *Etakamma/Aiṭugama* (etc.); *Paḫura/Piḫura/Puḫuru*; *Zitatna/Zatatna/Šutatna*; *Šaratum/Zurata*.

[5] E.g., Ugar. *updt* = Heb. *ʾaphudôt*; Ugar. *šu-la-mu* = Heb. *šālôm*; Ugar. *ulp* = Heb, *'allūph*, etc.

[6] The town-names *Ḫapatawa/Ḫubata(-u)/Ḫuppati*, *Gulbata*, *Šubani*, etc; the personal names *Aḫimana/Aḫimunu*, *Amatarunu/Amutaruna*, *Ḫuraṣana*,

The identification of ^{māt}*Dú-na-na-at* with ^{māt}*Da-nu-na*, extremely plausible from the linguistic point of view, is even more so from that of geopolitics. The anti-Hittite coalition, the formation of which is described in Akkizzi's letter, tried to resist Šuppiluliuma and sought help from Egypt instead of their former overlord Mitanni [1] which now had lost its importance. The king of Qaṭna, an old-time vassal of the Pharaoh, was probably the intermediary between the Northerners and the Egyptian court.[2] The coalition included, besides those cited by Akkizi (EA 53) Nuḫašše, Nii, Zinzar, Dunanat, and Qaṭna, also Mukiš (Alalaḫ), whose king Itur-Addu is known to have been defeated and deposed by Šuppiluliuma.[3] Dunanat (which we understand to be Eastern Cilicia) was contiguous to Mukiš which in its turn bordered, in the east, Nuḫašše and Nii, and in the south, Zinzar in the middle Orontes valley, which met Qaṭna farther to the south; the coalition thus formed a continuous territorial bloc. Since the letter of Akkizzi (EA 53) is roughly contemporary with that of Abimilki [4] (EA 151), it is possible to deduce that the acceptance of an Egyptian protectorate by Dunanat-Danuna induced Abimilki to include it within the limits of Canaan—a term which in the political geography of that time applied to the whole of the Syro-Palestinian dominions of Egypt.[5] It is also quite understandable why, after Šuppiluliuma's victory over his Syrian enemies, Danuna (the land of Adania) was divided between Ḫatti and Kizzuwatna.[6]

The country of *Dunanapa*, listed in a Hittite religious text,[7] is obviously identical with Dunanat. This Hittite text is an evocation to Cedar-gods in different countries that are divided in two main groups. The second group starts with the great powers of that

Gudarana, *Qutana* and many others, mostly Semitic. The Heb.-Phoen. *ḥarûṣ* "gold," compared to Akk. *ḫurâṣu*, is an example of many similar correspondences, where the second vowel retains its quantity, but interchanges its quality with the first vowel.

[1] XCIV, 43; CCCXCI, 32 ss.

[2] DLV, 130.

[3] CCCXCI, 32.

[4] CCLXXXVIIa, 45.

[5] Cf. n. 22 above; CCCLVII, 115 s.

[6] Exactly in the same way, the territory of another vanquished participant of the anti-Hittite coalition, Mukiš with its dependencies, was partitioned by Šuppiluliuma between the newly established kingdom of Aleppo, ruled by his son Telepinuš, and the Hittite ally, king Niqmad II of Ugarit (CCCXCI, 14 ss., 63 ss.).

[7] KUB XV: 34 and duplicates KUB XV: 33a; 33b; 38. Transl. CC, 351 ss.

time: Assyria, Babylon, Šanḫar (Šinʿar, the rest of Babylonia), Egypt, Alašia (Cyprus), and continues with the Anatolian countries in the direction from east to west. The first group includes the following North Mesopotamian and Syrian countries in the order: Mitanni, Kinza (Qadeš on the Orontes), Tunip, Ugarit, Zinzira,[1] Dunanapa, Idarukatta,[2] Gatanna,[3] Alalḫa, Kinnaḫḫi (Canaan), Amurru, Sidon, Tyre, Nuḫašši, Ugulzit,[4] Arrapḫa,[5] Zunzurḫi. We do not understand the relation between the forms *Dunanat* and *Dunanapa* in the same way as E. FORRER,[6] who has proposed to read in EA 53,43 *Tu-na-na-ab*. The reading *àb, àp* for the cuneiform sign No. 145 (*ad, aṭ, at*) existed only in the neo-Assyrian syllabary,[7] but cannot be presumed for the Amarna Age. We see in the ending *-pa* a frequent suffix of the Hurrian toponymics [8] which has replaced the Semitic feminine ending *-at*.

We have no grounds to suppose that Dunanat-Dunanapa was not Eastern Cilicia (Danuna), but an unknown country somewhere in Middle Syria, as it was possible to think before the discovery of the Karatepe inscription.[9] The political geography of the plain of Orontes and of the regions to the north and to the east of it hardly entitle us to postulate in that area the presence of another quite sizable state besides Qadeš, Qaṭna, Zinzar, Ugarit, Tunip, Alalaḫ, and Nuḫašše, not to speak of Amurru which had large possessions in this very region. There simply was no room for another state. It would be extremely strange if the existence of such a city-state in northern or middle Syria had left no trace

[1] = Zinzar on the Orontes; Zunzurḫi at the end of the list refers to Zuzzura in the former kingdom of Alalaḫ (AT 78: 5), Ṯunḏura of Thutmose III's list (No. 173), modern Zinǧar on the railroad from Aleppo to Homs (cf. XXXIX, No. 39). [2] Unidentified.

[3] Doubtless identical with Qaṭna (spelled Gatana in Old Babylonian texts, CDXXVI, III, 151).

[4] Or Ukulzat (CC, 318), capital of a vassal principality, established by Šuppiluliuma in a part of Nuhašše (CCLXXXVIIa, 44), appears as *Ú-ul-za-at* at Alalaḫ (XXXIX, No. 109).

[5] Most probably, not the city-state to the east of Tigris, but the North Syrian city later known as Arpad (CDLXVIII, 55; XXXIX, No. 114).

[6] CDXXVI, II, 239; followed by CCL, 183. [7] CCCVII, No. 145.

[8] Cf. in the kingdom of Alalaḫ: Ḫazinipa, Iatḫapa, Ippa, Iripa, Kappa, Qa-ri/tal-la-pa, Ṣinupa (DLII, index); in Hittite texts quoted in CCI: Ikkašipa (64 s.), Šallapa (57 and nn. 48 and 220); Zazlippa (44 ss., 72); Zizzilipa (72); quoted in CC: Ḫinašapa, Katapa, Taḫupa (205); Zalpa (CCXXXVII, 73, 179); the well-known Tušpa in Urartu; Ullaba in southern Armenia (CCCXCIX, 283); *Ḥlbbh* in Panamuwa's inscription (CCCXXXVI, 441).

[9] CDXXVI, II, 239.

either in the Egyptian and Assyrian topographical data or in the onomastics of the Hellenistic and Arab times. On the contrary, its identification with the land of Danuna (Adaniya) settles all questions. It is significant—at least in the absence of any negative argument—that the land of Adaniya, although well known to the Hittites, is not mentioned in the quoted text along with Dunanapa, which would have proved that they were indeed two different countries.

Thus, the information about Dunanat-Dunanapa fully harmonizes with what we have said above on the geopolitical and cultural attitude of Eastern Cilicia—her face toward Syria, her back toward Anatolia. According to the testimony of Akkizzi, Dunanat was hostile to the Hittites, and an ally of the Syrian Semitic states. The Hittite evocation to the Cedar-gods excludes Dunanapa from the complex of the Anatolian countries and includes her in the group of Syrian states. In the same way the above quoted Egyptian sources classify Qode: reckoning her among the Syrian territories and stating that as early as the first half of the XVth century she had been politically connected with the Canaanite states of the Orontes plain.—This same situation recurred, according to the Amarna letters, a century later and, according to Shalmaneser III and Zakir of Hamath, obtained again in the IXth-VIIIth centuries. Such constancy of foreign policy for the space of so many centuries could not have been merely fortuitous, but must have been the result of a fundamental geographic, economic and cultural unity between Eastern Cilicia and Syria.

Let us now briefly recapitulate the chronological milestones we have surmounted in the course of our preceding inquiry:

XVIIth century, the epoch of Amorite states in Syria and Mesopotamia: the city of *Adanat* is attested in a tablet from the neighboring Alalaḫ.

C. 1500 (Idri-mi): Eastern Cilicia is occupied by the Hittites, but attacked by Alalaḫ in behalf of Mitanni.

1482 (Thutmose III): Eastern Cilicia (Qode) is again under Mitannian overlordship; its contingent participates in the Mitannian army under Megiddo.

C. 1470 (Thutmose III): after the Egyptian conquest of North Syria, Qode pays tribute to the Pharaoh.[1]

[1] "Each of the Qode among them bore the tribute southward," LXXVIII, II, § 434.

C. 1460 (Telepinuš): the land of Adaniya is a separate state which resists the Hittite power.

C. 1365 (Akizzi): Dunanat joins the anti-Hittite coalition of Syrian states, and seeks protection of Egypt.

C. 1365 (Abimilki): Danuna is still independent, is reckoned as part of Canaan.

After 1365: Hittite occupation; wide penetration of Hittite ceramics and architecture.[1] Eastern Cilicia is divided between Ḫatti and Kizzuwatna.

1299 (Ramses II): Qode apparently restored as a Hittite vassal state; the Qode contingent in the battle of Qadeš listed among the Syrians.

C. 1260 (Ramses II): Qode ruled by a king, subject to Ḫatti.

C. 1200 (Ramses III): invasion and devastation of Eastern Cilicia, along with Asia Minor and Syria, by the Peoples of the Sea (confirmed by archaeological data).

After several "dark ages," the country of the Danunians (also known as Quê) emerges again as a typical North Syrian Hurro-Semitic state under neo-Hittite influence; it gravitates to the South Syrian coalition headed by Damascus.

Evidence of Early Cilician Toponymics

Proofs of the presence of an important Semitic element in the country of the Danunians are not limited to the language and pantheon of the Karatepe inscription. One finds them in large quantity in the East Cilician toponymics of the neo-Assyrian time and of the second millennium. In like manner to the other historical data, the toponymics show the mixed character of the East Cilician population. Many names of localities bear Hurrian features. But the multiplicity of Semitic toponyms shows that the Semitic

[1] Why was Eastern Cilicia conquered by Šuppiluliuma so late, after many victories in Syria, though she lay so close to the basic territory of Ḫatti? This is explained by geographical conditions. It was absolutely impossible to use the famous Cilician Gates in the Taurus if they were guarded by a hostile force. Two other passes from Central Anatolia to Cilicia were still less passable. See Xenophon, *Anabasis* I: II: 21, and geographical commentaries to this place, quoted CCCLII, 253 s. The Hittites used another route to Syria—through Kummanni to the upper flow of the Euphrates and to Carchemish (CLXXXIV, 53). Only after the conquest of Alalaḫ, when much easier roads through the Amanus were opened to Eastern Cilicia, was this country subdued by the Hittites.

population was numerous and had firmly taken root in the country.[1]

Let us begin with the epoch which is closer to the time of the Karatepe inscription. In this inscription a city named *p'r* is mentioned in the Phoenician text as the royal capital of the Plain of Adana. *P'r* corresponds to the Assyrian transcription *Paḫri*.[2] Isidore Lévy [3] identified it with the Greek *Pagrai*, modern Bağras in the Amanus; Bossert, on the other hand, with modern Misis, classical Mopsuhestia, situated near a mountain which was known to the Greeks as *Pagrika orê*.[4] It follows from these transcriptions that the guttural sound rendered by ayin in the Phoenician version of the name, was actually a ghayin (ġ). From Num. 23: 28 we know a locality *Baᶜal Peᶜôr* in southern Transjordan whose name is written in the same way as the Cilician *P'r* and where LXX also heard a ghayin, rendering it by *Beelphegor*.

The name *'dn*, preserved up to this day as Adana, is also Semitic and derives from *'adân* "lord" (which became in South Canaanite, including Hebrew, as a result of the shift *â* > *ô*, *'ādôn*), a frequent divine title, especially well known by the Greco-Phoenician Adonis and the Biblical *'ādôn*, *'ădōnāy*, applied to Yahwe. According to Stephanos of Byzantium, the eponymous founder of the city, Adanos, was a son of Uranos and Gê [5]—in other words a deity, naming cities after their patron deities being extremely widespread in the Semitic, and particularly in the W-S world.[6] That the inhabitants of Adana themselves felt the significance of their city's name in just this way, derives from another detail of Adanos's

[1] It should be supposed, in addition to everything else, that the Greeks had some reason, based on acquaintance with both peoples, when they declared Cilix a brother of Phoenix in their mythical genealogies.

[2] See p. 2, n. 4 above.

[3] CCCXXVIII, 105.

[4] LXXIV, III, 291.

[5] CDXXXIII, I, 66. It should not been thought that the presence of Uranos is proof of a late Hellenistic composition. According to CL, 187, Baᶜal-Šamêm, the "Sky-Lord," of the Karatepe inscription and other Syrian texts, is a separate deity, the personification of the sky, corresponding to Uranos of Philo's Phoenician theogony. Philo is confirmed by as ancient a document as the Hurrian Kumarbi myth (CCXL). There in a very old and precise testimony about the worship of the Sky as the god ᵈ*Šamû* as early as 1500 and as close to Karatepe as Alalaḫ (inscr. of Idri-mi, 1. 93: CDLXVIII, 22 s., 90).

[6] There is no need to enumerate such names. Adana or Adanat—i.e., the city of (god) Adân—should be compared with the Palestinian city Baᶜalā (Jos. 15: 9) or Baᶜalat (I Kings 9: 18). *Adân* and *Baᶜal* are semantically identical.

genealogy, as reported by Stephanos of Byzantium: he was the brother of Saros, the eponym of the river on whose banks Adana stands; this river was also known to the Greeks as *Koiranos*.[1] *Saros* (W-S *śar* "prince", Akk. *šarru* "king") is a good *pendant* to Adanos (W-S *'adân* "lord"), and one had to be a Semite to translate *śar* "prince" by the equivalent Greek (ultimately Anatolian [2]) title *koiranos*, even if this interpretation of the river's name was no more than popular etymology and it actually derived from another (but equally Semitic) root. The H-H form *Adanawa*, signifying "that of Adanas," [3] also shows quite clearly that *'Adân* was understood as a personal name.

We may also, with sufficient ground, consider Semitic the name of another large city—Tarsus. In Assyrian this name was *Tarzi*,[4] in Aramaic (e.g. on coins of the Achaemenid period) *Trz*.[5] In Arabic, the root *taraza* signifies "to be hard"—a fitting name for a fortress. The form *Tarzi* also coincides with Heb. *tirzā* (original reading **tarzā*), a kind of a tree (stone-oak?) Isaiah 44: 14. Naming cities after trees was very common in the W-S world.[6] True, the Hittite name of Tarsus was *Tarša*,[7] but the confusion of *z/ṣ/š* is in general characteristic for Hittite and Hurrianized Syrian cuneiforms of the second millennium,[8] and the Assyrian-Aramaic transcription correctly reproduces the original form of the name.

Two other names of Cilician strongholds, cited by Shalmaneser III, *Ta-na-kun* and *Ti-mu-ur*,[9] look Hurrian. In the first, we probably have the Hurrian roots *tan(a)* "to make" [10] and *kun/kunni*,[11]

[1] LXV, I, 178.

[2] Hitt. *kuiru̯ana* "sovereign, independent" (CLXIX, *s.v.*), applied to foreign rulers not admitted as equal by the king of Ḫatti.

[3] See p. 12 and n. 5 above.

[4] CCCXLV, I, § 583; II, § 286.

[5] CDXI, IV-A, 2, 2417. [A town *Trzy* lay near Ugarit, *PRU V*, No. 118:7]

[6] Cf. in the Bible: *'Êlôn* "oak, terebinth" Josh. 19: 43; *'Êlîm* (same plur.) Ex. 15: 27; *Tāmār* "palm" Ez. 47: 19; I Kings 9: 18; *Ta'ănat Šilô* "fig-tree of Shiloh" Josh. 16: 6; *Lûz* "almond-tree" Gen. 28: 19; Judg. 1: 23, 26; *Ritmā* "juniper" Num. 33: 18; *Rimmôn* "pomegranate-tree" Josh. 19: 7; Zech. 14: 10 and Josh. 19: 13; *Tappuaḥ* "apple-tree" Josh. 16: 8.

[7] See p. 27 above.

[8] Cf. in EA: Qadeš on the Orontes is named 1) *Ki-id-ši/Ki-id-ša*, 2) *Ki-in-za/Gi-iz-za*; *Ul-la-za/Ul-la-àš-za/Ul-la-áš-še*. The land called by the Hittites *Alše* or *Alziya* was always called *Alzi* by the Assyrians (CDXXVI, I, 88 s.); the Hittites made *Elkuniřša* out of the W-S *'El qônē 'arṣa* (see p. 207 below); and in Alalaḫ the sounds *z/ṣ/š* were interchangeable in writing (DLII, 19 s.)

[9] CCCXLV, I, § 582, 583.

[10] CDLXXIII, 83; CXCI, 262.

[11] CXCI, 229.

which we consider a loan-word from the Akkadian *kunnu* "to establish, to fortify." The second appears in the Nuzu name *Ar-ti-mu-ri.*[1] *Lamena*, captured by the same Assyrian king, is the same as *Lamiya* of the Hittite delimitation treaty; [2] it probably owes its name (along with other Cilician toponyms beginning with *Lam-*) to the Sumerian goddess *Lama* who "knew a great favor in the art of Cappadocia, Mitanni, Syria, Phoenicia during the whole second millennium." [3]

Turning to the evidence of the second millennium, we find, as mentioned, *Adanat* (Adana) as early as the XVIIth century. Then seven toponyms are cited by king Idri-mi of Alalaḫ as belonging to localities situated north of his own kingdom, which were by then occupied by the Hittites and which he plundered in a short raid.[4] This geopolitical conditions can only apply to a part of Eastern Cilicia immediately beyond the Amanus gates.[5] Those are:

1) *Pa-aš-ša-ḫe*—from Akk. *pašâḫu* "to be or to become quiet, to have peace, to be healed." The element *pašaḫ* appears in Hurrian names from Nuzu,[6] but it is certainly another of the many Akkadian name-forming elements borrowed by the Hurrian onomastica. The (haplographic) ending *-ḫe* is Hurrian.

2) *Da-ma-ru-ut-re'i* (SÌB)—appears in Thutmose III's North Syrian list (No. 222) as *Ka-ra-ta-m-ru-ta*, where *ka-ra* corresponds to Idri-mi's definition of the seven cities as GUR_7 = *karû*, for *kâru* "wall, embankment." [7] This is a clearly Semitic toponym. Sidney Smith derived it possibly from Arabic *damara* "to pass the night watching." [8] *Dmrn* occurs in Ugaritic, perhaps as a qualificative of Baal, reminding Philo's *Demarus*.[9] Cf. also the Phoenician river *Damuras* (Polyb. V: 68), now Nahr-Damur.[10]

[1] *Ibid.*, 35, 267.

[2] Cf. p. 26, n. 1 above.

[3] CDLXXVI, 84.

[4] CDLXVIII, 18-21, ll. 64-77a.

[5] Thus CDLXVIII, 67 ss., though all of the seven cities were not necessarily harbors, as he puts it; Idri-mi does not mention ships in describing his campaign.

[6] CXCI, 243.

[7] Cf. XXXIX, No. 69. For GUR_7, cf. CDLXVIII, 102, though *kâru* is there taken in its other sense "haven, port."

[8] CDLXVIII, 80. Arab. *damara* has the more common meaning "to destroy, to be destroyed."

[9] IIIa, No. 762.

[10] CCCLXXXIV, I, 661. Cf. also *Tadmôr* (Palmyra).

3) *Ḫu-luḫ-ḫa-an* — from Akk. *ḫuluḫḫu,* a mineral ("melted lead"), [1] with the toponymic suffix — *ân,* common in placenames of Amorite North Mesopotamia and North Syria.

4) *Zi-si*—Sidney SMITH identified it with Arabic *Sis,* cuneiform *Sizû,* known as early as the time of the Cappadocian tablets and then in the VIIth century,[2] the Byzantine *Sision* in Eastern Cilicia, between Anazarbus and the Taurus.[3] There is no reason to transfer it, with Sidney SMITH, to the lower flow of the Pyramus. This city was the farthest point of Idri-mi's advance to the north-west, and the three previous localities must accordingly be located between the Amanic Gates and Sision. Thence Idri-mi turned sharp to the south. If the common prototype of *Zi-si* and *Si-zu-u* is to be restored as **Zizu,* it may be Semitic (root *zwz,* Akk. *zâzu* "to erect, to raise").

5) *I-e*—Heb. *'î* "island" or (Is. 20: 6) "coast-land." It must consequently be located on the coast of the Gulf of Issus. Modern Ayas, situated on a narrow peninsula, may be considered for this site; its Hellenistic name *Aigai* "sea-shore" may have been a translation of *I-e.*[4]

6) *U-lu-zi*—bears a name very similar to that of the well-known North Phoenician city of *Ullaza* (mentioned many times in the Annals of Thutmose III and in the Amarna tablets), but can in no way be identified with it (as suggested by Sidney SMITH).

7) *Za/Ṣa-ru-na*—a typical W-S toponym both by the ending (cf. *Aialuna, Burquna, Ṣiduna* etc.) and the root (*ṣar* "narrow"). The name, expressing the idea of "narrows," "gorge," or "defile," suggests its location at the Syrian Gates, the strategic pass between Mount Amanus and the sea.[5] The place of Ṣaruna at the end of Idri-mi's enumeration agrees with this location: the king of Alalaḫ, having entered Eastern Cilicia through the Amanic Gates, returned home by the southern route through the Syrian Gates.

Thus the land to the east of Mount Amanus possessed, about 1500, cities with Akkadian, Hurro-Akkadian and, mostly, W-S names. The already quoted treaty of friendship and demarcation between

[1] LXXXLV, VI, 232. Cf. p. 387 below.

[2] CDLXVIII, 78; CCCXLV, II, § 513 (*Sizzû*), § 528 (*Sizû*). The first part of Idri-mi's itinerary may thus be traced roughly thus: Amanic Gates—Hierapolis Castabala—Anazarbus—Sis.

[3] CCCLXXIX, map.

[4] There even exists an islet near Ayas with ruins of a medieval Armenian castle. CDLXVIII, map, locates *I-e* on a narrow peninsula west of Ayas; but this alluvial strip of land hardly existed in early antiquity.

[5] XXXIX, No. 116. Cf. p. 387 below.

Šuppiluliuma of Ḫatti and Šunaššura of Kizzuwatna also contains several place-names of Eastern Cilicia, some of which are Hurrian, other Semitic. We shall begin by the latter.

1) ^{nâr}*Ša-am-ri*. Sidney Smith [1] has already correctly interpreted this river-name as "purely Semitic . . . (it derives) from the well-known Accadian root *šmr* and means 'the violent,'" and he identified it with the Greek name of modern Seyhan, Saros,[2] "through the form *Shaura*." We would rather suggest that the Greek *Saros* derived from the parallel Akkadian form *sâru* or *šâru* of the root *šamâru* "to dance, jump, batter, be violent, rage, storm." By popular etymology, explaining *Saros* as "prince," this led to the doublet *Koiranos*.[3]

2) *A-ru-u-na*—a typically W-S formation with the ending *-una* (cf. just above *Ṣaruna*). It may be compared to the middle Palestinian *ʿA-ru-na* in the Annals of Thutmose III.[4]

3) *Bi-tu-ra* (rather than *Pi-tu-ra* [5]), perhaps attested in Ugarit in the personal (gentilic-formed) name *Bn-Btry* listed next to *Bn-Adn* (inhabitant of Adana?), UM 152: rev. 6. The name is to be derived from the W-S root *bātar* "to dissect, to cut," whence *beter* "piece," with suffix *bitrô*; *hārê beter* Cant. 2:17 signifies, according to LXX, "mountains with ravines," and *bitrôn* II Sam. 2:29, "gorge, gully." Compare also the city of *Batruna* (EA 78 etc.) near Byblos.

4) *Še-ri-ig-ga*—here *g* probably corresponds to the Semitic *q* lacking in Hittite phonetics,[6] and if the reading *Šeriqqa* [7] is correct,

[1] cdlxvi, 46.

[2] Same identification cccxcvii, 230, n. 4. Cf. the characteristic declaration of Goetze, cci, 58, n. 237: "I need not stress that I do not agree with S. Smith's Semitic etymology of the name."

[3] Cf. p. 39 above.

[4] lxxvii, II, § 422. In North Syria, including Ugarit and Alalaḫ, the W-S ayin was dropped in Akkadian transliterations of native names. A pers. n. ^{f}*A-ru-u-na* is found at Nuzu (cxci, 36), but the onomastica of Nuzu was quite heterogenous, and there is no proof that this is to be considered a Hurrian name.

[5] cdlxvi, 45 transliterated *Bitura*. If one opts for the reading *Pitura*, this form is quite similar to the name of the North Syrian city on the Euphrates, Pitru or Pitura, cccxlv, I, §§ 463, 499, and of a locality in Edom, Phathur, ccclxiv, 376-380.

[6] The Hittites rendered the Semitic *q* either by *k* or by *g*. Cf. the name of wise woman from Kizzuwatna, written one time *Ma-aš-ti-ig-ga*, another time *Ma-aš-ti-ik-ka*, cci, 9, n. 23.

[7] clxxxiv, 60 identify Šerigga with the classical Serica on the left bank of the Saros.

it would equal the Akk. *šeriqtu, širiqtu* "gift, dowry, present," from the root *šarâqu* "to grant, to give away"; the signification would then be: "a town granted as a fief." [1]

5) *E-ri-im-ma*—cf. the city of *Eri-ma* in Middle Syria, EA 62 : 49. The name probably derives from the common Semitic root *ʿāram* "to be strong, powerful, terrific," and also "to heap up, pile up," whence many city-names in Mesopotamia, kingdom of Alalaḫ, and Ugarit.[2]

The city-names *A-na-mu-uš-ta, Zi-la-ap-pu-na, Zi-in-zi-lu-wa, Dur-pi-na* and Mount *Za-ba-ra-aš-na* in the same document, look Hurrian.[3]

The Hittite document Bo 4889 [4] (a list of land grants for temples, confirmed first by two kings of Kizzuwatna and then by a Hittite king) enumerates 16 toponyms. These are to be sought in Eastern Cilicia, since one of them is said to be situated near Tarša (Tarsus). Non-Semitic names prevail, but some toponyms may reasonably be taken as Semitic or having close analogies in Palestine:

1) The river ${}^{\mathrm{ID}}$*Pu-u-ru-na*, possibly named once more in the same text as ${}^{\mathrm{ID}}$*Pur-* . . . . In our opinion, this is the second main river of Eastern Cilicia, Ceyhan, the Greek *Pyramos* (with the frequent substitution of the final *-n-* by *-m-* [5]). The Heb. root *pārar* (alternate form *pur*) signifies "to break asunder," "to jerk, stir, shake," "to be untamed"—thus *Puruna*, exactly as *Šamri* (Saros), would express the idea of a violent mountain-stream.

2) *La-ak-ki-iš-*[*ši* ?]—cf. the well-known Palestinian city of

[1] This was the standard practice in the Hittite kingdom, in Alalaḫ, and in Ugarit. In Cilicia, as we are informed by the document Bo 4889 (which we shall see next), there existed many villages granted by the state to temples and priests.

[2] Cf. XXXIXa, n. 14. The gemination of the last consonant is normal for many Akkadian transcriptions of foreign geographical names.

[3] Cf. the Hurrian elements *an,- muš-, -ta, zilip-, zinzil-*, CXCI, 200, 235, 260, 278 s. *Zabar-* is probably Sumerian "bronze." *Dur-pi-na* should be compared with the Nuzu pers. n. *Dur-pu-un-na, ibid.* 269.

[4] CCI, 60-67.

[5] Like *Bêt-Hārān* Num. 32: 36 = *Bêt-Hārām* Josh. 13: 27, or *Geršôn* Gen. 46: 11 = *Geršôm* I Chr. 6 : 1. [This river appears as ${}^{\mathrm{ID}}$*Pu-u-ru-na* in the Hittite version of *Res Gesta* of Ḫattušiliš I, and as ${}^{\mathrm{nar}}$*Pu-u-ra-an* in its Akkadian version (H. Otten, *MDOG*, No. 91, December 1958, 82), in a context that makes its equation with the Pyramos very probable. The Hittite king crossed it on his way to North Syria—obviously in its upper stream, near Marash.]

Lākîš (Lachish), EA *La-ki-ši, La-ki-ša,* and the Phoenician colony in North Africa, *Lkš* (Latin Lixos).[1]

3) *Ši-i-na-mu*—cf. the well-known Palestinian city of *Šunêm,* EA 248a : 12, 21; 250 : 43 *Šu-na-ma,* and the Ugaritic *šnm,* both signifying "summit" (Arab. *sanām*).[2]

4) *Lu-u-bu-ru-na*—possibly a form with the suffix *-una* of Akk. *labâru* "to be old," D-stem *luburru* "to make old," perhaps with the sense of "ruins," as Ugaritic *mlbr.*[3]

The names *Ku-un-ni-ia-ra,*[4] *U-bar-ba-aš-ša,*[5] *Ik-ka$_4$-ši-pa, I-iz-zi-x, Ḫu-ul-la-aš-ša* and *Wa-aš-ti-ša* are Hurrian or Hurro-Akkadian;[6] Mount *Iš-ḫa-ra* bears the name of a Babylonian goddess;[7] *Ḫu-u-ra-a-li-ia-an-za* is mixed Hurro-Cassite;[8] *Al-za-ra* and *Mar-ga-an-na* are uncertain; [9] and the spring *Du-wa-at-ta-ri-na* (containing Hitt. *wātar* "water") is the only Hittite or Luwian name attested.

The conclusion from all these toponymic data is evident. The place-names of Eastern Cilicia in the second millennium were Hurrian, Akkadian and W-S, and they survived far into the first millennium. There is no difference, in this respect too, between Eastern Cilicia and the North Syrian states of Alalaḫ (with its vast dependencies) and Ugarit. It was, consequently, inhabited by the same population as North Syria, which in the middle and late second milennium was a mixture of W-S and Hurrian elements living in close symbiosis and ethnic harmony and sharing the same civiliza-

[1] EA 335: 10, 16; 328: 5; 329: 6; CCXLVI, 115.

[2] IIIa, No. 2651. Cf. *Šinamum* (Mari), Šinamu (neo-Assyrian texts) in Upper Mesopotamia (CCV, 123, 230, n. 1).

[3] *Ibid.,* No. 1443 (unless miswritten for *mdbr* "desert").

[4] Elements *kunni* and *iar* at Nuzu, though Hurrian origin uncertain (CXCI, 210, 229); *kunni* may be an Akkadian loan-word (*kunnu* "to establish, to set firm").

[5] The element *ubar* (cf. Nuzu *Ú-ba-ri-ia, Ú-pa-ru,* CXCI, 165) is Akkadian *ubâru* "client, sojourner," a legal term in Babylonia and Ugarit; cf. DXXXII, 371; CCCXXXII, 11 s.; XCVI, 206-211; RŠ 15.109 + 16.296 (CCCXC, 101); RŠ 16.132 (*ibid.,* 140); CDLXX, 163 s.; XXXVIII, 74 s.—*ba-aš-ša* may be compared to Hurrian *pašš-*"to send", CXCI, 243.

[6] See CXCI, 198-279, for the elements *ikk-, -še, -pa, izz-, ḫul-, -ašše, waš-,* and *-tiše.*

[7] Worshipped all over Mesopotamia (in a Hurrian mythological text cf. CCXL, 6) and in Ugarit (*Ušḫry, UM* § 20. 274).

[8] Hurrian element *ḫurr-* and god ^{d}*Ḫu-u-ur-ra,* cf. CXCI, 218; Kassite *ia-an-zi* "king," adopted in Nuzu Hurrian names, *ibid.,* 219.

[9] *Alz-* in *Al-za-ra* is reminiscent of the (Hurrian) land *Alzi* on upper Tigris. *Mar-ga-an-na* stands perhaps for *Marqanna,* from Akk. *raqû* "to hide, to hide oneself, to take shelter," cf. *marqîtu* "place of refuge."

tion.[1] One must add that in the Hittite text Bo 4889, quoted above, the great priestess (*entu*) who owned, together with the unnamed chief priest, number of the enumerated land estates in Eastern Cilicia, bore the name *Da-a-ni-ti*.[2] This is undoubtedly a Semitic name from the root *dîn* (W-S), *dânu* (Akk.) "to judge." [3] Such a name borne by the great priestess, one of the most prominent persons in the country, is very indicative: it shows, in accordance with the toponyms we have examined, what a great role the Semitic element played in the land of Adana.[4] Ruling dynasties could descend from foreign conquerors, but the leadership of the cult always remained in the hands of the local native priesthood.

The Semitism of the Name Danana/Danuna and its Relation to Greek Danaoi

Only an a priori conviction that it is impossible to expect Semites to be present in Eastern Cilicia [5] can explain the fact that, up to

[1] It is important to stress that documents from Alalaḫ and Ugarit do not reveal discrimination along ethnic lines in any social sphere. Any group of people, be it a village community, a guild, an army unit, a social estate up to the mariannu-aristocracy, always includes persons with both Semitic and Hurrian names. Cases where a man with a Hurrian name gave his son a Semitic name, and vice versa, are extremely common. Ugaritians with purely Hurrian names (*Ewr-žr, Ewr-šrm, Tlmyn*) wrote letters in W-S (UM 54; 89; 138; DXXIV, No. 12). Nor was Hurrian religion essentially different from that of their Semitic neighbors. According to E. Laroche, "the Hurrians, at the epoch when they make themselves known to us by abundant evidence, i.e., about the middle of the second millennium, possess a pantheon borrowed from Mesopotamia. But, in adopting it, they gave the Storm-god an outstanding place . . . It is probable that the presence of Adad with the West Semites played here a capital role. Hurrian religion, both in its pantheon and in its cult technique, widespread in Kizzuwatna, Ugarit, Aleppo, Mari, Assyria and Upper Euphrates (but not beyond the Antitaurus) is the product of a mixture in which I distinguish three principal elements: 1. an archaic Sumerian stock, 2. national divinities of the Hurrian mountaineers, 3. an Amorite influence" (CCCXXIIa, 133). Dussaud may have exaggerated when he drastically stated: "Grattez le khurrite et vous trouverez le sémite" (CXLVI, 180), but he was not far from truth.

[2] Ll. 39, 40, 76.

[3] Cf. Ugaritic *Mšt-Dnty*, wife of the king-judge Danel (to whom we shall return below); Biblical *Dînā*; whether *Dinîtu* is the correct reading of the Assyrian div. n. *Ištar* DI-*ni-tu* is uncertain. For the ending *-ti*, cf. 38 names with this ending at Alalaḫ, some of which are purely Semitic: *Aš-ra-at-ti*, *Aš-tar-ti*, *Aš-šu-ra-at-ti*, *Be-el-ti-ma-ti*; cf. also *A-na-ti* EA 170: 43. The Semitic name of the great priestess agrees with the fact that in the neighboring Kizzuwatna a priest bore the name *Ammi-ḫatna*, recognized by Goetze as Amorite (CCI, 8).

[4] For the name *Ú-ut-ti* in the same text, cf. p. 28 above.

[5] Cf. p. 42, n. 2 above.

now, not one of the numerous scholars having studied the Karatepe inscription and the problems connected with it has thought about the possibility of a Semitic character in the very name borne by the inhabitants of that country—Danunians. And though, if the name *Danuna* had been discovered not in Cilicia, but, let us say, in Palestine, there would hardly have been any doubts about the purely W-S origin both of the name and of its bearers.

The name *Danuna* clearly consists of the stem *dân* (*dan* before suffixes that carry away the accent) and the ending *-una*. As to the stem, it is purely Canaanite. We know in Palestine the tribe of *Dân* and a city of the same name. In addition, there was the pers. n. *Adda-dani* (EA 292: 3; 293: 3; 294: 3; 295: 3) in the Amarna Age,[1] the name of the Ugaritic sage Dan(i)el (*Dnil*), known also to the Hebrews (Ez. 14: 4), and used as well as a simple common name both in Ugarit [2] and Israel (a son of David, I Chr. 3 : 1). The same root is common in Assyrian onomastics (Aššurdân etc.). The ending *-una* (*-na*), again, is by no means specific for Hittite and Asianic languages, but exists—quite independently from them—in Greek and other Indo-European languages on the one hand, in all Semitic languages on the other.[3] As VIROLLEAUD has rightly remarked, "the ending *-n* (syllabic *u/ana*) expresses in Canaanite the idea of appurtenance."[4] It is one of the commonest gentilic suffixes in Ugarit (along with the nisbe *-y*), as in *Arwdn*, *Ṣrptn* and many, many others.[5] Especially significant is the Amarna onomastics relating to Palestine, South Syria and South Phoenicia—regions with a monogenous Canaanite population without Hurrian enclaves[6] —and having the ending *-una* attached to purely Semitic stems. This is shown by the following short enumeration; the Biblical

[1] EA 292: 3; 293: 3; 294: 3; 295: 3. Inasmuch as in EA 294: 3 the name is written phonetically *Ad-da-da-ni*, we do not share ALBRIGHT's view that the name must be read *Baʾli-šipṭi*.

[2] UM 314: 12.

[3] "Several typical suffixes, which are characteristic for native languages of Asia Minor, incidentally coincide with Indo-European suffixes," CCCXLIX, 4 s. The same is true for the Semitic languages, where the ending *-âna/-ânu/-ân* and its modification *-ûna/-ûnu/-ûn* belong to the common stock (LXXX, § 161.2), are common in Akkadian (DXXXI, § 56. r), in Canaanite and Hebrew (CDXCVII, § 121. iii. 2. a), and in Arabic.

[4] DXXVIII, 34.

[5] *l.c.*; CDXC, 100, 118; XXXVIII, 72.

[6] Except for a small and quickly assimilated group of Indo-Mitannian princes in some Palestinian cities.

forms (in their Masoretic spelling), where available, are cited in the opposite column:

AMARNA	BIBLE
A-ia-lu-na	*ʾAyyālôn*
Aš-qa-lu-na	*ʾAšqᵉlôn*
Bu-uṣ-ru-na	(cf. *biṣṣārôn* "fortress")
Bur-qu-na	
Bat-ru-na	(cf. *bitrôn* "gorge")
Gud-da-šu-na [1]	
Zi-du-na, Ṣi-du-na	*Ṣîdôn*
Ḫi-na-tu-na [2]	*Ḥannātôn*
Mu-ši-ḫu-na	
Ša-am-ḫu-na.	*Šimᵉᶜôn* [3]
Ša-ru-na	*Šārôn*

And still in the neo-Assyrian transcription:

Am-qar-ru-na	*ʿEqrôn* (LXX: *Akkarôn*)
Iš-qa-lu-un-na	*ʾAšqᵉlôn*
etc.	

Thus, in the XIVth century (and up to the VIIth), *-una* was the standard W-S (Canaaneo-Phoenician) form of the ending which became *-ôn* in Masoretic Hebrew. *Danuna* would be **Danôn* in Masoretic Hebrew, and would be quite as regular a derivative from *Dân* as *Šimšôn* (orig. **Šamšôn*) is from *Šemeš* (**Šamš*), *Ḥermôn* from *Ḥerem*, or—with a rarer ending form *-ûn*—as *Zᵉbūlûn* from *Zᵉbûl*.[4]

But the W-S name *Danuna* is not just a hypothetical construction: it is actually found in EA 117: 92 as a personal name; and it is known that W-S names of towns and tribes were often formed after the same models as those of persons and frequently coincided with them.[5] ᵐ*Da-nu-na* is mentioned by Rib-Addi, king of Byblos,

[1] For *Quddašuna*.

[2] Var. *Ḫi-in-na-tu-ni*.

[3] The name is identical with that of an Israelite tribe, but refers to a city in Galilee = *Simônias* of Josephus, *Vita* 24; LXX has *Simoôn* instead of Masoretic *Šimrôn* Josh. 11: 1.

[4] Šemeš, Ḥerem (in the Jewish Elephantine papyri) and Zebul (in Ugarit) are divine names.

[5] Thus Israel was an ethnic name with the Israelites and a personal name with the Ugaritians (DXXI, 65). A few other names with double usage: Ishmael, Manasse, Gad.

as an adversary of his; he could have been either a Byblian from among the opposition, or a commander of a detachment from the Amurru kingdom, but in either case a pure Semite. There is not a single non-Semitic name found among the people associated (as friends or enemies) with Rib-Addi and with his adversaries, the kings of Amurru.[1]

Another proof of the Semitism of the name *Danuna* is the family to which the bearer of this name belonged in Ugarit. His name, written alphabetically *Dnn*, is transcribed in syllabic cuneiforms as ^{m}*Da-na-na* and ^{m}*Da-na-nu*—with the alternative ending *-ana*. This *Dnn* is a brother of *Dnil*, and they are both sons of a man with the Canaanite name *Yṣr* (cf. clan name *Yēṣer* Gen. 46 : 24). [2] The parallelism (intended, of course) of the two brothers' names shows that the stem of the name *Dnn* is the same as that in *Dnil*, i.e. *dân*, and the name must be understood precisely as *Dan* + *ana*.

Danana alternates with *Danuna* in the ethno-geographical field also: it was found, many years ago, in the Assyrian geographical name $^{m\bar{a}t}$*Ia-ad-na-na* [3] or $^{m\bar{a}t}$*Ia-da-na-na*,[4] which undoubtedly

[1] GOETZE recently wrote: "I am of the opinion that the name Danuna is Ḫurrian. The formation *Danu* + *na* has its analogs in *Kinaḫ* + *na*, *Ḫatti* + *na*, *Api* + *na*, i.e. it ends, as many geographical names of the Ḫurrian period do, in the plural article *-na*. The element *tan(u)* is well known, and as a verb means 'to make' " (CXCIX, 52). Since Eastern Cilicia, as we have seen, possessed both Hurrian and W-S toponyms, GOETZE's claim is perfectly legitimate. However, we would expect an initial *t-* in the cuneiform, Phoenician, Egyptian and Greek transcriptions of the name: "alphabetic-syllabic correspondences show that in the Hurrian syllabary an initial dental is to be interpreted as voiceless, even though a given sign may contain *d-*" (CDLXXIII, 40). The ending *-na* is not peculiar for Hurrian: it is curious to note that ALBRIGHT quoted the same examples, *Ḫatti-na* and *Api-na*, as proof that *Danuna* was an Anatolian formation (XXV, 172); *Kinaḫ-na* is irrelevant, for the early epigraphic occurrences of the name of Canaan show that this name was W-S and not Hurrian (CCCLXXIII, 268). GOETZE further added (CXCIX, 52, n. 27): "Names like *Ṣidūna*, *Asqalūna* must be kept apart (despite LANDSBERGER, *Sam'al*, 1948, 57 fn. 144). They go back to *-ānu* which is excluded for *Danuna* because the *u* in this name is already attested in the Amarna age, i.e. before *-ānu* became *-ōn*." We do not really understand this surprising statement: are not "names like *Ṣidūna*, *Asqalūna*" and many more (some listed p. 47 above) precisely found in the Amarna letters?!. . .

[2] UM 314: 5, 12.

[3] In the inscription of Sargon II: 7 *šarrâni*$^{\text{MEŠ}ni}$ *ša* $^{m\bar{a}t}$*Ia-ʾ na-gi-e ša* $^{m\bar{a}t}$*Ia-ad-na-na* (in one version: *Ad-na-na*) *ša ma-lak* 7 *ûme*^{me} *i-na qabal tamtim e-rib* ^{d}*Šamši*$^{\check{S}i}$ *šit-ku-nu-ma ni-is-sat šu-bat-su-un* "seven kings of the country Ia', a district of *Ia-ad-na-na* which lies amidst the Western Sea at a distance of seven days, their habitations being far off" (transl. CCCXLV, II, § 186; CCCXCIX, 284).

[4] In the inscription of Esarhaddon, CCCXLV, II, § 710.

designated Cyprus. This large island, situated not far from Cilicia, is thus a third land of Danaans-Danunians, in addition to Mycenaean Greece and the Plain of Adana.[1] That *Iadnana* or *Iadanana* [2] must be understood as "Island of the Danaans" was stated, as it seems, for the first time by D. D. LUCKENBILL,[3] and, in apparent independence from him, by B. A. TURAEV.[4] ALBRIGHT [5] rejects the interpretation of the element *Ia* as W-S *'î* "island" through motives of "phonetic difficulties and the inherent improbability of such a mixture of tongues." He did not specify which "phonetic difficulties" he had in mind; but as to the "mixture of languages", it can exist only for those who do not see a Semitic name in *Danana/Danuna*. For us, though, both elements of *Iadanana* happen to belong to the same language—the Canaanite. ALBRIGHT [6] brings forward a different interpretation of *Ia*: "Though it has strangely escaped attention hitherto, it is obviously identical with Greek *Iā* in the name of the Ionians (*Iāones*, Iliad, with the well-known gentilic ending *-ŏnes*, sing. *-ōn*)." We regret to say that this possibility not only has not escaped attention prior to the publication of the quoted study, but was advanced as early as 1884 by Fr. LENORMANT,[7] who already identified the country of *Ia* (in *Ia-danana*) with the Gr. *Iās*, i.e. Ionian. But even the venerable age of this hypothesis does not make it very plausible; except for the city of Epeia, allegedly founded by Ionians from Attica, the Greek Cypriots were of

[1] Sidney SMITH rejected the accepted identification of Iad(a)nana with Cyprus and transferred it to the land of the Danunians, the Plain of Adana; he equated *Ia'* with Idri-mi's *I-e* (cf. p. 41 above) and the latter "with a long narrow peninsula south of the bay of Yumurtalic, or by the southern side of Ak Yatana" (CDLXVIII, 79 s.). The proposed peninsula is a narrow strip of alluvial soil, about 12 miles long and no wider that 0.6 mile. It is probably of relatively recent formation, but how could anyway a surface of about 7 square miles accomodate as many as seven kings? The inscription of Sargon II mentioning the surrender of the seven kings of Iadnana was found precisely in Cyprus, and Esarhaddon lists by name the vassal kings of Iadanana and their cities: the kings' names are Greek, and their cities are well-known Cypriot cities.

[2] The latter form is, no doubt, the primary one, and the former one is a case of dropping the unaccented vowel in a multisyllabic Akkadian word—cf. *Labnânu* from **Labanânu* (Lebanon).

[3] *ZA*, XXII (1913), 92-99, repeated CCCXLV, II, § 709, where the element *Ia-* is explained as Heb. *'î* "island". This was accepted by BOSSERT, then by others, e.g. FORRER, CDXXVI, I, 68 ("Danaer-Insel").

[4] CDXCVI, II, 48 (first published in 1913).

[5] XXV, 172, n. 39.

[6] XXV, 172.

[7] CCCXXIV, II, 2, 85 s.

Achaean origin and spoke a particular dialect, cognate, of all Greek dialects, with that of Arcadia.[1]

Nevertheless, the question remains from which Danunians did Cyprus receive its name "island of Danana," attested by Assyrian kings? Hitherto it had been taken for granted that it came from the Greek conquerors and colonists who, after 1200, seized more than half of the island. This is entirely possible and does not contradict any historical facts. But we know at present that, besides the Danaans (western Danunians), there also existed the eastern Danunians, separated from Cyprus only by a narrow strait. This distance is incomparably shorter than that dividing Cyprus from Greece. Many students of the ancient Cypriot civilization (specialists in Greek archaeology, by and large), are inclined to neglect the fact that Cyprus had preserved, up to very late antiquity, a massive Phoenician population which left numerous Phoenician inscriptions, coins, toponyms and especially cults, and that Cyprus' connection with the Syro-Semitic world was much older and longer than with the Greco-European world.[2] The scholar whom we have just quoted in the preceding footnote, has brought serious arguments in favor of the assumption that there had existed, since ancient times, a large Ugaritic colony in Cyprus, and that during the troubled time of 1650-1550, when Ugarit was almost completely destroyed, the ruling dynasty took refuge in its overseas dominions in Cyprus, and then returned home when the situation on the mainland had improved.[3] The letters of the king of Alašia-Cyprus in the Amarna archives belong entirely to the Syro-Palestinian circle, as much through their Akkadian as through their phraseology, style and

[1] E.g., CCCXLVIII, 176 ss.

[2] Here is how Cl. F. A. SCHAEFFER, the excavator of Ugarit and explorer of the Bronze Age strata of Enkomi on Cyprus, summarizes the characteristics of the most ancient Cypriot civilization: "The first settlers of the island must almost certainly have come from the neighboring coasts of Asia Minor and Syria. It is with . . . Anatolia . . . Syria . . . and Palestine that Cyprus shared her everyday life . . . Connections with the West, by the intermediary of sea commerce, could not change the predominantly Oriental character of the island and of its inhabitants. To make of it what it is now, an advanced post of Europe . . . the mass invasion of the late XIIIth century, followed by several similar waves, was needed . . ." (CDL, 328). "During these periods (third and second millennia), the ties of the island with Asia were still intact. They were not seriously menaced before the end of this period . . . the first European conquest which occurred since about 1250 . . ." (*ibid.*, 330). Actually, this invasion took place only after 1200, cf. p. 355, n. 6 below.

[3] Common conclusion of SCHAEFFER and NOUGAYROL, CCCLXXXVIII, 145 s.

religious background.[1] It is also very interesting that both main native royal-sacerdotal kins of Cyprus, the Kinyrads and the Tamirads (both with W-S names [2]) had even in classical time preserved a tradition regarding their eponymous ancestors' arrival from Cilicia.[3] The possibility that the population which had given Cyprus the name "Danana-island" had come directly from the country of the Danunians in Cilicia, can therefore be given as much credence as can its Greek origin. But it is difficult to decide between the two so long as the name *Danana* remains undiscovered in the epigraphic material of the island itself, whether it be Phoenician, Greek or Greco-Cypriot syllabic.

As to the alternation of the forms *Danuna/Danana*, it presents no difficulty if the W-S character of the name is assumed. ALBRIGHT, who, as we have seen, admitted this name to be of Hittite-Asianic formation, nevertheless, resorted to the evolution laws of Canaanite languages in order to prove the identity of the two variants: "The identification *Danāna* = *Danuna* (Amarna and Ramses III) is easy to explain: the original *Danāna* automatically became *Danōna* in Phoenicia and Western Palestine after about XVIth century," and the vowel *o* could not be rendered in hieroglyphics or cuneiforms otherwise than by *u*.[4] This is already half-way to the approach that has been expounded on these pages.

More serious, however, is the question of the linguistic correlation between the W-S *Danuna/Danana* and the Greek *Danaoi*. Since ALBRIGHT understands *Danana* as *Dana+na*, he explains the Greek form, too, as *Dana+oi*—the same base **Dănă* + the Greek plural ending *-oi* instead of the (Asianic) *-na*.[5] We, on the other hand,

[1] EA 35: 13, 37: "hand of Nergal" for pestilence. A Ugaritic text (to appear in *PRU* V as No. 8) cites "Baal, Eternal Sun, Astarte, Anath, all gods of Alašia." [As revealed by the recent excavations of P. DIKAIOS, a Horned God was worshipped in Enkomi in the XIIIth-XIIth centuries, cf. *Archäol. Anzeiger*, 1962, No. 1, 1-39. Horns as divine attribute is a purely Semitic idea.] Cf. CDXLVI, 68 s.: the oldest tomb (No. 11), discovered at Enkomi, dating from the first half of the second millennium, seems to have belonged to a Phoenician family; Kalopsida, 10 miles west of Famagusta, reveals a Phoenician center. Out of 14 extant Alašian names, preserved in records from Alalaḫ, Ugarit, Alašia itself (in archives of Ugarit and Amarna) and Egypt, 7 are W-S, 1 apparently W-S, 2 Hurrian, 1 Indo-Aryan, 1 Sumerian, 1 Akkadian, 2 probably Akkadian (or Hurrian), XXXIXa.

[2] They will be examined in another connection.

[3] Apollodoros, *Biblioth.* III: 14: 3; CCLIV, 75.

[4] XXV, 172.

[5] See p. 14 above.

divide the name in the (W-S) base *Dân* (becoming *Dan* before accented suffix) + (also W-S) ending *u/ana*. This seems to contradict the Greek form, which is *Danaoi*, while following from the base *Dan-* it would, at first glance, have been **Dan-oi*. However, the Greek form decomposes itself not in *Dana+oi*, but in *Dan+a(w)oi*, with an original digamma. We have an exact parallel to it in another archaic tribal name—*Kranaoi*, as the Attic Pelasgians are said to have been named, with their eponymous hero *Kranaos* (cf. *Danaos*). This name, interpreted by the Ancients as "rocky", is related to Gr. *kras* "head", *kranos* "helmet",[1] and its original form was *Kranawos*.[2] Before the disappearance of the digamma, the name *Danaoi* was also pronounced *Danawoi*, [3] and the newly deciphered Mycenaean tablets show that—as was expected—all Greek names which in their classical form end in *-aos*, *-aôn*, are spelled by *-awo-*.[4] Now the suffix *-av-*, denoting belonging, origin, property (and thus being semantically equivalent to Semitic *-u/ana*), is a common feature of several Indo-European languages, including Slavic,[5] Hittite, and Indian. We have already seen the H-H geographical name *Adanawa* (city of Adana), literally "that belonging to Adan" [6]—very close in its construction to our *Danawoi*. Still more similar by consonance (but no less fortuitous) is the Indian mythical name *Dânavâ*, epithet of the dragon *Vṛtra* in his quality of the son of *Dânu*, a female personage embodying the primordial water-element; in plural form *Dânavâs* it later became an appellation of ophiomorphous demons of Indian mythology.[7]

Thus the Gr. *Dana(w)oi* is a regular Hellenization of the Semitic ethnic name *Danuna* by way of replacing its gentilic ending *-una* (or *-ana*)with the Indo-European equivalent suffix *-aw-*. The linguistic evidence cited in this section consequently corroborates what we

[1] CDIII, *s.v.*

[2] LXXIII, 508, *s.v. krana[v]os*: "from the Indo-European root *qar* 'to be hard,' i.e. **q.r̥naṷo-s* (cf. *tana[v]os*)."

[3] CCCII, 34. (Some authors transliterate the digamma by *v*; we follow VENTRIS and CHADWICK in using *w*).

[4] DV, 99.

[5] E.g., *krov-av-*"bloody," from *krov'* "blood"; *luk-av-* "sly, arch," from *luk* "arch, bow," or in the form *-ov*, as in *Petr-ov* "belonging to Peter, descendant of Peter."

[6] See p. 12 above.

[7] CCCXCV, 112 s., 115; LXXXII, 281 s. KRETSCHMER's attempt to pronounce the Indian *Dânavâ* a real Scythian people of Central Asia and to make the Greek Danaans and the Syrian Danuna their descendants (CCCII, 15-36) has no support of facts whatsoever.

have systematically expounded in our preceding pages: that the Danunians, the basic inhabitants of Eastern Cilicia, were Western Semites in origin, language, culture and ethnic name; and that the name of the western Danunians, both in the form preserved in Egyptian sources of the XIIth century (Danuna) and in the Homeric form (Danaoi), coincides perfectly with the name of their eastern namesakes. As the Cilician Danunians could not have come from Greece, according to archaeologic and epigraphic data, the question of their relationship to the Greek Danaans can be settled only in one of two directions: either they had no more in common than, e.g., the Danaans and the Indian serpent demons *Dânavâs*; or, if they actually were related, the ancestors of the Greek Danaans must have come to Greece from the Semitic East.

Does Mopsos point to a Greek Conquest of Cilicia?

Besides the Danaans-Danunians, another remarkable onomastical coincidence exists between Greece and the Plain of Adana. As mentioned above, the Karatepe inscription cites *Bt-Mpš* as the royal house of the Danunian country. The name *Mpš* of the Phoen. text (the H-H text has the form *Muksas* [1]) is evidently identical with the Greek Mopsos. This name is frequently found in Greek mythology and toponymics, and in some variants it is, inter alia, associated with Eastern Cilicia. In the Hellenistic epoch two East Cilician towns, Mopsuhestia ("Mopsos' hearth") and Mopsucrene ("Mopsos' spring"), bore this name.[2] Mopsuhestia had a famous oracle shrine of Mopsos, where predictions were obtained by means of incubation. To Mopsos was also ascribed, together with another seer, Amphilochos, the foundation of Mallos on the East Cilician shore. He allegedly arrived in Cilicia with a detachment of Greek warriors after the Trojan war (we will examine these reports and other ones presently).

Thus, one more connecting link seems to be available, and its relevance must be scrutinized. For ALBRIGHT,[3] the presence of the "Dynasty of Mopsus" is proof "that in the first centuries of the

[1] Transliterated: *Mu-ka-sI-sI-*, BOSSERT *ap.* CLXXVII, 100; *Mu-g(a)-sa-sa-n*, CCCXXII, *suppl.*; *Mu-k(a)-sa-sa*, CCCXXI, Nos. 415, 433, 434.

[2] According to CDXI, XVI, 1, 243 ss., there is no mention of Mopsuhestia and Mopsucrene prior to the Hellenistic age. Strabo does not ascribe the foundation of Mopsuhestia to Mopsos; cf., however, Theopompos, frg. 103, (CCLXXII, II, B, 559).

[3] XXV, 170.

Iron Age *Danāna* or *Danōna* did refer to tribes of Greek affiliation". For DUPONT-SOMMER[1] the ancestor of the "Dynasty of Mopsos" is identical with Mopsos of the classical tradition. A. GRÉGOIRE [2] considers Mopsos a great Greek colonizer who came to Cilicia from Greece. BOSSERT [3] and DOBLHOFER [4] also consider Mopsos a historical character. BARNETT [5] sees in Mopsos an individual person and identifies him with *Muksus*, a man whose name (but nothing else) is found in a Boğazköy text from the last decades of the Hittite Empire.[6] HOUWINK TEN CATE [7] represents Mopsos as a great ruler of a South Anatolian empire after 1200.

The story of Mopsos, to which these scholars refer and which is but one among several others, runs as follows, if it is put together from references in ancient authors: [8]

1) *Mopsos the Clarian*. Manto, the daughter of the celebrated Theban prophet Teiresias, and herself a prophetess (as already her name shows), was given to the temple of Apollo in Delphi by the Epigons after they had taken and destroyed Thebes. From Delphi she was sent to Claros, another ancient center of Apollo's worship, near Colophon on the Aegean shore of Asia Minor. There she was captured together with her companions and became the wife of the Cretan Rhakios, the ruler of Claros. Their son was Mopsos, a prophet as his mother and grandfather (but others believed Apollo himself was his father). The foundation of Colophon was attributed to him. Now, after the end of the Trojan war, the chief seer of the Greek army, Calchas, came "on foot" to Claros with a troop of returning Greek warriors. He had a contest in divination with Mopsos and lost; then he died or killed himself from vexation. Mopsos took over his place and, together with the people who were with Calchas, crossed the Taurus. Some of his men stayed in Pamphylia, "others were scattered in Cilicia and Syria and as far even as Phoenicia." [9] According to others, Mopsos and Amphilochos

[1] CXXXII, 186.
[2] CCXXXI, 122 ss.
[3] LXXIV, III, 284.
[4] CXXI, 214.
[5] XLV, 142 s.
[6] CCCIII, 35, 146 transliterates *Mukšuš*.
[7] CCLXIII, 44-50.
[8] Main source: Strabo (XIV: 1: 27; 4: 3; 5: 16) who quotes named and unnamed earlier authors.
[9] This is the oldest variant of the story, told by Strabo after Callinos, an elegiac poet from Ephesos (early VIIth century). Neither Callinos nor Hero-

(another famous prophet), were the founders of Mallos, near the mouth of Pyramus; but in the struggle for power over the city they engaged in a single combat and killed each other. Both Amphilochos, who was the city patron, and Mopsos had oracles and a cult at Mallos.

These stories are supposed to be a trustworthy reminiscence of Greek conquest of Cilicia during the Peoples of the Sea's migration, and of the beginnings of the Mopsos dynasty there. As a matter of fact, the recognition of the Cilician *Mpš*'s Greek extraction does in no way modify our previous conclusion about the Semitism of the Cilician Danunians who lived there at least a couple of centuries prior to the traditional time of the Trojan war and the historically fixed time of the Peoples' of the Sea invasion. A priori it is not impossible that the "House of *Mpš*" was connected through its origins with Danaan participants of this invasion, some of whom could have stayed in Cilicia on their way to Egypt and later became absorbed by the native population. But an obstacle to recognizing the Cilician hero Mopsos as Greek colonizer is the great plurality, ubiquity and diffusiveness of his personality and the extreme discrepancy of what was told about him, his namesakes and his companions-in-arms. All of this can in no way be harmonized with the assumption of the historicity of Mopsos' deeds in Cilicia and of his having founded cities in that country. Besides the Mopsos we have just spoken about, one finds in Greek mythology and in ancient geography the following heroes and localities of the same name:

2) *Mopsos the Lapith,*[1] son of Ampycos from Thessaly (or Apollo) and the Nymph Chloris, also a soothsayer, but transferred by the myth into an earlier period than Mopsos, son of Manto. He was made a participant in all famous events of his generation: of the war of the Lapiths against the Centaurs, of the Calidon hunt, and of the Argonauts' expedition. While returning with the Argonauts, he died in Libya from a snake bite, was buried there and received a hero's cult and an oracle.[2] His essential identity with the

dotos (VII: 94) specify the tribal origin of these Greek intruders to Pamphylia; only later versions made them Lapiths, in order to harmonize the story with Mopsos No. 2 (see below).

[1] In inscriptions on West Greek vases: *Maophsos.*

[2] The animal that slays the god or the hero is often, in an earlier stage, identical with him. This is shown for the boar CLXXIV, VII, 22 ss.; the same may be true for the serpent—an age-old emblem of chthonic gods of fertility, healing and divination.

"younger" Mopsos cannot be doubted: not only have we the same essential characteristics, i.e., his being a great soothsayer, a son of Apollo, a traveller who dies abroad and then becomes a cultic hero and an oracle-giver, but the Greek warriors from Troy whom the "younger" Mopsos is said to have led to Pamphylia and Cilicia are expressly called Lapiths in some versions.[1]

3) *Mopsos and Rhodes.* According to Philostephanos of Cyrene,[2] Mopsos, after an oracle received by his mother Manto, sent the Lindian (or Argive) Lakios to found the city of Phaselis, a Rhodian colony in Eastern Lycia, near the border of Pamphylia; this Lakios was the brother of Antiphemos, the founder of the Sicilian Gela. Gela was founded in 690 or 689, and Phaselis about the same time, while Manto and Mopsos belong to the mythical generations of about the Trojan war. Lakios is, of course, the same name as Rhakios, the father of the Clarian Mopsos.

4) *Mopsos the Lydian.* According to Xanthos of Lydia, Mopsos was a son of Lydos and a brother of Torrhebos. The scene of his exploits is transferred to the Palestinian Ascalon, the city of the goddess Atargatis. He is said to have captured Atargatis with her son Ichthys and to have thrown them in the lake at Ascalon, where they were devoured by fish.[3] This Mopsos, too, is but a variant of the first one, since Colophon and Claros lay on the ancient territory of Lydia.[4] If the previously mentioned avatars of Mopsos enjoyed only a hero worship, the Lydian Mopsos, who acted so boldly with the greatest Syrian goddess, must certainly have belonged to the sphere of full gods.

5) *Moxos the Lydian.* The identity of the forms Moxos and Mopsos is ensured not only by what is told of both, but primarily by the Karatepe inscription, where Phoen. *Mpš* is rendered by *Muksas* in the H-H version. Nicolaos of Damascus [5] in his history of Lydia reports of a Lydian Moxos, who lived under king Meles,[6] achieved numerous and beautiful deeds, was famous for his gallantry and righteousness, and taught the Lydians to offer the gods a tithe of

[1] Sources listed CDXI, XXI, 2, 1827 ss., *s.v. Polypoites.*

[2] In his lost book on the foundations of cities in Asia, quoted in Athenaeus VII: 297e ss. Cf. CCXC, 249.

[3] Xanthos Lyd., *ap.* Athenaeus, VIII: 346e-f.

[4] Herod. I: 142.

[5] Frg. 16 (22), CCLXXII, II-A, 340.

[6] Meles is said to have been the predecessor of the last Lydian Heraclid king, Candaules, which puts him in the early VIIth century.

their belongings.[1] Then he besieged and took the city of Crabos (? — the text is corrupt), and threw its inhabitants into the nearby lake because of their atheism: this is but a further euhemerization of what Xanthos told about Mopsos the Lydian and Atargatis.

Now the name Mopsos/Moxos forms the base of several toponyms and ethnic names:

1) *Mopsion* was a town in Thessaly, named, according to Strabo IX: 5: 22, for Mopsos the Lapith.

2) *Mopsopia* was an old name for Attica, allegedly from an eponym Mopsopos, whom Strabo *ibid.* distinguishes from Mopsos. In reality, the suffix *-op-* was an old Greek ethnic ending,[2] perhaps connected with the Hurrian and Anatolian formative *-pa*.[3]

3) *Mopsopia,* to believe Pliny V : 96, was also the oldest name of Pamphylia, a country with which Mopsos the seer was associated.

4) *Moxianoi* or *Moxeanoi,* a tribe in western Phrygia, not far from the Lydian border; on coins written *Moxea* and *Moxeanon*.[4]

5) *Moxupolis,* a town in southern Phrygia or Cabalia.[5]

6) *Moxuene,* a region in Armenia.[6]

Thessalian Mopsion, Ionian Claros and Colophon, Lydia, Phrygia, Cabalia, Attica, Libya, Pamphylia, Lycian Phaselis, Palestinian Ascalon, Cilician Mallos—is it not too wide an arena for one life, are not there too many cities founded for one man? And was the tradition of Mopsos coming to Cilicia really so firm? It is noteworthy that Herodotos, speaking of Greeks in Pamphylia and Cilicia, ignores Mopsos. He knows about the Pamphylians (VII: 91) that "they descend from those who, returning from under Troy, were dispersed together with Amphilochos and Calchas." So, according to the legend he uses, Calchas himself, and not his victor Mopsos, was the one who had brought the Greeks to Pamphylia along with Amphilochos. Herodotos is also ignorant of the joint foundation of Mallos by Mopsos and Amphilochos; he ascribes to Amphilochos the foundation of another port town, the Syrian Posidion at the mouth of the Orontes (III : 91). However, the reports on Amphilo-

[1] Here the story of a drought that struck Lydia follows, and of how the Lydians asked the oracle about it. The exile of king Meles imposed by the oracle is told in other sources.

[2] Cf. CCCLXIII, II, 1, 270 s., with many examples.

[3] CXCI, 242; CLXXXIX, I, 54, 75; p. 35 above.

[4] CDXI, XVI, 1, 408.

[5] *Ibid.*, 409; CCIII, 140; CLXVI, 177.

[6] CDXI, XVI, 1, 409.

chos, Mopsos' mythical partner, are as contradictory as those on Mopsos himself, and it is worth while to dwell a little upon them, because they shed some light on the reliability of the Mopsos stories.

Amphilochos, a son of the great prophet Amphiaraos of Argos, and himself a prophet,[1] was considered not only the founder of Mallos or Posidion in the East, but of the Amphilochian Argos on the border of Epirus and Acarnania (Thucidides II : 68) as well. His popularity as city-founder reached as far as Spain.[2] "Hesiod says", reports Strabo (XIV: 5: 17), "that Amphilochos was killed by Apollo at Soli;[3] according to others, at the Aleian plain;[4] and others again say, in Syria, upon his quitting the Aleian plain on account of the quarrel" (with Mopsos). It is obvious that he was connected with all these localities on other than historical grounds. The truth is, that both he and Mopsos were famous ancient prophets, and no city could be founded without an oracle and supervision by a qualified soothsayer.[5] It was a matter of honor for a Greek city to trace its foundation to a great semi-divine personality of the mythical age.

The case of Mopsos in Cilicia must not be taken isolatedly, for it is not the only instance of this kind. We must give no more credence to the historical worth of the reports on Mopsos as the founder of Cilician towns than to the assertions of the same Greek sources that Tarsus was founded by Argives, led by Triptolemos (the famous hero of the Eleusinian agrarian myths) in search of Io (Strabo XIV: 5: 12; XVI: 2: 5), or by Perseus;[6] that the Cilician town of Olbe was founded by Ajax, son of Teucros, one of the heroes of the Trojan war (*ibid.* XIV: 4 : 2);[7] that the descendants of Triptolemos and his companions settled in the Plain of Orontes and were, many

[1] Properly, only an avatar of his father, CDXI, I, 2, 1887.

[2] *Ibid.*, 1940.

[3] In western part of East Cilicia.

[4] The plain of Eastern Cilicia.

[5] Even as late as the middle of the Vth century, the foundation of Thurii by Athens needed a favorable oracle from Delphi and the direct participation of Lampon, known as a theologist and interpreter of oracles, DIX, 278 s. Aristophanes, *Birds*, 959-991 mocks the custom of consulting diviners and oracle-collectors when founding cities.

[6] CDXI, IV-A, 2, 2415.

[7] The claim of the ruling priests in Olbe to descent from Teucros only shows influence from the neighboring Cyprus, where the founding of Salamis was ascribed to Teucros (with no other reason than his mythical origin from the island of Salamis near Attica).

generations later, incorporated into the inhabitants of the new city of Antioch (*ibid.* XVI: 2: 5); that the Arcadian Agapenor, another combatant of the Trojan war, founded the shrine of Aphrodite in Paphos (*ibid.* XIV: 6: 3), while this was an immemorial native temple. In the West, too, already Hesiod made the eponym of the Latins a son of Odysseus and Circe, and tales were invented which transferred to the West (Italy and Sicily) many other heroes of the Trojan war: Diomedes, Philoctetes, Idomeneus, Merion, Podaleirios, Epeios, Menestheus, Tlepolemos, and the Trojan Aeneas.[1] But the actual Greek colonization in the western Mediterranean began only in the second half of the VIIIth century.

If there were cases when groups of intruders tried to settle down in Cilicia and North Syria after the defeat of the Peoples' of the Sea invasion, these attempts were short-lived and bore no permanent results.[2] There was no continuity of Greek tradition in Cilicia between 1200 and the time of the Karatepe inscription. E. CAVAIGNAC had sufficient ground to conclude: "The Danuna of Cilicia do not present any trace of Hellenism"; [3] "Up to the present, one has not produced any positive indication of it" (of Greek infiltration in Cilicia); the mention of Mopsos at Karatepe is the only "small indication" of its possibility.[4] But we have seen how ambiguous the evidence of Mopsos is. There is another possible trace of Greek descent of the *Bt-Mpš* dynasty, noted in passing by BOSSERT: [5] he proposed to see in the title of *Bʿl Krntryš*, the dynastic deity of Azitawadd, the Greek word **krantorios*.[6] The presence of a pure Greek title in the Danunian inscription would be a much more decisive clue than the un-Greek, probably Anatolian, name of Mopsos. But the identity *Krntryš* = **krantorios* is anything but certain, and until there are more proofs available in its favor, it seems to be more consistent to look for the explanation of *Krntryš*

[1] Cf. CCCLXIII, III, 451 s.

[2] CCXLV, 141.

[3] XCV, 94.

[4] *Ibid.*, 100.

[5] LXXIV, IV, 183. He does not say in so many words that **krantoriịas* (as he writes it) is a *Greek* word; he simply speaks of "another Indo-European people in Cilicia, which pronounced the name Moxos 'Mopsos' and designated the storm-god as **krantoriịas*, 'the one who fulfills, who harkens' (cf. Greek *krantôr, krainô*)"; but the implication is clear.

[6] The double suffix *-tôr* + *-ios* is rather unusual in Greek; but cf. a formation which is very close both in sense and in shape: *anaktorios* "belonging to a king, a ruler" from *anaktôr* "king, ruler" (usually *anax*), from the root *anassô*. *Krantôr*, besides the sense preferred by BOSSERT, means also "ruler."

in the direction of the native Anatolian languages and pantheons, which offer close parallels.[1] In Cilicia, as elsewhere, the retrojection of the beginnings of Greek penetration on the mainland of Levant to the ancient heroic ages could have begun only after the actual start of this process; but there is no earlier date for it than about 700, i.e., in any case after Azitawadd.

It is true that Sir Leonard WOOLLEY takes on trust the version of Amphilochos as the founder of Posidion which he discovered and excavated at al-Mina near the mouth of the Orontes. He puts it thus: "After 1194: Re-founding of the port (Posideium) by Amphilochus." [2] Let us agree that under the conventional name of Amphilochos any Greek chieftain of about 1200 can be understood. But Sir Leonard WOOLLEY does not provide any archaeological data to support the dating of the Greek settlement in Posidion as early as the beginning of the XIIth century. On the contrary, according to his description and chronological table, there was a long gap between the level of Late Mycenaean ceramics (interrupted by the destruction at about 1194) and the next level of occupation, characterized by imported Greek ware of the period of 750-700. This was true not only in the harbor town itself—where the earlier strata could have been destroyed by the floods of the Orontes—but also in the Sabouni hill town, the residence part of the port.[3] The turning-point between the Bronze and the Iron Ages is characterized by a complete rupture of relations between the Aegean and the Orient; the prosperous cities of Alalaḫ and Ugarit were not rebuilt precisely because the trade with the Mycenaean world which made them rich suddenly stopped. It was only about 700 that WOOLLEY found traces of al-Mina's occupation and resettlement by Cypriot Greeks.[4]

[1] A god *Tarawa(š)* is met in Hittite texts among a group of deities connected with the city of Kaneš, CCII, 53, 134. In CCLIX, 53 s., *Krntryš* was explained as **kwirwan-tarayaš*, "the suzerain Tarayaš," *kwirwan* being a Hittite ruler-title (see p. 39, n. 2 above), and **Tarayaš*, a slightly modified form of *Tarawaš*. This explanation seems to be the most plausible one. Greek *koiranos* "suzerain" (already *Iliad* II: 206) certainly derived from Hittite *kuiru̯ana*, and it was used to translate the Phoenician *Bʿl mrqd* "lord of dancing" by *koiranos kômôn* (CCCLXIII, II, 2, 141). This agrees well with the construction *Bʿl Krntryš*. It is quite natural that Azitawadd, the only East Cilician ruler with a Luwian name, should have a Luwian deity as his special protector.

[2] DLV, 187, and more in detail 171 s.

[3] *Ibid.*, 172, 187.

[4] *Ibid.*, 173.

The date of 700 for the beginnings of Posidion as a Greek colony is quite in accord with the first historically attested Greek appearance in Cilicia. "As the Greeks landed in Cilicia and started a war, the Assyrian king Sennacherib went out to meet them, inflicted upon them a defeat and erected in memory thereof his image with an inscription," reports Berossus who has utilized cuneiform sources.[1] It is known from Sennacherib's own annals that in 696 this king suppressed a revolt by Kirua, the governor of Illubri in Eastern Cilicia, who had been joined by other Cilician towns, including the city of Tarsus; the Greeks thus came as the principal auxiliaries of the Cilician rebels, and notwithstanding their defeat, they managed to gain a foothold on the Cilician shore.[2] In the same years the Greek colony in Phaselis was established, whose foundation is connected in legend with Mopsos as the giver of the foundation oracle. It is to this period that one must attribute the rise of the tales that the new Greek settlements in the East Mediterranean had already been founded, back in legendary times, by the heroes of the Trojan war—or still earlier semi-divine characters.[3] This was, as seen, the general mechanism of legitimizing Greek or Hellenized cities on alien soil in the age of the Great Colonization (750-550).

Mopsos/Moxos: Greek and Anatolian

The Greek connection of Mopsos with Cilicia was facilitated by the fact that this name was known not only to the Greeks, but to the native inhabitants of Cilicia as well. Mopsos is clearly a local Anatolian character; our survey in the previous section showed that his name, both as a personal name or a toponymic is found mostly in Lydia and neighboring parts of Asia Minor. A man bearing the H-H form of his name, Mukšuš, is already mentioned in an important Hittite document from the late XIIIth century—the indictment of Madduwattaš, a Hittite vassal ruler from Western Anatolia.[4] Unfortunately, this name is cited only once in a com-

[1] Quoted by Eusebios, *Chron.* I: 27, and once again, by mistake, having taken the same event from Abydenos, *ibid.* I: 35.

[2] CCCLXIII, III, 65, 95, 424; CCCXCVI, 311 s.; CDLXVII, 69.

[3] "The tendency to derive the Cilician cities (including Mallos and Tarsus) from Argos is based on the vainglory of these early Hellenized cities which found a support in the legends of Amphilochos and Mopsos and Triptolemos and Io . . ." (CCCLXIII, III, 494).

[4] Published and commented: CCIII. The only mention of ^{m}*Mu-uk-šu-uš* is in § 33*: 76 (CCIII, 35; cf. 146).

pletely destroyed paragraph. We do not know whether he was a local chief as Madduwattaš himself, or an intruder. A la rigueur this Mukšuš could have been a Greek pirate-conqueror of the kind of Attariššiyaš from Aḫḫiyawā, whose deeds are abundantly described in the document. However, we have absolutely no hints as to the function, origin, nationality, and role of Mukšuš. In any case, his name is not a Greek one,[1] and its occurrence in central Anatolian regions, far from the sea, speaks against its introduction by the Greeks.

As shown by the Karatepe inscription and the Greek transcriptions, this name existed in Anatolian languages in two forms: *Mukšuš* and **Mupšuš*, which most probably corresponds to two Asianic languages—in one of them the old Indo-European *q* was preserved, in the other it shifted, as in classical Greek and in Umbro-Sabellian, to *p*.[2] This is evidence against the presumption of its import from outside. It may be recognized with Bossert that the coincidence of the H-H name of Asitawandas from Karatepe with the native name of the Pamphylian Aspendus, **Estwenda*, i.e., "(city) of Asitawandas," shows that the Danunian king bore an old royal name which may have occurred in his dynasty as early as in the second millenium.[3] But as Bossert himself considers the name of Asitawandas a purely H-H name, and as Aspendus did not

[1] Mopsos and other names with the suffix *-s-* (*-ss-*) are non-Greek (Asianic): ccxcix, 395, n. 1; cdxv, 416, n. 7; cccxi, 271 ss. The only attempt of a Greek etymology was to derive the name from a glosse in Hesychios: "*mopsos*: a stain on the hymation: Cypriots" (cf. cccxxx, 237). Gruppe tried to apply this to the "quite obscure" name: if its second part is *pus* ("foot"), **Mopsopus* would be "dirty foot," a synonym to *Melampus* ("black foot"), also a diviner; if it is *ops* "face," **Mopsops* would be a synonym to *Pêlops* ("muddy face"), ccxxxv, I, 552, n. 6. One could even compare the *Helloi* or *Selloi*, the prophets of Zeus in Dodona, who, according to *Iliad* XVI: 233-235, "do not wash their feet and sleep on naked earth." But the derivative of **Mopsopus* would be **Mopsopodia* (like *Melampus*: *Melampodia*, *Oidipus*: *Oidipodia*). The suffix *-op-* is found in many Grecian ethnic names (cf. p. 57 above) and has no relation to "face." Finally, Gruppe himself defines the dialect where the common noun *mopsos* signifies "a stain on a garment" as "vulgar Cypriot"; and in it, Semitic (Phoenician) loan-words abund; *mopsos* "stain" may be derived from the Semitic root *pšš*, Akk. *pašâšu* "to smear, to sprinkle with oil, fat, wine."

[2] On the latter: ccclxiii, III, 458, n. 1; on preservation of *q* in Mycenaean Greek: dv, 81; cccxlviii, 57, 100; on the passage $q > p$ in Luwian (Luwian *pippid* = Hittite *ku̯idku̯id*): xcv, 100, with reference to Forrer. The H-H language is considered by specialists to be Luwian (see cclxiii, xii s.); but, paradoxically, it is precisely the H-H version in Karatepe that has *Muksas*.

[3] lxxiv, III, 284.

become Hellenized before a comparatively late time, it follows from this that the *Mpš* dynasty included from earliest times bearers of H-H (and not Greek) names. Nor is there anything Greek in the attested names of the kings of Quê (Eastern Cilicia) in the IXth and VIIIth centuries: Katê, Kirri, Tulka, Urikki.

But it does not follow from this that I. Lévy was right in denying any relation between "Mupš, a truly Cilician character," and his Greek namesake, the prophet Mopsos, whom the Greeks have arbitrarily fused into one figure[1] (this is also the opinion of E. Laroche [2]). It is one and the same name, and the likelihood is that in both spheres there were similar mythological motifs connected with it. Nevertheless, the course of its dissemination must be imagined in an exactly opposite direction: not from Greece to Cilicia, but from Cilicia to Greece, whither it was brought as early as the Mycenaean epoch. In the documents in Linear B, both from Pylos and Cnossos, one finds a personal name written *Mo-qo-so*, i.e. *Moqsos* [3]—as in Hittite, H-H, and Lydian (in the Mycenaean dialect of Greek the transition $q > p$ was not yet accomplished). That this was the case and not the opposite, is a consequence first, of *Moqsos* being decidedly non-Greek, secondly, of the fact that there are no Greek names registered among the inhabitants of eastern states (Ḫatti, Alalaḫ, Ugarit), while the Mycenaean tablets include quite a number of Hittite, W-S and Hurrian names, and *Moqsos* is just one of them.[4]

Mopsos/Moxos is not the only name found both in the East of Asia Minor, where it is contiguous with Syria, and on her Aegean shore. Ed. Meyer [5] brought, many years ago, a few parallels to our case: thus the name of *Panamu(wa)*, king of Sam'al in the VIIIth century, occurs in Caria as *Panamyes*; the name of the Hittite king Muršiliš emerges in Lydia as the royal name Myrsilos (Herod. I: 7); the names with Tarku or Tarḫu, an East Anatolian god, are found not only in Cilicia, but also among Carians and Lycians (and as far as the Etruscans); the name of Tarḫundaraba, king of Arzawa in the XIVth century, returns in Caria as *Tarkondara*, a demos at Mylasa. In addition, there was the name of the Hittite king *Muwatalliš*, preserved in the state of Gurgum, adjacent to the Plain of

[1] CCCXXVIII, 105 ss.
[2] CCCXX, 263.
[3] DV, 421: *mo-qo-so* KN X 1497; *mo-qo-so-jo* (genitive) PY Sa 774.
[4] CCCXI, 271 ss.; CCCXLIX, 6, 7-9. See p. 358 below.
[5] CCCLXII, 624 s.

Adana, in the form of *Mutalli*, which also figures in Caria as *Motylos*, the legendary founder of the town of *Samylia*,[1] whose name, in turn, is remarkably like the name of another North Syrian state and city, *Śam'al*. The name of the mythical king of Mysia (during the Trojan war, of course), *Telephos*, was many times compared with *Telepinuš*, a name borne by a Hittite king and later by a Hittite royal prince and priest, who received from his father Šuppiluliuma the throne of Ḫalab (Aleppo).[2] Finally, let us quote the remarkable instance of the cult of the goddess Kubaba (Gr. *Kybêbê* Herod. V: 102, or more often *Kybêlê*), originally worshipped in North Syria (Carchemish and Ugarit), then in Cilicia, and in classical times the chief goddess of Lydia.[3]

We have seen in the preceding section that in the version of Xanthos of Lydia Mopsos still possesses relics of a divine nature. The question whether *all* heroes who received semi-divine honors were degraded gods may be debatable, but one thing seems to be certain: that oracles were always a prerogative of gods, and if there existed, along with the oracles of Zeus and Apollo, a few others that belonged to so-called heroes, these oracular heroes, at least, were real divine characters. They might have been regarded as mere heroes elsewhere, but in their own oracular shrines they were worshipped as gods: so it was with Amphiaraos at Oropos,[4] with his "son" Amphilochos at Mallos,[5] and with Trophonios at Leba-

[1] CCXXXVII, 57; CCC, 251; CCCI, 249. Mentioned only by Stephanos of Byzantium.

[2] E.g., CIII, 121 s.; CCLXIV, 210.

[3] Cf. V, 229 ss.; XX, II, 26, n. 1; CCII, 80, 133; CCCXVIII, 121; CCCXCI, 157. ALBRIGHT and NOUGAYROL are certainly right in connecting Kubaba with *Ku-ba-ú* or *Ku-ba-ba*$_6$, the mythical Sumerian ale-wife who became a queen of the legendary Kiš dynasty and reigned one hundred years. *Ku-ba-ba*$_6$ is actually the well-known Sumerian goddess *Ba-ba*$_6$ with the prefix *Ku* "holy" (XX, II, 26, n. 1). The legendary dynasties of Kiš and Uruk included other gods and demigods, as Etana, Dumuzi, Lugalbanda, Gilgameš. For the Hittites, Kubaḅa was a Hurrian goddess. She was early adopted in Cilicia; on the stele of Ordek -Burun (Xth-IXth century) she is mentioned twice, together with the specific deity of the neighboring Śam'al, the god Rekub-el. On the recently found Aramaic stele from Bahadurli, near Karatepe (Achaemenid time), Kubaba is the lady of several cities in Cilicia and in the Taurus (I owe this information to Prof. A. DUPONT-SOMMER).

[4] CDXI, I, 2, 1886 s.: "Amphiaraos . . . a chthonic god of prehistoric Greece. . ." "here in Oropos Amphiaraos was adored as a god." CCXLVII, 28: Zeus Amphiaraos; CCCXLIII, 392: "the chthonic image of Zeus Amphiaraos"; CCCLXIII, III, 397: "the prophetic hero Amphiaraos is the god of the Graeans in Oropos."

[5] On Mallos coins of the imperial time was the inscription: *Theü Amphilochu*, CDXI, XIV, 1, 916 s.

deia.[1] Since Mopsos also possessed his own oracular shrines, he certainly was originally a god. The very early occurrences of the name "Mopsos" as applied to persons (at Pylos, Cnossos, and Boğazköy) do not contradict the assumption of his original divinity. This duality is characteristic for Hittite onomastics, to which the name of Mopsos belongs. The above quoted Hittite royal names of Telepinuš and Muwatalliš were primarily names of gods: the former—of the well-known god whose disappearance and search are described in the Telepinuš myth,[2] the latter—of a god who was also designated by the ideogram NIR.GÁL.[3] Šandaš, the hero of the Hittite tale of the siege of Uršu and of a moralizing anecdote,[4] bore the name of the well-known Asianic god, also known as Sandon, which occurred frequently in the Cilicia of later ages as a personal name.[5] The name of the goddess Kubaba is met with as a Hittite feminine name (*Kupapaš*).[6] There also lived, under Muršiliš II, a Hittite general who bore the name of the god ^{d}KAL-*aš*.[7] Thus the Mukšuš (whoever he was) of the Madduwattaš text could have received his name in honor of the god of the same name.

In this way, the most likely conclusion about the relation of the Greek Mopsos to the Cilician *Mpš*/*Muksas* is the following. Mopsos is an East Anatolian name,[8] primarily, as it seems, a divine one

[1] CDXI, VII-A, I, 678: "Trophonios . . . or Zeus Trophonios . . . was an old, certainly pre-Greek god of chthonic character in the Boeotian Lebadeia, where he was consulted for oracles in a cave . . ." *ibid.*, 693: "his name, in Boeotian *Trephonios*, signifies 'the nourisher' "; *ibid.*, 694: "the divinities of the Nether World know how to predict the future . . . they know also the healing lore."

[2] Transl. CC, 126 ss.

[3] CCI, 60 ss., 64 ss., 67.

[4] CCXXXVII, 178 s.; CCI, 72, n. 284 (text 260 TU 12A I: 24).

[5] CCCLXII, 664.

[6] V, 230 (communicated by FRIEDRICH).

[7] CCI, 18. On the god KAL cf. CCXXXVIII, 161-164.

[8] We assumed this origin of the name on historical and geographical grounds, and linguistic considerations do not contradict it. However, from a purely linguistic point of view, the name *Mpš* could as well be W-S. It would then have come to Anatolia from Syria, along with Kubaba and other deities. We do not insist upon this possibility, but *Mpš* may be compared, with all reservations, to the word *mpšt* in a Phoenician inscription from Byblos, discussed by DUPONT-SOMMER (who dates it by the Xth or IXth century), CXXV. He writes on *mpšt* (CXXV, 164 s.): "We consider it a noun with the preformant *m*-, derived from the root *npš*. This root is attested in Judaeo-Aramaic with the sense of 'being numerous,' in Akkadian (*napâšu*) with the sense 'to extend, to be numerous,' in Arabic (*nafusa*) with the sense of 'being precious' . . . *munfasat* 'a precious thing,' *munfis* 'precious thing, fortune, good' . . . Morphologically, this word *mpšt*, where the *n* of the radical

(as the names of Telepinuš, Muwatalliš, Šandaš, Kupapaš, ᵈKAL-aš), which penetrated into the West of Asia Minor (Lydia, Claros, Rhodes) in the same way as the cult of the goddess Kubaba, and such names as Panamuwa, Mutallu, Muršiliš, Tarḫundara(ba). Since the shrine of Claros was pre-Hellenic,[1] Mopsos was probably also pre-Hellenic there. Together with other Asianic (and Semitic) names, Mopsos penetrated into European Greece as early as the Mycenaean age. Since the sharp distinction between "heroic" and "ordinary" names in Greek onomastics belongs only to the classical epoch,[2] Mopsos was adopted both as a human name (*Moqsos* of the tablets in Linear B) and as an oracular divine or semi-divine personage, and he became quite popular on both shores of the Aegean. Greek genealogies were created to connect him with European Greece: one proceeded from the existence of a town in Thessaly, called after him Mopsion, and made him a member of the old legendary tribe of the Thessalian Lapiths; the other one, whose center was the Hellenized Claros, linked him with the prophetic kin of Teiresias and Manto. As a famous soothsayer, he was made the legendary founder of several Greek colonies in Asia Minor. When the Greeks, shortly after 700, discovered him in his actual home-domain, they correctly identified him with the character of the same name whom they knew already, and Callinos from Ephesos (a city whose sanctuary almost formed one cultic unity with the neighboring Claros), a contemporary of the events, promptly put it into a story.

The history thus reconstructed of the penetration of the name (and probably of the essence) of the Anatolian Mopsos into Greece

is assimilated, as is normal in Phoenician, is the exact replica, in feminine form, of the Arabic *munfis*." In Akkadian, moreover, *napâšu* also signifies "to be abundant," especially in relation to the harvest. Both "precious thing, fortune" and "abundance, increase" are fitting names for a chthonic oracular deity similar to the fellow-oracle-givers Amphiaraos, Trophonios etc.

[1] CDXV, 46: "The *manteion* of Claros, substitute of the prophetic cave of Mother-Earth, where one still finds sherds of pre-Hellenic ceramics, seems to be quasi contemporary, in its origins, with the 'burned city' of Hissarlik"; Asiatic elements in the Claros cult, *ibid.*, 213; Creto-Carians, *ibid.*, 538-534; Hittite influence, *ibid.*, p. 554-572.

[2] In classical time up to the Hellenistic epoch, names of heroes were never given to people—they were, in a way, "taboo" (cf. CCCLXXXII, 190). But in the Mycenaean tablets one finds almost at every step names which later became "heroic." DV, 104 enumerate 58 names exactly paralleled in Homer, some of which were later counted as "heroic," e.g. *A-ki-re-u* Achilles, *A-pi-ja-re-wo* Amphiaraos (Boeotian *Amphiarēos*), *De-u-ka-ri-jo* Deucalion, *E-ko-to* Hector, *Ma-ka-wo* Machaon, *Te-se-u* Theseus, and many others.

with the wave of Oriental influence in the IId millenium, of his Hellenization, and then of his journey back into his old homeland with the advancement of the Greek colonization eastward about 700—is not exceptional in the history of cultural exchange between countries. Let us refer to one well-known example from medieval Europe. The motifs of the Nibelungen saga sprang up in the Frankish kingdom early in the Merovingian period, and very soon they penetrated through Germany into Norway; but after the conversion of the Saxons to Christianity the links between heathen Norway and Germany were severed for a long time, and the Nibelungen saga underwent a completely independent treatment in the two countries. In Norway, its heroes became typical Vikings, while in Germany they evolved into high feudal kings and knights. Then, after the first Crusades, relations between the two countries were restored, and secondary borrowings from the German Nibelungen Lied entered the Norwegian epic. Conversely, many centuries later, the German, Richard Wagner, created his Nibelungen cycle of operas mainly according to the Scandinavian version.[1]

The Hypachaeans of Herodotos

The necessity of exhausting all possible onomastical coincidences and ethnic links between Cilicia and Greece compells us to give consideration to an evidence from Herodotos, which has attracted much attention from several modern scholars. In his enumeration of the military contingents, provided by subject peoples to Xerxes' army and fleet, Herodotos (VII : 91) says about the Cilicians: "they were formerly called Hypachaeans (*Hypachaiaoi*); then they received their name from the Phoenician Cilix, son of Agenor". Because of the presence of the element *achaioi* in the name of the Hypachaeans, proof of very early colonization of Cilicia by Achaeans, as early as the time of the Hittite empire, was seen in this evidence.[2]

[1] Cf. CCCLXIII, II, 1, 288-296.

[2] CCC, 236 ss.: the Hypachaioi were Greek Achaeans from whom Eastern Cilicia took the name of *Qāwē*—cf. the Egyptian form *Aqaiwā(ša)*—with the Hittite elision of the initial *a*-; CDXCII, 30: "If the term *Aḫḫiyawā* had any relation to the Greek Achaeans, this was precisely to the inhabitants of those settlements (in Cilicia) who preserved . . . the name of Achaeans," with a reference to Herod. VII: 91. CDLXIX, 358 s., 378 also utilized the Hypachaeans to ascertain the location of *Aḫḫiyawā* in Pamphylia or Cilicia, but firmly believed that the *Aḫḫiyawā* of Asia Minor were quite distinct

The hypothesis that the kingdom of Aḫḫiyawā itself lay in Cilicia can now be considered completely abandoned.[1] But does the report of Herodotos at least hint that there were smaller Achaean settlements in Cilicia already in the Hittite epoch, or immediately after? This is not the only ethnonymical exercise of Herodotos; several others are included in this very same list of the peoples participating in Xerxes' army, or may be found in other parts of his History. His basic scheme is—that peoples change their names after prominent personages, who are in reality either mere eponyms, formed out of ethnic names, or fabular heroes with similarly sounding names, taken not even from the native, but from Greek mythology. The rôle of "the Phoenician Cilix, the son of Agenor" in the origin of the name of the Cilicians is exactly the same as that of "the Colchian woman Medea" in the case of the Medes (VII: 62), or that of "Perses, the son of Perseus" in the case of the Persians. In the first place, the ethnic name of the Cilicians is not Phoenician, secondly, it was brought to Cilicia (first Western, then Eastern) by the Anatolian tribe of Ḫilakku as late as the VIIIth and the VIth centuries. It was from this tribe that the united kingdom of the Syennesis dynasty received its name Cilicia. This occurred only about hundred years before Herodotos wrote his History.[2] Therefore, if the name of Hypachaeans preceded in Cilicia that of Cilicians, there is no reason to locate it as far back as the "Trojan war."

Though the name of the Hypachaeans is not found anywhere else, it was not invented by Herodotos—otherwise he would have supplied it with his own mythico-historical commentary. A very interesting suggestion was made by Isidore Lévy [3] who corrected *Hypachaioi* to *Hylachaioi*, a presumed Greek transcription of *Ḫilakku*, thus completely eliminating any relation of the name to the Achaeans. The only objections to this attractive hypothesis are: impossibility to prove that Herodotos' text is here corrupt, and difficulty to admit that the strong laryngal *ḫ* which in the parallel form was rendered by Greek *k* in *Kilikes*, should have been

from the Greek Achaeans; exactly the same is repeated LVII, 21, 44. CLXVI, 136 saw in the Hypachaeans post-Trojan, sub-Mycenaean Achaeans, half-barbarized and therefore called "half-Achaeans."

[1] First, because of the archaeological data (see p. 16 above), second, because the progress in reconstructing the geography of the Hittite Empire transferred Arzawa into the south-west of Asia Minor, and Aḫḫiyawā still farther to the West.

[2] DLIII, 39-42.

[3] *Ap. Mélanges Émile Boisacq*, II (1938), 119-127, quoted CCLIV, 34, n. 3.

attenuated into a mere spiritus rudus. We rather believe that Herodotos had in mind the Greek colonists from Cyprus who had established themselves in some localities along the Cilician shore under Sennacherib (first decade of the VIIIth century)—prior indeed to the coming of the Ḫilakku-Cilicians to Quê. The Cypriot Greeks considered themselves Achaeans,[1] so "Hypachaeans" signifies either "Lowland Achaeans," which is more probable, or "inferior Achaeans," not of pure blood.[2] After c. 540 they became, politically, Cilicians—that is what Herodotos, conforming to his scheme of ethnic name-shift, understood by "changing the name". The chronological sequence of events is correctly reported by Herodotos, but it has nothing to do either with the Aḫḫiyawā kingdom of the Hittite times, or with the imaginary colonization by Mopsos "right after the Trojan war."

Danaos and Danel: A Mythological Comparison

After these indispensable digressions on Mopsos and the Hypachaeans we return to the basic problem of this chapter, and one of the corner-stones of this entire study—to the relation of the Danaans to the Danunians. We have seen that in the light of the whole previous analysis the possibility of the Cilician Danunians' migration from Greece is eliminated. Therefore, there remain only two possibilities: either the two tribes had nothing in common except the fortuitous similarity of their names, or the Greek Danaans came to Greece from the Semitic East.

An examination of the Greek myths of King Danaos, the eponym of the Danaans, and of his kin, may help to find the way toward a solution. Up to now our investigation was based mainly on historical, archaeological, and epigraphical data, which were sometimes fragmentary and controversial, but had the advantage of offering positive facts. Now we must pass to the much more vague field of studying myths. We have learned from the sections dealing with Mopsos how little one can rely upon genealogical and foundation myths for the reconstruction of events that happened a thousand or more years before these myths were written down. In the absence of regular annalistic records and of uninterrupted continuity of written tradition, it is hard to expect that late constructions of

[1] Thus, seers were called *Achaiomanteis* at Cyprus, CCCLXIII, III, 363; the northern coast of Cyprus was known as the Achaean coast, CDXXVI, I, 68.

[2] CLXVI, 136; other explanations CCC, 216-219.

poets, mythographers and logographers should correctly render facts about the rise and political history of ancient tribes and realms which have perished long ago in historic changes and catastrophes.[1] The basic keepers of the tradition were priests and temple personnel, as the intellectually most developed class of that time—but, in conformity with their function of cult attendants, this tradition was not a political, but a religious one. What they kept and transmitted from generation to generation were myths, poems, and dramatic mysteries about gods and divine heroes with whom the cult of the given temples was connected. Such myths and legends had more chance of being preserved during the centuries. On the other hand, most myths—even if they are but tales about astral, elemental or chthonic deities—reflect in certain measure the historical epoch and the geographic environment where they were born. Precisely in this respect, in an indirect way, they are precious for the modern investigator. The details of the story may be, in the main, free creation of poets who worked on old mythical material; but the thematic pivot which often has analogies in the myths of other peoples can be separated, and its comparative analysis can reveal its origin.

Ancient historians perceived myths as reliable tales about real persons and events, and tried simply to free them from their supernatural elements and to rationalize them as much as possible. Of course, due to the lack of a critical approach and of a consistent methodology, such attempts were of a subjective, arbitrary and naïve character. Modern scholarship also tries to extract from myths the valuable kernels they contain. The best criteria here are the data of archaeology and epigraphics which are contemporary with the presumed time of the events depicted in a given myth. Mythological research has at its disposal another manner of treatment which helps to derive benefit from the very contents of the myth. This is the *method of relics*, developed in his time by

[1] From the methodological point of view, most of what Eduard MEYER formulated in CCCLXIII, II, 1, 251, n. 1, is still true: for historical remainders in the myths, only epic traditions can be consulted; the later genealogical and logographical arrangements are to be mistrusted, and "their entire pseudo-history of the Mycenaean epoch is without any worth, notwithstanding how often there were made attempts, in more recent times, to squeeze something out of it." But we shall see later that we find genuine ancient myths and epic traditions is some places where Ed. MEYER, due to the conditions of his time, saw late artificial combinations put together from disparate elements.

the prominent Polish Hellenist Prof. Tadeusz ZIELINSKI.[1] Its essence, applied to the questions which interest us, consists in analysing vestigial motifs which do not play a rôle in the preserved version of the myth and whose very occurrence there is not justified, but which do have a sense and a justification in other versions of the basic theme, known from other sources, earlier ones or those belonging to a different geographical milieu.[2]

Therefore, in our approach to the Danaos myth, we shall not begin by another attempt to reinterpret it as an historical relation.[3] Historical hints, preserved as relics in this myth, will be examined later. We should like to put the question in this way: if the Argive Danaans really had come from the Semitic East, and if the myth about their eponym Danaos really had been born among the Danaans themselves, then this myth must have had a close analogy to the W-S myths which were told in Syria, Phoenicia, and Palestine about the hero whose name the Cilician Danunians bore. According to our previous conclusions, that ethnic name derives from *Dân*. And a hero of that name actually did exist in the mythology of the Western Semites. This was Daniel or Danel,[4] hero of one of the largest W-S epic cycles discovered in the temple library of Ugarit. Judging from his having been mentioned twice by Ezechiel (14: 14; 28: 3), we can assume that he had been widely known, many centuries after the destruction of Ugarit, both in Judah and in Phoenicia (for in Ez. 28: 3 the ironical words, "thou art wiser than Daniel", are addressed to the king of Tyre).[5] For the subject of this study, the presence of the myth cycle on Danel in Ugarit is especially important, Ugarit having been the principal commercial link be-

[1] DLVII, book I: "De locis tragoediae rudimentalibus"; cf. CCCXLVI, 99, and CCCXLVII, 104 s.

[2] These may be strange-sounding names, already unintelligible to those who wrote the myth down, unusual rites and customs, petrified phrases and formulas, symbols and requisits and so on. Their discrepancy, and in many cases their straight contradiction of the attitudes and tendencies at the time the myth was written down, shows their relatively ancient age, and the adduction of variants in which these elements play a natural and justified rôle, helps restore the time and the place of the myth's origin.

[3] "Straightforward rationalist re-interpretation of a myth can only be detrimental to science," CCCXLVII, 105.

[4] Written *Dnil*, but twice *Dn.il*, with the word-divider, thence rather Dan-El, like e.g. the god Rekub-El at Śam'al. Both times when the name is found in Ezechiel, it is spelled in *scriptio defecta*: *Dn'l*, which is considered proof of its having been pronounced Danel, CXLVII, 69 ss.

[5] For the traces of the Danel story in Jewish legends, cf. CDLXXV.

tween Syria and the Aegean. Though this W-S epic (which the Ugaritian scribes called the *Aqht* poem after the name of Danel's son) is not fully preserved,[1] it can nonetheless help us to find W-S parellels to the Danaos myth.

Moreover, the hypothesis that the tribal name of the Danunians derives from the mythical hero Dan/Danel is corroborated by the existence of another W-S tribe with the same eponym—the Israelite tribe of Dan. Éd. Dhorme correctly compared the Ugaritic Danel with the eponym of the tribe of Dan,[2] both of whom are connected (not only by their names) with "judgment": the archaic Blessing of Jacob says, "Dan will judge his people as one of the tribes of Israel" (Gen. 49: 16), and Danel, sitting in the threshing-floor, "judges the case of the widow, adjudicates the cause of the fatherless" (1 Aqht: 24-25; 2 Aqht V: 7-8).[3] But the second saying of the Blessing of Jacob on Dan (Gen. 49: 17), comparing him to a serpent, is no less important in understanding his character. The serpent always was, among all ancient Mediterranean peoples, the symbol of the chthonic underworld gods, the givers of fertility, harvest, and healing (we shall discuss these functions of the serpent in our chapter III). And Danel is precisely such an agrarian-chthonic personage, according to the Ugaritic epic. He is a healer (*mt rpi*),[4] a soothsayer, a giver and a detainer of the harvest, his main activity is in cornfields and vineyards, and he is connected with the under-

[1] *Editio princeps*: DXVIII; other editions, translations and commentaries: CCXXXIV, 179-184; CCXXIII, 84-103; CXCVI, 149-155; CLXXXVI, 257-313; CCLII (with ample bibliography up to 1949); and others.

[2] "which is a hypocoristic of Dan-el, like Jacob > *Ya'aqōbh-'el,*" CXVII, 105.

[3] A full analogy to the origin of the tribal name of Dan from a divine figure of the same name is given by the names of some other Israelite tribes: Asher (cf. XIV, 99 s.), Gad, Zebulun, by many other W-S and Arabic tribes, clans, and towns. Danel's representation as an earthly king is not very important—there was no sharp dividing line between kings and gods (cf. CCXI, 208 s.) in mythology.

[4] Literally: "the man of healing" (genitive). In the extant text we have one reference to Danel's healing abilities: on his demand Baal breaks the wings of eagles and then, again on his demand, restores them. Magic rites, prayers, and exorcisms were an integral part of the practice of ancient Near Eastern healers. The ancient physician's task was primarily that of determining the transgression which caused the disease, or the god responsible for an illness, and this was ascertained through various methods of divination, including ornithomancy (cf. Calchas in *Iliad* I). When the "hand of Nergal" (pestilence) devastated Alašia, her king asked the Pharaoh to send him 1 ^{awil}*ša-i-li našrê* "one eagle-consulter" (EA 35: 26)—and Danel was precisely such a specialist in divination.

ground spirits, the Rephaim, who in addition to their other functions are invoked to come to the threshing-floors and vineyards—evidently to bless them. His son *Aqht*, a hunter with a remarkable bow, is at the same time a harvester (1 Aqht: 66-67, 73-74).

The Argive Danaos [1] is an analogous character—to judge from the relics in the myth. He and his daughters brought fertility to the Argive plain. His daughters found springs, and to them was also ascribed the introduction of the Thesmophoria—the principal feast of the agricultural goddess Demeter (Herod. II: 171). They were revered in Argos in classical times for having watered the country. In the later mythology the Danaides are represented as forever carrying water into a bottomless vessel, a punishment for having killed their husbands. But it was proven long ago that this motif had been transferred to the Danaides comparatively late, not until the Greeks had developed the idea of posthumous retribution. Even then the watercarriers of Hades did not immediately become identified with the Danaides, but were at first merely the souls of those uninitiated in the Orphic mysteries.[2] From the point of view of the iconologic or iconographic mythology, on which CLERMONT-GANNEAU wrote in his time,[3] the case is clear: the Danaides, the discoverers of wells, the irrigators, were pictured as carrying jugs on their shoulders; thence the later interpretation.

But exactly the same—literally—is said in the Ugaritic poem of Danel's daughter *Pġt*,[4] whose constant epithet is "who shoulders water, spreads the dew on the barley, knows the course of the stars"

[1] The classical Greek form of the name, *Danaos* (> *Danawos*) is constructed on analogy with the singular of the tribal name *Dana(w)oi*, and therefore it was believed to be merely an artificial eponym (CCCLXIV, 251). But the older form is attested in a Mycenaean tablet from Cnossos (KN Db 1324, V: 1631, DV, 417): *Da-na-jo*, i.e. *Danaios*, which corresponds to the Semitic extended form with the suffix *-aya*: EA *A-da-ia*, Alalaḫ *Pa-a-la-ia* (= *Baʿalaya*), *Ša-ma-ia*, *Ba-na-ia*, Ugarit *A-ba-ya*, *Ríq-da-ya*, *Ša-da-ya*, Biblical *Šimšay*, *ʾAbišay*, *Šešay*, *Yišay* etc.

[2] CCXLVIII, 613-623. "The Danaides of mythology were *well-nymphs* . . . Strabo (VIII. 256 [= 6 : 8]) preserves us a line from an epic poet, 'Argos, waterless once, the Danai [*Danaai*] made well-watered.' Long before the tragedy about their husbands, the Danaides were at work watering, fertilizing thirsty Argos. The Danaides as *merely Danaides*, might fitly be represented as filling a great well-*pithos*," *ibid.*, 619.

[3] Very often on has to seek "not in the image the translation of the myth, but in the myth the translation of the image," quoted LXII, 36.

[4] *Pġt* just signifies "girl" in Ugaritic; she has no personal name—precisely as the Danaides were originally nameless (they were later provided with banal standard names which vary from author to author).

(1 Aqht: 50-52; etc.). Moreover, the daughter of Danel is the heroine of a bloody vengeance drama, which corresponds to the tragedy involving the Danaides' husbands. She came forward as the avenger of her brother, the young hunter *Aqht*, who had been imprudent enough to insult the goddess Anath by refusing to cede her his wonderful bow and was thus killed by Anath's servant, the eagle-like *Yṭpn*. After the completion of seven years of mourning, *Pġt* declared to her father:

> Thou shalt bless me that I may go blessed,
> Protect me that I may go protected!
> I'll smite the smiter of my brother,
> Yea destroy the destroyer of my sibling! (1 Aqht: 194-197).

Danel eagerly approved his daughter's idea, and she put on a dress of a warrior, armed herself with a dagger, and concealed it under a woman's garb. Thus prepared, *Pġt* directed herself to her brother's murderer *Yṭpn*, who recognized her, received her in his abode, put into her hand a goblet of mixed wine (*msk*) which she drank, while he swore that "the hand that smote *Aqht* the hero will smite thousands of my lady's foes." Here the tablet ends, and the end of the episode remains unknown. GINSBERG, according to whose translation *Yṭpn* did not treat his guest with wine, but on the contrary, made her serve it to him (which is quite improbable), concludes: "The story . . . no doubt went on to relate that . . . Paghat killed Yatpan while he lay unconscious in the arms of Bacchus . . ." [1] GORDON, whose translation we have followed above, is not so certain, but he considers it "quite likely," that *Pġt* "avenged *Aqht* by slaying *Yṭpn*." [2] However, the first publisher of the *Aqht* epic, VIROLLEAUD, observed in his commentary to that passage: "The poem ends by a dialogue of Yṭpan and Paġat; they drink wine together and seem to be reconciled. It is known that the Legend of the Gracious and Beautiful Gods (SS) ends in the same way: by a kind of communion by the means of wine." [3] This variant seems to be more plausible, because 1) drinking wine together was a serious rite of fraternization, especially of the mixed drink (*msk*) which had magic properties; [4] 2) since, as most commentators presume, the

[1] CXCVI, 155.
[2] CCXXIII, 85.
[3] DXVIII, 181 s.
[4] With the Greeks, the "mixed drink" was known as *kykeon*, and it belonged to the basic ceremonies of initiation into the Eleusinian mysteries, CCXLVIII, 155 s. CLXXXVI, 311 recognized in the scene of *Yṭpn* treating *Pġt*

goddess Anath revived *Aqht* in the lost part of the poem,[1] the preliminary reconciliation between the family of the murdered and the entourage of the goddess would fit into this scheme very well.[2]

Essentially the same device is contained in the myth about Danaos and the Danaides. The daughters of Danaos, forced by their cousins, the sons of Aigyptos, to marry them, feigned agreement; but their father Danaos secretly armed each of them with a bronze dagger, and on the wedding-night each killed her husband, except the elder daughter, Hypermestra, who, inspired by the goddess Artemis, spared the life of her husband Lynceus. If one reconstructs the lost end of the *Aqht* poem according to VIROLLEAUD, *Pġt*'s abstention from killing *Yṭpn* is quite the same as Hypermestra's pardoning Lynceus. If one follows GINSBERG, the treacherous murder of *Yṭpn* corresponds to the bloody deed of the rest of the Danaides.

In the Ugaritic poem, Danel's and *Pġt*'s hate of *Yṭpn* stems from their desire for vengeance on behalf of their dead son and brother. In the Greek myth, this motive is replaced by the Danaides' repugnancy to the forced marriage with the Aigyptiads.[3] However, this motif is present in another W-S myth—this time a Hebrew one, the so-called "Shechem myth" (Gen. 34), which is remarkably close to the bloody wedding of the Danaides, and the heroine of which, moreover, bears the almost identical name Dinah (*Dînā*), a feminine form of Dan. Dinah is raped by Shechem, son of Hamor, the ruler of the city of Shechem;[4] he falls in love with her and, through his father Hamor, asks Jacob and his sons not only to give him Dinah for a wife, but to arrange a general intermarriage between the clan

with wine the "Semitic practice of concluding covenants by *commensality*, i.e. eating and drinking together," with several illustrations.

[1] CCXXIII, 85; CXCVI, 155.

[2] Especially so since it was seven years after her brother's death that *Pġt* undertook to fulfill her plan for vengeance. As proved CCXXIII, 4 s. and elsewhere, the disappearance of the "dying god" followed a seven-year pattern; thus we should expect *Aqht* to be revived by Anath precisely at that very time.

[3] Or by an oracle given to Danaos and warning him that this marriage threatens him with a danger (another variant: that one of the Aigyptiads would kill him). Reference to oracles is a common manner of justifying an action which, in itself, has already become unintelligible.

[4] Note that Shechem and Hamor are eponyms, respectively, of the city and of its ruling clan—just as Aigyptos is the eponym of Egypt. Why was Shechem, of all cities, chosen by the myth? We believe that one reason was the identity of its name (*škm*) with the standard epithet of *Pġt*: *škmt my* "who shoulders water."

of Jacob and the Shechemites (as, in the Argive myth, the collective marriage of the fifty sons of Aigyptos with the fifty daughters of Danaos). Jacob's sons pretend to agree, but demand, as a preliminary condition, that the prince and all males of the city become circumcised; and while they were suffering from the effects of the operation, Jacob's sons raid the city and kill all males in it. In this respect the Argive myth has followed the pattern of another W-S myth, but it still contains three important relics of the *Aqht* poem.

These are, first, the motif of a drought of many years, explained by the late mythographer quite arbitrarily: "The (Argive) country had no water, for Poseidon had dried the springs in anger against Inachos for his having testified about the country's appurtenance to Hera." [1] In the Ugaritic myth the seven-year drought plays an organic rôle and is described in detail; it is the consequence of *Aqht*'s murder, the punishment of the country for the shedding of innocent blood.[2] Secondly, the trial of Hypermestra for breaking the decision to kill all Aigyptiads; here Danaos, who organized the trial, is a judge—in conformity with the Semitic significance of his name and with his general correspondence to the Ugaritic Danel. Thirdly, Artemis' rôle in Hypermestra's mercy for Lynceus and in saving her life at the trial—a rôle so important that Hypermestra, after her acquittal, is said to have dedicated a temple to Artemis Peitho ("Persuasion").[3] Artemis corresponds here to Anath, the principal divine character of the *Aqht* poem, the hunter goddess who destroyed *Aqht* for not having ceded his marvellous hunting bow to her. That is all that remained from the rôle she played in the Ugaritic variant; in the Argive myth, she appears only in the last act, but her participation is significant. One could presume perhaps that Danel's wrath against his daughter for abandoning the vengeance design figured in the lost part of the *Aqht* poem—it was probably followed by Anath's intervention in favor of the girl, by reviving *Aqht* and by the return of general happiness.[4]

[1] (Pseudo-) Apollodoros, *Biblioth.* II: 1: 4. But according to the genealogy he accepts, Inachos was separated from Danaos by five generations.

[2] CCXXIII, 4 s., 84 s.

[3] Pausanias II: 21: 1, who also mentions a statue erected by Hypermestra to Aphrodite the Victorious (an alternative effort to find a Greek name for the goddess of the original myth).

[4] CDLXXV plausibly explains why Danel is mentioned along with Job by Ezechiel: Danel lost his son, and he was returned to him; the same motif (resurrection of Job's children) originally figured in the history of Job (instead of birth of new ones, as in the present form).

The closest relation of agriculture and justice—as in the figure of Danel—manifests itself also in the feast of Thesmophoria, allegedly introduced by the Danaides and dedicated to the agriculture goddess Demeter Thesmophoros—the "law-carrier" or "law-giver." [1] What is important is not the question of the historical reliability of that version,[2] but the very fact of the Danaides being associated with the main agrarian and chthonic feast of pre-Dorian Greek women. *Pġt*, "who knows the course of the stars," i.e. astrologer,[3] who masters the art of ornithomancy (I *Aqht* 28-37) and waters the fields, is precisely the type of a wise woman, expert in secret religious lore.

There can be no doubt: we have, at Argos and at Ugarit, the same basic myth; not only do the heroes' names coincide (Danaos and Dan-el), but their natures, the natures of their daughters, the essential plot, and the whole situation and circumstances as well. It is true that between the Ugaritic and the Greek version there is an interval of almost a thousand years: the *Aqht* poem was written down in the first half of the XIVth century, while the earliest coherent tale of Danaos and the Danaides we possess—Aeschylos' tragedy *The Suppliants*—was composed between 479 and 472.[4] This explains the two main points of divergence between them. First, the motif of *Aqht*'s murder, the principal line of the Ugaritic story, disappeared from the Argive myth, and was replaced by one of a forced marriage that turned into a bloodbath—also a W-S one

[1] CCXLVII, 145, à propos the name of the Thesmophoria: "The connection between primitive law and agriculture seems to have been very close. The name of the earliest laws recorded—they are rather precepts than in our sense laws—the 'Ploughman's curses'—speaks for itself . . . Other similar precepts, no doubt sanctioned by similar curses, have come down under the Thrice-Plougher *Triptolemos* . . ."—In a characteristic way, violent curses against the city near which *Aqht* was murdered, are put into the mouth of Danel, the agriculturer and judge.

[2] As FOUCART firmly believed in his otherwise very valuable CLXIX.

[3] We do not see why GASTER, CLXXXVI, 297, objects to the epithet "who knows the courses of the stars" being understood as referring to *Pġt*'s "proficiency in astronomy" (more correct: astrology). Astrology was known and popular not only in Babylonia, but also in Ugarit—cf. UM 143 and in the *Aqht* poem itself, Aqht 3: 9-10.

[4] But the myth of Danaos was already known to the iambic poet Archilochos early in the VIIth century—if the frg. 150, quoted by the Byzantine chronicler John Malalas, belongs to this bearer of that name: "Lynceus, according to wise Archilochos' account, made war on king Danaos and slew him and then took the kingdom and his daughter" (EDMONDS, *Elegy and Iambus*, III, 190 s., *Loeb Clas. Libr.*). For the name of Lynceus, see p. 193, n. 5 below.

and also onomastically centred around the root DN (Dinah!). However, in three parallel variants the motif of *Aqht*'s violent death is found in the myths of another Greek city, Thebes, in connection with another kin of Semitic origin, the Cadmids (see chapter II). Secondly, the figure of *Pǵt,* the heroine of the Ugaritic myth, the only daughter of Danel, was multiplied into fifty daughters of Danaos, of whom, however, only Hypermestra (and perhaps Amymona [1]) plays an individual rôle, while the others are needed only for quantity.

This exorbitant figure, very popular in Greek myths, has its explanation: it is the number of seven-day weeks in one lunar year ($50 \times 7 = 350$, the rounded number of days of a lunar year instead of the more exact 354). The proof is supplied by *Odyss.* XII: 129-130, where Helios is said to possess 7 herds of 50 cows each and 7 herds of 50 sheep each, a transparent allegory of the days and nights of the year. Selena, the Moon, also had from Endymion 50 daughters—it is the same motif. Further, Actaeon (as we will see, one of *Aqht*'s avatars) was torn to pieces by his 50 hounds; since he is a typical "harvest spirit," the figure 50 symbolizes the rotation of the year. Heracles has in one night deflowered and impregnated 50 daughters of king Thespios; since Heracles has all the characteristics of a sun-hero, here too the year-cycle is symbolized. As the Danaides were connected with the agricultural year-cycle, their representation as 50 sisters belongs to the same circle of ideas.[2] But in the final count, the symbolical figure 50 is also of Oriental origin; the Greeks did not count in seven-day weeks, while the Babylonians and the Western Semites did. Even more interesting is the Biblical agrarian jubilee cycle of 50 years ($7 \times 7 + 1$) to which the same chronological pattern applies. And in general, 50 was, with the West Semites and the Arabs, the standard number of a team, of a military unit.[3]

We have subjected the myth of Danaos and Danaides to comparative analysis, and we have ascertained its W-S origin. Taken in itself, this result could as well be interpreted as another of the very numerous cases of borrowing and assimilation by one people of the

[1] Amymona ("the blameless") became the beloved of Poseidon who struck for her the springs at Lerna out of a cliff.

[2] Then the figure 50 was indiscriminately applied to sons of various mythological personages: Arcadian king Lycaon, Attic king Pallas, Trojan king Priamos, etc.

[3] Cf. CCCLXIII, II, 2, 217.

literary works of another one—as, for instance, the Canaanite and Hurrian myths that we know in Hittite translation and adaptation. Even such a result would be not of small interest for the history of Greek culture. But we have here something more: the Argive myth on Danaos explains—in the usual mythological manner—how the tribe of the Danaans came to power in Argolis. That tribe is not a fictitious one—besides Homer, it is attested in authentic records of Egyptian eye-witnesses as one of the tribes of the Aegean basin. And since at the same time there existed, in the eastern Mediterranean, a W-S tribe of the Danunians, so the W-S nature of the myth on the Argive Danaos is an indubitable and very important connecting link between the eastern and the western Danunians which proves the oriental, Semitic origin of the latter, i.e., of the Homeric Danaans.

We have reached this conclusion on the basis of intrinsic data in the Argive myth itself, and we avoided completely the usual references to the myth's assertion that Danaos and his daughters came in a ship from the East, from Egypt. If that had been the whole content of the myth, it could be no more trusted than the notices of Greek authors about, e.g., the foundation of Tarsus by Triptolemos etc. But even without the data on Danaos' itinerary, the myth betrays its origin from the Semitic East—and so we have a right to recognize that this detail, too, reflects a genuine tradition of the Danaan migration from the eastern Mediterranean.[1] This is coupled with a circumstance of psychological order. It was only natural that the Greek colonies, freshly founded on barbarian shores, try to strengthen and extend their connections with the metropoly through the fiction of their having been founded, ages ago, by one of the famous ancient heroes from this same homeland. Yet is was contrary to the spirit of militant Greek expansion in the age of the great colonization

[1] A number of scholars considered correct the statement of the mythographers on Danaos' migration from Egypt (e.g. L. Holland, cclvi)—but they failed to bring any objective proof of it. Repeating the same myth over and again is not enough to make it historically reliable. By the way, Holland's reconstruction of the events behind the myths of Danaos, Europa and Cadmos is rather in discord with historical data. He was convinced, for instance, that the Philistines and the Ṯikar sat on the Palestinian shore long *before* the invasion of the Sea Peoples in 1200, and that there existed along the Phoenico-Palestinian coast an un-Semitic population, including Danuna; "Europa was born in Phoenicia,—though probably the Greeks never considered her of that Semitic Phoenician race they later knew" (cclvi, 88) and so on.

when it is recognized that the population and the oldest ruling dynasty of such a famous and immemorially Greek city as Argos was of foreign, un-Greek origin (the same applies to Thebes and other similar cases). Here is less chance of tendentious invention and more chance that there really was such a tradition in the city itself; especially so, if the main details, the personal names and the thematic motifs of the myth actually derive from the foreign country whose natives are said to have played a rôle in the foundation of the city or the dynasty. From this point of view we shall now approach the historico-geographic data of the myths of Danaos and his ancestors.

Near Eastern Roots and Parallels of the Io Myth

Ed. Meyer, who devoted a fundamental study to the Argive cycle of myths,[1] and briefly summarized his conclusions on a page of his capital comprehensive work,[2] attributed the origin of the myth of Io and her descendant Danaos to the period after 650, when under Psammetichos I Egypt was opened to the Greeks, and Greek merchants and mercenaries began their exciting acquaintance with the marvellous new country:

> The Egyptian religion, too, became known to the Greeks. They recognized in Isis the Argive Io, whom Hera had changed into a cow; they made the Apis bull into her son, under the name of Epaphos, and they found in these figures proof of the ancient tradition, which had already disappeared from the religion and was rooted in animal-worship, that Zeus, in the shape of a bull, had mated with Io. Thus sprang up the belief that Io had wandered to Egypt, that the two peoples of the Egyptians and the Danaans had originated from her descendants. . .The eponyms of the Egyptians and the Libyans, as well as those of the Cilicians and the Phoenicians, were included in the genealogical poetry; beside them stands Belos, who was derived from Beʿel, the god of the Aramaean merchants in Egypt.

The consistent scholarly critical method of Ed. Meyer is, of course, much preferable to most attempts to find exact historical information in a fairy tale—by applying shallow rationalization and subjective interpretation. But we now have at our disposal an incomparably greater amount of epigraphic and comparative mythological material than at the time of Ed. Meyer. We know,

[1] "Pelasgos in Argos. Io und die Danaiden. Der argivische Stammbaum," being the 4th chapter of "Die Pelasger," *ap.* cccLXI, 67-104.

[2] cccLXIII, III, 430 s.

thanks to the decipherment of the Mycenaean Greek tablets by Michael VENTRIS, that the Greeks knew Egypt as early as the Mycenaean epoch, and that among the personal names in these tablets not only *Misarajo* is found [1] (W-S *mṣry* [*miṣriyy*] "Egyptian"; as pers. n. at Ugarit *Mṣry, Mṣrn,*[2] at Nuzu *Muzru,*[3] *Muṣru*),[4] but as well *Aikupitijo* = *Aigyptios.*[5] This means that the Greek name for Egypt was borrowed from the East [6] as early as the Mycenaean epoch and was preserved unchanged through all the "Dark Ages" that followed the fall of Mycenaean culture. And not just this name, but several common names of W-S origin, too, which were believed up until now to have been borrowed from the Phoenicians in a much later period, in the Xth-VIIIth centuries.[7]

Since the personal name *Aikupitijo* (Aigyptios) is mentioned in Mycenaean texts of the same period as *Danajo* (Danaos), there is no reason to deny the possibility of a very ancient association of Danaos and Aigyptos in the myth we are dealing with. Aigyptos, as the brother and rival of Danaos, figures in all existing variants of the myth, as does the country of the same name, Egypt, but in different rôles. One version, transmitted by the real Apollodoros in the scholium to *Iliad* I: 42, apparently derives from the lost epic poem *Danaïs* or *Danaïdes* (attested in reliable sources),[8] and must therefore be considered older and more original than the genealogical catalogues which followed the epics. According to this version, the struggle for power and the hereditary domains of Belos between his sons had its place in Egypt; it was there, on Egyptian soil, that Danaos organized the murder of the Aigyptiads by his

1 Not included in DV. Cf. CCCXLIX, 8.

2 *UM*, § 20.1151.

3 CXCI, 101.

4 *Ibid.*, 308.

5 DV, 98, 414.

6 *Aigyptos* derives from the Egyptian name for Memphis, *Ḥ(t)-k3-Ptḥ*, through the Canaanite *Ḫikuptaḫ* (EA 84: 37; 139: 8) or Ugaritic *Ḥkpt* (var. *Ḥqkpt*), *UM*, § 20.629. Despite the absence of the final *ḥ*, GORDON's objection to its identity with Memphis (*UM*, *l.c.*; CCXXIII, 23, n. 1) is not shared by all scholars.

7 See pp. 337 s. below.

8 It is told in the two extant lines how the Danaides armed at the Nile shore—this already gives some notion about the plot which must have included the murder of the Aigyptiads in Egypt and the flight of Danaos and his daughters overseas to Argos. According to an ancient inscription, the epic had 6500 lines—half as long as the *Iliad.* It could not have been composed after the VIIth century, the end period of cyclic epic poetry. Cf. CDXI, IV, 2, 2091 s.

daughters, and then fled with them to the old homeland of his family, to Argos, where the ruling king Gelanor ceded to him his throne. Aeschylos, who utilized this version for his early play *The Suppliants*, performed soon after Xerxes' invasion of Greece, introduced in it the motif of a barbarian army's incursion into a Greek country; therefore the murder of the Aigyptiads happens (in the unpreserved second part of the trilogy, *The Egyptians* or *The Wedding-Makers*) not before, but after the flight from Egypt, and not in Egypt, but in Argos; this variant was followed by pseudo-Apollodoros in his *Bibliotheca*.[1]

Another variant is told by the scholiast to Euripides' *Hecabe* v. 886: Danaos and Aigyptos, direct sons of Io, were born and struggled for power in Argos itself; Danaos, from envy of the male descendancy of Aigyptos, expelled him with his sons to a country which derived from him its name of Egypt; when Aigyptos' sons had grown up, he invaded Argos with them, and it was there that the bloody wedding of the Aigyptiads with the Danaides took place. Some believed this variant to be the closest to the original version;[2] but, first, it is younger than Aeschylos—it already follows his representation of the Aigyptiads' invasion of Argos; second, it is not hard to notice that the version which makes Danaos never leave Argos was dictated by Greek chauvinism and contempt for barbarians, which developed since the second half of the Vth century and refused to accept the un-Greek origin of such a famous dynasty as the ancient Argive one.[3] We will thus make no mistake in considering the version of the scholiast to *Hecabe* as a late and tendentious modification of the Danaos myth. The Egyptian arena of action was certainly included in it since the beginning.

No doubt the well-composed genealogy which included, besides Danaos and Aigyptos, the eponyms of Libya, Phoenicia, and Cilicia,[4] was created relatively late (cf. Ed. MEYER, above, p. 80). Eponyms that are inserted only as inert filling and do not have any individuality or personal rôle in the story, are a late and artificial interpolation in the framework of an ancient myth; here also belong

[1] CDXI, IV, 2, 2094-2098, *s.v. Danaos.*

[2] *Ibid.*, 2095.

[3] On the anti-barbarian sentiments in Greece since the Peloponnesian war see CCCXLVII, 46-50.

[4] Libya, daughter of Epaphos, granddaughter of Io, bore from Poseidon Belos, father of Danaos and Aigyptos, and Agenor, father of Cadmos, Europa, Phoenix and Cilix.

such banal and un-individual Greek names as Agenor ("worthy, valiant") of the same genealogy. But such a conclusion is much more doubtful when applied to Belos who figures in the myth in the rôle of the father of Danaos and Aigyptos. This is, for one thing, not a geographical eponym, but the name of a god, Baal—a phenomenon of mythological order, on one level with Danaos-Danel. Ed. MEYER, as we have seen, put him beside the above mentioned eponyms and considered that "he was derived from Beʿel, the god of the Aramaean merchants in Egypt." But it can then be objected that the pronunciation *Bêlos* for Baʿal, instead of the expected **Bālos* (as in Ithobalos, Abibalos, contracted Asdrubas, Annibas, etc.) does not necessarily point to its late borrowing from the Aramaeans. Ed. MEYER himself noted in a different place,[1] speaking of the Phoenician Baal, that "in the Greek epics, in the genealogical trees of Hesiod and his followers, this became *Bêlos* in Ionian." This regular Ionic vowel shift *ā* > *ê* makes the assumption of Aramaean mediation unnecessary and, on the contrary, pleads for a long-standing occurrence of the name of **Bālos*/*Bêlos* in the Greek epic. Therefore *Bêlos* can with sufficient grounds also be considered as inherited from the remote W-S prototype of the Danaos myth. Let us remember, by the way, that Baal plays an important rôle in the Ugaritic *Aqht* poem (as the protector of Danel), and his worship was very important, too, in Egypt at a certain period—as we shall see presently.

In our time, we look quite differently on the Io myth than Ed. MEYER did in his. In view of the oriental myths that were discovered since his death, the Io myth no longer appears as a casual contamination of vestiges of Greek zoolatry with externally similar phenomena of the Egyptian religious iconography, but as a single whole of one piece, a tale with immemorially ancient roots in the religious ritual and symbols of the West Asian cultural complex.

The Io myth in its simplest form runs thus: Io, the daughter of the Argive river-god Inachos, first king of Argos (or the daughter of Phoroneus, or Iasos, or Argos, or Peiren, or Prometheus, or Arestor),[2]

[1] CCCLXIII, II, 2, 142, n. 1.

[2] A characteristic example of the inconsistency and arbitrariness of genealogical constructions. Since Io's father does not play any rôle in the myth (nor in its Oriental prototypes), mythographers had to supply his name by themselves—and were free to invent whatever they liked. It is important to stress this circumstance. DOBLHOFER (CXXI, 213) judges the reliability of the Greek tradition about Danaos having come from the East thus: he

was the priestess of Hera, the divine lady of Argos.[1] Zeus fell in love with her, and either he himself, to hide his love from his spouse Hera, or Hera through jealousy, turned her into a cow. We omit the episode with Argos Panoptes, who guarded Io the cow and was killed by Hermes, for he is probably only an aetiological conjecture to explain the constant epithet of Hermes, *Argeïphontês*, which became unintelligible. Io the cow, pregnant from Zeus, was expelled by Hera from Argos; Hera sent a gadfly to torment her, and stung and maddened by it, Io fled from country to country,[2] until she came to Egypt. There her ordeals ended; she recovered her human shape and bore Epaphos, who became king of Egypt and ancestor of Danaos.[3]

The ancients did not have any reliable etymology for the name of Io (this is usually a guarantee of the name's authenticity and antiquity). Some ancient authors presumed that *Iô* signified „moon" in Argos,[4] others derived the name from *iôn* "violet" and ac-accordingly made the cow Io not white, as in most records, but violet. Modern etymologies, whether from Greek or—as proposed by Victor Bérard [5]—from Heb. *yāʾā* (which he explained as "beautiful" and compared with the nymph Callisto, changed by Artemis into a she-bear) are hardly more convincing. The most plausible of the ancient etymologies is the derivation from *ienai* "to wander", and if one accepts it, *Iô* would be a good translation of W-S (Ugaritic) *arḫ*, Akk. *arḫu* "wild cow or heifer", from the root which is in Akk. *arâḫu* "to be quick, rapid, to hurry, to hasten, to move fast", Heb. *ʾāraḫ* "to wander, to travel". We will meet this word in W-S myths.

Already in the cylinder inscriptions of Gudea, the Sumerian ruler

was a son of Belos, and "one named Belos must have been an Oriental." That is true, but until one can prove that Belos organically belongs to the Danaos myth—which Doblhofer and others take for granted—this argument in itself has little value.

[1] In the list of the priestesses of Hera at Argos (the beginning of which is, of course, fictitious), Io is first.

[2] Their enumeration depended upon the imagination of each mythographer; cf. the long, entangled and contradictory itinerary of Io in Aeschylos' *Prometheus Bound*.

[3] "There is no certain clue for unravelling this myth," confessed Nilsson, CCCLXXXII, 62.

[4] This etymology has no confirmation, though in Sumero-Akkadian myths the godly cow is said to belong to the Moon-god. About this and other Greek etymologies cf. CDXI, IX, 2, 1749 s.

[5] LXV, I, 280 s.

of Lagaš, in the description of the marriage of the god Ningirsu with the goddess Ba-ú (or Ba-ba)—an annual rite to promote the fecundity of the earth—their wedding-room is called "a stable". Ba-ú is compared to "the Cow of the god Nanna" (Moon); Nanna himself is called "the mighty young bull of the heaven who lays down in his stable" (cyl. A), while in the cyl. B in the mouth of Ba-ú are put the words: "The holy Cow whom a woman has born (or "who [like] a woman was born") I am, the holy heroine, (that) of Ningirsu, who makes Lagaš resplendent, I am." [1] Thus, as early as in the time of Gudea, the image was widespread of a goddess who was at the same time a cow and a woman, and a special myth on the cow of the Moon-god.

This latter myth is preserved in Akkadian, in the form of a spell to ease the pains of birth.[2] It tells how the Moon-god Sin fell in love with a beautiful cow in his herd, whose name was Amat-Sin ("maidservant of the Moon-god"). The god's love drove her out of her senses. Then Sin copulated with her as a young fiery bull. The cow's delivery was very difficult, she suffered childbed pains, until Sin heard her call from heaven and sent to her two goddesses who eased her delivery. She gave birth to a son whom Sin named AMAR.GA, which Böhl renders by "suckling calf" (literally, "son [or "cub"] of milk"). Böhl was absolutely right in comparing this text with the Io myth.[3]

To the north of Babylonia this motif was adopted and developed in a peculiar manner by the Hurrians, but instead of the Moon-god, here it is the Sun-god who was fascinated by a heifer.[4] She gave birth to a human child, was amazed and indignant by so unnatural an offspring, but the Sun-god saved the child from his mother's anger, took it to heaven, and then ordered it deposited in a solitary place where birds took care of it, until it was found by a childless fisherman who adopted it and pretended it was the child of his wife; we do not know what happened to the child later.[5]

[1] CCLXXXI, 333-339.

[2] The text was found in Aššur; autography CLV, II/5, 74 s., No. 196, rev. II: 10-35; LXX, 110; translation and commentary LXXII, § 4, 204 s.

[3] LXXII, 202; he also compares the myth with that of Zeus and Europa, but Europa is never described or represented as a cow, so this comparison misses the point.

[4] CLXXVI, text No. 3.

[5] One finds here, besides, another myth known in the Danaan myth cycle: the fisherman Dictys who saved the new-born Perseus and his mother Danaë. For birds feeding an abandoned babe, cf. Gilgamos (Gilgameš) in Aelian

Farther to the West, this motif was extremely popular with the W-S Ugaritians, and is preserved in their literature in no less than four variants. In one of them, which is contained in the poem of Baal's hunt,[1] the heroine preserved the name of "maidservant of the Moongod", W-S *Amt-Yrḫ*,[2] but she is also *Amt-Aŝrt*, maidservant of the supreme goddess Asherah, wife of El.[3] El, the spouse of Asherah, orders her to go away into a desert and to give birth there to children whose names will be proclaimed by the gods. In the extant, very incomplete text, nothing is said about *Amt-Yrḫ* being a cow or a heifer. But her children are described as bulls with goodlike faces: "On them are horns like bulls, and humps like buffaloes, and on them is the face of Baal." [4] This would indicate that they were the fruit of the copulation of a god (El himself, most probably) with a cow. In the subsequent lines of the poem these monstrous creatures became the object of Baal's hunt and, somehow, the cause of his death.[5]

This myth has an indubitable resemblance to the story of Hagar in Genesis.[6] The heroine of the Hebrew tale flees to the desert from the oppression of her mistress Sara, being pregnant from Sara's husband Abraham; or is expelled by Abraham at the demand of Sara. After erring in the desert, she gives birth to Ishmael who is (if one takes the words about him in Gen. 16: 12 not in a metaphoric but a literal sense [7]), an onager-man, as the children of *Amt-Aŝrt* were bull-men. The heroine's name, Hagar, from Arabic *hağara* "to flee, to emigrate", is etymologically equivalent to *arḫ* "heifer" of the Ugaritic myths (from *arâḫu*) and to *Iô* (from *ienai*). The situation of the "matrimonial triangle" (El, Asherah, *Amt-Aŝrt*;

and Semiramis in Ctesias. Another example is *Trygôn* "turtle-dove," the wet-nurse of Asclepios (cf. p. 308 below).

[1] DXIII (BH) = UM 75. Translations: CCXXIII, 53 ss.; CXCV; CCXXVIII; CLXXXVI, 217-222.

[2] It remained unnoticed that *Amt-Yrḫ* = *Amat-Sin* of the Akkadian myth, and is a valuable connecting link between the two myths.

[3] Asherah, the spouse of the supreme god, corresponds in this context to the Greek Hera (Atargatis, a late form of Asherah, was also called Hera by the Greeks, cf. Lucian, *De Deâ Syriâ*). Io, too, is a priestess, i.e. a servant, of Hera.

[4] UM 75: I: 30-33. We follow the translation CCXXIII, 54.

[5] They bear in the poem the parallel names of *ʿqqm* (VIROLLEAUD, DXIII, 254, cites Akk. *uquqqu* "beast, brute," ideographically EME.DIB "one whose tongue was removed") and *aklm* "devourers."

[6] As observed CXCV, 140; XLII, 8 ss. (with further comparative details).

[7] Besides, who can tell where symbolism ends and direct sense starts in ancient myths?

Abraham, Sara, Hagar; Zeus, Hera, Io) and the expulsion of the heroine is the same in all of the three myths.[1] We do not know whether any importance should be attributed to Hagar being represented as an Egyptian, while her counterpart Io settled in Egypt.

But there existed as well in Ugarit a direct myth about the copulation of a god with a heifer or a cow. This myth is preserved in three variants: IV AB (= UM 76),[2] RŠ 1929, No. 6 (= UM 6),[3] and I* AB (= UM 67),[4] col. V. The god in all three of the texts is Baal, and the heifer or cow, according to rather transparent hints of the first text and a quite precise statement of the second, is none other than the goddess Anath. In the main corpus of the Baal and Anath epic she is represented as Baal's sister, but in the first two of the cited texts, which stand somewhat apart from the main corpus, she is his spouse.[5] Anath is said to be horned, which does not prevent her, in other places and on reliefs, from being depicted as having wings and flying.[6] In UM 76 Baal's uniting with a heifer (*arẖ*) happens in a region called *Aẖ Šmk mlat rumm*, "*Aẖ Šmk* which is full of buffaloes." Baal, aided by Anath, seeks and finds a heifer who then "bears a bull to Baal, yea a buffalo to the Rider of the Clouds," and after a long walk over different unknown mountains finally announces to Baal this joyous event, and Baal rejoices. But in the same text (its broken corner UM 132) [7] is depicted, with the utmost naturalism, the coupling of Baal with Anath, her pregnancy and someone's birth. Even without this fragment, one has the impression that it was Anath who turned herself temporarily into a heifer.[8]

The text UM 6 was skilfully collated and explained by H.

[1] Already in 1877, CDLX, 85, Hagar was compared to Io.

[2] DX; CCXXIII, 49 ss.; CXCVI, 141 s.

[3] CCXXIII, 51 s.; XCVII.

[4] DXIX, 789-792; CCXXIII, 41 s.; CXCVI, 139; CLXXXVI, 192 s.

[5] Thus also in the Aramaic inscription from Egypt published by DUPONT-SOMMER, CXXXVI, where *Bʿl bʿlʿnwt* is explained by this scholar as "Baal the husband of Anath" (82, 85 s.); he suggests that Anath could have been Baals sister from different mothers. Same view on the relation of Baal to Anath CCXXIII, 7.

[6] The Russian historian N. ROŽKOV defined this phenomenon as "chaotic concretism."

[7] CCXXIII, 53; CXCVI, 142.

[8] CXCVI, 142; CXL, 292. The scene of this episode, *Aẖ Šmk,* is probably identical with Josephus' *Samachonitis* = Lake Ḥule in Galilee, as proposed DX, 157; CXL, 283; CXCVI, 142, n. 2 (with a question-mark).

CAZELLES.[1] This is a hymn to Anath. In the very beginning, where Anath is invoked to massacre young men or servants (*ġlmm*), to shed their blood, to cut off their heads and hands (a well-known episode of the epic, V AB, B = ʿAnat, col. II), she is named "heifer" (*arẖ*) and it is said that she will have a child. Subsequently this is described more in detail; Anath is again named a heifer, and the son she bore to Baal is named "thy *mhr*,"[2] *zbl mlk* ("Royal Appointee"), *bkr zbl* ("first born appointee") and *ṣġr* ("the young one"). According to CAZELLES's well-founded suggestion, this young son of Baal and the heifer, the *mhr* of Anath, is the same "young one" (*ṣġr*) of the Rephaim text (III Rp = UM 124) who is named there *Rpu-Bʿl, mhr Bʿl w mhr ʿnt* and "thy son" (*bnk*), speaking of Anath. Other extremely important consequences of this text will be examined in chapter II. The rôle of the chief of the Rephaim, spirits of the Nether World, which is to all appearance played by the young *Rpu-Bʿl* ("healer of Baal" or "the healing lord," see chapter III) is a link connecting UM 6 with the last of the Ugaritic texts we are dealing with in this section—an episode in the poem of Baal's death.

Here the action apparently takes place in the Nether World—or on its threshold. I*AB (= UM 67), col. V, begins by somebody's impressive order to Baal, commanding him to descend into the underground world and to be counted among the dead. Then immediately follows (ll.17 ss.):

Aliyan Baal[3] hearkens.
He loves a heifer (*ʿglt*) in *Dbr*,[4]
A cow (*prt*) in the field of *Šẖlmmt*,[5]
He lies with her seventy-seven (times),
[Yea] eighty-eight (times).
And she conceives and bears *Mš*.
A coat (?) (*al*[l?]) she clad him.[6]

[1] See n. 436 above.

[2] CAZELLES considers that one of the words written *mhr* signifies "child, offspring," from the root *hry* "to conceive" (cf. Akk. *mâru* "son, child").

[3] Standard epithet of Baal in Ugaritic poems, usually translated "Mighty," "Puissant" (from *lʾy* "to be strong").

[4] *Dbr* here, probably, "pasture" (because of the parallelism with *šd* "field" followed by the still enigmatic qualificative *šẖlmmt*); but *dbr* (Heb. *dᵉbîr*) is also the "adyton," the dark and prohibited part of the Canaanite temples, adopted from Egyptian architecture and symbolizing perhaps the Nether World (DXXX, 103).

[5] In the col. VI of the same text it is said that Anath found Baal's corpse at this very spot—*arṣ dbr* // *šd šẖlmmt*.

[6] Clothing the new-born by his cow-mother is also found in the two other

(Then follow scarce remnants of two more lines and a gap of about 30 lines).

This Ugaritic myth bears a close resemblance to the much older Sumerian myth of Enlil and Ninlil,[1] which can help us in understanding it better. Enlil is banished by the gods into the Nether World for having deprived of innocence the young goddess Ninlil (who, however, following the advice of her mother, enticed him to it). Ninlil voluntarily entered the Nether World in search of Enlil. The latter, in order that Nanna (Sin) her offspring not be obliged to stay in Hell, takes the shape of an underground deity, the gatekeeper of the Nether World, and impregnates her with the chthonic god Ninazu as a substitute for Nanna. This is repeated twice more, Enlil taking respectively the shapes of the god of the underground river and of the ferryman over that river, and Ninlil conceiving two chthonic gods more—Nergal and one whose name did not subsist in the tablet. Now, though not in this very text, but in later Akkadian ones, Ninlil is described as "the lordly Wild-Cow, the most heroic among the goddesses," who "was butting my enemies with her mighty horns" [2]—a description which would fit Anath as well. *Rpu-Bʿl*, "the healing lord" or "Baal's healer," the son of Baal and the heifer Anath, conceived in the Nether World and chief of the underground spirits, corresponds exactly to Ninazu, "the lord healer", the old chthonic deity of healing. We believe that the other name of Baal's and the heifer's son, which he is called in I*AB (= UM 67)—*Mš̂*—inexplicable in Semitic, and for which an Egyptian origin was proposed,[3] may with no less probability be of Sumero-Babylonian origin and signify *Muš* "serpent" or "serpent-deity": as is well known, the serpent has everywhere been the symbol of the chthonic healing gods since the most ancient times.[4]

Thus in some variants the cow, impregnated by a god, bears a

Ugaritic myths of a heifer giving birth to a divine offspring. See p. 199 s. below.

[1] CCXCVI, 43-47; critical re-interpretation CCLXXI, 132 ss. and CCLXX, 165-170; new exposition CCXCV, 96 ss.

[2] Annals of Aššurbanipal (Cylinder Rassam IX: 75) *rîmtu ellilîtu*; translation CCCXCIX, 300.

[3] CCXXIV, § 20.1185, following III, § 21, takes *mš̂* as Egyptian *ms* "child" (was earlier suggested CDXXV, 153, n. 2.).

[4] The reasons for our etymology of the name *Mš̂* and of his feminine form *Mš̂t* are expounded pp. 229 ss. below. *Mš̂* is basically the same name as the Heb. *Môše*, Moses—and the close connection of Moses with the serpent-motif is well known.

calf, in other ones—a human child, in still other ones this child is a chthonic god of healing and is often symbolized by a serpent.[1] Something very similar must have existed in the archaic Hebrew mythology. Figuring among the ancestors of the Israelite people is Leah (*Lēʾā*), whose name is, since NÖLDEKE,[2] explained as a "wild cow", Akk. *liʾtu, littu* (feminine form of *liʾû* "wild bull"), which derives ultimately from the root *lʾy* "to be strong, mighty."[3] But at the same time this was the name or the epithet of a Canaanite goddess, as is shown by the name of *Abdi-liʾti*, the king of the Phoenician city of Arwad under Sennacherib,[4] "where *liʾt* 'the strong one', Hebrew *Lēʾā*, is probably an appelation of Astarte." [5] One of Leah's sons—perhaps originally her son *par excellence*, to whom the eponyms of other tribes could have been joined later, when a systematic national genealogy was established—was Levi (*Lēwî*), whose name strikingly resembles that of the mythical serpent Leviathan (*Liwyātān*) and was repeatedly explained as "serpent" (from the root *lwy* "to coil").[6] The Israelite priests, who were also oracle-explainers and physicians,[7] claimed descent

[1] The association of the divine symbols of bull (sky-god) and serpent (chthonic god) was common in the East Mediterranean world. In Sumer, Gugalanna "the great bull of heaven" was the slain husband of the infernal queen Ereškigal (CCXCIII, 5) who was herself identified with the "Serpent-star," mulMuš (constellation of Hydra, CCXXVI, No. 284). In Cyprus, "since the first Bronze Age, the Earth-Mother was . . . associated with the Bull-god . . . and with the Serpent, a chthonic god. The latter two personages seem to be intimately associated with each other" (CXX, 345 s.). In Crete, "there were three prominent features of ancient Cretan ritual, the procession carrying the serpent emblem of the chthonian god, the slaying and eating of the bull, and a warlike dance . . ." (CCXLII, 117). Cf. the Greek mystical saying: "For the Bull is the father of the Serpent, and the Serpent is the father of the Bull," quoted by Clemens of Alexandria (CCXLVII, 495).

[2] CCCLXXXIII, 167.

[3] NOTH, CCCLXXXVI, 83 supposed that Leah "the cow" personified the agricultural tribes of Israel, who raised cattle, and Rachel "the ewe," the half-nomadic sheep-raising tribes. But in reality it was just the opposite: the tribes of Ephraim, Manasse, and Benjamin (the "sons of Rachel") were settled farmers and possessed oxen, while Reuben, Simeon, and Judah (the "sons of Leah") were shepherd-tribes. Besides, *liʾû, liʾtu* never denoted domestic cattle, but only wild bulls and wild cows.

[4] Translation CCCXCIX, 287.

[5] CCXLVI, 30. See also CDXXVIII, 310, 476 ss. on the cult of Astarte as a sheep.

[6] CCVI, 226 ("'Sons of the Serpent,' Benê Lêvi"); exposed in detail and substantiated by B. LUTHER *ap.* CCCLXIV, 426.

[7] The Deuteronomic and Priestly laws of the Pentateuch especially stress their competence in cases of leprosy, Deut. 24: 8; Lev. 13-14, etc. On an

from Levi, and the most important of Levi's descendants, the head and organizer of the Levite priestdom, was Moses, the possessor of a miraculous serpent-staff and the creator of the healing bronze serpent on a stake. The sons of Leah migrated to Egypt—among them Levi—and were brought out from there by Moses, Levi's fourth generation descendant.

In the Israelitized vestige of the Canaanite myth of the cow-goddess we have seen above, the element of migration to Egypt occurs. In the analogous myth about the cow Io from remote Argos, Egypt may seem strange and inappropriate, but it is quite appropriate and natural in the neighboring Canaan, which during many centuries was in frequent political, cultural, and sometimes ethnic interdependence with Egypt. If we recognize, in the light of all that is said above, that the myth of Io was brought to Argos from the W-S world, then it becomes clear where Egypt came into it: this motif was already contained within its Canaanite prototype.[1]

The name of *Lēʾā* penetrated into Argolis in its original Semitic sound, too: with the Greek feminine ending *-is*,[2] in the form *Lêïs*, it is the name of the daughter of the mythical autochthonous founder of the city of Troizen, king Ôros. She bore a son from a god (in this instance, from Poseidon), and the name of this son, who inherited the throne of Troizen, was—in excellent harmony with the pattern we have just discussed—*Althêpos*,[3] "the healer" (from *althomai* "to be healed"). This is another valuable Greco-Semitic parallel to the myth of Io.[4]

earlier stage, I Sam. 6: 2-9, Philistine priests find magical remedies to stop pestilence.

[1] A close association of Egypt and Canaan existed as well in Egyptian myths, especially in the New Kingdom. Thus Bata in the "Story of the Two Brothers" flees to the Valley of the Pines (Lebanon), and the goddess Isis finds at Byblos the body of her slain husband Osiris.

[2] Cf. the Greek rendering of Egyptian names as *Isis, Nephtis, Nitokris*; of Semitic as *Semiramis, Derketis.*

[3] Paus. II: 30: 5.

[4] The Troizenians considered Ôros, the father of that Leïs, "the first man born in their country"; but Pausanias, II: 30: 5, reporting this tradition, noticed not without grounds, "Now in my opinion, Ôros is an Egyptian name and utterly un-Greek." And, indeed, this is the standard and correct Greek rendering of the name of the Egyptian falcon-god Horus (*Ḥr*), the personification of the Pharaonic power. The Canaanites very early adopted the cult of that god, as witnessed by the Ugaritic pers. n. *Ḥr* (UM 146: 8), [*Bn*]-*Ḥr* (UM 315: 13), *Bn-Abdḥr* ("Horus is eternal", UM 64: 36; 83: 11) and *Bn-ʿbdḥr* ("servant of Horus," to appear in Virolleaud *PRU V*,

We have examined in our preceding exposition eleven different variants of the Io myth, without counting that myth itself (3 Sumero-Akkadian, 1 Hurrian, 4 Ugaritic, 2 Hebrew, and 1 Greco-Semitic from Troizen). All of them originate from Western Asia, from the Sumero-Akkadian cultural center and from its Hurrian and W-S periphery. The closest to the Argive myths are the W-S versions, including characteristic details: banishment, wandering, Egypt, form or semantics of some personal names.[1] On the contrary, although the image of the cow-goddess was well known to the Egyptians since ancient times,[2] the thematic pivot of the fore-mentioned myths is not found in Egyptian mythology. Therefore, although Egypt is mentioned in the Io myth, it could not have been borrowed directly from Egypt.[3] A W-S land must necessarily be designated as its origin, and this agrees with and strongly corroborates the identical conclusion we have reached as to the myth of Io's descendants Danaos and the Danaides.

The Hyksos Background of the Danaan Myth Cycle.

However, if the myth of Io is W-S, as is its sequence, the myth of Danaos and the Danaides (as we have shown in the preceding section), why then did the Argive tradition connect both myths with Egypt? The answer is given by the fact that contemporary

No. 69:8 and No. 117: II: 35). Cf. also the Canaanite name *ʾÍ-ši-ḫa-ra* ("Man of Horus"), recorded among the Keftiu (Cretan) names in an Egyptian text of about 1500 (CDXII, 92; cf. XXXIXa, No. II: 1), and the Biblical *Ḥûr* (LXX: *Ôr*) associated with Moses Ex. 17: 10-12. Thus the Troizenian Ôros may be a genuine Canaanite-Egyptian relic. Moreover, "after Althêpos, Sarôn became king" (Paus. II: 30: 7)—a purely Canaanite eponym of the coastal plain along the gulf called Saronic after it: in Canaan, too, the coastal plain was called *Šārôn* (already EA 241: 4 *Šaruna*). One finds another mythological falcon-king in the region of the Saronic gulf: the Megarian Nisos (= *nēṣ*, as felicitously explained LXV, II, 395).

[1] The gadfly as a tool of divine wrath for chasing and persecuting somebody, also belongs to the images of W-S beliefs; according to Ex. 23: 28; Deut. 7: 20; Josh. 24: 12, the Canaanites were driven out from before the Israelites by hornets sent by Yahwe. As it was judiciously remarked, "even if this is but a metaphor representing panic, it supposes a popular belief attributing to this insect a demonic power" (CCCXLI, 583). In the Io episode of Aeschylos' *Prometheus Bound*, the gadfly is perceived precisely as a horrible demon, vaguely identified with the soul of the slain herdsman Argos.

[2] Cf., e.g., XXXIII, 17-22, 25, 30 s., 66; CCCLXXV, 37 s.

[3] Only during the New Kingdom, under Syrian influence, the cow-goddess Hathor assumed some features of the W-S Astarte (CCCLXXV, 39)—but not, as far as we know, anything of the motif of "a god's love-affair with a cow."

with the early phases of the Mycenaean civilization, Egypt was for a century and a half occupied by W-S conquerors whom it is customary, since Manetho, to call the Hyksos.[1] More than 120 years ago, F. C. MOVERS, the author of the first comprehensive and still interesting work on the Phoenicians, had rather by intuition than with the aid of the evidence at his disposal, recognized in the pivot of the myth of Danaos an echo of the expulsion of the Hyksos from Egypt, and perspicaciously observed: "The colonization of Danaos was not so much an Egyptian, as a Phoenician one . . . Danaos, the son not of an Egyptian, but of a Semitic ancestor Belos, flees before the sons of Aigyptos . . ." [2] We know now that the Hyksos kings were zealous worshippers of the Canaanite god Baal whom the Egyptians identified with their Seth or Suteẖ,[3] and whose cult was ostentatiously established in the Hyksos capital of Avaris-Tanis.[4] No wonder *Bêlos* in the myth of Danaos is represented as the king of Egypt.[5]

[1] There were several attempts to claim a non-Semitic (Hittite, Hurrian, or Indo-European) origin for the Hyksos (lately CCL, 102 ss.,) but without really convincing proof. On their Semitic origin cf., e.g., LXXVIII, 219 s.; CXLVIII, 38, 45; CXLVI, 180; CXXXVIII, 105 ss.; CDXLIV, 215 s; XLVII, 88; VIII, 84. It is worth while to quote here the latest statement (by J.-R. KUPPER) on the question whether the Hurrians were the moving power behind the Hyksos invasion: "At the time when these (the Hyksos) were moving into the Delta the Hurrians were just beginning to spread into Northern Syria, the only route they could have followed to Egypt. This being so, it is impossible, without pushing Hammurabi's date considerably farther back (KUPPER already accepts the higher of the two possible dates), to connect the Hyksos with the Hurrian migration. In the same way there can be no influence of the Indo-Aryans, who appeared distinctly later . . . The result is not simply negative; it gives the direction in which a solution to the Hyksos problem as a whole will be found" (CCCVI, 37 s.).

[2] CCCLXXIV, I, 46.

[3] On this, cf., e.g., CDLII, 104 ss. (the suggestion that the Hyksos Seth was modeled after Môt rather than Baal is unfounded).

[4] On the identity of Avaris with Tanis, cf. CCCLXIX; CCCLX. See, e.g., the inscription of the Hyksos king Apopi I on an altar: "He (Apopi) made it as a monument for his father Suteẖ, lord of Avaris, when he (Suteẖ) threw all lands under his (Apopi's) heel," LXXVIII, 220; and the famous "stele of 400th anniversary" of the installation of Seth's cult in Tanis (see following footnote).

[5] It is not necessary to look for a concrete Hyksos king as the original of Belos: it is precisely to the god Baal, the Egyptian Seth Nubti, that the "stele of 400 years" ascribes kingship over Egypt in standard expressions for a Pharaoh: "Year 400, 4th month of the third season, day 4, of the King of Upper and Lower Egypt: Seth-the-Great-of-Strength, the Son of Re, his beloved: The-Ombite [Eg.: Nubti], beloved of Re-Har-akhti, so that he exists for ever and ever" (translation DCXLIX, 253). Baal (Seth, Suteẖ) is both king of Egypt and father of the Hyksos Pharaoh (preceding note)—exactly like Belos.

In 1952, in an article "Les Hyksos et la légende d'Io," Jean Bérard proposed a felicitous interpretation of the name of Epaphos, the son of Io, who according to the myth was born and reigned in Egypt. The Greek authors did not understand any more the signification of that name and derived it from *epaptein* "to touch"; to explain this etymology an aetiological story was invented, that by the touch of his hand Zeus turned Io back into a woman, or even impregnated her in this manner. This etymology is very weak, but it shows that the name of Epaphos was not an invention of genealogists, but rather an un-Greek name preserved since old times. Jean Bérard discovered in *Epaphos* a slightly modified name *Apopi*,[1] borne by two or three Hyksos kings, and rendered by *Apophis, Aphophis*.[2] This discovery is another serious proof of the profound antiquity of the Io myth and of the whole Danaan cycle, and it confirms its creation in W-S circles which had just witnessed the dramatic history of their grandeur and later fall from power in Egypt.[3] We consider, by the way, the name *Apopi* no less Semitic than the other Hyksos names.[4]

[1] Egypt. *ip.p(y)*—not to be confused with *ʿ3pp* or *ʿpp*, the name of the mythical monster-serpent which the Greeks also called *Apophis*, CDXXIV, II, 162.

[2] LXI, 35.

[3] Jean Bérard, professor of the Sorbonne, tragically killed in 1957 in an automobile accident, was the son of Victor Bérard, the famous investigator of the *Odyssey* and of the Phoenician influence on Greece. Unfortunately, Jean Bérard's quoted study and other connected articles (as LX) are methodically on a low level. In their indiscriminate use of very disparate sources and treating myths as relating firm historical data, they curiously resemble the attempts of Hecataeos of Miletus to "rationalize" the Greek myths. His discovery of the Hyksos royal name Apopi in the Io myth was brilliant, but his further efforts to press into the Greek tale a few other Hyksos names were not crowned with success.

[4] Ranke considered the name *Apopi* Egyptian, but devoid of any meaning, simply a baby-language "Kosename" (or, as other German scholars call it, "Lallname"), CDXXIV, II, 162. However, as we hope to show in another work, *all* names of the Hyksos kings and their relatives and dignitaries are Semitic. A "Lallname" is not very probable to have been the only Egyptian name adopted by a Hyksos as his first name. The root *ʾpp* (Heb. *ʾāphaph*, Akk. *apâpu*) is perfectly Semitic and means "to embrace, to encircle, to bind"; a Hyksos predecessor of Apopi, the king Ḫiyan, called himself *inq t3.w* "the embracer of the Lands (Egypt)" in addition to *ḥq3 ḫ3s.wt* "ruler of foreign countries" (CDLXXXIa, 66); in Semitic, this gives *ʾapapu* (a perfect-formation), as Apopi's name has to be vocalized in agreement with the pronunciation before the Late Egyptian vowel-shift $a > o$. The name *A-pa-pa-a*, borne by a wife of king Niqmad II, existed in Ugarit in the XIVth century (CCCXC, RŠ 16.276).

Just as the Greek and the Germanic epics have reflected—though in a fragmentary, condensed and confused form—the conditions of two critical turning-point epochs, full of events of extraordinary significance and impact, two epochs of great migrations of peoples, so also the Hyksos epoch, the traces of which are visible in vestiges of the Danaan myth cycle, was a turning-point epoch for the whole of the Near East. We have very little written information on that epoch, but according to the archaeological data this was a time of enormous shocks, destructions, and displacements of entire populations. As the archaeologist Cl. SCHAEFFER summarized it, "it becomes more and more evident that the Hyksos movement was not just an episode of the Egyptian history and of its relations with Palestine. It was an event of a much larger bearing, which has profoundly modified the political and ethnic structure of the whole Western Asia. It had repercussions up to the island of Cyprus and probably even in Crete." [1] From the viewpoint of the Canaanites, the Hyksos age was the climax of their might and pride. "In the seventeenth century Palestine was the centre of a North-west-Semitic 'empire' controlled from the Hyksos capital at Avaris . . . At its height under Apophis and Khayana, this Hyksos state may have ruled from the Euphrates to southern Nubia." [2] "This was a time of great local prosperity . . . The preponderance of weapons and ornaments made in Egypt, or made after Egyptian models, suggests that much of the wealth was brought back to Palestine by warriors who had fought in Egypt on behalf of the Hyksos." [3] Such experiences must have left a deep trace in the entire Canaanite cultural circle in the form of legends about ancestors who had migrated to Egypt, ruled over her, and then were forced by the Egyptians to return back home, to Canaan.

Modern scholars excelled in excogitations how to explain historically the myth of Danaos, especially the statement on the double movement there and back, first from Argos to Egypt, then from Egypt back to Argos. The most singular of all was that of Sir John L. MYRES, which we feel obliged to quote verbatim:

> Manetho identified one of the numerous rulers of Egypt, in the anarchy that followed the death of Amenhotep IV, with the Danaus of Greek tradition, who quarreled with his brother Aegyptus and

[1] CDXLIV, 262 s.
[2] VIII, 86.
[3] *Ibid.*, 87.

was pursued by him as far as Argos, whence the family had come two[1] generations ago. What Egyptian evidence Manetho had for this story, is not now known; but the name Harmais which he gives to the Egyptian king who restored order in Egypt corresponds with that of Harmhab, the military adventurer who ended the period of confusion and founded the 19th dynasty in 1350. It is quite likely that one of the incidents of that obscure period may have been the expulsion of some corps of Danaan mercenaries who abused their position and had to be chased back home by Egyptian forces. The Greek traditional date for the arrival of Danaus in Argos from Egypt is rather earlier, and contemporary with the first mention of Danaan marauders in the correspondence of Amenhotep III.[2]

It is obvious that this famed scholar of early Greek history has never personally looked into the Manethonian excerpts or into the Amarna letters.[3]

SCHACHERMEYR also conjectured that the myth of Danaos hints at the presence of Danaan princes and mercenaries in Egypt, but he put it in a much earlier time than MYRES did, and it was not Danaos, but his brother Aigyptos, banished by Danaos from Argos according to the scholiast to *Hecabe*, who embodied the Greek

[1] We do not see how MYRES, a large part of whose voluminous book is devoted to a careful counting and confronting of mythical generations, arrived here at the figure "two." According to the mythographers, "the family of Danaos" had come to Egypt four generations earlier (five, including himself).

[2] CCCLXXVIII, 121.

[3] The relevant passage of Manetho, preserved by Josephus, *Contra Apionem* I: 15 (= 97-102), runs thus: ". . . Amenophis nineteen years and six months, and then Sethosis, also called Ramesses. The last-named king, who possessed an army of cavalry and a strong fleet, made his brother Harmais viceroy of Egypt . . . He then departed on a campaign against Cyprus and Phoenicia, and later against the Assyrians and Medes . . . Meanwhile, some time after his departure, Harmais, whom he left in Egypt, unscrupulously defied all his brother's injunctions . . . and rose in revolt against his brother . . . Sethosis instantly returned to Pelusium and recovered his kingdom; and the country was called after him Aigyptos. For Manetho states that Sethos was called Aigyptos and his brother Harmais Danaos." In a parallel quotation *ibid.* I: 26 (= 231): ". . . down to the two brothers, Sethos and Hermaios, the former of whom, he says, took the name of Aigyptos and the latter that of Danaos. Sethos, after expelling Hermaios, reigned fifty-nine years, and his eldest son Rampses, who succeeded him, sixty-six." —Now, abstraction made of how little all this has in common with the real course of Egyptian history, Manetho's Harmais, far from being the restorer of order and the banisher of Danaos, himself was the troublemaker and was —according to Manetho, or rather to one of his Greek vulgarizers—expelled under the name of Danaos! Besides, Haremheb was no "military adventurer," but the Egyptian commander-in-chief under Amenhotep IV and his successors, and never was a brother or a relative of Seti I. As to "the Danaan marauders in the correspondence of Amenhotep III", the only

(Danaan) mercenaries that helped the Egyptians against the Hyksos, and whose fellow-countrymen refused to receive back; the Egyptian queen Ah(hotep) who took part in the struggle with the Hyksos was perhaps hidden under the image of Io, but Io's wanderings relate not to those events, but to the migrations of the Danaans 400 years later, during the invasion of the Peoples of the Sea.[1] M. P. NILSSON made it more melodramatic: "If the myth goes back to the time when the Danaans raided Egypt,[2] its origin may be explainable under the conditions of this time. A crowd of Danaan women had been captured and made concubines of Egyptians; they slew their husbands and escaped." [3] Jean BÉRARD, applying methods of ancient logographers, relied on the parodistic story of Io invented by Herodotos I: 1 and considered her a real Argive princess, seduced and kidnapped by a Phoenician skipper and brought to Egypt.[4]

All these subjective conjectures which border on the genre of the historical novel not only have not helped to solve the problem since the time of MOVERS, but, on the contrary, have entangled it. The return home in the Danaan myth cycle is entirely borrowed—together with the whole of the cycle—from a Canaanite source: in the sagas of the power and fall of the Hyksos the element of the return home must have played an important rôle, but the homeland—it goes without saying—was Syria-Palestine. However, for the northwestern branch of the Canaanites, the Danunians, who as a result of their subsequent wanderings found a new homeland in the Peloponnese, the notion of "homeland" soon became identical with Argos. Besides, the reference to the more or less remote origin of the conquerors from the conquered country is a well-known way of legitimizing the conquest.[5]

Now in the Hellenistic epoch, when for the first time it became possible to compare and confront Greek, Jewish, and Egyptian

mention of Danuna in the Amarna letters is the report of Abimilki (EA 151: 52-55) which we repeat here once more: "The king of Danuna is dead, and his brother has become king in his stead, and his land is quiet"; thus myths are created even in our own days.

[1] CDXL, 146 s. It is hardly necessary to point out that there is absolutely no data whatsoever on the presence of any Greek mercenaries in Egypt up to the time of Psammetichos I (663-609).

[2] The invasion of the Peoples of the Sea is understood.

[3] CCCLXXXII, 66 s., cf. 64 s.

[4] LXI, 4, 14.

[5] E.g. the representation of the Dorian conquest of the Peloponnese as the "return of the Heraclids"; or the Egyptian fiction that Cambyses was the son of Pharaoh Apries' daughter (Herod. III: 2).

traditions and historical sources, both Greeks and Jews grew interested in the Egyptian data on the expulsion of the Hyksos—in the form in which it was accessible to them. Jews turned to it in search of confirmation for the Exodus story, Greeks distorted and caricatured it in order to vilify the national past of the Jews [1]—both approaches are preserved in Josephus' *Contra Apionem*. Greeks, too, found familiar features of their own Danaos myth in the Hyksos traditions. And already Hecataeos of Abdera represented both the Jewish Exodus and the Greek migration of Danaos and Cadmos as episodes of one and the same event—the expulsion of the Hyksos which he described after the late Egyptian fabular versions.[2] Thence the assertion—wherever it may have originated—that the Spartans (whose kings, through Heracles and Perseus, claimed descent from Danaos) are brothers of the Jews and descend from Abraham's kindred.[3] Among the modern scholars, H. BREASTED, Raymond WEILL, Salomo LURIA, René DUSSAUD and others also considered that at least part of the Biblical Exodus traditions originated as reminiscences of the Hyksos. For us, in this context, it is absolutely indifferent whether some tribes of the future Israelite confederation directly participated in the Hyksos invasion,[4] or the Israelites adopted these reminiscences from the real participants, the Canaanites,[5] or the Hyksos motifs were borrowed from the Egyptians themselves by Judaean settlers in Egypt since the VIIIth century,[6]—what interests us is the resemblance of the essential thematic skeletons.

Abstraction made from details and developments that have grown during the centuries of separate evolution of Argive and Hebrew legends about Egypt, their common thematic pivot can be summarized thus: the ancestor of the tribe migrates to Egypt, attains power there; his descendants stay in Egypt for four generations, but then the Egyptians prevail over the strangers, begin to oppress them, and they flee from Egypt; Egyptians pursue them, but

[1] Cf. DXLIII, 84-88, 95-145.

[2] Hecataeos' version is preserved in Diodorus Sic. XL: 3: 2.

[3] Letter written by the Spartan king Areus (309-265) to the High Priest Onias I, I Macc. 12: 7, which Ed. MEYER considers to be based on an authentic original. We have followed his explanation (CCCLXV, 30 s.) which first connected the contents of Areus' letter with the historical conception of Hecataeos.

[4] LXXVIII, 220.

[5] DXLIII, 185-191; CXLVIII, 45 s.

[6] CCCXLVI, 97.

perish; the fugitives safely return to their old home-country and again become its rulers. By an interesting coincidence, the number of generations spent in Egypt is the same in both cases: according to the scheme of Pentateuch, four generations—Levi, Qehat, Amram, Moses, and Exodus under the latter,[1] according to the genealogy of the Danaan dynasty, also four generations—Epaphos, Libya, Belos, Danaos, and flight from Egypt under the latter. Moreover, this roughly coincides with the real duration of the Hyksos rule over Egypt—approximately 150, maximum 160 years, from 1730 or 1720, when the cult of Baal was established in Tanis-Avaris, to 1580 or, according to some, 1570, when Ahmose I took Avaris, and the Hyksos retreated to Palestine. This is just four conventional generations of 40 years each, as was admitted both by the Bible and Greek logographers.[2] This may be a mere coincidence, but it may as well be a common literary feature reflecting a tradition that really existed with both peoples.

It must be said, that the heroes of the Exodus from Egypt in both versions—Moses in the Hebrew and Danaos in the Greek one—also have preserved some cognate features. Moses grows up at the court of the Egyptian king as a member of the royal family, and subsequently flees from Egypt after having slain an Egyptian—as Danaos, a member of the Egyptian ruling house, flees from the same country after the slaying of the Aigyptiads which he had arranged. The same number of generations separates Moses from Leah the "wild cow" and Danaos from the cow Io. Still more characteristic is that both Moses and Danaos find and create springs in a waterless region; the story how Poseidon, on the request of the Danaide Amymona, struck out with his trident springs from the Lerna rock, particularly resembles Moses producing a spring from a rock by the stroke of his staff. One discovers even more similar features if one takes, as a connecting link, the Ugaritic poem of Danel in which we have found the prototype of the Danaos myth.[3] The name of *Aqht*, the son of Danel, returns as *Q^{e}hāt*, the

[1] That is what was meant by Gen. 15: 16: "In the fourth generation will they return here." But a generation in the patriarchal age was supposed to last 100 years (cf. DXLV, 308), thence "400 years of oppression" in the same chapter, v. 13, and the figure of 430 years of the whole sojourn in Egypt (Ex. 12: 40): 400 years of oppression preceded by the happy period under Joseph.

[2] In particular, by Hecataeos of Miletus (CCLXI, 170).

[3] Two of the onomastical correspondences—namely, *Aqht—Q^{e}hāt* and *Pġt—Pûʿā*—were noticed by VIROLLEAUD in his *editio princeps*, DXVIII, 96,

grandfather of Moses. The name of the locality *Mrrt,* where *Aqht* was killed, figures in the gentilic form *Mᵉrarî* as the brother of *Qᵉhāt* in the Levite genealogy. The name of *Pġt,* the daughter of Danel and the devoted sister of *Aqht,* is met in the Moses story as *Pûʿā,* a midwife who saved the life of the new-born Moses. The very name of Moses, in the feminine form *Mšt,*[1] is, in the Ugaritic poem, the first half of Danel's wife's name, while the second half of her name, *Dnty,* corresponds to the name of Levi's sister Dinah. Dinah herself, as we have seen, is the heroine of a story analogous to the myth of the bloody wedding of her namesakes, the Danaides. *Dân,* the root of the names *Dnel, Dnty* (and also Dinah and Danaos), was the name of a tribe whose priests claimed to descend directly from Moses (Jud. 18: 30); and compare the serpent emblem of the tribe of Dan with the serpent staff of Moses and the bronze serpent he erected. Under the same name—Danaë—another Argive heroine of the Danaid stock is thrown into the sea in a chest with her new-born son—as Moses in his ark (*tēbā*)—and lands on the Serpent-island of Seriphos (Heb. *śārâph,* applied i.a. to the bronze serpent made by Moses). Moses, like Danel, is a healer, a prophet,[2] a miracle-worker—cf. Danel's staff (*mṭ*) which he extends while pronouncing curses against towns and localities, quite like Moses in Egypt; and especially, like Danel, he is a judge: in his sacred precinct, the Kadesh oasis, which was also called *ʿÊn-Mišpāṭ* "spring of judgment" (Gen. 14: 7), he created the springs of *Massā* ("ordeals"), *Mᵉrîbā* ("judicial arguments"), and *Mârā* ("bitter", cf. the "bitter water" for ordeals Num. 5: 18 ss.), and it was at *Mârā* that he "established for him (Israel) law and judgment (*ḥōq u-mišpāṭ*) and put him to ordeal (*nissāhû*)" Ex. 15: 25; he is constantly depicted as the supreme judge of Israel and the organizer of its judicial institutions (e.g. Ex. 18); and we have seen that in the myth of Danaos, too, a relic was preserved of Danaos being a judge.

These comparative observations may seem precarious, but the three myths—Ugaritic, Hebrew, and Greek—are so tightly inter-

99; but a more intimate and extended similarity between the two cycles, that of Danel and that of Moses, has not yet been discussed in the literature on the Ugaritic myths.

1 The masculine form, *Mš,* corresponding to *Môše,* also appears at Ugarit (cf. p. 89 above).

2 Danel's forecast of a seven-years drought is a typical prophecy, both in form and in essence.

woven, they contain so many common names, motifs, and situations, that their primordial cognacy looks very probable. True, in the Ugaritic myth (or at least in its extant parts) the Egyptian motif which plays so great a rôle in the two other myths is hardly present,[1] but this only shows that the W-S myth of Danel arose and existed in itself prior to the Hyksos invasion of Egypt, and the legendary reminiscences of the fate of the Hyksos rule in Egypt became only secondarily mingled with the motifs of this myth. But since this association had a place both in the Israelite traditions and in the Danaan myth cycle, it must have been done in a very remote antiquity, prior to the Danaans' migration to the West.

One should not be surprised that the events of the Hyksos epoch are presented in the myths in such a fabulous and un-historical way. This is a widely current phenomenon: where detailed chronicles are not kept—and often in spite of them, because they were only accessible to few—memories of real events soon lose all concrete historical detail and are confined to a familiar popular framework of traditional tale-patterns. Even the Egyptians themselves, a highly developed cultural nation with a millennial literary and annalistic tradition, the direct participants of the Hyksos drama on their own soil—even they, only four centuries after the expulsion of the Hyksos, little remembered the real events of the fight, and transformed the story of their oppression and liberation into a typical folk-tale of the kings Seknen-Re and Apopi with such a fantastic casus belli as the hippopotami whose splashing in the Theban pool prevented Apopi from sleeping at Avaris.[2] That Troy was destroyed, this is proved by excavations, and that this was done by Mycenaean Achaeans, is quite possible; but the myth of the Trojan war is built on the fabular international motif of the abduction of Helen which in its earlier Greek stages did not have anything in common with Troy,[3] and which already to Herodotos seemed to be too futile a cause for so great a war (II: 120). In the German Nibelungen epic, which mentions such historical characters as Attila, Theodoric, etc., the whole plot is founded on

[1] Except the association of the Canaanite artisan-god *Kšr-w-Ḫss* with Memphis (cf. p. 81, n. 6 above). The Canaanites apparently identified their god *Kšr* (*Kušarru* in cuneiform transcription, CCCLXXXVIIa, 168) with the Memphite Ptaḥ, as shown by Mochos' definition of *Chusôr* as "opener" (Ptaḥ understood as a derivation of the W-S root *ptḥ* "to open"); cf. CCCVIII, 374.

[2] Translation DXLIX, 231 s.

[3] CCCLXXXII, 73-76, 170 s.

fantastic fairy-tale elements: cursed treasure of underground dwarfs, fighting a dragon, invulnerable skin, thorn crown causing invisibility, the enchanted castle of Brunhild, and so on.

Does this mean that the Danunians whom we know as the inhabitants of the Cilician Plain of Adana, directly participated in the Hyksos conquest of Egypt? This assumption is not necessitated: the memory of the great Hyksos age and its end could have come to them from their southern neighbors as an all-Canaanite point of national pride. But it is quite possible, taking into account that the stormy movements of the transitory period between Middle and Late Bronze Ages have certainly embraced the whole of Syria. We have seen that the geopolitical interests of the Danuna country were always turned to the south and that she was an ally of Qadeš on the Orontes under Thutmose III, of Qaṭna under Amenhotep IV, of Damascus in the neo-Assyrian epoch. The bellicose youth of Danuna could have joined the Syrian and Palestinian warriors who went to Egypt with the Hyksos army and used to return with rich spoil. But it could have as well been that the Hyksos or their descendants hat settled in the Danuna country later, perhaps as a result of the Egyptian offensive in the South which was accompanied by destruction of many towns; [1] in the neighboring Ugarit, at least, the South Canaanite element began to increase sharply precisely in the first half of Late Bronze, between the end of the Hyksos epoch and the Amarna Age, as is shown by archaeological data; [2] and, to judge from name lists, many inhabitants of Ugarit in the XIVth century were migrants or descendants of migrants from South Phoenician and Palestinian cities.[3]

The Danaan cycle cannot be regarded as a mere literary borrowing made by Mycenaean Greeks in the East. If a people firmly believes some mythical characters to be its ancestors and makes them, in that quality, an object of reverence and worship, there can be but two explanations: either they belong to the fundamental fund of its own beliefs and traditions, or they have had the same place in the beliefs and traditions of the native population who had been conquered and assimilated by that people. But the plot, the geographical background and the onomastica of the Danaan mythological cycle are not Indo-European Greek and not Aegean pre-Greek;

[1] VIII, 87.
[2] CDXLIX, 252.
[3] XXXVIII, 72 ss.

they are W-S; consequently, the tribe that owned those myths was a W-S tribe which settled in Greece and gradually became Hellenized—quod erat demonstrandum.[1]

The Bases of Departure of West Semitic Penetration into Greece

The recognition of the Argive Danaans as a branch of the W-S people of the Danunians, whose other branch continued to live for many centuries in the Cilician Plain of Adana, is an important conclusion. It proves the real historical basis of Greek local traditions telling about the appearance in different places of mainland Greece and the Archipelago, in the Mycenaean age, of W.-S—Phoenician, according to Greek usage—settlers who brought with them their own un-Greek toponyms, divine names, and cults. It allows us, standing on the firm ground of the established identity of the Danaans with the Danunians, to approach in quite a different way the old controversial problem of "Phoenicians in Greece," which was for a long time, owing to the lack of sufficient sources, treated in a dilletante manner or on the plane of undemonstrable conjectures, speculations, and combinations, but which now can be investigated equipped with the new knowledge that has been acquired during the last three decades not only on the language, religion, mythology, and literature of the W-S world, but also on

[1] There are many more visible traces of Semitism in Argolis and the Peloponnese in general. Some of them were examined by V. Bérard in LXII (1894)—a book which, despite its obsoleteness, still contains a great deal of interesting facts and bright ideas. We shall mention some other in subsequent chapters. In this connection let us mention the information of Pausanias (II: 25: 10) that on the road to Epidauros, over the settlement Lessa, "there arises a mountain Arachneion, which in ancient times under Inachos bore the name of Sapyselaton. On it, there are altars to Zeus and Hera; when rain is needed, sacrifices are offered there to these gods." The name *Sapyselatôn* is inexplicable in Greek; but in Ugaritic it would have the aspect *Špš-ilt*, pronounced approximately *Šapš-ʾelat* or *Šapaš-ʾelat* "Šapšu the goddess." It is known that the Ugaritians considered the Sun not a god, but a goddess, and called her not by the common Semitic word for Sun, *šamš-*, but by a specific modification *šapš-*, which was also known in the neighboring Alalaḫ (in pers. n.) and even farther (cf. DXVII, 14 and CXI, No. 3214). Apparently, Pausanias was not wrong in ascribing to this toponym an immemorial antiquity. Its other name, Arachneion ("Spider-mountain"), may be purely Greek; but it may be reminiscent of *ʾAr-ʾaḫ*, the mythical abode of the Ugaritic goddess Pidray according to an Aramaic magic papyrus transliterated into Egyptian demotic (LXXVI, 227).

the hitherto unsuspected W-S state formations, their extension, population, and military potential.

When, at the end of the old and at the beginning of the current century, the data of the ancient authors on Phoenicians in Greece and the exaggerations of modern "Phoenico-maniacs" were put to severe criticism, even such scholars as Hugo WINCKLER and Eduard MEYER used to utterly underestimate the possibilities of Phoenician expansion. In that respect, strange as it may seem, the Orientalist WINCKLER stood exactly on the same positions that such radical "anti-Phoenicianists" as the initiator of that trend, the Hellenist BELOCH—though precisely from the viewpoint of his "Pan-Babylonism" the Phoenicians could have been utilized in the framework of this theory as the transmitters of the "Babylonian Weltanschauung" to the Greeks. He was decidedly against the hypothesis of Phoenician colonies in Greece; one cannot, he argued, make conclusions on the basis of a few toponyms; from all proposed Semitic etymologies he agreed to consider plausible just one—Melicertes-Melqart. The cause of his scepticism was considerations of a practical order: to establish colonies, strength is needed—and the Phoenician cities of the IId millenium simply did not have either the men or power to found colonies on alien ground. The Amarna letters, according to his opinion, depict Tyre and Sidon as insignificant towns, hardly able to survive and humbly depending on the Pharaoh's help.[1] Ed. MEYER was a little bit more indulgent: he kindly added to Melicertes one more Phoenician word, the Cabiri,[2] and, while categorically denying the possibility of any Phoenician establishments on the mainland, he agreed to the existence of tiny Phoenician commercial outposts on some Aegean islands, which peacefully disappeared as the Greek expansion progressed.[3]

Of course, WINCKLER's estimate even of Tyre's strength was very one-sided. He proceeded from the Amarna letters of Abimilki which depicted the situation of Tyre at the most critical moment, when this island-city was for a long time cut off from its possessions on the mainland and blocked on land and sea. If we had judged Athens only on the basis of the chapters in Xenophon's *Hellenica*

[1] DL. I, 421 ss.

[2] Mostly because of the correspondence *Kabeiroi-theoi megaloi*.

[3] CCCLXIII, II, 2, 113-122. He was sure that even in Cyprus the Greeks preceded the Phoenicians.

which describe the city's agony in 404, on the eve of capitulation, we would never be able to guess that a short time earlier Athens had been the strongest sea-power in Greece, and perhaps in the whole Mediterranean. But let us leave aside the city-states of classical Phoenicia, from Tyre to Arwad. One of the greatest revelations of archaeology in the thirties was the discovery of mighty W-S second millennium states to the north of classical Phoenicia—first of Ugarit, then of Alalaḫ, which were joined in the late forties by a third one—the Plain of Adana, whose epigraphical material, it is true, comes only from the IXth or the VIIIth century, but whose existence we have, in the first sections of this chapter, traced back to mid-second millennium. The Semitic population of those three states, according to its language and culture, could certainly have been considered "Phoenician" by aliens, including Greeks. The modern linguistical analysis of the Ugaritic language, from which the dialects of Alalaḫ [1] and Danuna [2] hardly differed in any significant measure, shows that it did not coincide in all points with the language of the Phoenicians and other South Canaanites; [3] but the differences between them were in any case much smaller than those between the Greek dialects. As shown by epigraphic evidence, and still more by the great amount of characteristic expressions, phrases and entire sentences which coincide in the Bible, in the Ugaritic literature of the XIVth century, and in the Danunian inscription of the IX-VIIIth century, the entire wide region from the Taurus to the borders of Egypt and Arabia has for many hundreds of years possessed a common spiritual culture and literature. But each of the three northwestern states surpassed beyond any comparison any city-state of Phoenicia, South Syria, and Palestine, and they represented a different type of state formation: not city-states, but feudal-territorial kingdoms.

Let us look at the kingdom of Ugarit. Its capital was, for its time, an enormous flourishing commercial and industrial city.

[1] Judging from personal names of W-S character. Such names as *Idri-mi* (where original *ḏ* > *d*, as in Ugaritic, instead of *z*, as in South Canaanite), or *Ša-ap-ša*, *Ša-ap-ši-abi* (with Ugaritic name for the Sun, *šapšu*, instead of Canaanite *šamšu*), show that phonetically the dialect of Alalaḫ was close to the Ugaritic.

[2] For the second millennium we can judge only by toponyms.

[3] Summarized CCXXIV, 120-123. As against CANTINEAU, LXXXVII, who emphasized the differences, cf. XXVI, 708; IX, 239; XXIX, 239; DXXI, 63, who stress the basic similarity between Ugaritic, second millennium South Canaanite, and Hebrew.

The royal palace of Ugarit was the most colossal edifice of the whole Near East outside Mesopotamia, far exceeding by its size not only the residences of other Syrian princes, but even—and by far—the palace of the mighty rulers of the vast Hittite empire at Ḫattušaš.[1] This bears witness to the tremendous economic and human resources of the kingdom. Unlike Tyre or Sidon, Ugarit possessed a wide hinterland, reaching the Orontes in the East, Mount Casios in the North, and bordering on Zinzar and Amurru in the South.[2] Administrative documents from the Ugaritic royal archives enumerate more than a hundred towns and settlements which were directly submitted to the central fiscal apparatus; but there were many more of them, for many towns with their districts were fiefs of individual vassals and were exempt from taxes by the crown.[3] The state possessed ships and provided them with military detachments.[4] It conducted a wide commerce—on land with Ḫatti and Assyria, on sea with Egypt and Palestine[5] (and through Palestine with South Arabia[6]), but especially with Cyprus and Mycenaean

[1] "The already cleared surface of the Ugarit palace, without counting the fortress in the west and the servants' buildings in the south, reaches 9000 square meters, and it will largely surpass this figure when the aisles east and south-east are excavated. In comparison, the palace of Atchana-Alalakh covers less than 2000 square meters; that of Boğazköy, even if we double the surface cleared so far, 3000 squatre meters," CDXLII, 251.

[2] After the defeat of the coalition Dunanat-Mukiš-Nuḫašše-Nii-Zinzar-Qaṭna (cf. p. 34 above) by Šuppiluliuma, aided by Niqmad II of Ugarit, the former rewarded the latter by incorporating an extensive territory of the abolished kingdom of Alalaḫ into the kingdom of Ugarit. The new borders of Ugarit reached the Ğebel Bariša in the north and then descended south about half-way between the Orontes and Aleppo. See the relevant cuneiform documents CCCXCI, 63 ss. and commentary, 10-18, and equations of several transferred localities with modern places, XXXIX, *pass.* Niqmad II styled himself after this increase of his kingdom not only *mlk Ugrt*, but also *adn Yrgb* (cf. XXXIX, No. 5: modern er-Ruğ) and *bʿl Šrmn* (correctly identified, as early as 1935, with mod. Sermin, CXXXVII, 228). For the treaty with Amurru, cf. CCCLXXXIX, 128 ss., CCCXCI, 284 ss.

[3] RŠ 16-239; 16.244; 15.114; 16.132 and others, published CCCXC; cf. BOYER, *Étude juridique, ibid.*, p. 294.

[4] RŠ 8.279 = UM 83. In RŠ 18.148 (to appear in *PRU* V), dating from the time of the Peoples of the Sea invasion, the last king of Ugarit is asked by one of his officers to equip 150 ships—a number surpassing the naval forces of any Greek state prior to 500 B.C.

[6] The tablet RŠ 18.31 (to appear in *PRU V*) tells about a Ugaritic ship going to Egypt with a load of merchandise and surprised by tempest in the neighborhood of Tyre and Akko. In Akkadian tablets, found in 1955, Akko, Ashdod and Ascalon are mentioned (CCCLXXXIX, 127).

[5] A merchant, whose name *Ybnn* seems to point to his origin from the South Palestinian city of *Yabne* (Iamnia), delivered, among other merchan-

Greece.[1] The scope of its enterprise and armaments is shown by an Ugaritic king's mission to his envoy in the region of Mount Amanus to buy 2,000 horses [2] (for comparison, let us point out that in the contemporary Amarna letters from Phoenicia and Palestine, claims for horses from Egypt—free of charge!—never exceed 50 pairs). It is difficult to determine the exact surface of the Ugaritic kingdom,[3] but speaking roughly, it was doubtless about three times as big as Attica and about twice as big as the whole of Argolis—and certainly much more thickly settled.

Even greater dimensions were reached by the kingdom of Alalaḫ. Alalaḫ (Mukiš) proper was already larger than the kingdom of Ugarit. But until the XVth century, up to the time of king Idri-mi, it formed a political entity with the regions of Ḫalab, Nuhašše, and Nii, in other words it enclosed the whole north of Syria almost up to the Euphrates, the modern Sancak of Iskenderun, and a strip of southern Turkey. In the XVIIIth century, in the early reign of Ḫammurapi, the kingdom of Iamḫad (as the state with Ḫalab for capital was then called) was estimated the strongest in the complex of Amorite powers of Syria and Mesopotamia, and its king had more vassal kings than Ḫammurapi of Babylon.[4] Even later Alalaḫ was a great military power (military detachments of a thousand or fourteen hundred men are frequent in the texts, and there were hundreds of chariots [5]), had ships, [6] and notwithstanding its being rather

dise, sandalwood (*almg*) and myrrh (*šmn mr*)—products of India and Yemen (UM 120).

[1] It is known that the harbor of Ugarit was one of the principal points of import of Mycenaean wares; but now there is proof that Ugaritians sailed on their own ships to the Aegean to bring this wares: the "dossier" of the rich merchant (*tamkar*) Sinaranu, son of Siginu, grandson of Milki-aḫu, possessor of wide estates in the kingdom of Ugarit, contains a document (RŠ 16.238, CCCXC, 107) about his ship returning from a cruise to Kaphtor ([māt] *Kaptu-ri*).

[2] RŠ 16.402 (DXXIV, 25 ss., No. 12).

[3] Until the reign of Niqmepa in Ugarit and Muršiliš II in Ḫatti, the kingdom of Ugarit included, as a vassal state, the principality of Siyannu and Ušnatu, the territory of which extended from Gibala (mod. Ğebeile) southward almost to Arwad. NOUGAYROL, CCCXCI, 17, estimated that the territory of the Ugaritic kingdom proper extended for 60 km from north to south and for the same distance from east to west. This equals 3,600 square km., or 1,390 sq. m., but NOUGAYROL underestimated the size of the territory annexed from Mukiš: under Niqmad II, the surface of his kingdom (not counting Siyannu and Ušnatu) must have been about 5,000 square km.

[4] CXXIV, 117 s.

[5] Cf. AT 183: 1,006 *šanannu*-warriors, 76 of whom are charioteers, and 1,436 Ḫabiru, including 80 charioteers (cf. AT 226).

[6] Idri-mi returned to Alalaḫ on ships (CDLXVIII, 16 s., lines 30b-35).

a military—feudal than a commercialized feudal state as Ugarit,[1] traded with the Aegean through its port, the future Posidion.[2]

Least of all we know of Danuna, or the kingdom of the Plain of Adana. But its territory, even if it was confined only to Lowland Cilicia, was larger than the territories of either Ugarit or Alalaḫ proper, and at least as large as the whole of the Peloponnese—but much more fertile. All three states together surpassed in size—and most probably in population, too—Peloponnese plus Middle Greece. Each of them was certainly able to send overseas detachments strong enough to take hold, if necessary, of some point or other in alien territory. Let us be just and ensure a fair trial to all parts. One does not see anything exceptional and impossible in sea raids and entire organized migrations of North-Western peoples to the Southeast of the Mediterranean; one coolly takes for granted that the half-wild Sardinians were good enough seamen to come in masses to Egypt, either for military service or for spoil; one accepts without a wink the presence of Sicilians among the Peoples of the Sea. That means that navigation was already developed in a measure to permit large military raids and migrations; but one agrees to it only as far as Europeans are concerned; as for Phoenician navigators, some scholars still find pleasure in reducing them almost to complete nonentity.[3] But the distance from Ugarit, Alalaḫ, or

[1] On the social differences between Alalaḫ and Ugarit, cf. CDLXX, 164.

[2] DLV, 151, 171.

[3] Thus Rhys CARPENTER, XCII (1958), one of the latest attempts to out-Beloch BELOCH not only in completely denying any Phoenician voyages into the Aegean before the VIIth century, but also in minimizing the extent and in reducing the age of Phoenician colonization in Africa, Sicily, Sardinia, and Spain. *Le mirage phénicien*, as he puts it, was due to Homer's "anachronistic" mentions of Phoenicians which Herodotos took on trust and purposely, only in order to confirm Homer, invented a series of fictitious stories about Phoenician settlements in Greece and Sicily (of which Homer, by the way, does not whisper a word). This article was published three years after the Ugaritic text RŠ 16.238 (seep. 107, n.1 above) telling about the ship of a Ugaritic merchant returning from Kaphtor (Crete) not in the VIIth, but in XIIIth century. We shall examine the arguments of CARPENTER's master BELOCH in chapter IV of this study. As to the background of their attitude, let us quote the investigator of the *Odyssey*, G. GERMAIN, by no means a "pro-Phoenicianist": "The European elements of the poem are not Oriental. But this does not imply that we assign therefore a 'Nordic' provenience to them, in the sense that certain Hellenists, mostly German, used, not without, as it seems, racial, if not 'racist,' implications . . . We cannot subscribe to the recent affirmations by Mr. Rhys CARPENTER (*Homeric Epics*, p. 17) that the Greek Muses were pure-blood Europeans, not having anything in common with the Creto-Mycenaean world" (CXCIII, 466).

Tarsus to the Aegean is by no means longer than in the opposite direction, and what was possible for Aegean peoples in 1200 did not present anything unachievable for West Semites, expert seafarers long since, a few centuries earlier. And if one objects, that the Peoples of the Sea were forced to sail away by some tremendous push of other populations (Dorians, Illyrians, or whoever they were), the same might be true for West Semites in the stormy Hyksos age and its aftermath.

All this was to show that, in contrast to what was believed a few decades ago, a West Semitic ("Phoenician") armed penetration into the Aegean basin, including Greece, was perfectly possible and feasible. And now we have proof that it was actually so—that an important branch of the W-S Danunians established itself in the Peloponnese and continued to bear the name of Danuna as late as the first decade of the XIIth century (in Homer, *Danuna* was Hellenized into *Dana(w)oi*). We are very glad to be able to insert in this place, before sending this work to the publisher, that the conception defended in it is now beginning to be shared even by classicists, as witnessed by the revised edition of volumes I and II of *Cambridge Ancient History*.[1]

When did the Danunians come to Argolis—this cannot be established, but if our analysis was correct, the terminus post quem is the fall of the Hyksos rule in Egypt, and the terminus ante quem is probably the rise of the unified Achaean state under the overlordship of Mycenae. This is roughly the period 1550-1450, and it may be curious to note that in one of the many ancient Greek attempts to elaborate a chronology for their Heroic Age, in the Parian Marble, the arrival of Danaos is fixed at 1520; of course, this result was obtained merely by counting back nine generations from the Trojan war (which the Parian Marble fixes at 1220) and attributing three generations to every hundred years. As to the road of the Danunians to Greece, this clearly led along the southern coast of Asia Minor,[2] through Rhodes. The myth of Danaos ascribed to him and his daughters a stop at Rhodes and the foundation of the temple of Athena in Lindos. This might well be an addition of a late mytho-

[1] See p. 331 below.

[2] V. Bérard, LXV, I, 174-191, enumerated several places along the South Anatolian coast, from Rocky Cilicia to Lycia, whose names seemed to him Semitic. Many equations are rather convincing, but since we have no other information on the origin of these settlements, we would not insist upon this evidence.

grapher, since he knew that one could not miss Rhodes on the way along the coast from the East. But in addition, Rhodian local historians of the classical time told stories about Phoenician establishments on their island, some of which ended only with the invasion of the Dorians.[1] For the "anti-Phoenicianist" school these stories were so many hollow words, but they are corroborated not only by some toponyms that already attracted the attention of Samuel Bochart, but also by intrinsic analysis of the Rhodian stories on the Phoenicians, which derive from W-S myths.[2] In the context of the Danunian migration, the traditions about Danaos or Phoenician kings in Rhodes take their proper stand.

We have so far positive data on only one base of departure for W-S penetration into Greece: the Cilician country of Danuna. But there are reasons to believe that the Danunians were not the only West Semites to enter the Aegean in the second millenium. The Ugaritians, who considered Kaphtor (Crete) as the residence of their artisan-god *Kŝr-w-Ḫss*,[3] actually knew the maritime road thither. If our etymology of the name of the East Argolian mountain Sapyselaton (see p. 103, n. 1) is correct, we have here a typical and peculiar Ugaritic name. And if Melicertes (to whose identity with Melqart even Ed. Meyer and H. Winckler agreed) was really introduced into Greece as early as the Mycenaean epoch,[4] this would point to the participation of southern Phoenicians, too, in the overseas expeditions. Besides, we know about Ugarit that in the XVth century a noticeable part of her inhabitants originated from Aradus, Byblos, Berytos, Sidon, Tyre, Sarepta, Acco, Ioppa, Gezer, Azotus, Iamnia.[5] One may imagine that Ugarit, like Miletus in the great age of Greek colonization, was the gathering-point of people

[1] Most of the scarce remainders of their works are quoted by Athenaeus and Diodorus Siculus; cf. CCCLXXIV, II, 250; CCXC, 71 s.

[2] To this we hope to return in a sequel to the present study.

[3] *Kptr ksu ŝbth, Ḥkpt arṣ nḥlth* "Kaphtor (Crete) is the throne of his sitting, Ḥikupta (Egypt) is the land of his inheritance," V AB (ʿnt) VI: 14-16.

[4] Melqart is not epigraphically attested before the first millennium; see p. 209 below.

[5] Cf. p. 102 above. In the eyes of the Mycenaean Greeks, the Ugaritians were as good "Phoenicians" as the Tyrians and Sidonians—not only linguistically and geographically, but in their character of "purple-makers" (the sense of "Phoenician") as well. The production of purple and purple-dyed wool was one of the main industries of Ugarit. See CDLXXXVIII (an Akkadian tablet from Ugarit about distribution of purple wool among a number of associates); RŠ 11.732 (DVIIIa, 253-260, heavy deliveries of purple wool and garments to the court of Ḫatti).

eager to go overseas—as merchants or settlers, depending on the conditions. We will, by the way, risk an assumption that the great rise of Tyre and Sidon since the end of the second millennium was caused not by the disappearance of the alleged Aegean competition on the seas—this did not prevent Ugarit from an extraordinary flourishing—but precisely by the total elimination of Ugarit and Alalaḫ who possessed until 1200 the quasi monopoly of trade with the West. We shall perhaps find traces of more than one W-S dialect in the Greco-Semitic personal names and toponyms which will be examined on subsequent pages. We also know that a large proportion of the population of Ugarit, Alalaḫ, Danuna, and Alašia [1] consisted of Hurrians, who actually formed one North Syrian political and cultural entity with the West Semites; we shall therefore not be surprised by traces of Hurrian onomastica being discovered in the Aegean.[2] We are certain that, along with the Syro-Phoenician influence, an important Hittite-Anatolian influence on Mycenaean Greece can be discerned, though it sometimes was exaggerated; [3] but this problem waits for a comprehensive study by a competent scholar.

All W-S populations of the second millennium, though having their own language, culture, and religion, were under the strongest influence of the mighty Babylonian civilization. Akkadian language was the main written language of the epoch (the Ugaritic cultivation of its native language was rather an exception—and even at Ugarit Akkadian prevailed outside the royal palace and the temple library). Akkadian religious, poetic, and legal texts were widespread and firmly implanted in W-S societies. A considerable syncretism reigned in religion; native gods often were assimilated with Babylonian ones or borrowed attributes from them. Accordingly, it is this mixed Canaaneo-Babylonian spiritual complex that will provide us with material for comparative work.

Our inquiry into the Danaan-Danunian problem has revealed the historical substratum of one interesting Greek myth cycle, and

[1] On Alašia, cf. p. 51, n. 1 above.

[2] See pp. 340-344, 347-351 below.

[3] F. Cornelius (cix, 302) made the brilliant remark that the murder of the Hittite king Muršiliš I, after his victorious return from Babylon, by Ḫantiliš, the lover of his wife (that is, according to him, the real bearing of the text) was transferred by Greek poets on Agamemnon. The scope of Cornelius' discovery is even wider; the myth claimed for Agamemnon the descent from the Anatolian king Tantalos, in whom many scholars saw the Hittite Tudḫaliyaš; Muršiliš I was a straight descendant of Tudḫaliyaš I.

it has given us the opportunity to try a method of approaching such myths. In the following chapters we will apply this method to some other myth cycles which classical Greece inherited from her remote Mycenaean past [1]—whether their heroes were labeled as Phoenicians or not. The Phoenician label may attract our attention towards a particular myth, but in itself it is not proof of real Phoenicianism; it is the contents of the myth that is decisive for our purpose.[2]

[1] Martin P. NILSSON's *The Mycenaean Origin of Greek Mythology* (1932) proves in a most convincing way the thesis forming its title. One may disagree with the savant author in many particular cases of mythological exegesis, and especially in his pro-Thracian and anti-Phoenician bias—but his systematic demonstration of the antiquity of Greek myths, of their reflecting many conditions, beliefs, and cults of the Mycenaean age, offers the preliminary basis for research attempts like the present study. More recently, T. B. L. WEBSTER adduced new evidence to prove that the epic poems of the Homeric age developed out of Mycenaean poetry, which itself grew on the rich ground of Oriental literature (DXXXVII, 64-90, 91-135).

[2] Alan J. V. WACE wrote in his Foreword to DV, XXVIII: "A fresh examination of the legends of early Greece must also be undertaken to estimate their archaeological and historical value."

CHAPTER TWO

CADMOS AND THE CADMIDS

MEMBLIAROS AND THE COSMOGONIC CYCLE OF THERA-ANAPHE

> With all the recognized weaknesses of Herodotus he still knew more about the Phoenicians than Beloch and his followers . . .
>
> ALBRIGHT [1].

Herodotos IV: 147 reports:

> There were in the island now called Thera, but then Calliste, descendants of Membliaros the son of Poikiles, a Phoenician; for Cadmos son of Agenor, in his search for Europa, had put in at the place now called Thera; and having put in, either because the land pleased him, or because for some other reason he desired so to do, he left in this island, among other Phoenicians, his own kinsman Membliaros. These dwelt in the island Calliste for eight generations before Theras came from Lacedaemon.

The name *Membliaros* is not an invention of Herodotos; it is a toponym turned into an eponymous ancestor, just as the name of the Laconian colonizer of Thera is but the name of the island supplied with a masculine ending. Stephanos of Byzantium reports that *Membliaros* or *Bliaros* was the old name of another island, Anaphe, the closest neighbor of Thera. It may seem strange that Herodotos associates Membliaros with Thera rather than with Anaphe, but we will presently see that the two islands formed a real cultic and mythological entity. Now the question is: did Herodotos really have any genuine local traditions regarding Phoenicians having settled in Thera or Anaphe a thousand years before his own time, or was it just a whimsical play of his fantasy, as is asserted by those who regard the Aegean as a prohibited zone for Phoenician ships?

Membliaros has no Greek etymology; the derivation from *memblomai*,[2] where *b* is secondary, is excluded by the independent occurrence

[1] XIX, 22. The article treats the problem of Phoenician colonies in the West Mediterranean, but its conclusion is true for our case as well.

[2] *Memblomai*, a secondary present medium of *melô* "to take care," formed out of the aorist medium *memelêtai* shortened to *membletai* with the regular Greek change of the cluster *ml* into *mbl*.

of the form *Bliaros* which retains the *b* and shows thus that *b* is an original consonant of the word. The same reason invalidates the Phoenician etymology proposed in the XIXth century by MOVERS [1] and H. LEWY.[2] But the name *is* W-S ("Phoenician"); it is a compound name, as shown by the parallel forms *Membliaros* and *Bliaros*, and it represents a very accurate transliteration of Ugaritic or archaic Phoenician *mêm-bli-ʾâr* "waters without light," [3] or, shorter, *bli-ʾâr* "without light = darkness." [4]

On first sight, such a name or toponym may seem extremely odd; but it immediately introduces us into the very heart of W-S mythical cosmogonic ideas. It is impossible, as soon as one has recognized the "waters of darkness" in the name of Membliaros, not to recall the famous description of the primordial chaos in Gen. 1: 2: "And the earth was a desert (*tōhū*) and a water-abyss (*bōhū*), and darkness was upon the face of the Deep (*tehôm*), and the spirit of God moved upon the face of the waters." Even if one agrees to a relatively late time (VIth or Vth century) of literary composition of the so-called priestly cosmogony, there can be no doubt that its author has only reproduced, in a stern and lapidary form, very old cos-

[1] CCCLXXIV, II, 2, 268.

[2] CCCXXX, 247 s.—Both MOVERS and LEWY proceeded from the parallel names attested for the island of Melos, situated in the same part of the Aegean sea: *Mimallis*, according to Callimachos, and *Memblis*, according to Aristides of Miletus (cf. CDXXIII, *s.v. Kadmos*); besides, Stephanos of Byzantium stated that Melos was a colony of the Phoenician Byblos. MOVERS and LEWY were probably right in deriving all three parallel forms from the Semitic root *mlʾ* "to be full": *Mêlos* = *mâlêʾ* "full," *Mimallis* = *memallêʾ* "filling, abundantly providing (rather than LEWY's reconstruction in passive: *memullāʾ* "filled"); and *Memblis* as a regular Greek contraction of *Mimallis*. If a river *Membles* also existed, this is not proof against the Semitism of the name (as in CDXXIII, *s.v. Membliaros*): a name like *memallêʾ* "abundantly providing" fits a river very well. But all these toponyms, interesting as they may be for the study of Semitic names in Greece, do not provide a real explanation of *Membliaros*: a) by neglecting its second part, *-ar(os)*, b) by failing to take into account the persistence of *b* in *Bliaros* (LEWY's assumption that *b* is a mutation of the initial *m* in a hypothetical **mli-aros*, is very unsatisfactory).

[3] "Light" is *ʾôr* in Hebrew, but Ugaritic has the older form *ar* (= *ʾâr*), *UM* § 20.76. The negation "without" is *beli* in Hebrew, with a šewā mobile between *b* and *l*, but the Greeks who dropped the first vowels in such Semitic loan-words as *chrysos* > *ḫarûṣ* "gold" and *mna* > *manā* "mina," probably disregarded the semi-vowel. For Ugaritic *bl* with the sense of Heb. *beli*, cf. *UM* § 12.4.

[4] Cf. Ugar. *blmt* "without death = immortality," *UM*, § 12.4, and also *u mlk u blmlk* UM 51: VII: 43, translated CCXXIII, 36 "whether king or commoner" (literally "non-king").

mogonic notions. The Phoenicians had basically the same cosmogonic pattern, as shown by the relics of Phoenician mythology presented by Philo of Byblos:[1] "As the beginning of all things he supposes dark and windy air, or a gust of dark air, and obscure,[2] Erebos-like chaos" *Praep. Ev.* I: 10: 1; and in a parallel fragment of cosmogony (ibid. I: 10: 7), he speaks of "the wind *Kolpia* and his wife *Baau* (which he explains as Night)." The wind, whatever origin its name *Kolpia*(*s*) might have,[3] corresponds to the "spirit (literally, wind) of God," and *Baau* (explained as Night, i.e. darkness) is the same word as *bōhū* in the cosmogony of Genesis.[4]

Now it is important to note that this same rare and specific word *bōhū*, the primaeval dark water-chaos, is met again, with the feminine ending *-t*,[5] in the form rendered in Latin transcription by *Boëth*, as the name of the sacred pool in the great Phoenician sanctuary of Astarte and Adonis in Aphaca.[6] It was believed that once a year the goddess descended into the pool as a fiery falling star, or that on solemn feast days, when people assembled in the shrine, a fire-globe was lit in the vicinity of the temple and probably

[1] The fragments of Philo Herrenius of Byblos (early IId century A.D.) are transmitted by Eusebius of Caesaraea in his *Praeparatio Evangelica*; one of their last editions is CII. We cannot mention here all the vast literature dedicated to Philo's work. Eusebius was right in defining Philo's approach to Phoenician cosmogony and mythology as "atheistic." Philo was an extreme euhemerist, and his awkward tendency to empty a religious story of all traces of religion by expelling the divine element from the creation story and by transforming Phoenician gods into mortal people highly degrades the worth of his reports; but under this pseudo-rationalist mask, relics of genuine old myths can be discerned.

[2] *Tholeros* "dirty, turpid, silty"; Philo needed such a description of the primaeval water-abyss in order to be able to explain in a "rationalist" way the formation of dry land out of water, "under the impact of the sun-heat."

[3] *Kolpia*(*s*) may be Phoenician (LII, I, 13: **qôl-piaḥ* "voice of blowing") or Greek (CCCVIII, 370: *kolpias* "winding, inflated"); but since it is put together with the Phoenician *Baau*, the Phoenician derivation seems more probable.

[4] As observed at least since MOVERS, CCCLXXIV, I, 279, 589, 666 s.; cf. LII, I, 12; CCCVIII, 370; CDX, 178.

[5] Cf. W-S *ʾarṣ* "earth" and Akk. *irṣitu* (*erṣetu*), W-S *teḥôm* (fem.) "ocean" and Akk. *tâmtu, tiâmat*.

[6] Germanicus (the nephew of Emperor Tiberius) ad Arati *Phaenomena* (which he translated into Latin) 20, 24; cf. CCCLXXIV, I, 591, 666 s.; LII, I, 12. Both MOVERS and BAUDISSIN compare *Ialdabaôth*, the Gnostic name of the world creator, explained as "born by *bāhôt*," the primordial water-chaos. ALBRIGHT (*ap.* CCV, 315, n. 15) recently suggested that *Ialdabaôth* was Phoenician rather than Aramaic, as supposed hitherto. For the vocalization *Boëth* instead of *Baôth*, cf. LXX *Noëma* for *Naʿamā*, *Noëmin* for *Nāʿomî*.

rolled down into the pool.[1] It is true that Astarte was worshipped, inter alia, as the planet Venus, but the rite described certainly had a much wider and more universal significance—it symbolized the bursting of the divine light into the primaeval dark water-chaos *bōhū* or *bāhôt* (Boëth), the first act of creation: "And God said: let there be light: and there was light" (Gen. 1: 3), or as Philo of Byblos expresses it in his clumsy "atheist" language: "And Môt [2] was shaped like an egg and burst forth into light" (*Praep. Ev.* I: 10: 2).

We see, thus, that a cosmogonic name like *mêm-bli-ʾâr* "waters without light" could well be attached to quite a real place, as *Bāhôt* "dark water-abyss" was in Aphaca.[3] We know in general that cosmogony, in the ancient East, was not a matter of abstract philosophic interest, but the central and essential subject of the ritual of the most important yearly festival—the New Year celebration. In Babylon, the great creation epic *Enuma Eliš* was not just a work for cosmologic references, but was solemnly read on the fourth day of Akitu, the New Year's festival.[4] The same, as recently

[1] Reported by early Christian authors: Sozomenos, II: 5; Zosimos, I: 58; cf. CCCLXXIV, I, 279, 589, 666 s.; CCCVIII, 158; CDXXVIII, 107, 175. According to Sozomenos, the fiery star in which Urania was embodied, fell into the river at Aphaca; but Zosimos speaks of an artificial pond at Aphaca connected with illumination festivals, and Germanicus, in his commentary to Aratos' *Phaenomena*, reports that the daughter of Venus Aphacitis had cast herself into the *stagnum Boëth*: this is obviously a contamination of Urania falling into the pond as a star and of the popular myth of Derceto drown or having drown herself in the pond of Ascalon or Hierapolis.

[2] As much as one can see from Eusebius' quotations of Philo, Mot was either a transfiguration of the primaeval wind, or the product of its mixing (with the water-chaos ?). The name is not clear; LII, I, 12 understood it as abstract of *mô* = *may* "water." Anyway, it has nothing in common with the Nether World god *Môt* (Ugar. *Mt*, Heb. *Māwet*), who figures in Philo as *Muth*.

[3] Aphaca properly signifies "spring, stream"; but cf. Ugar. *mbk nhrm qrb apq thmtm* (I AB = UM 49: I: 5-6, etc.) "the courses of the Two Rivers, the midst of the streams of the Two Deeps" (CCXXIII, 31, 44)—an expression with an evident cosmologic significance where *apq* (whence Aphaca) is associated with the Two Deeps (Apsu and Tiamat) of *Enuma Eliš*. For the pond symbolizing the water-deep, cf. Solomon's temple at Jerusalem, where, instead of a pond which was impossible because of the terrain, the Phoenician builders made a large copper basin with the significant name "sea" ("Sea", in Psalms and prophetic texts, is the adversary conquered by Yahwe). The reservoir for ritually pure water in Sumerian and Akkadian temples was also designated by the symbolic name *apsû* (CXVI, 32; LXXXIV).

[4] CCCXIII, 21-28; CDLXXI, 60; CLXXXVI, 34 ss.; CXVI, 246. The *akitu* festival could be celebrated at the vernal or the autumnal equinox.

revealed by careful analysis, was true for the Hebrew New Year, originally a part of the great autumnal festival of Sukkôt: [1] "indeed, it may be said that the New Year Festival was, as it were, a repetition of the Creation," and it was not without grounds that Rabbinical Judaism "discerned a relationship between the Feast of Tabernacles and the Creation." [2] It is very probable that not only psalms commemorating Yahwe's victory over the Sea and his enthronement as king, but the Hebrew cosmogonic epic as well, out of which the first chapter of Genesis was abridged, was a part of the New Year liturgy.

It is known [3] that on the first day of the feast of Tabernacles the great golden candelabra in the Women's Court of the Jerusalem Temple were lit, the whole court was brilliantly illuminated, and women performed a torch-dance to the accompaniment of music and songs all night long until the cock's crow when the crowd broke up. [4] OESTERLEY believed this to be a true relic of sun-worship —but in that case the festivity would last until sunrise, instead of ending long before it, with the first crow of the cock. In full harmony with the general cosmogonic character of the festival, its first night festivity with brilliant illumination and torch-dance symbolized the first act of creation: the appearance of light and the victory of light over primordial darkness. One can, with reason, identify the annual feast at Aphaca, where people assembled in masses, and lamps and fire-balls were lit around the temple and over the Boëth pool, with the great autumnal festival which most probably was common to the Hebrews and the Phoenicians.

Thus we come close to the idea that Membliaros was a Phoenician shrine in Anaphe where, in ancient times, the Phoenician cosmogonic myth about the first burst of light over the primordial dark water-chaos was annually performed through recitations and other ceremonies.

And this is not a gratuitous presumption. It is corroborated by the passage dedicated to Anaphe in the *Argonautica* of Apollonios of Rhodes. We will quote this passage in full—and after reading it

[1] CCCXCIV, 124-140; DXLVII, 197 s.; CLXXXVI, 36 ss.
[2] CCCXCIV, 124.
[3] From the Talmud—the Bible provides only indirect information on the way of celebrating Sukkot—but the Talmudic description is full of undoubtedly genuine and very old details and shows that under the Second Temple this festival was celebrated much as in earlier times.
[4] CCCXCIV, 134 s.

there will remain no doubt that Apollonios got his information directly from Anaphe and Thera. Originally this description had no relationship whatsoever to the Argonauts, and was only connected with their story, most probably, because noble families in Thera claimed to descend from them.[1]

Argonautica IV: 1694-1698:[2]

> But straightway as they sped over the wide Cretan sea night scared them, that night which they name the Pall of Darkness: the stars pierced not that fatal night nor the beams of the moon, but black chaos descended from heaven, or haply some other darkness came, rising from the nethermost depths.

This forceful description, so unlike the general, rather slack style of Apollonios, does not have an ordinary tempest as its subject; besides, a storm is not even mentioned there. It sounds like a highly poetic solemn cosmogonic myth, extraordinarily resembling Gen. 1: 2 and Philo of Byblos (in spite of the latter's unpoetic vulgarized form). The fragment speaks for itself; it operates with such notions, sacrified by liturgic tradition, as "black chaos" and "darkness rising from the nethermost depths," which reminds one of "the dark air" and "the obscure, Erebos-like chaos" of Philo, and "darkness upon the face of the Deep" of Gen. 1: 2. It is obvious that this description descends in a straight line from the common source of the other two versions: from an old Canaanite myth on the creation of the world. And then Apollonios passes to what can be defined as a counterpart of the following verse, Gen. 1: 3. After Jason's invocation to Phoebus Apollo (v. 1699-1705), the god comes to the rescue:

Argonautica IV: 1706-1718:

> And quickly, O son of Leto, swift to hear, didst thou come from heaven to the Melantian rocks, which lie there in the sea. Then darting upon one of the twin peaks, thou raisedst aloft in thy right hand thy golden bow; and the bow flashed a dazzling gleam all round. And to their sight appeared a small island of the Sporades, over against the tiny isle Hippuris, and there they cast anchor and stayed; and straightway dawn arose and gave them light; and they made for Apollo a glorious abode in a shady wood, and a shady altar, calling on Phoebus the "Gleamer" (*Aiglêtês*) because of the gleam far-seen; and that bare

[1] Herodotos IV: 145-149, repeating local Theraean traditions, makes the Laconian colonizers of Thera descend from the children whom the Argonauts begot with Lemnian women.

[2] Here and in further quotations from *Argonautica*, the translation of R. C. SEATON (Loeb Classical Library) is cited.

island they called Anaphe, for that Phoebus had revealed it to men sore bewildered.

We, thus, found what was to be proved—"dark waters" without any glimpse of light (the very *mêm-bli-'âr* we had discovered in *Membliaros*), and located, of all places, exactly at Membliaros-Anaphe. And the sudden appearance of light—of divine light with its source in itself, independent from sun, moon, or stars (a conception which later puzzled rationalist sceptics)—completely corresponds to the Biblical cosmogonic pattern. "And the bow flashed a dazzling gleam all round . . . and straightway dawn arose and gave them light" strongly resembles "And God said: let there be light! And there was light . . . And there was evening, and there was dawn: one day." Nor is the gleaming divine bow of the victorious creator god anything strange to the Biblical and Semitic cosmogonic idea. We know from Gen. 9: 11-14 that in a similar situation, after the Flood, when the waters of the Deep (*t^ehôm*) had once again retreated from the earth, Yahwe placed his bow on a cloud as a symbol of his covenant with the earth and all living beings. And in *Enuma Eliš* (a cosmogonic poem heavily overloaded with secondary details and additions, but basically related to the W-S creation myths), the bow is Marduk's principal weapon in his struggle with Tiamat (*t^ehôm*), the personified primordial water-chaos (tabl. IV: 35-38, 101-102). Apollo *Aiglêtês*, the "gleamer" or "light-giver," to whom Anaphe was dedicated,[1] is merely the Greek name of some older divine lord of Anaphe whose Semitic name was lost, but whose original rôle remained unchanged by the Dorian inhabitants of the little island.

In the following verses (1719-1730) Apollonios tells what peculiar offering the Argonauts brought to Apollo after their secure landing on Anaphe: not having anything else to offer, they poured water upon the altar. This made the Phaeacian maidservants of Medea laugh, and the Argonauts, in response, taunted the women and jested with them, and this double custom of pouring water on the altar and jesting with women was still observed by the Anaphaeans during the celebration of their main festival at the time of Apollonios.[2] The connection with the Argonauts and the origin of the rite

[1] Callimachos (quoted by Strabo X: 5: 1) gives the epithet "Aigletan" to Anaphe; inscriptions from Anaphe reveal the local cult of Apollo *Aiglêtês* (CLXII, IV, 365, No. 29).

[2] Same story briefly repeated by (pseudo-) Apollodoros, *Bibliotheca* I: 26: 1.

is an evident aetiology of the strange and no more understandable archaic rite; one may suppose that the very invention of twelve maidservants given to Medea by the Phaeacian queen was made by Apollonios or his precursor precisely in order to introduce the necessary female element in the all-male company of the Argonauts. Robert GRAVES (who usually turns to the Celts for parallels to Greek myths and rites) correctly noticed that "the water-sacrifice at Anaphe recalls that offered by the Jews on the Day of Willows, the climax of their festival of Tabernacles, when water was brought up in solemn procession from the Pool of Siloam . . . Tabernacles began as an autumn fertility feast and, according to the Talmud, the Pharisees found it difficult to curb the traditional 'lightheadedness' of the women." [1] Moreover, he specified that the custom described at Anaphe also belonged to the Autumn Festival of that island.[2] This presents another striking resemblance to the W-S New Year Festival which not only annually celebrated the creation of the world but also was a means of ensuring prosperity for the year ahead—by the traditional rain-charm to secure rain, and by hierogamic rites to stimulate fertility.[3] At Anaphe, as in Canaan, both aspects were integrally tied together.

Up to now, we have seen only the prologue to the world's creation —the dark primordial chaos—and its first act: "let there be light!"; but we have not yet answered the question why Herodotos located Membliaros at Thera and not at Anaphe. Both questions are resolved by the sequel to the Anaphe episode in Apollonios. Here we see the second act of the creation—the appearance of land from the primaeval waters—and this second act takes place at Thera. Its hero is no longer Apollo Aigletes, the divine patron of Anaphe, but the local hero of Thera, the mythical ancestor of the Battiad kings of Thera's colony Cyrene, Euphemos. He was included in the synthetic list of the Argonauts together with many other local heroes and mythical characters (as Mopsos, Orpheus, the Dioscuri, Meleagros, etc.),

[1] CCXXVII, II, 250, No. 9.

[2] *Ibid.*, 247, *i*. Unfortunately, we did not find any ancient sources for this timing—but it is very probable.

[3] Cf. the works quoted p. 117 n. 1 above. In particular, cf. the dances and the legendary abduction of the girls at Shiloh during the autumnal festival, Judg. 21: 21-23; the pouring of water on the altar as a rain-charm in the Elijah story, I Kings 18: 33 ss.; the pouring of water by Anath, also as a rain-charm, V AB (ʿnt): II: 39-42; and the prophetic complaints against sacral prostitution and general sexual dissoluteness during the great festivals.

but he is clearly a declassed god. *Euphêmos* was an epithet of Zeus at Lesbos, and probably elsewhere, also of Poseidon and Apollo.[1] Here is how Apollonios of Rhodes characterizes Euphemos the Argonaut (I: 179-184):

> After them from Taenarus came Euphemus whom, most swift-footed of men, Europa, daughter of mighty Tityus, bare to Poseidon. He was wont to skim the swell of the grey (or blue, *glaukoio*) sea, and wetted not his swift feet, but just dipping the tops of his toes was borne on the watery path.

This description—taking in account Euphemos' role of a genuine demiurge which will be shown presently—is evidently only a euhemerized paraphrase of the cosmogonic "Spirit (or wind) of God moving upon the face of the waters" and its counterparts in Philo's cosmogony. Not less characteristic are the names of Euphemos' parents. We will return to Europa in one of the next sections, dedicated to the Phoenician Europa, the sister of Cadmos; in this connection it is enough to mention that according to Greek lexicographers, *eurôpê* signified "darkness." [2] Here, Poseidon, the sea-god, can be called a modernization of the primordial water-element; he replaced some cosmogonic notion like, e.g., *Ôkeanos*, the father of all gods (*Iliad* XIV: 201), for since Euphemos became a representative of the heroic age, he could have had for divine father only one of the younger, Olympian gods. Thus Euphemos, the moving creative wind, has for parents the Darkness and the primaeval Ocean; he corresponds to Ialdabaôth "son of *bōhū*," as Gnostics called the world creator of the Old Testament; [3] and if the word *phêmê* in his name be taken in its signification of "voice," it may well be that he represents a Greek version of Philo's cosmic wind Kolpias = *qôl-pîăḥ* "voice of breath" or "audible blowing." [4]

A tradition transmitted not only by Apollonios (IV: 1551 ss.), but even by Pindar (*Pyth.* IV: 9 ss.), tells that Euphemos received, under the guise of a gift, a clod of earth from Triton in Libya; [5]

[1] CDXI, VI, 1, 1168.

[2] See p. 128 below.

[3] On Ialdabaoth, cf. lately CCV, 305, 315 ss., 318. The Gnostics, contemporaries of Philo of Byblos, combined Christianity with numerous elements of Semitic paganism.

[4] See p. 110, n. 3 above.

[5] Triton is a sea-deity; see following note. Libya is introduced because the Battiad dynasty of Cyrene claimed to descend from Euphemos through its Theraean ancestors.

and immediately after leaving Anaphe, he cast the clod into the sea —according to Pindar, inadvertently, according to Apollonios (IV: 1731-1755), on purpose, under the influence of a prophetic dream: "cheered by the prophecy, he cast the clod into the depths. Therefrom rose up an island, Calliste, sacred nurse of the sons of Euphemos," which was renamed Thera when Theras came there with the descendants of the Argonauts and in particular with those of Euphemos (IV: 1756-1764). This is an authentic relic of the creation of the earth out of the primitive ocean—a most natural organic sequel to the creation of light in the midst of the dark chaos.[1]

Thera is the counterpart of Anaphe. Anaphe-Membliaros symbolized the "waters without light," Thera, the miniature of the earth, formed after the creation of light, is her antonym: her name, quite probably, is the W-S *te'îrā* "lit, illuminated." Both islands were close neighbors; Strabo (X: 5: 1) mentions as closest to Thera not only Therasia which almost touched her, but in the same sentence Anaphe as well, and he quotes a verse of Callimachos: "Aigletan Anaphe, neighbor of the Laconian Thera." Both islands, or rather their ancient sanctuaries, must have formed a sort of cultic pair where cosmogonic epics had been ritually recited or dramatically performed during the New Year Festival: in Anaphe—the first part, dealing with the primaeval chaos and the victory of light over darkness, in Thera—the second part, describing the creation of dry land out of the boundless sea. This arrangement corresponds to a certain degree to the distribution of liturgic services between the two sacred mountains in Shechem: Gerizim, for blessings, and Ebal, for curses (Deut. 28: 12-13).

[1] This way of creating the earth out of a small clod of ground reminds us of a Babylonian cosmogony included in the ritual of the *kalû*-priest on the occasion of temple restoration (CDLXXXIX, 46 s., line 24 ss.; CXVI, 302 s.; full translation CDXXXVII, 341): "When Anu created the heaven, when Nudimmud (= Ea) created the *apsû* (Ocean), his abode, Ea took from the *apsû* a handful of clay, he created the god Kulla for the restoration of temples, created the reed-marsh and the forest for their construction-work," etc. It may be relevant that, according to the tradition, the Lemnian wife of Euphemos by whom he begot the ancestor of the Theraean and Cyrenean Euphemids, was named *Malachê* or *Lamachê*. The former name is evidently the W-S *malkā* "queen," and the latter, despite its Greek appearance, may well derive from the Semitic root *lmk* "to knead, to puddle" (Arab. *lamaka*, cf. Bibl. pers. myth. n. *Lemek*, LXX *Lamech*): in Akkadian myths, the mother-goddess Ninḫursag (Nintu, Mami, Aruru) formed the first man (or men) out of clay, as her partner Ea created in the same way the land, and his counterpart Euphemos the island Thera.

Poikiles and Related Problems

We can understand now why Herodotos made Membliaros, the eponym of Anaphe, a Phoenician and settled him on the more important of the two islands, Thera. It remains to elucidate, if possible, where he acquired the name of Membliaros' alleged father, Poikiles, and whether this name belongs to the cultic and onomastic entity of Thera-Anaphe. *Poikilês* seems to be a slight modification of the common Greek adjective *poikilos* "motley, variegated, multicolored, spotted, embroidered in colors," or figuratively "skillful, intricate, tangled, perfidious, cunning, sly." Both usages of the word fit very well to the Phoenicians as Greeks knew them in Homeric and archaic periods: they surely used to sell to the Greeks, among other merchandise, multicolored garments which were, in the same period, highly estimated in Assyria as Phoenician and Syrian products, and they had the reputation of sly and perfidious deceivers (e.g. *Odyss.* XIV: 288-290; XV: 415, 419). This would be a very simple explanation of Membliaros' patronymic *Poikilêo*; but certain indications seem to warn us against over-simplification in this case and rather to suggest that *Poikilês* might have been more intimately connected with Membliaros, Anaphe, and the whole cosmogonic cycle we have restored in the preceding section.

We can envisage three approaches to Poikiles, besides that mentioned above. One, which we will only hint in passing, is the possibility that *Poikilês* was a distorted *Kolpias* (with a metathesis), the name of the primaeval wind in Philo.

A second and much more serious possibility is that *Poikilês* was a translation of a misunderstood Semitic counterpart of the name *Anaphê*. This is correctly explained by Apollonios as a derivation of *anaphainô* "to appear, to reveal"—"for Phoebus had revealed it to men sorely bewildered" (IV: 1718); but the verb also has the meaning "to light (e.g. stars, fire)" ; it accords very well with the "fiat lux" myth connected with the island. Now the Akkadian liturgic term for divine appearance (theophany) was *nâmuru*,[1] and it is found many times in a Ugaritic hymn in the Akkadian language, but in Ugaritic alphabetic script, recognized, collated and translated by Éd. Dhorme,[2] e.g. *nâmur-ki linn*[*amer*] . . . [*bêl*]*etni*,

[1] Infinitive (verbal noun) N-stem of *amâru* "to see" (Assyrian form; Babylonian *nānmuru*).

[2] CXVIII.

nâmur-ki li[*nnamer*] "may thy appearance be seen, O our Lady, may thy appearance be seen." [1] *Anaphê* is a correct Greek translation of Akk. *nâmuru*; but in the native language of the West Semites who brought this term to the island, the same word signified "spotted" (cf. *nāmēr*, Heb. "leopard"), and it was accordingly translated once again in Greek when the knowledge of Akkadian went out of use in the W-S world after approximately 1200.[2]

A third and very interesting possibility is opened by comparing our reconstructed cosmogonic myth with the iconographic representation of a very similar myth inside a sanctuary in the Attic town of Phlya, which boasted that its mysteries were older than those of Eleusis. Hippolytus, the early Christian author of *Philosophumena* or *Refutatio Omnium Haeresium* describes one of the paintings of that sanctuary, which was restored and decorated by Themistocles after the Persian invasion and whose pictures thus reflect relatively ancient traditions: [3]

> There is in the gateway the picture of an old man, white-haired, winged (having his *pudendum erectum*); he is pursuing a blue-colored [4] woman who escapes. Above the man is written *phaos rhyentês*, above the woman *pereêphikola*. According to the doctrine of the Sethians, it seems that *phaos rhyentês* is "light" and that *phikola* is "dark water."

Jane HARRISON, speaking of this description, proposed to identify the old winged man with the *archaios erôs* of Orphic tradition, and assumed that his pursuit of the woman had an erotic character; the non-expurgated text of the fragment, indeed, shows it plainly. We have quoted Philo of Byblos who, in one of the variants of his cosmogony, put in the beginning of the world the wind Kolpia(s) and his wife Baau "darkness"; here we have the union of the "Rushing Light" (*phaos rhyentês*) with the "Dark Water of the

[1] CXVIII, 89, No. VIII (= UM 103): 23 s.

[2] Cf. the correspondence of *Poikilê petra* in Cilicia to its doublet *Anemurion* (LXV, I, 181).

[3] We quote after HARRISON, CCXLVII, 644, where the text and its translation are given. Miss HARRISON, however, omitted both in the text and in the translation the words which we have added in parentheses on the basis of the full edition of Hippolytus' work, CDXXVII, V, 67, our passage belonging to Book V, chapt. 15 of *Refutatio Omnium Haeresium*. Miss HARRISON referred to this work (discovered in 1842 among the manuscripts of Mount Athos Monastery) as "anonymous"; its authorship is, however, firmly established since its first publication in 1851.

[4] According to CDXXVIII, V, 67, n. 14, and CCXLVII, 644, n. 1, *kyanoeidê* ("blue-colored") is an emendation of *kynoeidê* ("dog-like") of the manuscripts.

beyond" (*pereê* + the mysterious *phikola*). Jane HARRISON herself made the remark: "We are reminded of the time when 'the Spirit of God moved upon the face of the waters'." But what does the word *phikola* for "dark water" represent? It certainly is not Greek and cannot be found in the most comprehensive and minute thesauri of the Greek language. On the other hand it curiously resembles *Poikilês*, the "father" of Membliaros—"the dark water." [1] The reference to the Sethians, one of the Gnostic sects (which have retained several relics of the old W-S paganism [2]), may point to a Semitic etymology, and only one can be proposed: *pî-kôl* "the mouth of all." [3] *Pe* (st. constr. *pî*) "mouth" as a metaphoric designation of an open bottomless abyss is common W-S; applied to the Nether World, it is found in Ugaritic mythologic poems [4] and in many poetic passages of the Bible.[5] The Babylonian creation epic *Enuma Eliš* IV: 97 tells about the mouth of Tiamat (the primordial water-abyss) which she opened to swallow Marduk. But the Akk. *pû* "mouth, orifice" is also used for "womb," and if this usage be admitted for W-S languages, the translation of *pî-kôl* by "the womb of all" would fit very well the primordial chaos whence all things and beings arose—exactly as in Enuma Eliš I: 4 it is said: "Mummu-Tiamat, she who bore them all," [6] or as in several passages of the Bible the Nether World or the earth are compared to the mother's womb.[7] Moreover, we actually find, in Akkadian cosmogonic poems, the epithet "Mother-Womb" attached to the mother-goddess Mami (or Nintu, or Ninḫursag), "the one who created mankind" and "the creatress of destiny." [8]

[1] It is known that as early as the Vth century *oi* was pronounced almost as *i*: *loimos* ("pestilence") and *limos* ("famine") had a practically identical pronunciation, Thucyd. II: 54.

[2] The previously mentioned Ialdabaoth; the serpent-worship of the Ophite (Naasene) gnostics; the cosmologic divine personage *Aiôn* (*Ulômos* "eternity" of the Phoenician cosmogony according to Damascius).

[3] This combination is not invented; it is actually found as a pers. n. *Pîkôl* Gen. 21: 22; 26: 26. (See p. 125, n. 1 below). In the second millennium, its W-S pronunciation would approximately have been *pî-kulli*.

[4] E.g. I* AB (= UM 67): II: 2-4: "A lip to earth, a lip to heaven, and tongue to the stars, so that Baal may enter his inwards, yea descend into his mouth" (translation CCXXIII, 39).

[5] See enumeration CLXXXVI, 189.

[6] *Mu-um-mu Ti-amat mu-al-li-da-at gim-ri-šú-nu.*

[7] Cf. LI, 20, n. 1.

[8] Old Babylonian poem of Atramḫasis (DXXXIV, 308 s.), I: iii: 2, 3, 7-8 (*at-ti-i-ma šà-as-sú-ru ba-ni-a-at a-wi-lu-tim*: "thou art the womb, the creatress of mankind"); I: iv: 15. Cf. CDLXXI, 99. In a Sumerian list of gods

Now Hippolytos himself leaves no doubt that our etymology of *phikola* as "the womb of all" is correct. His description of the Phlyan fresco quoted above is actually an illustration of what he says (*Refutatio* V: 15) about the Sethians: "For their doctrine concerning the womb is also the tenet of Orpheus." Earlier, V: 14, he so expounds their cosmogony which had its origin, along with the Orphism, in Phoenician systems:

> From the first great concourse, then, of the three principles, ensues a certain great form, a seal of heaven and earth. The heaven and the earth have a figure similar to the womb, having a navel in the midst; and if, he says, any one is desirous of bringing this figure under the organ of vision, let him artfully scrutinize the pregnant womb of whatsoever animal he wishes, and he will discover an image of the heaven and the earth, and of all the things which in the midst of all are unalterably situated underneath.
>
> . . . such a figure of heaven and earth as is similar to a womb after the first coition . . .
>
> From the water, therefore, has been produced a first begotten originating principle, viz., wind, (which is) violent and boisterous, and a cause of all generations . . .
>
> When, therefore, the waves that have been upreared from the waters have received within themselves the power of generation possessed by females, they contain, as in a certain womb, in different species, the infused radiance, so as that is visible in the case of all animals . . .

The original cosmogonic expression can thus be restored as *mêm-bli-'âr pî-kôl* "dark water, the womb of all." Thence the Greek transliteration *phikola* was understood as "dark water," and Herodotos (or his earlier logographic euhemerizing source) made from the two members of the formula a name and a patronymic, *Membliaros Poikilêo*. We must still explain how the epithet of the primordial water-chaos happened to figure in the patriarchal legend of the Genesis as *Pîkôl*, the army commander of the Philistine king Abimelech; our tentative explanation is given, as a brief excursus, in the footnote below.[1] We will submit elsewhere, in a different

(TRS 10: 36-37), "the goddess Nammu, written with the ideogram for 'sea,' is described as 'the mother, who gave birth to heaven and earth' (*ama-tu-an-ki*), and in another Sumerian text (TRS 71: i: 16) as 'the mother, the ancestress, who gave birth to all the gods" (CCXCVI, 39, 74, and n. 41). In Ugarit, in an Akkadian translation of a W-S list of gods, the epithet *sasuratum* "womb" is listed as a deity, corresponding probably to W-S *rḥm* "womb," already known from Ugaritic texts (CCCLXXXIXa, 82; DXLII, 170).

[1] The tentative suggestion that follows proceeds from two other hypothetical presumptions: a) the observation of S. A. Cook, CVII, 378: "The founder of the Judaean dynasty is a vassal of Achish, king of Gath . . . But the title of Ps. 34 calls the latter Abimelech, which is also the name of the

context, another possible Semitic etymology of the toponym Anaphe.[1]

Thus, having proceeded from Herodotos' report on Membliaros, we not only proved the W-S character of that name, but also uncovered several strong and vivid relics of W-S cults, rites, and epics on the islands of Thera and Anaphe. Our analysis established an important precedent as to the trustworthiness of Herodotos' information on Phoenicians inside his own Greek world. They obviously were not a product of his personal fantasy, but were based on local traditions, and these, far from being a result of misunderstanding, were rooted in the genuine presence of W-S ethnic elements which left a long-lasting impact upon the succeeding populations.[2] We do not know when these West Semites settled in Thera and Anaphe,[3] but this must have happened before the Dorian

'Philistine' with whom Abraham made a covenant at Beer-sheba (Gen. 21), while in a duplicate tradition it is Isaac who became powerful and entered into covenant-relations with Abimelech and the Philistines of Gerar . . ."; b) the presumption that the description of David's victory over Goliath (I Sam. 17) is a literary imitation of the myth of Marduks victory over Tiamat, as first suggested by WINCKLER ("The name Goliath-*galittu* = *tiâmat* is taken from Marduk's fight with Tiamat," DL, III, 51, n. 2; more in detail DLI, II, 173) and expounded in a striking comparison by STAPLES (CDLXXVII, 48-51). Now, Goliath was a Gittite, i.e. a subject of Achish, the contemporary king of Gath; and if Achish, under his parallel name of Abimelech, was the prototype of Abimelech in the patriarchal story, his foremost warrior, called Goliath in the legend, might also have been retrojected into the past under the parallel name of the hostile water-chaos, *Pî-kôl*. The acceptance of this explanation is not vital for the mythologo-semantic construction made in the text above. If it is rejected, this would only mean that another etymology has to be sought for the Biblical name *Pîkôl*, but not for *Poikilês* and *phikola*.

[1] See below.

[2] Rhys CARPENTER, XCII, 37, is very severe to the "generation of etymologizing geographers who took advantage of the triconsonantal structure of Semitic words and their vaporous (*sic*) vowels to extract Phoenician roots from Hellenic place-names everywhere in Greece and in the Aegean isles." Leaving aside the alleged "vaporosity" of Semitic vowels and the accidental fact that none of the Semitic words we have dealt with on the preceding pages was triconsonantal, we believe that in our approach we had the solid support of history of religions rather than that of external similarity of consonants.

[3] It is true that Herodotos speaks of eight generations during which Phoenicians lived on Thera from Membliaros to the arrival of Theras and the Minyans from Laconia; but this figure is calculated from the pedigree of Theras: Cadmos (contemporary with Membliaros)-Polydoros-Labdacos-Laios-Oedipus-Polynices-Thersandros-Tysamenos-Autesion-Theras. We have, however, a geological *terminus post quem*: the tremendous volcanic eruption that took away half of the original Thera and utterly destroyed every trace of life on the remaining part. According to the ceramics of the buried pre-

conquest, i.e. in the Mycenaean age. The form *'âr* for "light" (in *mêm-bli-'âr*) also points to the second millennium, when the northern W-S dialects still existed with their old Semitic *â*, not yet shifted to *ô*.

Europa, Tectamos, Hellotis

The well-known Greek myth of Europa tells how this Phoenician princess, daughter of Phoenix or Agenor and sister of Cadmos, was abducted across the sea to Crete by Zeus who took for that purpose the shape of a bull. Of course, this myth must be treated as a myth and not as a historical record. Even its indirect bearing is important enough: if the mythical character of Europa was indeed of Phoenician origin, this would be another example of W-S cultural penetration into Mycenaean Greece. Of course, since the end of the XIXth century most interpreters of Greek myths tried to deny Europa's Phoenicianism and to present her as a purely Greek (more precisely, Middle Grecian) character.[1] The name *Eurôpê*, taken in itself, is indeed a good Greek name: "wide-eyed" or "broad-faced." But this semantics does not explain how it happened that *Eurôpê* became the designation of the continent which still bears that name.[2] Hesychios reports following significations of the word *Eurôpê*: *chôra tês dyseôs, ê skoteinê* "land of sunset, or dark one," and of *eurôpon*: *skoteinon* "dark." This excellently accounts for the name of Europe in its geographic sense. But such semantics of *Eurôpê, eurôpon* can in no way be derived from the Greek language.[3] Only the old, many

eruption settlement, which imitated Late Minoan I types (CCLXVII, 302) the catastrophe occurred about 1550-1500. This is precisely the most likely period for the arrival of the Danunians and other West Semites into the Aegean (cf. p. 109 above and 331 below). It is easy to imagine that for those approaching Thera after the disaster, the aspect of the lifeless island covered with volcanic pumice suggested that it had just been created; thence the association of the creation myth with the resettled Thera.

[1] CDXI, VI, 1, 1287; CCCLXIII, II, 1, 254, n. 1.

[2] It was asserted (see preceding note) that in the *Homeric hymn to Apollo* 251, 291 the term "Europe" signified only Middle Greece, because it is contrasted not only with the islands, but with the Peloponnese as well. But the Peloponnese actually was considered an island (see above, p. 11. n. 5), and islands, even in the time of Herodotos, were not regarded as part of Europe; he states (IV: 45): "But it is known that this Europa was a native of Asia and she did in no ways come to the mainland which the Hellenes now call Europe, but from Phoenicia she came to Crete, and from Crete she moved to Lycia."

[3] The presumption that *eurôpos* "wide-eyed" had allegedly first metaphorically signified wide-open precipices, and then received the sense of "darkness" (CDXI, VI, 1, 1287), is quite improbable and contrived.

times abandoned and rejected hypothesis of this word's origin from the Semitic root *ʿrb* "to enter" or, speaking of the sun, "to set," (whence words for "evening" and "west"), and also "to be dark, black," [1] can explain its semantics.[2] Of course, one has to assume that this designation was first applied to Greece and neighboring continental territories by Phoenician seafarers, because it not only belongs to their language, but also corresponds to the viewpoint of comers from the East; and this is not the only case of the general name for a vast region being given by outsiders.[3]

Now *Eurôpê* cannot be considered a particularly accurate transliteration of a Semitic word signifying "evening," "west," or "darkness." Without Hesychios' testimony on *Eurôpê, eurôpon* there would be sufficient reason to be sceptical as to the relation of these words. But this testimony is incontestable, and it is necessary to proceed from it. Up to now, one used to accept or reject the theory of *Eurôpê*'s derivation from the root *ʿrb* without sufficient grounds or detailed examination; we will therefore try to elucidate whether this derivation is possible from the phonetico-morphological point of view, before passing to the mythological aspect of the problem.

The absence of the first radical consonant of *ʿrb,* the ʿayin, is quite normal and regular. Greeks did not render the Egypto-Semitic guttural ʿayin, except if it was pronounced ġayin; but the relevant root was spelled *ʿrb* also in Ugaritic, which preserved the Old Semitic ġayin; Arabic *ġrb* must be regarded as a deviation from the common Semitic pattern.[4] The third radical, *b,* is replaced by *p* in the Greek counterpart. But the interchange *b/p,* very common in Akkadian, is not infrequent in W-S languages [5] and is

[1] It was supposed by philologists that one of the roots with the consonantal composition *ʿrb* had the significance "to be black," whence Heb. *ʿôrēb,* Akk. *âribu* "raven" (CXCIV, 788). It seems to us that the two verbs are connected with each other: sunset, in the latitude of Palestine and Babylonia, is almost immediately followed by night and darkness. There is no evening in the sense of our middle latitudes; small wonder that *lîl* (*lêl*) is "night" in W-S and Arabic, and "evening" in Akkadian.

[2] Cf. *i.a.* CCCXXX, 139; XXXVI, 171; LXV, II, 360.

[3] The names of Africa, Hispania, and Iberia were probably given by the Phoenicians (on the two latter cf. LXIV, III, 292-299); comprehensive names such as Germania, Brittania, Albion were given by the Romans, Asia by the Greeks.

[4] The *ʿayin* is partially preserved in South Arabic: *ġrb* "to enter," but *mʿrb, mʿrby* "West, western."

[5] E.g. Heb. *nōphet* = Ugar. *nbt* "honey-comb"; Heb. *rôkēb bā-ʿărābôt* = Ugar. *rkb ʿrpt* "Rider of the Clouds"; Heb. and Aram. *peten* = Ugar. *bṯn* "serpent"; Heb. *barzel* = Ugar. *brḏl* = Aram. *parzel* = Akk. *parzillu* "iron";

observed in Greek.[1] What is more important, replacing *b* by *p* occurs in several Greek loan-words from Phoenician and Hebrew: *hyssôpos* from Heb. *'êzôb*; *elphos* "butter," *elpos* "oil, fat" in Cypriot Greek (Hesychios) from common W-S *ḥlb*; [2] most probably *harpê* "sickle-sword" from common W-S *ḥrb*, and cape *Pachynos* in Sicily from *baḫûn* "watch-tower." [3] Conversely, the Greeks perceived the Egyptian *p(r)* "house" as *b* in their transcriptions of Egyptian toponyms beginning with that word: *Bubastis, Busiris, Buto* (as against Hebrew transcriptions *Pî-Beset*, etc.).

From the point of view of vocalization it is obvious that *Eurôpê* cannot derive from the noun having in Masoretic Hebrew the aspect *'ereb* "evening", as is often stated in superficial studies,[4] since before the appearance of segolation that noun had to be pronounced *'arb*; nor from Akk. *erêbu, erêb šamši*,[5] for the change from *e* to *o* would be unaccountable. From Akk. *erêbu* most certainly derives Greek *erebos*, the dark realm of the dead which the Greeks, as did the Egyptians, fancied in the farthest west. The prototype of *Eurôpê* must be looked for in a different grammatical form. As shown by GORDON (*UM* § 9. 22), "we are dealing with an infinitive in *'rb špš* . . . = Acc. *erêb šamši*." The infinitive of the verb *'rb* sounded *'arâbu* in Ugaritic, but the W-S expression for "sunset" might have come to the Greeks through Southern Canaanites (Phoenicians), in whose language the shift from long accentuated *â* to *ô* took place relatively early,[6] and the infinitive, as in Hebrew, became *qāṭôl* (inf. abs.), *qăṭôl/qeṭôl* (inf. constr.), i.e., in our case, *'ărôb* (*šamši*).[7] This vocalization agrees with that of *Eurôpê*; the diphtong *eu* for the initial vowel was dictated by popular etymology

Heb./Ugar./Phoen./Akk. *npš* = Yaudian (Śam'al) *nbš* "soul, sepulchre"; Heb. *nāšap* = *nāšab* "to blow"; Ugar. *šbḥ* = *špḥ* "clan," *lbš* = *lpš* "garment," *ḫbṯ* = *ḫpṯ* "serves," *b'l* = *p'l* "to work."

[1] Besides the regular interchange *b/p* in conjugations of verbs, cf. *Ambrakia* = *Amprakia, Brasiai* = *Prasiai, Lebadeia* = *Lepadeia*.

[2] CDLIX, 86.

[3] *Ibid.*, 135; LXIV, IV, 472. Cf. also Heb. *'Akzib* = Gr. *Ekdippa*.

[4] E.g. XXXVI, 171: "Europe . . . grecianization of *ereb*."

[5] CCCXXX, 139.

[6] Already in the Canaanite glosses of EA; the shift took place in the XVIth century according to XXV, 172; in the XVIIIth century or earlier, according to CLXXXVII, 42 ss. As noted CCXX, 130, the native language of the Akkadian-writing scribes in Ugarit was South Canaanite rather than Ugaritic proper.

[7] Cf. *rāphâ hay-yôm la-'ărôb* "the day began to set down," Judg. 19: 9.

and perhaps also by the not infrequent phenomenon of substituting an additional vowel for a dropped weak consonant.[1]

Let us now examine the validity of this interpretation for the mythological role of Europa and her namesakes. Europa, sister of Cadmos, had as her center of worship the city of Gortyn near the southern shore of Crete; outside Crete, she was connected with the town of Teumessos in Boeotia, the legendary country of her brother Cadmos: a cave was shown there where Zeus was said to have hidden Europa from all gods and humans except himself.[2] The other two bearers of that name were both Boeotian. We have already seen one of the two: Europa, daughter of Tityos from Boeotian Orchomenos,[3] mother of Euphemos (above p. 121), and we have shown, in connection with the latter's rôle of demiurge, how well it fits him to be the son of Europa = "darkness" in the cosmological sense of the word.[4] Then in the Boeotian town of Lebadeia the goddess *Dêmêtêr Eurôpê* was worshipped.[5] If that goddess, as shown

[1] E.g. *Aërmôn* = *Ḥermôn*. For Greek *eu-* in foreign names, cf. *Euphratês* from Old Persian *Ufratu*, *Eulaios* from Akk. *Ulai*.

[2] Paus. IX: 39: 4-5; Antimachos *ap.* Steph. Byzant. *s.v. Teumessos.*

[3] Pindar *Pyth*, 4: 81.

[3] According to *Odyss.* XI: 576-581, Tityos was a son of the Earth. He "dealt violently with Leto, the famous bedfellow of Zeus," and was punished in the Hades by having his liver eternally torn by two vultures. Since, however, the idea of torments in Hell was relatively late in Greek mysteries religion, Tityos, the son of Earth, seems originally to have been a chthonic underground god, and the vultures, before they were re-interpreted as his tormentors, served as his symbolic attributes (on predatory birds as images of the Nether World see pp. 241 ss. below). From this point of view, his name may easily be derived from Akk. *ṭîṭu*, Heb. *ṭîṭ* "clay," which together with "dust" was the main characteristical feature of the Babylonian Inferno (see quotations on p. 242 below). And indeed, the recently discovered Ugaritic religious texts confirmed the existence of a W-S god *Ṭṭ*. In VIROLLEAUD's report to the Groupe Linguistique d'Études Chamito-Sémitiques, on February 21, 1962 (published in the Bulletin of GLECS, vol. IX, 50 s.), devoted to the lengthy text RŠ 24.244, the binomial *Ṭṭ w Kmš* appears among fifteen divine names, invoked in a conjuration against serpent-bites. "It is to be noted," added VIROLLEAUD, "that in RŠ 24.271: 5, one clearly reads *ʿṭ*, instead of *Ṭṭ*, accompanied, like here, by *Kmš*." Now *ʿṭ*, *Ṭṭ*'s alternate name, has a Hebrew and Akkadian etymology signifying "wrapped" or "dark" (Akk. *eṭû*, Heb. *ʿāṭâ*), and the Babylonian ghosts, we know, lived in *darkness* and nurished themselves with *clay*. Moreover, *Kmš* (the Moabite god Kemosh) appears in Akkadian divine lists as *Kammuš*, an avatar of the infernal god Nergal (see p. 278, n. 2 below). There can hardly be a reasonable doubt that the Ugaritic god *Ṭṭ* is the prototype of Greek Tityos, the father of Europa "the darkness." I express my profound gratitude to Professor VIROLLEAUD for having informed me about these unpublished texts.

[5] A name of the type of Zeus Belos, Zeus Ammon, Zeus Amphiaraos,

by her identification with Demeter, was a chthonic deity, a name signifying "dark" fits her well. In Arcadia, a country which preserved many archaic pre-Dorian cults and had many common cultic features precisely with Boeotia, Demeter had the epithet *Melaina* "black." [1] In Lebadeia, Demeter Europa was the mother of the local hero Trophonios, whose shrine was an absolutely dark underground cave where one descended to receive oracles; here again the Semitic semantics of the name *Eurôpê* correspond in the best way with the nature of its bearer.[2]

But did the Phoenicians themselves have a mythological personage with a name that could serve as the prototype of *Eurôpê* and signify "sunset"? The fact that Europa on her bull frequently appears on Sidonian coins since the time of Antiochos IV,[3] does not in itself prove Europa's origin in Sidon. The Phoenicians were by that time largely Hellenized and could readily have borrowed from Greek mythology a topic notoriously ascribed to one of their cities (Sidon or Tyre). The author of *De Deâ Syriâ* (Lucian or whoever he was) made special investigations on that subject in Sidon, but with little results; some of the priests identified Europa with their own Astarte (and perhaps not quite without reason), others denied it.[4] But it seems that we have succeeded in discovering the Semitic prototype of Europa in authentic religious texts which are at least fifteen hundred years older than Lucian and were contemporary with the Mycenaean epoch in Greece—the Ugaritic texts, and more precisely the first lot of tablets unearthed at Ras Shamra in 1929. In the text UM 9 (a list of sacrifices to Ugaritic gods and goddesses), in l. 9 there figures an offering for *ʿrb špš*, the personified sunset. The same deity is mentioned under a similar name in an analogous list of sacrifices UM 1: 12: *w l ll špš pgr* [5] "and to the Sun-Evening an offering/a stele." [6] W-S *ʿrb* is replaced here by Akk.

Zeus Trophonios, Artemis Iphigenia, Artemis Azzanatcona etc.—i.e., a superposition of a pan-Hellenic god over the name of a foreign or local deity.

[1] LXII, 105-109.

[2] On Gortynian coins, Europa was frequently pictured sitting on a willow. Hebrew for "willow" is *ʿărāb(ā)*; there originally may have been a word-play with *ʿarôb* "sunset" (= Europa), possible only in Semitic.

[3] XLIII, 126.

[4] Lucian, *De Deâ Syriâ* 4.

[5] *wlll* read by DUSSAUD, CXXXIX, 68 for *rgll* in the first autography by VIROLLEAUD, DXVI, pl. LXI (made before the decipherment), and explained by DHORME "and to the evening."

[6] *Pgr* explained as "offering" (CXLI, 177) or "stele" (*UM* § 25.1511).

lîlu "evening" (if this is not W-S *lêl* "night"); and the same name appears again, written very clearly, this time without being followed by *špš*, in a text of the same kind, UM 23: 7: *w. lll. ʿṣrm* "and for Evening (or Night), two birds." [1]

These short references undoubtedly establish the existence of a mythological entity—a deity of Sunset-Evening-Night. They do not reveal the sex of that deity, but this—and some other important information—we learn from one of the tablets of Ras Shamra, written in Akkadian with Ugaritic characters, which were identified as such and deciphered by Éd. DHORME.[2] This is No. IX of DHORME's series (= UM 104). DHORME directly declared it to be a transcription of tablet I of the well-known Babylonian series of magic conjurations, *Maqlû*,[3] but only the expressions of line 2 of the Babylonian text closely resemble those of line 2 of the Ugaritic tablet.[4] The rest presents little similarity. In *Maqlû* I, the gods of night are invoked first; then—in just one line—Night herself, and the text immediately turns to practical matters—to the request for protection against witchcraft. In UM 104, all extant lines are for celebrating (and not invoking) the goddess of Night alone, with poetic details that are absent from *Maqlû* I. UM 104 is a hymn to the goddess of Sunset and Night and not a magic spell; its Babylonian original is not identified as yet. [5] We cite the obverse [6] in the original Ugaritic form [7] and in DHORME's re-transcription into Akkadian and translation:

1.	*žmrk bltn il[t . . . .*]	*zamrâku bêlet-ni il[at . . . .*]
	mš̂ mš̂ty klt mk[ktmt i]	*mûši mušîti kallati muk[katimti*]
	n ll erbt ryb.l[ ]	*ina lîli erbêti rîba l[. . . . .*]

[1] The three groups of three vertical wedges each (*lll*) cannot stand for the figure "9." The Ugaritians wrote numerals in words.

[2] CXVIII.

[3] CXVIII, 84.

[4] *Mušîtum kallatum kutumtum* (*Maqlû* I: 2); *mûši mušîti kallati mukkatimti* (UM 104: 2).

[5] The tablet was written by one bearing the Akkadian name Ellil-aḫ[am-iddinna] (as DHORME restored his name).

[6] From the 4 lines of reverse, virtually nothing remains except the mutilated name of the scribe.

[7] In transliterating Ugaritic signs, we follow the system generally adopted in this book, and not that peculiar to the article of DHORME. The separation of words is introduced by us for the purpose of clarity; in the original, the word-divider signs are used only sporadically.

t ažmr. mʿnh.w[ ]	. . . *azamur. mʿnh w* [1][. . . .]
km ŝ tmr. mŝt klt]	*kîma ša tammiri mušîtu kallatu*[ ]
mŝty klt mkktm[*t . . . ir*]	*mušîti kallati mukkatim*[*ti . . . er-*]
bt ryb lžmrky[ ]	*-bêti rîba luzmur-ki*[ ]
uŝsk utllt. u[ ]	*ušassû-ki utullat* . . [ ]
[ ]*d u umam*(?)[ ]	[ ]. . . *û umâm* . . . [ ]
[ ]*l.im l mŝ*[ ]	[ ]. . . *ema lâ mašê* [,]
[*a*]*nu bly* [*ln*]	[*A*]*nu bêl i*[*lâni* . . .]
[*bl*]*nmq p*(?) [ ]	[*bêl*] *nêmeqi* . . [ ]

"I sing our Lady, the god[dess]
of the night, of the night, the vei[led] bride,
In evening thou enterst into the sunset[ ]
. . . I sing. *His answer is* . . . . [ ]
When thou hast shined, O Night, bride [. .]
of the night, veiled bride [. . . . thou en-]
terst into the sunset. May I sing thee [. . .]
They invoke thee, the herds of . . . . [ ]
[ ] . . . and the cattle of . . .[ ]
[ ] . . . not to forget [. .]
[. . . A]nu, the Lord of the g[ods]
[. . Lord] of Wisdom [2] . . . [ ]

We have before us the essence of the myth of Europa: the goddess of night, the veiled bride, who goes away into the sunset, as Europa (= Sunset/Evening) was carried away far westward, to Crete, and there became the mate of Zeus. Especially significant is the constant epithet of the Night-goddess: "veiled" (*kuttumtum, Maqlû* I: 2, part. N-stem *mukkatimtu* in the Ugaritic-Akkadian hymn, besides that in the Old Babylonian invocation to the gods of the night: "veiled is the night" [3]). It is also said about Ištar, in an Old Babylonian hymn to her: "She is glorious; veils are thrown over her head."[4] The veil is the standard iconographic attribute of Europa on coins of Gortyn and Sidon and in figurines.[5] It is usually represented blown out by the wind over Europa's head.[6] This feature appeared, it is true, in the Hellenistic epoch, but it was first introduced by

[1] *mʿnh w* . . . is a remark in Ugaritic language "his answer," i.e. that of the second half of the chorus, or of the second singer in the duet.

[2] A title of Ea.

[3] CDXXXVII, 390 s., line 10.

[4] CDLXXXI, 383, line 10.

[5] Cf. pictures in XLIII.

[6] XLIII, 126. The veil is usually represented as blown out by the wind over Europa's head. There is no reason to consider it a symbol of the heaven-vault, as suggested *ibid.*, 140.

the Sidonians—probably on the basis of their own traditions which are already found in the Ugaritic hymn of the XIVth century. In contrast to her two Boeotian namesakes, Europa is the goddess not of darkness as such, but of night full of bright heavenly luminaries. This is seen from l. 5: *kîma ša tammiri mušîtu kallatu mukkatimtu* "when thou hast shined, O Night, the veiled bride." The Babylonian "gods of the Night," invoked in Maqlû I: 1 and in the Prayer to the Gods of the Night, were gods of fire (Gibil and Nusku), of planets (Sin, Šamaš and Ištar), and of constellations.[1] As a shining star that goes away in the evening into the sunset, westward, the goddess *ʿrb špš*, alias Mušîtu, alias Europa, corresponds to the brilliant Evening Star (Venus) that lights after sunset on the quickly darkened sky. It is clear, thus, why she had the attribute of the veil (in common with Ištar, whose planet was Venus), and why the late Phoenicians allegedly identified her with their Astarte. It is also clear why the myth of Europa surrounds her with characters bearing astral names and actually being only reduplications of herself. Thus her mother is said to have been named Telephassa or Telephaëssa "the far-shining"; her Cretan double, Pasiphaë, another heroine of a love-story with a bull, bore a name signifying "shining for all"; her human husband was the Cretan king Asterios "the starry," actually only a euhemerized double of Zeus Asterios, worshipped in Crete. Minotauros, the fruit of Pasiphaë's passion for a bull, was also called Asterion.[2]

Moreover, the epithet of the Semitic counterpart of Europa, *kuttumtum* or *mukkatimtum* "veiled," is found in its original Semitic form in the Cretan mythological cycle related to Europa. The root *katâmu* "to veil" existed in W-S as well as in Akkadian, and it formed the base of Ugaritic pers. names *Aktmy* and *Ktmn* (*UM* § 20.106,981). In Crete, it appears as *Tektamos, i.e. *tiktam,* a personal name formed out of the 3d p. fem. sg. imperf.[3] signifying "she is veiled." In the late mythography the name *Tektamos* was used to create a father for Asterios, Europa's Cretan husband; but since the latter was only a degraded double of Zeus (Zeus Asterios)

[1] Cf. DXXXVI, 158.

[2] The evidence of ancient authors is collected CCCXLIII, 135.

[3] BROCKELMANN, LXXIX, I, 383, § 203. a. 1 thus defines (after BARTH) one of the categories of nouns with preformative *t*-: "Proper names, deriving from third person fem. sg. impf. like Arabic Tazīd, Taġlib, Tanūḫ, Hebrew Timnā, Tirṣā which, like the corresponding masculine forms, represent abridged sentences."

himself, this genealogical rôle is obviously artificial. Even more artificial is Tectamos' paternity: his father was Doros (the ancestor of the Dorians); he is said to have come to Crete from Thessaly at the head of Aeolians and Pelasgians (Diod. Sic. IV: 60: 2) or Dorians (*ibid.* V: 79: 3), but this is evidently a late invention aiming to harmonize *Odyss.* XIX: 177 which mentions Dorians in Crete before the Dorian invasion of Greece. The name *Tektamos,* however, is not one of the banal invented names; it only appears in this unique occurrence and looks genuine: the later mythographers simply took an epithet of Europa and, as customary, transformed it into a supplementary character to fill out a gap in the genealogy of mythical Cretan kings and to attach it to the ancestors of the Hellenic nation.

We do not know where Diodoros took that name from; but the mythographer Andron, quoted by Stephanos of Byzantium, spells it differently—*Tektaphos.* It is hardly plausible to ascribe the difference to a writing error, since graphically *my* cannot be mistaken for *phi.* This is rather another parallel Semitic epithet of Europa: **tiḫṭaph,* from the root *ḫāṭaph* (Arab. *ḫaṭafa*) "to seize, to carry off by force," used in the Biblical story of the kidnapping of the girls of Shiloh by Benjaminites (Judg. 21: 21). That is exactly what happened to Europa and what forms the central axis of the myth about her and Cadmos. This remarkable agreement speaks in favor of the proposed etymology and overweighs our usual reluctance to Greco-Semitic parallels with an incomplete identity of phonemes. This does not mean, however, that rendering an Oriental *ḫ* by the Greek *k* is anything unusual in Greek transcriptions. We will quote only three of several firmly established cases: North Syrian mountain *Ḫazi* > *Kasion, Ḫilakku* > *Kilikia,* South Cappadocian *Ḫubišna* > *Kybistra,* and one quite possible correspondence: *Ḫatti* > *Kêteioi* (*Odyss.* XI: 521).[1]

Now since the Evening Star goddess Europa-Pasiphaë is of Semitic provenance, there is reason to suppose that her lover, the divine bull, has the same mythological origin. In the W-S pantheon, as is known from Ugarit, the bull was the standard designation and image of the supreme god El.[2] Sexual union of a goddess with El was equivalent to an incest, since El was the father of all gods

[1] For *Ḫilakku* = *Kilikia,* cf. CCCXXII, 110, n. 33, with examples of the interchange *ḫ/k* in Hittite.

[2] *Ṡr Il, ṡr Il abh, ṡr Il dpid,* cf. *UM* § 20.2015.

and goddesses. But precisely such an incest is described in the Ugaritic ritual poem known as The Birth of the Good and Fair Gods (SS = UM 52). El enters there in a broadly described hierogamy with two female characters called "daughters of El" or "wives of El," and addressing El either "father" or "husband." The fruits of that hierogamy are *Šḥr* and *Šlm* "Dawn" and "Dusk"; we will see later what relation they may have to Cadmos and Europa. The scene takes place on the sea-shore (UM 52: 29-30), and the new-born good and fair gods are designated by the epithet *agzrym bn ym* (ibid. 61) which GORDON tentatively translates "*islanders*, sons of the sea." [1] The island *Kptr* (Kaphtor, Crete) was known not only to Ugaritic merchants, but also to the authors of Ugaritic mythological poems.[2] Does the term "islanders" refer, by any chance, to Crete? Our strong impression is that there must have existed a close relation between the W-S original of the myth of Europa-Pasiphaë and UM 52.

There are other examples of the incest motif in W-S mythology. Greek authors knew two basic versions about the birth of Adonis: according to one, Kinyras raped his daughter Myrrha (or Smyrna); [3] according to the other, as told by Panyasis, Myrrha deliberately made her father Theias drunk and became pregnant by him; when Theias recovered his senses, he wanted to kill his daughter, but the gods changed her into a myrrh tree which in due time gave birth to Adonis.[4] In the same way as in the latter story the daughters of Lot became pregnant by their father (Gen. 19: 30-38), and Tamar coupled by means of deception with her father-in-law Judah (Gen. 38: 14-30). In the story of Tamar two details attract, in that connection, our attention: her name, signifying "palm-tree" and suggesting an original end similar to that of Theias-Myrrha story; and the veil she put on her face when seducing Judah. Now *lôṭ* is Heb. for "veil" (Is. 25: 7, cf. root *lûṭ* "to veil, to wig, to cover" I Sam. 21: 10; I Kings 19: 13), and *b^enôt Lôṭ* might originally have referred to that same motif. That again reminds us of "Night, the veiled bride," of Europa's veil and of Tectamos-**tiktam*.[5] Moreover, in Gortynian Vth century coins, Europa was pictured sitting inside

[1] CCXXIII, 59 ss. (cf. Arab. *ǧezirē* "island").

[2] *Kptr* was the "throne of sitting" of the artificer god *Kšr-w-Ḫss*, V AB, E (= ʿnt: VI): 14.

[3] Ancient evidence is collected in CLXXV, V, 11, 43.

[4] *Ap.* (Ps.) Apollod. III: 14: 4; Anton. Liber. 34.

[5] For the symbolism and mythical occurrence of the veil, cf. CCLXXX.

a tree (a motif going back to a gem of the Middle Minoan III period [1]); her union with Zeus was consummated, according to Gortynian traditions, under the plane-tree that was devoted to her, or even on it; and on other coins, as already mentioned, she is associated with the willow. Does it point to an effaced motif of Europa being changed into a tree? Then on a Babylonian cylinder seal from Lagaš, on which CONTENAU ingeniously recognized the whole Theias-Myrrha story and the birth of Tammuz out of a tree, [2] the inscription runs *bît* NI.NI. This may be read *bît ì-lí* "house of god", but also *bît lí-lí*,[3] and we are inclined to understand it as "house of the Evening (goddess)," which would prove that according to the Babylonian original of the story by Panyasis, the name of the incestuous daughter transformed into a tree was *Lîlu* "evening," as the goddess of sunset was named in Ugarit alternately with *ʿrb špš* (= Europa).[4]

Another name for Europa in Gortyn was *Hellôtis*. There was an annual feast, called *Hellôtia*, in honor of Europa Hellotis of Gortyn. A feast of the same name was celebrated in Corinth in honor of a goddess Hellotis; it was accompanied by a race with torches, but the Corinthians no longer understood the names, the origin and the customs of that feast. They told contradictory aetiological stories and considered Hellotis either a pre-Dorian princess who perished during the Dorian conquest of Corinth, or identified her with Athena, who was called Athena Hellotis or Chalinitis, but also *Phoinikê*.[5] Athena Hellotis had also a temple at Marathon in Attica,

[1] CDXIII, 349.

[2] CIV, 44-47. The cylinder was published CLXXI, pl. XXIa, and reproduced CCXCVI, pl. VII, central figure.

[3] OPITZ, *AfO*, VIII (1932-33), 16 considered it possible that the woman under the tree was Lilith, associated with a tree in the Sumerian original of *Gilgameš* tabl. XII. But, as remarked by CONTENAU, CIV, 46, none of the persons depicted on the cylinder presents any resemblance to Gilgameš. The Sumerian she-demon Lilith (*Lilli*) has no etymologic relation to *lîlu* "evening."

[4] The existence of a goddess of that name is actually attested in Babylonia. CXI lists: No. 2011: ^{d}*Li-el-lum*, var. *Li-il-li*, *Li-lu* (distinct from Lilith); No. 2014: ^{d}*Li-li*; and No. 277: ^{d}*Ar-ka-a-a-i-tu*, apparently identified with ^{mul}*Li-li*. DEIMEL gave no comments on these names, but to us they appear quite intelligible: *arki* is Akk. for "behind, back," *arkû* "posterior, in the back," synonym of *aḫâru* "to be back," whence *aḫarru* "West"; the goddess *Arkaitu* is "the western," that is why she is identified with ^{mul}*Li-li* "evening star." See p. 153 below, on the designations of the four cardinal points.

[5] Steph. Byz. *s.v. Gortyn*; Athen. XV: 678A; *Etym. M.* 332: 40 "Phoenicians call virgins *Hellôtia*" (CCCXXX, 140 therefore wrongly: *Hellôtis* < **Helmot-is* < Phoen. *ʿalmat* "girl"); Hesych. *s.v. Hellôtia*; Tzetzes ad Lycophr. 659; cf. CCCLXXIV, I, 80 (*ʾelôtî*) "my goddess"); CDXI, VIII, 1, 197 s.

a place connected in mythology with Crete and the Cretan bull. [1] The name has no Greek explanation. Since Europa was the goddes of the Evening Star and the names connected with her tell about light and shining, the most natural etymology of *Hellôtis* is that of the W-S root *hālal* "to shine". The original W-S form probably was *hallat* + Greek fem. ending *-is*.[2] In Akkadian the epithet *ellêtu* "shining" (from the cognate verb *elêlu*) frequently designated Ištar.[3] In Arabic *hilâl* is the moon crescent (Ugar. *hll* may have the same meaning, cf. GORDON, *UM* § 20. 559), but in the fragment of an old Canaanite myth preserved in Is. 14: 12 ss., *Hêlēl* is the son of *Šaḥar*, the god of Dawn (now known from the Ugaritic poem mentioned above), and he was reasonably identified with the Morning Star by LXX. The difference of sex between *Hêlēl* and *Hellôtis* comes from the Babylonian astrology which considered the planet ^{mul}DIL.BAD (Venus) "female as evening star, male as morning star" [4]—an important formula to which we will soon return. The ending *-ôt* in *Hellôt*(*is*), instead of the expected *-at*, is a W-S dialectal variation: not only *ʿĂnāt* had also the form *ʿĂnôt* (Josh. 15: 59), but even *ʾÊlat* was written *ʾÊlôt* as well (I Kings 9 : 26).

PHOENIX AND THE PHOENICIANS

The best known form of the myth of Europa makes her and Cadmos (and also Cilix and Phoenix) children of the Phoenician king Agenor, whose banal Greek name "manly, bold" (a common Homeric epithet of heroes) betrays his relatively late character.[5] But according to the oldest mention, *Iliad* XIV: 321-2, the mother

[1] Inscriptional evidence: CDXI, VII, 1, 197 s.

[2] Relation with *hālal* already suggested XXXVI, 171 s., but as abstract *helelût* "shine, brilliance."—In Greek, no name could end in *-t* or *-th*; therefore the final *-t* in Semitic feminine names was either dropped altogether in Greek renderings, or supplied with a Greek feminine ending *-a, -ê, -ia, -is, -as, -ô*.

[3] LXXXV, IV, 105 (also about other gods).

[4] DXII, Ištar VIII: 8 ss.; CCCLVIII, II, 27 s.; CCXXVI, No. 109 (^{mul}DIL. BAD) : I: 5. We shall return to this important statement. Hesychios transcribed the Akkadian name of Venus (^{mul}DIL.BAD) by *Delephat*. Could it be assumed that the name of Europa's mother (her hypostase) *Têlephassa* (Attic pronunciation **Têlephatta*) "the far-shining," actually derived from *Delephat* through etymologizing interpretation ?

[5] H. LEWY, CCCXXX, 226, however, understood this *Agenôr* as a distortion of W-S *kinnôr* "lyre," occurring also in a more correct rendering as *Kinyras*, father of Adonis. *Knr*, the deified lyre, actually belonged to the Ugaritic pantheon (UM 17: 10, cf. CCCLXXXIXa, 82, DXLII, 170).

of Minos and Rhadamanthys, Europa, was the daughter of Phoenix. Beloch proclaimed Phoenix "a genuine Hellenic god, the blood-red morning-sun"; only because of the consonance of the names, he was mistaken for a Phoenician colonizer.[1] That explanation of Phoenix's mythical essence is a fine guess—but it must be proved by concrete evidence from the sources, as we brought, in the preceding section, proofs of an actual existence of a W-S goddess of the Evening Star and Sunset, whose name offers an etymology in keeping with all semantic and mythical features of the Greek Europa. Now, in all of Greek literature and epigraphy even the slightest allusion to Phoenix in the rôle of the "blood-red" morning-sun (or, for that matter, of the evening-sun) cannot be found.

On the contrary, wherever one finds Phoenix as a generalized representative of Phoenician colonization, this rôle can by no means be considered accidental or based on a misunderstanding. Stephanos of Byzantium, an assiduous and conscientious grammarian of early Byzantine times who compiled a long lexicon of ethnic names from a great number of historical and geographic works, ascribes the paternity of Itanos, Carnos, and Cytheros (eponyms, respectively, of the cities of Itanos, Carne, and Cythera) to Phoenix. Itanos, a port city on the eastern tip of Crete, presents many convincing signs of Phoenicianism. Its name is W-S: Heb. *ʾêtân* "strong, firm"; it derives, according to V. Bérard, from the expression *naḫal ʾêtân* (Amos 5: 24) "perennial brook," as the city indeed possessed one.[2] Immediately near Itanos there was the cape Salmonion, Salmone or Salmonis (Strabo II: 4: 3; Apoll. Rhod. IV: 1691,

[1] LVI, 127.

[2] CCCLXXIV, II, 1, 258; LXV, II, 337. XXXVI, 164 compared the Bibl. pers. n. *ʾEtân* and Heb. *ʾêtân* "strong, steady." CDXI, IX, 2, 2287 objected to it on the ground that that Semitic *taw* would allegedly require Greek *thêta* in transliteration. But this is true only for LXX; old Greek borrowings from Semitic did not observe that rule, cf. *k*^{e}*tôn(et)* > *chitôn*, *bêt-ʾēl* > *baitylos*, *keter* > *kitaris*; and conversely, the Semitic *ṭet* could be rendered by *thêta* which derived from it. Itanos appears in Linear A as *I-ta-nu* and in Linear B as *U-ta-no* (CDXIV, 39; DV, 147, 308). CDXI, IX, 2, 2287 s. enumerates "several names of places and rivers of non-Greek origin in the region of Itanos, many of which point to the Eteocretans of the neighborhood . . . : *Sedamnos*, *Karymai*, *Dorthanna*, *Atron*, *Mollos* . . . two frontier-places: *Ardaniton* and *Dāron* . . ." Most of these toponyms are recognizable as W-S: *Sedamnos* = *š*^{e}*dēmā* "plantation" or *śad ʾamnā* "field of the pillar"; *Karymai* = *k*^{e}*rāmîm* "vineyards"; *Dorthanna* = *dûr ṭanāʾ* "erected wall" (Phoen. root *ṭnʾ*); *Atron*, from the root *ʿāṭar* "to surround" (with walls), cf. Palestinian city-name *ʿAṭarôt*; *Mollos*, cf. Heb. *millôʾ*, Akk. *mulû* "earth-rampart, fortification"; *Ardaniton* = *ʿar dannîtu* "mighty city"; *Dāron*—cf. Arab. *dār* "abode," Ugar. *dr*, Heb.

even now Salmone), a name with a sharp Semitic sound which Assmann [1] identified with that of the mountain *Ṣalmôn* near Shechem (Judg. 9: 48; Ps. 68: 15). Commerce with the East flourished on the eastern coast of Crete during the Minoan and Mycenaean epochs; "if there is any point on the maritime route Phoenicia—Crete—Malta—Utica or Carthage, which can be supposed as having been visited by Phoenician mariners—this is, of course, Itanos," wrote Dussaud.[2] He then pointed, after V. Bérard, to the coins of that city which imitated those of the Phoenician Arados, and to the purple-dyeing establishments attested there by Herodotos IV: 151 for the VIIth century—a craft which was a purely Phoenician monopoly. We may add to it that the name of the purple-dyer who led the Theran colonists to Libya (and was, thus, not only a craftsman but also an expert seafarer), was *Korobios*—certainly not a Greek, but a Semitic name: *qārôb* "the near one, the intimate one," pronounced by Phoenicians *qōrôb*,[3] probably a hypocoristic of some theophorous name.[4] Finally, Dussaud explained the words *ʾš b ʿm ʾytnm* in a Punic inscription from Hadrumet [5] as "who (belongs) to the people of the Itanians," and identified *Bʿl rʾš* "Baal of the Cape" of the same inscription with the cape Itanon near Itanos (modern Placa).[6] He considered this inscription "a precious epigraphic argument in favor of the hypothesis of a contact between Itanos and the Phoenicians." [7]

dôr "encampment." This predominantly Semitic character of Eteocretan toponymics is in harmony with C. H. Gordon's identification of the Eteocretan language as W-S (see pp. 346 s. below).

[1] xxxvi, 164 s. [2] cxliii, 394.

[3] The Phoenician language went farther than Hebrew in shifting *a* to *ō*, even if it was unaccented (ccxlvi, 34, § 11). It resembled in that respect the Ashkenazic dialect of Hebrew which probably derived from Galilee, which borders on Phoenicia.

[4] Other Semitisms in Cyrene, probably due to the influence of Corobios and his companions: 1) the first settlement of the Therans in Libya was "Aziris, surrounded on right and left by two beautiful valleys and a river" (Herod. IV: 157), the name of which V. Bérard, lxv, I, 303, pertinently explained by W-S *ʾāzar* "to gird"; 2) the name of the spring which gave its name to the city of Cyrene—*Kyrê*, i.e. W-S *qûr* "spring"; 3) perhaps the Cyrenean agriculture god *Aptuchos*, whom Otto Blau, in 1865, interpreted as "the opener (of the soil)" and Goldziher, who quoted him (ccvi, 104), compared with *Yiphtaḥ* (here, however, the preservation of the W-S *ḥ* in Greek is abnormal).

[5] Published by J. Fevrier, *Bull. arch. du Com. des trav. histor.*, 1949, viii ss.

[6] And vice versa, a cape *Balithôn* existed in Carthaginian territory (Strabo XVII: 3: 16); it was compared with Cretan Itanos, xxxvi, 146.

[7] cxliii, 395.

Karnos is the eponym of the town of *Karnê* in Phoenicia proper, not far from Arados—it was named on its own coins *Qrn* "horn", and cf. the Latin translation on its coins of the Roman imperial age: *Cornu Phenices.*[1] Here Phoenix's rôle as father is more than natural. But there was in Greece, especially in Laconia, a pre-Dorian god, identified with Apollo as *Apollôn Karneios,* and this god was represented with a ram's horns; Greek authors explained it by *karnos* "ram." [2] But though Semitic *qarn* and Latin *cornu* form a remarkable pair, one of the very few Semito-Indo-European lexical coincidences, "horn" in Greek is *keras, -atos,* without the phoneme *n*; and therefore both *karnos* and *Karneios* must reasonably be considered Semitic loanwords (cf. the Palestinian town *ʿAštᵉrôt Qarnayim* Gen. 14: 5, "the horned Astarte").

Kythêros is the eponym of the island and city of Cythera between Crete and Laconia. The sea around the island was so rich in purple snails that Cythera was also named *Porphyrusa.*[3] A little bay there was called *Phoinikus.* Herodotos (I: 105) quite definitely states that the famous shrine of Aphrodite Urania in Cythera was founded by Phoenicians after the model of that goddess's temple at Ascalon. We made certain in the beginning of this chapter that Herodotos did not invent his reports on Phoenician settlements in the Aegean, but took them from reliable local sources (there are, in all, four such reports in Herodotos' work: Thera, Cythera, Thebes, and Thasos). There is absolutely no reason to disbelieve his information on the shrine of Cythera; he speaks of that particular temple, and not of the worship of Aphrodite in general which could be regarded as an exaggeration. Now there is an actual indubitable proof that Cythera had been visited, since very early times, by Phoenician or North Canaanite ships, and that the deity worshipped there was famous all over the Semitic East up to Mesopotamia.

A cuneiform dedication of Naram-Sin, son of Ibiq-Adad, king of Ešnunna, was found in Cythera as early as 1849.[4] This brings us

[1] CDXI, X, 2, 1964.

[2] *Ibid.*, 1989-1993.

[3] See the very instructive survey of the technological side of purple-snail fishing and preparation of purple (an old Phoenician monopoly) which necessarily required stable installations, harbors, and winter-quarters, LXV, I, 408-410.

[4] This inscription was partially deciphered by Hugo WINCKLER, then by E. UNGER, and finally by E. WEIDNER, DXLI. It is very short and badly damaged: (1) *a-na* ᵈ. . . . . [. . . . . .] (2) . . . . [. . . . . .] (3) ᵐ ᵈ*Na-ra-am-*ᵈ*Sin* [*šar Èš-nun-na*ᵏⁱ (4) *mâr* ᵈ*I-bi-iq-*ᵈ*Ad* [*ad šar Èš-nun-na*ᵏⁱ]

back to the epoch of Amorite domination all over Syria and Mesopotamia, to the XVIIIth century, when *Kaptara* (Kaphtor-Crete) already appeared in documents from Mari, and Ugarit began to be the link between Mesopotamia and the Aegean. The very name of *Kythêra*, "etymologically obscure" from the viewpoint of Greek language [1] was plausibly explained as Semitic by V. BÉRARD by applying his "method of doublets": as *Skandeia*, the harbor of Cythera, signifies "a kind of a head-dress" (Hesychios), similarly *keter, kōteret* is Heb. for "crown, tiara." [2]

An epigraphic mention of Phoenix also exists. It was found in a treaty between the small town of *Drêros* in the northeast of Crete, and the neighboring city of Cnossos, dating from 220. [3] It is this inscription which obviously was meant by Ed. MEYER when he asserted that Phoenix "was a prominent Cretan god": [4] there are no other data on that god to confirm his prominence. The context shows that Phoenix was regarded, at Dreros, on an equal level with gods—perhaps as the divine founder of the town. Now Dreros was situated on the eastern slope of Mount *Kadiston* in which name ASSMANN recognized—and it would be hard not to recognize—the Akk. *qadištu* (Heb. *qedeš, qᵉdēšā*) "hierodule" and also an epithet of the goddess Ištar to whom the hierodules were consecrated; that same scholar also derived the name of the nearby town of *Istros* or *Istron* from Ištar.[5] The name of Dreros has no Greek etymology [6]—but it may come from Heb. *dᵉrôr*, a bird, usually

(5) *a-na ba-la-ṭí-šu* [*i-qi-iš*]: "To the god .... Naram-Sin, [king of Ešnunna,] son of Ibiq-Ad[ad, king of Ešnunna,] for his life [erected]." Naram-Sin of Ešnunna occupied for a certain time the throne of Aššur and made conquests in Upper Mesopotamia (CCCV, 8, n. 1), which brought him close to the Syrian coast. Unfortunately, the name of the deity to whom his votive inscription of Cythera was consecrated, disappeared entirely. On the historical importance of the inscription, cf. DXXXVa, 59 s.; CCVII, 240.

[1] CDXI, XII, 1, 207.

[2] LXV, I, 207 s. A corporation of *ktrm*—probably hatters—figures in the administrative texts of Ugarit (UM 169: rev. 12). The original Semitic form of Cythera would have been **Kutara* (cf., for the vocalic pattern, such Ugaritic names as *Gu-pa-na, Gu-da-ra-na, Qu-ta-na*).

[3] Published CXXa, I, 769-774, No. 527. The following gods are invoked as witnesses of the treaty: Hestia in the prytaneion, Zeus Agoraios, Zeus Tallaios, Athanaia Poliuchos, Apellon Potios, Lato, Artemis, Ares, Aphordita, Hermas, Halios, Britomartis, Phoinix, Amphiona, Ga, Uranos.

[4] CCCLXIII, II, 1, 254, n. 3.

[5] XXXVI, 193 s.—For Ištar-*qadištu*, cf. CXI, No. 1617: III: 8; for the goddess *Qdšt* in Ugarit, cf. DXXIV, No. 4 (RŠ 15.130): 17.

[6] CDXI, V, 2, 1699.

identified with the swallow: "Ištar as the daughter of Sin manifested herself in the shape of a swallow." [1] Thus, here too, Phoenix is discovered in a place which betrays, by its toponymics, an Akkado-Phoenician impact. Moreover, C. H. GORDON's interpretation of the Greco-Eteocretan bilingual from Dreros shows that a W-S dialect continued to be used there about 600 B.C.[2] As a rule, wherever the eponym or toponym Phoenix is found, evident traces of Semitism are present. There was a port town Phoenix on the south-west shore of Crete, and it served as the harbor to the city of Araden —a name strongly reminiscent of Arados in Phoenicia.[3] Phoenix was considered the father of *Karmê*, whose daughter was the Cretan goddess Britomartis—but *Karmê* is obviously the W-S *karm* "vineyard," [4] and the second part of the name of Britomartis, explained by the ancients as "sweet maiden" (*brity*: *glyky*: *Krêtes*, Hesychios), is, as we believe, Akk. *mârtu* "daughter, maiden," or its W-S counterpart **mhrt* (attested in masculine form *mhr* "son" [5]).

The only character of this name on whom a story, and not just a mere mention in a genealogy, is available, is Phoenix son of Amyntor, the tutor of Achilles according to *Iliad* IX. The reason for his leaving his father's house is told thus (*Il.* IX: 445-456): on the request of his mother, he slept with the concubine of his father to make the old man odious to the girl, and was cursed by him as soon as he learned what had happened. It is exactly the same motif as in Gen. 35: 22: "During Israel's sojourn in that land, Reuben went and lay with Bilha, the concubine of his father; and Israel heard it"—here the story stops abruptly, but the sequel is supplied by the saying on Reuben of Jacob's Blessing Gen. 49 : 4: for having profaned the bed of his father, he was deprived of his primogeniture. As all heroes of the *Iliad*, Phoenix is completely humanized; there

[1] DXVIII, 105.—The occurrence of *ê* in *Drêros* would indicate a parallel form **darîru* for *darâru* > *d^e^rôr*. Or perhaps the older form of *Drêros* was **Drāros*.

[2] See pp. 346 s. below.

[3] XXXVI, 166.—The Phoenician name of Arados was *ʾArwad*, but the digamma would have been dropped in the case of the Cretan city as it was in the case of the Phoenician one. For the ending *-en*, cf. Heb. *garzen*, *ṣippōren* (CDXCVII, 45), *Yardēn*.

[4] XXXVI, 182.

[5] Cf. p. 88, n. 2 above.—There also was a harbor *Phoinikus* in the Ionian city of Erythrae—and again, that city possessed a statue of Heracles, which was said to have come from Tyre on a raft, and which (according to its representation on coins) really betrays a pure Phoenician Egyptianizing style—cf. p. 215 below.

is nothing semidivine in him, and no trace of Phoenicianism whatsoever. But it still is highly curious that the only parallel available to the story of a hero by the name of Phoenix is an episode of a W-S literary work—the book of Genesis.

Must Phoenix be considered merely an ethnic abstraction, a generalized eponym of the Phoenician nation, or does his mention among the gods of Dreros still allow us to consider him an individual entity of the pantheon? One does not contradict the other, if account is taken of an Ancient Eastern onomastical habit: calling the leading gods of alien peoples, even if they are adopted into the native religion, not (or not only) by their direct names, but by the title "god of this or that people," as a result of which the ethnic name becomes the name of the god. So the W-S god, known to the Sumerians as ^{d}Martu, and to the Akkadians as ^{d}Amurru, was originally named ^{d}*dingir Martu*, ^{d}*Il Amurrim* "^{god}God-of-Amurru." [1] In the same way, obviously, the ethnic name of the Cassites became the name of the god ^{d}*Kaššu*, cf. *Kaššu-nadin-aḫḫê*, the name of a Babylonian king c. 1000. There were "gods of the Ḫabiru," *ilâni Ḫabiri*,[2] but also a god ^{d}*Ḫabiru*.[3] and a goddess ^{d}*Sutîtum* "the Sutean," developed from ^{d}*Ištar Sutît*, "Ištar the Sutean." [4] The adjective "Phoenician" was already used by the Mycenaean Greeks as *ponike* (= *phoinika*).[5] It is known that ethnics might become official titles of deities; thus the family of the Athenian noble Isagoras sacrificed to *Zeus Karios*, the Carian Zeus (Herod. V: 66), and divine epithets often evolved into independent figures. It is therefore quite probable that *Phoinix* was an abbreviation of, let us say, *theos Phoinix* "the Phoenician god." Phoinix, the *father* of Europa, is precisely a relic of that ancient "Phoenician god," under which designation El, the head of the W-S pantheon, was probably understood.[6] But Phoenix, the *brother* of Europa in alternate genealogies, is a late secondary creation, merely a personi-

[1] CXIX, 62, where the god so styled is believed to have been El or Dagan.

[2] Cited in many Hittite treaties, cf. LXXV, Nos. 75-90.

[3] The god Ḫabiru is mentioned in the following texts *ap*. LXXV: No. 70 (Nuzu, pers. n. *Ḫabir-tilla* "Ḫabiru is the lord"); No. 89 (Boğazköy); No. 167 (neo-Assyrian).

[4] CCV, 143.

[5] DV, 344, 405.

[6] Phoenix, made Achilles' tutor by Homer, rather goes back to another W-S god, Baal, who, according to a Canaanite myth in Hittite translation, was tempted by his father's wife Ašertu (see p. 207 below). This is a related motif, not so close however as the story of Reuben and Bilha.

fication of the Carthaginians, as his brother Cilix is a personification of the Cilicians.

Until now, for the sake of simplicity, we did not dwell upon the linguistic provenance of the words *phoinix* and *phoinikes*, as if we shared the traditional view which regards them as purely Greek appellatives of "purple" and of the Canaanite "purple-makers." [1] It was admitted that *phoinix* derives from *phonos* "murder," through *phoinos* (**phon-io-s*) "murderous, sanguinary, blood-red," for which the Indo-European root was restored, on the basis of numerous cognates, as *g^u*hono-s*.[2] But the primitive sound g^u still existed in Mycenaean Greek as *q*. VENTRIS and CHADWICK, therefore, correctly stated about the Mycenaean Greek *po-ni-ke* and *po-ni-ki-ja* ("painted crimson, dyed crimson"): "Probably a loan-word; not from *phoinos* 'blood-red' which is from *g^u*hon-jos*." [3] The source of this loan-word must, consequently, be sought among the very people who were famous as crimson and purple dyers and whom the Greeks called *Phoinikes*. Now Heb. *puwwā*, Arab. *fuwwa*, is the name of *Rubia tinctorum L.* or dyer's madder, one of the most common sources of red dye and imitation purple in antiquity, a herbaceous plant at home in Syria, Palestine and Egypt.[4] A Hebrew clan of Galilee (which was contiguous to Phoenicia) bore the name of *Puwwā* (or *Pû'ā* [5]) and is quoted next to *Tôlā'* "crimson" (Gen. 46: 13; Num. 26: 23; I Chr. 7: 1 s.). The gentilic of *Puwwā* is *Pûnî* (Num. 26: 23), a form of the same aspect

[1] This view was accepted by SPEISER, CDLXXIV, who also showed that "red purple dye" was designated in the Akkadian documents from Nuzu with the term *kinaḫḫu*, which he correctly derived from [māt]*Kinaḫḫi* (cuneiform spelling of "Canaan"). ALBRIGHT believed for a certain time that *kinaḫḫu* was Hurrian for "red purple" and that "Canaan" was a Hurrian appellative: "land of purple-dye." Cf. CCCLI for references. More recent epigraphic discoveries proved that "Canaan" could not be Hurrian, but was a native W-S name; *kinaḫḫu* for "purple" owed its name to the land where purple was produced (CCCLXXIII). No plausible W-S etymology for "Canaan" has been suggested; ours is "sunset-land" (same meaning as Akkadian *Amurru*), from the root *kn'* "to bend down, to lower oneself." [See p. 387 below]

[2] LXXIII, 1032 s.

[3] DV, 136, 405.

[7] CCLXXXIX, 754; CLXIV, IV, 106, 131, 136.

[5] The mutual relation of the forms *Puwwā* and *Pû'ā* is the same as between Ugar. *hw* "he" (pronounced *huwwā*) and Heb. *hû'* (still pronounced *hû'ā* in the period of the Dead Sea Scrolls). The Ugar. pers. n. *Pwn* (UM 313: 8) may be related. [In RŠ 19.56 (to be published in *PRU* V as No. 51), *šmn.mat kbd pwt* (ll. 5-6) certainly means "eight hundred heavy (shekels) of madder-dyed fabric," especially since it is followed (l. 7) by *šmn mat pštm* "eight hundred (heavy shekels) of linen."]

as the adjectives *'ădmônî* "red," *qadmônî* "oriental," with the assimilation of the half-consonant *w* to the corresponding vowel *u* into a long *û*. This form *pûnî* provides us with the prototype of the Greek *phoin-ix* and Latin *Poenus, puni-cus.* It is even possible to prove that the other Greek word for "purple," *porphyra,* was of Semitic origin.[1]

The conclusion of this section is such: Phoenix being the mythical father of Europa does not refute, but on the contrary, strongly *corroborates* the Phoenician origin of her myth.

Scholars Reluctance to Admit the Semitism of Cadmos

Of all the heroes of Greek mythology, Cadmos, the founder of Thebes, was the Phoenician par excellence. The myths derived him from Phoenicia and the Greek tradition even (anachronistically) ascribed to him the introduction of the Phoenician alphabet in Greece.[2] Wherever local independent traditions about ancient Phoenician establishments existed (Rhodes, Thasos, Samothrace, and the previously mentioned Thera), effort was made to somehow link them with Cadmos. Moreover, his name is purely Phoenician —*qadm,* whatever exact semantics be given to it. But precisely because the case of Cadmos seemed to be the most certain of all, it became the target of particularly violent attacks of scholars

[1] To prepare purple-dye from purple-snails, two (according to Pliny, even nine) days of continuous boiling were necessary (CLXIV, IV, 114). The Greek *porphyrô* means "to rise seething" (LXXIII, 805 s.); Homer used it for the turbulent sea, but as early as in the Mycenaean tablets *popureja* (= *porphyrea*) applied to purple-dyed garments (DV, 321, 405). What connection was there between the notions of "seething" and "purple"? "Semantic connexion with *porphyrô,* "swirl,' is dubious," is said DV, 405. But V. BÉRARD, LXV, I, 409, in a most simple and convincing way, explained *porphyra* "purple" as "product of boiling," *porphyrô.* Now the root *porphyrô* itself, meaning "to swirl, whirl, seeth, jerk," is hardly related to Greek *phyrô* "to knead, to moisten," as the dictionaries usually pretend. Conversly, the Semitic root *pārar* II, mostly used in the pilpel form *parpar* (e.g. Arab. *farfara,* etc.), means "to jerk, flash, stir, rouse, be tossed to and fro, shake, bewilder" (CCLXXIX, 782); and there can be no doubt that Heb. *pārûr* "a pot for cooking" derives not from *pārar* I "to break" (*ibid.* 777 "breakable, therefore earthen"), but from *pārar* II (cf. also its non-geminated form *pûr* "to boil, ferment," CXCIV, 807). BOISACQ already remarked about *porphyra* "purple": "A Semitic origin is probable, though unknown" (LXXIII, 805).

[2] Herodot. V: 59-61. However, MARINATOS (CCCLV) envisages the possibility that the W-S (Proto-Phoenician) alphabet was known in Mycenaean Greece simultaneously with Linear B, and interprets in this sense the tradition about Cadmos as the importer of the Phoenician alphabet into Greece.

since the end of the XIXth century. Cadmos obviously was in their eyes the main stronghold of Phoenicianism on Greek soil, which they denied, and after reducing this central point of resistance, it would be easy to erase totally every trace of Phoenicians from the pages of Greek antiquity.

First of all, the name of Cadmos was declared non-Phoenician, and Greek etymologies were sought for it.[1] Some even severed his connection with Thebes and Boeotia: K. LATTE [2] made him a South Ionian hero from Miletos and Priene, the ancestor of the local family of Cadmids, who was at a late period transferred to Thebes. Other scholars did not go so far: the old citadel of Thebes was called Cadmeia, the Thebans appear in Homer only as Cadmeians, and all myths and sanctuaries connected with Cadmos were located in Thebes, not in Miletus. The participation of some of the Cadmeians, ousted from Thebes by the Boeotians proper during the Dorian invasion, in the colonization of Ionia, belonged to the Ionian tradition and is expressly stated by Herodotos I: 146. This is the best explanation for the appearance of Cadmids in Miletos; but since there never was a return movement from Ionia to Boeotia, the hypothesis of LATTE and his followers reverses the actual events.

But how and why was Cadmos believed to be a Phoenician if he was not one? As this study is not a history of the Greco-Semitic problem, we will limit ourselves to bringing the opinions of two outstanding scholars: Ed. MEYER (1928) and M. P. NILSSON (1932). Ed. MEYER reconstructed—in a purely speculative way—a com-

[1] WELCKER, quoted by CRUSIUS, "Kadmos," *ap.* CDXXXIII, II, 882, believed that the parallel form *Kassmos* was the original one, and equated it with Gr. *kosmos* "order," in Crete also "high state-official." CRUSIUS remarked that "this presents linguistic difficulties (because of the *d*)." BOISACQ, LXXXIII, 501, *s.v. kosmos*, warned against seeking connections with *Kadmos*. MOVERS, CCCLXXIV, I, 521 indicated that in Greek *d* before *m* often shifted to *s*, and so *Kadmilos* became *Kasmilos*. Here are some other examples: *asma* "song" from *adô*; *asmenos* "joyful, merry" from *êdomai*. But the opposite phenomenon, $s > d$, does not occur in Greek. Nonetheless, statements that *Kadmos* = *kosmos* are still uncritically repeated in some quite recent publications.—Another attempt to explain Cadmos as "a purely Greek word" is given CDXI, VII, 2, 2380 (*s.v. Harmonia*) by having recourse to a gloss by Hesychios: *kadmos*: *dory, lophos, aspis*: *Krêtes* ("*kadmos*: spear, helmet-crest, shield: Cretans"). Words peculiar to Crete, with its significant enclaves of non-Greek-speaking populations, hardly represent "pure Greek words"; in any case, *kadmos* does not have any Greek etymology in the sense given by Hesychios, either. But as a Semitic loan-word it does have a meaning, at least for "shield", which was carried *in front* (Semitic: *qadm*) of the warrior.

[2] *Ap.* CDXI, X, 2, 1460-1473, *s.v. Kadmos.*

plicated chain of gradual stages. As in the case of the myth of Io and Danaos, he arbitrarily dissected the living body of the myth and operated with disrupted mythological units. According to him, Cadmos originally was but the eponym of the tribe of *Kadmeioi* or *Kadmeiônes* in Boeotia; the numerous myths and, as he puts it, combinations connected with him were a later addition. Beside him stood the Boeotian earth-goddess Europa. In a certain, rather late stage, her cult was introduced in Crete, where she was identified with the Cretan goddess Hellotis of Gortyn. This made her a daughter of the prominent Cretan god Phoenix. Cadmos became Phoenix's brother and Europa's uncle. The later genealogies made Cadmos, Phoenix and Europa children of Agenor. So Cadmos and all his kin became Phoenicians. It was believed, and Thebes was considered a Phoenician colony, notwithstanding the location of Thebes in mid-continent, without access to the sea, which strongly contradicts it. [1]

But Ed. MEYER himself stated elsewhere that there existed a sharp distinction between the late schematic figures of genealogies and the old genuine characters of the heroic saga.[2] Cadmos, the hero of a very dramatic myth, saturated with adventures, events, and epic motifs, obviously belongs to the category of the latter. The relation between Cadmos, Cadmeia and the Cadmeians is the same as between Dan-Danel and the tribe and town of Dan and the people of Danaans-Danunians; as between the goddess Anath and the inhabitants of the towns ʿAnat (on the Euphrates), ʿĂnātôt and Bêt-ʿĂnāt (in Palestine); as between Astarte and the town of ʿAštarôt in Transjordan; or, in Greece, as between Athena and Athens,[3] Heracles and Heracleia. Then it cannot be proven that the worship of Europa was "secondarily" transferred to Crete from Boeotia; Europa certainly belonged to the original mythical figures of the

[1] CCCLXIII, II, 1, 254, n. 1. [See p. 387 below]

[2] CCCLXIV, 251: "Genuine myths and original sagas of gods . . . were transformed into genealogic-ethnographic tales reflecting the destinies of the corresponding tribes, tales in which along with purely genealogical figures as Tros and Ilos, Aegyptos and Danaos, Hellen, Doros, Ion, and their sons, stand much more ancient names of a different character, as Priamos and Aeneas, Danaë and Perseus, Deucalion and Erechtheus. . . . Myth and heroic saga which evolved from it are older than genealogic poetry."

[3] We share the opinion of NILSSON, CCCLXXXI, 490, that "the town *Athênai* is named after the goddess *Athênê*, not vice versa, the goddess after the town." Besides the arguments he brought *loc. cit.*, this opinion is confirmed by the worship of this goddess as early as the Mycenaean period, DV, 126.

pre-Dorian Crete, and her appearance both in Crete and in Boeotia can much more plausibly be ascribed to her simultaneous introduction from the East through a maritime route. We also have seen in the previous section that the excuse of Phoenix having allegedly been mistaken for a Phoenician is not valid: on the contrary, wherever Phoenix appears, either as a person or as a toponym, he is clearly connected with Semitic names, myths, and cults.

Ed. MEYER's final, and as he believed, decisive argument —Thebes' geographic situation—is based on an erroneous oversimplified view of Phoenicians as petty sea-peddlers never touching the ground beyond the beach. V. BÉRARD already removed the basis for such objections by his well-founded "theory of isthmuses"; he referred i.a. to the commercial and industrial activity of Hiram's Phoenicians not only in Jerusalem, but even in Elath, 280 miles distant from Tyre as the crow flies.[1] Thebes was situated on the crossing of the roads from the Gulf of Corinth to the Euripos and to Euboea, from the Peloponnese to Middle and Northern Greece. Her "situation in mid-continent," so emphasized by Ed. MEYER, is reduced, in plain figures, to merely 12 miles from the Gulf of Corinth and 15 miles from the Euripos. Nowadays, after the discovery of the large North Canaanite kingdoms of Ugarit, Alalaḫ, and Danuna, it became certain that none of their capitals was a seaport. While Ugarit was only 2 miles distant from her harbor, Alalaḫ, Adana, and Karatepe were separated from the sea-shore (in a straight line) by 25 miles and more—double that of Thebes. Nevertheless Alalaḫ possessed ships, and in the reliefs of Azitawadd's palace in Karatepe ships and sea-battles play a prominent rôle.[2] The topography of Thebes corresponds exactly to that of the capitals of the North Canaanite maritime states which, in the IId millenium, linked the Orient with the Aegean.

M. P. NILSSON, in a most convincing way, refuted the claims of a late introduction of Cadmos into Boeotia and proved that the Cadmeans, with whom Cadmos was linked inseparably, belonged to the oldest tribes known to epic poetry.[3] Moreover, "the myth of Cadmus is the foundation myth of Thebes in the strict sense of the word . . . The site of the town is determined by divine intervention, the origin of the people and of the noble families is explained. Such myths

[1] LXV, I, 49.
[2] CCCXXXIX, pl. 26.
[3] CCCLXXXII, 120 s.

are numerous, but they are almost always told of colonies or of towns, such as Rome and Carthage, put on an equality with them." [1] "If I am right, an old myth, of course handed down from Mycenaean times, told that Thebes was founded by the eponymous hero of the tribe which inhabited the town, the Cadmeans. The founder, Cadmus, came consequently from abroad." [2] So far NILSSON's reasoning offers strong support for the point of view which we believe to be correct. But for NILSSON, of course, that "abroad" can by no means be the Semitic Orient. Just in this unique point the myth which "is really a reminiscence of a historical fact," [3] needs be corrected. It was "a Mycenaean tribe" which "really founded a new town here." [4] "The old myth did not tell or had forgotten whence he (Cadmos) came, and the field was left open for guesses. At the beginning of the historical age the foreigners who constantly visited Greece were the Phoenicians. That is why the myth hit upon the idea of making Cadmus a Phoenician. At that time other foreigners were hardly known in Greece, and as Cadmus was acknowledged to be a foreigner, he became a Phoenician. The myth of his wanderings . . . and his genealogy were but consequences of his alleged Phoenician origin." [5]

How interesting it is that the myth remembered everything correctly, and the only gap of memory was whence the hero had come . . . And how deeply ignorant of other peoples the Greeks were: they simply could not imagine a foreigner other than a Phoenician! The myths managed, however, to find homelands other than Phoenicia for many a foreign founder of a city or a dynasty. Pelops, the eponym of the Peloponnese and ancestor of a Mycenaean royal house, was said to be a Lydian or a Phrygian; his sister Niobe was presented as the wife of Amphion, the hero of another foundation myth; many heroes of Middle Greece were described as Thracians; Teucros, the founder of Troy, was made a Cretan. If the whole point was to guess where Cadmos came from, why was he not rather made a good Greek migrant from Thessaly, the old home of Hellen and his sons, as the Aeolid kings of Elis and of the neighbor of Thebes, Orchomenos?

[1] *Ibid.*, 122.
[2] *Ibid.*, 126.
[3] *Ibid.*, 125.
[4] *Loc. cit.*
[5] *Ibid.*, 127.

A theory put forward in the beginning of this century [1] and emphatically taken over by Sir John L. Myres,[2] declared that the Cadmeians actually were Minoan settlers from Crete, called "Phoenicians" because of the red color of their skin; then, when the Minoan civilization fell into oblivion, that name was transferred to another "red-skin" people, the Semites of Canaan, and the two became confounded. But: 1. there hardly was a more marked difference in skin coloration between South Europeans and Levantines in the second millennium B.C. than at present; 2. the Phoenicians owed their name not to the color of their skins, but to their monopoly in producing the purple dye; [3] 3. there were two kinds of purple, deep dark red and bluish violet; the Greeks used the term *phoinix* for purple dye, but never for the color of a human skin; even a Red-skin Indian would not qualify for such a description; 4. the Minoan civilization of Crete was never completely forgotten by the later generations; Cretan thalassocracy, kingship, buildings, cults, myths, and customs survived with a surprising degree of accuracy in a number of Greek myths. There was absolutely no ground for confusion.

All these theories have one common feature: they conveniently eliminate the Greek reports on Phoenicians by shifting the blame onto some misunderstanding. None of their authors ever tried to compare the Greek myths of that category with Semitic myths and monuments in order to ascertain that there was no connection whatsoever; their minds were made up a priori. But we have seen that there was no misunderstanding in the case of Danaos, in the case of Membliaros, in the case of Europa. And how could an accidental misunderstanding provide not only Cadmos, but most of his family and environment with Semitic mythological names, and make them perform Semitic mythological tales on Greek soil? In order to make this evident, we shall turn to the intrinsic data of the Cadmeian cycle.

Mythological Essence of Cadmos

Cadmos was known to the Greeks as *Kadmos*, *Kadmôn*, and *Kadmaiôn*; the basic form corresponds to W-S *qdm* (*qadm*), the two others to W-S extended forms in *-n* (cf. Ugar. pers. n. *Qdmn*) and

[1] CCXLIII, 282.
[2] CCCLXXVIII, 321 s.
[3] Cf. p. 146, n. 1.

in *-yn* (cf. Ugar. *Špšyn,* from *špš,* and other names like *Agyn, Aḫyn, Iḫyn, Aryn, Iryn* etc.). Semantically, *qadm* may be interpreted in two ways. It literally means "in front"; applied to time, it signifies "formerly, earlier", thence a proposed explanation of *Kadmos, Kadmôn* as "the ancient one";[1] applied to space, it signifies "east," toward which the Semites turned their faces to establish the four cardinal points (whence the word "orientation"), as *'āḫôr* (Akk. *aḫarrû*) was "west," and accordingly *śᵉmôl,* "left," was "north," and *yāmîn,* "right," was "south." But the mythological essence of Cadmos cannot be understood without his relation to Europa. Only armchair scholars could believe that Europa's disappearance and Cadmos' unsuccessful search for her were an accidental contamination of myths, and not the basis of the entire plot. If Europa is the west, the Evening Star, then Cadmos, as shown by his name, is the east, the Morning Star. As Victor Bérard formulated it in one of the best chapters of his *Les Phéniciens et l'Odyssée,*[2] Cadmos and Europa are the two aspects of the planet Venus, the Morning and the Evening Stars, which were first believed to be two distinct luminaries and had different names in Greek. The Morning Star was *Heôsphoros,* "the bringer of the Dawn," the Evening Star was *Hesperos* (which, just as Semitic *ʿrb,* signified at the same time also "evening" and "west"). According to the Babylonian conception, the planet Venus as the Morning Star was male, as the Evening Star female.[3] That is exactly the situation with the sexes of Cadmos and Europa. The Evening Star goes away to the west (as was sung in the Ugaritic-Akkadian hymn), disappears beyond the sea; the Morning Star, her brother, rushes to her search, but the two can never meet.

Our task is now to show (as we did in the case of Europa) that Semites—and in particular the West Semites, whom the Greeks called "Phoenicians"—really possessed a god with a name and mythological essence corresponding to those of Cadmos and able to shed additional light upon the primordial form of his mythical story. A god ᵈ*Qa-ad-mu* is exactly attested in Babylonia,[4] and

[1] cccxxx, 214; lxxxi, 117.

[2] lxv, II, 359 ss.

[3] See p. 139, n. 4 above.—According to cxxviii, the occurrence of both a male deity *ʿAštar* and a female one *ʿAštart* in Ugaritic myths points to the same conception. This is possible, but thus far they have not been found connected with each other.

[4] cxi, No. 3002 ("oriens?"); cxii, IV, 1, No. 13: 2; lxvi, *s.v.*

though we have no information on his individuality, his occurrence makes it certain that the Semitic god Cadmos is not a mere scholarly speculation. The Ugaritic human name *Qdmn* [1] might have been formed out of this divine name, just as the human names *Bʿln*, *ʿntn*, *ʿṯtrn*, *Ṣdqn* derive respectively from the divine names *Bʿl*, *ʿnt*, *ʿṯtr*, *Ṣdq*. Very significant is the following place in the poem BH (= UM 75): I: 7-8, preserved incompletely, but sufficiently to establish the parallelism of the members:

]*p*/*h*(?)*rn. km. šḥr*
]*ltn. km. qdm*

It follows from the parallelism of the members and of their signification that *qdm* "east" was equivalent to *šḥr* "dawn", which is quite natural. Taking into account the attested polynomy of Canaanite gods, one may plausibly assume that *Qdm* was another name of the god *Šḥr*. We are much better informed about that god thanks to the Ugaritic poem SS (= UM 52),[2] where he heads the group of the good and fair gods and is the brother of *Šlm*, whose name literally means "peace", but has also, in some Semitic languages, the meaning "dusk." [3] This corresponds to the sibling-pair Cadmos-Europa, i.e., *qdm-ʿrb*. True, *Šlm* is apparently a god, not a goddess, in that poem; but the sex of deities, especially of the astral ones, was subject to change. Thus the Sun, a male deity with the Akkadians, was a female one with the Ugaritians, and *šemeš* is both masculine and feminine in Hebrew; *šaḥar*, the Dawn, was a male god with the Hebrews, judging by the name *ʾAḫišaḥar* (I Chr. 7: 10), but female, judging by the expression *ʾayyelet haš-šaḥar* (Ps. 22: 1) "the doe of the dawn." In the Middle Assyrian lists of divine names, a goddess ^{d}SILIM^{tu} (to be read ^{d}*Šulmitu*) or ^{d}SILIM$^{ni\text{-}tu}$ (^{d}*Šulmanitu*) is mentioned among W-S gods, and is defined as ^{d}*Ištar Uru-silim-ma*, Ištar of Jerusalem.[4] The fact that the W-S goddess *Šulmitu* was identified with Ištar, whose

[1] The bearer of this name, an inhabitant of the town *Ubrʿy*, had a son with the W-S name *Abmn* (UM 64: 40; 312: III: 3; 328: 3).

[2] Before the discovery of that poem, one could presume the existence of such a god on the basis of the mythical name *Hêlēl ben-Šaḥar* Is. 14: 12, and of the theophorous names *ʾAḫîšaḥar* I Chr. 7: 10, and *Šᵉḥaryā ibid.* 8: 26.

[3] Heb. hiphil *hišlim* "to bring to an end, to put an end to something"; hence perhaps—"completion, end of the day." Akk. *šalâm šamši, šulum šamši* "sunset," cf. VII, 195, n. 10; I, 308.

[4] LXXI, 380-383 (first published 1922), 517 s. (additions 1953).

planet was Venus, speaks for considering this *Šulmitu* as the female counterpart of the dusk-god *Šlm* in Ugarit, and one may easily imagine the variant *Šaḥar-Šulmitu* instead of *Šḥr-Šlm*.

Another rapprochement between Cadmos and the poem of the good and fair gods is permissible. *Šḥr* and *Šlm* were not the only members of that group; after the birth of the two, the hierogamy is repeated five times more (UM 52: 57), and again a message is brought of the birth of the gods, the *islanders*, the sons of the sea; thus their full number was seven. As most Semitic gods, they were not exclusive astral deities, but were connected, judging by the context, with fertility rites, were considered as sons of the sea and, probably, islanders. Now Cadmos was connected with a very similar group of gods, known to the Greeks under the Semitic name of *Kabeiroi, Kabiroi* (Heb. *Kabbîr* "great, mighty"). They were very mysterious divinities, and their individual names (except one) remain unknown; [1] besides, the five junior companions of *Šḥr* and *Šlm* in the Ugaritic poem are anonymous, too. The centers of their worship were Thebes, the Boeotian port of Anthedon, and, most prominently, the North Aegean island of Samothrace. Their original number seems to have been seven; in the Phoenician city of Berytos, too, according to Philo of Byblos, seven Cabiri were worshipped (whose eighth brother, not belonging to their group, was considered Asclepios-Ešmun).[2] The Babylonians also had a similar group of seven man-friendly protective gods, *ilani Sibitti*, together with their sister *Narûdu*.[3] The Cabiri were honored by mysteries, i.e. ritual dramatic performances, of which little is known except that they, as all other mysteries, had an agricultural background; let us also keep in mind that the Ugaritic "Birth of Gods" is not so much a poem as a script for such a dramatic play. The myth of Cadmos ascribed to him a visit to Samothrace on his way from Phoenicia to Boeotia; he allegedly buried his mother Telephassa there. This shows that the mythical personality of Cadmos was known on that island, too. And indeed, the only authentic extant name of one of the Cabiri is *Kadmilos, Kadmêlos* (also, with Greek sibilization of *d* before *m*, *Kasmilos*, and with further assimilation, *Kamilos*). This is a good W-S name, corres-

[1] The late information that their names were Axeros, Axiocerses and Axiocersa does not evoke confidence.—All ancient sources on the Samothracian cults are collected in CCCXXIX.

[2] Eusebius, *Praep. Evang.*, I: 10: 38.

[3] CCCLVIII, II, 203.

ponding to Heb. *Qadmi'ēl* Ezra 3: 9; but here it has to be understood not as "servant of god" (literally, "before the face of god"), [1] but as *Qadm-'ēl* (like *Dan-'ēl, Rekub-'ēl*), "Qadm the god." The Cabiri, originally chthonic fertility gods, were also revered as protectors of seamen and rescuers of shipwrecked—and the Ugaritic seven gods, headed by Dawn and Dusk, were both "good gods" and "sons of the sea." [2]

Cadmos himself, as is to be expected, was not only the god of morning dawn. His sharply expressed ophic character speaks for his connection with chthonic cults, which in no way contradicts his other mythological aspect. The ophism of Cadmos reveals itself in the myth's assertion that toward the end of his life both Cadmos and his wife Harmonia were changed into serpents and settled among Encheleians, whom later authors tried to locate in Illyria, but whose name signifies "eels," [3] snakelike fish. Now a couple of entwined, twisted serpents, a male and a female, in an attitude snakes assume only when copulating, was a very old fertility symbol (more about it in the subsequent sections) and the emblem of the Sumerian chthonic fertility god Ningišzida.[4] Thence also originated the caduceus, the attribute of Hermes, and that is perhaps one of the reasons why Cadmilos, Cadmos' Samothracian avatar, was sometimes taken for Hermes. Ningišzida used to be identified with the chthonic serpent-god Šeraḫ or Šaḫan and with the serpent-constellation mul*Muš* (Hydra); he was depicted as a man with serpents growing from his shoulders. [5] Another animal attribute of Ningišzida—which is often the animal conquered by the god [6]— was the dragon [7]—and the central episode of the myth of Cadmos is his victory over the dragon who lived on the very spot where he

[1] CCXXXV, II, 1327.

[2] Hesychios reports on a Samothracian cult of deities called *Aôoi* "those of the dawn," who were said to have come *ek dromu*. LXV, I, 68 emended it *ek Rhodu* "from Rhodes." But *dromos* may be a remnant of *dārôm*, Heb. "south."

[3] CDXI, VII, 2, 2385. Greek for "eel" is *enchelys*.

[4] CDXIX, II, 147; CCCLVIII, II, 35, 284; CLXXII, 10. On the significance of this emblem, its figuration and its geographical and chronological occurrence, cf. DIII, 40 ss.; D, 53-65.

[5] CXI, No. 2481: 12; CCXXVI, No. 284: I; DI, 60-89; CLXXII, 10-17.

[6] Thus the emblem of the god Ningirsu, according to Gudea, cyl. A: 4: 17; 5: 15; 13: 22 (CDXIX, II, 7, 8, 17) was the storm-bird Imdugud (Akk. *Zû*) whom he vanquished. For animals in the iconography of Ningirsu and Ningišzida and the reasons for them, cf. CLXXII, 10. s.

[7] CXI, No. 2481: 12: "Eius symbolum est 'draco angueus',"; CLXXII, 10 s.

erected Thebes. If we were sure that *ltn* in UM 75: I: 8 quoted above is preserved in full and no initial letters of the word had been broken off, we could suppose that *ltn. km. qdm* relates to Qadm in some connection with the famous dragon of Ugaritic mythology, *Ltn.*[1] It is very significant that the Sumerians also considered Ningišzida as the personification of the sunrise: according to Gudea,[2] the goddess Nanše revealed to him in his dream: "The sun which rose from the fruitful earth is thy god Ningizzida who, like the sun, rises for thee out of the fruitful earth." [3] On the other hand, Ningišzida was characterized as "the servant of the (fire-) god Gibil, he who drains the waters of the deep, who lays the foundation (*temen*) of the city and of the temple." [4] Serpent, dragon-victor, sunrise, city-founder—these four common motifs show that, though Cadmos' immediate prototype was the W-S god *Šḥr/Qdm*, the deeper roots of his image and essence go back (as many features in W-S religion) to the remote Sumerian past.

A W-S motif is also the oracle's order to Cadmos—to follow a young cow that had never worn a yoke and to build a city at the spot where she should lie down for rest.[5] It is found in I Sam. 6: 7-12 where the Philistine princes put the captive ark of Yahwe upon a new wagon driven by young cows who had never been yoked before

[1] The word]*p/hrn* in the preceding line, which stands in parallelism with *ltn* in line 8, may be restored *n*]*hrn*, extended form of *nhr* "river," the personification of which was notoriously represented as a dragon in Ugaritic poems (cf. V AB: D = ʿnt: IV: 35-39, pp. 291 s. below). Cf. p. 213 below, *f,* on the Theban dragon's connection with the river Ladon. No reasonable restoration has been proposed for]*ltn,* if this word be considered as incomplete.

[2] Cyl. A: 19-20 (CDXIX, II, 8 s.). We follow the translation of this passage CXV, 557 s. and XLVIII, 255.

[3] GRUPPE, CCXXXV, II, 1328, for insufficient reasons, compared Cadmos-Cadmilos with the Babylonian Uddušu-namir or Aṣušu-namir, created by Ea and sent to the Nether World to free Ištar. And, indeed, there is a resemblance, though not were GRUPPE saw it: the name *Aṣušu-namir* signifies "his rise is brilliant," it fits a god of the dawn, and the bearer of it was, moreover, sent to seek a disappeared goddess—like Cadmos. The Babylonians had a god of dawn, ᵈ*Šêrum,* but he did not play a noticeable rôle in their cult and mythology.

[4] CXI, No. 2481: 10, quoting Sargon Cyl. 61; *ibid.*, "conclusio." Gudea, Cyl. A: 18: 16-29, describes how Ningizzida helped him to build the temple of Ningirsu, and *ibid.*: 30: 23 he states of the temple: "Ningizzida built it on the underworld" (CDXIX, II, 22 s., 34).

[5] It is explicitly stressed that the cow, or heifer, has never been under a yoke, cf. Euripides *Phoenissae* 640; Ovid *Metam.* III: 10-11 (after earlier Greek sources).

and had calfs back home, and allowed them to go free; that would show the will of the deity; the princes followed the wagon until the cows brought the ark to Bêt-Šemeš, where the people sacrificed the cows to Yahwe as Cadmos sacrificed the guiding cow to Athena.[1] Another close parallel to I Sam. 6: 7-12 is Euripides' *Bacchae* 1333-1335: Dionysos announces to Cadmos that he and Harmonia will be changed into serpents and "in a wagon (driven) by heifers (*moschoi*), says Zeus' oracle, thou and thy wife shall lead barbarians." The word *moschos* could designate both a young bull and a heifer who did not yet wear the yoke, but Euripides (cf. *Phoen.* 640) uses it in the latter sense. The image is clear: the two serpents in the wagon do not really direct it; they were just a palladium as the ark was; the heifers drove the wagon obeying the mystic power emanating from the palladium, and the barbarians followed them as the Philistine princes did. In the extant form of the myth nothing is said about the ark; but the city founded on the spot providentially chosen by the cow bore the name of *Thêba* (so in Homer; later *Thêbai*) which has frequently been correctly identified with Heb. *tēbā* "ark, chest", synonym of *'ārôn*.[2] Sacred chests with mystical emblems, whose opening was strongly forbidden, played a great rôle in Greek mysteries celebration, and GRUPPE [3] derived the name of Thebes from such chests in the Cabiri mysteries. According to other hypotheses, the name originated from the ark in which the local Noah, King Ogygos, survived the flood.[4] Both motifs possibly played a rôle, for both the floating and the portable chest have a common cultic origin, though in Hebrew they were designated by different terms.

Such is the mythological essence of Cadmos. His name and almost all of his adventures and attributes are Oriental and originated in W-S myths of the god of sunrise, strongly influenced by the image of

[1] One may object: since the resource to cows is ascribed to Philistines, why not admit that the motif had been brought by them from the Aegean? However, the story is not a Philistine but an Israelite one, written from the Israelite Yahwist point of view *ad maiorem Dei gloriam*; the author operates with Israelite cultic terminology (*'ašām* etc.).

[2] Already Hesychios: *Thêba: polis Boiotias, kai kibôtôn; thêba: kibôtion.* The Greek word *thibê*, one of the many Semitisms in the Greek language, signified "chest." LXX translated *tēbā* in Noah's story by *kibôtos*, in Moses' story by *thibis*.

[3] CCXXXV, I, 61.

[4] NORK in his curious CCCLXXXIV, IV (1845), 365: "Thebes, according to its name, the Ship-city"; LXV, II, 368 s.

the Sumerian Ningišzida, the serpent-god of fertility, sunrise, and the building of cities, symbolized by entwined serpents and the dragon. Only the motif of armed men grown from the dragon's teeth which were sown by Cadmos, has no parallel in Oriental myths discovered so far, and is probably a local Greek addition aiming to satisfy the inhabitants' claim of descent from the aborigines. However, the idea of the first human beings having grown from the soil like plants is found, in a primitive form, in the Sumerian myth of Enlil and the pick-ax.[1] We shall now see that Cadmos is not an isolated figure, and that all characters linked with him by the myth have the same origin.

Harmonia

Cadmos' wife, Harmonia, was changed into a serpent together with him. She corresponds to the female in the couple of snakes twisted together in the magic symbol of fertility which was, in particular, the emblem of Ningišzida. Ovid (*Metam.* IV: 576-600), following older Greek poets, describes how Cadmos, changed into a serpent, twists around Harmonia who follows him in the metamorphosis. Her paternity in the Greek myth agrees with the essentially chthonic nature of Ningišzida: she is the daughter of Ares who "in ancient pre-Homeric times was a chthonic deity who could bring to humans both blessing and destruction", but mostly pestilence and war;[2] Ares was a kind of a Greek counterpart of Nergal. We have no indication as to who was the spouse of Qadm or Šaḥar in W-S mythology; as to the more ancient prototype of Cadmos, the Sumerian Ningišzida, his wife was sometimes the goddess Ba-ú (Ba-ba), sometimes the goddess called in Sumerian Geštinanna ("the heavenly vine"), in Akkadian Bêlit-ṣêri ("the lady of the steppe"). This latter goddess, notwithstanding her Sumerian name, was an underground chthonic deity and, in the classical system of the Babylonian pantheon, was assigned the function of the scribe of the Nether World, the secretary of the infernal queen Ereškigal, who registered not only the already dead, but also those who were doomed by the Nether World judges to die in the current year.[3] This reminds one of the fatal necklace and

[1] CCLXXI, 135 ss.
[2] CCCXLIV, s.v. *Ares*.
[3] CXI, No. 369. For the Nether World judges trying the living, not the dead, cf. CCLXXXVIII, 374-395.

peplos of Harmonia who caused destruction to whoever possessed them.

Like Cadmos, Harmonia was considered in Thebes, up to Roman times, as the founding heroine of shrines. To her was ascribed the erection of three archaic statues, *xoana*, of the triple Aphrodite —Urania "the heavenly," Pandemos "of the entire people," and Apostrophia "the returning" (Paus. IX: 16: 3), in whom V. BÉRARD[1] correctly recognized three attributes of Ištar—"queen of heaven," "ruler of all men," and she who returned from the Land Without Return. The Thebans asserted that the temple of Demeter Thesmophoros at Thebes had formerly been the house of Cadmos and Harmonia (Paus. IX: 16: 5). Harmonia was, thus, the owner of the house of the goddess. This allows us to recognize in her a Sumerian goddess who was also worshipped by the Akkadians and the West Semites. Her Sumerian name was *Nin-é-gal* "the lady of the palace," [2] sometimes also *Nin-uru* "the lady of the city." [3] Her name was translated into Akkadian as *Bêlit-êkallim*. In the divine family of the lunar cult in Ur, she followed immediately after Nin-gal, "the great lady," the wife of Sin. But in the Middle Syrian city of Qaṭna, which is supposed to have been a colony of Ur (during the IIId Ur dynasty), that secondary Babylonian goddess became the chief patron deity of the city.[4]

Both goddesses were also worshipped in Ugarit: Nin-gal under the Semitized name of Nikkal (*Nkl*),[5] and Nin-é-gal or Bêlit-êkallim under the W-S translated name of *Bʿlt-bt* or *Bʿlt-bhtm*,[6] where the plural *bhtm* signifies "palace." [7] It is interesting to note that the exact counterpart of *é-gal, êkallum* in W-S—*hkl* (Heb. *hêkāl*) was not used in the W-S translation of the goddess' name. Now if *êkallum* were translated not by *bt* or *bhtm*, but by another W-S word for "palace", *ʾarmôn*, the derivate of it would be *ʾArmônî*—which

[1] LXV, II, 364, 367.

[2] CXI, Nos. 2513, 2514.

[3] CCCLVIII, II, 30.

[4] DXXVII, 90 s.; DXVIII, 10. Nin-égal also belonged to the mixed Akkado-Amorite pantheon of Mari, CXXVII, 41 ss.

[5] Cf. the Ugaritic poem about the marriage of the Moon-god Yariḫ and the goddess Nikkal: NK (= UM 77).

[6] UM 1: 21 (*bʿlt bhtm*); 3: 37 (*bʿlt bt*); 33: 7 (*bʿlt b*[]); DXXIV, No. 2 (RŠ 16.394): 45 and No. 106 (RŠ 15.115): 33 (*bʿlt bhtm*); identification with Nin-é-gal *ibid.*, 140.

[7] I owe this interpretation of *bhtm* and its comparison with the analogous construction in Greek *dômata* to Prof. Cyrus H. Gordon. According to IIIa, No. 504 *bht*, as distinct from *bt*, means "magnificent house."

is actually attested II Sam. 21: 8 as the name of one of Saul's sons, a well-fitting name for a royal child. The feminine form of it would be *'*Armônit* or, with the ending of several female names in Ugarit, *'*Armônîyā*.[1]This is exactly the Greek name of *Harmônia*! The initial aspiration in the Greek name might be due to a possible descent from a phonetic variant of *'armôn*: *harmônā* (locative or feminine form?) Amos 4: 3; [2] or, more probably, to the same phenomenon which made *Hierosolyma* out of *Yerûšālêm* and *Hieromykês* out of *Yarmûk*: the Greek ear associated the first sounds of these names with *hieros* "holy," and in the same way *'Armônîyā* was perceived as Greek *harmônia* "fastening, tie, clamp," then "alliance, treaty," and finally "concord, harmony."

Did the theological scheme of any Mesopotamian city make Nin-é-gal the spouse of Ningišzida? This goddess is so little known that there are no precise data. It is known, however, that she was considered as the wife of the god Uraš,[3] a fertility-god of much the same nature as Ningišzida and the patron of the city of Dilbat,[4] the name of which is the same as that of the planet Venus. Besides, the month of Abu was devoted both to Ningišzida and Nin-é-gal.[5]

Teiresias

Snakes twisted together in the attitude of copulation, the symbol of Ningišzida playing a rôle in the myth of Cadmos and Harmonia, appear again in a very original and peculiar myth of their contemporary and fellow-townsman, the famous blind soothsayer Teiresias the Theban, so celebrated by the Odyssey and the great Athenian tragedies.

It is futile to look for a Semitic etymology for the name of

[1] There actually existed a god ^{d}*Ar-man-nu* in Babylonia, CXI, No. 278.

[2] This *hapax leg.* is traditionally translated as "palace"; however, CCLXXXIX, 243 consider it "unexplained."

[3] CCCLVIII, II, 30; CXI, No. 2513.

[4] CXI, No. 1495.

[5] CXI, Nos. 2481, 2513.—The goddess Nin-é-gal, or Belit-êkallim, penetrated into Greece in another avatar too: in the classical times, a little shrine in the Attic Mount Hymettos was devoted to *Hekalê* or *Hekalinê*, an effaced ancient goddess, who became in people's tradition a hospitable old woman, among whose guests Theseus figured (Callimachos, *Hecale* [R. Pfeiffer, *Callimachos*, I, frg. 230-264]; Plutarch, *Theseus*, 5 s., 14). *Hekalê* clearly derives from *hêkāl*, the W-S form of *êkallum*, and her rôle of a hospitable landlady is reminiscent of Harmonia with respect to Demeter Thesmophoros and of the Ugaritic *Bʿlt bt/bhtm*, "Lady of the House."

Teiresias, as did V. Bérard. [1] The Greek *teirea* (pl. tantum) "stars, constellations", cognate to *teras* "sign, omen, miracle, atmospheric phenomena as thunder, lightning or rainbow, dream etc. as signs of divine will and presage of future events", provides the best explanation for his name—actually a common name for a soothsayer, as his daughter's name Mantô signifies just the same.[2] But despite his non-Semitic name, the story of Teiresias is saturated with motifs from the Semitic East.

First, the image of Teiresias as a blind soothsayer. In the Ugaritic epic of King *Krt* (Krt: 99-100, 187-188) *ʿwr mzl ymzl* "a blind man consults the fate" is stated; the word *mazzālôt* II Kings 23: 5 signifies literally "constellations" or "planets," like *teirea*, the basis of the name of *Teiresias*, and in the Greco-Phoenician bilinguae *mzl* corresponds to *tychê* "luck," [3] as in post-Biblical Hebrew and Yiddish. The W-S word for "blind", which sounds *ʿiwwēr* in Hebrew, supplies a Semitic basis for the name of *Euêrês*, Teiresias' father according to the myth, but originally his own epithet.

Second, Teiresias' bisexuality. It is told that he was changed into a woman and became again a man after seven years of being a female. This brings us to Babylonia and Syria where bisexuality, uncertain sex and playing the rôle of the opposite sex were marked elements in beliefs and cultic practice. This was especially characteristic for gods of death and healing. Thus in Babylonia, Damu, a healing deity, one of the avatars of Tammuz, was considered sometimes a god, sometimes a goddess, the daughter of the goddess Gula and the god Pabil-sag.[4] Lagamal, the son of Uraš and Nin-é-gal, was also a goddess.[5] In the Hellenistic age Ešmun-Asclepios was identified with a Syrian deity who was sometimes Hadad's son Simios, sometimes Hadad's daughter Simia or Sima.[6] The same is perhaps true for *Mŝ* and *Mŝt* in Ugaritic mythology.[7] In the Syrian cultic center Hierapolis the castrated priests named Galli wore female cloths and behaved like women,[8] and in Babylonia, on the

[1] LXV, II, 366, from *dāraš* "to consult an oracle."

[2] DXXXVIII, 11 s. believed to find Teiresias as a god in a Linear B tablet from Cnossos, but this equation is dubious.

[3] CVIII, 82.

[4] God: CXI, No. 687; goddess: hymn to Ninkarrak KAR Nos. 15, 16 (CLV); CCLVIII, II, 170. As by-name of Dumuzi: CCCXVII, 299 ss., Tammuz No. I: 5.

[5] CCLVIII, II, 30.

[6] CXLIX, 130 s.

[7] Cf. p. 89 above and pp. 231 s. below.

[8] Lucian, *De Deâ Syriâ*, 27.

contrary, a special category of priestesses existed, sinnišat *zikrum*, i.e., "a woman who is a man," women playing the rôle of men and wearing men's clothes.[1] That such customs connected with the cult were known in Canaan as well is shown by the prohibition of transvestism in Deut. 22: 5. In line with this tradition was the notorious femininity of Dionysos, Cadmos' grandson, which originally was an actual bisexuality, *arsenothêlys*,[2] and probably the words of Bata, the Egypto-Phoenician dying god: "I am not a man, but a woman."[3]

The Greek myth tells the circumstances of Teiresias' double change of sex thus: once he came across two serpents in the act of copulation and killed one of them, the female, with his staff. Immediately he was transformed into a woman and remained so for seven years; some even add that he became a famous harlot (cf. the *qᵉdēšîm*, the male prostitutes of Canaanite and early Israelite temples). After seven years he again met two copulating serpents, that time killed the male, and became a man again.[4] The seven-year rhythm, the change of sex, and especially the symbol of the entwined serpents point to the East in an epoch which was quite remote in the scale of Greek history, for the emblem of interlaced snakes, very popular in earlier times, went out of use after the XIIIth century.[5]

Actaeon-Aqht

Cadmos and Harmonia had four daughters: Autonoë (mother of Actaeon), Semele (mother of Dionysos), Agave (mother of Pentheus),

[1] *Laws of Ḫammurapi*, §§ 178-180. The correct explanation of the term was given CXVI, 212.

[2] CDI, 163. Another interesting epithet of Dionysos was *pseudanôr* "the sham man," i.e. a woman in a man's garb (not the opposite, as stated CLXII, V, 161: this would have been *pseudo-gynê*), whose cult was introduced into Macedon by king Argeios and was performed by *Mimallones* (see p. 188, n. 5 below), girls who imitated men: Polyaenos 4: 3, cf. CLXII, V, 293, n. 61: d. According to (Ps.) Apollodoros, *Bibl.* III: 4: 3, the infant Dionysos was brought by Hermes to Athamas and Ino to be raised as a girl.

[3] So interpreted CDXXIX, *ad loc.* LEFEBVRE, CCCXXIII, 151, n. 48, denies it on the ground that Bata was married when he made this statement; but it is futile to look for strict logic in such types of magic tales, where sexual duality is a favorite motif.

[4] *Schol. ad Odyss.* X: 494, said to be an excerpt of an ancient epic *Melampodia*, published and translated by H. G. EVELYN-WHITE, *Hesiod etc.* (Loeb Classical Library), 268 s.

[5] DIII, 42. Two snakes, clearly recognizable as male and female, figure on the opposite sides of a votive stone-altar from Upper Galilee, which is also provided with a navel on its third side, so that the ensamble symbolizes fertility (CCLV); ALBRIGHT, in a note, considers the monument Phoenician.

and Ino (mother of Melicertes [1]). A son Polydoros was also ascribed to them, but he is just a name without a story, a genealogical filling, whose only purpose is to serve as the father of Labdacos and thus to link the famous Theban mythical dynasty of the Labdacids with Cadmos. This cannot be said of the daughters and especially of the grandsons of Cadmos, who are vivid individual mythological characters. Three of Cadmos' grandsons have this in common: they tragically perished in the prime of life; the fourth one, Dionysos, suffered this fate in his first incarnation. From the viewpoint of the ritual and mythical motif of their death, Actaeon, Pentheus and Dionysos form three avatars of the same dying god; the death of Ino and Melicertes, though related, belongs to a different ritual-myth cycle. In this way, the four (or five) grandsons of Cadmos are in fact reduced to two prototypes, and in accord with this only two of them, Dionysos and Melicertes, received divine honors, and their mothers, Semele and Ino, were granted immortality. And it is precisely Semele and Ino who bear rare and peculiar names defying Greek etymology, while Autonoë (approximately "one living by one's own reason") and Agave ("admirable, evoking deference") are normal Greek names, selected in conformity with the character of their sons, proud and wilful young men. We will see now that all mythological motifs and most names in the myths of Semele, Ino, and all four (or five) of Cadmos' grandsons are borrowed, with great accuracy, from W-S mythology.

We will begin with Actaeon, whose myth is in many respects the most typical of the series. Actaeon, the son of Autonoë, daughter of Cadmos, and of Aristaeos, was a famous hero and hunter. Once, while hunting in the Cithaeron mountains, he was changed by Artemis into a stag and torn asunder by his fifty hounds. According to one version, the wrath of the goddess was provoked by Actaeon having seen her bathing; [2] in later times, a rock was shown between Plateae and Megara from which Actaeon peeped on the goddess, and Actaeon's spring in which she bathed (Paus. IX: 2: 3). Accord-

[1] And of Learchos; but Learchos, as it will be shown below, is only a doublet of Melicertes.

[2] A similar offense was said to have been the cause of Teiresias' blindness. The goddess seen while bathing was, in the case of Teiresias, Athena. Blindness as a result of having seen a divine body in all its shining splendor fits well in the context of that story. The motif of a bathing goddess seems to be borrowed in the myth of Actaeon from the myth of Teiresias.

ing to another version, told i.a. by Euripides in his tragedy *Bacchae*:[1] 337-340, Actaeon was "rent limb from limb" by his "raw-ravening hounds" for having boasted that he excelled Artemis in hunting. His statues were erected on Boeotian mountains and cliffs in order to prevent drought and the pernicious consequences of summer heat: Pausanias still saw such a statue near Orchomenos (Paus. IX: 38: 4).

Almost everything in this myth goes back to the W-S myth which is evidenced in detail and with great art in the Ugaritic poem of *Aqht*. We already met its other heroes, Danel and his daughter *Pġt*, as the prototypes of Danaos and the Danaides; now we find in the Cadmeian cycle [2] its young hero *Aqht* who is absent from the Danaan myth. Th. H. Gaster [3] gave a well-documented and reasoned comparison of *Aqht* and the Boeotian hero Orion, but he did not once mention Actaeon who is much closer to *Aqht* in all respects, even in name.

1. There is substantial reason to believe that *Aktaiôn* derives from *Aqht*, or, more correctly, from one of the extended forms of that name. We have seen that the name of Cadmos existed with the Greeks in three versions, *Kadmos*, *Kadmôn* and *Kadmaiôn*, going back to W-S *Qdm*, *Qdmn* and **Qdmyn* (cf. *Špšyn* etc.). A shorter form of *Aktaiôn* is found in *Aktis*, one of the seven Heliads in Rhodes,[4] and in *Aktaios*, epithet of Dionysos in Chios. One may presume the existence of extended forms of *Aqht*: **Aqhtn* and **Aqhtyn* (cf. Ugar. *Krt* and once—UM 125: 39—*Krtn*). The W-S *h* in the middle of a word was never transcribed by the Greeks, as shown by *Qᵉhāt* = LXX *Kaath*, and *Maharbaʿal* = Greek *Merbalos* where the two vowels divided by *h* became one after it was dropped. The Greeks, of course, perceived their form of this W-S name as a purely Greek word formed out of *aktê* "shore, cape, peninsula"—which has no relation to the Boeotian Actaeon.

[1] Scholars agree that this tragedy, by its thoroughness of documentation and abundance of detail, is a precious source for understanding the essence of Bacchic cults. Its explanation for Actaeon's death may, therefore, be trusted as a genuine tradition.

[2] We understand by "Cadmeian cycle" the myths of Cadmos and his family, as distinct from "Theban cycle" (Oedipodia, Seven Against Thebes, Epigoni) which has no intrinsic connection with the first one and, in contrast to it, hardly contains any Semitic elements.

[3] CLXXXVI, 260-265.

[4] A link connecting the Cadmeian cycle with the Rhodian one is Leucothea, who was identified with Ino, daughter of Cadmos, in Boeotia, and with Halia, grandmother of the Heliads, in Rhodes.

2. Actaeon's father, Aristaeos (*Aristaios*), son of Uranos and Gê (as the patron of Cyrenaica—son of Apollo and Cyrene), is a very old god of abundance and soil fertility in various places of Greece. He was revered as protector of herds, game bees, agriculture, viticulture and olive-planting (Pindar, *Pyth.* IX: 5-65 gives him the titles of *Nomios, Agreus, Melisseus*). Thus, this deity resembles in all fundamental features *Aqht*'s father Danel, the giver of harvest and patron of agriculture.

3. *Aqht* received from his father a wonderful bow, made by the artificer-god *Kŝr*, and became, through it, a great hunter. The goddess Virgin Anath, a passionate huntress, tried to obtain this bow from *Aqht*, promising him all kinds of goods, even immortality. But *Aqht* refused—first courteously, proposing to supply the goddess with all necessary materials out of which *Kŝr* would manufacture another bow for her, and then more sharply: a bow is a thing for men, females have nothing to do with it. The goddess, insulted by his haughtiness, obtained from the supreme god El permission to kill *Aqht*. She fulfilled her plan by luring *Aqht* to a hunt and ordering her servant *Yṭpn*, who took the shape of an eagle, to soar in the midst of a flock of eagles over *Aqht* and to deliver the fatal blows upon him from above.

4. *Aqht* was torn asunder by the eagles, his corpse disappeared, and only in the inwards of the Mother of the Eagles did Danel find his remnants which he buried in an urn. What is important from the point of view of religious ritual is the fact of dismemberment and not who effected it. In the case of Actaeon this was done by his hounds, of Pentheus — by Theban women, of Orpheus — by Bacchants called Bassarids, of Dionysos-Zagreus—by the Titans. All of these symbolize one of the oldest rites of sacrifice, that of tearing or cutting asunder the victim (we will return to this and its origin). Actaeon's transformation into a stag also belongs here: there was a tradition that while dismembering a human victim, the performers of the horrible rite shouted that their victim was an animal; [1] and in a papyrus fragment of a Bacchic poem the killing and eating of a human victim disguised as a stag is explicitly

[1] Parents conducting their children to be sacrificed in Syrian Hierapolis shouted that those were not children but bulls (Lucian, *De Deâ Syriâ*: 58); Athamas killing his son Learchos shouted that this was a stag. Cf., however, *Gilgameš epic* V: 57-63, where Ištar turned one of her lovers into a wolf, "so that his own herd boys drove him off, and his dogs bit his thighs."

related.[1] The number of the hounds, fifty, which tore Actaeon into pieces is not accidental, but symbolizes the rotation of the year (see above, p. 78).

5. It is extremely important that Actaeon was connected in Boeotia with drought and rain. According to the Ugaritic myth, *Aqht*'s murder immediately provoked a cruel seven-year drought. His father Danel was a rain god, and his sister *Pǵt* sprayed dew upon the barley. The custom of erecting statues to Actaeon to prevent drought is easy to understand: they were a kind of propitiatory apotropy to atone for the country's automatic guilt for having been the scene of the murder [2] and to incline the spirit of the murdered to forgiveness.

6. Actaeon's spring in southern Boeotia where he committed the deed that caused his ruin (Paus. IX: 2: 3) is exactly comparable to the spring (*qr mym* 1 Aqht: 150 ss.) alongside which *Aqht* was killed, and which was therefore cursed by Danel along with the city near which the deed happened.

7. The parallel myths from neighboring regions of Greece, connected with Actaeon's name, are also significant:

a) There was a tale in Corinth (Diod. Sic. VIII: 10) of unrequited love by a member of the local Bacchiad aristocracy, Archias, to a beautiful boy Actaeon, son of Melissos. Desiring to possess him, Archias together with his friends broke into Actaeon's house and tried to kidnap him by force. The members of his family offered resistance, and during the fight for the boy, while he was pulled in opposite directions, he expired. Diodoros remarks: "He perished exactly as he whose name he bore." And indeed, the Corinthian myth is but a final humanized and degraded stage of the Boeotian. Even the father of the Corinthian Actaeon, Melissos, bears a name which is one of the epithets of the god Aristaeos, Boeotian Actaeon's father (*Melisseus*, patron of the bees). And the name of he who had caused his death, was *Archias*—a good Greek name, which in this context can, however, be traced back to the W-S *arḫ* "heifer" or "cow", epithet of the goddess Anath who destroyed *Aqht*.[3]

[1] This fragment is supposed to belong to *Bassarica* by Dionysios; see text in D. L. Pace, *Select Papyri*, III, no. 134 (Loeb Class. Libr.).

[2] "The town's responsibility for a crime perpetrated within its territory is . . . an institution attested in the Bible and cuneiform records, and persists in the modern Middle East", ccxxiii, 5.

[3] Though the principal reason for *Aqht*'s murder was his refusal to cede his bow to Anath, the motif of a goddess's love rejected by a mortal cannot be

b) In Attica confused myths about a king Actaeon existed, who was said to rule the country even before Cecrops. The simplest view is to see in him the eponym of Attica (originally Actica), but is it not remarkable that his daughter was named *Phoinikê* and that in her honor he gave to the letters he had invented the name of *phoinikeia grammata* (an Attic variant of the Phoenician Cadmos who allegedly introduced the Phoenician alphabet in Greece).

8. Finally, one should not neglect Actaeon's paternity, his being attributed to the family of Cadmos where there are so many genuine W-S motifs and names. Mythological clusters usually have a common origin.

The analogies between *Aqht* and another Boeotian hunter hero, Orion, drawn in detail by Th. H. GASTER, remain in force; thereby an indubitable similarity is established between Actaeon and Orion. But whereas in the myth of Actaeon *all* motifs go back to the Ugaritic poem of *Aqht*, the myth of Orion is incomparably more complex, and contains several outside motifs, including the episode with Oinopion and Merope, the blinding of Orion, the struggle with the scorpion, and even his slaying by Artemis by mistake and not because of her enmity towards him. Besides, much in the myth of Orion derives from Sumero-Babylonian models—from myths of Tammuz and his constellation *Sib-zi-an-na,* now called Orion, which had no noticeable influence upon the poem of *Aqht.* One must add a detail which Th. H. GASTER intentionally omitted: the myth of Orion, showing such a similarity to Babylonian and W-S myths, must have been borrowed from the East. The name of *Ôriôn* can most plausibly be derived from W-S *'ôr* "light" and explained as referring to the bright constellation with which the hero was identified. In Ugarit, a pers. name *Aryn* is attested which we derive from Ugaritic *'âr* (corresponding to south Canaan. *'ôr/'ûr,* cf. Greek variant *Uriôn*) + the name-forming suffix *-yn* (*-iyyân, -iyyôn*).[1]

completely ruled out. In 3 Aqht rev.: 24, Anath says: "Hear, O *Aqht* the Hero: Thou art my brother and I [am thy sister!]"—a standard Oriental love-formula.

[1] The name *Aqht,* in its Biblical variant (without the prothetic aleph) *Qᵉhāt,* LXX *Kaath,* also occurs in Theban mythology as *Kaaithos* or *Kaanthos,* "a very old-fashioned name, the proper form of which the tellers no longer knew" (CCLXXXVI, 34). However, this hero's rôle in the myth has nothing in common with that of *Aqht*: rather than murdered, he is himself a murderer, through whom fratricide came into the world.

Semele, the Eagle-Mother

The poem of *Aqht* permits us also to restore the original essence and to explain the name of Cadmos' daughter Semele, mother of Dionysos. Since *Semelê* has no Greek etymology, scholars looked for it in the Thracian language, for there a conviction prevailed that the cult of Dionysos had been brought to Greece from Thrace. But since the Thracian language is almost unknown, Paul Kretschmer turned to the language of Phrygia which is supposed to be cognate to Thracian; on Phrygian tombstones of about 200 and 300 A.D. the word *zemelo* stands beside that of *diôs* and *deus,*[1] and this word Kretschmer identified with the Russian *zemlja* "earth", proclaiming thus Semele an earth-goddess. [2] This etymology was almost universally accepted.[3] But the semantics of the Phrygian *zemelo* is far from being established; we do not exclude the possibility that it represents the Phrygian pronunciation of the Greek Semele, borrowed by the Phrygians from the Greeks to match their Zeus Sabazios who had been identified by the Greeks with Dionysos; Phrygia had been long since under a steady Greek influence.[4] As to the explanation of Semele by the Russian *zemlja,* every Slavic-speaker knows that the *l* in this word is secondary: the theme is *zem-*, the suffix *-ja,* and by dissimilation (which does not appear in most of the other Slavic languages)—modern Russian *zemlja,* but in derivatives, mostly *zem-* (*zemnoj, zemskij, ozem', nazem', černozem* etc.).[5]

Semele being affiliated with the Phoenician Cadmos, there were several propositions of a Semitic etymology; but all of them were more or less arbitrary, undemonstrable and provided nothing for

[1] Published by Ramsay in *Journ. Roy. Asiat. Soc.*, 1883, 120 ss., quoted CCXLVII, 403.

[2] CCXCVIII, 17.

[3] CCXLVII, 403 s., and theological theories created on that basis, 404-410; CLXII, V, 94; CCCLXXXI, 567, n. 19. Objections (not of linguistic character) CDI, 67.

[4] Cf., e.g., the inscription of the Phrygian king Midas, published by Ramsay (see n. 1 above), 138, No. 1, reproduced and explained CCCXLVIII, 218. It contains the peculiar Mycenaean titles *lawag(e)ta* (or *lawalta,* Phrygian variant) and *wanakta,* "duke" and "king," and its language is cognate to Greek (rather than to Slavic). Luria, CCCXLVIII, 209, considers that either the Phrygians were closely cognate with the Greeks, or they had been under a strong Mycenaean influence.

[5] See the best and most complete etymological dictionary of the Russian language, CDXVIII, I, 249 s., with exhaustive cognates from all Slavic and other Indo-European languages.

understanding the personality of Semele.[1] A way to the correct solution was hinted by VIROLLEAUD about 1935, though only orally and in passing.[2] He remarked that Semele, smitten by Zeus' thunder, corresponds to *Ṣml,* called *um nšrm* "the mother of the eagles" in the poem of *Aqht,* who fell to the ground after Baal, at Danel's request, had broken her wings. VIROLLEAUD never returned to this idea and similar Greco-Semitic comparisons. However, the putting together of Semele and *Ṣml* (which at first glance is hardly better justified than other Semitic etymologies), proves correct and fruitful in the light of the following investigation.

We have seen that according to the Ugaritic poem *Aqht* was killed by the eagle-shaped *Yṭpn* and torn to pieces by the rest of the eagle-flock. Danel, who could interpret the flight of birds, understood that his son's remnants were in the stomachs of the eagles. While the eagle-flock was flying over his head, Danel loudly invoked Baal: [3] "May Baal break the wings of the eagles, may Baal break their pinions that they may fall at my feet! I'll split their inwards and look: if there is fat, if there is bone, I shall weep and bury him, I'll put (him) in the *niche* [4] of the ghosts of the earth." Baal immediately fulfilled Danel's request: he broke the eagles' wings, they fell at the feet of Danel, but the dissection did not reveal the presence of *Aqht*'s remnants. Then Danel asked Baal to repair the wings of the eagles so they may fly away—i.e. to resurrect them, since they had been dissected—which also was fulfilled. Danel repeated the same procedure with *Hrgb ab nšrm, Hgrb* [5] the father of the eagles, but again without result, so *Hrgb,* too, was restored and flew away. But when Baal broke the wings of *Ṣml um nšrm, Ṣml* the mother of the

[1] R. BROWN in his very weak book LXXXI, 132 compared Semele with a non-existent Sumero-Akkadian deity ^{ilu}*Samela,* and *ibid.,* 135 with the Phoenician theophorous name *Pn-Smlt* from a bilingual inscription by a man from Cition, found at Piraeus (CCCXXXVI, 425). According to LIDZBARSKI, CCCXXXVI, 151, "in the Cyprus inscriptions, 'statue' is called *sml* if it represents a male person, *smlt,* if a female." Thus we have here an instance of deification of statues (like the ancient Arabic god Ṣalm), but not a mythological entity.—V. BÉRARD, LXV, II, 369, proceeding from the myth of Semele and Dionysos in a floating chest, strangely turned to Heb. *śimlā* "cloak" and *Śamlā,* a king of Edom; but both have nothing in common with the idea of being shut up in a chest, or with any other motif of the myth of Semele.

[2] See p. XIV above.

[3] I D (= I Aqht): 107-112. The following translation is that of CCXXIII, 96.

[4] *b ḫrt*; according to a more recent explanation, CCXXII, 102 s., "cemetery."

[5] DXVIII, 163 compared *Hrgb* with Akk. *argabu,* name of a bird.

eagles, Danel actually found in her inwards fat and bone, and identified them as those of his son. It is interesting that in this instance Danel did not ask Baal to restore *Ṣml* as well—she was killed permanently. Danel buried and bewailed *Aqht*'s remnants, for the performance of these ceremonies even over a fraction of the corpse insured that the spirit of the dead would have rest in the Nether World, and permitted hope for his resurrection in the flesh—which, most probably, happened after seven years.

But what in common can the she-eagle *Ṣml* [1] have had with Cadmos' daughter Semele? The commentators of the *Aqht* poem did not pay sufficient attention to the fact that *Ṣml* was one of the goddesses of the Ugaritic pantheon. In the above quoted list of Ugaritic gods and of the offerings they received (text UM 1), figures (line 14) *Ṣml,* recipient of "a large beast".[2] Her eagle-likeness, thus, does not preclude her being adored in human shape —as El was a bull, Baal a young bull, Anath a cow and a winged creature, her son Muš a serpent, Ḥoron a falcon, and so on.[3] The very fact of *Ṣml*'s being a part of the myth cycle of *Aqht* is sufficient for her to merit our close attention, for we have already seen that *Aqht* and the story of his death were included in the Cadmeian cycle as the myth of Actaeon, and Actaeon was not only a cousin but also an avatar of Dionysos-Zagreus who had perished by the same atrocious death. Like *Aqht,* Dionysos was killed, dismembered, eaten and again resurrected in a new incarnation through Semele—but not by an ordinary birth. As Baal did with the she-eagle *Ṣml,* Zeus killed Semele with his lightning and exorted from her womb the unborn babe Dionysos—as Danel extorted the remnants of *Aqht* from *Ṣml*'s inwards. The identity of *Ṣml* and Semele is definite-

[1] Its root is *ṣml,* Arab. *ṣamala* "to be hard, tough, rigid." It was used in Mishnaic Hebrew as a term. techn. for swelling and hardening of a girl's breast. In an economic text from Ugarit RŠ 15.62 (DXXIV, No. 127), the merchant *Ybnn* delivered, among other things, 5 talents of *ṣml* (an unknown merchandise) for 10 shekels. GASTER, in his translation of the Aqht epic *ap.* CLXXXVI, renders *Ṣml* by "Toughie"; this is quite an appropriate name for an eagle.

[2] In his transliteration of UM 1 : 14, GORDON put a question-mark after *l,* but in VIROLLEAUD's autography, DXVI, pl. LXI, *ṣml* is perfectly clear. In his translation of this text, CCXXIII, 112, GORDON italicized *Ṣml.* However, this mention of *Ṣml* is not included in his Glossary, UM § 20.1634, nor in AISTLEITNER's IIIa, No. 2326.

[3] In UM 1 : 14, *Ṣml* is mentioned after *Ušḫry* (the Sumerian goddess Išḫara) and *Ym* (the Sea-god Yamm), and before *Yrḫ* (the Moon-god Yariḫ). Thus, she cannot be considered an insignificant figure.

ly established by the following version told by Hyginus, *Fabulae* 167:[1]

> Liber (Latin name of Dionysos), son of Jupiter and Proserpine, was dismembered by the Titans. His heart, reduced into powder, was given by Jupiter in a beverage to Semele. And when Semele became pregnant because of it, Juno turned into Semele's nurse Beroë and said to her: "Child, ask Jupiter that he appear to you in the shape in which he appears to Juno: in order that you know how great is the pleasure to lie with a god." Semele, provoked by it, addressed such a request to Jupiter and was killed by lightning. Jupiter extracted Liber from her womb and gave him to Nysos to be raised, whence Liber received the name of Dionysos and began to be called "born by two mothers."

So a myth existed that Semele had eaten the heart of the dismembered Dionysos-Zagreus, as *Ṣml* had swallowed some of the remnants of *Aqht*! Hyginus' version not only is not a late one, but it goes back to immemorial archaic times when it was believed that pregnancy could be caused by absorbing magic food. It is easy to understand why it was not used by the tragedy-writers and mythographers of the classical Greek epoch: it was too naïve and primitive for their refined tastes. But in the second millennium this motif appears in Oriental literature. One may quote the Hurrian myth of Kumarbi who bit off and swallowed the genitalia of his father Anu and, though a male, became pregnant by them.[2] Still closer to our theme is one of the episodes of the famous Egypto-Phoenician tale of the two brothers, where Bata—another avatar of the dying and resurrected god—was killed in the shape of a bull at the demand of his treacherous wife who had become the wife of the Pharaoh; two persea trees grew up from drops of his blood, in which he was incarnated. When the treacherous wife learned of this, she ordered the perseas cut down, but while her order was being executed, a small fragment of wood accidentally flew into her mouth and was swallowed by her; it impregnated her and she bore a new incarnation of Bata who inherited the Pharaoh's throne.

The establishment of the identity of Semele, daughter of Cadmos and mother of Dionysos, with the Ugaritic goddess *Ṣml* is not only important for corroborating the Semitism of the Cadmeian cycle and its close dependence upon the epic literature of the West Semites: it also brings us closer to the recognition of important

[1] Hyginus, a writer of the Roman epoch, has collected many ancient and otherwise forgotten tales and variants.

[2] CCXXXIX, 124, I: 25-36.

and essential Semitic elements in the mighty cycle of Dionysiac myth and cult, where nobody earnestly looked for them.

Pentheus, the Doublet of Bacchos

Another grandson of Cadmos, his daughter Agave's son by Echion, was Pentheus. It was told—particularly in Euripides' *Bacchae*—that the old Cadmos ceded to him rule over Thebes, and that in his time Dionysos came to Thebes, claiming that he was the son of Semele and Zeus and introducing his orgiastic cult. Pentheus opposed it by all his means, but the Dionysiac madness seized Theban women, including his own mother and aunts, they ran away in frenzy to the Cithaeron mountains, rending animals and eating their flesh raw, and when Pentheus, disguised as a woman, went to see it, they mistook him for a lion and tore him to pieces.

Dismembering the victims (*sparagmos*) and eating them raw (*ômophagia*) belong to the essential elements of the Bacchic cult.[1] But the same is told, on the mythical plane, of the god himself in whose honor this rite was performed: the "first Dionysos," or Zagreus, was killed, torn asunder and eaten by the Titans. In the Bacchic cult, the sacrifice still remained in its first, magic stage, and did not evolve to its second, religious stage: the sacrifice was not a gift to the god, not his share at the sacrificial meal of the clan, but it represented the god himself, killed to maintain the world order and eaten in a sacramental communion in order that all participants may partake and absorb his divine essence.[2] The victim of the bloody Bacchic rites impersonated the god; god was sacrificed to himself. One of the most important personalities of the Dionysiac cult, Orpheus, perished the same death as Pentheus; and he has many features of a dying god, including his descent to and return from Hades. So Pentheus is a doublet of Dionysos, and their separation and the justification of Pentheus' death because of his enmity toward Dionysos is a common aetiological mode of mythology. Thus the boar who killed Adonis and was sacrificed to him in special cases, originally was Adonis himself, killed in the rite of communion; thus sacrificing goats to Dionysos was aetiologically

[1] Gilbert Murray, in his "Excursus on the Ritual Forms Preserved in Greek Tragedy," *ap.* CCXLVIII, 341-363, showed that the central element underlying Greek tragedy was the "unspoken" *sparagmos* of Dionysos. See also pp. 178 ss. below.

[2] As explained by Robertson Smith and Frazer.

motivated by Dionysos' hatred for the goats who damage the vines, although Dionysos himself was worshipped in the shape of a goat.[1]

Pentheus is a doublet of Dionysos-Zagreus not only in his death, but in his birth as well. As Zagreus was conceived by Persephone from Zeus who took the shape of a dragon,[2] as the Sumerian Tammuz (Dumuzi) was the son of Ningišzida, the serpent and dragon god,[3] so Pentheus, too, was the son of Echion "the serpent-man." As Euripides emphatically expresses it (*Bacchae* 537-544), "Pentheus betrays the chthonic race, brought up once by the dragon; begotten by the chthonic Echion, he is a grim-visaged monster and not a scion of mortals." And from his mother's side he was the grandson of Cadmos, changed into (i.e., symbolized by) a serpent.

The same is shown by the name Pentheus, which exactly fits a dying god. It comes from the verb *pentheô* "to grieve, to wail," noun *penthos* "sorrow, grief, weeping, wailing, cause of grief." Weeping for the dying gods was the essential rite of their liturgy. "For Tammuz, the lover of thy youth, thou hast ordained wailing (*bitakku*, root *bakû*) year after year," says Gilgameš to Ištar (*Gilg.* VI: 46-47), and still in the days of Ezechiel women wailed for (*m^ebakkôt*) Tammuz near the northern gate of the Jerusalem temple (Ez. 8: 14). Danel wept for (1 p. *abky*, 3d p. *ybky*) the slain *Aqht* for seven years, assisted by "weeping women" (*bkyt*) and "wailing women" (*mšspdt*). Phoenicians wept for Adonis, Greeks bewailed Dionysos by tragic threnodies.

But if Pentheus is a doublet of Dionysos, and if his name comes from "weeping, wailing" for a dying god, why not explain in the same way one of the most popular names of Dionysos himself—Bacchos (*Bakchos*, *Bakcheus*)? An unbiased man, not overwhelmed by the taboos of the Beloch school or by the postulate of the Thracian origin of the Dionysiac cult (see below) is brought step by step, almost against his own will, to an etymology of *Bakchos* from the common Semitic root *bky* (Akk. *bakû*, Ugar. *bky*, Heb.

[1] CLXXV, VII, 22 s. For Pentheus as originally Dionysos himself, cf. CLXII, V, 167 s.

[2] Zeus was Persephone's father; here again, the motif of incest, connected with the birth of Adonis, is present.

[3] Here too a case of incest may be implied. Geštinanna (Bêlit-ṣêri) was Ningišzida's wife, but she was also called Dumuzi's sister. She bears the name of a tree (*geštin* "vine"), as occurs in many related myths (Myrrha, Tamar, word-play Europa-willow). Was she perhaps transformed into a vine in some lost myth, as Myrrha into a myrrh-tree?

bākâ) "to weep, to wail." Both the sense and the analogy with *Bakcheus* suggest, as its W-S prototype, the passive part. which in Hebrew sounds *bākūy* "the bewailed." [1] It is hard to imagine a better epithet for the most typical dying and solemnly bewailed god of the Greek pantheon; and the only other explanation given to it was that it was nothing but an inarticulate cry.[2]

The historico-religious side of the problem will be treated in the next section. Here we will dwell on the linguistic and phonetic aspect of the suggested etymology. Could the Semitic *kaph* have been rendered by the Greek combination of the hard and the spirantized consonants *kch*? Not only could it have, but it actually and frequently was—and without direct relation to whether or not the *kaph* had a dageš (forte or lene). So *Zakāy* Neh. 7: 14 is transcribed in LXX by (genitive) *Zakchu*; *Zakkūr* ibid. 3: 2 etc. by *Zakchur*; *Sukkôt* Ex. 12: 37 and Judg. 8: 16 by *Sokchôt*, *Rekâb* II Sam 4: 6 by *Rekcha*. An analogous Greek rendering of the Egyptian royal name *Bokenranf* is *Bokchoris*. Another similar mode of transcribing the Semitic *kaph* (again without regard for gemination) is the Greek *gch*: thus *'Ākîš* I Sam. 21: 11 etc. becomes in LXX *Agchus*, Phoenician *Sakkun-yatōn* becomes Greek *Sagchuniathôn* (the Greeks, of course, read *gch* nasalized *nch*). Analogous to it is the transcription of the geminated Semitic *p* by Greek *pph*, e.g. *Ṣippôrā* Ex. 2: 21 becomes *Sepphora* in LXX; but ungeminated *p* in (*Ba'al*) — *Ṣephôn* Ex. 14: 2 becomes, too, (*Beel*) *Sepphôn*. There is, besides, clear and undeniable proof of the phonetic correctness of our etymology in a lexical statement by Hesychios: *bakchon*: *klauthmon*: *Phoinikes*; *klauthmon* or *klauthmos* means "weeping, howling, wailing, especially at a funeral." [3]

[1] There may be also another explanation. Not only the god was called *Bakchos*: his orgiasts, too, were *bakchoi* (sg. *bakchos*) if men, *bakchai* (sg. *bakchê*) if women. The god of the wailers may have received his epithet from them.

[2] E.g., CCXLVII, 413: "Iacchos and probably Bacchos itself, though they ultimately became proper names, were originally only cries." See pp. 192 ss. below.

[3] H. LEWY, CCCXXX, 138 did not detect in Hesychios' statement anything beyond the possibility of a "popular-etymological hint to Bacchos." V. BÉRARD passed by the cult of Dionysos in complete silence. R. BROWN, LXXXI, 137 assured that in his two-volume work, *The Great Dionysiac Myth* (1877-1878), he had "proved" the Semitic origin of *Bacchos* from . . . Melqart (*sic*), namely: *Mlqrt* > *Mlqr* > *Bkr* > *Bko* > *Bakchos*. It is easy to imagine what harm was done by that kind of book to the cause of Hellenosemitic research.

Semitic Elements in the Cult of Dionysos

> Greek religion was a many-sided thing. To the man of a studious age it appears rather to be a medley of religions, and as investigators we try to separate the threads and trace each one back to its own beginning.
>
> Guthrie.[1]

a) *The Alleged Thracian Origin*

There prevailed for a long time—and still prevails in books written in the pre-Ventris era—the conviction that Dionysos was not one of the fundamental Greek gods, that he was unknown not only in the Mycenaean, but even in the Homeric age, and was introduced into Greece from Thrace as late as in the VIIIth century.[2] We will not dwell on the precariousness of this approach from the standpoint of methodology, since the Thracian culture, religion and even the language are all but completely unknown. We will also postpone until later proof that the so-called Thracians of Middle Greece mentioned in Greek myths, had nothing in common with the historical inhabitants of the northeast of the Balkan peninsula. However, it must be mentioned that even at the time of the absolute rule of the Thracian theory, such prominent scholars in the field of Greek religion as O. Gruppe and W. Otto, on the basis of an objective investigation of the Greek materials, came to a diametrically opposite conclusion. Gruppe (1906) argued that Dionysos was one of the oldest deities in Greece, and that if the Thracians really adhered to his cult, it had been brought to Thrace by Greek settlers, and not vice versa.[3] Otto, in his instructive and absorbing book on Dionysos (1933), convincingly showed that the theories of the late penetration of Dionysos from Thrace into Greece are devoid of foundation; Dionysiac feasts go back to a very ancient epoch, before the Ionian settlement in Asia Minor; Homer knew Dionysos and most of the myths connected with him.[4]

Great importance was ascribed to Herodotos' evidence that the

[1] ccxlii, 6.

[2] This thesis was broadly expounded and defended ccxlvii, chapt. VIII, 363-463; cf. also dxlviii, II, 59-62; cclxxxvii, I, 206; cdxxxii, 256-260; clxii, V, 87-95; cdxi, V, 1, 1011 s.; ccclxxx, I, 564-568 ("The Ionians got acquainted with him from the Thracian tribes of Asia Minor"); ccclxxxi, 567-574; ccxli, 154. Mentions of Dionysos and Maenads in the *Iliad* (VI: 130 ss. and XIV: 325) were declared late interpolations.

[3] ccxxxv, II, 1409 s.

[4] cdi, 51-62.

Thracians worshipped Ares, Dionysos and Artemis (V: 7) and that the Thracian tribe of the Satrae possessed an oracle of Dionysos (VII: 10). But this is only the syncretic mode, so characteristic for Herodotos and other Greek authors, to name foreign deities by the names of Greek deities of a more or less similar nature. Neither Herodotos nor any other Greek author ever stated that the Thracians actually gave these names to their gods. On the contrary, modern scholars somehow closed their eyes completely to the same Herodotos who called the Egyptian Osiris, Dionysos (II: 41, 47, 48, 49, 144), an Ethiopian god, Dionysos (III: 97) and stated that the Arabs of the Sinai peninsula worshipped only Urania and Dionysos whom they called Alilat and Orotalt (III: 8). Great attention was also paid to the Thracian location by some authors of the fabulous land of Nysa where Dionysos was raised; but this location was no better than any other: Sophocles (*Antig.* 1131) and others located it in Boeotia, Herodotos (II: 146) in Ethiopia, Antimachos (ap. Diod. Sic. III: 65) in Arabia, the Homeric hymn to Dionysos (ibid. III: 66) in the mountains of Phoenicia, near the stream of Egypt.

The minority attitude of GRUPPE and OTTO was proven to be the only correct one. The excavations at Mycenaean Pylos and the decipherment of Mycenaean script by VENTRIS, revealed in a fragment of a Pylian inscription (Xa. 102) the name of Dionysos in genitive case: *Diwonusojo*.[1] But we have seen that the Mycenaean epoch was a time of appreciable Semitic ethnic and cultural penetration into Greece. The Greeks themselves unanimously attached their god Dionysos to the Phoenician family of Cadmos in Thebes. Boeotia was the main center for the propagation of the Dionysiac cult throughout Greece. We made sure in the previous sections that the Cadmeian myths of his mother, his birth, his avatars, contain a remarkable number not of circumstantial, but of direct proofs of the correctness of the Greek tradition. Let us continue our analysis in order to detect further Semitic parallels—not to the conception of the dying god in general which was a universal idea, and not with the aim of embracing the entirety of the enormous material concerning Dionysiac cults which certainly included

[1] DV, 127; XCIX, 124; CCCXLVIII, 291. Even if this is a human name (like the classical *Dionysios*), it anyway implicates the cult of the *god* Dionysos. [In a Linear B tablet from Pylos, discovered in 1960 (Xb 1419), *Di-wo-nu-so-jo* occurs again, accompanied by *wo-no-wa-ti-si*, a term composed with *wo-no* = *woinos* "wine", cf. A. HEUBECK, *Kadmos*, I/1, 62 s.]

elements of very heterogenous origin. Our purpose is more limited: we will try to show that quite a number of essential rites, mythical motifs, phraseological turns, technical terms, and proper names, which are peculiar to the Dionysiac cult, can be found and identified in the Semitic Orient.

b) *Dismemberment and Eating of Raw Meat*

The tearing to pieces (more correctly, and in more realistic terms, cutting or chopping asunder [1]) of the victim and eating it raw was the essential rite of the Bacchic orgies. One may doubt whether this was actually performed in practice in the classical period, but it remained extraordinarily vivid in the memory of all subsequent generations, it was reflected in the bright colors in all epics, dramas, hymns and myths, relating to the Dionysiac-Orphic cycle. For specious reasons, this rite was usually believed to be Thracian, though it was attested not among the Thracians, but mainly in Crete, where there were no Thracian settlements. On the contrary, it is very well known—both in ritual and in myth—in the Semitic East.

Jane HARRISON, one of the most convinced advocates of the Thracian theory, failed to find, however, a more salient and impressive example of *sparagmos* and *ômophagia* than the description of sacrifices among the Sinaitic Saracens given by Pseudo-Nilus, a Christian writer of the IVth century A.D.[2] And indeed, that ritual, already studied with much care by the investigators of Semitic religions, WELLHAUSEN [3] and ROBERTSON SMITH,[4] is extremely

[1] It must be specified that a man is unable to tear asunder with his bare hands an animal larger than a rabbit, and he is unable to bite through the hide of any animal, especially a large one. When Euripides writes (*Bacchae* 1125 ss.) that Agave tore out Pentheus' shoulder and so on, this is poetic licence, and Euripides himself ascribed such superhuman strength to direct participation of the god. Actually, as this is known from medieval practice, at least four horses are needed to dismember a man. Even the earliest man needed sharp tools in order to be able to consume the flesh of killed animals. Therefore, though poetic and ritual texts speak of "rending," it must be understood that the dismemberment used to be accomplished by means of cutting instruments (or horses, cf. p. 254 below).

[2] CCXLVII, 485 s., where the relevant text is translated in full. It is now proven that the work called *Narrationes* (whence the text is taken) was written not by St. Nilus, but by another Christian writer of the IVth century A.D.; but since the author was well acquainted with the customs of the Sinaitic Arabs of his time, this changes nothing in the reliability of his description. Cf. XLI, concluding note.

[3] DXLVI, 57 s.

[4] CDXXVIII, 282, 338, 491.

significant. The Saracens usually sacrificed handsome captive youths to their chief goddess, the Morning Star;[1] but if human victims were not available, a perfect white camel could be substituted. After having turned three times in a processional pace around the bound victim, the Arabs, following the example of the ceremonial leader, rushed on the camel, inflicted blows upon it with swords and knives, drank its warm blood, cut off from its quivering body piece after piece, and hurriedly ate them raw, so that by morning nothing would remain of the victim. Pseudo-Nilus' description agrees with an old Arabic term for a sacrifice brought by victorious warriors out of the spoils, *naqīʿa,* properly meaning "splitting" or "rending."[2]

There are, however, much older examples of this custom, namely in Israel. Under Saul (end of XIth century), Israelite warriors, after their victory over the Philistines, ate the raw flesh of animals taken as spoils—only the blood, at the insistence of the king, was poured on an improvised stone altar as the deity's share (I Sam. 14: 32-35). This happened at night, like the Arab omophagical sacrifice described by Pseudo-Nilus,—a fast having been proclaimed for the entire preceding day (until evening)—in order that the profane food should not mix in the stomachs with the sacred meat of the communion feast.[2] It is evident that this was a solemn sacrificial meal of victorious warriors. On another solemn occasion, in order to assemble an armed levy, the same Saul cut to pieces a pair of oxen and sent the pieces to all ends of the country—and it is very significant that he did it while being possessed by the spirit of God, i.e. in a state of ecstasy (I Sam. 11: 6-7). Again the same Saul saved the captive king of Amalek, Agag, for the purpose of sacrificing him to Yahwe, and this was performed by Samuel by cutting him to pieces (I Sam. 15: 33). All these rites and customs seemed already strange and archaic at the time when the stories mentioning

[1] South Arabs deified Venus as the god ʿAṯtar, but the corresponding deity of the North Arabs, ʿAtarsamain, was female. Herodotos (III: 8) cited her Arabic name Alilat ("the goddess") and correctly translated her epithet *-samain* "that of the heaven" by the Greek Urania. In Arabic-Aramaic inscriptions of the Vth century she is named (with the article *han-* instead of *ʾal-*) *han-Ilat* (CDXXIII, 2-8; CDXXII, 154). Isaac of Antioch, a Syriac Christian writer, calls this goddess *Kaukabta* "the female star." According to Herodotos (*loc. cit.*), she was the wife of the Arabic counterpart of Dionysos. Cf. XLI.

[2] CDXXVIII, 491.

[3] For this aetiology of fast, cf. CDXXVIII, 434.

them were written down; they were provided with aetiological explanations and often misunderstood.

Retreating further back, to the middle of the IId millennium, i.e. to the epoch contemporary with the Mycenaean age in Greece, many analogous motifs are found in the Ugaritic mythological literature. One example—the killing of *Aqht* and his being torn to pieces by eagles—has already been seen in connection with Dionysos' avatar Actaeon. It follows from the description of Anath killing the god of the Nether World Môt, depicted here as a typical "harvest spirit" (I AB = UM 49: II: 31-37), that Anath not only cleaved him with her sword, but chopped him to small pieces, for she winnows and sows him in the field.[1] Further, two descriptions of Anath's massacre of some people are relevant: she cuts off their heads and hands and bathes in their blood.[2] But the most startling text was found at the excavations of Ras Shamra in 1959 and published as RŠ 22.225.[3] It begins as follows:

(1) *ʿnt hlkt w šnwt*
(2) *tp aḫh w nʿm aḫh* (3) *k ysmsm*
tspi širh (4) 1 *bl ḥrb*
tšt dmh (5) *l bl ks*

(1) Anath goes and admires(?)
(2) her brother's timbrel and her brother's grace (3) as most beautiful.
She ate his flesh (4) without a knife,
She drank his blood (5) without a cup.

Anath's divine brother (Virolleaud does not doubt that this refers, as everywhere else in the Ugaritic myths, to Baal) was, thus, beating his timbrel (and perhaps singing, if "grace" stands here for "pleasant voice") when he was surprised by the goddess and became her victim. The timbrel was the sacred musical instrument peculiar

[1] Nilsson, ccclxxxi, 566 s., distinguished two independent elements in the Dionysiac cult: 1) "the trieteric orgia in which the god is dismembered and eaten in the shape of an animal," 2) "the conception of the new-born child in the winnowing-fan and of the death of the god; here he is clearly the spirit of vegetation." He declared the former element Thracian, the latter Phrygian. The Ugaritic myth, however, shows that the motifs of dismemberment and of the vegetation spirit were not mutually exclusive and might be applied to the same god.

[2] xcvii, 51.

[3] dxx (appeared in December 1961). I owe my earlier knowledge of the tablet to the kindness of Professor Virolleaud. For all details of the translation of the quoted lines and of their sequel, and for the general interpretation of the fragment, cf. xli.

to Bacchic festivals and mysteries. This close connection of the timbrel, sparagmos and omophagia in just five short lines of the Ugaritic fragment shows that Herodotos (II: 49) was on the right track in presuming that the Greeks "learned about the cult of Dionysos mostly from the Tyrian Cadmos and from those who came together with him from Phoenicia into the land which is now called Boeotia."

The tremendous importance of the Ugaritic evidence cannot be exaggerated. This is by far the closest analogy to the Dionysiac sanguinary cult known up to now. It is evident that these scenes reflect, on the mythological plane, the custom of personifying Baal himself in the slain and dismembered victim. It is hardly probable that sacral cannibalism was actually performed in the Syria of middle second millennium. It should rather be assumed that an animal was substituted in this ritual to be eaten raw. In the Ugaritic text, the conception of theophagy appears in the most naked form: the god is killed not by an enemy, and not as an enemy, but by his own sister, spouse and defender—as the adorers of Dionysos themselves killed and ate their god in order to partake of his divinity.[1]

c) *Ecstatic Cults and Mantics*

The most peculiar feature of Dionysiac feasts was their ecstatic character. The participants of the orgies, and especially the female ones, were supposed to bring themselves to "a hieratic state of holy madness"; [2] they were called the Maenads (*Mainades*) from *mainomenô* "to be in a frenzy," and designated by other names of similar signification. "The worshipers of Dionysos believed that they were possessed by god." [3] Having driven themselves to a frenzy by shrill music, dancing, shouting, running, jumping and whirling, they were supposed to perform strange and extraordinary acts in a state of complete temporary madness, without realizing or being responsible for their deeds. All this was so contrary to the renowned clarity,

[1] Already the ancients (Herodotos, Plutarch) felt the strong resemblance between Dionysos and Osiris. Otto, CDI, 181, correctly noticed: "In fact, the comparison of Dionysos to Osiris . . . is much more rational than the comparison with Thracian, Phrygian, and Minoan deities. But the myth of Osiris' death differs in too many important points from the Dionysiac," which he convincingly enumerates.

[2] CCXLVII, 395.

[3] *Ibid.*, 474.

serenity and rationalism of Greek genius, that the source of these customs was sought among the barbarian tribes of the northern Balkans or Asia Minor.

However, the classical land of religious ecstasy and cultic exaltation was the region of the West Semites, from the Mediterranean to the Euphrates. True, it was supposed that the Babylonian *maḫḫû*-priests were indubitable ecstatics and that their very name signified "madmen." [1] But this institution did not have a noticeable development in Babylonian life. On the contrary, in W-S Mari, as early as the XVIIIth century, possessed soothsayers called *muḫḫum* had a great influence.[2] In subsequent centuries ecstatic madness and cultic states of possession were characteristic of Phoenicia. Gustav Hölscher, in his *Die Profeten* (1914), collected much evidence on it, and connected it with the prophetic movement in Israel, especially in its earlier stages. We refer to his detailed summary and analysis of the ecstatic element in Israelite prophecy, for a wider exposition of that problem on these pages would be too great a digression from our immediate topic. But it is characteristic of the fundamental attitude of that time, which silently admitted the existence of some impenetrable barrier between Greece and the Semitic East, that in collecting parallels Hölscher did not pay any attention to Greek Bacchism. On the other hand, the renowned investigator of Greek religion, Erwin Rohde, posed the question: what was the real goal of the intentional Bacchic frenzy? and answered: "this madness," the state "of being overwhelmed, 'possessed' by a foreign power," "found effective application in the *mantic* and *telestic* arts"; [3] the *hieromania* was conducive to prophecy, "the *Mainads* are the official exponents of this *mantikê* of inspiration." [4] But he, on his part, did not even mention Hebrew parallels.

However, in Euripides' *Bacchae*, one of our best sources on the essence of Bacchism, the Bacchants directly call themselves

[1] cccxxxvii, 92 s.; dxxxiii, 400.

[2] dxxxiii, 401 ss.; ccc, 103 ss.; cdvii, 118.

[3] cdxxxii, 255.

[4] *Ibid.*, 260. Albright, xvi, 304 s. reported, it is true, earlier opinions regarding Israelite prophecy as an aspect of Dionysiac frenzy, but his unnamed predecessors and himself considered both as a phenomenon limited to the first millennium and ascribed the common origin of prophecy, Bacchism and the Assyrian *maḫḫû* to Asia Minor. We have learned since that the earliest occurrence of ecstatic prophets was as early as the XVIIIth century and as far from Asia Minor as Mari.

"prophets" (*prophêtai*) of Dionysos (l. 551), and the wise Teiresias defines Dionysos in this way (l. 298-301):

> A prophet (*mantis*) is this deity: the Bacchic frenzy and madness are full of prophecy (*mantikê*); for, when the god in his fullness enters their bodies, he makes his maddened ones tell the future.

Euripides' words are at the same time the most exhaustive definition of early prophecy among the Hebrews. Early Hebrew prophecy and Bacchism are identical both in their essence and in concrete details. All fundamental phenomena of Dionysiac ecstasy appear with the greatest clarity in Israel, which inherited ecstatic prophecy from the Canaanites,[1] and was the only W-S people to have left sufficient written evidence on it.

Here is a well-known place which is one of the principal pieces of evidence on the essence of ecstatic prophecy in archaïc Israel. Samuel says to Saul (I Sam. 10: 5b-6):

> when thou wilt enter the town, thou wilt meet a swarm of prophets descending the holy height, and in front of them are a harp, and a timbrel, and a flute, and a lyre, and they are prophesying. And thou wilt be seized by the spirit of Yahwe, and thou wilt prophesy with them, and thou wilt be changed into a different man.

The verb conventionally translated by "to prophesy" (*hitnabbē'*), a denominative from *nābî'* "prophet" (literally, "one called" by a god [2]), had not only the sense of foretelling the future, but also of "being crazy," "behaving like a madman." "To be among the prophets" for a respectable member of the aristocracy as Saul, was considered as strange and reprehensible (I Sam. 10: 11-12), just as Pentheus, in Euripides' representation, judged intolerable the participation of his mother and relatives in Bacchic frenzy.

How this "prophesying" looked in practice, is seen from another story about Saul, also explaining the origin of the phrase "is Saul, too, among the prophets?" I Sam. 19: 20-24. It shows that prophecy was a form of mass ecstasy and was very contagious, as hysterical phenomena usually are: many servants of Saul were "seized by the spirit of God," and finally "the spirit of God" seized Saul too, "and he too took off his clothes, and he too prophesied in front of Samuel, and he fell down naked, all that day and all night." Still, in the stories of Elijah and Elisha, describing the times of the IXth century, there is mention of the spirit of God which carries away

[1] CCLVII, first part; CCCXL, 221; cf. p. 182, n. 1 above.
[2] CCCXXXVII, 102; XLVI, II, 422, n. 1.

the prophets one does not know whither (I Kings 18: 12), far away into mountains and valleys (II Kings 2: 16),—as Bacchic rapture rushed male and female Bacchants into wild mountain woods (e.g. *Bacchae*: 114-119). Even at that time, the terms "prophet" (member of a prophetic brotherhood) and "madman" were synonyms (II Kings 9: 1, 11).[1]

Like the worshipers of Dionysos, the W-S ecstatic prophets usually acted not individually, but in considerable groups. We hear once of 450 Phoenician prophets of Baal assembled on Mount Carmel (I Kings 18: 22) and of 400 Israelite prophets of Yahwe (ibid. 22: 6-12). It is said of the former that while sacrificing to their god and calling to him for an apparition, they danced around the altar, shouted and wounded themselves with knives. One of the latter, while prophesying among the crowd of 400 prophets before King Ahab, fastened to his head iron horns (ibid. 22: 11),—as the women Bacchants on the Boeotian Mount Laphystos were called "horn-wearing women." [2] It is not easy to deduce from Greek poetic texts that the free-revelling Bacchants were organized into bands as the Israelite "sons of prophets" were; but in historical times, every city had its own college of women called *Thyiades* ("rushing ones") to perform the biennial orgies of Dionysos on Mount Parnassos.[3]

We are prone to associate the Bacchic ecstatic orgies with women, and the Hebrew prophetic movement with men. But the Bacchic revels were mixed—not only female *Bakchai*, but also male *Bakchoi* took part in them. Pentheus mistakes Dionysos for such a male Bacchant (*Bacchae*: 491), and considers that night festivals provide women with opportunities for lewdness (ibid. 222-225, 487). In the play *Ion*: 549-555, Euripides makes Xuthos participate in the night celebrations of the Bacchanals along with Maenads. On the other hand, women prophetesses existed among the Hebrews. As late as 622 B.C. the prophetess Hulda played an important rôle in Josiah's reform (II Kings 22: 14 ss.) A hundred years earlier, Isaiah speaks of a prophetess whom he approached on Yahwe's order—probably in a state of ecstasy—and who con-

[1] Conversely, the verb which in Hebrew means "to be mad" (*šāgaʿ*) has in Arabic (*sağaʿa*) the sense of uttering unclear and enigmatic prophecies in a state of possession, cf. CCLVII, 93, 130.

[2] *Schol. ad Lycophr.* 1237, cf. CDXXXII, 257 and n. 19.

[3] CCXLVII, 391-396; CLXII, V, 151-155 (both with extensive references to literary and epigraphic sources).

ceived from him and bore a son (Is. 8: 3). It is usually taken for granted that this prophetess was Isaiah's wife (as in French "Madame la générale"), but this assumption does not follow from anything in the text; [1] on the contrary, marital relations with one's own wife would hardly merit a special notice.

The more one goes back in time, the greater is the similarity with Greece. Two famous prophetesses, Deborah and Miriam, belong to the legendary heroic times. The former is named in Judg. 4: 4 *'ēšet Lappidôt* which is understood as "the wife of (a man called) Lappidot"—but we are inclined to see in this name simply a common noun, the plural of *lappîd* "torch," and to understand it as a relic of the nightly festivities with torches, so characteristic for the Greek Bacchanals (e.g. *Bacchae*: 146). According to Judg. 4: 5 "she sat under the palm-tree (or "pillar," *tômer*) of Deborah between Ramah and Bethel in the mountains of Ephraim"—which commentators identify with the tree mentioned in Gen. 35: 8: "And Deborah, the wet nurse of Rebecca, died and was buried below Bethel, under the terebinth; and he (Jacob) called it the 'terebinth of wailing' (*'allôn bākût*)." The two Deborahs, the prophetess and the nurse, are evidently the same figure; and in the oldest Greek literary mention of Dionysos and his Maenads (*Iliad* VI: 130 ss.) the latter are styled "nurses of the maddened Bacchos." *Bākût* "wailing" is—as shown above—the exact linguistic prototype of the Bacchanals. Moreover, *d*ᵉ*bôrā* is Hebrew for "bee"; the priestesses of the Ephesian Artemis (whose cult contained more than a few Semitic and Hittite features [2]) were called *melissai* "bees"; Thriae, the nurses of Hermes as the Maenads were nurses of Dionysos, prophesied in a state of holy madness and were represented as bees (*Hom. Hym. to Hermes*: 551-563).[3] As to Miriam, Ex. 15: 20 says about her: "And Miriam the prophetess, the sister of Aaron, took a timbrel in her hand, and all the women came out behind her with timbrels and dances." But for the proper names, this verse could easily be taken as a quotation from the *Bacchae*! The timbrel, by the way, was the sacral musical instrument of the Bacchants.[4]

[1] As to the definite article in *han-n*ᵉ*bî'ā*, cf. Amos 2: 7b *w*ᵉ*-'îš w*ᵉ*-'ābîw yēl*ᵉ*kû 'el-han-na'arā* "and a man and his father go to *a* girl," not to some specified particular girl.

[2] CDXV, 193 s., 213, 554-572; CDLXXXVI.

[3] CCXLVII, 441 ss.

[4] And of the dismembered and devoured god in the Ugaritic sparagmos-text (see p. 180 above). For music as a means of ecstatic inspiration, cf. II Kings 3: 15 and I Sam. 10: 5b-6 quoted p. 183 above.

d) *Attributes, Accessories, and Terms*

In things connected with Dionysos and his cult, strangely familiar Biblical symbolism and phraseology is found everywhere. Dionysos was the giver of water: near Messenian Cyparission a spring was said to have been struck from the soil by his wand (thyrsos) and was therefore named Dionysias (Paus. 4: 36: 7). The same faculty was ascribed to his Bacchants when possessed: they struck from cliffs streams of fresh water (Eurip. *Bacchae* 764 ss.), drew milk and honey from rivers (Plato *Ion*: 534a), and at their festivities, the earth ran with milk, wine, and honey (Eurip. *Bacchae*: 141).[1]

Like the Babylonian Tammuz,[2] the Phoenician Adonis and the Byblian god identified by the Egyptians with Osiris, Dionysos was thought to be within a tree; in Boeotia, he was named *Endendros* (Hesychios). His principal tree was the pine; [3] this relates him not only to Osiris, whose corpse grew into the trunk of a pine, but also to Bata, the hero of an Egypto-Phoenician myth,[4] who appears in the well-known "Tale of the Two Brothers," and presents a considerable similarity to many details of the myth of Dionysos. Bata, in this tale, places his heart among the cones of a pine and dies when the pine is cut. Of the animals, the favorite symbol of Dionysos was the bull; in Crete, he was killed in the shape of a bull both in myth as Zagreus, and in ritual in the rite of omophagy; Bata, too, transformed himself into a bull and was killed in its shape, but was revived as two persea-trees which grew from drops of blood of the slain bull.

The main sacral accessory of the Bacchanals were thyrsi—long wooden wands, wrapped with ivy-leaves and often topped with a

[1] Cf. also CDI, 89 s.

[2] Identified by FRANKFORT and CONTENAU on an Old Babylonian seal, cf. CIV, 46.

[3] CDI, 146.

[4] We insist on the presence of a strong Phoenician element in that tale, written under the XIXth dynasty, when several Phoenician myths (as that of Astarte and the Sea-god Yamm, CCCXXIII, 106-113) entered the Egyptian literature. The action of the tale takes place, for a great part, in the Valley of Pines (or Cedars), i.e. in the Lebanon. The magic role of the pine (cedar), which would have no reason in treeless Egypt, has strong analogies in the Gilgameš epic; the life of Ḫumbaba, the guardian of the cedar-forest in Lebanon (according to the Old Babylonian fragment LV, rev. 13) depends on a cedar which must be cut down before he can be killed. Furthermore, Bata's slander by an enamored woman and his self-castration are identical with the Syrian legend of Combabos (= Ḫumbaba!), told by Lucian, *De Deâ Syriâ*, 19-27.

pine-cone. *Thyrsos* has no Greek etymology. But Heb. *tirôš*, Ugar. *trš*,[1] Danunian (Karatepe) *trš* means "freshly pressed grape-juice", poetically "wine." In EA 228: 3 a king of Hazor Abdi-Tirši is mentioned; the same name, *Abdi-ti-ir-ši*, was identified by ALBRIGHT in an Akkadian tablet from Ugarit,[2] and this scholar drew the correct conclusion, that *Tiršu* was a W-S god or goddess: "This hitherto unknown divinity may perhaps have been a kind of Bacchus from whose name the Israelites [3] got the poetic word *tirōš* for 'wine'." [4] It does not follow from this, however, that the word's etymology from *wrṯ* (= *yrš*) "to trample down, to press (grapes)" [5] was incorrect: both grape-juice was *tirôš* "squeezed out" (a *tiqṭal* form) and the wine-goddess was *Tirôš* or *Tiršu* "the presser" (a name formed out of 3d fem. sg. impf.[6]). In Babylonia, too, the god (more often the goddess) of wine *Siris*, was known, whose name derives from the Assyr. *šerešu, serāšu, serāš* "wine" [7] and is evidently a distorted Š-form of the same root *yrš*. [8] Since *Tiršu* was a wine-deity, her name was given to the sacred wands in the cult of the wine-god, as the name of the goddess Asherah also became the name of the wooden poles which represented her.[9] Pictures are preserved where Dionysos is shown precisely as such a pole planted in the ground and provided with a human head;[10] and Pausanias tells about a log which was believed to have fallen from the sky and was erected as an image of Dionysos Cadmos (IX: 12: 4). From the symbolic viewpoint, the thyrsi were a sort of portable asherahs.[11]

[1] Also *mrš* (UM 124: 18) as qualification of *yn* "wine," Cf. Aram. *mêrtâ'* from the root *yᵉrēt* (= Heb. *yāraš*).

[2] RŠ 16.257: IV: 8 (CCCXC). However, this Ugaritic name is rather to be read *Abdi*[di]*-ir-ši*, with NOUGAYROL, because the same volume also contains such names as *A-bi-ir-ši* and *Abdi-ir-šu-na*.

[3] More correct: all West Semites.

[4] XXII, 18.

[5] CCLXXXIX, 406 s., 1027 s.

[6] See p. 135, no. 3 above.

[7] LXXIV, IV, 175.

[8] Akkadian for "wine-presser" was *sirašû* (CCCLVIII, I, 242). As viticulture in general, this term was borrowed from the West Semites. We understand it as Amorite pronunciation of the šaphel *šrš* (the Amorites pronounced Semitic *š* as [s], and *ś* as [sh]).

[9] We maintain that the name of the great Syrian godess Derceto derives from a synonymous verb *dārak* "to trample, to press" (grapes), see p. 206 below. Asherahs were erected in W-S sanctuaries as early as the XVIIIth century, at Mari (CDVI, 5).

[10] CLXII, V, 240 ss. We connect therewith Dionysos' epithet *Orthos* "straight," Athen. II: 38C. See p. 191, n. 4 below.

[11] In H-H, *tuwarsa* signified "vine" (CCCXXI, No. 160). According to BOSSERT, LXXIV, IV, 175-181, this was a W-S loan-word, *tirōš*, originally

The female attendants of Bacchic orgies had many names, most of which were Greek and qualified them as "mad" (*mainades*), "rushing" (*thyiades*), "wild" (*lênai* [1]), "destructive" (*oleiai* [2]). H. LEWY [3] tried to find a Semitic etymology for another one, *mimallones*,[4] but this name is probably Greek, too.[5] There is, however, one, rather widely used, which has no etymology in Greek: *bassarai* or *bassarides*. Aeschylos, in a lost tragedy *Bassarae*, called the Bacchants who dismembered Orpheus thus. Since Orpheus was supposed to be a Thracian, the action took place in Thrace. *Etym. Magn.* 191: 5 defines *bassarai* as multicolored chitons, reaching to the feet, worn by Thracian Bacchants and so named for Dionysos Bassareus; it quotes a line and a half from another lost tragedy by Aeschylos, *Edones*, where *bassarai* are Lydian chitons, reaching to the feet. This is repeated by Pollux 7: 59: *bassara* is a Lydian chiton, reaching to the feet, worn in the Dionysiac cult. The Latin writer Cornutus, *ad Persium* I: 101, reversed the situation: according to him, Dionysos was named Bassareus, and his Thracian Bacchants, Bassarides, because they wore long dresses made of fox-hides, and *bassara* is Thracian for "fox." [6]

This view gained an extraordinary popularity in modern litera-

meaning "wine." He quotes the opinion of HROZNY that *tuwarsa* (contracted to **tūrsa*) was the prototype of the Greek *thyrsos*: this word first signified "vine," then a wand from vine-wood. However, there is no evidence of thyrsi being made of vine-wood; on the contrary, the straight and smooth thyrsi in Greek pictures strongly contradict the assumption of their being made of knotty and curved vine-boughs. The word *thyrsoi* did not need Asia Minor as an intermediary to reach Greece.

[1] Cf. CLII, V, 154: (the Dionysiac feast) "*Lênaia*, which can only be derived from *Lênai* 'the wild women,' not from *lênos*, a 'wine-press.' "

[2] So called in Orchomenos, where they formed a special college. Name so explained CLII, V, 170, n. *a*.

[3] CCCXXX, 247.

[4] From *m^e^mullā'* "filled" (as he understood it, with wine). However, Bacchants are never described as drunken. Their frenzy had a different origin. The vocalization of *mimallôn* (if it be taken for Semitic) suggests rather "the filler."

[5] The *mimallones*, according to Polyaenos 4: 1, were girls who played the rôle (*mimêsin*) of men in the cult of Dionysos Pseudanôr, introduced into Macedon by king Argeios. Does not their name derive from *mimeomai* and *allos*: "those who play the rôle of others"? The custom itself, however, is Semitic, cf. p. 163 above.

[6] The entire Greek evidence is collected in CDLXXX, II, 180 ss. The quotation from Cornutus is given CLII, V, 293, ref. 61^{d}. A pers. n. *pa_2-sa-re-wo* (the last syllable badly preserved) in a Mycenaean tablet from Pylos, compared DV, 422, to *Bassareus*, definitely excludes all fantasies about the Thracian origin of the name.

ture, and most authors took it for granted, without even quoting its source—Cornutus. However, it is *per se* much more probable that sacramental garments dedicated to a god take their name from him rather than the opposite. If the Bacchanalian chitons were made of fox-hides, they could not, by definition, be multicolored (*poikiloi*). The wide Greek iconography of Dionysos, Bacchants and Bacchanals does not even present one instance of a person being dressed in a fur garb. Moreover, *bassara* being Thracian for "fox" is obviously due to Cornutus' blunder. The only Greek author who ever used a similar word for an animal was Herodotos. In a long list of Libyan wild beasts (IV: 192), some of which bear local unidentified names, he also mentions certain *bassaria* (plur.). Hesychios lists this word as Cyrenaean for "fox." Of course, neither Herodotos, a native of Halicarnassos, nor the Cyrenaeans in Libya can be supposed to use Thracian words.[1]

When defining the etymology of the term *bassara, bassaris*, one must keep in mind that Aeschylos, the oldest author whose mention of it is preserved, as well as other authors, connected the Bassarids with a definite mythical event—with their having torn Orpheus to pieces. It must also be remembered that the rite of dismembering the victim was central in Bacchic orgies. The word *bassara, bassaris* has to be derived from the Semitic root *bṣr* which in Hebrew (*bāṣar*) is used only in the specific sense of "cutting down grapes", "vintage," but in Aramaic means "to cut off," in Akkadian (*baṣâru*) "to cut, off, tear off, bite off," in D-form "to cut to pieces, to butcher," especially in relation to dogs' tearing a corpse to pieces, (e.g. *Maqlû* VIII: 87. 88), and the same in Ugaritic where (Hymn to Anath, UM 6: 5) *bṣr* is applied to cutting off hands and is parallel to *hrg* "kill" [2] in the scene of the massacre of certain youths or servants (*ġlmm*) by the goddess Anath. Moreover, the entire tablet, as we shall see, contains Dionysiac motifs. Thus *bassarides* are "the dismemberers," and one of the names of Dionysos himself, *Bassaros* or *Bassareus*, denotes the god in his rôle of the sanguinary "man-

[1] In Libya, we can expect rather to find Semitic words, brought there by the Phoenician settlers, Thus among the non-Greek names for Libyan animals, quoted by Herodotos in his list IV: 192, figure *boryes* (plur.), supposed to be a kind of gazelle: this is Heb. *bārîaḥ*, Phoen. **borîḥ* "runner." *Bassarion* for a carnivorous beast (a fox or a jackal) may well be linked to the Semitic root *bāṣar* which will be discussed in the text.

[2] So far the only occurrence of *hrg* (the common Hebrew word for "kill") at Ugarit.

tearing'' Dionysos *Anthrôporrhaistês,* as he was called in Tenedos.

The male participants of the fabled orgies of Dionysos, the companions of the Maenads, were the Satyrs. They were represented in Greek art not as normal human beings, but as half-goatlike or half-horselike demons. Jane HARRISON emphatically declared about the Satyrs:[1] "they are (what else should they, could they be?) the *Satrae*" (one of the Thracian tribes). Of course, the Satyrs *could* be some thing quite different. It is highly improbable that a real ethnic group should have been reinterpreted as a half-human demon-race; there are no other examples of such a phenomenon. On the contrary, the belief in goat-demons roaming over desert places existed among the Hebrews, very far from the Balkan home of the Satrae: they were called *ś^{ec}îrîm* "goats," were an object of worship in pagan times (Lev. 17: 7) and were believed to haunt abandoned ruins together with wild or fabulous animals and the famous Sumero-Babylonian she-demon Lilith (Is. 34: 14), and to dance there like true Bacchants (*ibid.* 13: 21). For the explanation of the name *satyros, satyroi* we must again turn to the grim rite of rending the victims so peculiar to Bacchic orgies. A common Semitic root *śtr* offers us a most natural and plausible etymology: Heb. *śātar* "to tear" (almost unused), Akk. *šatâru* "to ravage, to devastate," D-form *šutturu* "to pull down," Aram. *s^{e}tar* "to destroy," Arab. *šatara* "to split," S. Arab. *štr* "to destroy," Eth. *štr* "to rend". The masc. part. *śâtir* "destroyer, dismemberer" is an exact counterpart to the Bassarids.[2]

e) *Suggestions About Some Names of Dionysos*

No Greek god had so many names and surnames as Dionysos, whom Sophocles (*Antig.*: 1115) called "thou of the many names."[3] Most of them are intelligible Greek epithets, derived from the god's characteristics or from the places of his worship. It is still uncertain whether the very name of Dionysos, the second part of which has not yet been completely explained, may also be considered as Greek.[4] Some others certainly are not. We have proposed and sub-

[1] CCXLVII, 397.

[2] For *śâtir* > Gr. *satyros* (*i* > *y*), cf. *Bab-ili* > *Babylôn, bêt-ʾili* (*bêt-ʾēl*) > *baitylos, ʾêzôb* > *hyssôpos*, etc. See about the confusion of *i* and *y* in pre-Greek names adopted into Greek: DV, 77.

[3] Complete list CDXI, VI, 1, 1027 ss.

[4] The god's basic name is found in three principal variants: *Dionysos, Diônysos,* and *Dionnysos.* KRETSCHMER, CCXCVIII, 22 ss., showed that these

stantiated Semitic etymologies for two of his names, *Bakchos* (or *Bakcheus*) and *Bassaros* (or *Bassareus*). The Greek doublet of the latter is *Lyaios* or *Lysios*—not "looser" in the sense of liberator from bonds, as is usually understood,[1] but in a more cruel sense, from the other meaning of the verb *lyô*—"to tear asunder, to dismember, to disjoin"—cf. *Hippolytos* whose name signifies "torn by horses," and who was said to have perished precisely by such means.

forms go back to two types: "the Zeusian (or, as we would say, "divine") *nysos*" and "the *nysos* of Zeus." The Greeks treated the element *nysos* as separable. Out of it, they formed Nysa (or Nyseion), the god's fairyland, Nysos, his foster-father, Nysai, his nurses. But what does *nysos* mean? KRETSCHMER, *ibid.*, 19 claimed that *nysos* was Thracian or Phrygian for "son." This became a "generally accepted etymology" (CCCLXXXI, 567, n. 19). But already ROHDE, CDXXXII, 304, n. 1, showed that this hypothesis lacked the slightest support of facts. He believed that *Dionysos* was a purely Greek word. But if it were Greek, the Greeks would have known its meaning, which they did not. They tried to explain the god's name by his fairy-land Nysa, while the reverse was true (as another mythical land, Atlantis, received its name from Atlas, not vice versa). In an old book, full of fantastic, but sometimes very noteworthy ideas—Martin SCHULTZE's CDLX (1876), 230—we found a curious suggestion: that *Dio-nysos* derives from the Heb. *nēs* "stake, pole." This seems very queer, but let us try to apply this guess to what we know both about the cultic role of *nēs* in ancient Israel and the oldest iconography of Dionysos. The miraculous bronze serpent, created by Moses (Num. 21: 8) and still worshipped under Hezekiah (II Kings 18: 4) was raised on a *nēs*. An altar which Moses erected was named by him *Yahwe-nissī* (Ex. 17: 15). On the mutual relation of the two, cf. CCLVII, 112, 116; on the relation of Moses' *nēs* bearing the bronze serpent, to his staff which he could change into a serpent, cf. B. LUTHER *ap.* CCCLXIV, 426 s. On deification of wooden poles erected near altars in W-S religions, cf. p. 187, n. 9 above. On deification of cultic objects in general, cf. *ušḫt* (Akk. *šeḫtu* "censor") and *knr* (*kinnôr* "lyre," cf. Kinyras) in Ugaritic god-list UM 17: 9-10 (see DXLII). On the iconography of Dionysos: "We have literary record of sufficient authority, a verse of an oracle and a fragment from the *Antiope* of Euripides, both quoted by Clemens, to prove that this earliest agalma at Thebes was a mere fetish, an upright pillar; and simple villagers, even in the latest period, still attracted his beneficial power to the orchard by the consecration of a rude tree-stump," CLXII, V, 240, 281 ref. 8, 10, and 240 ss. on Dionysos commonly revered as a wooden pole, sometimes adorned with Bacchic symbols or the god's mask. On Dionysos Orthos ("straight"), cf. p. 187, n. 10 above. On Theban Dionysos Cadmos, a wooden log adorned with bronze, cf. p. 187 above. For the serpent on the *nēs*, cf. on the rôle of serpents in Bacchic orgies, p. 198, n. 2 below. For *ē* > *y*, cf. p. 190, n. 2 above; it is, however, probable that the original W-S form of *nēs* was **nussu*, cf. Heb. *šēm* = Amor. *sumu*, Akk. *šumu*, *bēn* = Amor., Ugar. and Akk. *bunu*, *beʾer* = Akk. *buru*, *ḥēṣ* = Akk. *uṣu* etc. The combination *Dio-nysos* resembles *Yahwe-nissī* quoted above; for its linguistically mixed character, cf. the god *Ppšr* in Ugarit (*UM* § 20.1568a) = Sumerian *Papsukkal*, where Sum. *sukkal* "vizir" is adequately translated by W-S *šr* "prince, minister."

[1] CDI, 90, 99, 105.

Some of Dionysos' names—*Bakchos, Iakchos* and *Euios*—were declared not real names, but personified exclamations. For Iacchos this already was asserted by *Etymol. Magnum*: from *iachê* "cry, howl" came *iachos,* and with a pleonastic kappa, *iakchos.* According to a popular opinion (ascribed to KRETSCHMER, but already found in BENSELER's dictionary), *Bakchos* originated from the same root (*w*)*iachein,* by reduplication **wiwachos.* As to *Bakchos,* this theory is quite improbable; the parallel forms, Lydian *Baki* [1] and Greek *Bakis,* originally a common noun designating a soothsayer,[2] show that kappa was the original. *Iakchos,* as early as 480 (Herod. VIII: 65), was not only a name of Dionysos (especially at Eleusis), but also a technical term for a particular mystic cry uttered during the performance of mysteries. Thence the idea that the divine name originated from the cry. The same idea was extended to other gods. So, according to T. B. L. WEBSTER,[3] "Enyalios, Ares, Paian were deifications of the battle cry, the melée, and the song of healing." This theory requires a serious revision.

Cries devoid of sensible meaning and serving only to express emotions, are extremely elementary and usually consist of vowels or a few open syllables (Oh! Ho! Oioioi! Alala! Boo! etc.). If, however, entire articulate words are shouted, they are sure to have an intrinsic semantic meaning to the persons who utter them. Battle-cries form no exception. "Hurrah" for a West European and "Ura" for a Russian may have no sensible etymology, but it is not so for those who brought this sound to Europe, for the Turco-Tartar tribes: in their language, "Ura!" means "strike!" and has a meaning quite adequate to its function. In the Middle Ages, the battle-cry of French chivalry was "Montjoy St. Denys!", and that of the Spanish, "Santiago de Campostella!", but it would hardly be reasonable to pretend that St. Denys and Santiago are battle-cries transformed into saints.

"How many people attach any precise significance to the thrice repeated .... 'Alleluia, Alleluia, Alleluia'?" asked Jane HARRISON,

[1] CDI, 58 (according to OTTO, this word could either have been borrowed, very early, by the Lydians from the Greeks, or taken by both nations from a common source).

[2] ROHDE, CDXXII, 292, 314 n. 58, showed that *bakis* was a common noun before becoming a pers. n., but did not connect it with Bacchos.

[3] DXXXVIII, 11. Enyalios and Paian certainly, and Ares possibly, were already independent gods in the Mycenaean period (DV, 126).

"They are a homage beyond articulate speech," [1] and further: " 'The Iacchos' was a ritual cry, one easily recognizable by an Athenian just as nowadays we should recognize Alleluia and Hosanna." [2] Miss HARRISON was perhaps more right than she herself supposed. For a modern European or American the W-S words Alleluia, Hosanna, or, for that matter, Amen, have no intrinsic meaning; but for the Hebrews who first began to use these words in liturgy they had a very precise sense: "praise Yahwe," "rescue us, pray," and "truly so." *Iakchos*, a word difficult to articulate, with an agglomeration of surd consonants, does not seem to have been a spontaneous emotional cry. Though it might not have independent significance for a Vth century Athenian, it might well have had one a thousand years earlier, in the same sphere from which Alleluia, Hosanna, and Amen came to Europe with another W-S religion. *Iakchos* can be explained on the basis of W-S vocabulary: it is *yakke*, 3d m. sg. impf. Piel of *nky* (Heb. *nākâ*) "to strike, to smite, to kill," i.e. "the smiter, the killer," [3] the Dionysos of the bloody human sacrifices, *Anthrôporrhaistês*, *Ômêstês*,[4] *Bassareus*.[5]

A specific salutatory cry in honor of Dionysos during Bacchic orgies was *euoi*, and among his numerous names and surnames *Euas* (Hesych.) and *Euios* also figure. It seemed certain that the nickname came from the cry. But what meaning has the cry? According to its function, it must correspond, more or less, to our "Hail!" Clemens of Alexandria heard in it the name of Eve (LXX *Eua*), "through whom sin came into the world," [6] and however erroneous

[1] CCXLVII, 413. [2] *Ibid.*, 542.

[3] One of the names, formed in the very common W-S and Arabic pattern from 3d pers. masc. sg. impf., as *Yiṣḥāq*, *Yiphtaḥ*, *Yaʿăqôb*, etc. YEIVIN, DLVI, 17 pertinently explained the Hyksos name written *Y-k-b-ʿ-r* not as a miswritten *Y-ʿ-q-b-ỉ-r* (*Yaʿqôb-ʾēl*), but as *Yakke-Baʿal* "Baal should strike"—or rather, we would say, "Baal strikes"—which is a good confirmation of our etymology for *Iakchos*.

[4] A human sacrifice to Dionysos Omestes was said to have been brought by Themistocles in 480, on the eve of the battle of Salamis, according to Plutarch *Themist.* 13; *Pelop.* 21; *Arist.* 9.

[5] Animals consecrated to Dionysos were the lynx and the panther. According to a judicious explanation by OTTO, CDI, 104 s., these beasts, more than any other felines, are distinguished by their sanguinary and murderous character—they rush upon their prey, tear it to pieces, hurriedly swalow the still warm flesh, as was ascribed to the Maenads. The ancients derived the name Lynceus (which we met in the Danaan cycle) from *lynx*; this probably shows that this Lynceus and his namesake in another Peloponnesian myth were faded avatars of Dionysos.

[6] Quoted *Protr.* II: 12; cf. CCXLVII, 483.

his identification was in substance, phonetically and semantically it is faultless. As *Eua, Euaioi* are the regular Greek transcriptions of Hebrew pers. n. *Ḥawwā*, ethnic name *Ḥiwwîm* (>**Ḥawwîm*) (both formed ultimately from the root *ḥwy* "to live" [1]) so also *euoi* renders W-S *ḥaw(w)ī* or *ḥaw(w)ay* [2] "live!"—imper. masc. sg. of the same root [3]—we would say "long live!" [4] And *Euios*, or *Euas*, accordingly, is *ḥawiyy* "living," the resurrected Dionysos, corresponding to Heb. *'ēl ḥayy*, "living god," an epithet genetically connected with the cult of dying and resurrecting gods.[5]

All these are, of course, hypotheses, but they may claim at least one thing in their favor: they explain unintelligible names and surnames of Dionysos not by invented, allegedly Thracian words, and not by declaring them mere cries which supposedly need not necessarily have any meaning, but by actually existing words from well-known languages, words with well-established meanings, which correspond both phonetically and semantically to various features and characteristics of Dionysos, and at the same time harmonize with the general conception, based on other facts, of the origin of Cadmeian and Bacchic cults.[6]

[1] The Greeks had no graphic means of rendering in their script the light aspiration of W-S languages, *ḥ*, so they dropped it altogether. This was consistently observed in LXX, e.g. *Ḥannā* > *Anna*, *Ḥamôr* > *Emôr*, *Nāḥûm* > *Naum*, etc., as against *Ḫebrôn* > *Chebrôn*, *Ḫôbāb* > *Chôbab*, *Naḫôr* > *Nachôr*, etc., and almost consistently in transcriptions of Phoenician and Punic names: *Ḥanniba'al* > *Annibas*, *Ḥannôn* > *Annôn*, etc. (exception: *Qart-ḥadašt* > *Karchêdôn*).

[2] On imperatives with the vowel *-a-*, cf. *UM* § 9.16.

[2] The root *ḥwy*, variation of *ḥyy*, is quite common (along with the latter) in Ugaritic, Phoenician, and Aramaic.

[4] In Hebrew, "long live!" is usually expressed by the jussive form (*yeḥî ham-melek*), but in Aramaic by the imperative (*malkâ' le-'âlmîn ḥeyi*), and Heb. *ḥay-Yahwe*! may also be an imperative.

[5] Cf. LI, 450-50: "Jahwe der lebendige Gott."

[6] We have by no means covered the wide area of Dionysiac cults. We are sure that they included many agricultural rites and customs which were not specifically Semitic and may be found everywhere, and we have therefore left aside the feasts of the tamed, regularized state-cult of Dionysos in classical times. We also left for a later occasion the cultic motif of the Dionysiac holy chest. Finally, here are a few other possible Semitisms in Dionysiac cults: 1) In Rhodes, cultic phalli consecrated to Dionysos were cut out of fig-wood and called *Thyônidai* (Hesych.), which MOVERS, CCCLXXXIV, I, 26 derived from Heb. *te'ēnā* "fig-tree" (cf. CDI, 147 on the association of figs, due to their shape, with phallic images). 2) In Attica, the first man to have received the gift of vine-planting from Dionysos, was said to be *Icarios*; the myth concerning him will be seen p. 260 s. below; his name clearly derives from the Akk. *ikkaru*, Heb. *'ikkār* "farmer, planter" (CCXXXV, II, 946 on his

The Myth of Zagreus in Ugarit

An opinion exists that Dionysos and Zagreus originally were distinct gods and were identified only by the Orphics.[1] But it was only Nonnos (500 A.D.) who consistently called by the name of Zagreus the first embodiment of Dionysos; all earlier authors, as well as the Orphic hymns, called the god's first incarnation by the same name of Dionysos. However, if they used the name Zagreus, it usually referred to the first incarnation. According to our conviction, the motif of Dionysos' double birth, of his resurrection in a new shape, belongs to the original core of the myth. We have observed this motif in the Ugaritic myth of *Aqht*, and in a still more pronounced form in the Egypto-Phoenician myth of Bata, and we have no doubt that the Greek epithets of Dionysos "twice born" and "he of two mothers" refer precisely to this myth. There certainly was some confusion raised by the strange motif of the prematurely born (or extorted from his dead mother's womb) Dionysos, having completed the months of gestation inside Zeus' thigh. It is true that male pregnancy appears in the Hurrian myth of Kumarbi which was known at Ugarit [2] and, judging from its use by Hesiod,[3] also in Boeotia. But why the thigh? We believe that we are dealing here with a literal translation of a W-S idiom which euphemistically designated begetting: "sprung from one's thigh" (*yōṣeʾ yᵉrēkô*, inaccurately translated in English Bibles by "loins") merely meant "begotten by one," his child.

Zagreus, according to numerous testimonies of ancient authors,[4] was a god with a particularly pronounced chthonic infernal charac-

name-sake Icaros, cf. pp. 271 ss. below). 3) "Probably not far from (Attic) Ikaria lay the deme called Semachidai, and this also claimed an ancestor Semachos, who was one of the first hosts of the stranger divinity; and his descendants also (as those of Icarios—M. A.) maintained special privileges, certain priestesses of Dionysos tracing their line from the daughters of Semachos," CLXII, V, 115. 299 ref. 69a. The name *Sêmachos* has hardly any Greek etymology (*sêma* "sign" and *achos* "pain, woe, sadness" give no acceptable meaning); but the Heb. *ṣemaḫ* means "plant" (cf. Ugar. pers. n. *Yṣmḫ* UM 10: 4), and was frequently used in poetic language to designate the mystic redeemer (Jer. 23: 5; 33: 15; Zach. 3: 8; 6: 12).

[1] E.g., CDXI, VI, 1, 1028.

[2] Kumarbi, along with other Hurrian divinities, is frequently named in a Hurrian text, with many Semitic words, written in Ugaritic script (UM 4), thus: *Il Kmrb*.

[3] As shown by Güterbock, pp. 217 ss. below.

[4] They are collected in a convenient way in CCCXLIII, 162-182; cf. also CCXLVII, 489-496; CCXLVIII, 1-74.

ter. His mother was Persephone,[1] the maiden who descended in the Nether World and became the queen of Hades. He was identified with Hades, or Pluto, or considered as the co-regent of Hades together with Pluto. Zeus begot him of Persephone, mating with her in the shape of a dragon, and she bore "a horned child." Barely born, Zagreus sat on Zeus' throne and took Zeus' royal insignia in his little hands.[2] Zeus appointed him his successor. But his reign was not long: still a child, he was perfidiously torn apart by his enemies. To Onomacritos, a poet of the VIth century, was ascribed the composition of a consistent story of Dionysos-Zagreus' death; Pausanias (VIII: 37: 5) repeats the opinion that he was the first to introduce in the mysteries of Dionysos the Titans as his murderers. Who had figured in this rôle in the primordial myth is impossible to establish, and it is not substantial: the myth is but an aetiology of the age-old custom of dismemberment (*sparagmos*), and only with the growth of consciousness did there arise the need for justification. In the myth of Osiris this rôle is played by his hostile brother Seth, in the myth of *Aqht*—by eagles at the instigation of Anath, in the myth of Actaeon—by hounds at the instigation of Artemis, in the above quoted Ugaritic theophagy myth—by Anath in person, in the myth of Bata his repeated slaying was accomplished each time at the request of his unfaithful wife. Accordingly, in extant versions of the myth of Dionysos-Zagreus' martyrdom, behind the immediate killers, the Titans, stands a goddess whom the Greeks identified with Hera and explained her cruelty by jealousy. The Titans, their faces whitened with gypsum,[3] distracted the

[1] Callimachos, frg. 171. In the systematized Greek pantheon, Persephone was Zeus' daughter. It is very possible that the Greek names of Zeus and Persephone have been applied to Oriental divinities of like character who, however, were not a father and a daughter. The motif of incest, on the other hand, was rather normal in the mythical sphere of dying gods.

[2] Frazer, clxxv, VII, 13 sees in this mythical feature the reflex of the archaic custom of sacrificing a royal child instead of the king himself by allegedly transferring to it the kingdom and then slaughtering it as a substitute.

[3] Harrison, ccxlvii, 493 proposed an apparently happy idea that the alleged Titans (*Titanes*) were originally only "white-clay-men" (*titanoi*). This thesis was fully accepted in clxii, V, 172, n.*d*. She herself, however, withdrew this etymology in later editions of her work (*loc. cit.*, n. 2)—as it seems, without real ground. Coloring the faces for performing ceremonies and murders is an immemorial custom. Gypsum was considered sacred by the Babylonians and was consecrated to the god Ninurta, ccclviii, II, 209. As for *titanos*, as "the ancients called dust and gypsum" (Eustathios ad *Iliad* II: 382: 36), or *tetanos* "dust, mortar, lime" (Hesychios), "its etymo-

child's attention with toys,[1] and suddenly rushed upon him. Zagreus, to escape the murderers, took different shapes, appeared as Zeus, as a serpent, as a lion, as a bull. In the shape of a bull he was finally overwhelmed by the Titans, torn to pieces and eaten.[2] We have seen in connection with Semele that the heart of the slain one was saved and than swallowed by Semele who conceived from it a new incarnation of Dionysos.

In the preceding chapter, in the section devoted to Oriental prototypes of the myth of Io, we have examined several Sumerian and Ugaritic myths treating the conception and birth of a chthonic god of the Nether World. The copulation of his father, the god of thunder and atmospheric phenomena (Enlil, Baal, cf. Zeus in the myth of Zagreus), with the gow-goddess takes place in Hell; the child born often has an ophic aspect. In the Ugaritic poem of the Rephaim (underground ghosts of the dead), III Rp B (= UM 124): 4, a god is mentioned by the nickname *ṣġr* "the little, or young, one." His other name is *Rpu-Bʿl* "the healing lord"; he is *mhr Bʿl w mhr ʿnt*, son of Baal and Anath, and he is the head of the Rephaim. His title is *zbl mlk* "deputy of the king," [3] followed by the unexplained epithet *ʿllmy* (ibid.: 10). We understand the latter as formed from *ʿllm* + the suffix of belonging -*y*,[4] and we see in *ʿllm* a plural formation for abstract nouns, from the root *ʿll* (Heb. Poel *ʿōlēl*) "to kill" (Judg. 20: 45), "to cut off to the end," of vintage (Lev. 19: 10; Jer. 6: 9 of extermination of Israel; cf. the same usage of *bṣr*!), "to inflict pain, to torment' (Lament. 1: 12; 2: 20; 3: 51; Ex. 10: 2, etc.), "to torture to death" (Jer. 38: 19; Judg. 19: 25). *ʿllmy*, thus, qualifies the "little one" either as the victim or as the instigator of cruel death (Dionysos was both). III Rp B (= UM 124): 2-4 is said:

hn bnk. hn [*bkrk*/*mhrk* ?]
bn. bn. aŝrk

logy is obscure," according to Boisacq (lxxiii, 972); should we regard it as a derivation of W-S and Akk. *ṭîṭu* "mud, clay"? (cf. p. 131, n. 3 above).

[1] The toys—apple, dice, tops, mirror, rattle—played a sacral role in Dionysiac mysteries.

[2] In some versions of the myth, omophagy is lacking: the Titans are said to have cooked the dismembered body of the Bull-Zagreus in a cauldron; in others, it is simply said that they ate him, without further specification.

[3] Akk. *zabâlu*—"to carry, to bring," in W-S apparently "to lift," thus *z*ᵉ*bûl* (vocalization given by the pers. names *Z*ᵉ*bûlûn* and *Z*ᵉ*bûl* and by *Beel-zebul* of the New Test.) is a part. pass., approx. "raised, appointed."

[4] Usually an ethnic (gentilic), but cf. *gt. mlkym* UM 1115: 5 "those of the royal wine-press"; for -*y* attached to plural form of nouns, cf. Danel's epithet *mt hrnmy* "the man of *Hrnm*."

hn ʿ[*nt. tuḫ*]*d ydk*
ṣġr. tnšq. špțk

"Behold thy son! behold, thy [first-born/offspring ?]!
The son, the son of thy shrine!
Behold, A[nath will se]ize thy hand,
O little one, she will kiss thy lips."

In the Ugaritic hymn to Anath (UM 6),[1] the goddess Anath, named *arḫ* "wild cow/heifer," bears a son designated as *zbl mlk, bkr zbl,* and *ṣġr*—this is obviously the same young god as in III Rp B (= UM 124). Before his birth, Anath kills and cuts certain "lads" or "servants" (*ġlmm*), or "a lad," if *-m* is here enclitic; the verbs used are *hrg* and *bṣr*. This is the motif of *sparagmos,* and the same verb is used from which we have derived the names Bassareus (for Dionysos) and Bassarids (for his Maenads who had dismembered Orpheus).

In the poem I*AB (= UM 67): V: 17-25, Baal, apparently already descended to the Nether World, copulates with a "cow" or a "heifer" (*prt,* ʿ*glt*), and she bears from him a son *Mš*. We have explained (above, p. 89) his name as Sumerian *Muš* "serpent." It is evident, that this Muš, son of Baal and the heifer, conceived in Hell, is identical with the "Little One" *Rpu-B*ʿ*l* from the two previously examined Ugaritic sources. The conception in Hell corresponds to the Sumerian myth of Enlil and Ninlil (see above, p. 89). It explains why "the Little One" was the head of the Rephaim, the underground ghosts, and is named *Rpu-B*ʿ*l* "lord healer." Identically the same name, *Ninazu,* "lord healer," is borne by the chthonic healer-god, the son of Enlil and Ninlil, conceived in the Nether World. And since "the Little One," the son of Baal and Anath the heifer, is also a healing god, this accounts for his being also named *Muš* "serpent," the immemorial emblem of physician gods.[2]

[1] Cf. XCVII.

[2] Ophic features were very pronounced not only in the myth, but in the ritual of Dionysos as well. Clemens of Alexandria, who knew the literature on Bacchic cults well, relates that Bacchants "are crowned with snakes. . and the symbol of their Bacchic orgies is a consecrated serpent" (quoted CCXLVII, 483). According to Euripides' *Bacchae* 697-698, the Bacchants gird themselves with snakes that did no harm to them. The bull-horned Dionysos was, since his very birth, crowned with a dragon, and in his honor his thyrsi-carrying Maenads crown their tresses in the same way (*ibid.*, 97-103). On pictures of Maenads, reproduced CCXLVII, 398 s., a Maenad is seen with a snake coiled around her hair (fig. 123), and another Maenad

We notice, furthermore, an interesting ritual detail in the Ugaritic myths telling of the cow giving birth to Baal's son: immediately after the delivery, the mother clothes and sometimes shoes him, even if he is described as a calf:

a) I*AB (= UM 67): V: 23: *al[l.t]šlbšn* "with a cloak she clothed him."

b) UM 6: 25: *k d lbšt. bir.mlak* "as thou hast clad the young one, the messenger"; *bir* is explained by CAZELLES, ad loc., by Akk. *bûru* "cub, child"; the use of *mlak* for a young god is not quite without parallels with the Biblical *mal'āk* "angel."

c) IV AB (= UM 76): III: 25-27:

(20) *arḫ. arḫ.* [ ]
ibr. tld. [*l b'l*] [1]
wrum. l[*rkb 'rpt*]
tḥbq.[ ]
tḥbq[ ]
(25) *wtksynn. b š̈n* (!) [2]
y[ ]*šrh.*[3] *wšḫph* [4]
[ ]*šḫp. ṣgrth*

which we translate: [5]

(20) "the heifer, the heifer[ ]
A bull she bears [to Baal]
Yea a buffalo to [the Rider of Clouds]
She embraces[ ]
She embraces [ ]
(25) And she covers him with scarlet
[ ] her child and she puts on him shoes
[ ] the shoe of his youth."

The dressing and shoeing of the calf, so persistently repeated in Ugaritic parallels to the Greek myth of Dionysos-Zagreus, is by no

is pictured with two huge serpents in her hands (fig. 124). Dionysos himself dances with a snake in his hand on the vase-representation reproduced in CLXII, V, p. XLV. By the way, there is nothing fantastic in it: for ceremonies, grass-snakes could be used—large, harmless and easily domesticated reptiles.

[1] Text completed after lines 36-37.

[2] On VIROLLEAUD's autography (DX), *š*(?)*n*(?) are discernible, as he put it into his transliteration. This supplies the well-fitting word *šn* "scarlet" (*UM* § 20.2046), Heb. *šānî*.

[3] We understand *šrh* ("her *šr*") as Akk. *šêru, šerru* "little one, child."

[4] *šḫp*, inf. abs. with the sense of a finite verb; the sense is supplied by Akk. *šuḫupatu*, with the determinative *mašak* "leather," an object always used in pairs, evidently—some kind of foot-wear. MEISSNER proved that mašak*šuḫupâtê* are shoes (of rawhide), cf. DLX, 275 for occurrences.

[5] Cf. also the translation in CCXXIII, 51.

means an accidental detail. In the Greek island of Tenedos, where many traces of ancient human sacrifices were remembered,[1] the following curious custom was observed: a cow with calf was devoted to Dionysos *Anthrôporrhaistes* "the man-tearing," and was treated like a woman in childbirth; the new-born calf was shoed in cothurns and then killed by one blow of an axe, and he who had delivered the blow was chased with stones up to the sea-shore.[2] The calf evidently symbolized the child Dionysos himself, the man who killed it was not only a performer of sacrifice but also a sacrilegious murderer, and the cothurns designated the victim's double nature —both a calf and a substitute for a human victim. Now we see that the texts examined bear evidence on this rite having already been performed in Ugarit!

Finally, in a fragment belonging to the cycle of Baal and Anath, UM 133, in spite of its brevity and damaged state, we can discern a fragment of the story of how the young (*ṣġr*) son of Baal and Anath, represented here too as a bull (*ibr*), was appointed Baal's deputy and successor: [3]

(rev., 1) *h*[ ]*rm. h*[ ]
yrmmh[ ]
mlk. gbʿh[ ]
ibr klhm. dlh [ ]
(5) *lytn lhm. tḥt bʿl* [4]
h. u qšt pn hdd.[5] *by*[*dh* ?]
ʿm. bym bʿl ysy [6] *y*[ ]
rmm. ḫnpm mḫl [*qm* [7]]

[1] Children were sacrificed there to Palaemon *Brephoktonos* ("the children-killer"), Lycophr. 229 with scholia; which Palaemon, according to a Cadmeian myth, was identical with Melicertes, son of Ino, grandson of Cadmos. See pp. 209 ss. below.

[2] Aelian, *Nat. anim.* 12: 34. Cf. CDI, 99, 178; CLXXV, VII, 33.

[3] Translation in CCXXIII, 15. Here follows our own tentative translation.

[4] *taḥat* can have the sense of "instead" in Hebrew, e.g. *hă-taḥat ʾĕlōhîm ʾânôki* "am I in the place of God?" Gen. 30: 2; *hûʾ yēšēb ʿal-kisseʾi taḥtay* "he will sit on my throne instead of me" I Kings 1: 30.

[5] *pn hdd* is translated below "before Hadad," but cf. Punic *Tnt pn bʿl* (goddess) "Tanit-Face-of-Baal"; thus *pn hdd* may here designate metaphorically Hadad's (= Baal's) consort, Anath.

[6] We understand *ysy* as 3d pers. masc. sg. impf. of *nsy* (Heb. *nāsâ*) "to test, put on ordeal." Perhaps the young god must be tested by Baal as to his efficiency in handling his bow in presence of Baal (or in handling the bow of Face-of-Hadad, i.e. Anath, the great archer), before he assume power.

[7] *ḫnpm*, cf. *UM* § 20.719, where this word is compared with Heb. *ḫanēph* "to be impious" and Akk. *ḫanâpu* "to perpetrate evil." Accordingly, we

mlk. nhr. -br[ ]
zbl bʿl. ġlm.[ ]
ṣġr hd wr[*ḥm* [1]] [*ʿnt* ?]
wlnhr nd [ ]
[ ]*il*

which may be translated:

. . . .
he raised him[ ]
the king, his hill[ ]
the bull of all of them who belong to him [ ]
let him be given to them in lieu of Baal
or a bow, before Hadad, in [his] ha[nd ?]
. . . in the sea will Baal test . . . [ ]
they arose, the impious, the evi[l-doers [2]]
the king, the river, he does . . . . [ ]
the deputy of Baal,[3] the lad [ ]
the Young One of Hadd and Mai[den (Anath ?)]
and to the river he went [ ]
[ ] god

We have, thus, in Ugaritic myths a very close correspondence to Greek myths on Dionysos-Zagreus, including his relation to the Nether World, his power over the ghosts, his double animal symbolism of a Bull and Serpent, his youth (particularly stressed), his rôle as first-born and heir of Baal, and even the peculiar custom of shoeing the sacrificial calf, the symbol of the child Dionysos. It is precisely to the Ugaritic myth that the epithet of Dionysos *bugenês* ,,cow-born'' can be traced,[4] which was used, characteristically, in Argos when invoking Dionysos from Hades, through the Alcyonian lake near Lerna.[5] We remember that in Argos another variant of the same conception was preserved—the myth of the cow Io who

restore the following word as *mḫl*[*qm*], part. masc. pl. piel from *ḫlq*, Akk. *ḫalâqu* "to perish"; in a Ugaritic text, *ḫlq* = Akk. *ḫulqu* = *lâ ṭâbu* "not good," *UM* § 20.710.

[1] We restore, according to the context, *r*[*ḥm*] (Heb. *raḥam* "girl"): *rḥm ʿnt* "Maiden Anath" (UM 49: II: 27) is a synonym of the more common *btlt ʿnt* "Virgin Anath" (*UM* § 20.176).

[2] Or, "the dest[royers]."

[3] *zbl bʿl* is elsewhere the title of Baal himself, and may be translated "Prince Baal"; but in the present instance, *zbl bʿl* must be taken as a stat. constr. and understood "the *zebul* of Baal," Baal's appointee.

[4] It was shown by Otto, CDI, 179 that this must be understood literally. He could not have known when he wrote it that Ugaritic texts would furnish direct confirmation.

[5] Plutarch *De Is. et Osir.* 35; Paus. II: 37: 5. Cf. CDXI, III, 1, 993; CDI, 176; CLXII, V, 126, 305 ref. 89; CLXXV, VII, 15.

had given birth, by Zeus, to the ancestor of the Danaan royal house. Another epithet of Dionysos, *Iatros* "the healer", goes back to the Ugaritic cow-born *Rpu-Bʿl.* Moreover, we have most probably detected in the Ugaritic myths of that series the very name of Zagreus.

Greek authors did not interpret or explain the name of Zagreus. Only *Etymol. Magn.* 406: 49 interpreted it as "great hunter": prefix *za-* "very" + *agreus* "hunter." This seems to be very plausible (such avatars of Dionysos as *Aqht* and Actaeon were famous hunters, the same is told of Adonis) and perhaps refers to the Bacchic wild rush for victims. There are, however, some difficulties: the prefix *za-* normally goes with adjectives and not with nouns, while *agreus* is a noun; [1] the mythological texts agree in stressing the extreme youth of Zagreus, his early childhood (though combined with divine might). Some modern investigators therefore regard the interpretation of Zagreus as "great hunter" as merely a popular etymology.[2] The famous student of Orphism, GUTHRIE, quoted as "more convincing than most etymologies" the hypothesis of Miss G. DAVIS [3] that Zagreus was an ethnic from Zagros, the mountain-chain in West Iran, and was brought to Greece by the Phoenicians.[4] As to the origin from the Zagros mountains, one should first have made sure that 1) the Zagros mountains had been so named in Semitic languages; 2) that in those mountains a well-known shrine of a god that might be compared to Zagreus had existed; 3) that any Oriental people, Babylonians, Hurrians, Hittites, or West Semites, had ever possessed some divine name connected with Zagros. None of these premises is fulfilled. But the idea of penetration through the Phoenicians does harmonize with the Ugaritic parallels to the myth of Zagreus we have just revealed.

We have seen, on the one hand, that the peculiar feature of Zagreus (the "first Dionysos") was his slaying as a *child*, and on the other hand, that the constant epithet of his Ugaritic counterpart was *ṣġr* "the Little or the Young One." *Ṣġr* (probably pronouneed *ṣaġru*, by analogy with Akk. *ṣeḫru*) provides a good semantic and phonetic basis for *Zagreus*, which name, in this way, simply signified

[1] Cf., on the contrary, *euagros* "the well-hunting one."

[2] CLXII, V, 129: "Hellenic philology has not been able to determine its meaning"; *ibid.*, n. *b*: "The explanation of the word as "the mighty hunter' . . . is not plausible on religious grounds."

[3] Quoted in CV, I, 651.

[4] CCXLII, 113.

"the Little, the Young One" before it was reinterpreted as *Za-agreus*, "the great hunter." [1] The transcription of Semitic ṣ by Greek *z* may be explained in two ways: either by hesitation in rendering the sound ṣ, quite alien to the Greek ear, which usually was transcribed by *s*, but in one significant case, at least, by *z*: the name of the town *Ṣōʿar*, from this very root, is rendered by LXX mostly through *Segor*, but in Gen. 13: 10 and Is. 48: 4, 34 through *Zogor*(*a*): here the entire consonantal composition of *Zagreus* is present. Another interesting case is the Greek *maza* "ritual dry barley-cakes" = Heb. *maṣṣā̆*.[2] Or it might be the phonetic waverings inside the Semitic languages themselves, where the sound ṣ was sometimes replaced by *z*, especially in transcriptions of W-S words and names in cuneiform documents of Canaanite origin.[3] It is also possible that the Semitic original of the name of Zagreus came to the Aegean not in its common form *ṣġr*, but in its dialectal variant *zġr*, observed in Hebrew along with it in the form *zeʿêr* "a little"; then the phonetic correspondence would be perfect.

As to the cruel death of Zagreus, we have reason to believe that his Ugaritic counterpart's title *ʿllmy* "that of killing, torture" revers to this motif. We have already cited exhaustive Ugaritic parallels contained in the myth of *Aqht* and in the scene of ritual sparagmos and omophagy performed by Anath. The poem of *Aqht* is connected by many links with the Dionysiac cycle, and it is certainly not by accident that the poem of the Rephaim, where the

[1] If a name such as "the little one" seems to be strange for a god, we may compare the Sumerian god ᵈ*Lugal-banda*, whose name signifies literally "the little king" (CXI, No. 1878). In particular, he was the husband of the "Wild-Cow Nin-sun," mother of Gilgameš, and to him was also ascribed the victory over the storm-bird Zû. Whether his image had any influence on the formation of the W-S god *ṣġr*, is unknown.

[2] The question which of the two is original, *maza* or *maṣṣā*, can be answered quite easily: *maza* has no Greek etymology, while *maṣṣā* has a good Semitic one: the usual derivation from the root *māṣaṣ* or *māṣâ* (Heb., Aram., Arab. "to drain, to drain out") seems to be quite satisfactory. In Laconia, the *maza*-cakes were used in the ritual of Ino, a goddess of Semitic origin (see next section), cf. Paus. III: 23: 8, and in Arcadian Phigalia, in a sacred meal, cf. LXV, II, 353.

[3] Not only in the case of *za*/*ṣa*, for which only one sign was available, but also in the cases od *zi* and *ṣi*, *zu* and *ṣu*, each written by a separate sign. Thus in the Amarna letters: *Ziduna* and *Ṣiduna*, *Zumur* and *Ṣumur*; *Naziba* for *Nᵉṣîb*, *Zuḫri* for *Ṣōʿar*; in Canaanite glosses: *yazini* from *yṣy* "to go out," *zipparatu* apparently for *ṣippôr* "bird," *zûnu* for *ṣôn* "small cattle," *zurya* for *ṣorî* "balsam," *kazira* for *qâsir* "harvest," *maḫzu* for *maḫaṣû* "they smote," etc.

"young" Ugaritic Zagreus appears, belongs to the cycle of *Aqht* and Danel. Because of the fragmentary nature of the texts, much is still obscure, but the suspicion arises: was not this young leader of the Rephaim not only the son of Baal and Anath, but also, perhaps, *Aqht*'s avatar or shadow in the Nether World? . . .[1] The new batch of mythological texts, unearthed at Ras Shamra late in 1961, perhaps will provide further parallels and elucidations.

Ino and Melicertes

The fourth daughter of Cadmos and Harmonia, Ino, and her sons Melicertes and Learchos (the latter is merely a doublet of the former) stand somewhat apart from the other three daughters and their sons. Those three grandsons of Cadmos, Actaeon, Pentheus, and Dionysos, are avatars of one and the same divine personage, Dionysos. The myth of Ino includes some Dionysiac motifs, but at the same time it belongs to a different category of Hellenosemitic myths and rituals—to those connected with the great W-S goddess Derceto-Atargatis and her prototype Asherah. They will be examined in a separate chapter of this study, and in order to avoid repetitions, we will now limit ourselves only to some aspects of the problem.

In myths devoted to Ino, she is depicted in gloomy colors. After her marriage with Athamas, king of Orchomenos, she revealed herself as a cruel stepmother. She tried to have Athamas' children from his union with the cloud Nephele, Phrixos and Helle, put to death. In the doublet of this myth she actually succeeded in arranging through a ruse the slaying of the two sons of her rival, another wife of Athamas, by that rival herself. In order to persuade the people that Phrixos must be sacrificed to Zeus Laphystios, she slandered him and artificially provoked a crop failure through parching the seed-corn. Her own sons were Melicertes and Learchos. Her husband Athamas, seized by a sudden madness, mistook the little Learchos for a stag, killed him, and then pursued Ino with Melicertes in her arms with his bare sword. Running away from Athamas, Ino, in despair, jumped together with Melicertes into the sea. Both were granted immortality. Melicertes was worshipped in Corinth both under his name (Paus, II: 2: 1) and under that of Palaemon (ibid. 3), and also, under that latter name, in Tenedos

[1] So is the opinion of Caquot, xc, 75 ss.: *Rpu Bʿl* was *Aqht*, resurrected after the seven-day banquet of the Rephaim.

where children used to be sacrificed to him (see p. 200, n. 1 above). Ino became a sea-goddess under the name of Leucothea, and a few shrines along the Laconian sea-coast were consecrated to her. Among these was "the water of Ino," a pond of the size of a small lake in Epidauros-Limera; on the feast of Ino, special ritual barley cakes named *maza* (Paus. III: 23: 8), were thrown into the water for divination.

If one looks behind these myths for their ritual essence, it becomes clear that Ino, before being represented as a mortial woman. had been a great goddess who was able to grant and to withhold harvest and whom it was necessary to propitiate with human sacrifices (the whole myth cycle, connected with the cult of Orchomenian Zeus Laphystios, is saturated with them). In the same Orchomenos, a custom was preserved up to a late time, according to which, during the celebration of the Agrionia feast, the priest of Dionysos pursued women belonging to the group of the *Oleiai* [1] and killed the first who failed to escape (Plut. *Quest. gr.* 38). The oldest literary mention of Dionysos, *Iliad* VI: 130 ss., tells how Lycurgos, son of Dryas, attacked the nurses of Dionysos and gravely injured them with his ox-goad; Dionysos saved himself by jumping into the sea.[2] Ino, the goddess of human sacrifices, was personified by the woman who was sacrificed to her, just as sacrificed children personified the very Palaemon-Melicertes to whom they were sacrificed. A particular kind of human sacrifice was the throwing of women into the sea or a pond. In Greece, its symbol was the suicidal jump of Ino, in Syria-Palestine it was personified in a number of myths about the goddess Derceto-Atargatis who either threw herself into the Ascalonian pond (or into the Euphrates), or was thrown into it, together with her son Ichthys, by Mopsos. This relates Ino to Derceto; but this is not the only point of resemblance: sacral ponds were consecrated to Derceto (like those of Ino) in both of her main sanctuaries, in Ascalon and in Hierapolis, and, at least in the latter, sacrifices were brought to her by throwing down from the cliffs wreathed animals [3]

[1] Cf. p. 188, n. 2 above.

[2] In the Laconian town of Brasiae, Ino was said to have been the nurse of Dionysos, Paus. V: 24: 4; according to Euripides' *Bacchae*, she took part in the dismemberment of Pentheus.

[3] The wreathes indicate that these animals were substitutes for human victims. In Achaia Phtiotis, according to Herodot. VII: 197, human victims from among the descendants of Athamas used to be led to the slaughter ornamented with wreathes over the whole body.

or children, of which pretense was made of their being bulls (Lucian *de Deâ Syriâ* 58). Moreover, Derceto, like Ino, was a sea-goddess and was represented—not in Hierapolis, it is true, but in Phoenicia—as half-woman, half-fish (ibid. 14).[1]

It should not be supposed that Derceto-Atargatis was a deity only of the Hellenistic age. She was simply a slightly modified form of the great mother-goddess of the old Canaanite pantheon, Lady Asherah of the Sea (*Rbt Aŝrt Ym*) of Ugaritic myths. *Derketô* is not a Greek distortion of Atargatis, but a completely correct W-S derivation from the root *dārak* "to trample, to press," especially grapes in wine-press. The first half of the compound name of Atargatis did not originally represent the Aramaic form of Astarte, as it is supposed, but derived in straight line from Asherah: W-S *'ŝr(t)* Aram. *'tr*, still preserved in the older variant *'tr'th* instead of the later, more common, syncretistic *'tr'th*. The second half, *'th*, explained as *'attâ*>*'antâ*, is most probably not the Aramaic form of the name of the goddess Anath, but a similarly sounding feminine formation from the root *'anâ* "to oppress, to crush," Akk. *enû* "to bend, to oppress, to squeeze"—semantically related to *dārak* in *Derketô*. *Tiršu* "the trampler," mentioned above (p. 187), was probably another name of the same goddess. Grape juice or wine, according to Semitic phraseology, was "blood of trees" (Ugar. *dm 'ṣm*) or "blood of grapes" (Gen. 49: 11 *dām 'ănābîm*), and the association of ideas between the trampling in the "blood" of grapes and in human blood was easy for the ancient mentality, both metaphorically and practically. Thus, Atargatis means "Asherah the oppressor," and we will discover this epithet, expressed by other equivalent Semitic roots, in the names of several Greek goddesses and heroines.[2]

Does this reconstruction agree with what is known about Asherah from the Ugaritic myths? She is represented there as the spouse of the supreme god, the Bull El, qualified as "merciful" (*lṭpn*) and "kind" (*d-pid*), but to whom, nevertheless (or rather precisely because of), Phoenicians and Carthaginians systematically sacrificed children, and occasionally adults too. Asherah's relation to Baal,

[1] The parallelism between Atargatis-Ichthys and Ino-Melicertes was already visible to KELLER, *Tiere des klass. Altert.*, 290, quoted in CDXXXIII, *s.v. Melikertes*. Same idea, LXII, 225 ss.

[2] Justification, references, and elaboration of these statements must be postponed for a separate chapter.

who seems not to have been her son, but her stepson,[1] was clearly hostile. True, bribed by an expensive gift, she agreed to intercede for Baal in order to obtain for him El's permission to have his own house; but Baal's death caused joy to her and her sons. The Hittite translation of a Canaanite myth may provide a clue in explaining the origin of that hostility.[2] Ašertu is described there as the unfaithful wife of the supreme god Elkunirša (apparently *'El qônē 'arṣa*, "El creator of the earth"); she tried to obtain the love of the Storm-god (i.e., Baal), threatening to prick him with her spindle if he refused.[3] The Storm-god, however, told the whole truth to his father Elkunirša—that Ašertu deceived her husband and continually sent her maidservants for him. Elkunirša ordered the Storm-god to insult Ašertu. He did so by coming to her and saying: "Of thy [. . . .], I killed seventy-seven, I killed eighty-eight." [4] Ašertu took great offence and became furious. She began to mourn for seven years. The gods (or the men?) languished, they drank abundantly, but—as OTTEN restores this place—they could not be sated and could not quench their thirst. At Ašertu's complaint, Elkunirša agreed to give up the Storm-god to her so that she could treat him according to her own discretion. Their talk was overheard by the ally of the Storm-god, the goddess designated by the ideogram ^{d}IŠTAR and corresponding, of course, to Baal's sister and companion-in-arms Anath. The end of this is not known—but this myth fits perfectly into the framework of the Ugaritic Baal and Anath cycle and explains a great deal in it.

This Canaanite myth in Hittite translation supplies us with an exact parallel to the myth of Ino. In that latter myth, too, Phrixos is presented as a handsome youth, slandered by a married woman who fell in love with him and was rejected—but for some reason, in the extant version, this rôle does not belong to Ino, who caused

[1] In Ugaritic poems, Baal is called *bn Dgn* "son of Dagan" (Bibl. Dagon), but there are no real reasons for supposing that El and Dagan were two distinct divine figures. El, "god" *par excellence*, was the title of Dagan (the god's proper name). Their having been mentioned separately in the same texts does not prove the contrary: each hypostase of El (and also of Baal, elsewhere of Ištar etc.) was listed apart.

[2] The following summary of the text is made on the basis of its publication by OTTEN, CD; he correctly identified all characters of the text with their Canaanite originals.

[3] Cf. the spindle (*plk*) in Asherah's hand, II AB (= UM 51): II: 3-4.

[4] Otten tentatively restores "[sons?]," and calls attention to the genuine Ugaritic number-pattern 77 // 88.

him to be sacrificed, but to Biadice, the wife of Athamas' brother Cretheus; she is, of course, Ino's doublet.[1] The heat and thirst caused by Ašertu for seven years in revenge for having been insulted by the Storm-god are also present: [2] in the myth of Ino, they are paralleled by the hunger she provoked by parching the seeds. Phrixos apparently retained quite few of the Storm-god Baal's characteristics, he was fully euhemerized; but nonetheless his association with his sister Helle reminds us of Baal and Anath, and his flight through the air on the back of the golden ram sent him by his mother Nephele, "cloud," is strongly reminiscent of Baal's most frequent epithet—*rkb ʿrpt*, "Rider of the Clouds." Helle's fall and death in the sea is another reflection of the custom of throwing women into the sea both as sacrifices to and symbols of the cruel sea-goddess.[3]

After this exposition, perhaps it will not seem arbitrary if we try to derive the name *Inô* from the root *ʿānâ*, Piel *ʿinnâ* "to oppress, to weigh heavy," with which we have also related *ʿattâ* < *ʿantâ* in the name of her Syrian (Aramaized) counterpart Atargatis (*ʾtr-ʿth*, later *ʿtr-ʿth*). The scarcity of evidence does not, however, allow us to reject completely the possibility of another Semitic etymology, proposed by V. Bérard—from W-S *ʿên* "spring." [4] He understood it, of course, in the spirit of his "toponymic" theory in mythology, and saw in Ino merely the personified abstraction of all numerous coastal springs which used to be visited by Phoenician seamen and purple-snail fishers. We made sure that Ino was an independent mythological figure, with her own epic story and a distinctive individuality. But a goddess *Bêlit-êni* "Lady of the Spring" is attested in a Ugaritic religious text, written in the Akkadian language but in Ugaritic alphabet. It appears presumably, but with a high degree of probability, in UM 105: 27-28 (a hymn to Ištar as a star), and quite clearly in UM 107: 1: *iš*[ ]*t blt in* which Dhorme [5] transcribed by Akkadian *ê šu*[*ʾe*]*tu bêlit êni* "O sovereign,

[1] Her name is very transparent: "she who judges by force." The names of Athamas' brothers, Cretheus and Salmoneus, are most certainly Semitic: the former is evidently *Krt*, the hero of a Ugaritic epic cycle, the latter has repeatedly been compared with *Śalmôn*, father of Boaz, Ruth 4: 21, and similar Biblical and Semitic names.

[2] Another example of the Canaanite seven-year pattern of fertile and sterile years, stressed by Gordon, ccxxiii, 4 and elsewhere.

[3] More about it—in chapt. III (pp. 282 ss.), in connection with the Argonauts myth.

[4] lxv, II, 401.

[5] cxviii, 90, 93.

Lady of the Spring!" The same goddess is further qualified as (again in DHORME's transcription) *bêlit [îm]ti ruḫi û šip[ti] bêltu [bâna]t kalama* "Lady of magic, witchcraft and incantation, Lady creatress of all." Who that goddess was is not known. But, on the other hand, springs do not play any rôle in the myth of Ino, and of all places associated with her cult, only in one shrine, near Thalamae, was there actually a spring of sweet water (Paus. III: 26: 1).

The name of the god *Melikertês*, Ino's son, was for a long time regarded as a good Greek transcription of the name of the well-known Phoenician god *Melqart* (for *Mlk-qrt* "king of the city"), the patron deity of Tyre. During the anti-Phoenician reaction, this name, too, had a hard time. MAASS [1] declared it a purely Greek name, from *meli* "honey" and *keirô* "to cut, to cut out," i.e. "the honey (-combs)-cutter." Even Ed. MEYER, who usually agreed with that general attitude, could not accept this view: "such a name is monstrous for a god," "not even the slightest hint of honey can be detected in the tradition." [2] He remained faithful to the identity of the *names* (not of the essences!) of *Melikertês* and *Melqart*, but made the reservation that the Greeks transferred the name of "Melicertes which was senseless for them" to the sea-demon Palaemon ("fighter") just so, without any motivation. Strange as it may seem, the identification of Melicertes with Melqart was recently opposed by such an enthusiast of Canaan as René DUSSAUD; [3] he asserted, besides, that Melqart was a late artificial product of syncretism, a synthesis of Baal and his adversary (in Ugaritic poems) Yamm, the Sea, created under Hiram I (i.e., in the Xth century). Of course, if DUSSAUD was right, the name of Melqart could not have penetrated into Greece in the Mycenaean age. If it is admitted, despite this, that Melicertes *was* the Greek form of Melqart, one would be compelled to regard this as an instance of the secondary reception of a Phoenician cult, somewhere closer to the middle of first millennium, through the binational milieu of Greco-Phoenician Cyprus—as happened with the popular cult of Adonis.

However, the difference between Adonis and Melicertes is very marked. Adonis was not integrated into the Greek heroic saga, he did not become a Greek character, but remained a foreigner (Assy-

[1] CCCL, 22-27.
[2] CCCLXIII, II, 2, 121 s.
[3] CXLIV, 210; CXLV, 2.

rian, Byblian, Phoenico-Cypriot). Melicertes was, for all Greek story-tellers and listeners, a local Greek hero—maybe, by his mother, of Phoenician origin, but living and dying in Greece, in an ancient royal city and family. In contrast to Adonis, Melicertes-Palaemon had both temples and cults in several Greek cities. This certainly proves that Melicertes had been assimilated very early, at the same time as Danaos and Cadmos. That Melicertes was Melqart, and not just some "honey-cutter," is shown by the splendid doublet, and even triplet, of his names, convincingly displayed by V. BÉRARD:[1] *Palaimôn*, or *Palemôn*, Melicertes' other name, is Phoenician *Baʿal-hāmôn* "lord of multitude," synonym of *Melk-qart* "king of the city," and *Learchos*, the brother and double of Melicertes, bears a name signifying in Greek "leader of the people," Greek doublet of *Baʿal-hāmôn*.[2]

The presumption that the god Melqart was first invented by the Tyrians in the Xth century is largely based on the information by Menandros of Ephesos, the Greek historian of Tyre (ap. Josephus *Antiqu.* VIII: 5: 3) that Hiram was the first to celebrate the awakening (*egersis*) of Heracles (= Melqart) in the month of Peritios (February-March). But this fragment refers rather to a change in the date of the feast, not to the introduction of a new feast, and still less to that of a new deity. The first epigraphic mention of Melqart belongs to the IXth century and occurs, characteristically, not in a Phoenician but in an Aramaic inscription of Bar-Hadad,

[1] LXV, II, 397 s.

[2] The softening of *b* into *p* is not exceptional in Greek transcriptions of Semitic words and names, and inside Semitic languages themselves, cf. above, p. 129 s. For the name of Baal, see the characteristic instances of spelling the names ^{m}*Ba-lum-me* (EA 8: 18) = ^{m}*Pa-a-lu-ú-ma* (EA 162: 76), and ^{m}*Baʿlu^{lu}ia* (EA 170: 2) = ^{m}*Pa-a-lu-ia* (EA 165: 9). R. EISLER explained *Palaimôn* as *Baʿal-Ḥammôn*, a well-known Phoenician god; but Baʿal-Ḥammon was not identified with Melqart, and the disadvantage of EISLER's interpretation is the loss of the excellent semantic correspondence pointed to by V. BÉRARD. The latter's reconstruction, *Baʿal-Hāmôn*, moreover, is not invented: a locality of that name really existed somewhere in Palestine, perhaps in the neighborhood of Jerusalem; there was a vineyard ascribed there to Solomon (Cant. 8: 11). Like Baʿal-Ṣ^{e}phon, Baʿal-Gâd, Baʿal-P^{e}ġôr etc., this place owed its name to a god. *Baʿal-Hāmôn*, "the Lord of Tumult", seems to have been a Dionysos-like figure, like *Balmarkodas* or *koiranos kômon* (*Baʿal-marqôd*, "the Lord that makes dance") of Arados. His name belongs to the same category as *Bromios* "tumultuous", a common epithet of Dionysos. Perhaps it is not by chance that the locality Baʿal-Hāmôn was famous for its vineyards. The Greeks, of course, could understand *Palaimôn* as "wrestler, fighter," from *palaiô*; but there are no traces whatsoever of a fighting-motif in his myth and cult.

king of Aram.[1] But no excavations were executed in Tyre and no early Tyrian inscriptions are available to confirm or to refute the worship of Melqart in Tyre prior to Hiram I; the priests of Melqart's temple in Tyre, for that matter, assured Herodotos (II: 4) that that temple existed since the foundation of the city, for 2,300 years. One cannot, of course, rely upon them, but it is suggested by the religious history of other Phoenician, Egyptian, Babylonian, and Greek cities, that the cult of local patron deities was very conservative and often went back to times immemorial. The stele of Bar-Hadad shows that the cult of Melqart was widespread far beyond the limits of the Tyrian kingdom and its possessions; this could have been true, to some degree, for a much earlier time, too. A very characteristic example of the relatively of epigraphic evidence is the case of the Babylonian god ^{d}*Da-ma-al-la*. Until recently he was known only by a unique mention in a cuneiform hymn from the Seleucid time;[2] in a quite surprising way he was discovered in a list of offerings to gods in the Ugaritic language, found during the 15th campaign of excavations at Ras Shamra.[3] Thus, it turned out that this god had been not only worshipped in Babylonia, at least since the middle of the second millennium, but had already succeeded in penetrating far to the West.

Melicertes and Learchos personify two modes of human sacrifices: the victims being slain by people in a state of temporary insanity and considered by them as stags, as described in the myths of Athamas, of Actaeon, or in the fragment of *Bassarika* mentioned above, p. 166, p. 167 n. 1; or being drowned in the sea or in a lake, which is peculiar not only to avatars of Derceto-Atargatis, but sometimes to Dionysos as well: besides his jump into the sea escaping Lycurgos (*Iliad* VI: 130 ss.), the Argives had an aetiological myth about Dionysos having been thrown by Perseus into the lake near Lerna from which he was solemnly evoked every year.[4] On the Isthmus of Corinth, the altar of Melicertes stood on the very shore of the sea, near a pine-tree consecrated to him, and it was told that a dolphin had brought the dead Melicertes there, and Sisyphos found and buried him and established the Isthmian games in his honor (Paus. II: 1: 3; Plut. *Quaest. conv.* 4: 3: 1). Again we are in the

[1] XXVIII; CCLI; CCCXXVII, with ALBRIGHT'S XXI.

[2] CXI, No. 686.

[3] DXXIV, No. 4 (RŠ 15.130): rev. 3: *l.dml*; identified with ^{d}*Da-ma-al-la* *ibid.*

[4] *Schol. T.Iliad* XIV: 319, *ap.* CDI, 73 s.; Plut. *De Is. et Os.* 35.

presence of the dying god's connection with the pine, as in the cult of Dionysos, the tale of Bata and the Byblian tradition that the dead body of Osiris came floating over the sea and grew into the stem of an evergreen tree (Plut. *de Is. et Osir.* 15, 16).

Other Evidence on Semitic Elements in Boeotia

In this section we shall enumerate briefly certain traces of Semitic toponymics and mythical onomastics in Boeotia, which are not directly connected with the great cycle of Cadmos and the Cadmids. Some of them were noticed by earlier scholars, some others, we hope, will be examined more in detail in connection with related myths.

a) *Ogygos* or *Ogygês*, ancient king of the region where Cadmos later built Thebes, and hero of the Boeotian flood myth. One of the seven gates of Thebes was named Ogygian after him. His name recalls that of the island of Ogygia where Odysseus saved himself from shipwreck. The motif of Odysseus escaping alone, while all his companions perished in the sea, may reasonably be compared with the motif of Ut-Napištim/Noah/Ogygos/Deucalion as the only mortals surviving the flood. On the other hand, the hero of the Egyptian Tale of the Shipwrecked Sailor, the only survivor of his ship's crew, landed on an island belonging to a serpent who threatened to reduce him into ashes and told him that all his family had been consumed by a fire that fell from heaven, and, moreover, that his island was doomed to disappear under the water. The international motif of flood is here implicated very clearly, and the serpent's fairy island may be called Island of Fire. Danaë and Perseus, cast into the sea in a chest, landed on the island of Seriphos (Heb. *śārâph* means both "serpent" and "blaze"). The island of Lesbos was, on the mythical plane, styled *Makaria* "Island of the Blessed" and also *Pyrrha* "fiery" and *Issa* (in which Bérard, *Phén. et Odyss.*, I, p. 166, recognized the Semitic doublet of *Pyrrha*, *'iš(t)* "fire"). The wife of Ogygos' counterpart Deucalion was named *Pyrrha*. This, and several other examples, show that the motif of *fire-island* was closely connected with that of universal flood or its reduced version, individual disaster in the sea. We derive therefore the name of the rescue-island Ogygia and of the flood-hero Ogygos from the Semitic root *'āgag* "to burn, to flame."

b) *Thêbê,* wife of Ogygos, the flood hero; or of Zethos, one of the founders of Thebes. The name signifies "ark,"[1] thence it passed to the city founded on the landing-spot, and from the city to its female eponym.

c) *Zêthos,* co-founder of Greater Thebes (with Amphion). W-S *zêt* (Heb. *zayit*) "olive-tree," cf. pers. n. *Zêtan* I Chr. 7: 10,[2] and perhaps the divine name *Sz-Zt* in the Canaanite incantation from Arslan Tash.[3]

d) *Dirkê,* name of a river near Thebes and of the cruel mythical queen of that city who wanted to kill her niece Antiope by tying her to the horns of a wild bull, but instead herself perished such a death. Her mutilated remnants were then thrown into the river which was thereupon named for her. She corresponds both in name and essence to Derceto, wife of the Bull-god El, goddess of human sacrifices, who was herself thrown into the pond of Ascalon. She resembles in many aspects Ino. On her tomb, the Boeotarchs used to offer mysterious nightly sacrifices.

e) *Ismênos,* river near Thebes. Its name has frequently been compared with that of the Phoenician healer-god Ešmun.[4] We see no reason to reject this etymology (cf. the river Adonis in Phoenicia). Ešmun, as other healing deities, was a serpent god, and the other name of the river Ismenos may have had this signification (see below, f). Apollo was worshipped in Thebes under the name of Apollo Ismenios, and Apollo, too, was a god of healing.

f) *Ladôn,* another name of Ismenos (Paus. IX: 10: 6). This was formed from the blood of the dragon killed by Cadmos. The dragon who guarded the golden apples of the Hesperides was also named

[1] See p. 158, n. 2 above.

[2] LXXXI, 140.

[3] CXXIX, 425, IV: 1, 5; VI, 9; CDXCIII, 27; CLXXXV, 187. None of these authors' very divergent explanations of *Sz-Zt* seems to solve this enigmatic word or name, Our suggestion is that the first part of it represents the Sumerian god ^{d}*Ša(g)-zu* "the heart-knower" (CXI, Nos. 3062, 3069), whose name was included among the 50 names of Marduk, *Enuma Eliš* VII, names Nos. 18-23 (CDLXXI, 70; LXXI, 296). In North Mesopotamia *Šazu* would be pronounced, in the Assyrian manner, *Sazu,* and his nature of a god "from whom the evil-doer cannot escape" (*Enuma Eliš, l.c.*) makes him fit the incantation against evil demons very well. The second part, *zt,* is the god of olive-trees, identified here with *Sazu.* Olive oil played a prominent rôle in Oriental medicine and magic (cf. CCLXXVI, 325 s.; CCLXXV, II, 2, 749 s.).

[4] CCCXXV, II, 334 s.; LXII, 232; LXV, II, 366.

Ladôn (Apoll. Rhod. IV: 1394).[1] It was said of the Syrian river Orontes that it arose from the remains of the wounded dragon Typhon who, before expiring, crawled into the source of that river.[2] The Ugaritic Prince Sea, alias Judge River, was represented as a dragon. In Libya, not far from the Lake Triton, was a river by the name of *Lathôn* or *Lêton*.[3] All this, taken together, permits us to see in the river and dragon Ladôn/Lathôn the dragon *Ltn* of the Ugaritic myths (Heb. *liwyātān*, Leviathan).

g) *Asôpos*, river in southern Boeotia. Cf. Heb. pers. n. *ʾĀsāph* (in Phoenician likely to be pronounced *ʾĀsōph*), legendary singer and seer; *ʾāsôph* "granary"; *ʾāsaph* "to gather, to collect," esp. grapes and fruits (same in Ugaritic). The river was probably named for a harvest-god.

h) Mount *Kithairôn*, convincingly explained by V. Bérard [4] by the Semitic root *qṭr*, Heb. Piel *qiṭṭēr* "to offer burnt sacrifices." We refer to his excellent comparison of the peculiar sacrificial ritual on Mount Cithaeron, described in detail by Pausanias IX: 3: 2-9, with the Syrian holocaust of Hierapolis described by Lucian, *de Deâ Syriâ* 49.

i) *Atalantê*, daughter of Iason, of Schoinus in Arcadia, or daughter of Schoinos of Boeotian Orchomenos, virgin huntress, heroine of the Calydonian hunt. She challenged those who wooed her to a footrace, overtook and killed them with her spear, until Melanion gained the race by a ruse. After her death she was changed into a lioness. She corresponds to the huntress Virgin Anath who did not suffer rivals, and to the man-slaying Babylonian Ištar. Her name, signifying in Greek "equal by weight," which hardly explains her nature, may rather be understood as *atal* (= Akk. *eṭlu* "hero") + *ʿAnta*, one of the W-S forms of the name of Anath.[5] A lioness-goddess

[1] On Ladon—river and dragon—cf. LXII, 232; CDXI, XI, 1, 382-395 (of course the name was transferred from the dragon to the river, not vice versa, as stated in the latter place).

[2] See sources listed CDXI, XVIII, 1, 1163.

[3] *Op. cit.*, XII, 1, 908.

[4] LXV, II, 411 ss.

[5] In the Beth-Shean inscriptions of Seti I, the goddess is called ʿAntit. XIV, 88 supposed the existence of a form *ʿ*Antat*, with a double feminine ending. Cf. the pers. name from Ugarit: *Abdi-an-ta* (RŠ 14.16:4) or *Abdi-an-tu* (*ibid.* 6, 9), i.e. *ʿbd-ʿnt* (DXXVI, 174, No. IV). In the Tanis inscriptions of Ramses II, the goddess is called *ʿAnta*, and the Pharaoh is described as her *mhr* (CCCLXXI, 2)—cf. *mhr ʿnt* at Ugarit p. 197 above.—If, however, we take the first element of the name *Atalantê* as Greek *atalos*, epic and poetic for "young, youthful," we obtain Atalanta = *btlt ʿnt* "Virgin Anath" or *rḥm ʿnt* "Maiden Anath," standard epithets of the goddess at Ugarit.

was worshipped in Ugarit, both under the W-S name *lbit*[1] and the Sumerian name *Prgl*[2] = *Piri(g)-gal,* "great lioness," adopted by the Hurrians as early as the time of the Agade dynasty.[3]

j) *Thisbê,* a city in Boeotia. This name, according to V. Bérard, "which has nothing Greek, belongs to the onomastics of the Scripture: *Tišbā,* LXX *Thisba.*"[4] More precisely, this locality appears only in Elijah's gentilic *hat-Tišbî*; it was located (I Kings 17: 1) somewhere in Gilead, but is not localized. However, since miraculous faculties of provoking drought and granting rain were ascribed to Elijah, he must have been largely assimilated with the Storm-god, whose name was *Teššub* among the Hurrians, who lived in a symbiosis with Semites in North Syria, and in the Amarna age even more to the south, in Palestine (in Ugaritic alphabetic transcription, UM § 20.1987, *Tšb*). So both the home-town of Elijah and the Boeotian city were named for that god.

k) Heracles in Thespiae. As reported by Pausanias (VII: 5: 5), there was an ancient temple of Heracles in the Boeotian city of Thespiae, with a strange statue of the hero, very different from the common Greek models, but of the same style as the statue of Heracles in Ionian Erythrae which was said to have come from Tyre on a raft (see above, p. 144, n. 5), *viz.*, with an Egyptian aspect. Indeed, on coins of Erythrae, a statue is represented in a style defined by archaeologists as "Egyptianizing Phoenician style." The hero is represented naked, without the lion-hide, his legs together, his right hand shaking a mace over his head, while the left grasps a scepter or a dagger.[5] Judging from this description, the statue was essentially like the well-known relief from Ugarit representing Baal,[6] and even more like a North Syrian bronze figurine conventionally designated as an image of Teššub.[7] And since Baal was

[1] Theophorous name *ʿbd-Lbit* UM 321: III: 38, cf. *UM* § 20.1000; CDXC, 105, who compares Akk. epithets of Ištar: *la-ab-bat* *^{d}I-gi-gi* and *la-ba-tu Ištar*. Same name *ʿbd-Lbʾt* on a javelin-head from Palestine (c. XIIth century), CCCLXVII, 6-9.

[2] UM 3: 50 *[d]bḥ. mlk. l. prgl* "the king's sacrifice (or "the *molk*-sacrifice") to *Prgl.*" *UM* § 20.1575: "n. of a divinity?" IIIa, No. 2263: "probably n. of a divinity."

[3] CDIX, 1 ss.: a temple to the goddess Pirigal built by Tisari, king of Urkeš, a Hurrian prince of Upper Mesopotamia.

[4] LXV, II, 376.

[5] *Ibid.*, 26, 377.

[6] CDXX, 168, fig. 490.

[7] CDXVI, 141, fig. 14: "a bronze figure of North Syrian Teshub, provenance unknown, now in Museum of Glasgow." Bronze and silver statuettes of the

identified by the IId millennium Syrians with the Hurrian Teššub (Ugar. *Tŝb*), the idea suggests itself that the name of Thespiai, before being understood as a derivation of *thespis* "inspired by god," itself bore the name of that god.[1]

l) *Tanagra*, a city in southeast Boeotia, had been settled, according to Herodotos (V: 57) by the Phoenician tribe of Gephyraeans (see below, m). The name is un-Greek. Since *nġr* is Ugaritic for "guard" (*UM* § 20.1260), **tanaġrā* would be a good Semitic toponym: "watch-tower, sentry-post." For the form, cf. Heb. *ta'ăwā* "lust" (from *'āwâ* "to desire"), *ta'ălā* "curse" (from *'ālâ* "to curse, to conjure"), *tabnît* "building" (from *bānâ* "to build"), *Tab^e'ērā* geogr. n. Num. 11: 3 (from *bā'ar* "to burn"), *taḫanôt* "encampment" (from *ḫānâ* "to camp") etc., etc.

m) *Gephyraioi*, ancient inhabitants of Tanagra, then an Attic clan with certain peculiar cults. Herodotos, who pretends to have made a personal investigation of their origin, claims that the Gephyraeans descended from Phoenician companions of Cadmos who had received Tanagra by lot (V: 57). If he is right, *Gephyraioi* may derive not from Greek *gephyra* "bridge," but from the root *ġpr*, Arab. *ġafara* "to cover, veil, hide, or conceal," *ġafr*, *ġifarat* "veil," Ugaritic *ġprt* "veil,"[2] *yġpr* NK (= UM 77): 28 "he will cover with a veil."[3] Thus *Gephyraioi* may go back to *ġaphûrā*, part. pass. fem.: "the veiled one," epithet of a goddess, cf. the veil of Europa, her by-name *tiktam* "she is veiled," and her rôle of the mythical sister of Cadmos.

n) *Elieus*, epithet of Zeus in Thebes (Hesych.). Already Samuel BOCHART, *Chanaan*, I, cap. 17, recognized the Phoenician divine name *Eliun* in it, recorded by Philo as equivalent to Greek *Hypsistos* "the Most-High,"[4] (Heb. *'Ēl 'Elyôn* Gen. 14: 18 etc.). For the change of ending, cf. *Typhôn* (certainly from W-S Ṣaphôn), variant

same type, obviously produced "in a Phoenician or North Syrian factory," were "very popular imports into Crete and Greece in the Late Minoan III period," CCLXVII, 311 s., and fig. 63. This may be indicative as to the age of the statue in Thespiae.

[1] The passage of *b* to *p* may be due to a secondary process, as frequently observed in Greek.

[2] DXXIV, No. 106 (RŠ 15.115): 7.

[3] This verb has not been recognized by the translators of this passage, but it fits very well, since the passage deals with preparing a young goddess for wedding.

[4] CCCXXV, II, 334; LXII, 64.

Typhôeus.[1] As noted by LENORMANT, *Zeus Elieus* of Thebes is evidently identical with *Zeus Hypsistos* who had a temple in the same city and gave his name to one of the city's gates (Paus. IX: 8: 3).

Each of these rapprochements may seem unimportant and fortuitous by itself, but taken together, added to the great Cadmid cycle, this agglomeration of Semitic elements in one relatively small area cannot fail to make a certain impression.[2]

THE THEOGONY OF HESIOD AND THE MYTH OF KUMARBI

After the publication of the Hittite translation of the Hurrian myth of "the kingdom of heaven" (usually named the Kumarbi myth), its astonishing resemblance to the beginning of Hesiod's *Theogony* made it quite certain that Hesiod had "Oriental forerunners," whose works he used. "How did these myths reach the Greeks?" asked H. G. GÜTERBOCK in his remarkable comparative study to which we refer for the essence of the problem.[3] Having rejected the theory of E. FORRER [4] that they came to the Greeks from Ḫatti, through Western Anatolia, many centuries after the fall of Hittite Empire, GÜTERBOCK declares:

> Another explanation, which was first proposed by B. LANDSBERGER, seems more likely to me: that these myths reached the Greeks by the way of Phoenicia. Not only did the Greeks consider the Phoenicians as their masters, but through the discovery of the epic texts of Ras Shamra (ancient Ugarit), we know that a literature of this kind had flourished in Phoenicia at the time of the Hittite Empire . . . Before the discovery of the Ras Shamra and Boğazköy texts, scholars used to

[1] Or else, in a simpler way, the W-S original of *Elieus* could have been a shorter form, *ʿly*, an epithet of Baal UM 126: III: 6-7, 8-9. Cf. *UM* § 20.1402, quoting and discussing DAHOOD's "The Divine Name *ʿēlî* in the Psalms."

[2] Pausanias IX: 12: 2 affirmed that *Onga* (spelled *Ogga*), the name of Athena in Thebes, whose altar was attributed to Cadmos, was a Phoenician name. Other authors spell it *Onka* (*Ogka*). Unfortunately, none of them transmitted the meaning that was ascribed to it, and the ambiguity of transcription makes it very difficult to propose any Semitic etymology (one of the several suggested ones is that of V. BÉRARD, LXV, II, 367, from *ḥuqqā* "law"). A Boeotian name occurring in two or three variants (*Ergynos*, father of Trophonios in Lebadeia; *Erginos*, mythical king of Orchomenos; *Argynnis*, epithet of Aphrodite) resembles the Ugaritic pers. n. *Irgn* UM 151: 13, but the resemblance may be accidental. In no case can the Ugaritic *Irgn* be considered as a Greek name: *Erginos/Ergynos*, taken as Greek, are usually derived from *ergô* "to work"—but in pre-classical times this root began by a digamma: *wergô*.

[3] CCXL, 110 ss.; CCXXXIX, 133.

[4] CLXV, 711.

> distrust Philo who, according to them, had taken this story from Hesiod. That this accusation was wrong now becomes clear from our texts. Especially the fact that Philo still has a generation preceding Ouranos, which was omitted in Greek mythology, is a strong argument for the assumption that he got his material not from Hesiod but from an old source. The question of whether or not the Greeks got their mythology from Phoenicia can now be answered in the affirmative. But the Phoenicians were not the inventors of these myths; they were merely intermediaries between the Hurrians and the Greeks.[1]

The last statement of H. G. GÜTERBOCK is subject to caution. One of the principal episodes of the text he has published and commented on takes place on Mount Ḫazi = Casius, Mount *Ṣpn* of the Ugaritic myths, in Semitic territory, where the Hurrians had settled only toward the middle of the second millennium.[2] The monster Ullikumi, begotten by Kumarbi to fight with the Storm-god, appears from the sea beneath Mount Casius, i.e. from the Mediterranean Sea, long familiar to West Semites, but entirely strange to the purely continental Hurrians. In another Hurrian myth, that of Ištar and the mountain Pišaiša, the latter is listed by the Hittites among the mountains of Syria.[3] It should be admitted rather that the myth of Kumarbi, besides purely Hurrian elements, contains many Sumero-Babylonian motifs and characters (Alalu, Anu, etc.) and also distinctive borrowings from West Semites. Apart from this remark, we agree unconditionally with GÜTERBOCK's conclusion: "The relation of the latter [= the Greek epic] to the oriental world can now, I think, be regarded as well established." [4] This is a first-rate contribution to the problem of Hellenosemitica.

It must be noted in the context of this chapter, largely devoted to Boeotia, that Hesiod was an inhabitant of the Boeotian Ascra, near Mount Helicon, as he himself stated in his *Erga*: 639. True,

[1] CCXXXIX, 133. LANDSBERGER's article, to which GÜTERBOCK referred, was published in Turkish in 1942 (see CCXL, 111, n. 56). Another author who immediately after the first publication of the Kumarbi text compared it to Hesiod and Philo was F. DORNSEIFF; cf. his article republished in CXXII, 35-69 (written 1937).

[2] Cf. CLXXXVII, 40.

[3] CCXL, 122; CD, 147. The name of Kumarbi's vizir, *Mukišanu*, is a W-S gentilic of Mukiš, the northern neighbor of Ugarit. On the general relation between the Hurrian and the W-S religions, cf. LAROCHE, quoted p. 45, n. 1 above.

[4] CCXXXIX, 134. Cf. OTTEN's endorsement of the important rôle ascribed to Canaanites and to Phoenicians in particular in transmitting Oriental myths to the Greeks, CD, 149.

some historians of Greek literature do not believe that the *Theogony* and *Erga* were written by the same author; they try to draw a distinction between the learned theologist of the former and the simple peasant of the latter.[1] But Robert VIPPER, the author of an excellent *History of Greece* (1916), who, by the way, never doubted that both poems were written by Hesiod,[2] made the following fine remark about the accusatory speeches in *Erga*: "Where did Hesiod take the right and the courage to speak in such a preaching tone? . . . In the poem *Works and Days* many aphorisms, omens, admonitions are scattered, which could have been learned by Hesiod only in a school directed by priests and seers. The poet has mastered well the religious wisdom of his time . . . The priestly philosophy of history betrays itself in many ideas and images of Hesiod." [3] Besides, it is said in the *Theogony* itself, that this poem was written near Helicon (*Theog.* 22-23). The story of the first generations of gods is only the most significant, but not a unique instance of Hesiod's dependence on oriental models. The sharp invectives of Hesiod against the abuses of the kings and their unjust trials, written "in the style of Old Testament prophets," [4] certainly go back in their style and contents to the Canaanite precursors of the social demands of the Hebrew prophets, of which a remarkable sample forms the end of the Ugaritic poem of Keret.[5] The myth of the golden age at the dawn of mankind, of the flood which destroyed the second, silver generation, of the chest of Pandora, who caused, through her curiosity, pains and sufferings to humanity, and many

[1] Cf. on this problem and its history RZACH, "Hesiodos," CDXI, VIII, I, esp. 1187-1201.

[2] DIX, 59.

[3] *Ibid.*, 68.

[4] *Loc. cit.*

[5] For comparison: Hesiod *Erga* 267-269: "Remember my words, ye kings, devourers of gifts (*dôrophagoi*); judge according to the conscience; never ordain an unjust sentence. Zeus' eye sees everything, knows everything; he looks upon you, when he wants to, he knows how judgment is done in the midst of the cities"; II K (= UM 127): 43-54 (our translation differs in some details from CCXXIII, 82 s., CXCVI, 149, CCXXIX, 25): "Hear, O *Krt-Ṡ*ʿ!/Listen and incline (?) (thy) ear! / Like the worst of plunderers thou rulest / And (like) an offender thou governest. / Thou hast let thy hand fall into destruction (or distress). / Thou judgest not the cause of the widow, / Thou adjudicatest not the case of the wretched, / Thou drivest not out those who prey on the poor. / Before thy face, thou feedest not the orphan, / (Nor) behind thy back, the widow. / Like (thy) bedfellow is the sickness, / (Like thy) concubine, the disease. / Descend from the kingship — I shall reign, / From thy sovereignty—I shall sit upon it."

other details in *Erga* can be traced back to Sumerian and Babylonian myths,[1] adopted and elaborated by West Semites and known to us from the first eleven chapters of Genesis.

All this allows us to make certain conclusions as to the circumstances in which Oriental myths in Boeotia were transformed and incorporated into the poems of Hesiod. This was not a result of recent borrowings from the Phoenicians, as, let us say the Orientalizing style in art. It was not from the Phoenician merchants who sold *athyrmata* (trinkets, *Odyss.* XV: 416) that Greek priests and religious poets could learn the deepest secrets of oriental theology, mythology, and social-ethical programs. And the last candidate to be closely acquainted with Phoenician traders was, of course, Hesiod, the thrifty, severe, puritan peasant from a remote village, resembling his older contemporary Amos from Tekoa; he certainly disliked the Phoenicians as much as did the prophets of Israel and Judah. All his wisdom and theological lore was certainly received in the local Boeotian priestly circles; and if his works are so integrally saturated with oriental elements, this means that oriental wisdom and mythology were carefully preserved and transmitted from generation to generation by the Boeotian clergy—since the very time of Cadmeian colonization, when the W-S element in Boeotia was represented not by the sporadic appearance of retail merchants, but by seagoing conquerors, kings, warriors, city-founders, who were accompanied by their priests, seers, singers, the transmitters of the age-old religious tradition.

A Glance at the Tribe of the Cadmeians

We have established that from the point of view of historical background the myth of Cadmos is not different from that of Danaos: it preserved only the bare statement that the ancestor-eponym had come from the Semitic East,—which is confirmed by the comparative analysis of the myth. But, as to the details of the story, all of them, without exception, reflect not the actual events of the tribe's migration from Phoenicia and its establishment in Boeotia, but repeat the fabulous motifs inherent to the eponymous hero in his quality as a mythical entity, a god or a demigod, and consolidated by the consecrated epic religious tradition. It is precisely the presence of such a great quantity of W-S and Mesopo-

[1] E.g. the Sumerian myth of the Golden Age, cf. CCXCVI, 107, n. 2.

tamian personal names, toponyms, cults and myths in Thebes and the rest of Boeotia that speaks convincingly for the settlement of a large and strong W-S group in Boeotia, which was the origin of the tribe of Cadmeians and of their fortress, Cadmeia.

Up to now, we have regarded Cadmos as an individual mythical hero. But his rôle as the eponym of a real tribe (Cadmeians) also agrees with W-S usage.[1] In a Ugaritic poem from the Baal cycle, II AB (= UM 51): VII: 34, mention is already made of certain *qdmym*, a word formed of the stem *qdm* + ethnic suffix plur. *-ym*.[2] Directly before that line, the text is broken for a few lines, and the context is therefore very unclear, but immediately after it follow intelligible lines: "The enemies of Baal seize the forests, the foes of Hadd, the fringes of the mountain" [3]—and this allows us to venture a rapprochement with V AB (= ʿnt): II: 7-8, where Anath, sister and defender of Baal, "smites the people of the seashore, destroys mankind of the sunrise." If *qdmym* be understood as "easterners", they would correspond to "mankind of the sunrise" (*adm ṣat špš*); "westerners"—perhaps here called *ʿrbym* or *mʿrbym*, corresponding to "the people of the seashore" (*lim ḫp y*[*m*])—might have figured in the badly damaged line 51: VII: 33, in parallelism to *qdmym* and probably in connection with *ʿmq* "valley," as *qdmym* are put in connection with *bmt* "hill." Here, of course, the poem means by *qdmym* the inhabitants of the East in general, not a concrete tribe. But in other instances the meaning might have been narrower and more concrete. Thus, there existed in the Ugaritic kingdom a town named *Mʿrby* "western," whose inhabitants were *mʿrbym* (*UM* § 20.1445).[4] In North Mesopotamia in the XVIIIth century, two confederations of W-S nomadic tribes existed, *Benê-Iamina* "sons of the South" and *Benê-Simʾâl* "sons of the North"; later the same names (and probably the same tribes) appear as the tribe of Ben-

[1] Lenormant, cccxxv, II, 322 grasped the essence of the problem: "In the personality of Cadmos, two ideas, two distinct figures melt into one. Cadmos is at the same time the *Oriental*, the chief of the principal Phoenician colony in Greece, and *one of the gods* whose cult was introduced by that colony."

[2] Gordon, ccxxiii, 36 translates *qdmym* by "the early ones," but in *UM* § 20.1662 puts it off "for further studies."

[3] Translation ccxxiii, 36.

[4] In the tablet RŠ 11.790: 11 rendered ideographically [ālGIŠ.ŠU (SILAN) = *erêb šamši* (dxxix, 125, 145), usually written in Akk. [āl]*Ma-ʾ-ra-bá*, [āl]*Ma-ra-bá* (dxxii, 50, 52, No. XXVIII: III: 30). A settlement [āl]*Ma-ra-ba* (perhaps the same) also belonged to the kingdom of Alalaḫ, AT 269: 18.

jamin in Palestine and the city and state Śam'âl in North Syria. So the cardinal points of West, North, and South could well provide names for real tribes and cities.

The matter was not different for the East, *qdm*. As early as the Egyptian tale of Sinuhe (time of the XIIth dynasty) there is mention of a region *Qdm* somewhere in Syria, apparently not far from Byblos.[1] A town *Qa-du-me* existed in the kingdom of Alalaḫ (mod. Qadimiye near Aleppo).[2] The Bible calls the nomadic tribes to the east of Palestine by the general name of *Beⁿê-Qedem*, and mentions once (Gen. 15: 19) a tribe of Qadmonites (collective sing. *haq-Qadmônî*) after the Negeb tribes of Qenites and Qenizzites. The ending *-n* (*-ôn, -ân*) served in Ugarit as an ethnic, along with *-y*, and sometimes took the extended form *-yn* (*-iyyôn, -iyyân*), e.g. *nġšyn* "Nuḫaššean". Both forms of the Greek name of the Cadmeians, *Kadmeioi* and *Kadmeiônes*, being Greek in construction, at the same time strictly reproduce W-S *qdmym* (*Qadmiyyîm*) and **qdmynm* (**Qadmiyyônîm*), and the name of the fortress *Kadmeia* corresponds to W-S toponyms in *-y* (*-iyya*) which were common in Ugarit and to which also belongs the Danunian *'ztwdy*.

The question put by Ed. MEYER (above, p. 149)—which comes from which: the ethnonym *Kadmeioi* from the toponym *Kadmeia*, or vice versa—can hardly be solved with certitude. Speaking in general, in spite of Ed. MEYER's opinion, the archaic tribes of Greece, reminiscences of which were preserved in the *Iliad*, did not pass on their names to the cities they inhabited.[3] One can envisage two possible variants of the origin of the ethnonym *Kadmeioi*. Either the colonizers of Thebes were in the main natives of some Syrian region named *Qdm*—for instance, that mentioned in the story of Sinuhe; then the introduction of the ethnic *qdmym* into Boeotia would be analogous to the introduction of the ethnic *dnnym*, Danunians, into Argolis. Or (which is perhaps more plausible) the evolution was the same as e.g., in the case of the goddess ʿAštart > the city ʿAštarôt > the ethnic ʿAštarôtî, or the god Ḥôrôn > the city Bêt-Ḥôrôn > the ethnic Ḥôrônî. In both cases, the eponymous hero and the ideal founder of the city was the homo-

[1] Translation DXLIX, 19. The term may have been less vague than WILSON (DXLIX, 19, n. 10) and HELCK (CCL, 45) consider it.

[2] Frequently mentioned, cf. DLII, 155 (index); XXXIX, No. 149.

[3] We know the tribes of Abantes in Euboea, Epeians in Elis, Lapiths and Myrmidons in Thessaly, Danaans in Argolis, but they never named their cities and their territories with their tribal names.

nymous god Qadm, the W-S personification of sunrise, dawn, and morning-star, the head of the group of the "good gods," protectors of seamen and givers of fertility, who had absorbed the essential characteristics of the Sumerian serpent-god and dragon-fighter Ningišzida. It is possible that the founders of Cadmeia had a special predilection for the god Qadm (Šaḥar) even in their old home, and it is equally possible that, since every city must have had its patron deity, they chose Qadm precisely because he reminded them of their eastern homeland and they felt themselves Easterners in the new and strange land of the West, *'arôb-šamši*—Europe. In any case, Cadmeians and Cadmeia fully correspond onomastically to such ethnonyms and toponyms as Benê-Iamina, Benjamin, and Edomite Têmân for the South,[1] Benê-Sim'âl, Śam'âl, and Mount Ṣaphôn for the North,[2] *M'rby* and *m'rbym* for the West,[3] not to speak of the exactly equivalent *Qdm*, Qadume, Bᵉnê-Qedem, and Qadmônîm.[4]

The myth, centered on the individual hero and not on the tribe, paid little attention to the Phoenician companions of Cadmos. It even made all of them perish in the jaws of the dragon, to make room for the autochthonous warriors grown from the dragon's teeth. But Greek historians regarded the coming of the Phoenicians to Boeotia as an important mass migration. Herodotos V: 57 tells about partitioning the whole of Boeotia among the Phoenicians who came with Cadmos, and about Tanagra having fallen to the Gephyraeans. All this is, of course, his own guess, and he betrays himself by the anachronistic attribution to Cadmos of the introduction of Phoenician letters into Greece (V: 58).[5] Still more precise data, half a millennium later, are brought by Pausanias (IX: 5: 1). He plainly tells of an invasion by a whole Phoenician army headed by Cadmos, which defeated the native tribes of Aones and Hyantes; the former surrendered to the Phoenicians, the latter preferred to leave for neighboring Phocis. He probably based his report on works of

[1] And even now Yemen ("South") in South Arabia.

[2] And even now eš-Šâm ("North"), the Arabic name of Syria.

[3] And even now Maġrib (Morocco and North-West Africa generally).

[4] We found somewhere in the recent literature the following singular objection (already made by BELOCH, LVI, 129): how could people from the East call themselves, in their own language, "Easterners"? Well, the Norsemen called themselves Norsemen or Normans ("men from the North") wherever their settled: in Normandy, in England, in South Italy, and in Sicily, and their descendants still call their country Norway (Norge).

[5] Cf., however, the suggestion made by MARINATOS, p. 147, n. 2 above.

earlier Boeotian historians, who certainly did not possess reliable data on events so remote, but who, on the other hand, made their deductions, as did Herodotos, from observing the numerous remnants of Phoenicianism in the Boeotia of their own time. The analysis of Boeotian toponymics, mythology, and local traditions shows, indeed, that the guesses of Herodotos and Pausanias did not disagree, in their main outlines, with what really must have happened some time back in the Mycenaean age.[1] Without many men and a lasting domination over the country, the Semitic newcomers would not have been able to impose on Boeotia, so thoroughly and for so long a time, so many of their names, vocabulary, beliefs, and cults.

[1] The only modern scholar to accept these statements of Herodotos and Pausanias is, so far as we know, TJUMENEV, CDXCII, 33.

CHAPTER THREE

BELLEROPHON AND OTHER GRECO-SEMITIC HEALER-HEROES

PART A

Onomastica and Attributes of Healing Gods

Is Bellerophon a Semitic Name?

Greek mythical characters of Semitic origin may be found not only within large cycles as the Danaan or the Cadmeian whose Oriental or direct Phoenician origin was admitted by the Greeks themselves. The sound of some name often attracts attention by its apparent Semitic coloring. The possibility of suggesting a more or less fitting Semitic etymology for such a name seemed to many scholars of former generations to be the solution of the question. Actually, however, it is not quite so simple. The establishment of an etymology is only the first step; the principal work is thereby only begun.

One of such names is *Bellerophôn*. The bearer of it was the hero of a vivid, dramatic myth which, in Euripides' treatment,[1] received a bold theomachist tendency. Yet the signification of his sonorous distinctive name was totally unintelligible even to the ancient Greeks themselves. They were compelled to have recourse to etymological guesses and to construct aetiological stories. The name *Bellerophôn, -ontos,* was reinterpreted into *Bellerophontês,* the second half of which was understood as "slayer" (like in *Argeïphontês* "killer of Argos," surname of Hermes). Thence the naïve guess that, accordingly, *Bellerophontês* had killed a certain *Belleros* and was therefore compelled to flee from Corinth. Homer, in his story of Bellerophon, does not know anything about it. The Byzantine archbishop Eustathios (632: 7; 635: 5) reports the existence of another form of this name, *Ellerophontês,* and interprets it as

[1] Euripides, frg. 297 from the lost tragedy *Bellerophon*; though fragmentary, it gives a notion of the tragedy's conception.

phoneus kakias "slayer of evil."[1] In the XIXth century, several attempts were made to give an Aryan (Sanscrit) etymology to the element *Belleros*, e.g. through the derivation *Belleros* < **Belteros* < **Velteros* > *Vr̥tra*, the monstrous serpent killed by Indra in the Vedic religion, so that Bellerophon turned out to be an avatar of Indra.[2] All these etymologies proved to be quite untenable and have been abandoned long ago, without being replaced by better ones.

It seems that H. LEWY was the first to turn toward Semitic languages in order to explain this name.[3] Many of the etymologies proposed in his book are so forced and elaborate that they do not evoke any confidence. This one, however, raises thoughtful attention. H. LEWY understood *Bellerophôn* as *Beʿel-rāphôn* "Baal of healing, salvation," like *Bʿl-mrpʾ* in the Phoenician inscription CIS I, No. 41. The form *Beʿel* instead of *Baʿal* he explained as Aramaic, and *rāphôn*—as a formation from the root *rāphâ* (for *rāphâʾ* "to heal"), an abstract notion like *gāʾôn* "grandeur," *hāmôn* "tumult, crowd," *ḥāzôn* "vision." He reconstructed, for the alleged variant *Ellerophontês*, the original *ʾĒl-Rāphôn*, comparing it to Raphael and referring to the parallelism *Baʿal-b^erît* = *ʾEl-b^erît* Judg. 9: 4. 46, *B^eʿelyādâ* I Chr. 14: 7 = *ʾElyādâ* II Sam. 5: 16, *Baʿal-Ḥammôn* and *ʾEl-Ḥammôn* in Phoenician inscriptions. The vowel *e* slipped in between *ll* and *r*. The rest is popular etymology.

Let us examine, for the time being, H. LEWY's etymology from its purely linguistic side.

1) There is absolutely no need to derive *-rophôn* from *rāphâ* (i.e., *rpy*) instead of *rāphâʾ* (i.e., *rpʾ*). Only the latter means "to treat for an illness, to heal," while the former signifies "to sink, to weaken," and does not fit for a name with the presumed sense of "Baal of healing." A formation in *-n* from the root *rpʾ* is actually attested in W-S: this is the Ugaritic pers. n. *Rpan* (UM 91: 7; 150: 4; 300: rev. 14), in Akk. transcription ^m*Rap-a-na*,[4] which in Phoenician

[1] BETHE, "Bellerophon", *ap.* CDXI, III, 1, 241 suspected that the variant *Ellerophontês* was specially invented for etymological purposes. And indeed, despite Bellerophon's popularity, this variant does not occur anywhere else. We may therefore disregard it in our investigation.

[2] Cf. CCXXXVI, 105, where other odd etymologies are also quoted.

[3] CCCXXX, 190-193, and earlier in *N. Jahrb. f. Philol.*, 1892, 185. This etymology was promptly adopted by V. BÉRARD, LXII, 116; LXV, I, 192.

[4] CCCXC, 164, RŠ 16.363: 11'. It may be worthwhile to quote the pseudo-epigraphic *Testament of Solomon*, according to which Solomon built temples to Baal and Raphan (CXCVII, IV, 153 s.). *Raphan* is exactly the Ugaritic *Rpan* = *Rap-a-na*; there probably still was a healing-god of that name in

would have been pronounced **Roph'ôn*.[1] It must be taken not as an abstract noun "healing," but as a personal name in *-n* with the sense "healer", like Ugar. divine names and surnames like *Lṭpn*, *Škmn*, pers. n. like *Ubln*, *Bʿln*, *Brqn*, *Ḫrpn*, *Ktmn*, *Nʿmn*, and dozens of other similar, or like Heb. pers. n. *Gidʿôn*, *Naḥšôn*, *Šimšôn* etc.

2) There is no need, either, to resort the Aramaic pronunciation of *Bʿl* as *Beʿel* in order to explain the first *epsilon* in *Bellerophon*. Aramaic influence began to be felt outside Syria much to late to be taken in account for this name. Reduction of *a* to *e* is quite common in Greek renderings of Semitic names, as *Ekdippa* for *'Akzib*, *Melchisedek* for *Malkiṣedeq*, *Semiramis* for *Sammuramat* etc. One may also compare Tiglathpileser III's spellings *Sibitti-bi-'-il* (a king of Byblos) and *Matan-bi-'-il* (a king of Arados), along with more common *Ba-'-li-Ṣa-pu-na*,[2] and much earlier, in the Amarna Age, the W-S name of an Alašian: *Be-el-ša-am-ma* (EA 37: 26).[3]

3) The double lambda does not necessarily point to gemination in the Semitic original. Here are a few proper names—pers. and geogr.—with geminated consonants in LXX transcription, while there is none in the Hebrew text: *Sennaar* Gen. 10: 10 (*Šinᵉʿār*), *Balla* Gen. 14: 2 (*Belaʿ*, on a wrong place), *Balla* Gen. 30: 4 (*Bilhā*, originally **Balhā*), *Basemmath* Gen. 36: 2 (*Baśᵉmat*), *Mannachath* ibid.: 23 (*Mānaḫat*), *Bamma* II Sam. 4: 6 (*Baʿanā*) etc., and besides LXX, *Ioppa* (Heb. *Yaphô*, Akk. *Iapu*). In many cases, the gemination compensated for the dropping of an aspirate or laryngal (*h* or ʿ).

Thus, with the preceding emendations, the derivation of *Bellerophôn* from **Baʿal-rāphôn* is quite possible and regular. However, *comparaison n'est pas raison*. In our previous research into the Danaan and Cadmeian cycles we were guided by the rule that can briefly be formulated thus: the principal and essential stress is put on the similarity and relationship not of *names*, but of mythical motifs. As for the names, they are compared only under the condition that the functional role of their bearers and not merely their sound is identical or analogous. Neither H. LEWY, nor

Syria toward the end of the pre-Christian era; and the sequence "to Baal and Raphan" is reminiscent of the reconstructed form Baʿal-rāph'ôn.

[1] Even if, under the influence of the aleph, it were pronounced *Rᵉphō'ôn*, it would become *rophôn* in Greek: the šᵉwā mobile would repeat the following full vowel, as in LXX, and the ending *-aôn*/*-oôn* or *-an* would shift to *-ôn* in classical Greek: cf. Posidaôn-Potidan-Poseidôn.

[2] CCCXLV, I, §§ 770, 772, 800.

[3] This name may be understood as *Baʿal-šammâ* "Baal is an object of fear."

V. BÉRARD found it necessary to support the Semitic etymology of the name of Bellerophon by a comparative study of his myth. We shall take up this task, but in a wider scope. In order to elucidate the character of Bellerophon, we shall have to take into consideration a number of other personages which, at first sight, have very little if anything in common with him. This will prove worthwhile, because in this way we shall get acquainted with one more cycle of Greco-Semitic mythical heroes, united this time not by common genealogy or location, but by their being part of the important category of healing heroes and gods.

SUMERIAN AND SEMITIC PARALLELS TO THE NAME OF BELLEROPHON

Are there, in Semitic mythology, any names similar to the hypothetical prototype of the name of Bellerophon? A combination that fully coincides—i.e., **Bʿl-rpʾn*—has not yet been found in epigraphics, though *Rpʾn* (*Rpan*) itself is attested in Ugaritic human onomastics. However, very similar names are commonly encountered in the mythology and epigraphics of Syria, Phoenicia, and Mesopotamia.

a) Ninazu and Ningišzida

These Sumerian gods, whom we have met in previous chapters, fell to the rank of secondary divinities in their homeland after the end of the last neo-Sumerian IIId Dynasty of Ur. However, Sumerian culture left a very strong impact upon the Western Semites—not only through the Akkadians as a part of general Babylonian culture, but directly, through the Sumerian colonies on the middle Euphrates (Mari) and in Syria (Qaṭna). In art, this is demonstrated by a bronze portrait head from Alalaḫ (XVIIth century) which goes back to Sumerian models of late third millennium, and even by the much more primitive statue of Idri-mi of Alalaḫ (XVth century).[1] In religion, this manifests itself by the continuity of symbols, iconography, and sometimes of onomastica. Deities who had lost their importance in Babylonia, had their

[1] WOOLLEY, Introduction to CDLXVIII, 8; DLV, 77 s. He sees in the clumsy statue of Idri-mi "a complete break from the Sumerian-influenced school that produced the magnificent portrait head of Yarim-Lim" (CDLXVIII, 8); its general style, however, is reminiscent of Sumerianized peripheral art, especially that of early Mari, and DUSSAUD, CLII, 157 was right in considering this statue a specimen of "Sumerian art which survived in provincial surrounding."

independent development in the W-S territories. As convincingly shown by STARCKY in his excellent study,[1] Ninazu was, most probably, the prototype of many, if not of all, W-S healing gods. His name literally means "Lord Physician" and, translated into W-S, is actually found in different variants. We have already examined the Sumerian myth of his conception in Hades, and seen that this myth was apparently reproduced in Ugaritic poetry (above, pp. 87 ss.).

Ninazu was considered the father of the god Ningišzida (^{d}*Nin-giš-zi(d)-da, Nin-giz-zi(d)-da*), who was also endowed with the virtue of healing.[2] His symbol was a snake or two entwined snakes; he was depicted as a man with serpents growing out of his shoulders, and identified with the serpent-deity Šeraḫ (Šaḫan) and the constellation of Hydra (^{mul}*Muš*). The semantics of his name are subject to discussion, but it is clear that he was related by his name with "tree," or "wooden pole," as the symbol of the vegetation-spirit.[3]

b) Muš and Ugaritic Mŝ/Mŝt

We saw (above, p. 89,198) that the Ugaritic *Mŝ*, the son of Baal and the heifer-goddess (Anath) conceived in Hades, corresponds to Ninazu in the plane of mythological motifs, and that his name, which has no Semitic etymology,[4] has to be explained rather as a Sumerian than as an Egyptian name. Now, in the context of other chthonic deities, it is time to substantiate our identification of Ugaritic *Mŝ* with Sumerian *Muš* "serpent."

Phonetically, the correspondence of *Mŝ* to *Muš* is flawless. There simply could be no other transliteration of *Muš* by means of Ugaritic alphabetic signs. The Ugaritic letter *ŝ*, though genetically derived

[1] CDLXXVIII, 73 s. [2] DI, 69.

[3] According to CXV, 557-560, *Nin-giš-zi-da* = *bêl iṣ kitti* "Lord of the Tree of Truth"; according to XLVIII, 255 = "Lady of the Tree of Life"; according to CDLVII, 176 = "Lady of the Upright Pole." *Nin* may be "lord" as well as "lady"; *giš* may be both "tree" and "wooden object"; *zi*, as shown by the last sign *da*, the Sumerian genitive suffix which repeats the closing consonant of the preceding syllable, cannot be ZI = *napištu* "life," but must be understood as ZI(D) = *imnu* "upright" or *kênu* "faithful, sure, normal." Thus "Lord of the Upright Pole" seems to be the most plausible translation. See also p. 312 below.

[4] Some understand *Mŝ* and *Mŝt* as, respectively, "son" and "daughter" (CDXXV, 153, n. 2), or "lad" and "lass" (*UM* § 20.1185), both authors (and III, § 21) comparing Egyptian *ms* "child" or "born"; others, without any comparative reasons, as "lord" and "lady" (XIII, 17) or "male one" and "damsel" (CCXXX, 50, 105).

from Proto-Semitic *ṯ*, was actually pronounced exactly like its correspondents in Hebrew, Amorite and Akkadian: [sh]. It occupies the place of the Hebreo-Phoenician *šin* in the sequence of the Ugaritic ABC,[1] and it is transliterated by the Akkadian sign *ša* in the comparative chart composed by Ugaritic scribes.[2] All proper names written with *š* in Akkadian have this sound rendered by the Ugaritic *ṡ*, eg., *Alašia* = *Alṡy*, *Šubaru* = *Ṡbr*, *Aššuraia* = *Aṡrym*, *Šuppiluliuma* = *Ṡpllm*. In the Akkadian texts transliterated with Ugaritic signs, the Akkadian *š* is rendered by *ṡ*, even if there is a *š* in cognate Ugaritic words, e.g. *šumu* = *ṡm* (Ugar. *šm*), *lišlim* = *lṡlm* (Ugar. *šlm*), *šarru* = *ṡr* (Ugar. *šr*). Akkadian *mûši mušîti* "Night, O Night," is transliterated in Ugaritic by *mṡy mṡty*; [3] *mûšu* "night" has no relation to *muš* "serpent", but they are homonyms.

The following considerations speak against the Egyptian origin both of *Mṡ* and of the Hebrew name *Môše*, similar in appearance. Though in the cuneiform transcription of XVth-XIIIth centuries the Egyptian element *ms*(*w*) or *mś*(*w*) is rendered by *ma-ša*,[4] in Hebrew the Egyptian *s*/*ś* is rendered by *samek*: *R*ʿ-*ms-sw* = *Ra*ʿ*amses*, *p*3-*nḥs* = *Pinḥas*, *T-ḥ-p*3-*nḥsj* = *Taḥpanḥes*. *Môše* does not harmonize with it, and this disharmony has not yet been explained satisfactorily.[5] It is therefore preferable to detach *Môše* from Egyptian loan-names. The same applies to *Mṡ*, though we do not know of even one Ugaritic transliteration of an Egyptian name containing the sound *s*/*ś*, in order to make a comparison. More important than linguistic considerations, however, seems to be, in this instance, a historic one. In spite of Ugarit's submission to Egypt under the XVIIIth dynasty and of the lively commercial and political relations between the two countries even afterward, not a single borrowing from Egyptian divine or human onomastica could be detected in the entire mass of Ugaritic texts. On the

[1] DXXII, 22 s.; *UM* § 3.1.
[2] DXXI, 65 s. (RŠ 19.159 = DXXIV, No. 189).
[3] Cf. p. 133 above.
[4] Cf. XII, Nos. 3, 11, *17, 48, 60.
[5] According to CCXXXIV, 230 s., *Ra*ʿ*amsēs* was a late form in Hebrew. But *Pinḥas* was obviously borrowed from Egyptian not later than the XIth century, and probably earlier—so why does it have a *samek*, not a *šin*? ALBRIGHT gave contradictory explanations to this phenomenon: in 1925, he interpreted the form *Pinḥas* as the result of the local Ephraimite pronunciation (*sibbôlet* instead of *šibbôlet*, Judg. 12: 6), XIV, 84, n. 1; in 1950, on the contrary, he considered the form *Môše* "a inner Hebrew development," XXV, 171, n. 33.

contrary, the Sumerian element is very noticeable in the Ugaritic pantheon and mythology. Sumerian names of deities often appear in Ugarit in a partially Semitized form, which reveals the long duration of their taking root in W-S religion. *Nkl-w-Ib*, i.e. *Nikkal* < *Ningal* + *Ib* < Akk. *enbu* "fruit," epithet of Sin,[1] is not the unique Sumerian divinity at Ugarit. To it must be joined: 2) *Ušḫry*, the Sumerian healing goddess *Išḫara*; 3) *Prgl*, the Sumerian *Piri*(*g*)-*gal*, "Great Lioness" (cf. above, p. 215); 4) *Ppšr*, "*Pp* the Prince", i.e. the Sumerian *Pap-sukkal*, "Pap the vizier", with *sukkal* replaced by the equivalent *šr* (cf. p. 190, n. 4 above); 5) *Pbl-mlk* in the Poem of *Krt*, i.e. the Sumerian god *Pa-bil-sag* (cf. below, p. 300 s.); 6) *Bʿlt-bhtm*, corresponding in her name and essence to the Sumerian goddess *Nin-é-gal*, Mistress of the Syrian city of Qaṭna (cf. above, p. 160). Including *Mš*, this would make as many as seven Sumerian gods—a proportionally large number in the relatively small Ugaritic pantheon. This permits us to consider the presence of the Sumerian serpent-god in Ugaritic mythology not as an uncommon or rare exception, but as a normal phenomenon, attested many times.

Such an interpretation of *Mš*, the son of Baal and Anath the heifer, is corroborated by the other Ugaritic variant which gives him the name of *Rpu-Bʿl* "Healing Lord" = *Ninazu*, the chthonic healer-god, normally symbolized by a serpent. For the Hebrew *Môše*, too, the association with the Canaaneo-Sumerian serpent-god seems to be much more convincing than with the pale banal Egyptian hypocoristic from some name composed with *ms*(*w*) "born." The ophic features of Moses are very pronounced: his sacred emblems are the serpent-wand and the bronze serpent on a pole; his tribe is Levi, whose name also signifies "serpent" and who was the son of Leah, the "cow" (cf. above, p. 90 s.); he is a healer in the full sense of this word, knowing both how to cause and to heal diseases. Moreover, the gentilic from *Môše*, preserved in the name of the Levite clan of *Mûšî*,[2] proves that the original vowel was not *a*,[3] but *u*.[4]

However, if *Mš* = *Muš* "serpent", how should one understand the feminine from *Mšt* which figures in the names of two Ugaritic

[1] *UM* § 20.7; CDXCV, 61 s.

[2] DXLV, 143.

[3] XXV, 171, n. 33: "*Môše* (Egypt. *Māšĕ*, later *Mōšĕ*)."

[4] The Greek transcription *Môusês* reflects *û*, not *ô*, and *ôu* was originally read *û*, not *oÿ*: cf. Heb. *Gûnî* > LXX *Gôuni* Gen. 46: 24; Akk. *Mummu* > Damascius *Môumis*.

mythical heroines: *Mšt-Dnty*, the wife of Danel, and *Mšt-Ḥry*, the wife of *Krt*? [1] In the same way as *Mš*—it is also "serpent," but with a feminine ending (cf. Heb. pers. name, masc. *Nāḥāš* I Sam. 11: 11 etc., fem. *Neḥuštâ'* II Kings 24: 8). The Sumerian serpent-deity could be both male and female.[2] The constellation mul*Muš* was identified not only with the god Ningišzida, but with the goddess Ereškigal as well.[3] For the wife of Danel *mt rpi* "man of healing," whose namesake, Dan, was a serpent (cf. above, p. 72), the name of *Mšt* "she-serpent" fits in the best way. *Mšt-Ḥry*, the wife of *Krt*, was also the daughter of *Pbl-mlk*, i.e. of the Sumerian god Pabilsag, mentioned above, husband of the healer-goddess Ninkarrak, father of the healing-goddess (or god) Damu. The Sumerian word for "serpent," with the Semitic feminine flexion, is also quite natural for her.[4] The second part of her name, *Ḥry*, is not merely a common noun or adjective:[5] a goddess *Ḥrt'* existed in Palmyra,[6] and the same Syrian goddess was, many centuries earlier, mentioned in Egyptian inscriptions of the New Kingdom. Her name was apparently given to a locality near the Sinaitic border, *Pî-hā-ḥirôt* of Ex. 14: 2 = **Pî-Ḥ-r-t* "temple of the goddess *Ḥ-r-t*." [7] We derive *Ḥry* from *ḥārar* "to flame, to blaze," [8] so that *Mšt-Ḥry* would signify "fiery serpent." From very numerous examples of association between serpent and fire, we will limit ourselves here only to Heb. *śārâph* "serpent" from the root *śāraph* "to burn," and to the Sume-

[1] Commonly translated, without proof, "lady,"; but to be certain, one should have detected this vocable in a context where it would be used as a common noun, detached from the personal names of the heroines of the Aqht and Krt epics.

[2] The deity dKA.DI (now certain to be read d*Sataran*), identified with d*Muš* (CXII, IV, 1, No. 15: 46) was considered a goddess (DLVIII, 505), but also a god (DXXXIX, 98 s.).

[3] CCXXVI, No. 284.

[4] See p. 301 below.

[5] DXVII, 89: *ḥry* is parallel to *ġlmt* "young woman" and *ašt* "wife"; *UM* § 20.660: "free"; CCXXX, 104 s.: "a Hurrian" (but "Hurrian," as it might be expected, is *ḫry* in Ugaritic).

[6] Cited in one inscription with the goddess Nanai and the god Rešeph, also on tesseras, LXXXVIII, 268 ss.

[7] XV, 16. A daughter of the Hyksos king Apopi was named *Ḥ-r-ta*, CCL, 102. As we hope to show elsewhere, names with semantics connected with "flame," "blaze" and the like were unusually popular among the Hyksos rulers.

[8] *UM* § 20.660 and IIIa, No. 974 also derive this name from *ḥrr*, but with the sense of "being free" (as in South Arabic); morphologically, however, this makes no difference.

rian incantation to the Great Serpent: "Great Serpent, seed of fire!" [1] We interpret the line *ḥr.bšnm.uḫd.bʿl-m* in the mythological Fragment RŠ 15. 134: 6,[2] in the same sense, which VIROLLEAUD translated "Baal will seize the hole of the serpents." Though the Arabic *ḥaur* is, indeed, "hole," in Ugaritic, Hebrew, and Akkadian words containing the sounds *ḫr* were used.[3] Thus, here we have rather "glaze, flame of the serpents." Finally, if ALBRIGHT's decipherment of the Old Sinaitic inscriptions can be taken as definitive, in many of them *mš* is preceded by *dt bšnm* "that of the serpents" and is never found without it.[4]

c) *Rpu-Bʿl*

We are already thoroughly acquainted with *Rpu-Bʿl*, son of Baal and the heifer, a chthonic deity identical with *Mš* (see above, p. 197-202). Let us now look upon him from the viewpoint of the direct signification of his name: "Healing Baal" or "Lord Healer." This is an exact translation of the Sumerian *Ninazu* and, at the same time, it fully corresponds to the prototype of the name of Bellerophon, **Bʿl-rp*ʾ(*n*). Both components stand here in reverse order, but according to the rules of Semitic onomastica this has no importance whatsoever for the meaning of the name.[5]

d) *the Rephaim*

The Ugaritic *Rpu-Bʿl* appears in close connection with figures called *rpum*. They are obviously identical with the Phoenician *rp*ʾ*m*, Hebrew *r*ᵉ*phā*ʾ*îm*—the ghosts of the dead in the Nether World. The re-interpretation of the *r*ᵉ*phā*ʾ*îm* as a mythical ancient giant people who allegedly inhabited Palestine before the Canaanites is a secondary development. Their name puzzled scholars; they could see no relationship between spirits of the dead and the notion of medicine, implicated in the root of their name—*rāphâ*ʾ "to heal," whence *rōphe*ʾ "physician" (Hebrew and Phoenician). There were proposals to derive their name from the root *rāphâ* "to be weak, to go down," which was believed to indicate the weakness and immateriality of

[1] CCLXXXII, 56.
[2] DXXIV, 3, No. 1.
[3] Akk. *ḫurru* "hole," Ugar. *b-ḫrt* "in the holes," *ḫr* "Underworld," Arab. *ḫurr*.
[4] XIII, Nos. 351, 353, 360, 361.
[5] Cf. *Beelzebul* (*Baʿal-Z*ᵉ*bûl*) and Ugar. *Zbl Bʿl*, Heb. *ʾĒliyâhū* and *Yôʾēl*, *ʿAmmiʾēl* and *ʾEliʿamm* (same man), *Y*ᵉ*hôyākîn* and *Y*ᵉ*kôniyâhū* (same man), Ugar. *Ibnkl* and *Nkl-w-Ib* (same goddess), etc.

the shadows in Hades. But there is no need to distort the root, depriving it of its third radical aleph. Those who are amazed by the etymology of Rephaim from *rāphâ'* "to heal," simply do not understand the organic association between the notions of the Nether World—the chthonic cycle—and of healing, i.e. granting health, strength, fertility, and fecundity.

In the Ugaritic invocation to the Rephaim, they are invited to mount their horse-driven chariots and to visit treshing-floors and plantations: *mġy rpum l grnt* [*w ilnym*[1] *l*] *mṭ't*, I Rp. (= UM 121): I: 6-7.[2] It was, consequently, expected that their presence would have a wholesome effect on the crops and the vineyards. The dead were considered the natural givers of harvest: the earth where they lay germinates the seeds cast into its bosom, and nourishes the roots which penetrate it. Thence follows one line of association with medicine: the prosperity of human beings is equated with that of vegetation. The second line of association proceeds from an idea which is diametrically opposed to health and preservation of life —from the idea of death. The primitive mentality had no doubts that whoever is capable of taking life away is its full master; accordingly, if he is duly propitiated, he may grant life as well. Hence the phenomenon which seems strange for the modern mind: the common worship of poisonous and deadly creatures as symbols of health, prosperity, and healing. The underground gods (and the ghosts were actually considered as belonging to them), precisely because they had power over the living and could at any moment call them into their dark abode, were by this very reason propitiated as givers and preserves of life. Hence both the dread of the dead and the desire to win them over.

e) *Dnil mt rpi*

It is not by accident that the Ugaritic texts on the Rephaim adjoin the epic of Danel and *Aqht*. Danel, as mentioned earlier (cf. p. 72, n. 4 above), was a giver and withholder of harvest and a typical magician-healer. There is no doubt that his permanent epithet *mt rpi* signifies "man of healing," although there may be some hesitation

[1] *Ilnym*—one of the names for underground ghosts, cf. *UM* § 20.128; literally—"gods," cf. Phoen. *'lnm* (CCXLVI, 77).

[2] Completed after parallel passages. In spite of the text's lack of clarity, the impression is that their number was 7/8, the favorite figures-combination at Ugarit. CDLXXVIII, 79 compares them to the beneficient heptad of the Babylonian spirits (*sibitti*).

as to what the Ugaritians themselves associated with these words. Was there not a portion of truth in the first interpretation of Danel's title by VIROLLEAUD [1] and DHORME [2] who, in 1936, understood it as identical with *Mt* (= *Môt*), the god of death and the Nether World? Certainly, Danel is far from being dead, but his qualification as *mt* expresses his belonging to the cycle of chthonic fertility-gods.[3] Mot himself, Baal's adversary, is depicted in the moment of his death as a typical "spirit of the harvest," "the last sheaf," and in the poem UM 52 he is magically equated with a vine. FRAZER brought many examples from the European agrarian ritual from which it follows that the visual personification of Death in seasonal ceremonies was considered dangerous, but at the same time beneficial, as a giver of harvest and fertility.[4] If our reasoning is correct, Danel personified this salutary aspect of Death.

In the epic of Danel, as we noted, many details are related to ophic motifs. One of the more significant of these details is the association of Danel with eagles as a hostile power who killed and devoured his son. Eagle and serpent form a very common symbolic pair.[5] This motif is expressed in the clearest way in the Babylonian myth of Etana. The eagle treacherously devoured the serpent's young, and the serpent, in revenge, broke the eagle's wings and threw him into a pit, where he was doomed to perish. Etana found and healed the eagle, and the latter, as a reward, took him into heaven to bring down from there the "plant of birth," without which Etana could have no son. All these motifs, except the flight to heaven, appear in the Danel cycle, although in a different arrangement. On the other hand, the motif of flight to heaven, first

[1] DXVIII, 87 s.

[2] CXVII, 106 s.

[3] According to CDXCIV, 45, the two antediluvian names containing the element *mt-* (*M^etušelaḥ* and *M^etuša'ēl*—the only of their kind in the Bible) are composed, respectively, with *Šelaḥ*, the name of the Canaanite underworld river, and *Še'ôl* "Hades."

[4] CLXXV, IV, 233-240, 246-254.

[5] Beside the myth of Etana, it is found in *Iliad* XII: 200-209 (an eagle holding in his talons a huge serpent who finished by biting him—the apparition considered an ominous portent); in Aristophanes *Equites* 218-222 (parodying an oracle about a serpent's victory over an eagle); in Plutarch *Vita Themist.* 26 (Themistocles' dream of a serpent which was entwined around him, changed itself into an eagle, carried him away and deposited on a golden wand of a herald). A synthesis of the two was achieved by inventing winged dragons, especially popular in the desert of Sinai, where they were mentioned as real beings by Isaiah 30: 6 and Herodot. II: 75.

described in the myth of Etana, gained very wide diffusion,[1] and we shall meet it frequently throughout the present chapter, including in the myth of Bellerophon.

f) Raphael

VIROLLEAUD correctly compared the name *Rpu-Bʿl* with Raphael (*R*^{e}*phâʾel*) in Jewish angelology.[2] Not only his name is parallel to that of *Rpu-Bʿl*, but in essence, too, he remained even in the Judaism of the Second Temple epoch and of later times a degraded (mediatized [3]) chthonic healer-god. In the book of Tobit, Raphael is the angel who healed Tobit from blindness. In one midrash it is said directly that God was so pleased by a group of angels that he changed its leader's name from Labbiel into Raphael, appointed him Angel of Leechcraft, and handed him over all kinds of drugs and remedies.[4] At the same time, Raphael—like his Sumero-Babylonian prototypes and the Canaanite *Rpu-Bʿl*—was the Prince of Hades (I Enoch 20: 2 s.; 22: 106).[5] It seems that even his parallel name of Labbiel is very ancient and characteristic. The Babylonians reported on the constellation of Serpent (i.e., Hydra) that it was the image of the dragon *Labbu*.[6] Thus, *Labbiʾēl* signifies—if one proceeds from Akkadian—"serpent-god," and Raphael's symbol as a Jewish angel was precisely a serpent.[7] The constellation ^{mul}*Muš*, as already mentioned, represented both Ningišzida, the chthonic healer-god, and Ereškigal, the queen of Hades.

g) Šd-rpʾ

For details we refer to the excellent comparative monograph by

[1] Cf. *inter alia* Yahwe's words in the Exodus legend (Ex. 19: 4): "I lifted you on wings of eagles and brought you to me"—a very clear echo of the Etana myth.

[2] DXVIII, 88, n. 1.

[4] The term "mediatization" was used in Germany, when Napoleon deprived scores of small princes, counts and barons of their territorial sovereignty and included their domains within the states of larger rulers. We conventionally apply this term to the mechanism of transforming former gods into angels, changing them from free and rather independent vassals of a supreme god into courtiers and officials of the unique God.

[4] CXCVII, I, 54; V, 70 s. (sources: Midrāšîm Konen 26-27, and Yeraḥmeʾēl 14-15).

[5] CXCVII, V, 71, with a pertinent analysis which, however, misses the relationship between Rephaim and healing.

[6] CCCLVIII, II, 410.

[7] Celsus, quoted by Origen, *Against Celsus* VI: 30, who quotes analogous conceptions of the Ophite gnostics (CDXXVII, IV, 586 s.).

Jean Starcky,[1] who understands this name as *Šed-râphe'*, "genius-healer." The cult of this god was widespread at Palmyra, where his permanent attributes on numerous extant representations [2]—the serpent and the scorpion—clearly show that he was a healer-god not only by his name. One of the patterns of his iconography—serpents growing from his shoulders—goes directly back to the iconography of Ningišzida in the third millennium and illustrates the extreme conservatism and long-lasting continuity of his image among West Semites. He was worshipped by the Phoenicians much earlier than by the Palmyrenes: the stele of Amrit (ancient Marathos, on the coast opposite Arwad) with his image was sculpted no later than the Vth century. Inscriptions in honor of *Šed-râphe'* were discovered in Punic Africa,[3] and this, as correctly indicated by Starcky,[4] shows that his cult was introduced by the first Phoenician colonizers of Africa, which pushes back the beginning of his worship to at least the beginning of the first millennium. In the Puno-Latin bilingual from Leptis, *'dn šdrp'* is parallelled by the Latin *Liber Pater*; thus, in the Roman epoch this god was equated with the Italic form of Dionysos—and this is a tolerably correct identification in light of what we deduced in the preceding chapter about the relationship of Dionysos to *Rpu-B'l*. On the much older Phoenician stele from Amrit, inscribed *Šdrp'*, this god is depicted as a victorious god, standing on a lion and holding a vanquished lion, like Gilgameš.[5] However, Starcky shows that there is no contradiction in this. According to Frankfort, the ancient Sumerian fertility-god could present himself as the victorious hero over a leonine monster, and this aspect was elaborated into the type of the god Ninurta, originally another chthonic god.[6] On a cylinder from the epoch of Agade the chthonic god is designated as such by being ornated with barley-ears, but his attributes (bow, club, lion-hide) are the same as those ascribed later to Heracles, the victor over the Nemaean lion and other monsters.[7] Ningišzida, too, could be represented on certain seals as the victor over a griffin.[8] We can thus draw an important

[1] CDLXXVIII.
[2] Cf. their list in CDLXXVIII, 70 ss.
[3] At Carthage, published XCVIII, II, 193-199, and at Leptis, published CCCXXVI, 31.
[4] CDLXXVIII, 84.
[5] *Ibid.*, 77.
[6] CLXXII, 14 and pl. IIIa.
[7] CLXXI, 115.
[8] CDLXXVIII, 77.

conclusion: the beneficial and friendly character of the chthonic healer-god could express itself in mythology and iconography in the motif of victory over a lion, dragon, griffin or other real or fantastic monster—as was ascribed to Bellerophon.

Besides Amrit, Carthaginian Africa, and Palmyra, the cult of Šed-râphe' is attested in Byblos, and in Hellenistic time also in Cilicia.[1] In Hebrew, *šed* signified a demon only in the evil sense of the word, but an indubitable proof exists that originally *šed* was a good spirit with the West Semites, as *šêdu* was with the Akkadians. Namely, in Egypt, beginning with the XVIIIth dynasty, a god *Šed* was known as a benign deity, a protector and healer; his cult was brought from Syria.[2] What is especially interesting for our topic is that CLERMONT-GANNEAU,[3] almost a hundred years ago, detected Šed-râphe' in the god Satrapes, worshipped at Elis (Paus. VI: 25: 6), and proved that his name had nothing to do with the well-known Persian title, but was a modification of the Semitic name. According to Pausanias, in Elis, Satrapes was equated with Poseidon, and this seems strange, but he immediately adds: "*Satrapês* is a surname of *Korybas,*" and this is quite a different matter. The Corybants were ancient deities or genii in the Cretan cult of Rhea, who helped to raise the infant Zeus. They were identified by the ancients with the Curetes (*kurês,* from *kuros* "lad," "servant") and the Cabiri. It was remembered that there were seven of them. ASSMANN[4] derived *korybas* from W-S *Qarub-ba'al* "attendant of Baal" (like *Ḥanniba'al* > *Annibas,* etc.). V. BÉRARD, who enthusiastically accepted and developed this etymology, identified the Corybants with the Curetes (transl. of W-S *na'ar,* both "lad" and "servant").[5] And actually, the Corybants were chthonic gods like Šed-râphe': on a low relief from Boeotian Lebadeia, a serpent stands in front of three Corybants.[6] The Ugaritic myth I*AB (= UM 67): V: 8-9 revealed that Baal was accompanied to the Nether World by his "seven lads, eight boars." These seven lads, apparently, correspond, to a certain extent, to the seven *Rpum* and the seven Corybants ("attendants of Baal"), and their leader, *Korybas* par excellence,

[1] CDLXI, 169 s.
[2] LXXXIX, 74-88.
[3] *Le dieu Satrape et les Phéniciens dans le Peloponnèse* (1868).
[4] XXXVI, 177.
[5] LXV, II, 266 ss.
[6] CDLXXVIII, 80.

corresponds to *Rpu-Bʿl.*[1] It is clear why in Elis, Satrapes (*Šed-râphe*ʾ) was identified with Corybas (*Qarub-Baʿal*). So the second important conclusion from the above is—that a divine figure of the same type and almost of the same name as *Rpu-Bʿl* (or, if one prefers, *Bʿl-Rpu*(*n*) = Bellerophon) actually penetrated into Greece and had his own cult there.

h) *Bʿl-mrp*ʾ

This divine name appears on a broken Phoenician inscription from Cyprus, published in *CIS*, I, No. 41, and it was the only one to which H. Lewy could refer as a real Semitic parallel to the Semitic original of *Bellerophon* which he had reconstructed. Since then, as we saw, several other parallels were discovered. The editors of CIS translated this name by "Baal Sanator," [2] which supposes the vocalization *Baʿal-merappê*ʾ; it is also possible to read *Baʿal-marpê*ʾ "Baal of healing." [3] Semantically, if not morphologically, this name actually corresponds to **Bʿl-rp*ʾ(*n*). The word *mrp*ʾ penetrated into Greece in a very ancient epoch. It figures, in the form *Marapijo*, in a Mycenaean tablet.[4] V. Bérard, following his "method of doublets," found that the Aegean island of Siphnos had two other names: *Meropiê* or *Meropê*, and *Akis*. Since *akeô* is "to treat a sick person," and *akos* is "remedy," so *Akis* is "recovery, sanatorium"; thus Greek *Akis* = Semitic *merappâ*ʾ (from *rāpâ*ʾ "to heal") = *Meropê*.[5] This conclusion must be remembered; the occurrence of *Meropê* or *Meropiê* in this very sense is not limited to Siphnos, and we shall trace it in other parts of Greece, including an instance where it appears in direct relation to Bellerophon. We shall also see that the form *marpe*ʾ, too, appears in Greek mythology, and again in a situation which has much in common with Bellerophon.

Such are the Oriental parallels to the name of Bellerophon, interpreted as a Semitic one. It follows from their examination that certain names of this type really penetrated into Greece, and that a

[1] Clermont-Ganneau already compared Satrapes-Šed-râpheʾ to the Rephaim.

[2] cx, 61.

[3] cdlxxviii, 78.

[4] Landau, ccxi, 80 (KN Dw 1296), which he tentatively equates with *Melambios* or *Melampios* but on p. 215 s. irrelevantly compares with the Persian tribe of *Maraphioi*, Herod. I: 125. It is most probably W-S, *marpe*ʾ or *merappe*ʾ.

[5] lxv, I, 157.

name like **Baʿal-rāphʾôn* agrees excellently with the pattern of their formation.

PRINCIPAL ANIMAL SYMBOLS OF HEALING DEITIES

The preceding survey of several healing gods acquainted us with two of their most favorite attributes: the serpent and the scorpion. The serpent's intimate connection with medicine survives in traditional emblems up to this day. The cause of this connection was believed to be the changing of skin by snakes, after which they were supposed to become young and regenerated.[1] This justification is possible, but it was not the principal one. The same rôle played by the scorpion and its close association with the serpent in the iconography of healing gods shows that the important fact was the poisonous and deadly nature of both. An animal that inflicts death so rapidly and cruelly must also possess the ability to prevent it.

We saw the serpent as the attribute of healing gods in Mesopotamia, Israel (the bronze serpent), Phoenicia (Ešmun), Palmyra (Šed-râpheʾ), Greece (Asclepios and Dionysos). One may also compare the South Arabic (Minaean) god *Naḥas-ṭâb* "the good serpent,"[2] and the statement in Ugaritic poem II K (= UM 126): III: 9 which we read, with VIROLLEAUD, [3] *nʿm lḥṭt bŝn* "the serpent is good for the wheat." Along with the serpent, a considerable role is played by the scorpion.[4] It was one of the symbols of Šed-râpheʾ, but even much earlier—of the Sumerian goddess Išḫara, the patronness of the consummation of marriage and the goddess who warded off evil.[5] Her other symbol was the serpent or dragon (*bašmu*),[6] and her constellation was the Scorpion.[7] It is known that Išhara belonged to the Ugaritic pantheon (under the name of *Ušḫry*).

The constellation of Sagittarius is situated next to the Scorpion. The Babylonians represented it as scorpion-man shooting with a bow, and identified it with the god Pa-bil-sag,[8] whose title was "vicegerent of the Nether World," [9] and who was the husband of

[1] E.g., CCCLVIII, II, 284.
[2] CCLXXIII, 77.
[3] DXXV, II, 198.
[4] DII.
[5] *Op. cit., pass.*
[6] CCCLVIII, II, 26; DII, 5.
[7] CCCLVIII, II, 26; DII, 1, 17.
[8] CCXXVI, NOS. 356-358; CCLXXV, II, 2, 681; CCCIV, I, 261.
[9] CCCLVIII, II, 33.

several healing goddesses: Gula [1] (usually the wife of Ninurta), "the great physician" who "by the touch of her pure hand makes the dead living"; [2] *En-annun*, and *Nin-isinna* or *Nin-karrak*, [3] an avatar of Gula, who was, like Ninurta's wife, "the great physician" (*Šurpu* IV: 86), but could also inflict pain upon her enemies, as well as diseases, incurable sufferings, loss of potency (*Cod. Ḫammurapi*, rev. xxviii: 50-69). Pa-bil-sag's and Nin-karrak's son was Damu who (*Šurpu* VII: 78 s.) bears the title of *âšipu rabû* "great exorcist"; [4] but in the Hymn to Ninkarrak, Damu is said to be their *daughter*.[5] In the Amarna Age, Pabilsag became a character in a Ugaritic epic (see below, p. 301).

Gula's constellation was Aquarius,[6] and her animal emblem, the dog.[7] Water was an important element of magic medicine—both as the source of fertility and because it was used for divination. Ea, the god of the ocean, was the "specialist of magic art, and in particular, through his artful incantations and his beneficial water-cult, he brought recovery from diseases caused by demons." [8] The incantation-priests (*âšipu, mašmašu*), who fought evil demons, were "adepts of Ea's art." [9] The very name for "physician" in Sumerian, *a-zu*, literally signified "who knows water." Išḫara was styled "Išḫara of the sea." [10] We shall see sea-gods as healers in Greece, too.

Another symbol of the healing gods was the bird, especially predatory and nocturnal birds, *viz.*, eagles, hawks, and owls. As to eagles, vultures and other birds of prey, in hot countries they devour

[1] *dam* ᵈ*Gu-la-ge* . . . CXI, No. 2945.

[2] CCCLVIII, II, 31.

[3] *KAR* No. 15 = 16: 11 ss.; CCCLVIII, II, 33, 170.

[4] CCCLVIII, II, 33; CXI, No. 687. In earlier texts, Damu was styled *a-zu* "physician," CCCLXXVIII, No. 5: 5, 8, 9; cf. CCLXXVII, 166 s.: he is a god of Hades, according to texts of the early Old Babylonian period; his abode is Arallu (Nether World), "the vaste cave"; he sends thunderstorms and is associated with ᵈIM (Storm-god). As a chthonic god, he became more or less equated with Dumuzi, CCCXVII, 300 s., line 5.

[5] CCCLVIII, II, 33, 170.

[6] *Ibid.*, 31, 406; CCCIV, I, 262; CCXXVI, Nos. 81 (ᵐᵘˡGU.LA) and 82 (ᵐᵘˡ ᵈGU.LA) which were perhaps not identical, according to GÖSSMANN; the former was represented as a man (or a horned bearded man with bull's or horse's legs) pouring water from a vessel; the latter as the goddess on her throne, mostly with her emblematic dog.

[7] CCCLVIII, II, 31, 206.

[8] *Ibid.*, 201.

[9] *Loc. cit.*

[10] CCCLVIII, II, 26; DII, 5 s.

unburied corpses, and, consequently, according to primitive notions, the souls of the dead pass into their bodies—and the souls of the dead were at the same time chthonic gods (*ilm arṣ*), deities (*ilnym*) and healers (*rpum*). Following the association of soil fertility with subterranean ghosts, and of the latter—with birds of prey, the fertility-spritis of date-palms were represented on Assyrian reliefs as winged and eagle-headed.[1] The seven winged Babylonian spirits, carrying panicles of the date-palm, were gods of fertility and of health in general.[2] They were identified with the seven sons of Enmešarra, the king of the Nether World, known under the general name of *Sibitti* (heptad), and described as prisoners in Hades,[3] and on the other hand with the *Sibitti* of propitious gods who were fighting hostile demons and were styled *ilâni rabûti* "great gods." [4] It was an eagle who knew where the magic "plant of birth" was to be sought and carried Etana into heaven to get it. It may seem strange that birds symbolize not only the sky, but the underground abode of the dead as well, but such was the ancient Oriental conception: the ghosts in Hell had the aspect of birds:

> Where dust is their fare and clay their food,
> (where) they see no light, residing in darkness,
> (where) they are clothed like birds, with wings
> for garments.
> (*Descent of Ištar*, obv. 8-10).[5]

And almost in the same words:

> To the house wherein the dwellers are bereft of light,
> Where dust is their fare and clay their food,
> They are clothed like birds, with wings for garments,
> And see no light, residing in darkness.
> (*Gilgameš* VII: iv: 36-39).[6]

[1] Cf., e.g., the reproduction in LXVII, 97, fig. 77. Cf. also the mythological image in Ezech. 17: 7 about an eagle who planted and watered a mystical vine.

[2] CCCLVIII, II, 49.

[3] *Ibid.*, 6; WEIDNER, "Enmešarra," *ap.* CDXXVI, II, 396 ss.; CDLXXVIII, 79.

[4] CDLXXVIII, 79 pertinently compares them to the Cabiri whom the Greeks called *theoi megaloi* "great gods" (this is also the meaning of W-S *kabbîrîm*).

[5] Translat. CDLXXI, 107.

[6] *Ibid.*, 87.—The Greeks, too, imagined the souls of the dead as winged. In *Odyss.* XXIV: 5-9 they are compared to bats. HARRISON, CCXLVII, 200 s., remarked: "The notion of the soul a human-faced bird is familiar in Egyptian, but rare in Greek, art" (one indubitable instance follows). "The persistent anthropomorphism of the Greeks stripped the bird-soul of

The ghosts were, moreover, not just birds, but birds of prey: Ištar threatened to free the dead from Hell so that they would eat the living (*Desc. of Ištar*, obv. 19). Birds, residing in darkness, never seeing light, are, of course, *owls*. And, indeed, the owl (we shall meet it in Greek cults later in this chapter) was a favorite emblem of healing gods. Already in Babylonia, a connection existed between the notions of "owl" and "magic medicine," which, although disregarded until now, is necessary to examine here.

The Akkadian root (*w*)*ašâpu* "to conjure, to exorcise" is the basis of many terms, connected with priesthood and magic: *âšipu* "incantation-priest who also receives repentance," fem. *âšiptu* "incantress," but also "witch"; *šeppu* (or *šeppû*), a kind of priest, according to *CAD* 4, p. 371,[1] "the exorciser . . .: an ecstatic with evil magic power"; "the Sumerian designation of the *eššepû* AN.NI.BA.-TU 'one who has been entered by a divine power' refers to an ecstatic"; —*eššepu*, fem. *eššēputu* "belonging to the priesthood; a special category of priest";—*šiptu* "incantation";—*muššepu* "repentance-priest" (before whom confessions were made).[2]

But from the very same root the word for "owl" *eššepu* is derived, identical with one of the priestly terms listed above.[3] According to *CAD* 4, p. 370, *eššepu* (*eššepû*, *iššepu*, *iššepû*, fem. *eššepitu*) is "a bird of evil portent," usually named in omina texts between *qadû* "owl" and *anpatu*, or immediately before the latter; and further, p. 371: "a number of indications seem to suggest that *eššepu* (*eššepû*) refers to a nocturnal bird of ill portent, related to the owl"; "the relationship between the person *eššepû* and the bird *eššepu* remains obscure, although the hairdo of the exorcist may have been likened to the bird's appearance."

Of course, the point is not in the hairdo. The relationship of the *eššepu*-priest to the bird of the same name had a more intrinsic

all but its wings," Cf. FRANKFORT, CLXX, 134 s., where he, with certainty, defines the winged and bird-like beings in Mesopotamian art as belonging to the Land of Death. It is important to note that the beautiful winged and taloned female figure on the Burney Relief (to which we shall return later) is flanked by two huge *owls*—cf. our immediately following text.

[1] In *CAD* (LXXXV) the root and its derivatives are transliterated with *b* instead of *p*, as in the dictionaries of BEZOLD, MUSS-ARNOLT, VON SODEN, in the works of MEISSNER, and practically in all Assyriological editions. To avoid confusion, we have normalized the spelling even in quotations from *CAD*.

[2] Cf. LXXXV, IV, 370 ss. and LXVI, 74.

[3] CCCVII, No. 515: NINNÁ *eššepu* "owl"; NINNÁ.NINNÁ = NINNÁ. MUŠEN *eššepu* "owl."

nature. What are an "exorcist" and a "repentance-priest"? They are, first of all, healers: the *âšipu*-priest expells diseases, impurity, sins.[1] Damu, the son of the healing goddess Ninkarrak, was *âšipu rabû* "great exorcist." According to ancient conceptions, a disease is caused either by an evil spirit who enters a man's body, or by the man's own sin. The priest, after hearing the patient's confession, diagnosed which one of his deeds caused the gods' anger, and advised him how to propitiate them. The magico-medical rôle of confession is well-known: cf. one of the letters of Rib-Addi, king of Byblos: "I am old, and my body is afflicted with a severe disease. And let the king, my lord, know that the gods of Gubla are angry, and (consequently) the disease is worse, and I have acknowledged my sins to the gods" (EA 137: 29-33). It is known from the Bible that ecstatic prophets, who where also, like the *eššepu*, "ones who have been entered by a divine power," were believed to have the magic power of healing the worst diseases, and even, like the goddess Gula, able to revive the dead. The bird *eššepu* was not an exclusively evil omen: according to the excerpt of an omina-collection, quoted in *CAD* 4, p. 370, if this bird traces circles over a house, the house will have an abundance of food. Consequently, the attitude toward it was dual: like the spirits of the dead, whom the owl personifies, it is considered both a giver of abundance and an object of fright. *Âšiptu* is both an incantress and a witch, an evil sorceress who inflicts all kinds of sufferings on people.

Thus, a bird of the owl family, an *owl*, had the name of an *exorcist-priest*. We observe a similar semantic doublet in the name of another kind of owl-bird, *qadû*, quoted in portent texts along with *eššepu*. The root *qadû*, from which this name derives, may be considered a parallel form of the geminated verb[2] *qadâdu* "to stoop, to waver, to bend oneself." *Qadâdu appa* "to fall with the face down,"[3] is equivalent to *labânu appa* "prostrate"—one of the essential ceremonies of priestly liturgy. The well-known W-S term for "priest," Heb. *kômer*, Aram. *kᵉmar*, sporadically in Akkadian

[1] CCCLVIII, II, 65.

[2] Cf. DXXXI, 146, § 105.a: "Verbs ultima *ī*, along with verbs media geminata, are formed from some biconsonantal roots (cf. *ḫerûm* 'to dig' beside *ḫarārum* 'to dig ditches'; *redûm* 'to follow' beside *radādu* 'to persecute')."

[3] Same in Hebrew: *qādad* "to fall down, to prostrate," with *ʾappayim* "face": *way-yiqqōd Dawid ʾappayim ʾarṣâ way-yištāḥû* "and David fell with his face to the earth and did obeisance"; cf. I Kings I: 31; Ex. 4: 31.

(Cappadocian *kumra*,[1] Babylonian *kamîru* EA 1: 15, *kameru*[2]), also derives from the root *kamâru* with the same meaning as *labânu*: "to press, to lie flatly, to fall down, etc." [3] Another owl-bird, listed in parallelism with *qadû*, was *akû*, defined as *iṣṣûr muši* "nocturnal bird." The root *akû* is parallel to *dalâlu* "A: to proclaim, to glorify (a king or a god) . . . B: to perform a ritual . . ." [4] whence *dullu*" . . . 3) work, 4) ritual, 5) medical treatment".[5] Thus *akû*, equivalent to *dalâlu*, is again connected with priestly ritual and medicine.

To the same category of nocturnal and desert birds of omen belong: *kâsu* (= Heb. *kôs* "owl", translated in Targum by *qadyâ*, i.e. *qadû*), *bûṣu* = *iṣṣûr ḫurri*, a bird living in caves, and *anpatu* (Heb. *'ănāphā*), who had the same Sumerian correspondence as *eššepu*.[6]

Let us keep in mind this connection of the *owl* with priesthood and medicine: it will help us to understand many things in the names and natures of several Greek healer-heroes, including Asclepios, the principal one. Now we shall dwell on an interesting myth cycle from the island of Cos, where we shall discover a number of names and motifs which have already been seen on Babylonian soil. It will serve as a good introduction to the Greek pattern of healing gods.

Cos-Meropia and its Family of Bird-Heroes

The Greek island of Cos near the south-western coast of Asia Minor was one of the two principal centers for the worship of Asclepios (along with Epidauros). This rôle of Cos predisposes us to be particularly attentive to its second name, or surname, attested in ancient sources: *Meropiê*.[7] We saw above (p. 239) that V. Bérard deduced from the doublet *Akis* // *Merop(i)ê* (parallel names of the island of Siphnos) the signification *M^e^rappâ'* "healing" (fem.) for

[1] Cf. cccxxxiv, 42 ss.
[2] Cf. lxvi, 143; ccclx, 3.
[3] The prayer ritual, performed by the priests in Babylonian temples, included: "raising the hands", *našû ša qâti*, "opening the palms", *petû ša upnâ*, "kneeling", *kamâsu*, and "prostration", *šukênu* or *labân appi*, ccclviii, II, 80.
[4] lxxxv, III, 46 s.
[5] *Ibid.*, 173.
[6] Should we, moreover, try to derive the very word *anpatu* from the Sumerian counterpart of *eššepu*—not as a bird, but as a priest: *an-ni-ba-tu*?
[7] The common derivation from *meropos* "human, mortal" does not fit here at all; which island of the Archipelago was not one of human beings?

Meropê. Such an interpretation fits Cos, the sacred island of the healing-god Asclepios, even better. But the similarity between Siphnos and Cos goes farther. We have seen immediately above that among the ominous night-birds which were connected semantically with the magico-medical rite of expelling diseases, the birds *kâsu* (Heb. *kôs*) and *akû* are found. These names provide an additional doublet, to which a third parallel from the same island of Cos may be added:

1) *Meropiê* = *Akis* (> *akû* "owl")
2) *Meropiê* = *Kôs* (> *kôs*, Akk. *kâsu*, "owl")
3) *Meropis* from *Kôs*, changed into an *owl.*

It is therefore evident that the island of Cos (*Kôs*) owed its name to a W-S word associated with the owl (*kôs*). Westward from Cos lies the island of Anaphe. Above, p. 123 s., we dwelt on the Greek semantics of its name, and we connected it with the W-S cosmogonic myth associated, according to our restoration, with this island. However, the Greek mind could have interpreted in the spirit of its language and in accordance with the local myth a word which originally was un-Greek. From the external point of view, *Anaphê* coincides in a most ideal way with the Hebrew name of the bird *'ănāphā* = Akkadian *anpatu.* Already BOCHART noticed that the name of the bird *anopaia* in *Odyss.* I: 319 (a hapax) derives from Hebrew *'ănāphā*;[1] and it is noteworthy that it was Athena (whose symbol was the owl) who turned into this bird; but *Anaphê* reproduces the W-S original still more closely. Another association of *kôs* and *'ănāphā* may be observed in Syracuse.[2]

A myth preserved in the transmission of Antoninus Liberalis,[3]

[1] BOCHART, *Hierozoicon*, III, 99, cf. CCCXXX, 9 s.; LXV, I, 438.

[2] V. BÉRARD, LXIV, IV, 472 (cf. also LXV, I, 440) basing himself on the statement by Thucidides VI: 2 "Phoenicians occupied the capes and neighboring islands (in Sicily), in order to trade with the Siculi," identified several Greco-Sicilian toponyms as originally Phoenician, among others *Syrakusai* or *Syrakosai* as **sûr hak-kûsîm* (we would prefer **sur hak-kôs* "owl-cliff"). To this we may add that the river of Syracuse was named *Anapos* (Thuc. VI: 66), and an island in the Syracusan harbor bore the name of *Ortygia* "quail"—another magico-medical bird, cf. the myth of how Iolaos returned to life Heracles, slain by Typhon, by putting a quail under his-nose (Eudoxos of Cnidos, quoted by Athenaeus IX: 392: d. e) . . *Ortygia* "quail-island" was also a parallel name of the holy island of Delos in the Cyclades. For toponyms formed out of bird-names, cf. the town ^{al}*Iṣṣûru* in the kingdom of Ugarit.

[3] A writer of the IId century A.D., the author of a myth collection *Metamorphôseôn synagôgê.*

but which is undoubtedly extremely ancient, is connected with the island of Cos. It tells that the oldest king of the island was *Merops*; after the sudden death of his wife, the nymph Echemeia, slain by Artemis, he attempted suicide, but was changed by Hera into an eagle and placed in the sky as the constellation *Aquila.* We have seen the rôle of the eagle in belief connected with magic medicine, and we have no doubt that this Merops, like his island, got his name from W-S *m^{e}rappê'* "healer." His son Eumelos and the three children of the latter worshipped only the Earth and did not recognize any other gods; they insulted Hermes, Athena and Artemis, who visited them, and were therefore changed into birds. Worshiping the Earth alone is an obvious relic of the chthonic nature of the entire Meropid family. The type of birds they were changed into is very significant.

Eumelos became a "night raven," *nyktikorax*: by this term LXX translates the Hebrew *kôs*, it is accordingly a kind of owl.[1] Thus the king of Cos was changed into the very bird whose name his island bore. His son Agron became a *charadrios*, which is usually translated by "plover," but this is far from being certain. LXX renders by *charadrios* the Hebrew *'ănāphā*, which is, in turn, identical with Akk. *anpatu*, associated with the owl-species *qadû* and *eššepu* and sharing with the latter a common Sumerian designation: it is, accordingly, another night-bird. Its Greek name derives from *charadra* "a cleft, a fissure in the ground," which corresponds to the Akkadian epithet for another nocturnal bird, *bûṣu*: *iṣṣûr ḫurri* "bird from the pit." One of Eumelos' daughters, Meropis (i.e. W-S for "healer") was changed, as could be expected, into an owl (*glaux*). The other, *Byssa*, having kept her name, became a bird of the same denomination, also known as "the bird of Leucothea." According to Antoninus Liberalis, Hesychios and other ancient authors, *byssa* was a kind of owl (*glaux*),[2] presenting thus a full

[1] Cf. Nicarchos ap. *Anthol. Palat.* XI: 186: 1: *nyktikorax adei thanatêphoron*—it was, thus, considered a bird of evil portent. Aristotle, *Hist. Anim.* 8: 3 enumerates *nyktikorax*, *glaux* ("owl"), *byas* ("eagle-owl") among *nykterinôn* ("night-birds"). See the documentation in CDLXXX, VI, 1593 s.

[2] Cf. CDLXXX, III, 459: "Byssa, Eumeli filia, in ululam mutata, de qua Antonin. Liber. 15, p. 106, *Hê de (Athêna) autên epoiêsen ornithôn glauka*; *byssa de tô autô onomati legetai, kai esti Leucotheas ornis*. Alia forma *byza*." *Byssa/byza* is not merely the feminine form of *byas* "eagle-owl," Lat. *bubo*; the hesitation in the sibilant *ss/z* points to a transcription of the Semitic *ṣ*.

coincidence with *bûṣu* or *iṣṣûr ḫurri*. It is obviously an Akkadian loan-word.[1]

To this must be added the daughter of Eurypylos,[2] who came to Cos after the transformation of the Meropids into birds. Her name was *Chalkiôpê*, yet in this instance it is derived not from *chalkos* "copper, bronze", but from *chalkis* which—in the "language of the gods"—designated the "night-hawk" (corresponding to *kymindis* in ordinary, "human" language). Thus our Coan collection of nocturnal bird-heroes increases by another unit. Still another Chalciope, in a different heroic family named after birds of prey, will be found in a later part of this chapter.[3]

This local myth from the island of Asclepios is very significant. It not only reveals its Semitic toponymics, but also shows how strong the Semitic impact was precisely in the cycle referring to the sphere of chthonic healing-spirits, personified in Cos—as in Babylonia—as nocturnal birds of prey. At the same time, it underlines the rôle of the owl in Greek mythology. The Coan pattern convincingly shows that the owl (*glaux*) did not become Athena's symbol by accident; and also not—as NILSSON in an oversimplified way decided [4]—because many small owls live even now on the Athenian Acropolis.[5] "As far as I know," stated NILSSON, *loc. cit.*, "the owl does not occur in Minoan and Mycenaean monuments, and we know nothing about its prophylactic value in this early age." Our survey

[1] *Bûṣu* translated "bat," CCCVII, No. 79* (with a question mark); in the vocabulary (p. 298) without it. LXVI and CCCLXXVI, *s.v.*, translated *bûṣu* . . ., "falco peregrinus?" probably on the basis of Arab. *bâz* "falcon", but the phonetic similarity is rather a remote one.

[2] We understand *Eurypylos* "of the wide gates" as a surname of Hades whose gates, according to Greek notions, were open wide to all comers. Cf. *Têlepylos*, epithet of the mythical city of the anthropophagic Laestrygones in *Odyss.* X: 81, another variant of the dead-city motif, and the fight of Heracles with Hades in *pylos*, among the dead, *Iliad* V: 395 ss., cf. CCCLXXXII, 203.

[3] Cf. *Iliad* XIV: 291: "the immortal gods call (him) *chalkis*, but men call him *kymindis*." Hesychios: *chalkis*: *eidos orneu, hê glaux*; Schol. Aristoph. *Aves*: 262 interpreting Homeric *chalkida* by *tên glauka*, etc. Cf. complete evidence CDLXXX, IX, 1269 s. There was an islet *Chalkê* near Cos (Thucid. VIII: 44)—another "bird-island" in the Archipelago, and in a very significant neighborhood. Cf. also p. 294 below.

[4] CCCLXXXI, 494.

[5] Owls, as was known to the authors of the Babylonian portent-texts and of several Biblical passages mentioning them, like to live in uninhabited ruins; there certainly were much fewer of them in the Acropolis before it became a ruin, and it is hard to imagine that this particular spot was at any time a special gathering-place for owls.

of this particular division of Babylonian ornithology, confronted with Coan cycle, points to the opposite. The owl was an emblem of recovery and prosperity exactly as Athena's other emblem, the serpent, was. Athena herself was originally imagined as an owl—it's in this sense that her surname *glaukôpis* has to be understood: it means precisely "owl-eyed," or "owl-faced," or "owl-shaped," and not "grey-eyed," as usually translated, and she inherited it from the East, where there were many bird-goddesses. The healer-heroes of Greek myths carrying the names of *Glaukos* also derive from the "owl," and not from the "grey sea." We shall meet one of them in Bellerophon's family, as closely associated with Merope as we have already noted in the remarkable triple doublet cited earlier in this section.

Let us now return to the Siphnian toponymic doublet *Merop(i)ê/Akis*. The first member, in Cos and elsewhere, could also be a mythical human name: masc. *Merops*, fem. *Meropis* or *Meropê*. The same is true for the second member, *Akis*. This myth reached us in a late Sicilian version (Ovid *Met.* XIII: 750-897). Acis is depicted as a handsome youth, loved by the sea-goddess Galatea (*Galateia*), daughter of Nereus. The jealous Cyclops Polyphemos smashed him with a fragment of a cliff, and Galatea changed him into the source of the river Acis. Everything in this myth goes back to the Semitic East (it was, of course, brought to Sicily by Greek settlers). Galatea, the sea-goddess, is not "milk-white," as the Greek interpretation would suggest, but the personification of the agitated sea (the standard Akkadian epithet of the sea is *tâmtu gallatu*, cf. also Heb. *gal* "wave"). Her father Nereus, as suggested long ago, is W-S *nāhār* "river," [1] which in Ugaritic myths is a parallel name of the Sea-god, Yamm. A goddess's love for a beautiful youth who perishes in the prime of life is common in Oriental mythology: cf. Ištar and Tammuz, Aphrodite (Astarte) and Adonis, Astronome (*ʿAštart-naʿamā*) and Ešmun. The young lover's murder out of jealousy figures in the myth of Adonis who was also changed into the river named after him. Tammuz, in the Ḫarranian version of his myth, was smashed among stones. Ešmun was a healer—so was Acis, according to his name. And even the image of the Cyclops is proven archaeologically to be an invention of Babylonian fantasy.[2]

[1] E.g., LXII, 494.

[2] Henri FRANKFORT discovered at Khafaje (Diyala region) a clay-plaquette from about 2000 showing a god with a bow and quiver slung over shoulders,

PART B

Bellerophon, His Family, and His Adventures

Bellerophon's Genealogy

In order that the personality and the mythical appurtenance of Bellerophon appear with the desired prominence, it is necessary to examine him against the background of all his kindred—especially so because one of our objectives is to show that the Semitic sound of his name is not accidental. One of the methodological instructions of Victor Bérard was that names which are the object of a systematic study must be classified according to their historical or legendary kinship.[1] Of course, one may meet an artificial combination of late mythographers and genealogists, but the suspiciousness of many former scholars was to a large degree exaggerated. We have already seen in the analysis of the Danaan and the Cadmeian cycles that each really forms an organic entity, and late additions of genealogical character can easily be recognized and eliminated. However, without limiting ourselves to this, we will keep to our principle of putting the main accent on community of mythical motifs.

a) *Sisyphos*

The pedigree of Bellerophon, presented in *Iliad* VI: 152-155, starts with Sisyphos, son of Aeolos, a man renowned for his wisdom, who lived at Ephyra ,a city of Argos. We have shown above (p. 208, n. 1) that two brothers of Sisyphos, Cretheus and Salmoneus, bore obviously Semitic names, and a third brother, Athamas,[2] was the husband of the Semitic goddess Ino and the father of Melicertes-

slaying a demon with a broad dagger; the demon has a round face surrounded by 12 triangular rays, and in the middle of his forehead is a diamond-shaped incision, certainly representing an eye, as recognized by Frankfort; there are no traces of eyes where they are expected to be carved (cf. *AfO*, XI, 1934-1936, 265 and fig. 8; CLXX, 128 and n. 3). The god with the bow reminds us of Apollo and his slaying the Cyclopes (explained by the Greek myth as revenge for their having prepared the thunderbolt with which Zeus smote Apollo's son Asclepios). Before having knowledge of this plaquette, we presumed the Oriental origin of the Cyclops image by methods of comparative philology and mythology; but to this we hope to return at another opportunity.

[1] LXV, I, 123.

[2] LXXXI, 145 suggested that *Athamas*, Ionian *Tammas*, derives from *Tammuz*, but this combination is convincing neither from phonetic nor mythological grounds.

Palaemon (Semitic *Melqart* and *Baʿal-hāmôn*). There are other Semitisms in the first and the next generation of the Aeolids.[1] This is not proof of the Semitism of Sisyphos himself, but it does indicate the possibility of Semitic origin.

From all that has been told about Sisyphos in antiquity, the myth of his descent to Hades and his return to the world of the living must be considered the most ancient and authentic information. It immediately shows that Sisyphos was originally a chthonic infernal god. Proceeding from this, it is possible, first of all, to explain the name of his city *Ephyra*. It was identified with Corinth, but was located elsewhere as well; it apparently was a mythical city. We shall see that in *Odyss.* I: 254 Ephyra is connected with a character bearing a Semitic divine name who is an expert in poisons—or, by the previous expounded analogy with the serpent and the scorpion, a healer as well. So a suggestion imposes itself—to understand *Ephyra* as W-S *ʿăphurā* "dusty" (from *ʿāphār* "dust"). It is a very fitting name for the underground Nether World, whose main feature, according to Akkadian beliefs, was its utter dustiness: "over door and bolt dust is spread," *eli* ^{is}*daltu û* ^{is}*sikkuri šapûḫ epru* (*Desc. of Ištar*, obv. 11); in *Gilgameš* VII: iv: 40 the Nether World is called "House of Dust," *Bît epri*; and in both texts the spirits of the dead—and even the queen of Hades, Ereškigal, herself—nourish themselves with dust and clay. In the Bible, too, *ʿāphār* is the synonym of the realm of the dead (Ps. 30: 10); cf. *yōr*^{e}*dê ʿāphār* "those who descended into dust" Ps. 22: 30, and *y*^{e}*šēnê ʾadmat ʿāphār* "those who sleep in the earth of dust" Dan. 12: 2.

Was Sisyphos a healer? Yes, he was, and the greatest one, too —no matter that he became one neither by leechcraft nor remedies, but by pure magic. He was said to have chained Death (who had

[1] Of the five daughters of Aeolos, four have quite normal Greek names, but the fifth, *Kanakê*, has a non-Greek one, reminiscent of the Akk. root *kanâku* "to seal"; for the semantics of this root as applied to a woman, cf. Cant. 8: 6 "put me like a seal upon thy heart"; cf. also the pers. n. *Ḥôtâm* "seal" I Chr. 7: 32; 11: 44. Another guess would be the derivation from Akk. *kanâktu* "olibanum oil," a fragrance used in ancient Eastern perfumery and medicine (cf. XXXV, VII, 178). *Tyrô*, daughter of Salmoneus, wife of Cretheus, is connected by her name to the city of Tyre (she possibly derives from a divine "Lady of Tyre"). *Amythaôn*, son of Cretheus, father of the prophet Melampus (ancestor of a family of diviners) may be compared to the Biblical *ʾAmittay* (from *ʾemet* "truth"), father of the (probably legendary) prophet Jonah. *Aphareus*, son of Perieros, father of Idas and Lynceus, has to be related to *ʿāphār* "dust," by extension "Nether World."

been sent for him) through a ruse so that a long time after nobody died on earth, until Ares [1] delivered Death from his bonds. Victory over Death, prolongation of human life was the greatest that was expected from a healing god. We have seen that the healer-god Damu was "the great exorcist," *âšipu rabû,* that the priests bearing the cognate names of *âšipu, eššepu,* and *muššepu* expelled disease, freed the patient from evil spirits, found out which action of the sick had caused the anger of the gods. The name of *Sisyphos,*[2] incomprehensible for etymologists (who wanted to see in it a derivation from *sophos* "wise" [3]) must be derived from the same root. By analogy with the root *(w)ašabu* "to sit," the permansive of which in Š-stem (III: 1) is *šušub* in Babylonian, *šešub* in Assyrian dialect, the Š-permansive of *(w)ašapu* would have been, in Assyrian pronunciation, *šešup* "the one producing incantations, producing witchcraft." This would be a literal correspondence to *Sisyphos* both in form and essence.[4] It finds confirmation in the names of Sisyphos' wife and sons.

b) *Merope*

After what we have seen in Cos and in Siphnos, it will be easy for us to recognize in Sisyphos' wife Merope, one of the seven Pleiads, the daughters of Atlas, the W-S *m^erappâ'* "(fem.) healer." With the Babylonians, the Pleiads were considered as a collective deity *Sibittu* "the Heptad," defenders of humans from evil spirits. Upon two *kudurru* (border-stones) of the Cassite epoch, this Heptad, in the form of the Pleiads, is located near the Scorpion,[5] which was a

[1] Ares originally was a chthonic god of pestilence, very similar to Nergal or Namtar.

[2] Hesychios also quoted a variant *Sesephos.*

[3] Eustathios explained *Si-syphos* as *theo-sophos* "divinely wise." Modern scholars suppose a reduplication of *sophos,* meaning "Very Very Wise One," CCXLVII, 608.

[4] Sisyphos is famous for his "sisyphean toil"—his sentence in Hades was to roll uphill a heavy stone which, the moment it reached the summit, rolled back (already in the *Nekyê* interpolation, *Odyss.* XI: 593-600). This could not belong to the ancient myth, because the idea of posthumous retribution was utterly strange to archaic Greek religion. It was interpreted as an allegory of the sun's movement up and down the celestial vault (recently repeated CCXXVII, I, 219, No. 2). However, no solar motifs are noticeable in the figure of Sisyphos. If the "sisyphean toil" goes back to some ancient models, it could have been a misinterpretation of a picture representing Sisyphos or somebody else rolling a stone uphill with the intention of erecting it there as an orthostat.

[5] CDLXXVIII, 79.

powerful medical apotropy and the constellation of the healer-goddess Išḫara. Atlas, the father of Merope and the other Pleiads, originally was the wise god of the sea depths (*Odyss.* I: 51). Philo of Byblos used his name for one of the five avatars of the Phoenician El, all five of whom are one and the same god. The Greeks rendered by their divine name of Cronos both the Phoenician El and the Babylonian Ea, and El is cognate with Ea in ways besides this. Atlas is the W-S El in the role of the ruler of the Ocean; *Il mbk nhrm b apq thmtm,* "El who pours the (two?) rivers into the stream of the two oceans," corresponds to Ea, whose abode also was at the mouth of the rivers, at Eridu. We have seen Ea's relation to medicine, with the very term for "physician," *a-zu* "one who knows water." As to the Pleiads in particular, Hesiod, in extant fragments, called them only *Peleiades,* i.e. "doves"; the myth of the doves carrying ambrosia, the food of immortality, to Zeus referred to them. This was another motif of possession of a remedy against death.

Merope was a "healer" not only by her name. According to the attenuated, but still recognizable myth of Sisyphos, the latter, when he was forced to go to Hades, took the precaution of instructing his wife not to perform any funeral rites for him. This gave him the opportunity to ask Persephone for leave from Hades—allegedly to remind his wife of her duties, but actually in order not to return to the Nether World. In all this, the ancient core is evident: Sisyphos is resurrected thanks to his wife: she, like Gula or another Sumerian goddess, Entinnuga, knew how to return dead men to life. She merits the name of "healer" to no less an extent than Ešmun-Iolaos who magically revived Melqart-Heracles.[1]

c) *Glaucos*

1. Sisyphos' son, according to *Iliad* VI: 156, was Glaucos. We are already prepared by the analysis of the Coan bird-cycle for the

[1] Here is a list of other heroes and heroines of this name: 1) Merope (in Hyginus)—an Oceanid, mother of Phaëthon, a hero who in many respects reminds us of Bellerophon (see pp. 268 ss. below); 2) Merops, king of Ethiopia, husband of Clymene, mother of Phaëthon; 3) Merope, wife of Polybos, foster-mother of Oedipus; since he was brought to her with wounded feet, the name signifying "healer" is not out of place here; 4) Merops, king of Cos, discussed p. 247 above; 5) Merops, king of Percote in Hellespontian Phrygia, a cunning diviner, probably a doublet of the Coan Merops; his grandson, the son of Priamos, the dream-interpreter *Aisakos,* after the death of his wife *Asteropê* leapt into the sea, but was changed by the gods into a diving bird (a fate similar to that of the Meropids of Cos).

derivation of this name from *glaux* "owl," corresponding to the Akkadian *eššepu*—both "owl" and "exorcist-priest, or sorcerer," cognate to his father's name *Sisyphos* (*šešup*). According to Pausanias II: 4: 3: "Sisyphos had not only one son Glaucos, the father of Bellerophontes, but also a second one, Ornytion." GRAVES understands this name as "bird" (= *ornithion*).[1] If correct, this etymology would provide a fine doublet for *Glaukos*, confirming the latter's bird-nature.

The myth of Glaucos tells that during the funeral games in honor of Pelias at Iolcos he was torn by his maddened horses (or even devoured by them). He was worshipped at Corinth as the demon who frightens horses during races (*Taraxippos*). Hippolytos perished in the same way—his very name confirms the story of his death. Glaucos' son, Bellerophon, was thrown from the sky by his winged horse. Phaëthon's heavenly horses bolted, too, and he fell to the earth dead. Lycurgos son of Dryas (the same who, according to *Iliad* VI: 130 ss., attacked Dionysos and his nurses the Maenads) provoked, according to other myths, a drought by killing his son, and, in order to stop it, he was condemned to death and was dismembered by horses on Mount Pangaeos. Diomedes, in a myth of the Heracles cycle, used to feed his mares with human flesh and was himself given as food to his own mares. The same mares dismembered Abderos, the eponym of the city of Abdera. Such constancy of motifs caused GRAVES to deduce "that the pre-Hellenic sacred king was torn in pieces at the close of his reign by women disguised as mares." [2] Of course, neither women nor even robust men could dismember an adult man with nothing but bare hands. The participation of horses in dismembering the victim (*sparagmos*) —a rite we have discussed earlier in connection with Bacchic cults— must be understood literally, as in the medieval putting to death by quartering. The victim's flesh, if it really became a ritual food, was, of course, consumed not by the horses, but by the human participants of the rite. This rôle of horses in the technical side of *sparagmos* was the reason for ascribing equine features to the Bacchic Satyrs—i.e. "dismemberers" (see above, p. 190). We have seen, however, that the victim who was torn to pieces was originally identified with the god himself. Consequently, Glaucos was a

[1] CCXXVII, II, 402.
[2] *Ibid.*, I, 232, No. 1.

chthonic god, related in nature to Zagreus and his W-S prototype *Rpu-B'l*. This closes the circle of analogies.[1]

2. This Glaucos was probably identical with the Boeotian sea-god of the same name—and this accounts for the doublet of Bellerophon's pedigree which made him a son not of Glaucos, but of Poseidon himself. We found in the Boeotian Glaucos some features which complete the personality of his Corinthian namesake. He was worshipped in the Boeotian city of Anthedon, a purely maritime city, without agricultural suburbs, whose inhabitants were occupied only with sea-trades, fishing, and catching purple-snails. This, together with the cult of the Cabiri in Anthedon, and the strong Semitic influence in the whole of Boeotia, predisposes us to expect the presence of some Phoenician impact there. The already euhemerized myth that was told about Glaucos in Anthedon, made him a fisherman and a diver. Once, while he threw the fish he had caught on the shore, he noticed that those touching a certain grass revived. This grass was sown by Cronos back in the Golden Age. Then he himself tasted this grass and was overwhelmed by the desire to throw himself into the sea, which he thereupon did. Oceanos and his wife Tethys then made him a god and bestowed the gift of prophecy upon him. Glaucos was depicted as an old man with long dishevelled hair and a fishtail. Thus, motifs connected with the Babylonian Oannes, prevail in the personality of this Glaucos: he is a sea-god and is represented, as are Oannes and the sea-gods on coins of Ascalon and Arados, with a fishtail; he is a giver of oracles, i.e. expert in divination and knower of divine secrets; and he is a healer, for he possesses the magic "plant of life" which, according to *Gilgameš* XI: 265-276, grew in the sea.

3. The motif of magic healing appears still more distinctly in the myth of the Cretan Glaucos, son of Minos.[2] As a child, running after a mouse, he fell, head first, into a great jar with honey standing in one of the palace basements, and drowned. Nobody knew where his body was. Minos entrusted his search to the Argive (or Corinthian) seer Polyeides ("the much-knowing"). He found the fatal honey-jar through the help of an *owl* that was sitting at the entrance of the basement and had frightened away a swarm of bees. Minos

[1] Glaucos as a charioteer-hero may be compared to the Ugaritic Rephaim who ride in horse-driven chariots.

[2] (Ps.) Apollod. *Bibl.* III: 3: 1; Hygin. *Fabulae* 136.

then ordered that Polyeides revive Glaucos, and shut him together with the corpse in an underground grave. A serpent crept into the grave, Polyeides killed it; then another serpent came, touched the dead one with some herb, and restored it to life. Polyeides took hold of the herb and revived Glaucos. Then Minos requested that Polyeides teach Glaucos his art of divination, and he was obliged to consent. But at the moment of sailing away, he told the boy to spit into his open mouth. Glaucos obeyed, and forgot at that very moment all he had learned from Polyeides.

Everything here is of Oriental origin. In clay vessels filled with honey rich Babylonians were buried. The serpent appears as the giver of life and possessor of the magic herb of life. In *Gilgameš* XI: 287-289, a serpent stole from Gilgameš the plant of life which he had obtained from the bottom of the sea. An owl shows the way to the mystery of Glaucos' whereabouts. The motif of the drowned Glaucos who was revived by a magic herb and became a soothsayer is basically identical with that of the Anthedonian Glaucos. And again, with the Babylonians, saliva (*îmtu*) was the synonym for magic and sorcery.[1]

So the pedigree of Bellerophon demonstrates the presence of Semitic names and mythical motifs, connected precisely with healing deities.

Bellerophon and Anteia

The crucial motif of the Bellerophon myth is his conflict with Anteia, King Proitos' wife. Later on, in order to explain how Bellerophon (believed to be a Corinthian) found himself at the court of Proitos (believed to have lived at Tiryns), the variant of Bellerophon's name, *Bellerophontês*, was interpreted as "the slayer of Belleros," and a story was invented to the effect that he was forced to flee his native city because he had killed Belleros, a Corinthian. This version has no support in Homer, who makes Bellerophon meet Proitos without leaving Ephyra. Therefore, another variant was invented (Paus. II: 4: 3)—that this Proitos was not the descendant of Danaos, the brother of Acrisios, but his

[1] In the presence of such a prevalence of Babylonian motifs in both variants of the Glaucos myth, one is obliged to recognize V. Bérard's (lxv, II, 253 s.) attempts to present the myth of Glaucos son of Minos as a description of the Egyptian underground kingdom of the god Sokar, as completely missing the point.

namesake, Bellerophon's cousin, the son of Thersandros, Glaucos' brother. However, it follows from the *Iliad* that the Proitos of the Bellerophon story was the very same Proitos, the strongest ruler of Argos (Argolis or the entire Peloponnese), and Ephyra was a part of his dominions (by the way, there is no hint whatever that Sisyphos and Glaucos were *kings*). The exact location of Proitos' kingdom is quite unimportant for our topic, for the myth of Bellerophon and Anteia is a very widespread mythical motif which could be associated arbitrarily with this or that locality. Here is the myth as told in *Iliad* VI: 156-170: [1]

> To Bellerophontes the gods granted beauty and desirable manhood; but Proitos in anger devised evil things against him, and drove him out of his own domain,[2] since he was far greater, from the Argive country Zeus had broken to the sway of his sceptre. Beautiful Anteia the wife of Proitos was stricken with passion to lie in love with him, and yet she could not beguile valiant Bellerophontes, whose will was virtuous. So she went to Proitos the king and uttered her falsehood: "Would you be killed, o Proitos? Then murder Bellerophontes who tried to lie with me in love, though I was unwilling." So she spoke, and anger took hold of the king at her story. He shrank from killing him, since his heart was awed by such action, but sent him away to Lykia, and handed him murderous symbols, which he inscribed in a folding tablet, enough to destroy life, and told him to show it to his wife's father, that he might perish.

The Greeks told myths with the same plot about Hippolytos and his stepmother Phaedra, and about Peleus and Astydamia (or Cretheïs), wife of king Acastos.[3] BETHE was perfectly right when,

[1] We quote the translation by Richmond LATTIMORE, 157, disregarding, however, his attempt to imitate the Homeric division in hexameters.

[2] LATTIMORE's translation of v. 158 may cause the impression that Bellerophon had his own domain from which he was expelled. The original has no possessive pronoun at all, it merely reads: *hos rh' ek dêmu elassen* "he expelled him from the people."

[3] On the possible Semitism of the name of Phaedra, cf. p. 267, n. 2 below. As to Cretheïs, this seems fairly certain. When Peleus took revenge, conquered Iolcos and slew Acastos and Cretheis, he cut Cretheïs' body in twain, put it in the city-gates and introduced his army into the city between the two bloody halves. The meaning of the rite to pass between pieces of a cleaved victim, which was widely known in Israel and in Greece, is explained in detail by FRAZER, CLXXIV, I, 391-428. Cutting the victim for ritual purposes had a special name *kārat* "to hew, to chop," whence *k^erōt b^erît* "to conclude an alliance." Now *Kretheïs* exactly means in W-S "the dismembered" (approx. *k^erîtā*). This cannot be an accidental coincidence. In other variants of this myth (Apollod. III: 13: 7), she is called *Astydamia* which we understand as Hellenized W-S *ʾašt-dāmîm*, feminine of *ʾîš-dāmîm* Ps. 5: 7; II Sam. 16: 8 "a man stained with innocent blood." The same story was also told of Phrixos (see p. 207 above) and Tennes of Tenedos (Paus. X: 14: 1 s.).

despite all his antipathy to Semitizing Bellerophon, he nevertheless declared that "both story-motifs, that of the shy youth slandered by the rejected woman, and that of the Uriah-letter" had an Asiatic origin.[1] He was only wrong in considering these motifs as secondary additions to the Argive myth of Bellerophon, while they form its principal pivot; and in not going farther than Lycia in his search for the place of their origin, for it must be sought much farther to the East. Indeed, the *Iliad* itself (VI: 200-202) makes Bellerophon live, toward the end of his life, in the Aleian Plain, i.e. in Lowland Cilicia, the old homeland of the Danaans-Danunians.

In the W-S world, the motif of "the chaste youth" was very widespread. A classical example of it is the corresponding episode of Joseph's story in Egypt, Gen. 39: 7-20. After the discovery of the papyrus d'Orbiney, a quite similar plot was revealed in the Egyptian tale of the two brothers, and it was supposed that the Biblical story of Joseph had borrowed it from there. But it is more probable that the Egyptian story itself is an adaptation of a Phoenician topic.[2] Bata, its hero, slandered by his sister-in-law and pursued by his angry brother, emasculated himself to prove his innocence. The same was told in Phoenicia of the young healer-god Ešmun, pursued by the love of the goddess Astronoë or Astronome (= ʿAštart-naʿamā); and in Syrian Hierapolis, of Combabos, the builder of the Atargatis temple, with whom Queen Stratonice, the wife of an Assyrian king, fell in love. (Pseudo?) Lucian who transmitted this story to us, identified her with the wife of one of the Seleucids (*De Deâ Syriâ* 17), but actually, as even demonstrated by her name, she was another avatar of Astarte.[3] This Combabos can easily be recognized as *Ḫumbaba* (or *Ḫubaba*,[4] *Ḫuwawa*) of the Gilgameš epic, the guardsman of the cedar-forest of Lebanon, in the middle of which was situated the temple of Irnini, a hypostasis of Ištar. He is a local

On the Semitism of the Phrixos myth, cf. p. 207 above and pp. 282 s. below. On Semitic influence in Tenedos, cf. p. 200 above.

[1] Bethe, "Bellerophon," cxci, III, 1, 246.

[2] See p. 186, n. 4 above.

[3] Phoenician kings bearing theophorous names composed with *ʿAštart*, Hellenized them into *Stratôn*.

[4] This is a W-S name, a quṭal-form of *ḥābab* "to love," probably "the beloved," cf. the names *Ḥôbâb*, father-in-law of Moses, and *Ḥbb*, head of scribes at Ugarit (UM 73: rev. 4). Benveniste, lviii, 250 agreed that taken in itself, *Kombabos* is a transcription of *Ḫumbaba*, but he objected that "these personages are as dissimilar as possible," and preferred to derive *Kombabos* from the goddess *Kubaba* (p. 251). He did not, of course, utilize Bata as *tertium comparationis*.

W-S personage, borrowed by the Mesopotamians together with the motif of the divine cedar-forest. In the Sumerian and Akkadian poems he appears as Gilgameš's enemy and is depicted in odious terms, while in the Phoenico-Egyptian version his counterpart Bata [1] is the protagonist and is described sympathetically. However, the motif of self-castration is not a necessary part of the story. In the Canaanite myth of Ašertu and the Storm-god (Baal), which came to us in a Hittite translation (above, p. 207 s.), the motif of rejected love and vengeance on the part of the insulted goddess appears with classical clarity, but without self-castration. The same motif also appears in the Gilgameš epic, tabl. VI, where Ištar fell in love with Gilgameš and, after having been rudely rejected by him, turned herself to the supreme god Anu with a request to punish the hero.

All these heroes have this in common that they belong to the cycle of the "dying gods" of fertility. It is known that Gilgameš was appointed by Enlil the judge of the Nether World as compensation for immortality, which he could not obtain.[2] There is no need to dwell upon Baal as a giver of fertility and his descent to the Nether World. It has already been repeatedly demonstrated that most of the motifs in the Joseph story are more or less euhemerized motifs of the Tammuz-Adonis myth.[3] Bata is a typical "vegetative spirit," slain and revived, embodied in trees (cedar/pine and persea) and in a bull. Ešmun, a figure close to Adonis, and in addition, the principal Phoenician healer-god, is another link to Bellerophon-*Ba'al-rāph'ôn*. As in the cases of Bata and Joseph, Bellerophon's beauty

[1] The points of resemblance are: 1) location, 2) cedar-forest, 3) dependence of the hero's life on a cedar which must be cut down in order to kill the hero, 4) self-castration of Bata = self-castration of Combabos, in the same circumstances, while the name of Combabos = Ḫumbaba. Bata is not a Phoenician name; the hero of the cedar-forest was assimilated, in the Egyptian version of the story, with Bata, an obscure provincial god, worshipped together with the much better known funeral god Anubis in the small town of Saka in Upper Egypt (CDXXIX, 333 s.; CLX, 61).

[2] Cf. "The Death of Gilgameš," a Sumerian fragment, published by KRAMER, CCXCII and CCXCV, 50 ss. Cf. also LAMBERT, CCCX, 207 s., who emphasizes Gilgameš's "rule of Hell" and his being the "beloved of Ereškigal."

[3] In short: the motif of being slain by a wild beast; that of descent into a pit (= Hades), paralleled by prison; that of a seven-year cycle of abundance and famine; that of a mummy carried in a portable coffin; the name signifying "the multiplier." Cf. CCVI, 126; CDLX, 51-60; DXXX, 76, 101; DLI, II, 75 ss., 287.

and innocence are stressed. Like Bata and Joseph, Bellerophon leaves his country, settles and marries in a remote land, and like Bata, he is an invincible hero, killing all his enemies.[1] Like Gilgameš, he is forced to fight a terrible monster because of rejected love. Later on we shall speak of the resemblances with Hippolytos.

The goddess who persecutes the godly hero, is Asherah in the myth of Baal, Astarte (according to the Greek rendering of her name) in the myths of Combabos and Ešmun, Ištar in the myth of Gilgameš; in the stories of Bata and Joseph she is fully humanized and has lost her personal name. In the Ugaritic myth of *Aqht* (already mentioned many times above), the motif of rejected love is all but absent, but apart from that, the rôle of Anath taking vengeance upon the youth *Aqht* who had insulted her, is quite analogous. Besides, Anath was not fully differentiated from Astarte. In the Hittite translation of the Baal and Ašertu myth, it is precisely Anath, the sister and defender of Baal, who is designated by the ideogram ^{d}IŠTAR. The wife of Proitos who slandered Bellerophon is called *Anteia* in the *Iliad*: this is a correct and precise rendering of the name of Anath—ʿAnat, ʿAntit, or ʿAnta. This is confirmed by the doublet of Proitos' wife's name, used by the tragedians instead of the Homeric Anteia: *Stheneboia*. This name signifies in Greek "the mighty cow," and is a perfect epithet for Anath. We have already seen that the cow was Anath's animal symbol and double, and that one of the W-S surnames of the goddess—*L'ʾt* (Leah)—signified both "cow" and "mighty" (above, p. 90).

A further corroboration is given in the name of Proitos' and Anteia's daughter: *Maira*.[2] In order to understand its functional-semantic rôle, let us see where else it occurs in Greek mythology. In the Attic myth of Icarios, he is described as the first to receive Dionysos in all Attica. As a reward, Dionysos taught him viticulture and wine-making. When Icarios treated herdsmen with wine, they thought themselves to be poisoned, and killed him. His daughter Erigone, helped by the dog Maira, found her father's body and, grief-stricken, hung herself from the pine tree beneath which her father had been buried. Dionysos took Icarios, Erigone and Maira into heaven and made them into the constellations of Boötes, Virgin,

[1] "But those who were sent to the Cedar Valley, did not come back, for Bata had killed them. He left only one of them, to carry the news to His Majesty," *Pap. d' Orbiney*, § 11 (CDXXIX, 96).

[2] Cf. CDXXXIII, *s.v. Anteia*.

and Greater (or Lesser) Dog.[1] Icarios, as already mentioned,[2] is W-S *'ikkâr* (> Akk. *ikkaru*) "farmer," *Êrigônê* "the early born" is the Dawn (cf. *êrigeneia*, the standard epithet for *Êôs* in Homer and in Hesiod's *Theogony* 381), and *Maira*, changed into a star, is evidently the W-S part. fem. hiph. of *'ûr* "to light": *ma'îrā* "the shining one." Since Anath, the Queen of Heaven, was identified with Venus (*Kaukabtā*) and, under the name of *'Uzzā* "the strong one," was worshipped by the Sinaitic Saracenes as the Morning Star (above, p. 179), the name of Maira is quite in place for a daughter (originally perhaps a reduplication) of Anteia.

Chimaera and Pegasos

The first and foremost exploit of Bellerophon was his victory over the monster Chimaera which in *Iliad* VI: 178-183 is described thus: [3]

> Then after he had been given his son-in-law's wicked symbols, first he sent him away with orders to kill the Chimaera none might approach; a thing of immortal make, not human, lion-fronted and snake behind, a goat in the middle, and snorting out the breath of the terrible flame of bright fire. He killed the Chimaera, obeying the portents of the immortals.[4]

In later antiquity, the Chimaera used to be aetiologically interpreted as the personification of a volcanic crater in the Solymian Mountains in Lycia.[5] However, the Chimaera was well-known in places considerably remote from Lycia; so Sicyon stamped her since archaic times on its coins. She was clearly transferred to Lycia together with Bellerophon. Apparently, a Greek princely house which claimed descent from Glaucos, Bellerophon's grandson, actually gained a foothold in Lycia; its other representatives ruled in Ionian cities of neighboring Caria (Herod. I: 147). As all "Mischgestalten" of Greek art and imagination, the image of the Chimaera came to Greece from the Mesopotamian-North Syrian cultural circle.[6] A representation of a monster, strikingly resembling the

[1] Cf. the ancient sources *ap*. CCXXVII, I, 262 s.

[2] Cf. p. 194, n. 6 above. Etymology suggested LXV, I, 282.

[3] Translat. by Richmond LATTIMORE, 158.

[4] Hesiod *Theog*. 319-322 specified that the Chimaera had three heads: a lion's, a goat's, and a serpent's. She was also represented so in plastic art.

[5] Cf. LXV, I, 191; CLXVIII, 91.

[6] It is a common-place in archaeology that the Greek notion of the famous Theban Sphinx—half-woman, half-lion, winged—reproduces the Syro-Phoenician type, very different from the Egyptian. As to the Chimaera, the

Chimaera, was discovered at Carchemish;[1] it belongs to "neo-Hittite" art, but since nothing similar has been discovered in Ḫatti-land proper, we do not see why it should be considered a Hittite import rather than a native Syrian motif, influenced by the inexhaustible fantasy developed by Sumer and Akkad in inventing bizarre hybrid monsters.

Bellerophon's victory over the lion-headed Chimaera corresponds to the victory of his analog, the Phoenician healer Šed-râphe', over the lion depicted on the stele of Marathos (Amrit). Victory over monsters—dragons, lions, hydras and other "Mischgestalten'—was an obligatory feature of myths about savior gods, the givers of fertility, prosperity, and health. In this respect, the myth of Bellerophon and the Chimaera presents many Oriental features. Its partial prototype is the Babylonian Enlil's victory over the monster Labbu. Labbu was considered a dragon and was identified with the constellation ${}^{\mathrm{mul}}$*Muš* "serpent" (even now Hydra, i.e. sea-serpent), but its name literally means "lion"—it was, accordingly, a combination of a lion and a dragon, may be a leontocephalic dragon.[2] The third ingredient of the mixed nature of the Chimaera was the goat. If it originally belonged here (which may be doubted), it also comes from Babylonia and symbolizes the sea: the "goat-fish" (a goat with a fishtail) was the animal symbol of the Babylonian sea-god Ea. Its astral counterpart was the constellation of

Oriental origin of this motif, occurring *inter alia* in the Luristan bronzes, is established CDXXX. See also following note.

[1] BURN, LXXXIII, 130 s. compares "a veritable Chimaera" on a relief from Carchemish, which shows "a winged lion, with its tail raised aloft and ending in a serpent head, and a human head in a conical helmet rising from the lion's shoulders, in place of that of the goat." This fantastic creature is reproduced on pl. X of the quoted work, and CCCXXXIX, pl. 17. The absence of the goat's head should not surprise us; we shall present reasons for assuming that the Greeks introduced the goat in the Chimaera's composition because of their having misunderstood her name. Moreover, a creature of the same peculiar type as the monster of Carchemish is actually represented on a Greek (Protocorinthian) vase which shows a lion (wingless) with a male bearded head growing from his back, CDXXXI, 22, fig. 1.

[2] Cf. the lion-headed eagle in the coat-of-arms of Lagaš. Labbu is said to be "the progeniture of the river," and the god that vanquished him descended from heaven in a cloud, in the midst of a storm, holding the seal of life (*kunukku napišti*) before his face. Cf. translation CDXCVIII, 62. Pegasos, according to Hesiod *Theog.* 283, 286, flew away from Bellerophon to the immortal gods and carried ever since thunder and lightning for Zeus. He thus personified the thunder-cloud, cf. the epithet of the Ugaritic Storm-god Baal "Rider of the Clouds" and p. 265, n. 1 below.

Capricorn, which the Greeks borrowed from Babylonia exactly in this shape. With the West Semites, the monster vanquished by a god was the seven-headed sea-dragon Leviathan (in Ugaritic spelling *Ltn*). In Ugaritic myths his victor was Baal (or, sometimes, Anath), and in several passages of the Bible he was destroyed or harnessed by Yahwe. This is the ancient motif of victory over the hostile water-element.

Fire-breathing monsters were well-known in the ancient East. So the heavenly bull in the Gilgameš epic killed hundreds of people with his first two snorts (VI: 114-129). Fire-breathing monsters are depicted on many Babylonian cylinder seals.[1] The serpent on the fairy island in the Egyptian tale of the shipwrecked sailor was also fire-breathing—he threatened to reduce the sailor to ashes.[2] However, the most important literary evidence for harmonizing the presumable water-nature of the Chimaera with her fiery breath is the description of the notoriously pelagic dragon Leviathan in Job 41: 11-13: "Out of his mouth go burning torches, and sparks of fire leap forth. Out of his nostrils goes smoke, as out of a burning pot or cauldron. His breath kindles coals and a flame goes out of his mouth." This parallel makes it absolutely unnecessary to have recourse to the volcanic theory in order to explain the image of the Chimaera.

Now a question arises: did the *Chimaira* get her name from being one-third goat, or conversely, was the ill-fitting goat-ingredient introduced because of a misinterpretation of her name? *Chimaira* was indeed a common term designating a she-goat, as *chimaros* was one for a he-goat, but their connection with goats was secondary: the Greeks themselves explained them as technical terms for "winter-born" goats.[3] *Chimaira* was, accordingly, the "wintry" (from *cheimos*) in the primary meaning of her name; some modern scholars preferred to see in her the personification of the wintry colds and storms. However, if the etymology proceding from "goat" is abandoned, it is logical to turn for the origin of the Chimaera's name to the place whence both her image and the image and name of her victor had come—the Semitic East. V. BÉRARD, proceeding mistakenly from the Chimaera's identity with a volcano, accepted

[1] The fire-breathing mouth of the Chimaera is an Assyro-Babylonian motif, CXXX, 1168. Same comparison CLXVIII, 91, but the author still inconsistenly maintained that the Chimaera personified a volcano in Lycia.

[2] CDXXIX, 19.

[3] Cf. the full evidence CDLXXX, IX, 1501 ss.

an etymology from Heb. *ḫāmar* which he incorrectly translated "to bubble, to boil." [1] Actually, this root is never applied to the bubbling of boiling water, but only to wine (Ps. 75: 9) and the sea (Ps. 46: 4; Habak. 3: 15), where heating by fire is excluded; it has to be translated "to heave, to foam" —hence the noun *ḫemer* (Ugar. *ḫmr*) "a frothy drink," poetically "wine," and *ḫomêr* "agitation," speaking of the sea. Thus the etymology from *ḫāmar*, if correctly understood, is very appropriate for a dragon personifying the sea. The use of the word *ḫômer* in the psalm which forms chapt. 3 of the Book of Habakkuk is very significant. It is a mythological hymn on the theme of Yahwe's victory over the water-element, treated several times elsewhere in the Bible. Especially interesting are v. 8: "Is it against the rivers that Yahwe is angry, is thy wrath against the rivers, is thy fury against the sea, that thou dost ride upon thy horses, thy victorious chariot?" and v. 15: "Thou hast trodden the sea with thy horses, the foaming of the great waters" (*ḫômer mayim rabbîm*). U. CASSUTO [2] detected in the psalm of Habakkuk a close similarity to the Ugaritic poem III AB, A (= UM 68) chanting Baal's victory over the personification of the water-element, named *Zbl Ym* // *Šp̈t Nhr* "Prince Sea" // "Judge River."

Like Yahwe in the psalm of Habakkuk against the sea, so, too, Bellerophon, attacking the Chimaera, had a combat-horse: Pegasos. The Homeric exposition of the myth does not mention Pegasos, but there is no doubt that his association with Bellerophon was a primary one. Homer hints vaguely of "portents" or "miracles" of gods which helped Bellerophon to kill the Chimaera (*Iliad* VI: 183), and the marvellous winged horse, sent to him by the gods, might well be considered one of them. As remarked by BURN,[3] the narrative of Bellerophon:

> is a curious one, and not quite like anything else in Homer. It is clearly not inserted from a delight in story-telling, for the stories of Bellerophon's adventures are not *told*; they are merely made the subject of allusions . . . The allusive style . . . seems to indicate the existence of an audience which enjoyed merely being reminded of stories which it knew.

[1] LXV, I, 191; CCCXXX, 191 quotes FISCHER, *Bellerophon*, 93, as the first to have proposed this etymology. More recently, cf. CXXX, 1169: Chimaera —"goat"—is perhaps a popular etymology of some Semitic word.

[2] XCIII; cf. CCLXIX.

[3] LXXXIII, 128.

The image of the winged horse is Oriental. Thus, on a beautiful Assyrian seal one sees a graceful winged horse engaged in a combat with a monstrous gigantic lion.[1] It seems that a certain unpublished text of Ras Shamra, RŠ 24.244 (whose knowledge I owe to the kindness of Professor VIROLLEAUD), indicates the presence of divinized horses in the Ugaritic mythology: *um pḥl pḥlt bt ʿn bt abn bt šmm w thm qrit l špš umh* (lines 1-2). *Pḥlt*, poetically qualified as "daughter of the water-spring, daughter of the stone, daughter of the Heavens and the Ocean," is a daughter of the Sun-goddess *Špš* (whom she "encounters," *qrit*), and herself the mother of *Pḥl*. Now *pḥl* (Arab. *faḥil*, Assyr. *puḫâlu*) is Ugaritic for "stallion" (*UM* § 20. 1533), [2] and *pḥlt*, accordingly, should signify "mare." [3] We must not be surprised by the Sun-goddess being represented as the mother of a "mare" and the grand-mother of a "stallion": horses were traditionally consecrated to the Sun,[4] and, moreover, the goddess Demeter was imaged in the Arcadian Phigalia with a horse's head, and it was said that she bore, in the shape of a mare, the divine stallion Arion,[5] who was sometimes assimilated to Pegasos.[6]

The winged horse is, in a certain aspect, a mythico-iconographic synthesis of the destructive horse and of the eagle who carried Etana to heaven in order to get the "plant of birth," without which he could have no offspring. However, Etana did not reach the upper

[1] CDV, 159, fig. 200; 310, No. 200; cf. CXXX, 1171.—It is interesting to note that Babylonian astronomy named a constellation both ^{mul} ^{d}IM. DUGUD^{MUŠEN} "the divine Storm-bird" and ^{mul}ANŠU.KUR.RA = ^{kakkab}*sîsû* "horse" (CCXXVI, Nos. 32 and 196), which suggests that they had a notion of a mixed fabulous creature, half bird, half horse, corresponding to Pegasos, but astronomically not identical with the Greek and modern constellation of this name.

[2] In the extant Ugaritic myths, this word is used for "jackass," in parallelism with *ʿr* "ass," but for the matter of that, the Akk. cognate of W-S *ʿr*, *urû*, also meant "stallion." Evidently, with the introduction of the horse the older asinine terminology was largely transferred on it.

[3] Cf. Akk. *urû* "stallion," *urîtu* "mare," or Heb. *sûs* "horse," *sûsā* "mare."

[4] Cf. the sacral horses of the Sun in the Jerusalem temple, II Kings 23: 11; Šamaš standing on a horse in the procession of Assyrian gods at Malatya, CDXX, 181, fig. 537; the horses in the chariot of Helios.

[5] Paus. VIII: 25: 3-5; (Ps.) Apollod. III: 6: 8; LXII, 108 ss.

[6] On some Etruscan representations, over the winged horse is written *Ario*, over his master—*Melerpanta* (Bellerophontes), CXXX, 1172.—To return to the Ugaritic text, two of the epithets of the "mare" *Pḥlt*, mother of the "stallion" *Pḥl*, *viz.*, "daughter of the source" and "daughter of the Ocean," are reminiscent of what Hesiod told about Pegasos having been born "near the sources (*pêgai*, whence *Pêgasos*) of the Ocean (*Theogony* 281 s.)."

heaven of Ištar: he was frightened by the tremendous height and ordered the eagle to carry him down. The descent ended in a fall —the eagle was bruised, and what happened to Etana is, unfortunately, lost. It is usually believed that Etana, too, was killed, but SPEISER expresses his strong doubt about that: his opinion is that Etana survived the catastrophe, for Sumerian lists of kings mention Etana's son Baliḫ—so he finally did have a son.[1]

Etana's flight to heaven for the "plant of birth," the secret of which is known to the eagle, certainly belongs to the cycle of healing-motifs. (Let us recall the childlessness of Danel *mt rpi* and the rôle —though an utterly different one—of eagles in the poem about him). Bellerophon's flight to heaven on the back of Pegasos, which had so disastrous a result for him, goes back to the same pattern. What motivated Bellerophon, after a series of victories, after becoming the husband of the Lycian king's daughter and an heir to his throne—is not known for sure. In the dramatic version by Euripides, Bellerophon learned from his dying father-in-law the whole truth about Stheneboea's slander and the perfidious letter of her husband —and rebelled against the injustice of the gods who gave luck and happiness to cruel and treacherous tyrants and abandoned pious cities to the mercy of villains. "And after all that, people are still saying that there are gods in heaven? They are not there, they are not there, unless people want madly to believe in old stories!" [2] And he decided to prove it by ascending to heaven. Of course, this sermon on atheism reflects the ideology of certain sceptical circles in the later Vth century and could not have figured in the original old myth. It is possible that in the ancient version the already humanized Bellerophon—like Gilgameš—was seized by a craving for immortality and decided to obtain it from the place where it was available—from heaven, where (according to the Babylonian Adapa myth) Anu had treated Adapa with the food and water of life, but he refused them by mistake. However,

> When the gods created mankind,
> Death for mankind they set aside,
> Life in their own hands retaining.[3]

The very idea of humans reaching heaven is odious to gods (Gen. 11:

[1] CDLXXI, 114, 118 n. 50.
[2] Euripides frg. 293; cf. DIX, 293 s.
[3] *Gilgameš* X (Old Babyl. Vers.): iii: 3-5, translat. CDLXXI, 90.

1-9). The Bellerophon story in the *Iliad* does not mention Pegasos and the ascension to heaven, but again it vaguely states that at the end "he became hateful to all the gods" (VI: 200)—the same expression which, in the very same conversation between Diomedes and Glaucos, is applied to Lycurgos who had attacked Dionysos (VI: 138). Thus, the author knew of some sacrilegious deed by Bellerophon.[1] According to post-Homeric expositions of the myth, Pegasos threw down Bellerophon when he ordered him to fly still higher, or Zeus sent a gadfly which stung the winged horse and caused the rider's fall. Anyway, Bellerophon fell to the earth, remained alive, but was badly mutilated and spent the rest of his life in solitude and gloom, as stated by Homer. These myths relate to the heroized stage, but originally, when Bellerophon was still conceived as a god, his flight to heaven must have been understood as the rebellion of a god against the established rule of the supreme god, as will become clear from the examination of parallel myths seen in the next section.

Parallels with Hippolytos and Phaëthon

The myth of Hippolytos is very close to that of Bellerophon. Like Bellerophon, he was slandered by Phaedra whom he had rejected.[2]

[1] Harrison, ccxlvii, 220 explained Bellerophon's self-exile to the Aleian plain and his madness (as she understood it) as a consequence of the manslaughter which he, according to the aetiological story explaining his name, had involuntarily committed in Corinth before he fled to Proitos. But it would be quite unnatural to think that such an offense, easily placated by purification rites, would have such grave consequences and that these would have manifested themselves so late, toward the end of Bellerophon's life.

[2] Phaedra originally was identical with Aphrodite (clxxv, I, 25). This follows from Paus. II: 32: 3 that there was at Troezen a temple of Peeping Aphrodite, "for from here, when Hippolytos practiced his exercises, Phaedra, who was in love with him, used to gaze upon him." Is the name *Phaidra* connected with that of the Ugaritic goddess *Pdry* (pronounced *Pí-id-ra-i*, RŠ 17.116: 3, cccxci), as suggested by Graves, ccxxvii, 1, 306, No. 1: "Phaedra occurs in South Palestinian (*sic*) inscriptions as *Pdri*." In Ugarit, she was one of the three daughters of Baal, but in an Assyrian list of gods, *Pi-id-di-ri* [ ] is one of the names of Ištar (cxi, No. 2988), compared with the Ugaritic goddess dxiv, 9, n. 1. But *phaidros* "luminous, clear, radiant, brilliant," figuratively "gay, joyous," is a good Greek word with Greek etymology (cognate to *phaos*, *phôs*, *phainô*, etc.), and this is all the more strange since in Ugarit *Pdry* was named *bt ar* "daughter of light." However, consideration of *Pdry* as a Greek loan-name in Ugaritic is prevented by its occurrence in Assyria; besides, it has a good Semitic etymology, to which we hope to return in a different connection. The Greek genealogical myths considered Phaedra a granddaughter of the Phoenician Europa.

Like Glaucos, Bellerophon's father, he was rent by his maddened horses—and Bellerophon himself, too, was thrown down and crippled by his horse. Sir J. G. Frazer deduced with undisputable clarity from the cult of Hippolytos at Troezen and elsewhere that Hippolytos was one of the avatars of the beautiful young dying god, whose classical image is presented by Adonis.[1] On the other hand, the hunter Hippolytos, the companion of Artemis, is not devoid of resemblance to the Boeotian hunter-heroes Orion and especially Actaeon, both of whom are of Semitic origin, as was shown in Chapt. II. The name of Hippolytos is a Greek one, and has a very transparent significance. It means "rent by horses" and indicates the circumstances of the hero's death. It was perhaps his surname instead of his genuine lost name.[2] The image of Hippolytos which resembles that of Bellerophon, permits us to reconstruct some features of the latter which are less noticeable in the extant versions of his myth, namely his relation with the Adonis type of nature-gods.

Bellerophon's similarity to Phaëthon is less obvious. The myths at our disposal tell us that he was the son of Helios and Merope (or Clymene, or Rhode), and that he forced his father to promise that he would allow him to make one ride through heaven on his sun-chariot. But once in heaven, he lost control of the horses which went astray, rushed blindly, and caused terrible heat and drought. Zeus was obliged to strike Phaëthon with lightning, and his corpse fell to earth near the mythical river Eridanos, where it was bewailed by his sisters the Heliads (who became poplars or alders). The same motifs appear in this myth as in the story of Bellerophon: ascension to heaven with horses, loss of control over them, the wrath of gods and the hero's fall to earth. Phaëthon's disaster caused by bolted horses is identical with the death of Glaucos and Hippolytos. Finally, his death by Zeus' thunder is reminiscent of that of Asclepios, the healer-god.

There is no doubt that the myth of Phaëthon is entirely adopted from W-S mythology. Gruppe[3] showed as early as 1906, and

[1] CLXXV, I, 28-40.

[2] The Greeks themselves were conscious of this, and some authors gave a second name to Hippolytos—Demophoon, known from the *Homeric Hymn to Demeter* (son of the Eleusinian king Celeus, nursed by Demeter). But it does not make an impression of a genuine ancient name, either.

[3] CCXXXV, II, 943.

Grelot [1] developed in detail fifty years later, the fact that the name, image, and myth of Phaëthon go back to the Canaanite myth of *Hêlēl ben Šaḥar* "Shining One, sun of Dawn," preserved as a fragment in Isaiah 14: 12-15. The name *Phaëthôn* "the shining, glittering" is an exact translation of *Hêlēl.* According to Hesiod's *Theogony* 986-991, Phaëthon was the son of Eos, the Dawn, from Cephalos, and was ravished by Aphrodite to become the night-guardian of her temple. Grelot compares this passage with another one in the *Theogony* 378-382 (which he believes to be the more authentic of the two): that Eos bore to Astraeos, Zephyros (west wind), Boreas (north wind), Notos (south wind) and the star Heosphoros, i.e., the morning star, replacing the absent Euros (east wind).[2] From these parallel passages it follows that Phaëthon, in addition to the significance of his name, was, like Hêlēl (correctly translated *Heôsphoros* in LXX and *Lucifer* in the Vulgate) both the Morning Star and the son of Dawn. The reference to him by the author of Is. 14 runs as follows: [3]

(12) How art thou fallen from heaven,
  O Morning Star, son of Dawn!
Thrown down to the earth,
  Who laidst the nations low!
(13) And thou saidst in thy heart:
  "I will ascend into heaven,
Above the stars of God
  Will I exalt my throne,
And I will sit upon the Mountain of Assembly,
  In the uttermost parts of the North;
I will ascend above the heights of the clouds,
  I will be like the Most High."
(14) Yet thou wast brought down to the Nether World,
  To the uttermost parts of the pit.

In this highly poetic fragment, the religious phraseology and the images of Ugaritic mythology are preserved intact. The Mountain of Assembly in the farthest North is the holy mountain *Ṣpn* (*Ṣāphôn*) and the *ġr pḫr* of the Ugaritic poems, where all the gods meet to hold council under the chairmanship of El. The Most

[1] ccxxxii.

[2] ccxxxii, 27 ss.—To this one of the names given to Phaëthon's mother may also be compared: *Rhôdê*, most certainly meaning the "rosy" dawn (*rhôdodaktylos Êôs*, the "rosy-fingered Dawn" of Homer).

[3] This fragment of an old myth is quoted by the author of Is. 14 as a poetic image, to which the fall of the Babylonian king is metaphorically compared. We follow the Masoretic text in writing *Hêlēl*, but the correct pronunciation is assumed to have been *Hilâl*.

High (*ʿElyôn*) is the Phoenician Eliun, the oldest god to reign in heaven, corresponding to the Sumero-Hurrian Alalu of the Kumarbi myth. Baal used to ride over the "heights of the clouds." We have before us a remarkable sample of an ancient Hebreo-Canaanite myth of the arrogant young god who daringly decided to rise to heaven, and to take by force the world throne, and thus to become the supreme god; but who was precipitated from heaven and thrown into Hades instead. However, this myth (in its lost Phoenico-Canaanite original) is not only at the base of the Greek myth of Phaëthon. The names and paternity of Hêlēl and Phaëthon are the same, but not their intentions. No trace is left in the extant versions of the Phaëthon myth of the haughty design to seize the throne of heaven. GRUPPE and GRELOT overlooked the thematically even greater similarity of Hêlēl to the proud theomachist Bellerophon, whose rebellion was artfully presented by Euripides in such a way that he earned the dangerous distinction of being known as an atheist.[1]

There are some other traces of Semitism in the myth of Phaëthon. Merope, his mother, has the same name as Bellerophon's grandmother—or perhaps originally his mother, since Glaucos gives the impression of a double. Horses and chariots were consecrated to the Sun in the temple of Jerusalem until the reform of Josiah (II Kings 23: 11). We shall meet the motif of a flying chariot and point to its W-S parallel. The mythical river Eridanos, where Phaëthon fell, was later identified by Greek geographers with the Po, or the Rhône, or even with the Rhine (so apparently Herod. III: 115). However, the Greeks also located it in Hades[2]—and this is, of course, the original variant: the Canaanite prototype of Phaëthon, Hêlēl, fell from heaven directly into the Nether World (*Šeʾôl*). The Babylonians called the river of the Nether World, which the dead had to cross, by the name *Ḫubur*; the same name also belonged to Tiamat, the personification of primordial water chaos (*Enuma Eliš* I: 132 and *pass.*), and also to a

[1] GRELOT, in addition, wanted to find the prototype of Hêlēl-Phaëthon in the Ugaritic *ʿAṡtar*, who in South Arabia was the male Venus-star—but there is nothing similar between the two, at least in the extant Ugaritic texts. ʿAṡtar did occupy Baal's throne, but not in a bold rebellion, as intended by Hêlēl: he was peaceful and legally named king in lieu of the dead Baal by the supreme divine couple El and Asherah, and not against them.

[2] Schol. Eurip. *Orest.* 982, and several Latin authors, enumerated CDXI, VI, 1, 446 ss., § 3.

goddess who was the female counterpart of Ea, the ocean-god.[1] Since Ea's sacred city and residence was Eridu (which in the third millennium was situated on the shore of the Persian gulf), it seems permissible to derive *Eridanos* from *Eridu* (with an ending as in *Iardanos*, another river name).[2]

Three more Flying Heroes

a) *Icaros*

The most famous of the flying heroes of Greek mythology, the one who became the symbol of human age-old striving for flight and the patron of all those who ever tried to liberate man from being bound to the earth, is Icaros, the son of the celebrated craftsman and inventor Daedalos. There is no need to recount the well-known myth about him. In the Icaros myth, we meet a new means of flight: not on an eagle's back, not riding a winged horse, not in a magic chariot, but with the help of self-made attached wings. Iconographically, the motif of winged human beings is very frequent on Old Babylonian cylinder seals; they often depict bird-men before the throne of a god, like captive enemies or defendants brought for trial. They were, for the most part, believed to represent the bird-god Zû, the myth concerning whom we shall examine later on; but we still are inadequately informed about most of the tremendous mass of Sumerian and Old Akkadian myths, which are reflected plastically on ancient seals, but are not preserved in extant literary documents.[3] However, it seems fairly plausible to presume that the bold leap of imagination toward the idea of artificially-made, detachable wings was originally Greek.

Gruppe[4] recognized in the name *Ikaros* the Hebrew *ʾikkār*

[1] cdlxxi, 62, n. 41; cdlxxii, 12, on possible association of *ḫubur* with *šubur*/*šubar* which signified a) Subartu (country) and b) "earth."

[2] Eridu had its astral counterpart in the constellation which the Babylonians called ^{mul}NUN^{ki} (= Eridu) ^{d}*É-a*; Kugler, for astronomic reasons, identified it with the Greek (and modern) constellation of Eridanus plus Vela and southern part of Puppis, and remarked: "Even the name testifies to the Babylonian origin of this constellation," ccciv, *Suppl.*, 67. Thus our derivation of *Eridanos* from *Eridu*, reached by mythological methods, is corroborated from quite a different side.

[3] Perhaps these bird-men represent spirits of the dead according to their description in *The Descent of Ištar* and *Gilgameš*. Cf. Enkidu's dream in *Gilgameš* VII: iv: 31-32: ". . . he transformed me, so that my arms were [ ] like those of a bird," before he was brought to the Nether World.

[4] ccxxxv, II, 946.

"farmer, ploughman" (actually, it goes back to Akk. *ikkaru* which, in its turn, derives from the Sumerian ENGAR). He saw in Icaros the personification of Orion, whose descent under the horizon was allegorically represented as the hero's fall into the sea. The importance of Orion's appearance and disappearance from the sky for the timing of farming operations is well known from Hesiod's *Works and Days*. Independent of this astral interpretation, the etymology of Icaros' name is corroborated by the role of his Attic namesake Icarios, the first vinegrower and wine-maker (above, p. 194, n. 6; p. 260). The myth of Icarios includes not only agrarian motifs, but chthonic-infernal ones as well (let us recall that the goddess ^{d}*Geštinanna* "heavenly vine" was the scribe of the Babylonian Hades). The hanging of Erigone ("the early born"—Dawn or Morning Star) reminds us of the fate of Inanna, the Sumerian Ištar, in the oldest version of her descent to the Nether World: she was killed there, and her corpse was hanged from a stake.[1] The pestilence which struck the country after Erigone's hanging and stopped after establishing the feast of "swings" in her honor (pestilence is "Nergal's hand," EA 35: 37) also belongs here. Erigone is responsible for the spread and cure of epidemics as a typical Babylonian healing goddess; no wonder she is associated in the myth with a dog: the dog was the animal symbol of the greatest healer, the goddess Gula. In Icaros, again, the motif of Hêlēl-Bellerophon's insolent heavenward flight, punished by precipitation into the sea (in the myth of Hêlēl—directly to the Nether World) finds its expression.[2]

b) *Marpessa and Idas*

The mighty boxer Idas, son of Aphareus and brother of the sharp-eyed Lynceus, was a flying hero—he possessed a winged chariot. He carried away in this chariot Marpessa, daughter of the river Evenos, with whom Apollo himself fell in love. Zeus, acting as arbitrator between Apollo and Idas, left the choice to Marpessa. She chose Idas, for she knew that Apollo would forsake her when she grew old.

The name *Marpêssa* is usually derive from *marptô* "to seize, to

[1] CCXCV, 55, lines, 167 s. (the translation is not quite certain). The rite of hanging human expiatory victims is well attested in W-S religion, cf. II Sam. 21: 6.

[2] The third bearer of this name, Icarios father of Penelope, belonged to a mythical kin rich in Semitic names (cf. p. 274 s. below).

grasp, to catch, to embrace"; GRAVES [1] translates "snatcher." This would apparently point to her being originally conceived as a bird of prey—and she actually was a flier even in the extant version: she flew with Idas in his winged chariot. On the other hand, we have seen that birds of prey were one of the symbols of the healing gods. Taking into account that the names of the flying heroes we have met until now were Semitic (Bellerophon, Icaros, Phaëthon = Hêlēl), we consider as possible and probable that the name *Marpessa* was a W-S one, reinterpreted by the Greeks, namely *marpe'* (cf. *B'l-mrp'*) + Greek feminine ending *-ssa*. We even believe that the name of the mythical heroine to whom the Greeks ascribed the foundation of Carthage, *Elissa* (a name whose Semitic original was vainly sought [2]), is an exactly similar Greco-Semitic formation: *'Ēl* "god" + *—issa*, i.e. "goddess." [3]

We consider the name of Marpessa's husband, Idas of the flying chariot, as Semitic, too. Its stem is *Ida-*, declinable according to the first declension. It may well derive from the Semitic root *yd'* "to know, to learn, to apprehend", Akk. *idû*, Heb. perf. *yāda'*, but in some proper names (*'Ăbidâ'* Gen. 25:4, *Šᵉmidâ'* Num. 26: 32)—*yidâ'*. This form was, apparently, quite ancient, for in W-S (Amorite) names of early IId millennium it is found even in the beginning of a name, as *Idamaraṣ*, a tribe and a country in Mesopotamia.[4] This latter name is very interesting in itself: Akk. *marâṣu*, Ugar. *mrṣ* (cf. Arab. *maraḍa*) means "to be, or to become, ill"; as a noun, Akk. *marṣu* (st. abs. *maraṣ*), Ugar. *mrṣ* is "disease". However, this vocable figures in other Amorite names of theophoric type: *Iamruṣ-il, Abimaraṣ, Adamaraṣ, Aḫimaraṣ, Atamaraṣ*.[5] Thus, *maraṣ* is

[1] CCXXXV, II, 399.

[2] Ed. MEYER, CCCLXIII, II, 2, 111, asserted that *'Elīšā*, the oldest son of *Yāwân* in the Table of Nations, Gen. 10: 4, represented Carthage, allegedly for its mythical founder heroine Elissa. This does not explain, however, the origin of the latter's name. (As a curiosity and an illustration of total ignorance of things Semitic by many prominent Classicists, let us quote from Th. ZIELIŃSKI, *Iz žizni idej*, I [1908], 389: "Elissa, a Phoenician name; cf. Hebrew Elisa-beth"—which is actually composed of *'Eli* + *šeba'*!) The equation of *'Elišā* with Carthage is highly improbable: *'Elišā* was an island (Ezech. 27: 7), and the compiler of the Table of Nations would not have mistaken the Phoenician Carthage for a Greek tribe. *'Elīšā* is rather Alašia-Cyprus (CXIII, 44 = CXV, 184 s.).

[3] There was a mountain Marpessa in the island of Paros. This shows that her cult was fairly widespread.

[4] CCCV, index.

[5] CCCLXXXV, 23.

the name of a god who inflicts diseases—but who, accordingly, also has the power of curing them. *Ida-maraṣ* can only mean "he knows the disease," or rather "Maraṣ (the diseases-god) knows." Of course, knowledge of the secret of causes of the sickness and of the no less secret procedures of cure belonged to the first duties of a medicine-man. The Akkadian word for "physician," *asû*, derived directly from Sumerian *a-zu* "who knows water," and the Akkadians called the divine storm-bird who stole the "tablets of fate" from Enlil by the name *Zû* (^{d}*Zu-u*), Akkadianized Sumerian *zu* "who knows." Indeed, by appropriating the "tablets of fate", the bird must have acquired all the mysterious knowledge of the gods. We shall return later on to Greek reflections of the Zû myth, but, to a certain degree, Idas was one of Zû's avatars—by his name ("who knows"), by his ability to fly, by his theomachy (expressed in the Greek myth by his ravishing the girl whom Apollo loved), and by his end: all myths agree that Zeus struck him with his thunder. This is explained as punishment for the slaying of Zeus' son Polydeuces, but the explanation is purely aetiological: another hero of a heavenly chariot, Phaëthon, perished in the same way, as did Iasion ("healer" by his name), and the classical paragon of Greek healer-gods, Asclepios. Idas, "the one who knows," is an appropriate husband for Marpessa, "the healer." [1]

Like all healer-heroes and bird-heroes, Idas is connected with the Nether World. As to his partial prototype, the bird-god Zû, one may agree with the opinion of E. A. Speiser: [2] "It is probable that Zû belongs to the realm of the nether world." A number of underworld demons have the head, hands, feet or face of Zû.[3] As Frankfort stated about the widespread type of male and female creatures with wings and talons of a predatory bird in Babylonian art, "the texts suggest that these creatures are inhabitants of the land of the dead.[4] The name of Idas' father, Aphareus, clearly derives from W-S *ʿāphār* "dust", metaphorically "the Nether World" (above, p. 251). The chance of an accidental consonance is excluded by the names of Aphareus' kinsmen: his half-brothers by

[1] We leave aside the question whether the *Idaioi Daktyloi*, the mythical inventors of iron smelting, could be connected with the same root.

[2] CDLXXI, 111; earlier very convincingly expounded by Fish, CLXIII, 162, 168 ss.

[3] "A Vision of the Nether World," an Assyrian tablet of the VIIth century, translat. CDLXXI, 109 s.

[4] CLXX, 134.

his mother were Icarios and Tyndareus, sons of Oebalos. We have met *Ikarios* = *'ikkâr* earlier in this section. *Tyndareus* or *Tindareôs* may correspond to a W-S tiqṭal-form from *nādar* "to vow," with preservation of the first radical *n* like in the Shechemite XVth century name *Ia-an-ti-na-du* = *Iantin-Addu*,[1] or in the name of a Byblian king about 1730, *Iantin-ḫammu*.[2] For *Oibalos*, cf. *'Êbâl*, the name of the sacred mountain in Shechem, and of a Horite clan in Seir, Gen. 36: 23. A very noticeable Semitic impact upon pre-Dorian Laconia may certainly be discerned. This applies especially to the oldest Laconian cult-center, the city of Amyclae with its shrine of Apollo Amyclos. It must now be considered proven that this god is none other than the Canaanite god *Ršp Mkl*, to whom we shall return later in this chapter.[3]

c) Abaris

A very striking example of a flying healer-hero with a purely Semitic name is presented in the person of *Abaris*—a miracle-working priest of Apollo, said to have been a Scythian or a Hyperborean, i.e., a native of a fabulous paradise land in the extreme North (cf. *yarkᵉtê ṣāphôn* in the myth of Hêlēl). Later authors tried to fix the dates of his life in the VIIIth or even VIth century, but there is nothing historical about him. He recieved, according to Iamblichos (*Vita Pyth.* 19: 28), a golden arrow from Apollo on which he used to fly in the air (*aithrobatês*). He passed through all Greece with oracles, he healed diseases with one word, he composed many dedicatory and purificatory formulas, he lived without food (Herod. VI: 36), he saved Sparta from pestilence and built there the temple of *Korê sôteira*, Persephone the Savior (Paus. III: 13: 2).

The derivation of the name *Abaris* from Heb. *'ābar* "to fly, to soar in the air," imposes itself. V. Bérard, indeed, explained it in this way.[4] In another place, he derived the name of *Abrotê*, the wife of the mythical Megaraean king *Nisos* who was changed into a sea-eagle (and whose name he explained as Heb. *nēṣ* "hawk"), from the same W-S root *'ābar*, quoting as proof the gloss by Hesy-

[1] CCCLXXXV, 29; cf. Babylonian Amorite *Ia-an-ti-in-ilu*, CXV, 86.

[2] XVII, 9.

[3] We have already referred to Apollo *Karneios* and to Cythera (p. 142 above); cf. also LXV, I, 197-203, where three toponyms of the eastern coast of Laconia are explained as Phoenician. (Lynceus, brother of Idas, like his name-sake in the myth of Danaos, owes his name to the lynx, the animal symbol of Dionysos).

[4] LXII, 179.

chios: *abartai*: *ptênai*: *Kyprioi*.[1] The figure and the name of Abaris illustrate, once more, the source of Greek notions on healing heroes, and help to restore their general pattern.

PART C

Jason and the Bird-Heroes of Aia

Iasion and other Heroes connected with Demeter

a) *Iasion*

We shall start with the hero who bore an almost identical name to that of Jason: *Iasiôn*, or Iasios. The significance of the name does not rouse the slightest doubts: it derives from *iaomai* ' to heal," *iasis* "healing, recovery." The genealogists made him, either with or without grounds, a brother of Dardanos, who was the hero of several flood myths and the mythical founder of the Cabiri worship at Samothrace. Iasion himself was also said to have been connected with the Samothracian Cabiri mysteries.[2] The oldest poetical sources make him a lover of Demeter, the goddess of agriculture. According to *Odyssey* V: 125-128,[3]

> . . . when fair-tressed Demeter yielded to her love, and lay with Iasion in the thrice-ploughed fallow field, Zeus was not long without tidings thereof, and cast at him with his white bolt and slew him.

Hesiod *Theog.* 969-974 specifies: [4]

> Demeter, bright goddess, was joined in sweet love with the hero Iasion in a thrice-ploughed fallow (*neiô eni tripolô*) in the rich land of Crete, and bare Plutos, a kindly god who goes everywhere over land and the sea's wide back, and him who finds him and into whose hands he comes he makes rich, bestowing great wealth upon him.

Here the description is given of the well-known and widespread agrarian rite of *hieros gamos* [5]—the sexual act performed in a

[1] LXV, II, 405; already in CCCXXX, 8, with reference to Hamaker, *Misc. Phoen.*, 301.

[2] He was there considered the father of Corybas, i.e. *Qarûb-baʿal*, identified elsewhere with *Satrapês* = *Šed-râpheʾ*, cf. p. 238 above. For ancient statements, cf. CCCXXIX, 65.

[3] Transl. by S. H. Butcher and A. Lang.

[4] Transl. by Hugh G. Evelyn-White.

[5] On Sumerian and Old Akkadian cylinder seals, scenes, of *hieros gamos* are frequently accompanied by images of a *scorpion*—the chthonic symbol of fertility and health, cf. DII, 14; XXXI, 114. On a Canaanite cylinder of the XIVth or XIIIth century, an extremely naturalistic scene of *hieros*

freshly ploughed field, whose purpose was to secure a rich harvest through magic which, in this instance, was both homeopathic and contagious. The fruit of Demeter's union with Iasion is Plutos, i.e., "wealth"; his name almost coincides with Pluto, surname of the great King of Hades. Gods of earth and underworld were considered rich, because of their disposition of underground treasures and of their function as givers of harvest. The example of Iasion shows in relief the organic connection of the chthonic fertility-gods with healing, which often was an essential feature of their character, as has already been traced in many Oriental heroes and gods and in the Rephaim.

Iasion's death from Zeus' thunderbolt is explained by the *Odyssey* as an instance of divine prohibition for a mortal to be the lover of a goddess. But the same motif is repeated with Phaëthon, Idas, Asclepios—every time with a different reason. It was obviously inherent to the cycle itself.

b) Triptolemos

It must be considered highly probable that originally the fruit of Demeter's union with Iasion in a thrice-ploughed fallow was not the abstract Plutos, but the well-known hero of the Eleusinian cycle, Triptolemos, whose name precisely signifies "thrice-ploughed" or "thrice-plougher." No extant literary source states it, but the Greeks nevertheless joined Triptolemos with Iasion and, for instance, there was a version that the constellation of Gemini represents them. In the extant versions of myths about Demeter, Triptolemos is the goddess's foster-child (in the Homeric Hymn to Demeter this rôle is played by Demophoon, and Triptolemos figures among the rulers of Eleusis and the founders of the mysteries, but on monuments of art Triptolemos is represented as a young boy [1].). Demeter handed over to him a flying chariot driven by serpents (or dragons, which is one and the same in Greek) [2]—to fly over all the earth and

gamos is depicted, with a scorpion under the marital bed, CDLXII, 38 ss. and pl. IV, fig. 3.

[1] "The old matriarchal couple, the Mother and the Maid, who though they were two persons were yet but one goddess, had for their foster-child now one local hero, now another, now Demophoon, now and chiefly Triptolemos," CCXLVII, 562. Miss HARRISON is, however, mistaken in saying that "Triptolemos . . . descended from his high estate as local chieftain to become a beautiful boy in a chariot drawn by snakes" (*loc. cit.*); on the contrary, in this respect, it was the *Hymn to Demeter* which modified the genuine Eleusinian tradition.

[2] CCXLVII, 555, fig. 156.

to spread agriculture among men. In more general expressions, the same is said by Hesiod on Plutos, the son of Demeter and Iasion. Thus we again meet the flying chariot, but this time with still more pronounced chthonic attributes—serpents and the spreading of agriculture.

The custom of ploughing thrice was common for Greece and Syria. It was so routine in the latter, that the Ugaritic verb *ŝlŝ*, formed from the numeral *ŝlŝ* "three," signified "to plough" and was equivalent with the regular verb for it, *ḥrŝ* (*UM* § 20. 2037). Apparently, in this sense the toponym *Baʿal-Šališā*, a settlement in the Mountains of Ephraim, II Kings 4: 42, should be understood. The god after whom it was named was, it may be assumed, a ploughman, like Triptolemos. It is perhaps not by chance that this town in mentioned in one of the marvellous stories of the prophet Elisha as the place whence, after a most cruel famine, someone brought twenty barley loaves and a bagful of ears for Elisha and his disciples. These miraculously satisfied the hunger of a hundred men, and there was even some food remaining. In the Homeric Hymn to Demeter, too, a general cessation of crops is described, and the renewal of soil fertility started by the Rharian plain in Eleusis.

The book of Ruth tells—in a fully euhemerized form—the Hebrew version of the Eleusis myth.[1] A more thoroughly comparative survey must be left for another opportunity. The rôle of Eleusis is played there by Bethlehem, the "House of bread." [2] The arrival therein of the old Naomi, depressed by the loss of her sons, and her talk with the local women resembles amazingly Demeter's coming to Eleusis after her loss of Cora (*Hom. Hymn to Dem.* 90-117). In Judaea as in Greece, the harvest-goddess split in two:

[1] Already SCHULTZE, CDLX, 120, wrote: "The connection of the later legend with the ancient myth of seasonal change can hardly be traced in the Old Testament as clearly as in the lovely idyl of Ruth the Moabite." WINCKLER, DL, III, 65-78, saw Ištar in Ruth, and Marduk-Tammuz in Boaz; but their prototypes are Canaanite rather than Babylonian. A systematic study of the Book of Ruth from the point of view of agrarian mythology must be left for later; here, we must confine ourselves to the bare outlines of this problem.

[2] Moab plays the rôle of the Nether World whence Ruth and Naomi return to Bethlehem after a long famine. The association of Moab with the Nether World may be explained by Moab being the country of Kemoš (Inscr. of Mešaʿ 5-6), the Moabites—the people of Kemoš (Num. 21: 29), and Kemoš himself—one of the names of the Hades king Nergal: *Kammuš* (CCLXXIX, 235 ss.; XXI, 32; CCLXXXIX, 441; CXI, No. 1628).

the old one (Naomi, Demeter) and the young one (Ruth, Cora).[1] Here, too, the agrarian rite of hierogamy is described—not in a freshly ploughed field, but in a threshing-floor, on freshly harvested crops (which had the same purpose)—between Boaz, i.e., *Ba'al-'Oz*, "strong Baal," [2] and Ruth,[3] and their son received the name of *'Ôbēd* "laborer," specifically used in the sense of "tiller" (*'ôbēd 'ădāmā* "tiller of ground" Gen. 4: 2, cf. *la-'ăbōd 'et-hā-'ădāmā* "to till the ground" Gen. 2: 5). Though he was the son of Ruth, the women neighbors said "there is a son born to Naomi" (Ruth 4: 17), and Naomi became his nurse (ibid. 16). All this, including the details, corresponds to Demeter's relationship to Triptolemos.[4]

c) *Musaeos*

Another figure, connected with the Eleusinian cult of Demeter, was that of the mythical pre-Homeric poet Musaeos. He was described not only as a poet but as a priest, prophet, and physician as well. Later antiquity knew many religious poems ascribed to him—prayers, hymns, instructions in medicine and purifications, but, of course, they were all counterfeits. The well-known Orphic writer of the VIth century, Onomacıitos, published a collection of his prophecies, and was exposed by the poet Lasos from Hermione as having added his own falsifications (Herod. VII: 6). But the very desire to pass off one's works under the renowned name of Musaeos proves the antiquity of his reputation. Herodotos himself ascribed to him many prophecies which came true. He was believed to be one of the fundamental religious teachers of mankind—at least it was so at the time of Celsus. After all the above, we should not be surprised that this healer, soothsayer, and servant of the agrarian-chthonic cult of Demeter was supposed to have been able to fly. Pausanias (I: 22: 7) read in a poem which he believed to be a work of Onomacritos, that Boreas, the North Wind, had granted him the art of flying.

[1] On Demeter and Cora as two aspects of the corn-goddess, cf. CLXXV, VII, 39 s.; CCXLVII, 271-276.

[2] As noticed by BAUER, LIII, 73 s.

[3] The name of Ruth is currently derived from *rāwâ* "to drench, to irrigate," and that of Naomi is a variant of *Na'ămā* "the lovely," epithet of W-S goddesses. We derive *Maḥlôn*, the name of Ruth's first husband, from *meḥillā* "cave, underground" (= the Nether World).

[4] It is noteworthy that Boaz descended from *Naḥšôn*, the "serpent-man," Ruth 4: 20.

His name, of course, was, and still is, understood as derived from the Muses. However, Artapanos, an Alexandrian Jew of the IId century, affirmed in his *Jewish History*,[1] that Musaeos was none other than Moses, *Musaios* being only a modification of *Môusês*, and that he was the teacher of Orpheus. This is, naturally, nothing more than an extreme example of the Judaeo-Hellenic polemics of the Lagid period on the problem of which of the two peoples could claim cultural priority. It is, nonetheless, quite possible that there was something more behind the similarity of the names and natures of the two personages than simple fortuity. We may now suspect what could not be guessed by Jewish propagandists more than two thousand years ago: that both Musaeos and Moses had developed from a common Canaanite prototype, the chthonic and ophic healer Muš whom we know from Ugaritic mythology (above, p. 230). The image of a flying serpent should not seem strange: we have already seen how widely this synthesis of bird and serpent was represented in myths of this category, in particular at Canaan. Besides, Boreas, who taught Musaeos to fly, was considered and depicted as a serpent or serpent-man (Paus. V: 19: 1).

Jason and the Golden Fleece

By his name, Jason (*Iasôn*) is almost identical with Iasion; his name also signifies "healer," and it was understood so by the ancients. In what did Jason's healer-character consist? There is, apparently, little left of it in the extant versions of his myths. The ancients interpreted his name in the sense that he had freed, purified, i.e. healed, the Athamantid clan from the curse that hung over it: the obligation of sacrificing the first-born in atonement for Phrixos. It is true that according to the very reliable information by Herodotos (VII: 197), this custom subsisted, at least in theory, up to his own time. According to the first version, however, the purification was accomplished by returning the Golden Fleece from Aia. Why the fleece should play such a rôle is not explained by the myths, but the ritual side of this plot is quite genuine and very ancient.

The fleece—i.e., the hide together with the wool—of the freshly killed victims, played one of the most important rôles in the rite of purification. Jane Harrison collected many testimonies of

[1] Quoted by Alexander Polyhistor frg. 14 (Euseb. *Praep. Evang.* IX: 27); cf. CDXL, XVI, 1, 758.

Greek authors on this subject.[1] The person to be purified stood with his left foot on the fleece of a freshly killed victim, or the hides of the victims were kept until a special ceremonial day, when they were stretched under the feet of the polluted. Those who wanted to obtain an oracle through incubation (namely from Amphiaraos), had to be purified, and this was attained by sleeping on the hides of sacrificed rams. HARRISON correctly summarized: "The fleece is not divine in our sense, not definitely either for blessing or for cursing; it is taboo, it is 'medicine,' it is magical. As magical medicine it has power to purify, i.e. in the ancient sense, not to cleanse physically or purge morally, but to rid one of evil influences, or ghostly infection." [2] Strangely enough, she did not mention in this connection Jason the "physician" and his magic fleece.

The magic idea underneath this rite apparently consisted in the supposition that the fleece (especially if it was fresh, hardly cooled) would absorb or suck in the impurity. So in Babylonia, the purification of the temple for the Akitu feast was performed by rubbing its walls with the body of a beheaded sheep.[3] In Babylonia also, the hides of sacrificial animals were even more connected with medicine in general than they were in Greece. Among the "visible medical remedies" used by the Babylonian magic physicians, MEISSNER [4] mentions the "sheep of repentance" (*mašḫulduppû*) and the "Fleece of the Great Bull" (*sugugallu*). The "visible medical objects" were deified,[5] and the "Fleece of the Great Bull" was identified with Anu himself or with a goddess *Nindagud*.

Thus Jason, before he became in the epic the personification of the ideal of ancient Greek knights-errant, a kind of chairman of the Hellenic Round Table, had first of all been a healer-hero, a magic expeller of evil. This is hinted in his education by the wise physician, the Centaur Cheiron, an honor he shared with Asclepios himself, but even more so by his being the husband of such a typical magician, physician, and poisoner, as Medea, whom we shall

[1] CCXLVII, 23-28; CDXXVIII, 473 ss.

[2] CCXLVII, 28.

[3] CCCXIII, 24; CLXXXVI, 35 s.

[4] CCCLVIII, II, 209.

[5] Among them, the censer; in Ugarit, it figured, with the lyre (*knr*), in a list of gods (cf. p. 190, n. 4 above). On the healing rôle of the lyre (*kinnôr*) in expelling an evil spirit, cf. I Sam. 16: 23; incense and fumigation for purification and expelling of evil spirits have been known since remotest antiquity to this day.

examine later. His heroic deeds do not exclude his being a healer-hero, they rather complete it: we have seen that victory over monsters was a standard attribute of Oriental healer-gods.

However, the complicated and dramatic myth of the Argonauts is not exhausted by this. Why was this particular fleece needed? Why was it necessary to search for it in the remote fabulous country of Aia, on a dangerous voyage, to a deadly fight? Why was it necessary to take it away from King Aietes, how did it come to him, and what mythological image is to be sought underneath this grim king? The epic absorbed and synthesized several other, though cognate, motifs. It took for its point of departure the myth of Athamas, Ino, and Phrixos, the purely W-S character of which we have shown on pp. 204-212 above. Its continuation, forming the introduction to the myth of Jason and the Argonauts, proves to be of the same character.

We have seen that Phrixos, the son of King Athamas, had to be sacrificed to stop drought and famine. It was the same in the archaic times of Israel; seven sons of King Saul were sacrificed in order to save the country from a three-year famine (II Sam. 21: 1-10).[1] Like Isaac in the Genesis story, Phrixos was rescued by divine interference and the miraculous appearance of a ram as his substitute.[2] Attention must be payed to another very important coincidence: the name *Phrixos* stems from the verb *phrissô* "to tremble, to fear, to dread," and it is quite appropriate to the ordeal he went through; now the specific epithet of Yahwe as the deity of Isaac (who narrowly escaped being slaughtered as a victim) was *paḫad Yiṣḥāq* "the terror of Isaac," Gen. 31: 42, 53.

Then the familiar motif of air-flight follows—this time on the back of a ram with golden fleece—and Helle's fall into the sea: the motif of drowning women or girls in the sea or another water-reservoir as a rain-charm, but at the same time the fate of several flying heroes such as Icaros, Bellerophon, and the Canaaneo-Hebrew Hêlēl ben Šaḥar. The name *Hellê* certainly is a feminine form of the latter, as the Cretan Europa-*Hellôtis* (in the former instance, the feminine Semitic ending *-t* was dropped altogether in the Greek as in Hebrew; in the latter it was completed by the

[1] It is perhaps not irrelevant that the mother of two of them, who took care of the bodies of all seven, was named Riṣpā, daughter of ʾAyyā: Aia was the country where Phrixos fled.

[2] Phrixos sacrificed him personally after reaching Aia, and not on the spot, but this is a secondary variant.

Greek feminine ending *-is*). Moreover, Helle was carried away across the sea by a ram, as Europa was by a bull.[1] A ram with golden fleece appears again in the myth of the struggle between Atreus and Thyestes; there it is the symbol of domination over Mycenae: the man who owns it is the legal king. Atreus' unfaithful wife Aërope stole the ram (or its golden fleece) from her husband and handed it over to Thyestes; Atreus ordered Aërope cast into the sea (or, according to another version, her own father Catreus had the intention of drowning her in the sea, but sold her abroad instead [2]). *Aëropê* is obviously a variant of the name *Eurôpê,* among whose descendants she belonged; some authors even call her *Eurôpê,* i.e., Evening Star (above, p. 128 ss.); but the re-interpretation of her name with the introduction of *aêr* "air" clearly shows that a myth must have existed of her flight in the air like Helle, with whom she shares the remaining motifs in her myth.

The myth of Phrixos ends by his arrival in the land of Aia, ruled by King Aietes (*Aiêtês*), whose name signifies "eagle." There he married Aietes' daughter Chalciope, who was not only the daughter of an "eagle," but herself bore the name "hawk-faced" (see above, p. 248). In the same way Moses, the hero of a Hebrew legend, to save himself from death in Egypt, fled to the land of Midian and there married the daughter of the local wise priest; her name was *Ṣippôrā,* i.e., "bird." After his death, the golden fleece of the ram whom he had sacrificed, fell into the hands of Aietes who placed it under the guard of a never-sleeping dragon.

Aietes, Circe, and the Land of Aia

The land of Aia never had a real geographical existence. It is one of those fantastic countries at the edge of the world which include the Isles of the Blessed, the Gardens of the Hesperids, the island of Erytheia, the mythical Ethiopia, most of the countries visited by Odysseus, the Dionysiac Nysa, Plato's Atlantis, etc. With the growth of rationalism, attempts were made to identify all these fantastic places with concrete countries. Since Aia was imagined to lie somewhere in the North (cf. the rôle of North in Semitic

[1] On the rôle of the sheep as a symbol of Astarte, and on ram-gods, cf. CDXXVIII, 310, 469-479.

[2] A typical example of "motivated substitution" in systematization and harmonization of earlier independent myths—a literary device, on which cf. CCCXLVII, 104 s.

myths [1]) and at the same time in the East (closer to sunrise), she was finally identified with Colchis (now the coast of Georgia)—but this happened only in the Vth century.[2] The word *aia* is found in poetic speech with the signification of "earth, country"—but, of course, a fabulous region must have borne a less abstract, a more expressive proper name. Moreover, the *Odyssey* describes another locality with a very similar name, the island of *Aiaiê*, where Aietes' sister, the sorceress Circe lived. It is clear that the explanation of one of these two names will provide an answer as to the significance of the other.[3]

The clue to a correct solution was given by V. Bérard.[4] He recognized in *Kirkê*, the sister of *Aiêtês* the "eagle," a feminine form of Greek *kirkos* "hawk," and accordingly interpreted the name of her island as *ʾAy-ʾayyā*, W-S "island of the Hawk." We would rather divide *Aiaiê* thus: *Aia* + *iê* (Greek fem. adject. ending), i.e. "that of the Hawk," for the pronunciation **ʾay* for W-S*ʾî*, *ʾîa* "island" is not attested. Of course, we cannot agree with the toponymic theory of V. Bérard. He accepted the identification of the island Aiaie with the cape Circaeum in Latium, as it was believed by the Romans; near it he found the river *Vulturnus* "vulturine" and the island *Astura* "of the hawk." He believed that these places had received their Latin and Phoenician names because of the abundance of predatory birds in them. Circe was a personification of a toponym, and she was made the sister of Aietes simply because a "she-hawk" fits well as an "eagle's" sister. Helios was made her father because the hawk was Apollo's bird, and her mother was named *Persê* because, in Hebrew, *peres* is the name of a bird of prey—as V. Bérard explained it, the sea-eagle, *Haliaeetus ossifragus*.[5] Such a simplified approach contradicts the facts. Circe is a mythical personage of full stature, a genuine personality, not a dry personification of a toponym. Eagle-gods and hawk-gods are well-known in the East: Egyptian Horus, Babylonian Zû, Canaanite Ḥoron (falcon-god) and *Ṣml* (eagle-goddess), Arabic Nasr, etc. In Lydia, the cult

[1] E.g. Baal's residence in *ṣrrt Ṣpn*.

[2] The first to identify Aia with Colchis were Eumelos of Corinth and Herodotos, cf. CDXXXIII, *s.v. Aia*.

[3] The interpretation of *Aiaiê*, Circe's island, as an onomatopoeic name "(island of) wailing" (CCXXVII, II, 367, No. 5) is unconvincing.

[4] LXIV, IV, 283-315.

[5] *Ibid.*, 313. This is the current identification of the bird *peres*. However, LXX translates it by *gryps*.

of a hawk-goddess was widespread, "whose origin"—according to Ch. PICARD [1]—"must be sought in Egypt, in Mesopotamian Asia." The Lydian dynasty of the Mermnads, founded in 687 by Gyges the "sea-eagle," got its name from *mermnos* "hawk"; they were the "hawk-kings." [2] The *mermnos*, according to Aelian *Nat. Anim.* 12: 4, was the emblem of the Mother of Gods, i.e., of Cybele or Kubaba. The H-H inscriptions from Carchemish write the name of Kubaba by the ideogram of a hawk.[3] In Etruria, too, the hawk played an important rôle in religious symbolism.[4] And since the Etruscans (as was believed in antiquity and is considered even more nowadays) came to Italy from Lydia, it becomes clear whence the notion of the hawk-goddess was introduced into Latium, which was subject to Etruscan domination and influence for a long time.[5] The sequence of events must be restored in just the opposite order to that believed by V. BÉRARD: precisely because the Etruscans, migrants from Asia Minor, worshipped a hawk-goddess, several localities, including Mount Circaeum, received names connected with her; and precisely because of that the Greeks from neighboring Cumae, who, in their turn, had great influence upon the tribes of Latium, located the fabulous island of Homeric Circe there. Moreover, we know that the cult of Cybele-Kubaba came to Asia Minor from Syria and, in the final analysis, from Sumer (cf. p. 64, esp. n. 3, above). It is therefore clear why the island of her avatar Circe bore the Semitic name of Aiaie. This is not the only Semitic name in her family.[6]

V. BÉRARD, absorbed by the *Odyssey* and by his toponymic theory of the origin of its fabulous personages, neglected the myth

[1] CDXV, 491.

[2] *Ibid.*, 493; XLIV, 22 s.

[3] XLIV, *loc. cit.*

[4] CDXV, 494 s.

[5] We found in one of the studies of the eminent Russian authority in comparative literature, A. VESELOVSKIJ, the exposition of a medieval Tuscan tale, which is an original variation of the Odysseus and Circe story. In it, the jealous Circe changed Odysseus' daughter Melissa into a hawk; this shows that Circe's relation to the hawk was known in Tuscany (former Etruria), though nothing suggests it in the *Odyssey*, and it could not possibly be deduced from Circe's name by Latin-speaking people.

[6] A bird-name, very like Greek *kirkos* "hawk," existed in Sumerian (KUR.GI^{MUŠEN}), whence Akk. *kurkû*, Aram. *kurkyâ*, Arab. *kurkī*. However, the latter two refer to the crane, and TALLQVIST, CDLXXXV, convincingly showed that the Sumerian and the Akkadian names had the same meaning. This paper was brought to my attention by Dr. A. Leo OPPENHEIM.

of the Argonauts which is considerably older, and was widely known when the Odyssey was composed.[7] Like many features in the Odyssey, Circe's island Aiaie was transferred into this epic from the lost pre-Homeric songs of Argo, where, even in the extant retellings, it figures under the name Aia. Naturally, Aietes' and Circe's connection with the Sun was caused by more profound motives than the necessity of providing them with a father, to which end the hawk's consecration to Apollo had been used. First of all, Apollo usurped Helios' place quite late; in the *Odyssey*, in the *Homeric hymn to Demeter* and other older works, Apollo has no relation to the sun, and Helios is an independent divine character. Second, the iconographic idea of personifying the sun by a hawk penetrated from Egypt all over the ancient Near East. The sun-disc provided with hawk's wings was adopted by Hurrians, Hittites, Assyrians. There is reason to suppose that the Western Semites were, moreover, influenced by the consonance of their word for "hawk", *ʾayyā*, with the name of the Babylonian goddess *Aia*, the spouse of the Sun-god Šamaš. The West Semites had *ʾAyyā* ("hawk") as a proper name: a Horite clan in Edom was similarly named (Gen. 36: 24), as was also the father of Saul's concubine Riṣpa (II Sam. 3: 7; 21: 8); but it apparently was a divine name as well, as shown by the name of the Edomite king *Aiarammu* [2] and some others.[3] *Aia* ("hawk") as the Sun-country, and *Persê* (another bird of prey) as the Sun-god's wife—both of these W-S names go back to this combined Egypto-Babylonian influence.

To this another reason was added for considering the Sun-god the father of Circe, Aietes and his family. We have already made sure that predatory birds—eagles, hawks, owls—were symbols not of celestial, but of chthonic and infernal spirits, demons, and gods.

[1] *Odyss.* XII: 70 quotes the itinerary of "Argo, that is in all men's minds, on her voyage from Aietes." *Iliad* VII: 467 ss. names Jason as a generally known personage and is acquainted with the episode of his visit to Lemnos and his begetting of a son by Hypsipyle there.

[2] Sennacherib, Hexag. Prism. II: 54. Translat. CCCXCIX, 287.

[3] On the other hand, the attempt of AISTLEITNER, I, 302 and IIIa, No. 159, to find a god *Ay* in several Ugaritic mythological poems and in *ʾi*, initial element of several Phoenician and Hebrew names, misses the point. It should also be noted that AISTLEITNER regarded the alleged god *Ay* as identical with the Sea-god Yamm; yet in a recently found Ugaritic lexical text (quoted CCCLXXXVIIa, 168), ᵈA.A (*Aia*) is, unexpectedly, equated with the Ugaritic god *Ku-šar-ru*, i.e. *Kšr*, the artificer god who provided Baal with magic arms to vanquish precisely the Sea-god Yamm.

And according to an association which is strange for us, but perfectly comprehensible for the ancient mentality, the Sun-god was considered the ruler and patron of the inhabitants of Hades. So Idri-mi, King of Alalaḫ, promising a blessing to those who would treat his statue well, wrote: "May the Sun-god, the lord of what is above and what is below, the very lord, avert the shades from him." [1] Commenting on these words, S. SMITH noticed: "This aspect is known from other documents. In L. W. KING, *Babylonian Magic and Sorcery*, No. 53, a prayer is addressed to the Sun-god for release from ills caused by ghosts. In *Cuneiform Texts* XXXII: 18: 36 the Sun-god is called *šar eṭimme* 'king of the shades'," etc.[2] The same idea is clearly expressed in the Ugaritic poem I AB: VI (= UM 62, rev.): 44b-49: [3]

špš (45) *rpim. tḥtk* [4]
(46) *špš. tḥtk. ilnym* [5]
(47) *ʿdk.* [6] *ilm.* [7]
hn. mtm. (48) *ʿdk.*

[1] d*Šamaš bêl e-lu-ti ù šap-li-ti bêlu*lu-u*e-ṭim-mi lu u-ti-ra-šu*, Inscr. of Idri-mi 100-101, CDLXVIII, 22 s.

[2] *Ibid.*, 91 s.

[3] Our division in verses and translation may be compared with DXV (*editio princeps*), 238; CCXXIII, 48; CXCVI, 141; CLXXXVI, 205.

[4] Since so many nouns end here in *-k* "thy," *tḥtk* must also be understood as 2d person—but whether *tḥt-k* "under thee," as VIROLLEAUD, or *t-ḥtk*, 2d (not 3d)!) pers. of a verb *ḥtk*—is not easy to decide. The translation "O Šapaš, the Rephaim are under thee" (i.e., under they power) is excellent from the religious point of view, but meets with an apparent grammatical obstacle: *rpim* is an oblique case, they must therefore be the direct object of the action. However, in the poem of the Rephaim, Rp. (= UM 121, 122, 123, 124), the forms *rpum* (nominative) and *rpim* apparently do not follow any logical order, and in GORDON's translation, CCXXIII, 101 ss., both are translated by nominative (or vocative). Nevertheless, it may be preferable to observe the strict indication of the case forms, and to take *rpim* as accusative. For the root *ḥtk*, GORDON, CCXXIII, 48, translated it tentatively "*looks after*"; in *UM* § 20.673 he compared Arab. *ḥataka* "to walk quickly," but this verb is intransitive. We understand it as Heb. *ḥātak* "to cut," figuratively "to decide, to order" (same semantic phenomenon as with *gāzar*), cf. Dan. 9: 24 *šâbûʿîm šibʿîm neḥtak ʿal-ʿammᵉkâ* "sevently weeks are decreed for thy people," and especially the emblematic saw-knife of the Akkadian Sun-god with which he "cuts decisions" (CLXXII, 18, n. 2).

[5] *Ilnym* is a synonym of *rpum* in the poem Rp.; we translate "manes."

[6] *ʿd* is rather a parallel form of *ʿdt* "assembly, congregation" than "witness."

[7] *Ilm* "gods," cf. *ilm arṣ* "chthonic gods" in I D (= 1 Aqht), and *ʾĕlôhîm* applied to the ghost of Samuel I Sam. 28: 13. *Ilm* are parallel to *mtm* "the dead" (Heb. *mêtîm*, Akk. *mîtûti* in *Desc. of Ištar*).

kšrm, ḥbrk [1]
(49) *w ḫss. dʿtk* [2]

(O) *Špš* (Sun-goddess), over the Rephaim thou decidest!
(O) *Špš*, thou decidest over the manes!
Thy assembly are the (chthonic) gods!
Behold, the dead are thy assembly!
Kšr is thy companion,
And *Ḫss* thy (man of) understanding!

In other words, the Sun-goddess is accorded power over the shades of the dead, and the wise god *Kšr-w-Ḫss* has to be her adviser. In another Ugaritic poem, III K (= UM 128): V: 18-20b the words:

ʿrb. špš. lymǵ (19) *krt*
ṣbia. špš (20) *bʿlny*

the sunset, verily, will reach *Krt*,
the host of *Špš*, our lord.

—are put in such a context ("ye shall weep over *Krt*," l. 12; "the dead ye shall weep," l. 14; "dead," l. 16; *b ḫr* "in the Pit," l. 22) that, as pointed out by AISTLEITNER,[3] the idioms "to reach the sunset" and "to enter the host of the Sun" obviously signified "to die."

The origin of the idea of the Sun's power over the ghosts of the Nether World is probably the following: at night, when all gods, identified with stars and planets, are in the sky, the Sun travels his path underground from West to East, to appear again at the eastern horizon in the morning. The name of the Babylonian Sun-god's wife, *Aia* (spelled A.A) properly means "waters"; she is supposed to have been "the personification of the waters which Šamaš traverses from the western to the eastern gate during the night."[4] Aia, thus, is really an underground deity. The image of the cruel Circe who changes men into animals was explained as an ancient goddess of death, disposing of the souls of the dead which she puts in other, animal, bodies.[5]

[1] *Kšrm* = *Kšr* + enclitic *-m*.

[2] *Ḫss*, epithet of *Kšr*, signifies "intelligent." *Dʿt* "understanding, intelligence" is a feminine noun for an abstract notion, but with the meaning "man of understanding": cf. Ugar. *ṣrt* "enmity" in parallelism to *ib* "foe," thus used in the sense of "enemy."

[3] II, 7.

[4] CXII, IV, 1, No. 949: 162.

[5] CLXXXI.—A notion of how Circe could have been imagined in the earliest times, may be given by a terra-cotta relief (the so-called Burney Relief) of the epoch of the First Dynasty of Babylon, published and described

The Plot of the Argonauts Epic and the Myth of Zu

We may now return to the Golden Fleece. Aietes, the Eagle, the "destructive-thinking" or "of baneful mind" (*oloophrôn, Odyss.* X: 137), took hold of it and refused to surrender it. But it was necessary for Jason to deliver it to King Pelias, so the latter could cede his throne to him. It follows from the parallel myth of Atreus and Thyestes that the Golden Fleece was the symbol and attribute of kingship: the man who owned it was recognized as king. But to retrieve it from the redoubtable Aietes was an exploit of unparalleled hardship, and Jason would never have succeeded without the help of Aietes' daughter Medea.

This plot of the Argonaut myth is entirely borrowed from the Babylonian one of the theft of the Tablets of Destinies by the bird-god Zû.[1] The Tablets of Destinies were the magic attribute of divine kingship; they were a kind of a pectoral worn by the supreme ruler of the world. In early times, before the creation of the world, the oldest goddess Tiamat handed over the Tablets of Destinies to Kingu, the commander-in-chief of her army of monsters; by this token he was "elevated to the rank of Anu" (*Enuma eliš* I: 156-158). We recall that the "Fleece of the Great Bull" was magically identified with Anu (p. 281), and this clarifies why the Golden Fleece plays the rôle of the Babylonian Tablets of Destinies in the Argonaut myth and its Pelopid parallel. After his victory over Tiamat and

by CCCXCVIII, 351, fig. 1, and CLXX, 130, fig. 1 (also reproduced CDV, 287, fig. 358). It is one of the most beautiful representations of woman's body in all of Babylonian art. A nude goddess, of very gracious proportions, with a full, handsome face, wearing a divine tiara of four rows of horns, stands on two lions. Behind her shoulders are two wings; instead of feet she has talons of a predatory bird. Huge owls stand on both sides of her. CCXCI, 16 ss. sees in her Lilith. This is a creature of the same kind as Circe the "she-hawk," a fatal predatory goddess, beautiful and cruel, dominating wild animals (cf. the tame lions in Circe's garden), in whom FRANKFORT (CLXX, 134 s.) saw an inhabitant of the Land of Death.

[1] The Akkadians called Zû: "doer of evil, to one who raises the head of evil"; no other divine being was so described (CLXIII, 166). Aietes' epithet *oloophrôn* "of baneful mind" should be compared to this. In a Sumerian myth entitled by KRAMER "Gilgamesh, Enkidu, and the Nether World" (CCXCVI, 30), Zû settled on the top of a tree planted by Inanna, while in its middle Lilith, "the maid of desolation," built her house, and under its roots a serpent "who knows no charm" made its nest. Zû was also associated with a serpent in Gudea's Cyl. A: 27: 19 and in an Akkadian text CT XXII, pl. 48: obv. 5 (CLXIII, 164). Lilith was a she-demon very much like Circe, Aietes' sister, cf. preceding note. Aietes had an immortal dragon in his service. Zû lived in a "faraway mountain" (in the Lugalbanda myth named *Sa-a-bu* or *Za-bu*^{ki}, DLIV, 30, 36), as Aietes resided in the farthest of inhabited lands.

her host, Marduk took away the Tablets of Destinies from Kingu and put them on his own breast (*Enuma Eliš* IV: 121-122). But Marduk plays the rôle of creator of the world and supreme lord only in the version which was composed in the city of Babylon in order to glorify the local patron-god. Originally, in the third millennium, the supreme god was Enlil—and this he remained outside the theology of Babylon; the expression "Enlilship" (*enlilûtu, ellilûtu*) signified "supreme power," and this "Enlilship" was identified with the Tablets of Destinies, worn by Enlil.[1] Zû was the guardian of the temple Duranki ("bond of Heaven and Earth") where Enlil lived, and, constantly observing the supreme god, he conceived the plan of stealing from him the Tablets of Destinies and so to become the "master of the norms" and to "direct the totality of all the Igigi" (heaven-gods). Profiting from the moment when Enlil had taken off his crown and the Tablets of Destinies in order to wash, Zû seized the Tablets of Destinies and flew away to his mountain. "The norms were suspended," i.e., there was no rule in the world. It was urgently necessary to bring back the Tablets of Destinies. Anu exhorted the gods to fight Zû, but they refused, one after another. Then Ningirsu according to one version, Ninurta according to another, went out to fight Zû, but he was invincible: arrows that were shot into him were magically rejected. In the end, Zû was vanquished, and his image became the coat-of-arms of Ningirsu at Lagaš, but it is not known how this happened. An incomplete tablet is preserved in which the Sumerian god Lugalbanda ("the little king") [2] is described as the final victor. It follows from this that he prevailed by a ruse. The text tells that he invited Zû's wife and son to a banquet with the intention of seducing the former and of intoxicating Zû; this plan succeeded, Zû was caught in nooses upon his own nest and strangulated himself, his young perished with him, and only his wife survived to bewail their death.[3]

[1] The Old Babylonian and Assyrian versions of the myth of Zû are published in translation CDLXXI, 111-113, 515-516, with extensive bibliography.

[2] CT XV, pl. 41-43. Transliter. and translation: DLIV.

[3] Cf. CXVI, 314; CLXIII, 163; CDLXXI, 113; CDXCVIII, 154 (a short fragment of the Lugalbanda epic); DLIV (full edition and translation of the Lugalbanda epic).—Traces of a mythic creature, reminiscent of both Zû and Aietes, are perhaps discernible in a recently discovered and "horribly mutilated" (as VIROLLEAUD described it in a letter to the author) Ugaritic fragment RŠ 24.251, where we meet a hitherto unknown personage named *Ḳl-bl*, a son

We find all this in the myth of Aietes, the Eagle of the Golden Fleece. Aietes' daughter Medea assisted Jason and abducted her brother Apsyrtos. In the parallel Greek myth of the struggle for the Golden Fleece, the similarity is still closer: here the Golden Fleece is seized by Thyestes from Atreus with the help of the latter's wife Aërope. Intoxication as a means of obtaining the Golden Fleece also figures in the Argonaut myth, but here it is applied not to Aietes himself, but to the dragon whom he had guard the Golden Fleece: Medea made him drink a soporific beverage. A dragon guarding gold belongs to the most common of mythological motifs, and is found, in particular, in the Ugaritic poem of Baal V AB: D (= *ʿnt*: III): 35-44 in a context which presents considerable interest for the central plot of the Argonaut myth. The goddess Anath declares there:

l mḫšt. mdd (36) *il ym.*
l klt. nhr. il rbm
(37) *l ištbm. tnn. išbm(?)n(?)h* [1]
(38) *mḫšt. bšn. ʿqltn*
(39) *šlyṭ.*[2] *d. šbʿt. rašm*
(40) *mḫšt. mdd. ilm. ar* [*ṣ*/*š*] [3]

of the Sun-goddess Šapaš, about whom we only learn that he "wept like a boy and shed tears like a child" (*ybky km nʿr ydmʿ km ṣǵr*), one does not know why. His name can hardly be explained otherwise than "voice (or thunder) of destruction" (*qôl-beli*; *beli* "detrition, destruction" Is. 38: 17, Akk. *balû* in D-stem "to destroy, uproot, annihilate, extinguish [fire or life]"). This fits the destructive thunder-bird Zû in the best way; the Akkadian myth states that Zû's shouting drove back arrows aimed at him (CDLXXI, 515). Like Zû's Greek counterpart Aietes, *Ql-bl* is a son of the Sun-deity.

[1] VIROLLEAUD, in *editio princeps*, DXIV, 53, with remarkable ingenuity explained the verb *šbm* by Arab. *šabama* "to muzzle" and compared Job 40: 25-26, where the image of muzzling the Leviathan is developed in more detail.

[2] In CCXXIII, 20 GORDON translated *šlyṭ* "the accursed one," from Aram. *lyṭ* "to curse," but in *UM* § 20.1389 he agreed with III, § 80 in translating "powerful" (so earlier VIROLLEAUD in I* AB: I: 1 and in this passage, explaining *-y-* as a pejorative formation of adjectives, DXIV, 54).

[3] VIROLLEAUD restored a *ṣ* at the end of line 40; GORDON in his transliteration (CCXXIV, 180) divides *ṣmt* in the beginning of line 41 into *ṣ*, which he attaches to *ar* at the end of line 140 (obtaining *arṣ*), and *mt* = the god Môt, to whom he attributes the qualification "the calf of Il—." We prefer the restoration of VIROLLEAUD, but we would like to suggest that the presumably missing letter after *ar* could have been *š*, obtaining thus *mdd ilm arš* "the beloved of the gods, *Arš*," a monster of the same kind as Tannin, cf. *b ym arš w tnn*, I AB: VI (= UM 62: rev.): 50, "in the sea, there are *Arš* and Tannin."

(41) *ṣmt. ʿgl. il. ʿtk* [1]
(42) *mḫšt. klbt. ilm. išt*
(43) *klt. bt. il. žbb* [2]
imtḫṣ w (44) *itrš. ḫrṣ*

Did I not crush El's Darling, Sea?
Nor destroy River, the great god?
Nor muzzle Tannin full well?
I crushed the writhing serpent,
The powerful one of seven heads,
I crushed the darling of the gods of the ear[th], [3]
I exterminated the young bull, the rushing god, [4]
I crushed the bitch of the gods, Fire.
I destroyed the daughter of El-*Žbb*.
I fought and I inherited gold.

"It is interesting to note," said Gordon in a footnote to this passage,[5] "that by fighting one (or more) of the foregoing dragons, 'Anat obtained gold, which was evidently guarded by the dragon(s)," and Virolleaud [6] compared "the garden of the Hesperids with the *golden* apples guarded by a dragon,[7] or the *Golden* Fleece far in the north" and reminded us that according to Job. 37: 22 "from the North comes gold." [8] In order to get hold of the gold, Anath vanquished not only a dragon,[9] but a young bull and Fire (personified as "the bitch of the gods") as well. Jason, too, in order to obtain the Golden Fleece, had to prevail over fire-breathing bulls, created by Hephaestos. On the other hand, these fire-breathing brazen-footed bulls are connected with the motif of the heavenly bull with his mortal snort, vanquished by Gilgameš, and to some extent, too,

[1] *Ṣmt*—1st pers. perf. of *ṣmt. ʿtk* (hardly the town of *ʿAtāk* in Negeb, I Sam. 30: 30), probably the name or qualification of the calf (or young bull), was derived by Virolleaud, dxiv, 17, from Arab. *ʿataka* "to rush upon, to attack." Cf. Behemoth along with Leviathan in Job, and *šôr hab-bār* ("bull of the steppe") in the same association in Aggada and Jewish folklore.

[2] *Il žbb* = Baʿal-Zebûb? (cf. *UM* § 20.523).

[3] Or, rather, "I crushed the darling of the gods, *Arš*," cf. p. 291, n. 3 above.

[4] Or, ". . . the young bull of the Rushing God."

[5] ccxxiii, 20, n. 1.

[6] dxiv, 54.

[7] That dragons name, *Ladôn*—through the intermediate forms *Lathôn*, *Lêton*—undoubtedly goes back to Ugar. *Ltn* (= Heb. *Liwyātān*), cf. p. 214 above. He is not named in the quoted passage, but in I* AB (= UM 67): I: 1-3 the qualifications *bšn ʿqltn* "the writhing serpent" and *šlyṭ d šbʿt rašm* (together with a third one, *bšn brḥ* "the running serpent," cf. Is. 27: 1) explicitly designate *Ltn*.

[8] dxiv, 56.

[9] The victory over Leviathan was also ascribed by the Ugaritic cycle AB to Baal himself.

with the brazen bull-shaped idols in which Phoenicians and Carthaginians used to burn their sacrifices (including human ones).[1] The magic plant which preserved Jason from the fiery breath of the bulls, directly corresponds to "the plant to put out poison" which was grasped in Marduk's hand when he went forth to battle Tiamat (*Enuma Eliš* IV: 62). The remaining episodes of the Argonaut myth, as it is expounded by Apollonios Rhodios, are either quite independent local myths (as the episode of Anaphe and Thera, cf. above, p. 117 ss.), or borrowings from other famous cycles (as the sowing of dragon's teeth from the myth of Cadmos, the visit of Circe from the *Odyssey*), or simply free inventions of tellers and poets to fill the itinerary of the heroes with adventures.[2]

Semitisms in the Bird-Family of Aietes

a) *Aietes*

So the antagonist of Jason the "healer", the one from whom the Golden Fleece which he had illegally appropriated had to be extorted, corresponds both in name and mythological function to the Babylonian bird-god Zû. The name *Zu-u,* though used by the Akkadians (the Sumerians called him, most commonly, ^{d}IM.DUGUD MUŠEN), is evidently of Sumerian origin and signifies "the one who knows." [3] It is very characteristic that Aietes' wife was called *Idyia* (Hesiod *Theog.* 960), epic dialectal form of *Eidyia,* i.e. "the one (fem.) who knows"—an adequate wife of a hero whose prototype

[1] CCXXVII, II, 240, cf. CLXXV, IV, 74 s. for such interpretation of the Cretan Minotauros and Talos.

[2] A note on the Argonauts' visit to Lemnos, the island stained by the massacre of all males. Herodotos VI: 138, having told a legend about how the Lemnian Pelasgians had murdered all their Attic wives and their children, adds: "Because of this deed, and also of a more ancient one committed by the Lemnian women who had massacred their husbands together with Thoas, it became a habit in Hellas to call 'Lemnian' all criminal actions " (*lêmnia erga*). In Akkadian, *limnu, lemnu* = "an evil one," *limuttu,* plur. *limnûtu* "evil, evil deed, impurity." It seems that both stories on mass crimes in the island of Lemnos are aetiological myths to explain the Akkadianism (brought by West Semites) *lêmnios* = *lemnu* "evil."—It seems also that the name of the strong-man *Amykos,* vanquished in fist-fight by Polydeuces, derives from W-S *ʿmq* "strong," (*UM* § 20.1413), Akk. *emûqu* "strength, power," *emqu* "strong."

[3] DEIMEL, CXI, No. 1327, asked: "Num *Zû* cum *Zu-en* (Sin) cohaeret?" (*Zu-en,* or *En-zu* "lord of knowledge" was the Sumerian name of the Moon-god). CCXXVI, No. 172: "^{mul} ^{d}ZU, the star of the 'knowing god' . . . (^{d}ZU = ^{il}*Zû*?)." Philologically, there is no difficulty whatever.

was Zû (Sum. ZU = Akk. *idû* "to know"). Was it not possible that her Semitic prototype bore a similar sounding name, which had in Semitic the same meaning as *Idyia* did in Greek (cf. p. 274)? The name of Aietes himself was sometimes considered a Semitic one: BOCHART, *Hierozoicon*, II, p. 743, derived the Greek word for "eagle", *aëtos* or *aiêtos* (whence *Aiêtês*) from Hebrew *ʿayiṭ* "a bird of prey: eagle, hawk or the like."[1] (Cf. Is. 46: 11 figuratively of Cyrus). Since *aëtos* "eagle" is a common name in Greek, its possible W-S origin is interesting as another instance of a W-S loan-word in Greek, but whether it is accepted or rejected, it does not change our restoration of the mythological origin of Aietes.

However, the name of Aietes' and Circe's mother, *Persê* (*Odyss.* X: 139) or *Persêis* (Hesiod *Theog.* 956), which V. BÉRARD derived from W-S *peres* "sea-eagle" (or, with LXX, griffon-vulture), combined with the name of the land of Aia, proves undoubtedly and unequivocally the presence not only of mythical motifs of Oriental origin, but of Semitic names in Aietes' family as well. We may also add to them the following names, which, in fact, include all the rest of the Heliads of Aia.

b) Chalciope

We have already met this name on the other bird-island, Cos, and we derived it not from the commonly known noun *chalkos* "copper, bronze," but from *chalkis*, a word from the "language of gods," equivalent to *kymindis* "night-hawk." This name harmonizes in meaning with the entire onomastica of the fabulous Aia, and at the same time it comes from a word which appears in every way Semitic. Although a predatory bird of this name is not registered in the lists of impure birds Lev. 11: 13-19 and Deut. 14: 12-18, its name may easily be derived from *ḫalâqu*, Akk. and Ugar. "to perish," in D-stem "to destroy," or from Heb. *ḥālaq* "smooth, hairless," which would point to the bald head of some eagles and vultures—cf. Micha 1: 16: "widen thy bald spot like an eagle." The "language of the gods," distinct from Greek, in some cases proves to be Semitic—the forgotten hieratic language of the ancient "Phoenician" colonists. Thus, the miraculous plant, given to Odysseus by Hermes to protect him from Circe's charms, was called in "the language of the gods" *moly* (*Odyss.* X: 305). V. BÉRARD[2] explained it as Heb.

[1] Thus also LXV, I, 438.
[2] LXV, II, index, s.v. *moly*; LXIV, III, 173.

mallûăh (*Artiplex halimus*), from *melah* "salt", but it may still better be derived from the root of those words, *mlḥ* (cf. *UM* § 20. 1117): "good". [1]

c) *Cytissoros*

So, according to Herodotos VII: 197, the son of Phrixos and Chalciope was called, who returned to his father's homeland just in time to save his grandfather Athamas from being sacrificed. Since then, as punishment for this interference, a similar fate threatens every oldest among his descendants who dared enter the prytaneion (city-hall) of Alos in Achaia Phtiotis. Apollonios Rhodios (II: 1155-1156) added three more brothers to his family, whose banal names (Argeus, Phrontis, and Melas) betray their artificial nature. The name *Kytissôros* is quite different and very singular. Its second part, *-issôros*, renders in a very precise way the Ugar. *ʿṣr*, Akk. *iṣṣûru* "bird." Its location at the end of the name agrees with the cuneiform habit of putting the determinative ḪU (= MUŠEN) = *iṣṣûru* after the name of the bird. Or else it may be another instance of putting the qualificative after the proper name, as in Ugar. *Yṣb-ġlm*, *Krt-ŝʿ*, *Bʿl-šr*, *Pbl-mlk*. We hesitate to explain the first part of the name, the element *Kyt-*—not because convenient Semitic etymologies are lacking, but because of the duality of both consonants (Greek *kappa* = both *k* and *q*, *tau* = both *ṭ* and *t*), which supplies too many possible etymologies.

d) *Absyrtos*

This is the Latin spelling of the name—the Greeks wrote *Apsyrtos*, but they were, in any case, unable to render the combination *abs-* otherwise than through *aps-* (e.g., *Araps*, plur. *Arabes*). He was abducted by his sister Medea when she fled with Jason, slain, cut to pieces, and the pieces were scattered in order to hinder Aietes' pursuit. Here again we are in the presence of the rite of sparagmos,[2] and we have here perhaps the same Semitic root from which we derived the surname of Dionysos, *Bassareus*, and the name of his man-tearing Bassarids: *baṣâru* "to cut, to tear to pieces."

[1] For salt as antidote against bewitchment, cf. the Babylonian incantation *Maqlû* VI: 111-119 (translat. CCLXX, 143).

[2] Dismemberment of a brother by his sister: cf. the Ugaritic fragment RŠ 22.225, p. 180 above.

The name would, then, be divided into the elements *A-bsyr-tos*: prothetic *a-* + *baṣur* part. pass. of *bṣr* "the dismembered" + the Greek suffix *-tos*.

e) Medea

Medea, the younger daughter of Aietes, became the wife of Jason "the healer." A ritual comparative analysis was necessary in order to detect the elements of Jason's "healer" character, but as for Medea, she possessed it in a very conspicuous degree. In Sumero-Akkadian mythology, the wives of healer-gods usually were healer-goddesses.[1] It was not by chance that Jason "the healer" was married to a heroine who was a salient representative of magic medicine, who knew medical plants, poisons, incantations, who was able to produce soporific beverages, to make one fire-resistant, to grant fecundity (Eurip. *Medea* 717 s.), and even to return youth to old men and to revive the dead. The evolution of the myth left to her, out of the couple of healer-heroes, the art of magic and leechcraft, and perhaps it made it even more spectacular. Circe, "the she-hawk," the ruler of Aiaie, Aietes' sister, is described in the *Odyssey* as a similar magician and expert in mysterious drugs.

The name *Mêdeia* was, of course, understood by the Greeks as a derivative from *mêdomai*, epic and poetic for "to discuss, to invent, to plan" (especially evil things), *ta mêdea* "thoughts, plans, intentions," and also "wit, slyness." When they became acquainted with the Medes (*Mêdes*), fictions appeared based on the similarity of their name to hers (Herod. VII: 62). But, probably, even the first etymology was based on a Greco-Semitic play of words. In accordance with the Semitic origin and the specific semantics of the names of all her kinspeople, the root of her name has to be sought among Semitic names for various predatory birds, or verbs for "flying." Besides, she really used to fly upon her dragon-spanned chariot (see immediately below). We derive her name from the W-S root *d'y* "to fly," Heb. *dā'â*, whence Heb. *dā'ā* (or *dayyā*), a bird of prey, translated by LXX Lev. 11: 14 *gyps* (a type of vulture), Ugar. *diy*, plur. *diym* || *nšrm* "eagles." *Mêdeia*, according to this interpretation, derives from Part. sg. fem. Piel of *d'y*; this would be in Ugar. **mdiyt* (**madiyat*), in Heb. **m^{e}dē'(y)ā*. Part. Piel of the rare verb *dā'â* is not attested, but cf. the verb *'ûph*, identical in meaning,

[1] P. 241 above.

and used with the sense of "flying" in Piel (more correctly, Polel) *ʿôphēph*, whence "flying": *meʿôphēph*, e.g. *ʿôph meʿôphēph* "flying bird," *śārâph meʿôphēph* "flying serpent"; the same applies to the verb *rāḫaph* "to soar," whence *meraḫephet* "soaring" in the famous verset Gen. 1: 2.

f) The Motif of the Flying Chariot

We find in the myth of Medea the already familiar motif of a flying chariot, driven by dragons. On it Medea escaped from Ephyra after the perfidious and cruel murder of her rival, the princess Glauce. The name of the latter, by the way, signifies "owl" and is typologically well connected both with Ephyra ("region of dust" = Nether World, cf. p. 251) and with the healer-heroes Medea and Jason. This is the fourth occurrence of a flying chariot, the first three having been those of Phaëthon, Idas, and Triptolemos.

However, this is by no means a Greek invention. This motif, too, is found in the W-S world, namely in the story of Elijah's ascension in the presence of Elisha (II Kings 2: 11): "And as they still went on and talked, behold, a chariot of fire and horses of fire separated the two of them. And Elijah went up by whirlwind into heaven." Many ancient myths were embodied in the person of Elijah. He has attributes of the Storm-god (cf. p. 215), and as such, he is the heir of Baal, the "Rider of Clouds," *rkb ʿrpt* (it is not known how this was imagined: mounted on a winged horse, like Bellerophon, or on a chariot, like Yahwe in the psalm of Habakkuk 3: 8, 15). Moreover, Elijah was the greatest healer in Hebrew legend, whose miracles even included resurrecting the dead (I Kings 17: 17-24)—which was also the maximal expectation from Sumerian healer-deities. It is more than probable that the Greeks of the Mycenaean Age, having borrowed the personages of their myths about healer gods and heroes from the East, have also simultaneously borrowed the motif of a flying chariot, too.

g) Mermeros and Ilos

It is said in *Odyss.* I: 254-259 that Odysseus once

> came up out of Ephyra from Ilos son of Mermeros. For even thither had Odysseus gone on his swift ship to seek a deadly drug, that he might have wherewithal to smear his bronze-shod arrows: but Ilos would in no wise give it him, for he had in awe the everliving gods.[1]

[1] Transl. by BUTCHER and LANG.

Ilos, son of Mermeros, lived in the city of Ephyra—the same name as the city of Sisyphos, Glaucos, and Bellerophon, with which the myth of Medea is also connected. It is a question of secondary interest to seek its precise location; it might have been, for the author of the passage, some conventional vague region, but, if he identified it with a real city in Greece, this most probably was Corinth, as in the myths of Sisyphos and of Medea. In the Bellerophon episode in *Iliad* VI: 152-153 it is located in the Peloponnese. We already pointed to the chthonic significance of the name of Ephyra. Of course, an expert in preparing poisons fits well as an inhabitant of such a city. The further pedigree of Ilos is not traced in the *Odyssey*, but later mythographers considered Mermeros and Pheres as the sons of Jason and Medea, and made Mermeros the father of Ilos to a son of Pheres and a nephew of the first Mermeros. According to some authors, Mermeros and Pheres were killed by the Corinthians after Medea's treacherous murder of Glauce; according to others, including Euripides (who, however, did not mention their names) they were slaughtered by Medea herself.[1]

Whether the descent of Mermeros from Medea is original, or whether it was inspired by the characteristics of his son Ilos in *Odyss.* I: 254 ss.—in either case, it remains a fact that he is a figure of the same cycle. The name of Mermeros has a purely Greek explanation: *mermeros* in epic poetry means "causing anxiety, heavy, difficult, terrible"; *mermera* "frightening, terrible deeds." But, nevertheless, the association of Mermeros with Ilos in the formula "Ilos son of Mermeros" betrays the Oriental origin of both names.

The god ^{d}*Mermer* was the national deity of the kingdom of Ḫana on the middle Euphrates, and especially of its capital Mari. His name is a reduplication of ^{d}*Mêr*, which derives from Sumerian *mer*, *mir* "wind." In Mari, and then in Terqa, the capital of the second kingdom of Ḫana, he was usually called by the compound name ^{d}*I-tur-Me-er* "Mer is propitious." Still at the end of the second millennium there was a king in Ḫana by the name of *Tukulti*^{ti}-^{d}*Me-er*. The worship of the god ^{d}*Mêr* is attested from the dynasty of Agade to the end of the Assyrian empire. In the god-lists of Aššurbanipal's library, he is listed under the names *Ilumer*, *Iluwer*,

[1] Cf. the variants and their sources in ccxxvii, II, 254 s. The rest of the names of the children, ascribed to Jason and Medea, were obviously invented. They are trivial names, or Thessalian eponyms.

and *Mermeri*, and is identified with Adad, which corresponds to the Sumerian meaning of his name. The name *Iluwer*, spelled alphabetically *'lwr*, figures in the inscription of Zakir of Hamath (early VIIIth century) as his personal patron-deity. DOSSIN, on whose data this summary is based,[1] derives the name of the city of Mari (originally *Me-er*^{ki} or *Me-ra*^{ki}) from its patron god. To this must be added the fact that the cult of this god penetrated into Syria not later than the middle of the second millennium, for a king of Tunip in the valley of the Orontes, about 1450, apparently bore the name of *Ir-Mermer*.[2] The fact that *Ilu* + *Mêr* have formed a single divine name *Ilumer/Iluwer*, stresses the organic connection of *Ilos* and *Mermeros*, taken over from the Semites as a binomial and decomposed by the Greeks into two names.

It seems that at the time of Mari, *Mêr* (*Iturmer*) was not yet fully identified with Adad (or was his independent avatar). Now, when we know that Adad, i.e., the W-S Hadad-Hadd (= Baal), was a dying god and spent some of his time in the underworld, we should not be surprised by his avatar Mermeros' association with Ephyra and mortal poisons.[3]

PART D

Cheiron and Asclepios

CHEIRON, PABILSAG, AND PBL-MLK

Jason (the "healer") was a disciple of the wise Centaur Cheiron. As is known, Cheiron was also the teacher of Achilles, the hero of the Trojan war, the paragon of a bellicose prince as perceived by the Greeks of the Homeric age. The writers of the classical period described in detail the many-sided education given by Cheiron to Achilles, they transformed it into a synthesis of pedagogic ideals of their own time. Homer, however, mentions only one subject which Cheiron taught Achilles. In *Iliad* XI: 827-831 the wounded Eurypylos implores Achilles' friend Patroclos: [4]

[1] CXXV, 153-159.

[2] CDLVIII, 89.

[3] It may be significant that another *Ilos* is the brother of *Assarakos* in *Iliad* XX: 232. The Assyrian character of these names was assumed by LENORMANT in 1879. We would understand *Assarakos* as ^{d}*Asaru* (one of the 50 names of Marduk) with the Akk. ending *-aku*.

[4] Transl. by Richmond LATTIMORE.

> But help save me now at least, leading me away to my black ship, and cut the arrow out of my thigh, wash the dark blood running out of it with warm water, and put kind medicines on it, good ones, which they say you have been told of by Achilles, since Cheiron, most righteous of the Centaurs, told him about them.

Achilles in the rôle of a surgeon and physician seems unfamiliar, but he, too, like many other strong heroes and gallant warriors, preserved in his character something of the nature of the old Oriental monster-fighters who were, at the same time, healers.[1] However, Cheiron's authority as a great teacher of medical art went still further. The god of medicine par excellence, Asclepios, owed his proficiency to the same master. *Iliad* IV: 217-219 tells that Machaon, a son of Asclepios and chief surgeon of the Achaean army, "sucked the blood and skillfully laid healing medicines on it that Cheiron in friendship long ago had given to his father."

Comparative astrology shows that Cheiron was fully entitled to such a reputation. The Greeks considered the zodiacal constellation of Sagittarius his heavenly image, which they represented as a centaur (a horse with a human torso, arms, and head) drawing a bow. They had borrowed this iconography (as most of their notions of stars and constellations) from the Babylonians. The latter sometimes represented Sagittarius in the same way as the Greeks, i.e., as a hippocentaur with a drawn bow, but more often as a scorpion-man shooting, with the hind part of the body being that of a scorpion instead of a horse. The Babylonians kept for the constellation of Sagittarius the Sumerian name of the god ^{d}*Pa-bil-sag*, sometimes shortened to ^{d}*Pa-bil*, ^{d}*Pa*.[2] We have already met this god as the husband of several healing-goddesses (above, p. 240), and we have seen that the scorpion, like the serpent, was a symbol of healing, fecundity, and prosperity, and a widespread apotropy throughout the ancient Near East, and later, in Greece and Rome. The Babylonian astronomers cunningly put together images of healing gods in their sky: next to the scorpion-man Pabilsag (Sagittarius) they

[1] Achilles' medical abilities were not always described in so rationalistic a way as by the realistic author of the *Iliad* who only recognizes drugs and does not want to know anything about magic (in the *Odyssey*, though later, blood running from a wound is still "stayed with a song of healing," XIX: 457). In the *Cypria*, though composed after the *Iliad*, an older approach to medical art is preserved: there Achilles heals the incurable wound of Telephos, which he himself had inflicted, with rust scraped from his spear.

[2] CCLXXV, II, 681 s.; CCCIV, I, 261; CXI, Nos. 2941-2945; CCXXVI, Nos. 356-358.

situated the constellation which even now bears the name of Scorpio, which the Babylonians identified with the "great physician"-goddess Išḫara, and next to Scorpio lies the constellation of Hydra (i.e., water-serpent, ^{mul}*Muš* of the Babylonians), which in Mesopotamian astrology represented the god Ningišzida. A glance at the sky explains why Cheiron-Sagittarius was considered the teacher of the ophic healer-god Asclepios, a remote product of evolution of the serpent-deity Ningišzida.

There can be no doubts as to the road by which the Babylonian astral symbolism of Pabilsag-Cheiron penetrated into Greece. This happened by the maritime way, through the West Semites. It is proven by the fact that Pabilsag had been adopted and included in mythological poetry by the Ugaritians who were located in the most important point of contact between the Syro-Mesopotamian cultural cycle and the Aegean. *Pbl-mlk,* king of *Udm,* figures in the epic of King *Krt,* and it was his beautiful elder daughter [1] *Mšt-Ḥry* whom *Krt* married. The strange and apparently non-Semitic name *Pbl* puzzled the scholars. ALBRIGHT [2] saw in it the personification of Babylon (by dissimilation from *Bâbel*), and compared with it the Hittite name for Babylon, *Pabili.* GRAY adopted the line of least resistance in interpreting unintelligible names: "We regard *pbl* not as real proper name, but as an onomatopoeic name as the Hebrew *bâbēl* in the popular etymology of Gen. XI, 7, or the Greek *barbaros.*" [3] The name was, however, unraveled with perfect correctness by VIROLLEAUD in the *editio princeps* of I Krt: "*Pbl* is the Sumerian *Pabil-sag* 'Pabil (is) the chief (or the head)'." [4] Unfortunately, other scholars did not pay any attention to this clue, and VIROLLEAUD himself did not elaborate his idea. He did not go beyond a reference to the book by Ch.-F. JEAN,[5] where, strangely enough, the learned French Assyriologist, contrary to the facts,

[1] *nʿmt šph bkrk,* I K (= Krt): 144, 290, may also be understood as "the most gracious of the offspring of thy first-born," i.e. *Pbl-mlk*'s granddaughter.

[2] XVIII, 30, n. 55.

[3] CCXXX, 104, n. 4; he continues: "The reference is to the non-Semitic character of the king in the *Krt* text, which we regard as commemorating a decisive phase in the amalgamation of Semite and Hurrian in North Syria." He understands *Ḥry* in the name of *Pbl*'s daughter as "the Hurrian," though this ethnic name is spelled *Ḫry* in Ugaritic (UM 2: 21). Moreover, *Pbl* is located by the *Krt* poem not in North Syria, but somewhere south of Tyre and Sidon, and the most probable identification of his country *Udm* is with Edom, *Udumu* in Assyrian spelling.

[4] DXVII, 11 s.

[5] CCLXXVIII, 102.

stated that nothing was known of the god Pabilsag besides his name. We have seen that he is known well enough for us to have quite a distinct notion of him. Besides what was said above, it may be added that in the monotheistic Babylonian list of gods, in which all of them are declared merely various names of the unique deity Marduk, Pabilsag is included in "the ogdoad of the great gods." [1] In another interesting list, also with a monotheistic tendency, in which all gods are considered parts of the body of Ninurta, Pabilsag is this god's "tongue." [2] According to LANGDON, the Babylonians called Sagittarius *ûmû daprûti* "destructive spirits", in plur. majestatis.[3] It is known in what redoubtable colors scorpion-men are described in *Gilgameš* IX: ii: 7: "whose terror is awesome and whose glance is death". [4] We are again in the presence of the dual attitude towards chthonic gods: they are both destructive and beneficent.

As distinct from the other personal names in the Ugaritic epic which may or may not be accompanied by epithets and qualifications, *Pbl* is never met without being followed by *mlk*. VIROLLEAUD considered therefore, that *mlk* "king" substituted for *sag* "head" of the Sumerian original, and regarded *Pbl-mlk* as "a hybrid name, unique at Ras Shamra." [5] The Ugaritic texts revealed since then another similar Sumero-Semitic hybrid name: *Ppšr* for *Papsukkal* (see above, p. 190 s., note 4 and p. 231). However, since the Babylonians also wrote, in shorter form, ᵈ*Pa-bil*,[6] *mlk* may also be considered a title or qualification, placed after the name, as happens in Ugaritic texts (cf. p. 295). Since *Pbl* turns out to be a Sumerian god with an image projected into the starry sky, this harmonizes perfectly with the name of his daughter, *Mšt-Ḥry*, a "hybrid" Sumero-Semitic name signifying "fiery serpent" (probably to be read *Mušt-Ḥarayyā) and astrologically referring to the constellation of Hydra. Her being "fiery" is not only immanently connected with the essence of "serpent" (Heb. *śārâph* includes both notions—of "fire" and of "serpent"), but also agrees with the element *bil* "fire" in the name of *Pa-bil-sag*.[7]

[1] CLIV, 329 s.
[2] *Ibid.*, 331.
[3] CCCXVI, 282.
[4] Translat. CDLXXI, 88.
[5] DXVII, 12.
[6] CXI, No. 2944; CCXXVI, No. 357.
[7] The meaning of the name is probably "the wand with a fiery head." PA = *ḫaṭṭu* "wand, staff. scepter," cf. the variant *Pa-giš-bil-sag*, CXI, No. 2948; PA is also = ᵈḪENDUR = ᵈ*Išum* "fire."

It may seem strange that a Sumerian astral god appears in a Ugaritic poem without any divine attributes, simply as a king of the earthly land of *Udm*. But exactly the same phenomenon of very early euhemerization is found in the Sumerian texts, too. In the list of the antediluvian kings of the chronological prism W-B 444, the very first of them, *Á-lu-lim*, king of Eridu, bears the name of the god ᵈ*En-lulim*, i.e., of the divine deer-herd Ninurta (Gudea, Cyl. B: 10: 7)[1] and of the star ᵐᵘˡ*lu-lim*, identified with Enmešarra, a chthonic deity.[2] The fifth antediluvian king is the god ᵈ*Dumuzi*, the sixth, *En-síb-zi-an-na* "faithful herdsman of heaven," an epithet of the god Dumuzi and the name of the constellation of Orion.[3] In the first postdiluvian dynasty, that of Kiš, we find a king *Zuqaqip* "Scorpion," Etana "a shepherd, he who ascended to heaven"; in the next one, that of Uruk, we find the god ᵈ*Lugalbanda*, the god ᵈ*Dumuzi*, the god (originally) ᵈ*Gilgameš*. One should not take in all good faith this euhemerization, returning thus to the methodology of Philo Herrenius and Diodorus Siculus in expounding and interpreting myths.[4]

The name *Cheirôn* is believed to be a hypocoristicon from some name composed with *cheir* "hand" and having the meaning "surgeon."[5] This is, of course, the only possible Greek etymology for *Cheirôn*. It is, however, strongly contradicted by the persistent spelling of this name as *Chirôn* on Attic vases, though "hand," *cheir*, may assume the form *cher-* in some dialectal variants, but never **chir*. The Athenians would not have spelled Cheiron's name in this way if they had any feeling of its connections with "hand," "hand-work." Besides, such a name for a healer-god seems to be a good deal too rationalistic for an ancient mythical image. Since the figure of Cheiron comes from the East, it would be rather advisable to search there for its etymology. We eliminate the derivation from *ḥārar* "to flame," *ḥārôn* "burning," which would harmonize with *bil* "fire" in the name of Cheiron's prototype Pabilsag and with his identification with ᵈ*Išum*, the firegod,[6]

[1] CCCXIV, 8, n. 1; CDXXVI, II, 394. [2] V R: 46a: 31, CCCXIV, *loc. cit.*

[3] *En* is only the title of the supreme priest, added to the proper name, cf. names of supreme priests under the IIId dynasty of Ur: *En-nir-gal-an-na*, *En-nir-zid-an-na*, etc., CCCIX, 59.

[4] This view of the personality of Dumuzi is now presented as the last word of scholarship by KRAMER, CCXCIV, 10 s.

[5] CDXI, III, 2, 2302.

[6] PA = ᵈḪENDUR = ᵈ*Išum*, CCCVII, No. 295; ᵈ*Pa-sag-ga* = ᵈ*Išum na-gir su-qi ša-qu-um-mi* "ᵈIšum praefectus viarum desertarum," CXI, No. 2954.

but which is contradicted by the nature of its first radical, doomed to disappear in Greek transcription. We do not pretend, either, that the name of Cheiron reflects Pabilsag's being "the vicegerent of the Nether World," through Heb. *ḫôr* "cave," Ugar. *ḫr* same sense, with implication of Hades,[1] Akk. *ḫirîtu* "cemetery." We would rather equate *Cheirôn* with the Ugaritic personal name *Ḫyrn* (UM 323: III: 11; IV: 11) which VIROLLEAUD [2] compared to m*Ḫa-i-ra-an-nu* from Nuzu; [3] this name is, of course, not a Hurrian but a Semitic one (the Ugaritic *Ḫyrn* was the father of *Mnḥm* and *Iḫyn*, in which *iḫ* = *aḫ* "brother"). For its etymology, we envisage two possibilities, both of which perfectly agree with the nature of Pabilsag-Cheiron:

1. Either it derives from the root *ḫyr* "to choose" (Arab. *ḫāra*, Akk. *ḫâru*), whence Akk. *ḫâwiru* or *ḫâ'iru* "husband," fem. *ḫirtu* "(first or principal) wife." Pabilsag was the husband of the goddess Ninkarrak (Nin-isinna); their hierogamy was a popular feast at Isin.[4] Pabilsag was a scorpion-man, and scorpions, because of their conspicuous love-games, were considered as the symbol of mating and copulation; the scorpion-goddess Išḫara was the patronness of the consummation of marriage, the guardian of the sacred room of the *hieros gamos*.[5] VON SODEN considers that a god d*Ḫâwiru*/d*Ḫâ'iru*, the "husband-god" par excellence, spouse of the grain-goddess Nisaba, had a statue in the neo-Assyrian temple of Adad.[6] It may be relevant to note that in the curious *hieros gamos* story of Judah and Tamar (Gen. 38), Judah's friend *Ḫira'* very prominently plays the rôle of matchmaker; that Peleus seized hold of the goddess Thetis following the advice of Cheiron; and that their magnificent wedding, in which all the gods participated, was celebrated outside Cheiron's cave.[7] These fragmentary vestiges, put together, may pro-

[1] Cf. UM 5: 1 *kt'rb 'štrt ḫr* "when Astarte enters the cave" (an allusion to Istar's descent to the Nether World); *ḫr* as the place where *Krt* will be after his death, II K: V (= UM 128): 22.

[2] DXXIII, index of pers. n.

[3] Now included in CXCI, 50, and explained *ibid.* 304: "bridegroom."

[4] CCCLVIII, II, 101.

[5] DII, 1, 8, 14-17.

[6] *Ap.* LXXV, 135. The text referred to is KAV No. 42: II: 8-11 (autography in CDLVIII); the god's name is actually spelled d*Ḫa-bi-ru*, and was plausibly believed to derive from the population group of the Ḫabiru. One may agree or not with the interpretation of VON SODEN, but it points, in any case, to the possibility of d*Ḫâ'iru* as a divine name.

[7] Cf. the sources *ap.* CCXXVII, I, 271.

vide a clue to understanding Pabilsag-Cheiron as the patron of marriage, a male counterpart of Išḫara.

2. Or it derives from a word cognate to the Arab. *ḫair* "good, excellent, etc.; good thing, blessing; wealth, property; liberal, open-handed etc.; beneficent, benevolent; benign, gracious, kind": an excellent name for a god of health, fertility, abundance, and help to humans. In the forms *Ḫyr, Ḫyr', Ḫyrw, Ḫyrn,* it appears as personal names in ancient Aramaic inscriptions from Sinai and Palmyra.[1]

Asclepios: Myth and Symbolism

Towards the end of our survey of healer-heroes, we come to the one who enjoyed the greatest reverence as a healer and physician god. The main center of his worship in European Greece was Epidauros on the eastern coast of Argolis, and in Asiatic Greece this rôle was played by the island of Cos (which we have discussed above, p. 245 ss.), but Thessalians, Messenians, Arcadians and others also had claims that he was their fellow-countryman.[2] The question of what Asclepios was originally: a god, or a hero who was later deified,[3] is hardly important; there was a permanent fluctuation between the two categories both in Greece and the Ancient Near East. However, in this particular case, it seems almost certain that Asclepios started his career in Greece as a god, but, as many pre-Hellenic or non-Hellenic deities, he was for a certain time driven back by more powerful pan-Hellenic gods, especially by Apollo, but only to take his revenge later. The often-quoted fact that his sons, Machaon and Podaleirios, are treated in the *Iliad* as simple warrior-princes of the heroic age, having only medical knowledge in addition, is not proof of the opposite. The sons of goddesses, Achilles and Aeneas, as well as the son of Zeus himself, Sarpedon, are also described in exactly the same way, i.e., as completely human beings. In general, though Homer is the oldest written source in Greek literature, he advanced quite far toward scepticism and rationalism in his relatively secular treatment of the myths.

Asclepios' emblem was the immemorial Sumerian symbol of a

[1] CCCXXXVI, 273 s.

[2] The ancient evidence on Asclepios is comprehensively collected and commented on in the two-volume work CLVI.

[3] Discussed in detail in CLVI.

serpent, wound around a staff, an attribute of chthonic healer-gods. This very emblem—a bronze serpent on a staff—was worshipped in the temple of Jerusalem until about 700; its creation was ascribed to the great thaumaturge and healer, the ophic hero Moses, and it had healing properties (II Kings 18: 4; Num. 21: 8). Thus the way, by which the old Sumerian emblem penetrated into Greece, is clear here too. At the same time, the cult of the bronze serpent in Judaea long before the beginning of Hellenic influence upon Syria shows, that the serpent around a staff as the symbol of the healer-god Ešmun on Phoenician coins, and the serpent, coiled around the spear of Šed-râphe' at Palmyra, are not borrowings from Greece, but an indigenous Syro-Phoenician motif.

In sculpture of the classical epoch, Asclepios was represented with ancient and clear attributes. The statue of Asclepios in Sicyon, by Calamis, showed the god holding a scepter in one hand and a pine-cone in the other (Paus. II: 30: 3). The pine-cone was an emblem of Dionysos (one of whose epithets was *iatros* "physician"), and in the Egypto-Phoenician Tale of the two brothers Bata placed his heart among the cones of a pine (some translate "cedar") as a guarantee of his life's security. The Sicyonians had a tradition that Asclepios had come to their city from Epidauros, in the shape of a serpent (Paus., *loc. cit.*). In his shrine at Epidauros, tame serpents were kept (Paus. II: 28: 1). His statue at Epidauros represented him sitting on a throne, with a staff in one hand, and the other reposing on the head of a serpent, and a dog lying beneath the throne (Paus. II: 27: 2). The authors of the monograph on Asclepios asked themselves why the dog was associated with this god, and answered: he inherited it from the Epidaurean hero Maleatas,[1] who "was a hunter and was fond of dogs. His sanctuary was situated on the hill *Kynortion* and itself was called Kyon . . .[2] It is also possible that . . . the dog was regarded as the animal which had nursed the babe Asclepios after he was exposed by his mother." [3] The explanation must rather be sought in the ancient Near Eastern cult of healing deities. The goddess Gula, "the great physician," "she who by the touch of her pure hand revives the dead" (as

[1] However, it is by no means probable that (Apollo) Maleatas preceded Asclepios in the cult of Epidauros. His name, conversely, shows that he was originally worshipped on cape Malea, the southmost point of Laconia.

[2] Kynortas, too, was a Laconian pre-Dorian hero.

[3] CLVI, I, 227.

Asclepos did!), had the dog for her emblem.[1] Clay figurines of magic dogs with inscribed names as "he who bites his adversaries" or "catcher of enemies" were popular Babylonian talismans against diseases.[2]

Several ancient relics were preserved in the myths on his birth. All myths make Apollo his father, and most make Coronis, daughter of Phlegyas, his mother. According to one myth (Paus. II: 26: 6) [3]

> Coronis, they say, when with child with Asclepios, had intercourse with Ischys son of Elatos. She was killed by Artemis to punish her for the insult done to Apollo, but when the pyre was already lighted Hermes is said to have snatched the child from the flames.

This reminds us of the birth-story of Dionysos. According to the Epidaurian version (Paus. II: 26: 3-5), Coronis

> all along had kept hidden from her father that she was with child by Apollo. In the country of the Epidaurians she bore a son, and exposed him on the mountain called Nipple (*Titthion*) at the present day, but then named Myrtium (*Myrtion*). As the child lay exposed he was given milk by one of the goats that pastured about the mountain, and was guarded by the watchdog of the herd. And . . . Aresthanas (for this was the herdsman's name) . . . on finding the child desired to take him up. As he drew near, he saw lightning that flashed from the child, and, thinking that it was something divine, as in fact it was, he turned away. Presently it was reported over every land and sea that Asclepios was discovering everything he wished to heal the sick, and that he was raising dead men to life.

Exposure of a miraculous child by his mother is an old Oriental motif. It had already been well-known, when the Babylonians transferred it to King Sargon I of Agade.[4] Here also belongs the legend of Cyrus which Herodotos (I: 110, 122) apparently wrote down after the tales of the Persians (to judge by the usage of the genuine Iranian word *Spakô* "bitch"). Still nearer to the legend of Sargon is that of Moses (Ex. 2). For being nursed by a goat, cf. the Sumerian god Ningirsu: "eius mater est capra sacra, quae nutrit capras *lulimu*."[5] In Arcadia, on the shore of the river Ladon,[6] the temple of the Child Asclepios was situated, and nearby was the grave of

[1] CCCLVIII, II, 31. She is depicted on kudurrus (border-stones) of Cassite epoch exactly as Asclepios in Epidauros: sitting on a throne, with her dog at her feet, cf. CDLV, pl. 18 (kudurru of Nazimaruttaš).

[2] Cf. photographs LXVII, 90, fig. 72; 91, fig. 73, and the description of their use *ibid.*, 104.

[3] Transl. by W. H. S. Jones (Loeb Class. Libr.).

[4] Transl. CDLXXI, 119.

[5] CXI, 201: 2.

[6] On the ophic meaning of the name Ladon, see pp. 213 s. above.

Trygon, his nurse (Paus. VIII: 25: 11). *Trygôn*—a detail not noted by commentators—is Greek for "turtle-dove": nursing of an exposed babe by doves transfers us to Ascalon, where such a legend was told about Semiramis (Diod. Sic. II: 4, 5). In the Hurrian myth of the Sun-god's son born by a cow and saved by the god (p. 85 above), the babe was exposed and fed by two kinds of birds (their names cannot be identified), until it was found by a fisherman.[1] Adonis, born of Myrrha after her transformation into a myrrh-tree, was found by Aphrodite who put him into a chest and entrusted him to Persephone (cf. the chests of Sargon I and Moses).

In connection with the latter myth, we would wish to point to a possible onomastic correspondence between the birth-story of Adonis and that of Asclepios. The mountains above the precinct of Asclepios at Epidauros were called Titthion (Nipple) and Cynortion (Paus. II: 27: 7); the former, on which Asclepios was said to be exposed after his birth, had a more ancient name, Myrtion. Each of them has its own etymology—one derives from the myrtle, the other, it is believed, is related to *kyon, kynos* "dog"—but when such names as *Myrtion* and *Kynortion* are found together, they evoke a vivid association with *Myrrha* and *Kinyras,* the parents of Adonis, whose names are purely Semitic ("myrrh" and deified "lyre"). Besides, the pers. n. *Kynortas* figures in the mythical genealogy of the pre-Dorian kings of Laconia in a very significant surrounding: he was the grandson of *Amyklos* (= Canaanite god *Ršp Mkl,* see below, p. 311) and the father of *Oibalos* (= the sacred mountain *ʿÊbāl* near Shechem). *Kynortas* may be understood as W-S *kinnor* "lyre" + Dorian suffix *-tas* (Attic and Ionian *-tês*), designating origin, occupation, etc., e.g. *auletês* "flutist."[2] If this is really so, it is all the more significant since nothing is known about any cult of Adonis at Epidauros, and, consequently, these W-S names belonged, since very ancient times, to the cult of Asclepios. And since the Greeks, as a rule, identified Asclepios with the Phoenician healer-god Ešmun, the Adoniac names in Asclepios' holy precinct indirectly confirm the original relationship between, or identity of, the Phoenician Adonis and Ešmun.

Asclepios' bringing dead men to life evoked upon him the wrath of the gods. Following a complaint by Hades that Asclepios was

[1] On Coronis as a possible "cow," see p. 309 below.

[2] The interchange *i/y* in Greek renderings of foreign words and names is rather common, cf. p. 190, n. 2 above.

robbing his realm of its inhabitants, Zeus killed Asclepios with his thunderbolt. He was resurrected, however, and became a god. This is a standard end of healers in Greek mythology; we have already seen several instances of it, each time with a different justification.

This is, properly speaking, the entire story of Asclepios as it is usually rendered by the mythographers. Actually, however, the myth of Asclepios is far from being limited to this. Several variants are preserved which are not usually considered as being related to Asclepios, but comparative analysis reveals their close connection with him, enriches our knowledge of his nature and origin, and helps gain an understanding of his strange name. The myths of his father, mother, and grandfather are also significant.

Coronis and Phlegyas, Ares and Apollo

The name of Asclepios' mother, *Korônis,* is usually derived from the Greek *korônê* "crow." [1] After what we have written in this chapter on birds as personifications of chthonic spirits and gods of healing, this etymology should not seem inappropriate, though the crow is not found among the typical birds connected with magic, portents, and medicine. The name of Coronis' father, Phlegyas, accords better with the general pattern of bird-symbolism: *phlegyas* was a Greek word for "eagle," already used in the Hesiodic *Scutum Herc.* 134.[2] Thus Asclepios, like the heroes of his island Cos, descended from a family of predatory birds.

On the other hand, *korônis,* exactly identical with the name of Asclepios' mother, was an epithet of ships in Homer, which some ancient linguists interpreted as "black" (crow-colored), while others pretended it meant "in which the summits are inflexed" or "in which the stern is concavely curved," and the adjective *korônios,* according to Hesychios, signified "a cow with concave and crescent-shaped horns." [3] Putting aside the question whether this word may have derived from Semitic *qarn* "horn," it must be said that it has the same semantic as W-S *'Aštart Qarnayim,* the "two-horned Astarte" Gen. 14: 5. If so, the birth of the healer-god

[1] "Coronis may signify a crow, the symbol of longevity, cf. Preller-Robert, *Mythology,* I, p. 515, n. 3," CLVI, I, 34, n. 44.

[2] Suidas: *phlegyas*: *ho aëtos*; Hesych.: *phlegyas*: *aëtos xanthos, oxys.* Hesiod *Scut. Her.* 134 speaks of feathers of a dark (or brown) eagle: *morphnoio phlegyao.* Cf. CDLXXX, IX, 934.

[3] Cf. the evidence *ap.* CDLXXX, V, 1859.

by the "curved-horned" Coronis would coincide exactly with the Ugaritic myth, expounded many times above, of the cow-goddess giving birth to *Rpu-B'l* "lord-healer," also named Muš "serpent." The Epidaurian Isyllos pretended that the real name of Coronis was *Aigla*; [1] if this name goes back to a genuine tradition, *Aigla* could have been a misinterpreted (as "shining") W-S *'glt* (Heb. *'eglā*) "heifer," one of the designations of the cow-goddess in Ugaritic mythology: it would then be a parallel to *Korônis* "the curved- horned." [2]

Besides the meaning "eagle," the name of Coronis' father Phlegyas can also be derived from the root *phlegô* "to burn, to flame." It would then be semantically equivalent to the name of the Canaanite god Rešeph (Heb. *rešeph* "flame, lightning, inflammation, fever"), who corresponded to the Sumero-Akkadian god of pestilence, the underworld, and war, Nergal.[3] This is still more underlined by Phlegyas' mythical paternity which makes him a son of Ares—a god who is also very similar to Rešeph and Nergal according to his original nature (cf. p. 159). Phlegyas was said to have been the king of Orchomenos in Boeotia: now in the Catalogue of the Ships, *Iliad* II: 512, the chiefs of the Orchomenians in the Trojan War are named Ascalaphos and Ialmenos, sons of Ares and Astyoche, daughter of Actor. Strangely enough, Hellenists have not paid any visible attention to the coincidence of the names *Askalaphos* and *Asklêpios*; [4] they are, however, too close to each other to consider the rôle of Ares in the respective genealogies of their bearers as a fortuity. We shall later see what light Ascalaphos sheds on the mythology of Asclepios. Meanwhile we are in the presence of a characteristic doublet: one variant makes Asclepios the son of Apollo, the other—of Ares. Actually, the two variants are reduced to one: there is no essential difference, but only onomastic hesitation

[1] *Inscr. Graecae* IV², 1, No. 128: IV: 48-50, quoted CLVI, II, 19 s., testimony No. 18 (same inscription *ibid.*, 24, testimony No. 32).

[2] Cf. the glosses by Hesychios: *Aiglaêr*: *ho Asklêpios*; *Aglaopês*: *ho Asklêpios*: *Lakônes*; CCXXXVI, 702. Cf. in the neighboring Troizen the mythical hero *Althêpos* ("healer"), son of *Leïs* ("cow"), grandson of *Ôros* ("falcon"), see p. 91, n. 4 above.

[3] On Rešeph, cf. CXV, 747 s.; VII, 79; CDLXIV; XCI. On the identification of Rešeph with Nergal at Ugarit, cf. the correspondence of *Ršp* in the list of gods UM 17: 5 to Nergal in its Akkadian translation RŠ 20.24 (CCCLXXXIXa, p. 82).

[4] This was noticed CDLX, 131, with the remark "perhaps" and without elaboration.

in translating the original *Rešeph* into Greek through identifying him with a similar Hellenic deity. Rešeph was notoriously identified by the Greeks with their Apollo,[1] an especially salient instance thereof being a Cypriot billingual in Greek (Cypriot syllabic) and Phoenician,[2] in which *Ršp Mkl* corresponds to Greek *Apoloni Amukoloi* (Apollo Amyclos).

Amyklai was the oldest capital of Laconia and remained till the end of antiquity its main sacral place, the cultic center of Apollo Amyclos. When the Cypriot bilingual became known, it was believed (through lack of more data and the false conviction that Phoenicians came to Cyprus later than the Greeks) that *Mkl* as epithet of Rešeph (equated with Apollo) was simply a transcription of the Greek *Amyklos*, whose cult had been brought to Cyprus from Greece.[3] However, this very same god *Mkl* was later discovered in the Beth-Shean inscription of Seti I (end of the XIVth century) as the principal god of this Canaanite city. It then became clear that (as formulated by ALBRIGHT) "the cult of this Canaanite divinity wandered westward to Greece in the later part of the Bronze Age," and that it was not *Mkl* that derived from *Amyklos*, but, on the contrary, *Amyklos* derived from *Mkl* with a prothetic *a*, and the city of *Amyklai* got its name from the god *Amyklos* just like *Athênai* from the goddess Athena.[4]

The etymology of the name *Mkl*, if it be considered as W-S, is obscure; several W-S roots are possible, but all of them are not very convincing. ALBRIGHT's derivation of *Mkl* from a Sumerian (Emesal dialect) title of Nergal: *Umun-urugalla(k)* "Lord of the Great City" (i.e. Hades) [5] is very attractive from the point of view of both gods' essences, but it requires us to postulate the elision of too many vowels and especially consonants. However, *Mkl* looks very similar to two other indubitable Sumerianisms in W-S languages: *Nkl* (*Nikkal*) < *Nin-gal*, name of the Moon-goddess, and *hkl* (*hêkāl*) < *é-gal* "palace". We suggest a much simpler Sumerian derivation for the divine name *Mkl* which, judging by the vocaliza-

[1] VII, 79. Cf. CXV, 747 s. that the Palestinian Apollonia preserves its old name, derived from *Rešeph*, in her modern Arabic name *Arsuf*.

[2] CIS, I, No. 89 (CX, 104 ss.).

[3] CCCLXIII, II, 1, 253, n. 2.

[4] XXI, 33; VII, 79.

[5] XXI, 33 s.; he explains that the name was presumably read *Umunerigalla*, *eri* being Emesal for *uru*; Akk. *Irkalla* "Hades" goes back to Emesal *erigalla*; the name Nergal, written NE.ERI.GAL, means approximately "Mighty One of the Underworld."

tion of its Greek counterpart, was most probably pronounced *Mukol* (according to ALBRIGHT) or rather *Mûkāl* (cf. *hêkāl*). *Mu* is Emesal for the standard Sumerian *giš* "tree, wood"; [1] so, for instance, standard Sumerian *dNin-giš-zi(d)-da* becomes in Emesal *dUmun-mu-zi(d)-da*.[2] This name also appears without the title *nin* "lord/lady," simply *dGiš-zi-da*, *dGiz-zi-da*,[3] and apparently signifies "straight tree" or "straight wooden pole." [4] Deification of trees and/or wooden pillars was immensely popular in the ancient Near East, and no less than 61 Sumerian divine names begin by *dGiš*, with 5 more having *giš* contained within them.[5] The name of Gilgameš, the judge of the Nether World, was originally spelled *dGiš-gín-maš* (*Gišgimmaš*) and simply *dGiš*. Moreover, there was a god—an infernal one, as shown by his name—called *dGiš-gál-e-nu-gi-e*,[6] and another one, whose name was phonetically spelled *dGiš-ka-la*,[7] which goes back to Sum. *giš-gal* "great tree" or *giš-gál* "standing pole." In Emesal, this would give *mu-gál*, and we actually find a divine name *dMu-gal-la*,[8] which would regularly become *Mûkāl* in Semitic.[9]

When we turn now to Amyclae, we find that the statue of the local Apollo Amyclos—as represented on Laconian coins—actually has the remarkable and significant shape of a pillar turned with its narrower end downward (as was normal for Minoan and Mycenaean columns, originally made of tree-trunks), and provided with a

[1] Cf., e.g., CCCVII, No. 61.

[2] CXI, No. 2481: 8.

[3] So in the Adapa myth (CDLXXI, 101), and in the Sumerian lamentation over Dumuzi, CCCXVII, 300 s., line 6.

[4] Cf. p. 229, n. 4 above.

[5] CXII, IV, 1, No. 561.

[6] *Ibid.*, No. 561: 19. GÁL = *ga-al* = *ka-a-nu* "to be firm; to stand; to be stable" (*ibid.*, No. 80: 7); thus *giš-gál* = *giš-zid* "upright tree/pole," and the combined ideogram GIŠGAL = *manzâzu* "standing, place of standing," then "position, post" (CCCVII, No. 49*). DEIMEL did not explain the expression *e-nu-gi-e*, nor list it under the sign *e* (No. 308) in the general part of his *Šumer. Lex.*; we presume, however, that the initial *e* = KUR "mountain, land" (CXII, II, 2, No. 308: 10), and the closing *e* is the Sumerian case ending; *gi* probably stands for gi_4 = *târu* "return"; thus *e-nu-gi-e* = *kur-nu-*gi_4*-a* = *erṣet lâ târi* "the land without return," a common designation of the Nether World.

[7] d giš-ka-la [. . .], CXII, IV, 1, No. 561: 6. The ideogram whereof this was the phonetic complement, is erased; it might have been GIŠGAL, see preceding note.

[8] *Ibid.*, No. 102: 6; CXI, No. 2162.

[9] The frequent Babylonian name *Mu-kal-la*, *Mu-kal-li*, *Mu-kal-lim* (CIA, 108) may well be related.

helmeted human head and two arms holding a bow and a spear.[1] This iconography is a striking confirmation of the deduction chain presented above, and, consequently, of a continuous uninterrupted chain of cultural connections between regions as distant as Sumer in the East and the Peloponnese in the West, with North Mesopotamia, Syria, Phoenicia, Cilicia, Cyprus, and Crete as intermediary links.

Apollo, according to archaic notions, was first of all the god of pestilence (*Iliad* I: 43-52), and he remained so even at the time of the Peloponnesian war (Thuc. II: 54). In the same time, he also was a healing god; this duality, which we have already disclosed in the images of several Oriental deities and in the symbols of the serpent and scorpion, is well formulated by ALBRIGHT: "The god who brought death through disease was also best fitted to heal the ills which he had inflicted." [2] Apollo was a relative late-comer in Greece; his name does not yet appear in Mycenaean texts; he is believed to have come from Asia Minor.[3] He was superimposed over a number of earlier divinities of a similar nature. Thus, *Paian* (also *Paiôn* and *Paiêôn*), the ancient healer-god already worshipped in the Mycenaean age (*Pa-ia-wo*, i.e., *Paia[w]ôn*, in Linear B texts [4]), and still an independent god in *Iliad* V: 401, 899-904, became an early epithet of Apollo (e.g. *Hom. Hymn to Apol. Pyth.* 272; Soph. *Oed. Tyr.* 154).[5] In the Peloponnese, he annexed the names of the Semitic gods *Karneios* (above, p. 142) and *Rešeph Mûkāl,* just discussed. In the same way he annexed—indirectly, as his son—the healer-god Asclepios. But Rešeph was also identified with another Greek god of fire, war, pestilence, and death—Ares, already known

[1] CLXII, IV, 309. Now it is very curious that Beth-Shean, the city of the god Mukal, called itself *Nysa* in the Hellenistic period and had *a bronze pillar* as one of its principal sacral landmarks (see evidence *ap.* XLIIa, 126). Can it be only a coincidence that 1) the name *Mûkāl* means "standing pole," 2) his Laconian avatar Apollo Amyclos was represented as a standing pillar, 3) Dionysos was represented in the same way, 4) *nysos* in his name probably stands for *nussu* "pole" (cf. n. 308 to chapt. II), 5) Beth-Shean (Scythopolis) called itself *Nysa* and pretended to have been founded by Dionysos, 6) it possessed a sacral bronze pole?

[2] VII, 80.

[3] Cf. CCCI, 250; CCCLXXX, I, 558-564 (largely on the basis of HROZNÝ's H-H readings, completely refuted since then by LAROCHE, CCCXIX, 113 and n. 59).

[4] DV, 127; XCIX, 124; CCCXLVIII, 290 s.

[5] But also of Asclepios, Dionysos, and even of Thanatos (Death), Euripides *Hippolyt.* 1373.

in the Mycenaean epoch [1] and later drawn still nearer to Nergal by the consecration of the planet Mars to him.[2] Thence the double genealogy of Asclepios: he is the son of Apollo, but the grandson of Phlegyas (another avatar of Rešeph), the great-grandson of Ares; or, in Phlegyas' city of Orchomenos, he is, under the name of Ascalaphos, the direct son of Ares.

The Myths of Ascalaphos

Nothing noteworthy is told about the Orchomenian king Ascalaphos who figures in the Catalogue of the Ships with his brother Ialmenos,[3] except that he was also included into the list of the Argonauts (quite anachronistically, from the point of view of the count of mythical generations). However, besides this pale and completely euhemerized avatar of the god, a very colorful myth is preserved on another Ascalaphos—who is, as might be expected, one of the deities of the Nether World (Apollod. I: 5: 3). This Ascalaphos was the son of Acheron, the god of the river of Hades, and his mother is called either *Gorgyrê* (a common noun signifying "underground," "subterranean prison") or *Orphnê* ("darkness")—thus, his infernal origin is put in sharp relief. He spied upon and denounced Persephone (who had been carried away by Hades into the Nether World). He said she had consumed a pomegranate seed and thus doomed herself to stay there forever. The angry Demeter, Persephone's mother, threw him into a hole and placed a heavy rock over him. When Heracles rolled it away, he found Ascalaphos turned into a short-eared owl which the Greeks called *askalaphos*.

The notion of the Nether World's river—as almost all the Greek notions of the world beyond the grave—was borrowed from the Babylonians through the West Semites. The Sumerians and Akkadians called the river of their Hades *Ḫubur*, and the Greek name *Acherôn*, as was pointed out long ago, derives from the W-S *'aḫărôn* "western,"[4] since Hades was thought to be in the Far West (cf. one of the Greek names of the Nether World, *erebos* =

[1] XCIX, 124.

[2] The identification of Rešeph with the planet Mars is indirectly proven by the astrological tablet from Ugarit UM 143, cf. DXXII, 25 ss.

[3] *Ialmenos* has a Semitic touch. Was this name perhaps connected with the root *hālam* "to smite" or with the precious stone *yahălôm* Ex. 28: 18, translated by LXX: *adamas* "diamond"?

[4] CCCXXX, 229. Cf. CDXCIV, where the belief in an infernal river is traced in the Hebrew and Phoenician religions.

Akk. *erêbu* "sunset"). Let us now return to the Sumerian myth of Ninlil's descent to the Nether World, already expounded, in another connection, p. 89. In order to obtain acceptance into Hell, she was obliged to surrender herself, in turn, to the gatekeeper of the underworld, to the god of the subterranean river, and to the ferryman over that river.[1] The gatekeeper impregnated her with Meslamtaea (Nergal), the subterranean river-god—with Ninazu, the "Lord Physician," the most typical of the chthonic healer-gods (see above, p. 229); the name of her third son, begotten by the ferryman, is erased. Ascalaphos, the son of the Hades-river Acheron, thus fully corresponds to Ninazu, the prototype of many W-S healer-gods, from whom, in turn several analogous Greek personages derived. This striking correspondence finally establishes beyond any doubt the identity Asclepios = Ascalaphos = Ninazu.

The image of the owl as a chthonic healer-god has already been elucidated, deciphered, and illustrated with examples above. Ascalaphos the Owl is the most significant of these examples. The owl apparently does not figure in the cult of Asclepios himself, and so its occurrence in this parallel mythological offshoot is all the more interesting; but the island of Asclepios, Cos, and some of its heroes got their names from the owl. However, Ascalaphos was identified not only with this nocturnal bird; another, less significant, variant of his transformation by the angry Demeter exists. The action again takes place at Eleusis, and he appears under a slightly modified name *Askalabos*. His mother Misme [2] gave water (or barley-water) to Demeter, and when he mocked the greediness with which the thirsty goddess drank, she splashed the rest of her drink on him, changing him into a lizard.[3] His change into a lizard instead of the expected serpent may be explained thus: the species of serpents used by the Greeks for worship as symbols or personifications of Zeus Meilichios, Asclepios, dead heroes, and other chthonic personages, was *Coelopeltis lacertina*, a large serpent up to 6 feet long, poisonous, but not dangerous for people because of the rear location of its

[1] It is supposed that it was really Enlil who, in turn, assumed the aspect of the three infernal personages, but this might have been a modification in order to attribute the chthonic gods to Enlil's progeniture.

[2] Misme seems to be an ancient chthonic goddess (cf. the god *Mismos* on a gnostic gem), probably identical with *Misê*, who was connected with Cora, often conceived as an androgynous deity, worshipped at Eleusis, Phrygia, Cyprus, etc. CDXI, XV, 2, 2040 s., 2050.

[3] CDXXXIII, *s.v. Askalabos*. CDLXXX, II, 2173 s.

poison fangs; it is distinguished from all other serpents by its lizardlike head.[1] However, *askalabos* was also taken for a real serpent.[2] Thus the image of Asclepios' double, Ascalaphos-Ascalabos, impersonates both the serpent and the owl—the symbolic animals, which occur together in the emblems of Athena.

The Name of Asclepios

The name of Asclepios absolutely does not surrender to even the remotest Greek etymology.[3] The ancients were not able to give it any acceptable explanation. They understood the second part of it as *êpios* "the mild," but the first part was unintelligible. The ancient authors were forced to invent an Epidaurian tyrant Ascles whom Asclepios allegedly cured of an eye-disease, and from whom he derived his name, or, to compose wholly senseless etymologies, as from *a* "not" and *skelê* "leg," i.e. "something dry," so that *Asklêpios* = "non-dry" = "humid," and so on.[4]

In the years when Semitic etymologies for non-Hellenic Grecian names were fairly popular, some were also tried for Asclepios. Of them, the one by Martin Schultze may be quoted: *ʾEškôl-ʾâb* "Father Grape-Cluster," the deified grape-cluster, cf. pers. n. of a legendary ruler of Hebron *ʾEškôl* Gen. 14: 13.[5] We have here a very close phonetic correspondence;[6] and if the grape-cluster be considered as a symbol for Dionysos, it should be remembered that the name of the Phoenician healer-god Šed-râpheʾ was translated into Latin by *Liber Pater* (Italian counterpart of Dionysos) in a North African

[1] ccxlvii, 327 s., on the basis of the conclusion "by an eminent authority on snakes, Dr. Hans Gadow" who has studied the monuments.

[2] cdxxxiii, *s.v. Asklepios.*—For the phenomenon of an *owl* and a *lizard* being called by the same name (*askalaphos/askalabos*), cf. the same semantic dualism in Hebrew and Aramaic: Heb. *tinšemet* designates in Lev. 11: 18 an *owl* (cclxxxix, 1035: "white owl, *Tyto alba*"), and in Lev. 11: 30, a *lizard* (*loc. cit.*: "chameleon"); Targum Onkelos translated it in both cases by *bâʾwât* (from *byt* "to spend a night"), cclxxiv, I, 135.

[3] "The name is thoroughly obscure," cdxxxiii, *s.v. Asklepios.* Its dialectal forms: *Aschlapios, Aischlapios, Aischlabios* etc. (ccxxxvi, 146, n. 17) do not make its etymology any easier.

[4] Cf. clvi, I, 80 s.; II, testimonies Nos. 267-273.

[5] cdlx, 131.

[6] This cannot be said of Schultze's alternative etymology, *loc. cit.*, "*ʾEškôl-râphâʾ* ʾEškol the Giant' which became *-rôpêʾ* 'healer.' " The cluster *-lr-* would rather follow a progressive assimilation *-rr-* than regressive *-ll-* (the geminated *l* never appears in any variant of the name). The same phenomenon of progressive assimilation is true for the cluster *-rl-* in the Cilician city-name *Marlos* > *Mallos*.

bilingual (above, p. 237), and that there a certain similarity exists between Asclepios and Dionysos. Unfortunately, the grape-cluster does not occur among the extremely numerous epithets and surnames of Dionysos, except for a unique case of *Dionysos Botrys* in "a half-barbaric inscription of the Roman period at Philippi." [1] It is even less so for Asclepios: not even the least hint of grapes, vines, or wine can be detected in any myth about either him or his doublets—nor in his iconography and symbolism.

Our opinion is that the clue to the name of Asclepios-Ascalaphos is provided by the transfer of this name to the owl—the symbolic bird of his sacred island, Cos. We have carefully traced (above, pp. 243 ss.) the original phenomenon of Akkadian lexicology, in which names, connected with priestly, cultic, and magic medicine, were transferred to several birds of the owl-family, which played an important rôle in magical portents. Thus, *eššepu* was the name not only of the exorcist-priest, who by his incantations expelled evil spirits from his patient's body, but of the owl *eššepu* as well. Another species of owls from the same category of magic birds, *qadû*, apparently got its name from *qadâdu appa* "to prostrate oneself"—one of the essential rites of the priestly temple-ceremonial. The name of a third owl-species of the same category, *akû*, derives from a root signifying "to be oppressed," [2] but the synonym of which, *dalâlu*, meant "to perform a ritual," with a derivative *dullu* meaning "medical treatment". The essential term for prayer-prostration before the god, obligatory for every priest, was *labânu appi* "to fall with the face down," literally "to flatten one's nose." [3] The ritual term "to fall with the face down" is a very ancient and persistent one. It goes back to Sumerian KA.SU.GAL, from KA = *appu* "nose, face" and SU.GAL = *labânu*, and survived in late Hebrew *n^ephilat ʾappayim* "(prayer-) prostration." [4]

The most common Ugaritic verb for "to fall" is the biliteral root *ql* (*qll*? cf. *UM* § 20.1683), Šaphel *šql* "to cause to fall, to throw down," by extension "to kill" (in Akkadian, too, *dâku* "to kill"

[1] CLXII, V, 296 and 289 (evidence 45[k]). To this may be added that, according to Clemens of Alexandria, *Protr. P.* 22, the Thebans called Dionysos *ampelos* (quoted *ibid.*, *loc. cit.*)—a statement which has no confirmation in Greek literary and epigraphic texts.

[2] Whence *akû*, *ekû* "orphan, pauper, beggar, cripple"—same semantic phenomenon as in Hebrew, *ʿânî* "pauper," literally "oppressed," from *ʿânâ*.

[3] *Kômer*, *k^emar* "priest" also derives from *kamâru* // *labanu*.

[4] LIX, VIII, 3721.

is often parallel to *labânu* [1]). Replacing the verb in the phrase *labânu appi* by the Ugaritic *šql*, we obtain, in 1st pers. impf., **ašql-ap* "I prostrate myself" (literally: "I cause my face to fall down"): cf. II K (= UM 127: 32, 44) *šqlt bġlt ydk* "thou hast let thy hand to fall into distress" [2]—the verb-form *šql* applied, as in our reconstruction, to a part of one's own body. As to the name being formed from the 1st pers. impf. instead of the 3d, as is usual, cf. at Ugarit the title of Baal *Aliyn*, from the root *l'y*,[3] or the *a* could have been a prothetic one. Our hypothesis is strongly corroborated by the personal name from Alalaḫ: *A-aš-qa-li-ia*,[4] being a hypocoristic of some longer name precisely constructed with the 1st pers. impf. of *šql*: *'ašqal*. Our restoration presents a full coincidence with *Askalaphos*, and, consequently, with *Asklêpios* (the other dialectal forms are distortions of the unintelligible name, made on Greek ground). It harmonizes with the symbol of Asclepios, with the Mesopotamo-Syrian origin of all details of his image, myth, pedigree, symbols, with the Akkadian terminology and rôle of priesthood and of owl-birds associated with it, and with the entire body of healing heroes and gods who came to Greece from the East.

The family that was associated with Asclepios, consists of abstract personifications of different aspects of health and healing, none of whom are living mythological images. The surgeon-kings Machaon and Podaleirios, Asclepios' sons in the *Iliad*, are an exception. On Podaleirios, virtually nothing can be said.[5] The name of his brother, *Machaôn*, is commonly derived from *machomai* and explained as "the one who cuts with a knife" = a surgeon. But *machomai* means "to fight, struggle, wage war, counteract," and not "to cut." Besides, according to *Iliad* IV: 217-219, Machaon healed the wound not by surgery, but by applying drugs (see quotation on p. 300). It is rather another of the countless Greek names composed with *-machos*, like Aristomachos, Lysimachos, Machanidas, etc. This name would then have no more relation to its bearer's paternity than the names of all the numerous sons of Zeus have

[1] And vice versa, Akk. *dâku* "to kill" = Heb. *dākâ* "to bend, press."

[2] For the meaning of *ġlt*, cf. *UM* § 20.1481; IIIa, No. 2143; CXCVI, 149 (divergent interpretations); ours is based on Arabic *ġalla, ġāla*.

[3] Explained VII, 195, n. 11 as an abbreviation of the full title *aliy qrdm qryy b arṣ mlḥmt* "I prevail over the heroes who meet me in the land of battle."

[4] AT 139: 16.

[5] The etymology of his name in CCXXVII, II, 405 "without lilies where he treads, i.e., discouraging death" appears over-artificial.

to the supreme god of the Greeks. It is possible, however, to suggest a W-S etymology which proceeds from the ability to revive dead men ascribed to Asclepios and several Oriental healer-gods. Part. Piel of *ḥwy* "to live" is *mḥwy* or *mḥw*,[1] and with the suffix *-n*, common in pers. n., *mḥwn*. This would be pronounced approximately **Maḥawwôn*, which corresponds to the Mycenaean pers. n. *Ma-ka-wo*,[2] = *Macha(w)ôn*. The difficulty in accepting this etymology consists in the irregular preservation of *ḥ*, which was usually dropped in Greek transcriptions. We have, however, already noted that this phoneme was preserved in *Karchêdôn* < *Qart-ḥadašt*; the Ugaritic *ḥ* sometimes rendered an alien *ḫ*, e.g., *ḥtš* = Hittite *ḫatuš*, whence Akk. *ḫattum* "silver." [3] Might not the preservation of *ḥ* in the Greek stage of **Maḥawwon* be due to an instinctive avoidance of an hiatus? . . . These are the arguments *pro* and *contra* considering *Macha(w)ôn* as W-S **Maḥawwôn* "reviver," and let this possibility be noted on these pages.

Conclusion on Healer-Heroes

Our investigation of the Greco-Semitic healer-heroes is closed. We started with Bellerophon and showed that the Semitic sound of his name (W-S *Ba'al-rāph'ôn* "Lord-healer") was not fortuitous, but that this hero actually was a personage of the Canaanite cycle of healing gods. All essential parts of the plot in the myth of Bellerophon were borrowed from the East, i.e., from Canaan or, through Canaan, from Mesopotamia. We extended our analysis on several other heroes of Greek mythology whose adventures or names were similar to those of Bellerophon, and we detected obvious signs of Semitic origin in them too, in names, plots, symbols, and other details of their myths. In some cases, certain names appear in Greek translation, but there are always other, untranslated names

[1] Cf. II D (= 2 Aqht): VI: 32-33 where Anath declares: *ap a!nk aḥwy aq[ht ġz]r* "I will even immortalize (literally, "cause to live") *Aqht* the Hero," and I D (= 1 Aqht): 15-16: *hw l aḥw* "him would I not have kept alive" (or: "him would I surely cause to live").

[2] DV, 104; CCCXI, 79. As it is known, the Mycenaean syllabary rendered *ch* by *k* and dropped the *n* at the end of syllables.

[3] On *ḫattum* as "silver" in Old Assyrian (Cappadocian) texts, on Hittite spelling of URU*Ḫa-at-ti* by URUKU.BABBAR*ti* ("silver") and the identity of this term with *ḥtš* in Ugaritic, see CCCXXXI, 379 s.; XLVIII, 48. On Ugar. *ḥ* = foreign *ḫ*, cf. CCLIII, 161. It is also relevant that the Ugaritic scribes found the Akk. sign *ku* the closest equivalent of their *ḥ*, RŠ 19.159, DXXI, 65.

available in the same stories, or other evident signs allowing us to determine their appurtenance and origin.

We found that some of the characters examined ultimately derived from different avatars of the Sumerian chthonic serpent-god (also worshipped as a wooden pole), some—from another favorite symbol of Sumerian healer-gods: owls, eagles, and other predatory birds, and one, the Centaur Cheiron, from the Sumerian scorpion-man, the god Pabilsag, representing still another popular symbol of the same significance, the scorpion. Never before in our study, despite frequent references to Sumero-Akkadian parallels, have we met such a dense and compact influence of the great Mesopotamian culture upon West Semites, and through them—upon Greece. No wonder it was so: fear of disease and death belongs among the strongest impulses of human nature, and it is natural, when seeking help and comfort, to turn towards countries with an immemorially ancient civilization and an age-old reputation of possessing great and mysterious wisdom. To our modern intellect, the Babylonian obsession with demons and myriads of wild superstitions may seem the highest degree of delusion and backwardness—to their less civilized neighbors West of the Euphrates, and to the oversea neighbors of the latter, the enormous scope of all that pseudo-science seemed an imposing arsenal of weapons against evil. Long before the "Chaldean"—the magician and astrologist—was received with honor in Roman society, Sumero-Akkadian magic medicine, half-assimilated and refashioned by the Phoenicians and North Syrians, made its first invasion on the continent of Europe. This happened at the same time and through the same agents as the ecstatic cult of Bacchus; but if in ecstatic prophecy the Canaanites set the tone to the surrounding world of those times, they were only the disciples of the Babylonians in magic medicine and in mantic arts, based on pseudo-scientific observations and cold technical interpretations.

We consider especially important that in those cases when borrowing from Babylonia is beyond doubt, we were always able to establish that the link between Babylonia and Greece had been Canaan (in the widest sense of this term). Sometimes, no precise epigraphic evidence was extant on Canaanite ground—but the W-S mediation manifested itself in proper names. Thus, we do not know any close parallels to the myth of Zû with the W-S peoples—but the names of the participants of its very elaborate Greek version, the myth of the Argonauts, are W-S (besides those which were translated into Greek). The river of the underworld existed in the religion of Sumerians and Babylonians on one hand, and in Greek religion on the other hand; its presence in the religion of the Hebrews or other West Semites can only be surmised on the basis of very slight vestiges; however, the Greeks called this river not by a name derived from Sumero-Akkadian *Ḫubur*, but by a W-S name *Acherôn*. The same applies to the Ugaritic *Pbl-mlk* as a link between the Sumerian Pabilsag and the Greek Cheiron, etc., etc. And how many specifically Canaanite motifs, not attested in Mesopotamia, have we detected in the myths discussed in this chapter!

An example provided by archaeology is instructive. Jean NOUGAYROL, in one of his reports to the French Academy of Inscriptions,[1] spoke about Babylonian and Etruscan haruspicy. He established that haruspicy of the Babylonian type was practiced at Mari, Boğazköy, Tarsus, Alalaḫ, Megiddo—it had, thus, reached the Mediterranean shore not later than the XIIIth century. The hepatoscopic nomenclatures of Babylonia and classical Greece coincide in a remarkable way, as shown by comparison of the relevant glosses of Hesychios with the terminology of the cuneiform haruspicy texts. It is also known that, in Italy, the Etruscans were great specialists in this sort of mantic examination. A clay model of a liver similar to those used in the East, was found in Falerii Veteres, near Rome. How did this lore come from Babylonia to the neighborhood of Rome, asked NOUGAYROL. The two models excavated at Megiddo, in Palestine, bear the same characteristic elements as the model of Falerii, while those used by the Babylonians and Hittites differ from them in form. Thus, concluded NOUGAYROL, Phoenicia was probably the center from which this practice diffused toward the West, to which DHORME added,[2] that the Syrians rather than the Phoenicians were the intermediaries.

W. F. ALBRIGHT, in 1941, made the following concluding statement on Canaanite mythology as it appeared after the discovery of Ugaritic documents: "Canaanite mythology stands just about where one might have placed it *a priori*, in an intermediate position among Mesopotamian, Egyptian, Anatolian and Aegean. The Canaanite pantheon reminds one almost equally of Mesopotamian and of Homeric conceptions . . . The mythology of Ugarit strikes

[1] CCCXCII, 509-518.
[2] *Ibid.*, 518.

a happy medium between Babylonia and the Aegean scarcely resembling the former any more than the latter." [1] Our study, and in particular this chapter, gives a concrete picture of how this dynamic rôle of a "happy medium" (or rather, "happy intermediary") worked in practice. We have pointed to Canaanite and Canaaneo-Mesopotamian roots of a number of Greeks gods, heroes, beliefs and myths; we leave it to those whose love for Greek poetry and art we share, to continue our work from the position of comparative literature and aesthetics, and to determine the rôle of Greek genius in their evolution.

[1] VIII, 91.

CHAPTER FOUR

EVIDENCE OF ARCHAEOLOGY AND EPIGRAPHY

Does Archaeology contradict Semitic Penetration into the Aegean?

We approach the temporary end of our investigation. The portion of our research which is presented here does not cover all of the detectable Semitic elements in the earliest ancient Greece which were vestigially preserved in the religion, mythology, toponymics, and literary monuments of the classical time. We hope that the elaboration, documentation and systematic exposition of the rest of our preliminary notes and sketches will soon follow this study. The general image, however, appears even from the preceding three chapters. Single details may be changed or rejected, but the abundance of close parallels and of identical names and features in analogous places leaves no doubt that the Mycenaean, and after it, the Homeric and classical Greece owed to the West Semites and to their Mesopotamian teachers a very significant and important part of its spiritual culture.

However, before this conclusion can be made with a sufficient degree of certitude, the question put in the title of this section must still be resolved. Any kind of historical deductions, based upon the study of written documents, may be declared insufficient if they are not corroborated by archaeological data, by material proofs. We observed this rule when trying to establish the ethnic and cultural origins of the East Cilician Danunians. What about the presumed new home of the Danunians and kindred tribes—the islands and coasts of the Aegean? Since the appearance of Beloch's *Die Phoeniker am aegaeischen Meer* (which had a baneful influence out of proportion to its modest size), the argument of the alleged lack of archaeological evidence in support of Semitic presence in the Aegean has been repeatedly adduced against any attempt to establish the real facts about a Greco-Semitic relationship. Seventy years have elapsed since Beloch published his article; historical knowledge, especially archaeological documentation, both of ancient Greece and the ancient Near East, has made enormous progress; and nevertheless, the adversaries of the conception shared by the present author were unable to invent any new arguments against it.[1]

BELOCH categorically stated that the Phoenicians never visited the Aegean before the VIIIth century, even as merchants.[2] They simply could not have done so—their ships were too small for trips of that length.[3] The origin of the Mycenaean style is a riddle, but the overwhelming probability is against its connection with Phoenicia.[4] If a couple of Semitic words have slipped into the Greek language (which BELOCH did not believe), this could only have happened, if at all, by the land-route, through Asia Minor.[5] And the concluding sentence was: "The last word belongs here, as everywhere in prehistoric questions, to the monuments." [6]

Now, in our own time, BELOCH's argumentation makes an almost ridiculous impression. What did he know about ancient navigation and the minimum size of a ship able to sustain a voyage from Syria to Crete? [7] What could he have known of Mycenaean and Phoenician style before the discovery of the Minoan civilization in Crete and the start of excavations in Syria and Phoenicia? How could he pronounce judgments about Semitic words and toponyms in Greek, if, according to his own confession, he did not know any Semitic language? But, unfortunately, his attitude, though obviously refuted by the development of archaeology, is very die-hard. Well, then, let the monuments have the last word.[8]

The famous archaeologist and historian of civilization V. Gordon CHILDE wrote about the transition from Neolithic to Bronze in Crete: [9]

> The 'neolithic' phase was ended by a 'quickening impulse from the Nile, which permeated the rude island culture and transformed it' into the Minoan civilization . . . At the same time even more explicitly Asiatic traits can be detected among the innovations distinguishing the 'Metal Age' from the 'Neolithic' civilization. . . . Minoan metallurgy is

[1] It suffices to compare BELOCH's LVI and CARPENTER's XCII.
[2] LVI, 111 s.
[3] *Ibid.*, 116.
[4] *Ibid.*, 114.
[5] *Ibid.*, 125 s.
[6] *Ibid.*, 131.
[7] See pp. 352 ss. below.
[8] A systematic comparative archaeological survey of Syria and the Aegean would require a voluminous study by a specialist. We must limit ourselves to a few references.
[9] C, 19.

> based entirely on Asiatic traditions; the coppersmith cast axe-heads with a hole through the head for shafting in the Mesopotamian manner, the artists treated rosettes and similar figures in the Asiatic, not in the Egyptian style.

He remarks in another place: "Metallurgy and other discoveries could be diffused in the Aegean from Egypt or Phoenicia without passing over the Anatolian plateau," [1] i.e., by sea—as early as the third millennium. As for the Cretan burial customs, "The clay coffins have early parallels both in Mesopotamia and Egypt, whereas jar burial is a specifically Anatolian-Syrian rite." [2] "How far fresh Anatolian or Syrian colonists—merchants or artisans—joined with Egyptian refugees in founding Minoan cities is for us a secondary question," [3] concluded CHILDE; for us, however, the archaeologically deduced presence of Syrian settlers in ancient Minoan Crete is a conclusion of primary importance, confirming a very early ethnic connection between Syria and the Aegean.

Another outstanding archaeologist, Claude F.-A. SCHAEFFER, made a remarkable discovery at Ras Shamra. He had no preconceived ideas about Phoenician influence in the West when he found in the middle strata of Ugarit bronze weapons and adornments which were characteristic for Central European Early Bronze. He believed, in 1939, that they witnessed the "coming of the first Europeans" to Ugarit.[4] Ten years later, after a thorough study of the materials and cautious checking of synchronisms, he came to a diametrically opposite conclusion. We refer to his study which is saturated with facts and eloquent pictures.[5] The essence of his discovery consists in the following. He found a specific population group in the Middle Ugarit I period (2100-1900), who had probably originated in the mountain countries to the north of the Fertile Crescent and possessed a remarkable skill in bronze metallurgy. Their distinctive metal wares consisted of three types of weapons: triangular daggers with hilts finished in crescents, spears with sockets, and flat axes with blades pierced by large "windows," and specific ornaments: massive bronze neck rings (so-called "torques"), toggle-pins, and wire spirals. All these peculiar objects are also found, in the same assortment, in another main center of

[1] CI, 242.
[2] C, 24.
[3] *Ibid.*, 20.
[4] CDLI, 18.
[5] CDLII, 49-120.

this group—at Byblos, and also, more sporadically, at Qaṭna, Megiddo, Sidon, Gezer etc. The same assortment of bronze wares is found in numerous sites of Central Europe of Early Bronze which started there about 1800-1700.[1] MONTELIUS proved that the technique of bronze came to neolithic Europe from the ancient East by two routes: the western, along the coasts of Spain and France to the British Isles and the coast of the North Sea, and the eastern, along the Adriatic Sea, through the Balkan peninsula, to the Danube basin, and thence, along the great rivers, up to the Baltic Sea, North Sea, and Scandinavia. The "torques" and the characteristic wares which accompany them are dispersed along the eastern route. They were not brought by commerce, but were cast on the spot by specialists in mining and metallurgy who prospected new deposits of copper and especially of tin, rare and indispensable for bronze fabrication.[2] But how did these instructors reach Hungary and Bohemia? SCHAEFFER [3] convincingly proved that

> According to the investigations, the Torque-Bearers did not take the land route—the 'torque' is lacking on this route [i.e., in West Anatolia and the Balkans]. This compels us to admit that the Torque-Bearers of Syria, the prospectors and artisans of metal, took the sea. Following the south coasts of Anatolia, the islands of the Aegean, and the shores of the Adriatic, they seem to have advanced directly toward Central Europe where they must have provoked the prodigious development of mines and metal industry of Bohemia and Hungary which marks the beginning of the Bronze Age.

Other types of Syrian weapons followed the same route: bronze axes of Syrian type were found in Albania and Dalmatia, and their unexpected presence was immediately compared with the Greek myth which made Cadmos end his life in Illyria.[4]

SCHAEFFER, who first discovered these wares in his native Alsace, and then at Ras Shamra, excludes any possibility of a mistake. Every layman can check the correctness of his conclusions comparing the pictures of the European specimens with their Syrian counterparts.[5] What were "the causes of the dispersion of the Torque-Bearers and of the diffusion of metallurgic knowledge in

[1] *Ibid.*, 112.

[2] This opinion was advanced by MONTELIUS and accepted by CHILDE, C, 128 s., 301.

[3] CDLII, 115.

[4] *Ibid.*, 116.

[5] CI, 242, expresses his full agreement with the views of SCHAEFFER.

prehistoric Europe," asks SCHAEFFER, and he answers: "The principal cause was the impoverishment of copper and tin mines in Western Asia and the need to find other ones." [1] Then he summarizes:

> The Torque-Bearers were originally no Semites, but they rapidly became Semitized after their establishment in Syria. And, certainly, without the commercial genius of the Proto-Phoenicians, without their experience of the seas, they would not have been able to traverse the Mediterranean and to penetrate toward the virgin layers of copper and tin ore of Central Europe.
>
> We see thus that the ancestors of the Phoenicians must have been, as early as the beginning of the second millennium, bold seafarers and enterprising intermediaries. They fulfilled, as early as that time, the rôle which we have discovered them fulfilling at the time of their prosperity, in the XVth-XIVth centuries...
>
> To so many missions accomplished by this industrious and gifted people, the Phoenicians, or rather their ancestors of the early second millennium, added that of having transmitted, from Orient to Occident, the knowledge of bronze, the first known industrial metal. We have seen that the merit of having taught the secrets of this discovery so rich in consequences to the Neolithic people of southern, central, and northern Europe belongs, in particular, to these Torque-Bearers revealed by my discoveries at Ras Shamra and those of Byblos and elsewhere in Syria.[2]

It is, thus, established by palpable monuments that the inhabitants of the Syro-Phoenician coast made systematic sea-voyages across the Mediterranean as early as the beginning of the second millennium. Their route traversed the Aegean and doubled the shores of Greece. The Akkadian votive inscription from the XVIIIth century, discovered at Cythera,[3] which is contemporary with Middle Ugarit II, corroborates the data of archaeology. The mention of Kaphtor (*Kap-ta-ra*) in the contemporary documents from Mari confirms the mutual relations between Crete and Mesopotamia via the cities of the North Syrian coast.[4] For the Syro-Cretan con-

[1] CDLII, 119.

[2] *Ibid.*, 120.

[3] Cf. pp. 142 s. above.

[4] There are four mentions of artifacts from Kaptara in the Mari texts, CXXIII, 111 s. The geographical text *KAV* No. 92 brings another proof that the oversea road to Crete and Greece was known in Mesopotamia early in the second millennium. *A-na-kù*^{KI} and *Kap-ta-ra*^{KI} figure there (l. 41) as *mâtâti ebirti tâmti elîti* "lands beyond the Upper (Mediterranean) sea." *Kaptara* is Crete and *Anaku* (phonetic spelling of the Akkadian word for "lead" or "tin") most probably refers to Greece. Cf. CDLVIII, 67 s. (autography of the text); X, 195 s. (transliteration), 236 s. (on *Kaptara* and *Anaku* as Crete and Greece); CDXXVI, 239 s.; DXXXVa, 62; CCVII, 239. The text is a neo-Assyrian copy of an Old Babylonian text describing the world empire

nections during the Middle Minoan time, let us quote still another great archaeologist, Sir Leonard WOOLLEY, one of whose last accomplishments was the digging up of Alalaḫ. After having excavated the palace of King Yarim-Lim in the Level VII of Tell Aṭšana, he was able to trace "unmistakable connexions with Crete." He found that "the methods of construction employed in Yarim-Lim's palace are the same as those of Knossos" (a detailed comparison follows) "and the frescoes are identical in colouring, technique, and style." [1] He decidedly ascribed priority to the palace of Yarim-Lim which he believed to have "antedated by more than a century the Cretan examples in the same style." Here, owing to his use of the "middle chronology" for the Old Babylonian period and to his locating Yarim-Lim of Alalaḫ a generation too early,[2] he was wrong; but he correctly stated that "Yarim-Lim's palace (was) in the old tradition," while "in Crete all this appears suddenly." The earliest specimens of the Cnossos-style frescoes appear in the palace of Zimri-Lim at Mari (c. 1730), which was the object of admiration and imitation by the contemporary kings of North Syria; [3] the author of the latest comprehensive work on prehistoric Crete, R. W. HUTCHINSON, indicates that "the Mari frescoes, however, appear to be over a hundred years earlier than the miniature frescoes of Knossos (which may well have been influenced by them rather than have influenced them)," and he notes without objecting that "it has been suggested also that Minoan frescoes were influenced by those of Level VII at Atchana (intermediate both geographically and chronologically between those of Mari and of Crete)." [4] Now we can return to WOOLLEY's significant conclusion:

> There can be no doubt but that Crete owes the best of its architecture, and its frescoes, to the Asiatic mainland. And we can say more than this. The exchange of goods by international trade is one thing, and a most important thing, but it has its limits; one cannot export a palace on board ship, nor is the "art and mystery" of fresco-working a form of merchandise. These professional techniques require direct contacts,

of King Sargon. The author had in mind the great conqueror Sargon of Agade, already a legendary figure by that time, but his geography is that of the XVIIIth century.

[1] DLV, 74 s.

[2] The relative chronology of Level VII is established in CCCVI, 33, 34 ss.

[3] The king of Ugarit, through the intermediary of king Ḫammurapi (of Yamḫad-Aleppo), asked Zimri-Lim of Mari the permission to see the palace of Mari, CXXIV, 125.

[4] CCLXVII, 179.

> and we are bound to believe that trained experts, members of the Architects' and Painters' Guilds, were invited to travel overseas from Asia. . .[1]

The same view of the Middle Minoan period was given by V. Gordon CHILDE:

> The native population would be swelled by the immigration of craftsmen attracted by the wealth of Minoan courts and towns. So professional potters from Asia may have introduced the potter's wheel and trained native apprentices in its use. And other specialists such as fresco-painters may have arrived to minister to courtly desire for refinement.[2]

SCHAEFFER was of the opinion that WOOLEY's statement on the scope of Syrian influence upon Middle Minoan Crete was "exaggerated." [3] However, the architectural material from Ugarit caused him to revaluate one of his earlier views. When he first found, in 1938-1939, the fortress guarding the access to the gigantic royal palace of Ugarit, he did not hesitate to see in it "a strong influence of Mycenaean architecture," and still a greater resemblance to the walls of Homeric Troy.[4] But after the excavations of 1948-1950 he declared in a different tone:

> Besides, I must immediately exclude here the hypothesis of dependence on Hittite military architecture. It seems to me more probable that the Anatolians [5] have borrowed the essential elements of their fortification system from North Syria, to which they were indebted for so much other knowledge . . . [The wall] reminds us evidently of analogous defense walls of Tiryns and Mycenae.[6]

This would imply, in this context, that Tiryns and Mycenae, too, followed the North Syrian fortifications pattern, which requires to assume the presence of trained North Syrian architects and builders in the construction of Mycenaean defense walls. On more than one page of R. W. HUTCHINSON's recent survey architectural and artistic parallels between Minoan Crete and Syria-Palestine may be found.[7]

The style of weapons in the Middle Minoan age continued to follow closely the Syrian and Mesopotamian patterns. The famous two-edged Double Axe, which became a sacral symbol in Crete,

[1] DLV, 74.
[2] C, 26 s.
[3] CDXLIX, 328 s.; CDL, 105.
[4] CDXLV, 292.
[5] Anatolia, of course, includes Troy.
[6] CDXLVIII, 4 s.
[7] CCLXVII, 166-169, 181, 213, 218, 219, 225, 311 s., etc.

was borrowed from the Sumerians.[1] The rapier from the Middle Minoan I period, found in the palace of Mallia, is shown to be a development of Sumerian types.[2] A particular type of Late Minoan dagger, characterized by an "inlaid handle enclosed by a flanged tang," was "probably invented by some Hyksos swordsmith, and spread gradually along the trade-routes from Knossos, Mycenae, Byblos, and Ras Shamra"; "the earliest is certainly that of *Nḥmn* the servant of Apepi I found at Dahshur." [3]

The spiral decorative motif was long considered an invention peculiar to the Aegean. When the spiral was found in the palace of Mari, it was supposed that it had been brought there by Aegean masters who took back to Crete oriental motifs—capricorns, lions, griffins.[4] However, recent comparative study showed that this motif was of Sumerian origin, and penetrated thence to Syria.[5] A very minute study of the Aegean seals, gems, and other small art objects, made by M. L. and H. ERLENMEYER, convincingly proved that these were closely dependent upon Mesopotamian and Syrian models. Thus, the images of cervids on Aegean seals, which appear especially from the middle of the IId millennium, were clearly connected with Mesopotamian representations, known there since immemorial times and related to the cult of Inanna-Ištar; Syria, too, preserved the tradition of cervid images.[6] A more comprehensive analysis of decorative motifs and styles led the same scholars to the deduction that the passage from Middle Minoan I (pre-Palace Period) to Middle Minoan II (early Palace Period) was "connected with immigration from the eastern mainland," and the home-country of those new-comers was mainly Syria.[7] In particular, M. L. and H. ERLENMEYER detected (and illustrated with numerous pictures) specific North Syrian and Hurrian motifs since Middle Minoan II, and especially in Late Minoan since the middle of the XVIth

[1] C, 28.

[2] *Ibid.*, 29.

[3] CCLXVIIa, 169 s. (note the W-S name *Nḥmn*). CDXXXIX, 20 ss. distinguishes two types of Aegean swords: A—a long sword with a midrib—doubtlessly of Near Eastern origin, was adopted by the Cretans while visiting Phoenician harbors (Ugarit, Byblos etc.) and further developed; B—a short one with shoulders and tangs, the invention of which, as we have seen, was ascribed to the Hyksos.

[4] P. DEMARGNE, quoted CXLII, 233.

[5] CDXVII.

[6] CLVIII, II, 321 ss., 338.

[7] CLIX, III, 269.

century.[1] This agrees excellently with the chronology we have deduced from quite different sources (above, p. 109 s.).

T. B. L. Webster, a classicist, devoted an excellent detailed chapter to "Mycenaean Art in its Setting," showing its constant and close borrowing from Near Eastern art;[2] he stated in particular:

> It is certain that many themes were borrowed by Aegean art from Asia and Egypt; the master of animals, the mistress of animals and snakes, antithetic pairs of animals, groups of lion tearing bull, are known from Sumerian art of the third millennium . . . [There exist] Syrian parallels for the goddess with a mirror on the ivory mirror-handle from the tomb of Klytaemnestra . . . The evidence for internationalism in art is overwhelming.[3]

Another classicist, Frank H. Stubbings went even farther, thus summarizing his conclusion from the archaeological data in his recent chapter on the chronology of the Aegean Bronze Age:

> Thus we can firmly date the beginnings of Late Minoan I and Late Helladic I as contemporary. As will be argued in another chapter, there is a case for inferring the arrival in Greece at this time of new rulers from abroad, such as are indeed ascribed by legend to the beginnings of the first heroic age. Some of those immigrant founder heroes are of origins too improbable to be fictitious—Danaus, for example, from Egypt; Cadmus from Syria. The only probable juncture for such immigration which can be recognized in the archaeological record is at the transition from Middle Helladic to Late Helladic; while in terms of external history no time is so likely as the period of the expulsion of the Hyksos overlords from Egypt. It seems more than fortuitous coincidence that the heroic era of Athens, according to the *Marmor Parium*, begins at 1582 B.C., and that Danaus is in that document placed at least in the same century. Several, consequently, of the principal legends of the earlier heroic age may be set in relation to the archaeological history as events of the period of settlement in Greece after the first immigrations, a period of internal conflict leading ultimately to the supremacy of Mycenae.[4]

By the somewhat peculiar expression: "origins too improbable to be fictitious"—Stubbings probably understood: "improbable from the point of view of Greek nationalist attitude toward non-Greeks"; there is nothing more improbable in an immigration from the Levant to Greece than in an immigration from Greece to the Levant (e.g., Philistines). We wait for the promised chapter where the author's point will be explained more in detail.

[1] *Ibid.*, 270 s., 289 ss.
[2] DXXXVII, 27-63.
[3] *Ibid.*, 30 s.
[4] CDLXXXIII, 74.

Can one always rely upon Ceramic Data?

The general archaeological picture presented, on the basis of statements by competent specialists, in the preceding section, is diametrically opposed to what was pretended by Beloch in 1894. The false, unnatural image of the Aegean hermetically cut off from the Eastern Mediterranean and growing in "splendid isolation" until the "Greek miracle" blossomed out, ceded its place to the conviction that Mycenaean society was "a particular variant of Eastern Mediterranean society, of which clear traces can be seen in the Homeric epic." [1] However, in the same year, 1958, when these words were published, another specialist in Homer repeated sharply (almost verbatim) the claims of Beloch and asked for the only archaeological evidence he recognized as valid: the presence of "Phoenician" ceramic sherds in the excavated sites.[2] This attitude, which may be called fetishism of ceramics, is characteristic for a certain kind of archaeologist. From an auxiliary method of determining the chronological sequence of levels in an excavated mound in the absence of written documents or individualized pieces of art, the study of potsherds became a goal in itself. Data of toponymics, onomastics, religious cults, historical texts, even of architecture, glyptics, and painting, are pitilessly rejected if they cannot be justified by the testimony of ceramics. This extreme devotion to the evidence of material remainders could have been justified and even laudable as a consistent application of a strictly scientific method, if this approach were always faultless. But in practice it is not always so.

Before elaborating this point, let us first clarify the fact that the frequent claim of the total absence of "Phoenician" ceramics in Mycenaean sites is not correct. Large clay vessels of pure Canaanite style and manufacture were discovered in Mycenaean cities; it is supposed that they had arrived with Oriental spices.[3] This, at least, proves the existence of a Syro-Mycenaean trade, if not the direct presence of Syrians and Phoenicians on Greek soil. But here is how a world authority in archaeology warns us against over-esti-

[1] DXXXVII, 91. The text bears "East Aegean," but this is obviously a writing-error, for the Mycenaean civilization originated and centered on the *Western* side of the Aegean. We corrected it on the basis of analogous statements *ibid.*, 22 and 64.

[2] XCII, esp. 37 s., 39 s., 53.

[3] DXXXVII, 66; CCLXVIII, 13.

mating the value of ceramic data even for prehistory, where few other data are available:

> Farming must of course have started in South-West Asia. But in tracing its primary expansion thence, it must now be remembered that the first farmers were not necessarily also potters; the first peasant colonists to reach Europe may not have left a trail of potsherds to mark their tracks! And these tracks were not necessarily on land.[1]

In historical times, we meet more than once the presence of a sharply individualized ethnic group on a certain territory, proven beyond any doubt by the evidence of epigraphic and historic monuments, but having no corroboration in ceramic data. Since we are speaking of the westernmost group of the Canaanites, who we believe to have penetrated into the Aegean and left a deep trace in the toponymics and religious life of this region, the best analogy would be provided by another branch of the Canaanites—the eastern one which had, a few centuries earlier, and on a far greater scale, invaded and conquered all of Mesopotamia.

As is known, West Semitic tribes, commonly designated as Amorites (Akk. *Amurru*), took hold, early in the second millennium, of Assyria, Mari, Babylon, Larsa, Isin, Ešnunna and of all other states of Babylonia and Upper Mesopotamia. The Amorite invasion entailed not only a general change of dynasties, but also the appearance of a numerous foreign ruling class in Akkadian cities, the penetration of W-S nomadic tribes in the very midst of Sumerian and Akkadian agricultural districts, a noticeable linguistic influence and the introduction of new deities into the Babylonian pantheon. This entire immense process, however, became known exclusively through onomastic data. The Assyriologists remarked that a great number of personal names of a new type appear, early in the second millennium, in the cuneiform documents. These names were Semitic, but not Akkadian, and their linguistic analysis proved that they belonged to the W-S (or "Canaanite" in the wide sense of the term) group of languages. New written sources, in particular those of the Mari archives, later shed additional light on the history, rôle, and nature of these W-S invaders. But archaeology—if epigraphy is excluded from its proper scope—is silent about their arrival and power over an enormous cultural region. No potsherds marked their trail from Syria up to South Babylonia. Neither Theo BAUER,[2]

[1] C, 16.
[2] LIV.

nor Dhorme,[1] nor Kupper,[2] authors of the most comprehensive works on these "Amorites" or "East Canaanites," ever referred to archaeological data as proof of the presence of a new ethnic group in Mesopotamia. All their conclusions are exclusively based on philological data; the first two of the mentioned studies, published before the discovery of the Mari archives, have used only the testimony of personal names. The situation is no different when one turns from these historico-philological works to purely archaeological surveys of Mesopotamia.[3] The transition from "Ur III" to "Old Babylon," i.e., from neo-Sumerian to Amorite domination, is established without any ceramic contribution.

Now, with respect to East Canaanites on Mesopotamian ground, onomastics provides the most reliable material, and nobody demands that sherds of some specific "Amorite" ceramics be presented as covering vouchers of W-S presence in Mesopotamia. The Amorite conquerors and rulers are admitted as real people who left a bright trace in history without having to confirm the fact of their existence by specific potsherds in order to satisfy future archaeologists. However, when it comes to their western kinsmen in the Aegean, the attitude changes drastically. They are not accepted as real beings without first producing their ceramic passports.

Scholarship, however, cannot tolerate any bias. What is found possible with respect to East Canaanites in Mesopotamia, cannot be refused to West Canaanites in the Aegean. The example of the Amorite conquerors of Mesopotamia, who left for posterity the names of their tribes, gods, kings, men, and women, but no traces of material civilization, explains why immigrants from Syria and Phoenicia cannot be detected on Greek soil by narrow methods of ceramic analysis, and why data of onomastics and mythology are quite sufficient for unconditional acceptance of their historic reality—especially since this is confirmed by other archaeological proofs, quoted in the preceding section.

The same refers to the Indo-Aryan penetration into Mesopotamia, Syria, and Palestine towards the middle of the IId millennium.

[1] "Les Amorrhéens" (1928-1931), reprinted *ap*. cxv, 81-160.

[2] cccv.

[3] E.g., cdiv, II, 40 s.: in Mesopotamia, "one does not speak of 'Bronze Age' or 'Iron Age' with their divisions (Early, Middle, Late) and subdivisions (1, 2, 3), but one enumerates, from top to bottom, the encountered epochs or periods," *viz.*, Sassanid, Parthian, Seleucid, Achaemenid, Neo-Babylonian, etc.

This penetration is established not by material remains, but exclusively by proper names (human and divine) and a few linguistic traces.[1] Let us quote another striking example. René DUSSAUD, speaking of Nelson GLUECK's discoveries in Transjordan, made the following important observation:

> A rather curious problem posed itself before Mr. Nelson GLUECK who had been the first to uncover the very original Nabataean ceramics. In spite of all his research, he did not find the least trace of Nabataean ceramics at Umm-el-Djemal, which had been occupied by the Nabataeans for no less than three centuries, and he does not hide his embarrasment (p. 13). This example shows us how cautious one must be in historical utilization of ceramics. Its presence brings a precious indication, but its absence does not allow us to make a conclusion with certitude. Here, it seems that Nabataean ceramics came into collision with local pottery. Nelson GLUECK came to the conclusion (p. 23) that "the Nabataeans introduced their religion and their script and their architecture into the Syrian part of their kingdom, but not their pottery." [2]

This remark is entirely applicable to our case. Minoan and Mycenaean ceramic wares dominated all the markets of Syria and Palestine between, roughly, 1500 and 1200. They were imported in great quantities and imitated in local workshops. It is hard to imagine that W-S migrants to the Aegean, the homeland of the beautiful pottery then in general fashion, would carry with them their own inferior wares which they did not want to use even at home. To import ceramics to the Aegean would have been equal to "carrying owls to Athens" or "coal to Newcastle." We know from several Phoenician inscriptions found in the Piraeus that a noticeable Phoenician community, with an internal organization, existed there in the Vth-IVth centuries. And how many Phoenician potsherds were excavated in Attica, the greatest exporter of artistic ceramics? [3]

[1] Cf., e.g., the appendix on Indo-Aryan names in Mesopotamia and Syria by P. E. DUMONT *ap.* CCCXCIII.

[2] CLI, 149. Cf. CXCVIII, 13, 23.

[3] Cf. CVI, 179: if no ceramics are found outside the place of their production, it does not point to an absence of trade, but simply indicates that these particular ceramics, because of their low commercial value, were not exported. It is also relevant to quote from this recent article on principles of using archaeology for restoration of history: "Written records often provide checks on conclusions that might be suggested by the material evidence." The distribution of Greek dialects, the background of Homeric poems, the data of tradition firmly show that the Dorian invasion really took place. "But although it is eighty years since archaeologists began looking for relics

We shall conclude this section with the words of A. DUPONT-SOMMER:

> However useful archaeology may be, however thorough its methods may be today, it remains an auxiliary science of history; and history is constructed essentially with texts: when archaeological exploration does not possess any text to guide and elucidate it, it most often can only grope along and present inaccurate or uncertain conclusions.[1]

DATA OF THE MYCENAEAN TABLETS (LINEAR B)

Happily, the Mycenaean age recently ceased to be the exclusive domain of descriptive archaeology, and becomes more and more the field of history. As formulated by the prominent archaeologist A. PARROT, "history starts at the moment when, with the appearance of writing, proper names (of individuals, cities, deities) are written down and thus conserved for posterity . . . History cannot establish solid bases otherwise than upon written documents, and we can pretend to have seized it only with texts in our hands, and only then." [2] Since the decipherment of the Mycenaean Linear B texts by Michael VENTRIS, the Mycenaean civilization has become, to a certain degree, a literate one. It is true that the system of Mycenaean writing was technically imperfect and appalingly ambiguous; it is true that literacy does not seem to have widely permeated Mycenaean society, and was used, as far as the now available documents allow us to judge, to very limited purposes; but they do contain proper names—human, divine, and geographical—and thus qualify as historical monuments. Moreover, they reveal the social organization of the early Greek world, and the methods of administration and recording.

The system of recording betrays a well-developed, standardized chancellery style, with uniform formulas and accounting devices. The similarity of the official Mycenaean style to that of the ad-

of the invading Dorians, they have not found them . . . There is in fact so far no material evidence that is certainly characteristic of the Dorians themselves . . . Here, too, is an example of an important invasion that has no positive archaeological record" (*ibid.*, 177). "In conclusion it appears to me that many archaeologists, both Classical and Prehistoric, are not critical enough when they try to reconstruct a society from its material remains, and further that they tend to exaggerate the significance of particular objects" (*ibid.*, 179). Other analogous examples and opinions are quoted CDII, 163.

[1] CXXXIII, 54.

[2] CDIV, II, 292.

ministrative and economic tablets of Ugarit and Alalaḫ is beyond any doubt, and was recognized, elucidated and commented by the editors of the first corpus of transliterated Mycenaean inscriptions, VENTRIS and CHADWICK,[1] as well as by the scholars who applied the data of those documents for comprehensive attempts of Mycenaean age synthesis.[2] Of course, the chancellery methods and style in different countries of the ancient Near East had much in common and depended on the highly developed traditions of Sumer and Akkad. But the Mycenaean documents stand closest to those of North Syria. They look like simplified imitation of the latter which, in their turn, were significantly less elaborate than Mesopotamian accounting tablets. This corresponds exactly both to the gradation of cultural levels of the three regions and to their geographical situation. T. B. L. WEBSTER concluded:

> If records are largely alike, the civilizations which produce them are likely to have large common elements.[3] . . . Thus the records fully agree with the material remains in showing that the rich, elaborate, and highly centralized Mycenaean civilization was much more akin to contemporary Near Eastern kingdoms than to the city-states of archaic and classical Greece.[4]

The Mycenaean vocabulary provided by the Linear B tablets is very restricted, owing to the uniformity of their contents; it includes, according to VENTRIS and CHADWICK, only 630 lexical units.[5] Nevertheless, these scholars name several Mycenaean borrowings from the Semitic languages, which were formerly believed to have been adopted much later:

kuruso (= *chrysos*) "gold," from *ḫarûṣ;*
kito (= *chitôn*) "chiton," from Ug. *ktn, ktnt,* Heb. *kᵉtōnet;*
kumino (= *kyminon*) "caraway seed," from Akk. *kammûnu,* Heb. *kammôn;*
sasama (= *sesama*) "sesame," from Akk. *šamaššammu,* Ug. *ššmn;*
kuparo (= *kypairos*) "cyperus," from Heb. *kôpher,* Ug. *kpr;*[6]
ponike, ponikija (= *phoinikai, phoinikia*) dyes and other products

[1] DV, 106 s., 113, 133.
[2] DXXXVII, 7-26 (chapt. I: "Records of Society in the Second Millennium"); CCCXLIX, 9-16.
[3] DXXXVII, 7.
[4] *Ibid.*, 22 s.
[5] DV, 385.
[6] These five words are listed DV, 135 s. For Ugar. *kpr* = *kôpher* = "henna" (cyperus), cf. CLXXXVI, 211; IIIa, No. 1369.

imported from Phoenicia, a loan-word in Greek;[1] we have shown above, p. 146 s., that the loan-word was taken from Phoenician;

rewo (= *lewôn,* i.e. *leôn*) "lion," as to which they share the old assumption that this word derived from Semitic *lb'* (Akk. *labbu,* Ug. *lbu,* Heb. *lābî'*.[2] This is phonetically improbable,[3] unless some inner Greek development (interchange *bêta*/-*digamma,* occurring sometime between the Greek dialects) is presumed to have been responsible.

erepa (= *elephas*) "ivory, elephant," though provided with the Asianic suffix *-nt-*, ultimately originates from Semitic *'lp* (Akk. *alpu,* Ug. *alp*) "ox".[4]

Three more Mycenaean words should be added:

rita (= *lita*) Homeric "garment, linen," was long ago derived from Heb. *lôṭ* "veil, covering,"[5] has now a much closer analogy in the Assyrian form of this word, *lîṭu* or *lêṭu*;[6]

damokoro, name of a function; E. R. LACHEMAN convincingly identified it with Akk. *tamkâru,* "merchant" or "royal commercial agent";[7]

temeno (= *temenos*), temple-precinct or royal domain on public land; from Sum. *temen,* Akk. *temmenu* (Ug. *tmn*?[8]) "sacral foundation of a temple," by extension the temple itself.[9]

These loan-words point primarily to commercial relations with the Semitic East, and their evidence is important enough: "commercial relations must not be underestimated, most influences from one country to another take place through them."[10] But the presence of *temeno* shows, in addition, a religious influence; were we in

[1] DV, 136, 405. The alternative Greek word for "purple," *porphyra,* formerly believed to be post-Homeric, appears in the Mycenaean texts as *popureja* "(garments) of purple," *popuro,* DV, 321, 405. If our derivation of this word (see p. 147 above) is correct, we have here another Semitic loan-word in Mycenaean Greek.

[2] DV, 346.

[3] Semitic *b* could not have been spirantized so early; however, the interchange *b* | *w* is very common in Hurrian spelling.

[4] DV, 346. For H-H *uluba(n)das* "ivory," with head of a bull as determinative (elephants were considered as a kind of bulls), cf. XLIV, 6.

[5] LXV, I, 376.

[6] DLX, 274 s.

[7] Quoted CCX, 53, n. 2.

[8] IIIa, No. 2773.

[9] CCX, 53, n. 2.

[10] CCL, I.

presence of temple-archives instead of royal accountance, the number of such loan-words may have been more considerable.

The Linear B tablets are very rich in personal names. It must be remembered that the very defective nature of the Mycenaean syllabary makes the recognition of personal names quite uncertain. "We can only be confident of our solution when we have clear parallels in classical Greek and the name is long enough to exclude alternative interpretation," says CHADWICK,[1] and we know that most W-S names are rather short. "We have reason to believe that a number of names are not of Greek type, and thus we have nothing by which to identify them," says further CHADWICK.[2] Perhaps the richly preserved onomastica of ancient Syria can be helpful in this respect. One must, however, take into account that the Pylian tablets were composed immediately before the destruction of the palace and kingdom of Pylos, at the very end of the XIIth century. Even if any Semitic or Hurrian elements had penetrated into Messenia in the earlier centuries, they would probably have been assimilated by so late a date. Therefore, the relatively small number of personal names in the Pylian tablets that present possible traits of Oriental origin is quite expected; the bare fact of their presence is significant enough.

The Cnossian tablets contain a comparatively larger proportion of names which may reasonably be taken as Semitic or Hurrian. It is believed that the Linear B tablets from Cnossos, unlike their Pylian counterparts, dated from a period before 1400. Recently, however, first Carl BLEGEN,[3] then Leonard PALMER[4] brought forward an impressive amount of evidence and interpretation to the effect that Sir Arthur EVANS' stratigraphic attribution of the Cnossian tablets in Linear B was erroneous, and that those tablets were really contemporary to those of Pylos, from which they are practically undistinguishable by their script and language. If this controversial claim is founded, the Cnossian tablets are also a relatively late evidence, having been written after two centuries of Greek domination. Moreover, Cnossos, as the residence of the Greco-Mycenaean conquerors, was more Hellenized than the rest of the island. If, nevertheless, Semitic and Hurrian names are

[1] XCIX, 98.
[2] *Ibid., l.c.*
[3] LXIX.
[4] CDII, *passim,* esp. 20-28, 156-225.

present in Cnossian tablets, this proves that before the Achaean conquest of Crete, or in the provincial cities, their relative importance must have been much greater.

The following short list, by no means complete, provides analogies from Syria to some names from Pylos (PY), Cnossos (KN) and Mycenae (MY).[1] The reader will notice that Greek parallels, adduced by Ventris and Chadwick (in brackets), often require the restitution (more or less haphazard) of many presumably omitted consonants, or are obviously of non-Greek provenance (Aphareus, Assarakos, Katanê, Kakkabos and so on).

a-di-ri-jo KN [*Andrios*? *Andriôn*?] W-S *'addîr* "mighty, noble" (*UM*, § 20.57). Cf. Ugar. *Adrdn* (= *'Addir-dân*).

ai-ku-pi-ti-jo KN [*Aigyptios*] "Egyptian," from Ugar. *Ḥkpt* "Egypt," cf. *mi-si-ra-jo* below.

a-ka-to KN [*Akanthos*; *Agathos*; *Agathôn*] Ugar. *Aqht*?

a-ka-ta-jo KN, PY [*Aktaios*] Perhaps Ugar. *Aqht* + *-y*, cf. p. 165.

a-mu?*-ta-wo* PY [*Amytaôn*] Cf. *Amût-pî-el*, king of Qaṭna, c. 1730.

a-na-te-u PY From the div. n. *'Anat* (like many pers. n. in Syria).

a-no-po PY Egypt. div. n. *inpw* (Anubis)? Or the bird *'anāphā*, whence Homeric *anopaia*, cf. p. 246.

a-pa-re-u KN [*Aphareus*] A hypocoristic of a W-S name composed of *'āphār* + div. n., like *'pr-Ršp*, *'pr-B'l*, etc.

a-ra-da-jo KN A hypocoristic of a name constructed with Akk. *arad-* "sevant of ..."; cf. Ugar. *A-ra-ad-ni*, Alal. *A-ra-ta*, *A-ra-ti*. Or gentilic of the city of *Arwad* (Gr. *Arados*), cf. Ugar. *Arwdn*.

a-ra-na-ro KN Hurrian: *alla-* "Lady" + *-nar*,[2] cf. Alal. *Al-li-ni-ri*, Ugar. *Alnr*, and other similar names at Nuzu. Also in Linear A.

a-ra-si-jo KN [*Alêsios* founder of *Alêsion* in Elis] "Alašian," cf. Alal. pers. n. *A-la-ši-ia*, gentilic *a-la-ši-i*; Ugar. pers. n. *Alšn*, gentilics *alšy*, *alšyy*.

a-ri-ke-u KN [*Halikeus*? *Haliskeus*? should be *wal-* from *haliskomai*] Ugar. *Ark*, Alal. *A-ri-ku*, i.e. W-S *'arîk* "long, longeval."

a-sa-mi KN Hurrian element *ašm-*, cf. Alal. *Aš-ma*, *Aš-ma-a-du*, *Aš-ma-an*, *Aš-mi-šarri*, *Aš-mu* etc.

[1] In order not to extend the list beyond reasonable limits, no references as to tablet and line are given for the quoted names. They may be conveniently found: Mycenaean—in the index of pers. n., DV, 414-427, and CCCXI; Ugaritic alphabetic—in CCXXIV, IIIa and DXXIV, 217-226, or in CDXCIX; Ugaritic cuneiform—mostly in CCCXC, 238-264 and CCCXCI, 244-252; Alalaḫ—DLII, 125-153; Nuzu—CXCI. Identifications by Ventris and Chadwick, if any, are put in brackets.

[2] CXCI, 199, 238.

a-sa-ro KN [cf. *Assarakos*] Ugar. *Asrn, Aśrn.*

a-ta-no KN [*Antānôr*] Cf. Ugar. *Atn, Atnb, Atn-Prln, At-ta-nu*; Alal. *A-ta-na-be-(en)-di, A-ta-na-bi-ti.* Also Linear A.

da-na-jo KN [*Danaios?*] W-S *dan-* + suffix *-ay(a)*, cf. n. 377 to chapt. I.

du-ni-jo KN, PY Cf. Ugar. *Du-nu-ib-ri,* Alal. *Du-u-na,* Akk. *dunnu* "strong."

i-da-i-jo KN, PY [Not from Mount Ida, which is written with initial *w* in Mycenaean] Alal. *I-da-at-*[?], *Id-du-wa*; probably from Akk. *idû* "to know," *ida-* in Amorite names.

i-mi-ri-jo KN [*Himerios?*] Ugar. *Imrt* (fem.), Alal. *Im-me-ri* (Akk. and W-S *'immêr* "lamb").

ja-sa-no KN Heb. *yāšān* "old, ancient," cf. Ugar. *Yšn, Ia-ši-nu,* Alal. *Ia-šu-na.*

ja-sa-ro KN Heb. *yāšār* "straight, righteous," Ugar. *Yšr, Ia-ši-ra,* Alal. *Ia-še-ri-na, Ia-aš-šar-ḫu, Ia-aš-ri-e-da.*

ka-da-no KN [*Chaldanos?*] Ugar. *Kdn* (Akk. *kadânu* "to hide, to protect").

ka-da-si-jo PY [cf. *Chadêsiai,* name of the Amazons] Common Semitic root *qādaš* "to be, or to make holy." Cf. Ugar. div. n. *Qdš-w-Amrr,* pers. n. *Bn-Qdšt,* guild *qdšm.*

ka-ka-po PY [*Kakkabos*] Akk. *kakkabu,* Heb. *kôkāb* "star," Babylonian pers. n. *Ka-ak-ka-ba-a.*

ka-mo KN [*Skamôn, Kamôn?*] Ugar. *Kmy, Kmn,* Alal. *Ka-a-mi, Kam-mu.*

ka-mo-ni-jo KN [*Skamonios?*] Ugar. *Kmn*; Akk. *kamânu* "to embrace."

ka-pa$_3$*?-no* KN [*Karbanos*] Cf. Ugar. n. div. *Gpn,* pers. n. *Gu-pa-na* (W-S *gpn* "vine").

ka-pa-ra$_2$ PY Akk. *kapâru* "to wipe, to cleanse," Heb. *kāpar* "to coat, to propitiate, to pardon," Aramaic pers. n. *Kapara.* The Mycenaean spelling may, moreover, correspond to any of the following Ugar. pers. n.: *Gbrn, Gbry, Kbl, Kbr.*

ka-ra-pi PY [*Krambis?*] Cf. Ugar. *Grbn, Grp, Gur-pa-na,* and *glb* (Heb. *gallāb,* Akk. *gallabu*) "barber," the variant *Mglb* as a pers. n.

ka-ra-su-no PY LANDAU: = *Garašunu*;[1] cf. Heb. *Geršôn,* Ugar. *Tgrš* (root *gāraš* "to expell").

[1] With reference to I. J. GELB, *Inscriptions from Alişar,* 70.

ka-ta-no KN, PY [cf. place-name *Katanê*[1]] W-S *qāṭān* "small," Ugar. pers. n. *Qṭn*. Or Ugar. *Gtn* (from *gat* "wine-press").

ke-re-no PY, MY [*Gerēnos*?] Cf. perhaps Ugar. *Kran, Ki-ir-ru-na*.

ke-re-te-u PY [*Kretheus*] Cf. Ugar. *Krt, Krtn*.

ke-ro-wo PY [*Keraos* < **Kerowos*?] Ugar. *Krw, Krwn, Qrwn* (UYECHI: Hurrian div. n. *Kurwe*[2]).

ke-ti-ro KN, PY Ugar. *Ktr* (W-S *ktr* "crown, hat").

ke-wo-no-jo PY Ugar. *Kwn, Ka-wa-na* (Semit. root *kwn* "to be, to establish," *UM*, § 20.899, cf. Heb. *kawwân*, a cultic cake).

ki-e-u PY [ethnic adj. *Skieus, Chieus*?] Ugar. *Ky, Kyn*, Nuzu *Ki-ia*.

ki-ri-ja-i-jo PY [*Killaios*?] Ugar. *Kryn, Ki-ir-ia-na*, Alal. *Ki-ri-ia-an*.

ko-do-ro PY [*Kodros*] LANDAU: = Alal. *Ku-du-ru*. Cf. Ugar. *Kdrn*, Akk. *kadru* "mighty, proud, fiery."

ko-ka-ro PY [*Kôkalos*] Ugar. *Kkln*.

ko-tu-ro₂ PY [*Kotylos*] Ugar. *Ktr, Ktln, Ku?-ti-la-na*.

ko-za-ro PY Nuzu *Ku-uz-za-ri, Ku-za-ri-ia*; or Ugar. *Bn-Gzl* (Akk. *guzalû*).

ku-ne-u KN [*Kuneus*?] A very common onomastic pattern in the Near East. Cf. Old Babylonian *Ku-un-na-a*, Middle Babylonian *Ku-un-na, Ku-un-nu* etc., Nuzu *Ku-un-na, Kun-nu-ia* etc., Alal. *Ku-ni-ia, Ku-un-ni* etc., Ugar. *Ku-ni-ya* etc., Alašian XIVth century *Ku-ni-e-a*.[3]

ku-ra-no KN [*Kyllênos*] Ugar. *Kur-wa-na*.

ku-ta-i-jo KN *Kytaios*? Cf. Hurrian onomastic element *kut-*.[4]

ma-ra-pi-jo KN [*Maraphios*] Cf. W-S *marpe'* "healing," *merappe'* "healer," p. 249 above.

mi-ka-ri-jo PY [*Mikkaliôn*] Cf. Heb. *Mîkâl*.

mi-sa-ra-jo KN W-S for "Egyptian," Ugar. gentilic *mṣry*, pers. n. *Mṣry, Mi-iṣ-ri-ya, Mṣrn*, Alal. *Mi-iz-ru*.

mo-da KN, PY See following name.

mu-da KN Akk. *mûdû*, honorific title: "notable," "known (to the king)," "knowing," widely used at Ugarit.

mu-ka-ra (fem.) KN [*Mykalê*, a cape in Asia Minor] Akk. pers. n. *Mu-kal-la, Mu-kal-lim* (Sumer. div. n. *Mu-gál-la*), Ugar. *Mkl*, Canaan. div. n. *Mkl* (Bet-Shean), *Ršp Mkl* (Cyprus).[5]

[1] This Sicilian name is non-Greek. V. BÉRARD, LXIV, IV, 472, plausibly explained it as Phoen. *qaṭanā* "little," along with some other East Sicilian toponyms (cf. now the Syrian *Qaṭanum* = *Qaṭna*).

[2] CXCL, 188, 230.

[3] XXXIXa, No. I: 5.

[4] CXCI, 231.

[5] CIA, 108, and cf. pp. 311 ss. above.

mu-ta-pi KN W-S **Mût-'abi,* cf. Ugarit *Mtb'l,* Amarna *Mut-Baḫlu,* Alal. *Mu-u-ta, Mu-ut-ta, Mu-ut-tu.*

na-ru KN Ugar. *Nrn, Nryn,* Alal. *Na-ra-ḫi,* Nuzu *Na-ra-a-a, Na-ri-ia.*

na-ta-ra-ma MY Alal. *Na-ta-ru-ma.*

o-ku-ka PY [*Ôgygos, Ôgygia*] Sem. *'āgag* "to burn, to flame," cf. Bibl. *'Ăgāg* and above, p. 212.

pa-da-ro KN [*Pandaros*] Ugar. *Pdrn, Pdr-mlk, 'bd-pdr,* and div. n. *Pdry*; for *Pandaros,* cf. Ugar. *Pndr,* Alal. *Pa-an-tar-aš-šu-ra* (Hurrian *pand-* "right").

pa-di-jo KN [*Pandiôn*] Ugar. *Pdy, Pa-di-ia, Pdyn,* from the common Semitic root *pādâ* "to ransom, to redeem."

pa-ja-ni-jo KN [*Paianios*] Ugar. *Pyn.*

pa-pa-jo PY [*Pamphaios*] Ugar. *Ppn, Pa-pa-na,* Alal. *Pa-pa-e, Pa-pa-ia,* etc. (Hurrian *pab/p* "mountain").

pa-pa-ro and *pa$_2$-pa$_2$-ro* KN [*barbaros*? place name *Paparos*?] Ugar. *P[p]rn, Prpr.*

pa$_2$-ra-jo KN [Pharaios?] Alal. *Pa-a-la-ia,* for *Ba'alaya* (cf. *ibid. Ba-a-la* and *Pa-a-la* etc.); cf. Amarna and Ugar. *Ba'luya.*

pa-ra-ko KN [*Phalaikos,* mount *Plakos*] Ugar. *Prk,* Alal. *Pa-ra-ak-ki* (Akk. *parakku* "shrine").

pa-ra-ti-jo KN [*Pallantios*] Ugar. *Prt, Prtn, Prtwn,* Alal. *Pa-ra-at-ti.*

pa-ra-to KN [*Platôn*?] Cf. preceding name.

pa-wi-no KN [*Phaennos, Phaïnos*] Ugar. *Pwn.*

pe-ri-ta KN [*Peritas*] Perhaps Ugar. *Birtn* "Berytian"?

pe-te-u KN [Not *Pentheus*] Ugar. *Pity* (Ugar. *pit,* Heb. *pe'ā* "edge, out-skirt")?

pu-ko-ro-PY [*Purkolos*] Cf. Ugar. *Pqr.*

pu-re-wa KN [*Phyleus*] Cf. Ugar. *Plwn* or Alal. *Pu-ra-wa-ma.*

ru-ta$_2$-no (fem.) KN Perhaps Ugar. *ltn* "dragon"?

sa-ke-re-u PY [GEORGIEV: *Zagreus*] Ugar. *Sgryn, Sqrn,* or *Ṣġr* (*ṣġr* "small," cf. pp. 202 s. above, as prototype of *Zagreus*).

sa-ke-re-wo PY Variant of preceding.

si-da-jo KN [*Sidaios*] Ugar. *Sdy, S̈dy, Šdyn.*

si-ra-no KN [*Silānos*] Ugar. *Sln, S̀rn, S̈rn.*

si-ri-jo PY [*Sirios*?] Ugar. *S̈ryn,* Alal. (fem.) *Si-ri-ia.*

si-za KN Ugar. *S̀z, Szn.*

su-ke-re KN Hurrian: Ugar. *Su-uk-ri-ya-nu,* Alal. *Šu-uk-ri,* Nuzu: several names with this element.

u-ra-jo KN [*Hylaios, Hyraios?*] Ugar. *Uryn,* Alal. *U-ra-an,* (fem.) *U-ra-ia.*

u-ra-mo-no KN [*Hylamnos?*] Ugar. *Urm,* Alal. *U-ru-me* (place-name), Alašia [*U*]*r-ru-um-ma.*[1]

However ambiguous some of these equations may be, the preceding list shows that at least a certain part of the non-Greek names borne by inhabitants of Crete and the Peloponnese of the late Mycenaean age were Syrian (W-S and Hurrian). Syrians, thus, came to the Aegean not only as sailors and merchants, but as permanent settlers as well.

Evidence of the Minoan and Eteocretan Inscriptions

Tablets from Hagia Triada (near Phaistos) and inscriptions on votive objects, written in Linear A, demonstrate the presence of a Syrian, Semitic-speaking ethnic element in Minoan Crete. The decipherment of Linear A by Ventris permitted us to look into the cognate writing of Linear A ("Minoan"). Their language proved not to be Greek. After establishing the syllabic values for most of the Linear A signs, scholars began to investigate the language. One school tried to recognize there certain features of the Luwian language. Cyrus H. Gordon, in 1957, was stricken by the Semitic character of the names of different vessels in the HT (Hagia Triada) tablet 31, which were accompanied by pictographic determinatives of the corresponding vessels. The brevity and limited vocabulary of the HT tablets made it difficult to proceed with the analysis of their language; nevertheless, in the same year 1957 Gordon was able to announce that it was Semitic. His first impression was that the Minoan language belonged to the W-S group; [2] then he worked for several years under the conviction that it was East Semitic (Akkadian); [3] until in 1962, a new careful edition of Linear A inscriptions on stone [4] provided him with a sufficient amount of new material to firmly recognize again the predominantly W-S character of the "Minoan" language.[5] The progress of Gordon's study can best be learned from his own publications.

As in most cases of new conceptions, which radically alter tradi-

[1] EA 37: 24; for restoration cf. xxxixa, No. I: 7.
[2] ccxix.
[3] ccvii; ccxvii; ccxvi.
[4] W. C. Brice, *Inscriptions in the Minoan Script of Class A*, London, 1961.
[5] ccxviii.

tionally accepted views, GORDON's discovery was met with an understandable degree of caution. Later, however, even non-Semitist students in the Minoan-Mycenaean field had to agree that at least "it seems to be a fact that certain words in Linear A resemble equivalent terms in Semitic languages." [1] Scholars who disagreed with GORDON identified, this notwithstanding, new Semitic words in Linear A.[2] What must be stressed, is the fact that not merely single nouns, but words of other grammatical categories (verbs, prepositions, conjunctions) in Linear A proved to be W-S, and that an entire sentence (a dedication) is composed in perfect agreement with West Semitic vocabulary and grammar. This indicates that we are in presence not just of a few Semitic loan-words for exotic goods, but that the Minoan scribes actually thought and wrote in a W-S language.

As long as GORDON emphasized the Akkadian character of the HT tablets, a question could arise: why were they not written in standard Akkadian cuneiform? True, it was already known that the use of one writing-system to render a language usually written in another system is by no means a unique phenomenon. Thus, Hurrian and Akkadian texts in Ugarit were sometimes written in the native alphabetic script, devised for a W-S language; [3] an Aramaic magic text was transliterated in Egyptian demotic; [4] Aramaic incantations were written down in Akkadian cuneiform;[5] Canaanites of early second millennium apparently tried to write their language in Egyptian hieroglyphs.[6] However, the recognition of the W-S character of the Linear A texts clarified the situation. They were composed before the end of the XVth century (and started considerably earlier), i.e. prior to the Ugaritic alphabetic texts and to the spreading of the Canaanite alphabetical system in Syria and Phoenicia. The W-S population came to Crete not having yet a writing of its own. It adopted the Cretan Linear A (locally developed from earlier hieroglyphic script) for writing in

[1] XCIX, 151.

[2] Maurice POPE, the first to accept the theory of HT language as Semitic, though disagreeing with many of GORDON's readings, identified *ku-ni-su* as Akk. *ku-ni-šu* "emmer wheat"; PERUZZI recognized *sa-mu-ku* = *ṣimmu-qîm* "cakes of day raisins."

[3] Hurrian: the long text UM 4, and a few shorter ones; Akkadian: UM 102-105. [See p. 388 below].

[4] LXXVI.

[5] CCVIII; CCXII.

[6] CCL, 612.

Canaanite, just as its modified form, Linear B, became the writing medium for Mycenaean Greek.

The linguistic and onomastic milieu [1] as revealed by the Linear A texts is exactly the same as in Ugarit, where a mixed W-S and Hurrian Semitized population lived in a state of perfect symbiosis. While names of Syrian origin in the Mycenaean (Linear B) texts form only a minority in a predominantly Greek milieu, the Minoan (Linear A) onomastica known so far is practically all Syrian. This betrays the existence of a solid and compact Semitic population in the eastern and central parts of Crete.[2] It was by far more important than mere commercial foreign enclaves in harbor cities, because Semitic speech in Crete survived the Linear A texts by a thousand years. This results from another important discovery made by Cyrus H. GORDON in 1962. Greek authors stated that Eteocretans ("true Cretans"), the remainder of the pre-Greek population of the island, continued to exist as a distinct, non-Greek-speaking population of the eastern part of Crete late in classical time. A few extant inscriptions, written in Greek characters, but in an utterly un-Greek, incomprehensible language, were identified as Eteocretan (three from Praisos, one from Psychro, one—a Greco-Eteocretan bilingual—from Dreros). They were epigraphically attributed to about 600, 500 and 300 B.C. GORDON established that their language, though now written in the more convenient Greek alphabet instead of the clumsy Minoan syllabary, continued to be W-S. GORDON conventionally calls it "Phoenician," as "the ancient Greeks would have called" them, or "Alphabetic Minoan." [3] Notwithstanding the very bad state of preservation and the rather bewildering orthography of the inscriptions, he was able to discern such Semitic sentences as *me y mar krk o kl es y es* (Text III: 3-4) = *mi hûʾ mar krak ʾô kol ʾîš we-ʾîš* "whosoever (whether) son of the city or any man at all"; *onadesi emetipi mit* = *ʾntš* (pers. n. in

[1] For onomastica, cf. also XCIa; CDXIV; CDXIVa.

[2] An extra-Cretan source on Cretan second millennium onomastica is provided by an Egyptian writing-board of about 1500 with the heading, "To make names of Keftiu." It was first published by W. Max MÜLLER, *MVAG* 1900, 1, 6-9, then revised and published again by T. E. PEET, CDXII (1927). According to our investigation, the fourteen names preserved belong to the Syrian onomastica of that epoch; they include W-S, Akkadian, and Hurrian names (XXXIXa).

[3] CCXIV, 213. [See also C. H. GORDON, "Toward a Grammar of Minoan," *Orientalia*, NS XXXII (1963), 292-297.]

Cypriot Phoenician) *ham-meṯṯibi mêt* "O., the benefactor, has died"; *mosel os phraiso* = *môšel ʿoz Prays-* "the mighty ruler of Praisos", and other.[1] In the bilingual, he found a factual correspondence between the Greek and the Eteocretan versions.[2] We refer for details to GORDON's two articles.

What is, in particular, important from the historical point of view is the fact that the Eteocretans, contrary to the Phoenician colonies in the West, did not use the Phoenician alphabet for their inscriptions. This proves that they were not recent migrants from Phoenicia, but direct descendants of the W-S Minoans from mid-second millennium, who settled in Crete *before* the invention of the Phoenician alphabet and were cut off from their Levantine kinsmen by the temporary rupture of maritime relations after 1200. They have also preserved even in Greek script the Minoan disregard for distinguishing voiced and unvoiced consonants. Semitic presence in the easternmost part of Crete could be deduced from the local personal and geographical names (see p. 140 above); it is interesting to trace down Eteocretan Semitic epigraphy as far west as Psychro.

When BELOCH tendentiously tried to ridicule Phoenician presence in any spot of Greece, he ironically asked: if there were Phoenicians in Crete, why are they not listed among the five peoples of the island according to *Odyss.* XIX: 175-177: Achaeans, Eteocretans, Cydonians, Dorians, and Pelasgians? [3] Now C. H. GORDON demonstrated that precisely one of those five peoples, the Eteocretans, were Phoenicians! This revelation came too late to convince BELOCH and his generation, too late to support the efforts of Victor BÉRARD, but not too late to remove the survivals of the spell cast by BELOCH and his school upon Hellenic studies.

EPIGRAPHIC EVIDENCE FOR SYRO-AEGEAN MARITIME RELATIONS IN THE SECOND MILLENNIUM

A few words must be devoted to another of BELOCH's assertions: that the Phoenicians simply could not reach the Aegean before the VIIIth century, because their ships were too small for such voyages (above, p. 324). Nobody denies now that the Levantine coast and the Aegean were connected by lively relations as early as the

[1] *Ibid.*, 212 ss.
[2] CCXIII.
[3] LVI, 127.

second millennium, but something of BELOCH's obsolete attitude still remains: the Phoenicians of the second millennium are considered as an immobile, passive element, never venturing away from their coast-strip, while all merits of mastering the seas and establishing trade-relations with the East are ascribed to the Minoans and Achaeans.

This is, of course, completely invalidated by archaeological and epigraphic proofs of Semitic penetration into the Aegean, but beside this indirect data we possess direct epigraphic information on the level of Ugaritic ship-building and the scope of Ugaritic maritime travels in the IId millennium. Among the most recent epigraphic discoveries at Ras Shamra figures the Akkadian tablet RŠ 20.212, a letter from the Hittite court to a Ugaritic king of the late XIIth century with the request to furnish one large ship for transporting 2,000 measures of grain from the land of Mukiš (northern neighbor of Ugarit) to the city of Ura (in Cilicia) in order to save the local population from famine. The letter states that all this cargo would require one, at most two trips.[1] NOUGAYROL, in his recently published report on new Akkadian texts from Ras Shamra, tries to evaluate the capacity of that ship. Since the unit of volume is here, as elsewhere, certainly the *kor* = 300 *qa* = about 300 liters, the total cargo makes about 6,000 hectoliters of grain, or *450 metric tons*. "The author of the letter," says NOUGAYROL, "admitted thus that the king of Ugarit disposed, or could dispose, of ships capable of carrying about 500 tons, or perhaps even more, if one takes into account the containers. This very high figure is not improbable, according to the informations which we have on the Egyptian fleet of that time, or on the later Phoenician, then Greco-Roman fleets."[2] A vessel of 500 tons—even half as big—certainly could even cross the Atlantic,[3] not only the short sea-distances on the route: Ugarit—Cyprus—Southwest Asia Minor—Crete.

Ugaritic ships actually performed such trips. We have already mentioned the text RŠ 16.238 speaking of a Ugaritic merchant who returned with his ship from Kapturi (Crete).[4] Another very impor-

[1] CCCLXXXVIIa, 165.

[2] *Loc. cit.*

[3] *Santa Maria*, the largest ship in Columbus' first expedition, was 233 tons; his two other vessels were much smaller. The light boats of the Vikings crossed the North Atlantic from Norway to Iceland, Greenland and the mainland of North America.

[4] CCCXC, 107 (cf. p. 107, n. 1 above).

tant letter figures among the newly discovered texts of Ras Shamra (RŠ 20.238). It is a copy of a message sent by a king of Ugarit to a king of Alašia, and it depicts conditions on the eve of the great eastward push of the Sea Peoples. Pirate ships of the enemy already made ravaging raids upon the shores of the Ugaritic kingdom. "Does not my father know," writes the king of Ugarit, "that all my troops . . . are now in the Hittite country, and all my ships are in the Lycian country?"[1] Certainly, Ugarit and other vassal states of the Hittite empire did their best to bar the road to the invading Peoples of the Sea, whose final break-through caused the destruction and disappearance of both Ḫatti and Ugarit. But where did the Ugaritic fleet try to defeat and stop the redoubtable invaders? Not in the coast-waters of Syria, not even near the shores of Cilicia, but at the farthest advanced defences of the Mediterranean main, in Lycia, at the very entrance into the Aegean.

The myth that the Phoenicians did not become a people of experienced sailors before the first millennium must disappear forever. They certainly sailed to the Aegean, and beyond it, at least a thousand years earlier, as shown by the Phoenician Middle Bronze Age weapons and ornaments in Illyria, the penetration of the Torque-Bearers (above, p. 326) and the Akkadian inscription of Cythera (p. 142). We have now documentary proof that Ugaritic trading ships and warships went to the Aegean in the XIVth and the XIIIth centuries.[2]

[1] CCCLXXXVIIa, 166.

[2] The new technique of underwater archaeology made recently an important contribution toward restoring the scope of Syrian maritime ventures westward. The Museum of the University of Pennsylvania expedition found an ancient wreck just off Cape Gelidonya in Lycia. This was a small ship heavily loaded with copper ingots from Cyprus (stamped with Cypro-Minoan signs) and bronze scrap, and "it is almost certain that a smith traveled on board the ship" to produce new tools (L, 247). Pottery sherds date the shipwreck around 1200. Though the cargo was taken in Cyprus, the main producer of ancient Mediterranean copper, the scarabs, the oil-lamp and the skipper's seal are Syrian, and the analysis of the wood also shows that the ship "was probably made with Syrian wood" (*ibid.*, 248). We are in presence of a Syrian vessel which not only carried copper to the Aegean, but also served as an ambulant metallurgic workship to supply with tools the harbors it visited. This ship was by no means exceptional; closely similar tools have been found, about forty years ago, in the Acropolis hoard in Athens: "this would suggest only that the latter objects had been brought to Greece in a vessel such as ours," concludes George F. Bass (XLIX, 276), who directed this underwater "excavation" and described its results (XLIX and L).

The Theory of Dussaud vs. Bérard

Victor Bérard died in 1931, two years after the discovery of Ras Shamra. The first excavations there, which revealed masses of Mycenaean ceramics and Mycenaean-style sepulchral vaults, led to the assumption that a veritable Mycenaean colonization took place at Ugarit in the XIVth and XVth centuries. This enabled Dussaud to reverse the theory defended by Bérard; he concluded his obituary of this scholar thus: "The typical legend of Cadmos is best explained as that of a group having come from the Greek mainland and infiltrated into Phoenicia, which stayed there a certain time, then returned to Greece and brought thither new techniques, namely writing." [1]

Much later the same opinion as to the ways of Oriental cultural penetration into Mycenaean Greece was advanced by T. B. L. Webster. For him, the strong Oriental background of the Mycenaean myths and stories transmitted to the Homeric age was beyond doubt. But, in order to explain this dependence, he again took recourse to the assumption of Mycenaean settlers in Ugarit and Alalaḫ: "I hope to make plausible (that) they also transmitted local stories home"; [2] "in Ugarit, a Mycenaean settlement is almost certain"; [3] and in the "Conclusion and Summary": [4]

> Mycenaean establishments in Cyprus, Ugarit, Alalakh and elsewhere [5] were open to literary and artistic ideas from the East, quite apart from what the Mycenaeans in Knossos must have absorbed from the Minoans. Traders may have been responsible for the loan words for clothing and spices; but princes, warriors, poets, and master craftsmen also journeyed between the Mycenaean world and the East, and their commerce was ideas and art forms.

Could such means of cultural transmission have taken place? Theoretically—yes, even if only as a secondary factor in the process of Semitic cultural expansion into the Aegean. Has this theory, however, any firm historical confirmation?

There are no archaeological proofs of Mycenaean settlements in Cyprus prior to its conquest by the Peoples of the Sea; the abundance of Mycenaean wares is due to import and local imitations.[6] The

[1] CLIII, 393.
[2] DXXXVII, 37.
[3] *Op. cit.*, 66; note the restriction "almost."
[4] *Op. cit.*, 284 s.
[5] Where else, for instance?
[6] Immerwahr, CCLXVIII, 12, concludes that Cyprus was not really colonized by Mycenaeans: there were only traders' points and perhaps a prince in

island passed under Hittite sovereignty from about 1300, and fought the Aegean invaders as a traditional ally of Ugarit.[1] A recent study of the so-called Cypro-Minoan syllabary [2] led to the conclusion that it does not derive from Cretan Linear B, and its resemblance to Linear A is not much pronounced; it did not come directly from Crete, but more probably from Syria where it had been invented, perhaps in imitation of the Cretan Linear A, which became known to the Syrians before 1400.[3]

Enkomi. The assumption that a Mycenaean prince already ruled in the ancient capital of Alašia before the Greek installation on the island was advanced by SCHAEFFER, CDLXIII, 323-343. It was based on the observation that the last two men to have been buried in the grave-vault beneath the most important building of Enkomi were exceptionally tall, and one of them had at his side a bronze sword of a type known all over Europe at the end of the Bronze Age, but having probably originated in Mycenaean Greece. Exceptional stature was not, however, peculiar for the race of the Mycenaean Greeks. As to the evidence of the sword, we now know that Mycenaean swords imitated Oriental models (CCLXVIIa; CDXXXIX). SCHAEFFER himself (CDXLIII, 339) mentions that a few samples of the same type of weapon as that found in the Enkomi vault, were discovered in Egypt, and that one of them carried the cartouche of the Pharaoh Seti II (1215-1210). If Pharaoh Seti II was not declared a Mycenaean because of possessing such a sword, why should the person buried in the Enkomi vault be? Moreover, in 1953, SCHAEFFER discovered at Ras Shamra a bronze sword of exactly the same type, engraved with the cartouche of Pharaoh Merneptah and manifestly manufactured in the metallurgic shops of Ugarit (CDLIII, 169-177). SCHAEFFER (CDXLIII, 335 s.) defined that the ruler's residence of Enkomi (so-called Building 18) was built between 1350 and 1250—as he believed it, by a foreigner, according to the architectural style reminiscent of certain details at Cnossos, Tiryns and Mycenae (*ibid.*, 342 s.). We know, however, from the Hittite indictment of Maduwwattaš, written shortly before 1200 (CCIII, 157 s.), that Alašia ([URU]*A-la-ši-ya-wa*) was indeed attacked by Attaršiyaš of Aḫḫiya and his ally "the man of Piggaya," but they were repulsed by their rival, the unruly Hittite vassal Madduwattaš (CCIII, § 36).

[1] "The country of Alašia is a country of the Sun (= Hittite king) and pays him tribute," states Arnuwandaš, the last but one king of Ḫatti, in the "dossier" of Madduwattaš, § 36. The recently discovered correspondence between the king of Ugarit and the king (or the "great intendant") of Alašia, belonging to the time of maritime invasions from the West, depicts Alašia as a steady ally of Ugarit against the raiding flotillas (RŠ 20. 238 and 20.18, CCCLXXXVIIa, 165). The "great intendant" of Alašia bears the name *E-šu-wa-ra*—a typical Indo-Aryan name (composed with Indian *súvar* "sun"), one of the many introduced into the Hurrian environment after 1500.

[2] CCLXXV.

[3] *Op. cit.*, esp. 15-19. DUSSAUD, ap. CDXLIII, 4, even wrote about the Cypro-Minoan tablets: "One may suppose that it was invented by the scribes of the king of Alasia in imitation of the script of Ugarit." This goes too far: the Ugaritic script is alphabetic, while the Cypro-Minoan is syllabic. Since, however, the Minoan Linear A from Crete was used to transcribe a W-S speach (p. 344 ss. above), its principles may very easily have been learned

"At Alalakh," says Sir Leonard WOOLLEY who headed its excavations, "there was no colony of Mycenaean merchants such as at this time existed at Ugarit [1] . . . but Ugarit was a harbour town whereas Alalakh lies well inland; it is likely enough that there was a colony of the sort at al Mina, the port of Alalakh . . .",[2] but since all the ancient strata of al Mina had been washed away by the Orontes,[3] nothing is left to make this likelihood more substantial, except the old a priori view that if Mycenaean wares were imported to Syria, this could have been done by none other than "agents of Greek firms."

The question of Ugarit remains. The impression of the first excavations was so strong that, early in the thirties, some scholars assumed that the Ugaritic king *Nqmd* was the Greek *Nikomêdês*, that the geographical name *Yman* (UM 2: 19) was Ionia (Assyr. *Iaman*, pronounced *Iawan*, Heb. *Yāwān*), and the alleged deity *Ršp Ddm* was Apollo Didymaeus.[4] But it was soon clarified that *Nqmd* (*Niqmadu*) was a pure W-S name signifying "Hadd is the avenger," [5] and that the land of *Yman*, "where there are buffaloes by myriads" (UM 51: I: 43) was a district somewhere in Syria, not far from Amurru, according to the context. Later, it also became clear that there was no such deity as *Ršp Ddm*, but two distinct deities, *Ršp* and *Ddmš*.[6] A recently discovered Sumero-Hurro-Ugaritic list of gods proved, moreover, that *Ddmš* (*Da-ad-mi-iš*) was not a god, but a goddess.[7] The date of the presumed conquest of

by the Syrian cousins of the Eteocretans (before they invented their alphabetic systems) and transmitted by them to the Cypriots.

[1] We shall presently see whether the existence of a Mycenaean colony at Ugarit is really certain or even, as WEBSTER (cf. p. 355 above) put it more cautiously, "almost certain."

[2] DLV, 151.

[3] *Ibid.*, 166.

[4] CXIV, 32-56; CXVII, 110; CCLXVI, 169-178.

[5] CXXVI; DXI.

[6] CCCLXXXIXa, 82, (RŠ 20.24); Akk. transcription *Da-ad-mi-iš*.

[7] CCCLXXXVIIa, 168: ᵈ*šu-zi-an-na*: *ta-at-mi-i*[*š*: *da-ad-mi-iš*]. The Sumerian ᵈ*Šuzianna* was "the younger wife of Enlil, the wet nurse of Sin," and was identified with the healing goddess Gula (CXII, II, 3, No. 354: 146; *ibid.*, IV, 1, No. 651: 19). On the other hand, another Sumerian healing goddess, Išḫara, bore the surname *bêlit da-ad-me* "Lady of the Dwelling" (CXI, No. 1494; DII, 4). We may thus consider *Dadmiš* a derivation of Akk. *dadmu* "dwelling." It is interesting to quote CDXV, 397, n. 2: "A. BOUCHÉ-LECLERCQ remarked that the etymology of Apollo Didymaeus explained by the epithet 'twin' is a late sacerdotal gloss. The name of Didymes seems to be pre-Hellenic . . ."

Ugarit by the Mycenaeans was lowered to the period immediately *after* Niqmadu, i.e., to about 1350—a hundred and fifty years prior to the historic invasion of the Peoples of the Sea.[1] But the uncovering of the royal archives of Ugarit showed that the Semitic dynasty of Niqmadu and his predecessors continued to rule Ugarit until its ultimate destruction by the Peoples of the Sea about 1200, and that its last king bore the glorious W-S name of ʿAmmurapi.[2] The strong artistic influence of the Mycenaean world upon Ugarit proved not to have had any political background there.

This does not favor the admission of the presence of Mycenaean "princes and warriors" in Ugarit, unless they came there for studies, as the legendary Scythian prince Anacharsis was said to have come to Greece, many centuries later, in order to learn Greek wisdom. We know, however, from the newly discovered Ugaritic documents (as we already knew from the Hittite materials on the Aḫḫiyawā) that those "princes and warriors" used to come to the shores of Cyprus and Syria with much less idealistic goals. An establishment of Mycenaean traders and potters is much easier to assume. Ugarit was a truly international city; besides the native Canaanite and Hurrian population it included multinational elements from many cities and countries. As we have pointed elsewhere,[3] foreigners were not discriminated against or restricted in Ugarit; they had the same rights and the same duties as the natives, belonged to municipal units and vocational corporations, served in the armed forces of the kingdom and could be raised to the highest social status—to the rank of *mariannu* or even to the position of an autonomous vassal ruler. The administrative tablets from Ugarit mention hundreds, perhaps over a thousand, personal names borne by the inhabitants of the kingdom and its neighbors and visitors, but none similar to those listed in the Linear B tablets can be identified as Mycenaean Greek. The entire Ugaritic onomastica is either W-S or Hurrian, with a few Hittite and other Anatolian names, one or two Indo-Mitannian, and several Akkadian or Akkadianized.

Furthermore, the Ugaritic administrative texts frequently mention foreigners by their ethnic names. They appear as organized groups, like the Assyrian and Egyptian residents of Ugarit, or as individuals. Among the latter we again find Assyrians and Egyp-

[1] DXVIII, 64 s.; CDLI, 99 ss.
[2] CCCXC, XXXVII s.
[3] XXXVIII, 71-74.

tians, then Subaraeans, Mittanites, Hittites, Arzawians, Hurrians, Amorites, Canaanites, Nuḫaššeans, Alašiots, and natives of several Phoenician and Palestinian cities: Aradus, Berytus, Byblos, Sidon, Tyre, Sarepta, Acco, Gezer, Iamnia (Yabne), Azotus (Ašdod), Ioppa (Yaphô). One Lycian (*Bn-Lky*) figures in a Ugaritic tablet, but there is no mention of any natives of the Aegean. No Achaeans, Aeolians, Ionians, Cretans, Caphtorians, Cnossians, Rhodians or any other ethnic or geographical names of the Greco-Aegean world can be found in Ugaritic texts.[1]

These indications are quite precise. They prove that no Mycenaean settlement existed at Ugarit in the XIVth and XIIIth centuries, though Ugarit was the principal link between the Near East and the Aegean and the greatest importer of Mycenaean wares. These were most probably brought by Ugaritic merchants who went to Crete for them (or perhaps even farther); if some of the Mycenaean artifacts came on Mycenaean trade ships (of which we have no proof), the Greek merchants and sailors did not stay at Ugarit for any appreciable time. "The agents of the Greek firms would have no business in the interior because when once goods had been landed from aboard ship their land transport would naturally be the affair of Asiatic carriers," said Sir Leonard WOOLLEY about the hypothetical Mycenaean tradesmen at the port of Alalaḫ; [2] this is true for their counterparts at Ugarit as well. In any case, they were not at all integrated into Ugaritic society, and this completely excludes any possibility of their having learned so much of the W-S and Akkadian religious and poetic literature that this study could have comprehensibly and profoundly influenced the entire Greek spiritual culture for centuries to come.

Of course, the Ugaritic god *Kŝr* (*Kušarru* in syllabic cuneiform) was supposed to have Kaphtor for his throne. But this does not signify that *Kŝr* was a native Cretan deity, imported to Ugarit by Aegean settlers. *Kŝr* is a good W-S name: "the appropriate, the useful, the one who adjusts things"—a most fitting name for the artisan and artist of the divine family (cf. Akk. *kešêru* "to bring in order, to support, to restore"). If Kaphtor was assigned to him as his domain, this was because Crete, before it was conquered by the Greeks, was considered a part of the Canaanite world. No, the

[1] We pointed to these facts XL, 193 s. SCHACHERMEYR, CDXLI, 377, and LIVERANI, CCCLXXXVIII, 52 s. came to the same conclusions.

[2] DLV, 151.

"princes, warriors, poets" (and priests, too) who "journeyed between the Mycenaean world and the East" and imported into the former "ideas and forms" (p. 350) were not Greeks; they were, as the Greeks called them, Phoenicians, who landed on the Greek islands and mainland, founded cities with Phoenician names, established Phoenician dynasties, introduced Phoenician cults and taught the secrets of Oriental magic, religion, and poetry to the natives who were eager to learn and to memorize them.

Circumcision among the Achaeans

There is a remarkable epigraphic testimony of how strong and deep the Semitic religious impact upon the Achaeans and other Aegean peoples was. This is an Egyptian text, contemporary with the Late Mycenaean period. There has been much writing and controversy about it, but it obtains its real significance in the context of this study.

The famous inscription of Merneptah which describes this Pharaoh's victory over the Libyans and their allies, the Peoples of the Sea (about 1225), states that the following carnal trophies were taken from the slain enemies: from the dead Libyans, the phalli were cut off, for they had *qrn·t,* and from the dead Šardana, Šak(a)ruša, Turuša, and 'Aqiyawaša, "who had no *qrn·t,*" the hands were cut off (the Ruku, or Lycians, are not mentioned in this connection).[1] Now, *qrn·t,* as was finally proved, signifies "foreskin," which is confirmed by pictures illustrating Merneptah's triumphal inscription and representing the Libyan phalli of a characteristic uncircumcised shape, as well as by the phonetic correspondence between Egypt. *qrn·t* and Heb. *'orlā* (<*ġrlt*) "foreskin."[2] The fact of being circumcised is specifically stated about the Achaeans: "['*A-qi-*]*ya-wa-ša* who had no foreskins, slain, whose hands were carried off, (for) they had no [foreskins]," and with less emphasis about the other three Peoples of the Sea.[3] According to Breasted, "the question of the homes of these peoples is in greater uncertainty

[1] LXXVIII, III, §§ 587 s.
[2] *Ibid.*, § 587, n. *h*. Indeed, the Semitic *ġ* was regularly transcribed by the Egyptians as *q* (sometimes *g*), and the Semitic *l*, especially after another liquid, frequently dissimilated (or spelled) to *n*. The explanation of *qrn·t* as "foreskin" was first proposed by Brugsch. The interpretation of *qrn·t* as "phallus-bag" (goulfic) is now abandoned. Cf. CCCXLIII, II, I, 558 s.
[3] LXXVII, III, § 588.

that the rendering of *qrn·t*, and should be decided by this rendering rather than the reverse."[1] For, as remarked by Ed. MEYER,[2]

> it is very amazing to meet circumcision here, in the maritime world. Circumcision was at home in Egypt since the oldest time, and from there it was adopted by the Israelites and the Phoenicians.[3] It is imaginable that the Šardana and the tribes connected with them have also borrowed this custom from Egypt. (But what about the ʾAqiyawaša) ?) Should one admit that the Achaeans shared it temporarily, at least in the colonial region ? Or are the Aqaiwaša nevertheless a quite different people, and then perhaps identical with the Aḫḫiyawa, and the latter not being Achaeans ?

We see how difficult it was to accept that a Greek tribe could ever have observed so un-Greek a rite as circumcision. There can, however, be no doubt that *ʾAqiyawaša* = *Aḫḫiyawā* = *Achai(w)oi*, and that they invaded Egypt not from some hypothetical "colonial region,"[4] but from the Aegean itself. One is bound to recognize that circumcision prevailed among them in the Mycenaean age, as well as among the Tyrrhenians (from Lemnos or Lydia) and the unidentified, but probably Aegean, tribe of Šak(a)ruša. Circumcision in the ancient world was, indeed, limited to Egypt and the Western and Southern Semites. Whether the Semites borrowed it from the Egyptians, or it had been introduced into Egypt by the Proto-Semitic element of the Egyptian population in the pre-dynastic period—this we do not intend to decide.[5] But outside the Egypto-Syro-Arabian circle it could exist only as a borrowing from there.

[1] *Ibid.*, § 587, n. *h*.

[2] CCCLXIII, II, 1, 559.

[3] MEYER, *loc. cit.*, n. 1 quotes Josh. 5: 9 and Herod. II: 104 as evidence that the Israelites and the Phoenicians adopted this custom from Egypt. Cf., however, n. 5 below.

[4] It was supposed for some time that the Achaean "colonial power" was located in Pamphylia. Even if this were true, this could not have been the cause for observing the rite of circumcision: it was not known in Anatolia. SCHAEFFER, CDXLIII, 352, n. 3, tried to explain the adaptation of circumcision by the Achaeans by admitting their sojourn at Cyprus, in an Oriental environment; he believed that Cyprus must have been an indispensable base for any maritime invasion of the Delta. However, A. GJERSTAD, A. FURUMARK, and F. MATZ, in studies quoted *op. cit.*, 354, n. 1, are opposed to the assumption of Mycenaean colonization in Cyprus prior to 1200 (which agrees with epigraphic evidence, cf. p. 355, n. 6 and p. 356, n. 1). The Achaeans and their allies at the time of Merneptah landed in Libya, to the west of the Delta, as auxiliaries of the Libyans; Cyprus lies in quite a different direction, while the straight distance between Crete and Libya is only about 170 miles, less than from Cyprus to the coast of the Delta.

[5] In any case, Eg. *qrn·t* is the adaptation of Sem. *ġrlt*, not the opposite (cf. XXVII, IX: A: 8).

Besides, we cannot ascribe it to the influence of individual missionaries who simply did not exist at that time. Only the settlement in Greece of an important group of population whose religious and ritual principles would be adopted by large masses of the people, could have introduced the general spread of circumcision among the Achaeans. And we have already seen in the first chapter of this study that the tribe of the Danaans which dominated the Peloponnese was of W-S origin, and that the ethnic notions of the Achaeans and Danaans essentially coincided. Circumcision among the Achaeans, attested by the eye-witness Merneptah, shows most convincingly how strongly W-S ritual customs became rooted among them. Circumcision is not an easy and pleasant operation, and in later centuries it has scared away many potential proselytes from Judaism. Yet the Achaeans and the Aegean Tyrrhenians adopted it.[1] The complete breakdown of the Mycenaean state-system and civilization, and wide ethnic shifts in Greece were needed to cause the disappearance of that custom.

Greece and the Semitic East: Concluding Remarks

We have seen that important W-S settlements existed in at least three parts of Mycenaean Greece, and smaller colonies were established in several other places in that region. For Crete, the fact of a strong Semitic penetration was suspected on the basis of local toponymics and survivals in mythical names and motifs; now it is confirmed by epigraphic data as a result of C. H. Gordon's decipherment of the Minoan and Eteocretan inscriptions. The Semitic origin of the Danaans of Argolis was demonstrated by our analysis and confrontation of the Phoenician, Egyptian, and Hittite historical data on the people and country of Danuna with the intrinsic evidence of the Danaan myth cycle. For the Cadmeians of Boeotia, we have corroborated the statement of the Greek tradition on their Phoenician origin by exploring the evidence of Cadmeian religion, mythical onomastics, and geographical names. Similar data clearly points to W-S (Phoenician) presence in Laconia, the islands Thera, Anaphe, Cythera, Cos, Thasos, Tenedos, Rhodes and other places. Not only was Phoenician spoken in several parts of Mycenaean Greece,[2] but the entire Mycenaean civilization was

[1] The Philistines, however, as emphasized in the Bible, did not observe circumcision even after their having settled in a W-S milieu.

[2] Beloch, LVI, 129, trying to deride the Phoenician origin of the name

essentially a peripheral culture of the Ancient East, its westernmost extension. It is interesting to quote in this connection the recent opinion of an archaeologist on the causes of the collapse of Mycenaean civilization: [1]

> . . . it is clearly not the Mycenaeans who disappeared, but Mycenaean civilization. The strength of that civilization depended greatly upon invigorating contact with Crete and the East, from the time of the Shaft Graves onward. When contact was broken, Mycenaean culture drifted so far in sterility that it is hard to recognize.[2]

What made for the depth and breadth of the W-S impact upon Mycenaean Greece? Why did so great a number of Semitic names, motifs, terms, rites and customs survive the fall of the Mycenaean political system and preserve itself as a very significant part of the Hellenic cultural heritage? In order that one culture may be able to influence another, there must exist a certain internal similarity and correspondence between the ways of life of their bearers. Egypt, for example, has exercised a strong influence upon W-S art and architecture, but a rather insignificant one upon W-S spiritual culture—beneath any comparison to the impact of Mesopotamia. W-S influence upon Egypt, again, was quite superficial and did not survive the epoch of the New Kingdom. One of the causes thereof was probably the extremely isolated and original character of the Egyptian social and political order, whose principles of strict centralization and subordination were quite unlike the free world of the numerous small Syro-Palestinian states and city-states. Egypt, the prototype of many totalitarian statist systems of modern time, and the unruly, divided Syria were extreme contrasts.

Conversely, Greece and Syria-Palestine were very similar in their geographical and natural conditions. Both were broken, geographically dismembered territories without a central organizing axis. This brought about similar state formations and internal orders. And indeed, from the viewpoint of the social and political regime,

Kadmos, wrote with what he believed to be irony: "They must have been learned people, those ancient Thebans, who understood even Canaanite!" This is the plain truth, though . . .

[1] DVII, 74.

[2] This recognition of an "invigorating contact with Crete *and the East*" sounds rather different from what was written by another archaeologist only 13 years earlier, whose special study on the Aegean and the Orient explored exclusively "the influence of the vigorous and creative Western culture upon the civilizations of Levant" (CCLXXXIV, 3). Nowadays, the connections between the Aegean and the Levant are no more considered a one-way road.

the limit between the Ancient East and West did not coincide with the division between Europe and Asia, but lay much more to the East. In this respect, the Greek and the W-S worlds formed a common circle of small states, incapable of unification and centralization, unless if conquered by some outside empire. The Greek polis is usually contrasted to the Oriental military-bureaucratic despotisms of Egypt and Mesopotamia [1]—but the Canaanite city-states belonged to the former category, not to the latter. The ancient Greeks themselves realized this in regard to the Phoenician cities and Carthage. It would be one-sided to consider the Greek polis, evolved from the conditions of the Homeric age, as something exclusively Greek, and to oppose it to the Mycenaean order, which is characterized as Asiatic, the latter being indiscriminately defined as absolute rule of deified kings.[2] Canaanite cities, as early as the Amarna Age, were far from being despotic bureaucratic monarchies. The king's power was limited by the aristocracy, and in some cases the oligarchic city-council could rule the city without the king. The political way of life as described in the Homeric poems, presents a resemblance to the Canaanite states of the second and first millennium to no less a degree than the Mycenaean order.[3] The

[1] Strictly speaking, this is correct only in part: Mesopotamia started from the stage of city-states, and strong survivals of municipal autonomy of larger cities existed even under the truly despotic neo-Assyrian empire. But even Assyria started as an almost republican city-state. The closest so far parallel of the Mycenaean diarchy of *wanaka* ("lord") and *lawageta* ("leader of the people, commander") is the dual rule of the Old Assyrian state by *iššakkum* (Akkadianized *ensi,* the priestly ruler of the Sumerian city-states) and *ukullum* (Sumerian *ugula* "who raises the people").

[2] Thus WEBSTER, DXXXVII, II, We cannot agree with his interpretation of the Homeric phrase "honored by the people like a god" as literally meaning that the king enjoyed the status of a god—let us say, like the kings of the Agade or Ur III dynasties in the third millennium. (In the second millennium, during the existence of the Mycenaean civilization, deification of kings went out of use). Of course, kingship was always considered more or less sacred, due to its remote origin. But the quoted phrase is a standard metaphore just meaning "to honor very much." In the Amarna letter EA 21:24-26, Tušratta of Mitanni writes to his "brother," Pharaoh Amenhotep III: "Manê, my brother's messenger, and Ḫanê, the interpreter, I have honored like a god" (*ki-i i-li ur-te-i*[*b-bi-ma*]). When one of the greatest monarchs of the epoch speaks so about commoners, there can be no doubt that the phrase did not have any religious implications.

[3] "The king (in Homer) is far from undertaking personal decisions, and the secondary chiefs who surround him bear no resemblance to functionaries. All important decisions are taken after deliberation; the poems mention the basileus' closest council, *bulê,* and the general assembly, *agorê,*" DIX, 51. Agamemnon and Priam are surrounded by seven superior counselors each;

Canaanite kings of the Amarna Age are not earthly gods, ruling above the submissive mass of the population. They are real Homeric warrior-kings, *primi inter pares*, always ready personally to mount the chariot and to lead their fellow-charioteers into the battle.[1]

ROBERTSON SMITH, many decades ago, had a correct presentiment of the facts when he wrote:

> Up to this point the progress of society was much alike in the East and in the West, and the progress of religion . . . followed that of society in general. But . . . the independent evolution of Semitic religion was arrested at an early stage . . . The northern Semites . . . whose progress up to the eighth century B.C. certainly did not lag behind that of the Greeks, were deprived of political independence, and so cut short in their national development, by the advance from the Tigris to the Mediterranean of the great Assyrian monarchs . . . From this time onward the difference between the Syrian or Palestinian and the Greek was not one of race alone; it was the difference between a free citizen and a slave of an Oriental despotism.[2]

But even under the pressure of Babylonian and Persian rule the Phoenician cities preserved their autonomous municipal government. They were granted wide privileges by the kings of Persia whose sea-power entirely depended on them, and their situation was essentially the same as the conditions of Greek cities in Asia Minor, submitted to the same Persian overlordship.[3]

We believe that this essential similarity and parallel development of the state life of the West Semites and the Greeks, caused by similar geopolitical conditions, was the principal cause of the easy and fundamental adaptability of the Cretans, Achaeans and other tribes of Greece to the influence of the W-S settlers who arrived among them in the period of the greatest rise of W-S civilization and political might. In turn, a great part of the West Semites adopted the Hellenistic civilization easier and more thoroughly than any other Oriental population when, twelve centuries later, the Orient was conquered by Hellenism.[4]

this reminds us of the city administration of Succoth consisting of seventy-seven princes and elders (Judg. 8: 14), to be understood as an assembly of seventy elders headed by a closer board of seven princes.

[1] Cf. the phraseological parallels between Homeric poems and the poetic works of the Canaanite circle, CCXV; CCXXV, 101-122; CCX, 218-277.

[2] CDXXVIII, 34 s.

[3] VIPPER, DIX, 560 s., speaking of Alexander of Macedon's conquest of Phoenicia, notes: "Phoenicia turned out to resemble Greece—a country of autonomous city-cantons living in discord with each other."

[4] The most Hellenized regions of the Hellenistic Asia were North Syria with such cities as Antioch, Seleucia, Laodicea (region of former Ugarit and

These were the two greatest swings of the East Mediterranean pendulum. Chronologically, the swings from East to West preceded those from West to East. Long before Hellenism imposed itself over the ancient civilizations of the East, Semitism had exercised no less an impact upon the young civilization of Greece. Hellenism became the epilogue of the Oriental civilizations, but Semitism was the prologue of Greek civilization.

Alalaḫ), Eastern Cilicia, many cities of Central and South Syria, Transjordan, Scythopolis and Samaria in Central Palestine, and the entire Philistine coast. The Phoenician cities eagerly adopted the Greek language and Greek names, combining them with reverence of old sacral traditions, and a strong Hellenistic party arose even among the less adaptable Jews in the hills of southern Palestine. Phoenicians from Cyprus and the mainland, Cilicians and Syrians became prominent among the leading Greek philosophers.

ABBREVIATIONS OF SERIALS AND PERIODICALS

AASOR	*Annual of the American Schools of Oriental Research.*
AcOr	*Acta Orientalia.*
AfO	*Archiv für Orientforschung.*
AJA	*American Journal of Archaeology.*
AJSL	*American Journal of Semitic Languages and Literatures.*
AnOr	*Analecta Orientalia.*
AO	*Der Alte Orient.*
AOS	*American Oriental Series.*
ArOr	*Archiv Orientální.*
BASOR	*Bulletin of the American Schools of Oriental Research.*
*CAH*²	*Cambridge Ancient History, Revised Edition of Volumes I and II* (appearing in fascicles).
CRAI	*Comptes-rendus de l'Académie des Inscriptions et Belles-Lettres.*
DMOA	*Documenta et Monumenta Orientis Antiqui.*
EOL	*Jaarbericht van het Voor-Aziatisch-Egyptisch Gezelschap ,,Ex Oriente Lux''.*
HBAW	*Handbuch der Altertumswissenschaft.*
HSCP	*Harvard Studies in Classical Philology.*
HUCA	*Hebrew Union College Annual.*
IEJ	*Israel Exploration Journal.*
JAOS	*Journal of the American Oriental Society.*
JAs	*Journal Asiatique.*
JCS	*Journal of Cuneiform Studies.*
JEA	*Journal of Egyptian Archaeology.*
JHS	*Journal of Hellenic Studies*
JKF	*Jahrbuch für kleinasiatische Forschungen.*
JNES	*Journal of Near Eastern Studies.*
JPOS	*Journal of the Palestine Oriental Society.*
JSS	*Journal of Semitic Studies.*
MAPS	*Memoirs of the American Philosophical Society.*
MIO	*Mitteilungen des Instituts für Orientforschung.*
MVAG	*Mitteilungen der Vorderasiatischen Gesellschaft.*
MVAÄG	*Mitteilungen der Vorderasiatisch-Ägyptischen Gesellschaft.*
PEQ	*Palestine Exploration Quarterly.*
PRU	*Le palais royal d'Ugarit*
PSBA	*Proceedings of the Society of Biblical Archaeology.*
RA	*Revue d'Assyriologie et d'Archéologie Orientale.*
RAr	*Revue d'Archéologie.*
RB	*Revue Biblique.*
RHPR	*Revue d'Histoire et de Philosophie Religieuses.*
RHR	*Revue de l'Histoire des Religions.*
StOr	*Studia Orientalia.*
VDI	*Vestnik Drevnej Istorii.*
VT	*Vetus Testamentum.*
WO	*Die Welt des Orients.*
YOS	*Yale Orientale Series.*
ZA	*Zeitschrift für Assyriologie.*
ZAW	*Zeitschrift für die alttestamentliche Wissenschaft.*
ZDMG	*Zeitschrift der deutschen morgenländischen Gesellschaft.*

BIBLIOGRAPHY

(only works directly referred to are included)

I. Joseph AISTLEITNER, "Götterzeugung in Ugarit und Dilmun (SS und Ni. 4561)." *AcOr*, III (1953), 285-311.

II. — "Ein Opfertext aus Ugarit (1929 No. 2)." *AcOr*, IV (1954), 259-270.

III. — *Untersuchungen zur Grammatik des Ugaritischen* (= *Berichte . . . der Sächs. Akad. d. Wiss. zu Leipzig, Phil.-Hist. Kl.*, B. 100, Heft 6). Berlin, 1954.

IIIa. — *Wörterbuch der ugaritischen Sprache*, herausgegeben von Otto EISSFELDT. (Same series, B. 106, Heft 3). Berlin, 1963.

IV. Ekrem AKURGAL, *The Art of the Hittites*. Photographs by Max HIRMER. London, 1962.

V. William F. ALBRIGHT, "The Anatolian Goddess Kubaba." *AfO*, V (1928-29), 229-231.

VI. — "An Aramaic Magical Text in Hebrew From the Seventh Century B.C." *BASOR* No. 76 (Dec., 1939), 5-11.

VII. — *Archaeology and the Religion of Israel*. Fourth Edition. Baltimore, 1956.

VIII. — *The Archaeology of Palestine*. Revised and reprinted. Harmondsworth, 1960.

IX. — "An Archaic Hebrew Proverb in an Amarna Letter from Central Palestine." *BASOR* No. 89 (Feb., 1943), 29-32.

X. — "A Babylonian Geographical Treatise on Sargon of Akkad's Empire." *JAOS*, XLV (1925), 193-245, 1 map.

XI. — "The Biblical Period." *Ap. The Jews: their History, Culture, and Religion*, ed. by Louis FINKELSTEIN, Vol. I, New York, 1949, 3-69.

XII. — "Cuneiform Material for Egyptian Prosopography 1500-1200 B.C." *JNES*, V (1946), 7-25.

XIII. — "The Early Alphabetic Inscriptions from Sinai and their Decipherment." *BASOR* No. 110 (Apr., 1948), 6-22.

XIV. — "The Evolution of the West-Semitic Divinity ʿAn-ʿAnat-ʿAttâ." *AJSL*, XLI (1925), 73-101.

XV. — "Exploring in Sinai with the University of California African Expedition." *BASOR* No. 109 (Feb., 1948), 5-20.

XVI. — *From the Stone Age to Christianity*. Second Edition. Garden City, N.Y., 1957.

XVII. — "An Indirect Synchronism Between Egypt and Mesopotamia cir. 1730 B.C." *BASOR* No. 99 (Oct., 1945), 9-18.

XVIII. — "New Canaanite Historical and Mythological Data." *BASOR* No. 63 (Oct., 1936), 23-32.

XIX. — "New Light on the Early History of Phoenician Colonization." *BASOR* No. 83 (Oct., 1941), 14-22.

XX. — "New Light on the History of Western Asia in the Second Millennium B.C." *BASOR* No. 77 (Feb., 1940), 20-32; No. 78 (Apr., 1940), 23-31.

XXI. — "Post-scriptum" (to LEVI DELLA VIDA, "Stele of Ben-Hadad"). *BASOR* No. 90 (Apr., 1943), 32-34.

XXII. — "Recent Books on Archaeology and Ancient History." *BASOR* No. 139 (Oct., 1955), 14-25.

XXIII. — Review of A. GOETZE, *Kleinasien*. *AJA*, LXV (1961), 399-400.

XXIV. — "Some Important Recent Discoveries: Alphabetic Origins and the Idrimi Statue." *BASOR* No. 118 (Apr., 1950), 11-20.

XXV. — "Some Oriental Glosses on the Homeric Problem." *AJA*, LIV (1950), 162-176.

XXVI. — "Two Little Understood Amarna Letters from the Middle Jordan Valley." *BASOR* No. 89 (Feb., 1943), 7-17.

XXVII. — *The Vocalization of the Egyptian Syllabic Orthography* (= *AOS*, 5). New Haven, 1934.

XXVIII. — "A Votive Stele Erected by Ben-Hadad I of Damascus to the god Melcarth." *BASOR* No. 87 (Oct., 1942), 23-29.

XXIX. — and William L. MORAN, "A Re-Interpretation of an Amarna Letter from Byblos." *JCS*, II (1948), 239-248.

XXX. Albrecht ALT, "Die phönizischen Inschriften aus Kilikien." *WO* (1949), 272-287.

XXXI. Pierre AMIET, "Le symbolisme cosmique du répertoire animalier en Mésopotamie." *RA*, L (1956), 113-126.

XXXII. *Ancient Near Eastern Texts Relating to the Old Testament*, edited by James B. PRITCHARD. Second edition. Princeton, 1955.

XXXIII. Rudolf ANTHES, "Mythology in Ancient Egypt." *Ap.* CCXCIV, 15-92.

XXXIV. *Archaeologia Orientalia in Memoriam Ernst Herzfeld*. George C. MILES, Editor. Locust Valley, N.Y., 1952.

XXXV. *Archives royales de Mari*. Transliterations and translations, I-IX. Published and translated by G. DOSSIN, Ch.-F. JEAN, J.-R. KUPPER, J. BOTTÉRO, G. BOYER. Vol. XV: *Répertoire analytique des tomes I à V*, by J. BOTTÉRO and A. FINET. Paris, 1941-1960.

XXXVI. Ernst ASSMANN, "Zur Vorgeschichte von Kreta." *Philologus*, LXVII (1908), 161-201.

XXXVII. Michael C. ASTOUR, "Benê-Iamina et Jéricho." *Semitica*, IX (1959), 5-20.

XXXVIII. — "Les étrangers à Ugarit et le statut juridique des Ḫabiru." *RA*, LIII (1959), 70-76.

XXXIX. — "Place-Names from the Kingdom of Alalaḫ in the North Syrian List of Thutmose III." *JNES*, XXII (1963), 220-241, 1 map.

XXXIXa. — "Second Millennium B.C. Cypriot and Cretan Onomastica Reconsidered." To be published in *JAOS*, LXXXIV (1964).

XL. — "Semitic Names in the Greek World and Greek Names in the Semitic World." *Scripta Mediterranea*, presented to Cyrus H. GORDON, Waltham, Mass., 1962, 45-62 (priv. circ.); reprinted in *JNES*, XXIII (1964), 193-201.

XLI. — "Un texte d'Ugarit récemment découvert et ses rapports avec l'origine des cultes bachiques grecs." *RHR*, CLXIV (1963), 1-15.

XLII. — "Tradycja biblijna jako źródło prehistorii hebrajskiej." *Biuletyn ZIH* No. 22 (1957), 3-25.

XLIIa. M. AVI-YONA, "Scythopolis." *IEJ*, XII (1963), 123-34.
XLIII. Jean BABELON, "Le voile d'Europè." *RAr*, 6th series, XX (Oct.-Dec., 1942-43), 125-140.
XLIV. R. D. BARNETT, "Early Greek and Oriental Ivories." *JHS*, LXVIII (1948), 1-25.
XLV. — "Mopsos." *JHS*, LXXIII (1953), 140-143.
XLVI. A.-G. Barrois, *Manuel d'archéologie biblique*. Paris, vol. I, 1939; vol. II, 1953.
XLVII. — Review of Flinders PETRIE, *Ancient Gaza*, IV. *Syria*, XVII (1936), 86-88.
XLVIII. George Aaron BARTON, *Semitic and Hamitic Origins*. Philadelphia, 1934.
XLIX. George F. BASS, "The Cape Gelidonya Wreck: Preliminary Report." *AJA*, LXV (1961), 267-286, plates 83-90.
L. — "The Promise of Underwater Archaeology." *The American Scholar*, XXXII (1963), 241-254.
LI. Wolf Wilhelm BAUDISSIN, *Adonis und Esmun. Eine Untersuchung zur Geschichte des Glaubens an Auferstehungsgötter und Heilgötter*. Leipzig, 1911.
LII. — *Studien zur Semitischen Religionsgeschichte*. Leipzig, I, 1876; II, 1878.
LIII. Hans BAUER, *Das Alphabet von Ras Schamra. Seine Entzifferung und seine Gestalt*. Halle/Saale, 1932.
LIV. Theo BAUER, *Die Ostkanaanäer. Eine philologisch-historische Untersuchung über die Wanderschicht der sogenannten "Amoriter" in Babylonien*. Leipzig, 1926.
LV. — "Ein viertes altbabylonisches Fragment des Gilgameš-Epos." *JNES*, XVI (1957), 254-262.
LVI. Julius BELOCH, "Die Phoeniker am aegaeischen Meer." *Rheinisches Museum für Philologie*, NF XLIX (1894), 111-132.
LVII. Hermann BENGTSON, *Geschichte Griechenlands* (= *HBAW*, III: IV). Munich, 1950.
LVIII. Émile BENVENISTE, "La légende de Kombabos." *Ap*. CCCLIX, 249-258.
LIX. Elieser BEN YEHUDA, *Thesaurus totius hebraitatis, et veteris et recentioris*. No date. Vol. I-VIII, Berlin. Vol. IX-XIV, Jerusalem. Vol. XV, New York.
LX. Jean BÉRARD, "De la légende grecque à la Bible: Phaéton et les sept vaches maigres." *RHR*, CLI (1957), 221-228.
LXI. — "Les Hyksos et la légende d'Io. Recherches sur la période prémycenienne." *Syria*, XXIX (1952), 1-43.
LXII. Victor BÉRARD, *De l'origine des cultes arcadiens. Essai de méthode en mythologie grecque*. Paris, 1894.
LXIII. — *Did Homer Live*? Transl. by Brian RHYS. New York, 1931.
LXIV. — *Les navigations d'Ulysse*. Paris, vol. I, 1927; II, 1928; III and IV, 1929.
LXV. — *Les Phéniciens et l'Odyssée*. Second edition. Two volumes. Paris, 1927.
LXVI. Carl BEZOLD, *Babylonisch-Assyrisches Glossar*. Posthumously published by A. GOETZE. Heidelberg, 1926.
LXVII. — *Ninive and Babylon*. Third edition (= *Monographien zur Weltgeschichte*, 18). Bielefeld and Leipzig, 1909.

LXVIII. E. BILGIÇ, "Die Ortsnamen der 'kappadokischen' Urkunden im Rahmen der alten Sprachen Anatoliens." *AfO*, XV (1945-51), 1-37.

LXIX. Carl BLEGEN, "A Chronological Problem." *Ap.* CCCLXVIII, 61-66.

LXX. Franz Marius Theodor de Liagre BÖHL, *Akkadian Chrestomathy*. Vol. I. Leiden, 1947.

LXXI. — *Opera Minora. Studies en bijdragen op assyriologisch en oudtestamentisch terrein*. Groningen-Djakarta, 1953.

LXXII. — "Oud-Babylonische Mythen." *EOL* No. 4 (1936), 194-204.

LXXIII. Émile BOISACQ, *Dictionnaire étymologique de la langue grecque étudiée dans ses rapports avec les autres langues indo-européennes*. Heidelberg and Paris, 1923.

LXXIV. Helmuth Th. BOSSERT, "Die phönizisch-hethitischen Bilinguen." I: *Oriens*, I (1948), 163-192; II: *ArOr*, XVIII, 3 (1950), 10-42; III: *JKF*, I (1950-51), 264-295; IV: *ibid.*, II (1952-53), 167-188, 293-339.

LXXV. Jean BOTTÉRO, *Le problème des Ḫabiru à la 4e rencontre assyriologique internationale*. Paris, 1954.

LXXVI. Raymond A. BOWMAN, "An Aramaic Religious Text in Demotic Script." *JNES*, III (1944), 219-231.

LXXVII. James Henry BREASTED, *Ancient Records of Egypt. Historical Documents from the Earliest Times to the Persian Conquest, collected, edited and translated by*... Five volumes. Chicago, 1906.

LXXVIII. — *A History of Egypt, from the Earliest Times to the Persian Conquest*. Second edition, New York, 1912.

LXXIX. Carl BROCKELMANN, *Grundriss der vergleichenden Grammatik der semitischen Sprachen*. Berlin. Vol. I, 1908; vol. II, 1913.

LXXX. — *Semitische Sprachwissenschaft*. Leipzig, 1906.

LXXXI. Robert BROWN, Jun. *Semitic Influence in Hellenic Mythology*. London, 1898.

LXXXII. W. Norman BROWN, "Mythology of India." *Ap.* CCXCIV, 277-330.

LXXXIII. A. R. BURN, *Minoans, Philistines, and Greeks B.C. 1400-900*. London, 1930.

LXXXIV. Eric BURROWS, "Problems of the abzu." *Orientalia*, NS I (1932), 231-256.

LXXXV. *CAD*: *The Assyrian Dictionary of the Oriental Institute of the University of Chicago*. Editorial Board: Ignace J. GELB, Thorkild JACOBSEN, Benno LANDSBERGER, A. Leo OPPENHEIM. Chicago and Glückstadt, 1956 and on. Published so far volumes 1 (p. I), 3, 4, 5, 6, 7, 16 and 21.

LXXXVI. *The Cambridge Ancient History*. Edited by J. B. BURY, S. A. COOK, F. E. ADCOCK. Twelve volumes of text, five volumes of plates. Cambridge, 1925-1939.

LXXXVII. Jean CANTINEAU, "La langue de Ras Shamra." I: *Syria*, XIII (1932), 164-170; II: *ibid.*, XXI (1940), 38-61.

LXXXVIII. — "Tadmorea." *Syria*, XVII (1936), 267-282, 346-355.

LXXXIX. André CAQUOT, "Chadrapha. A propos de quelques articles récents." *Syria*, XXIX (1952), 74-88.

XC. — "Les Rephaïm ougaritiques." *Syria*, XXXVII (1960), 75-93.

xci. — "Sur quelques démons de l'Ancien Testament (Reshep, Qeteb, Deber)." *Semitica,* VI (1956), 53-68.

xcia. Giovanni Pugliese CARATELLI, "Sulle epigrafi in Lineare A di caractere sacrale." *Minos,* V (1957), 163-173.

xcii. Rhys CARPENTER, "Phoenicians in the West." *AJA,* LXII (1958), 25-53.

xciii. Umberto CASSUTO, "Il capitolo 3 di Habaquq e i testi di Ras Shamra." *Annuario di Studi Ebraici,* II (1935-37), 7-22.

xcix. E. CAVAIGNAC, "L'Égypte et les Hittites de 1370 à 1345." *Syria,* XXXIII (1956), 42-48.

xcv. — *Les Hittites.* Paris, 1950.

xcvi. Henri CAZELLES, "Hébreu, Ubru et Ḫapiru." *Syria,* XXXV (1958), 198-217.

xcvii. — "L'hymne ugaritique à Anat." *Syria,* XXXIII (1956), 49-57.

xcviii. J. B. CHABOT, "Mélanges épigraphiques, II." *JAs,* 11th series, XVII (1921), 177-199.

xcix. John CHADWICK, *The Decipherment of Linear B.* New York, 1959.

xcixa. — "Minoan Linear A: A Provisional Balance Sheet". *Antiquity,* XXXIII (1959), 269-278.

c. V. Gordon CHILDE, *The Dawn of European Civilization.* Sixth edition, revised. New York, 1958.

ci. — *New Light on the Most Ancient East.* Rewritten in 1952. New York, 1953.

cia. ALBERT T. CLAY, *Personal Names from Cuneiform Inscriptions of the Cassite Period* (= *YOS,* I). New Haven, 1912.

cii. Carl CLEMEN, *Die Phönikische Religion nach Philo von Byblos* (= *MVAÄG,* 42, 3). Berlin, 1939.

ciii. Georges CONTENAU, *La civilisation des Hittites et des Hurrites du Mitanni.* Nouvelle édition, revue et augmentée. Paris, 1948.

cix. — "Monuments: XIX. 'Allatu under the bent tree'?" *RA,* XXXVIII (1941), 44-47.

cv. Arthur Bernard COOK, *Zeus: a Study in Ancient Religion.* Three volumes (five books). Cambridge, 1914-1940.

cvi. R. N. COOK, "Archaeological Argument: Some Principles." *Antiquity,* XXXIV (1960), 177-179.

cvii. Stanley Arthur COOK, "Syria and Palestine in the Light of External Evidence.—The Rise of Israel." *Ap.* LXXXVI, II, 296-406.

cviii. G. A. COOKE, *A Text-Book of North-Semitic Inscriptions. Moabite, Hebrew, Phoenician, Aramaic, Palmyrene, Jewish.* Cambridge, 1903.

cix. Friedrich CORNELIUS, "Die Chronologie des Vorderen Orients im 2. Jahrtausend v. Chr." *AfO,* XVII (1954-56), 294-309.

cx. *Corpus Inscriptionum Semiticarum, ab Academia Inscriptionum et Litterarum Humaniorum conditum atque digestum. Pars prima, inscriptiones Phoenicas continens. Tomus primus.* Paris, 1881.

cxi. Anton DEIMEL, *Pantheon Babylonicum. Nomina deorum e textibus cuneiformibus excerpta et ordine alphabetico distributa.* Rome, 1914.

CXII. — *Šumerisches Lexikon*. Four volumes in nine books. Rome, 1927-1950.

CXIII. Édouard DHORME, "Les peuples issus de Japhet d'après le chapître X de la Genèse." *Syria*, XIII (1932), 28-49.

CXIV. — "Première traduction des textes phéniciens de Ras Shamra." *RB*, XL (1931), 32-56.

CXV. — *Recueil Édouard Dhorme. Études bibliques et orientales.* Paris, 1951.

CXVI. — *Les religions de Babylonie et d'Assyrie* (= "*Mana*," I, II). Paris, 1949.

CXVII. — Revue of Ch. VIROLLEAUD, *La légende phénicienne de Danel.* *Syria*, XVIII (1937), 104-113.

CXVIII. — "Textes accadiens transcrits en écriture alphabétique de Ras Shamra." *RA*, XXXVII (1940), 83-96.

CXIX. I. M. DIAKONOV, "Amorei." *VDI*, 1939, No. 4, 60-69.

CXX. P. DIKAIOS, "Les cultes préhistoriques dans l'île de Chypre." *Syria*, XIII (1932), 345-354.

CXXa. Guilelmus DITTENBERGER, *Sylloge inscriptionum graecarum.* Four Volumes. Fourth edition (offset reprint of the third ed., 1915). Hildersheim, 1960.

CXXI. Ernst DOBLHOFER, *Zeichen und Wunder. Die Entzifferung verschollener Schriften und Sprachen.* Vienna-Berlin-Stuttgart, 1957.

CXXII. Franz DORNSEIFF, *Antike und Alter Orient. Interpretationen* (= *Kleine Schriften*, I). Leipzig, 1956.

CXXIII. Georges DOSSIN, "Les archives économiques du palais de Mari." *Syria*, XX (1939), 97-113.

CXXIV. — "Les archives épistolaires du palais de Mari." *Syria*, XIX (1938), 105-126.

CXXV. — "Inscriptions de fondation provenant de Mari." *Syria*, XXI (1940), 152-169.

CXXVI. — "Nqmd et Niqme-Ḫad." *Syria*, XX (1939), 169-176.

CXXVII. — "Le panthéon de Mari." *Ap.* CDLXXXIV, 41-50.

CXXVIII. DU MESNIL DU BUISSON, "ʿAštart et ʿAštar à Ras Shamra." *EOL*, III (1946-48), No. 10, 406.

CXXIX. — "Une tablette magique de la région du Moyen Euphrate." *Ap.* CCCLIX, 421-434.

CXXX. J. J. DUNBABIN, "Bellerophon, Herakles and Chimaera." *Ap. Studies Presented to David M. Robinson*, vol. II, St. Louis, Mo., 1953, 1155-1163.

CXXXI. André DUPONT-SOMMER, *Les Araméens*. Paris, 1949.

CXXXII. — "Azitawadda, roi des Danouniens. Étude sur les inscriptions phéniciennes de Karatepe." *RA*, XLII (1948), 161-188.

CXXXIII. — *Les écrits esséniens découverts près de la mer Morte.* Paris, 1959.

CXXXIV. — "Étude du texte phénicien des inscriptions de Karatepe." I: *Oriens*, I (1948), 193-197; II: *ArOr*, XVIII, 3 (1950), 43-47; III: *JKF*, I (1950-51), 296-308; IV: *ibid.*, II (1952-53), 189-200.

CXXXV. — "L'inscription phénicienne de la spatule dite d'Asdrubal." *ArOr*, XVII (1949), I, 158-167.

CXXXVI. — "Une stèle araméenne d'un prêtre de Baal trouvée en Égypte." *Syria*, XXXIII (1956), 79-87.

CXXXVII. René DUSSAUD, "A propos de la Table dite généalogique de Ras Shamra (TG)." *Syria*, XVI (1935), 227-228.

CXXXVIII. — "A propos de la venue des Hittites et des Hourrites en Syrie." *JKF*, I (1950-51), 105-107.

CXXXIX. — "Brèves remarques sur les tablettes de Ras Shamra." *Syria*, XII (1931), 67-77.

CXL. — "Cultes cananéens aux sources du Jourdain d'après les textes de Ras Shamra." *Syria*, XVII (1936), 283-295.

CXLI. — "Deux stèles de Ras Shamra, portant une dédicace au dieu Dagon." *Syria*, XVI (1935), 177-180.

CXLII. — "L'influence orientale en Crète." *Syria*, XVIII (1937), 233.

CXLIII. — "Itanos." *Syria*, XXVI (1949), 394-395.

CXLIV. — "Melqart." *Syria*, XXV (1946-48), 205-230.

CXLV. — "Melqart, d'après des récents travaux." *RHR*, CLI (1957), 1-21.

CXLVI. — "Nouveaux textes égyptiens d'exécration contre les peuples syriens." *Syria*, XXI (1940), 170-182.

CXLVII. — "Un nouvel example de rehabilitation du texte massorétitique." *Ap.* XXXIV, 69-71.

CXLVIII. — "L'origine de l'alphabet et son évolution première d'après les découvertes de Byblos." *Syria*, XXV (1946-48), 36-52.

CXLIX. — "Peut-on identifier l'Apollon barbu de Hiérapolis de Syrie?" *RHR*, CXXVI (1942-43), 128-149.

CL. — Review of A. DUPONT-SOMMER, "Azitawadda, roi des Danouniens." *Syria*, XXVII (1951), 185-187.

CLI. — Review of Nelson GLUECK, *Explorations in Eastern Palestine, IV. Syria*, XXIX (1952), 149.

CLII. — Review of Sidney SMITH, *The Statue of Idri-mi, Syria*, XXVII (1950), 157-160.

CLIII. — "Victor Bérard (necrologue)." *Syria*, XII (1931), 392-393.

CLIV. Erich EBELING, "Babylonisch-Assyrische Texte." Ap. CCXXXIII.

CLV. — *Keilinschrifttexte aus Assur religiösen Inhalts*. Two fascicles. Leipzig, 1915.

CLVI. Emma J. EDELSTEIN and Ludwig EDELSTEIN, *Asclepius. A Collection and Interpretation of the Testimonies.* (= *Publ. of the Inst. of Hist. of Medicine, The Johns Hopkins Univ. Second Series: Texts and Docum.*, II). Two volumes. Baltimore, 1945.

CLVII. William F. EDGERTON and John A. WILSON, *Historical Records of Ramses III. The Texts of Medinet Habu.* Two volumes. Chicago, 1936.

CLVIII. M. L. ERLENMEYER—H. ERLENMEYER, "Cerviden-Darstellungen auf altorientalischen und ägäischen Siegeln." I: *Orientalia*, NS XXV (1956), 149-153; II: *ibid.*, NS XXVI (1957), 321-339.

CLIX. — "Uber Philister und Kreter." I: *Orientalia*, NS XXIX (1960), 121-150; II: *ibid.*, same vol., 241-272; III: *ibid.*, NS XXX (1961), 269-293.

CLX. Adolf ERMAN, *Die Religion der Ägypter.* Berlin, 1934.

CLXI. Margarete Falkner, "Studien zur Geographie des alten Mesopotamien." *AfO*, XVIII (1957), 1-37.

CLXII. Lewis Richard FARNELL, *The Cults of the Greek States*. Five volumes. Oxford, 1896-1909.

CLXIII. T. FISH, "The Zu Bird." *Bulletin of the John Rylands Library*, XXXI (1948), 162-171.

CLXIV. R. J. FORBES, *Studies in Ancient Technology*. Seven volumes. Leiden, 1955-1963.

CLXV. Emil FORRER, "Eine Geschichte des Götterkönigtums aus dem Hatti-Reiche." *Ap. Mélanges Franz Cumont*, 1936, 667-713.

CLXVI. — "Kilikien zur Zeit des Hatti-Reiches." *Klio*, XXX (1937), 135-186, 2 maps.

CLXVII. — *Die Provinzeinteilung des assyrischen Reiches*. Leipzig, 1920.

CLXVIII. John FORSDYKE, *Greece Before Homer. Ancient Chronology and Mythology*. New York, 1957.

CLXIX. Paul Foucart, *Les mystères d'Eleusis*. Paris, 1914.

CLXX. Henri FRANKFORT, "The Burney Relief." *AfO*, XII (1937-39), 128-135.

CLXXI. — *Cylinder Seals. A Documentary Essay in the Art and Religion of the Ancient Near East*. London, 1939.

CLXXII. — "Gods and Myths on Sargonid Seals." *Iraq*, I (1934), 2-29.

CLXXIII. —, Mrs. H. A. FRANKFORT, John A. WILSON, Thorkild JACOBSEN, *Before Philosophy: The Intellectual Adventure of Ancient Man. An Essay on Speculative Thought in the Ancient Near East*. Harmondsworth, 1959.

CLXXIV. James George FRAZER, *Folk-lore in the Old Testament. Studies in Comparative Religion, Legend and Law*. Three Volumes. London, 1919.

CLXXV. — *The Golden Bough. A Study in Magic and Religion*. Third edition. Twelve volumes. London, 1912.

CLXXVI. Johannes Friedrich, "Churritische Märchen und Sagen in hethitischer Sprache." *ZA*, NF XV (1950), 213-255.

CLXXVII. — *Extinct Languages*. Transl. by Frank GAYNOR. New York, 1957.

CLXXVIII. — *Hethitisches Elementarbuch*, I: *Kurzgefasste Grammatik*. Heidelberg, 1940.

CLXXIX. — *Hethitisches Wörterbuch. Kurzgefasste kritische Sammlung der Deutungen hethitischer Wörter*. Heidelberg, 1952.

CLXXX. — *Phönizisch-Punische Grammatik* (= *AnOr*, 32). Rome, 1951.

CLXXXI. Ryszard GANSZYNIEC, "Homer i Odyssea." *Ap. Odyssea*, Polish transl. by Józef WITTLIN, Second edition. Warsaw, 1930.

CLXXXII. John GARSTANG, *Prehistoric Mersin*. Oxford, 1953.

CLXXXIII. — "Where East Meets West: An Ancient Village in Cilicia." *ArOr*, XVII (1949), I, 270-274.

CLXXXIV. — and O. R. GURNEY, *The Geography of the Hittite Empire* (= *Occasional Public. of the British Inst. of Arch. in Ankara*, No. 5). London, 1959.

CLXXXV. Theodor H. Gaster, "The Magical Inscription from Arslan Tash." *JNES*, VI (1947), 186-188.

CLXXXVI. — *Thespis. Ritual, Myth, and Drama in the Ancient Near East*. Foreword by Gilbert MURRAY. New York, 1950.

CLXXXVII. Ignace J. GELB, "The Early History of the West Semitic Peoples." *JCS*, XV (1961), 27-47.

CLXXXVIII. — *Glossary of Old Akkadian*. Chicago, 1957.

CLXXXIX. — *Hittite Hieroglyphs*. Chicago. Vol. I, 1931; vol. II, 1935; vol. III, 1942.

CXC. — "Studies in the Topography of Western Asia." *AJSL*, LV (1938), 66-85.

CXCI. —, Pierre M. PURVES and Allan A. MACRAE, *Nuzi Personal Names*. Chicago, 1943.

CXCII. Vladimir GEORGIEV, "Istorija ègejskogo mira vo II tysjačeletii do n.è. v svete minojskix nadpisej." *VDI*, 1950, No. 4, 48-68.

CXCIII. Gabriel GERMAIN, *Genèse de l'Odyssée. Le fantastique et le sacré*. Paris, 1954.

CXCIV. William GESENIUS, *A Hebrew and English Lexicon of the Old Testament, with an Appendix Containing the Biblical Aramaic*. . . . Edited . . . by Francis BROWN, S. R. DRIVER and Charles A. BRIGGS. Corrected impression. Oxford, 1952.

CXCV. Harold L. GINSBERG, "Baʿlu and His Brethren." *JPOS*, XVI (1936), 138-150.

CXCVI. — "Ugaritic Myths, Epics, and Legends." *Ap*. XXXII, 129-155.

CXCVII. Louis GINZBERG, *The Legends of the Jews*. Transl. by Henrietta SZOLD and Paul RADIN. Index by Boaz COHEN. Seven volumes, Philadelphia, 1946-47.

CXCVIII. Nelson GLUECK, *Explorations in Eastern Palestine, IV*. (= *AASOR*, XXV-XXVIII, 1945-49). Part I: Text. New Haven, 1951.

CXCIX. Albrecht GOETZE, "Cilicians." *JCS*, XVI (1962), 48-58.

CC. — "Hittite Texts." Ap. XXXII, *passim*.

CCI. — *Kizzuwatna and the Problem of Hittite Geography* (= *YOS*, *Researches*, XXII). New Haven, 1940.

CCII. — *Kleinasien*. Second edition (= *HBAW*, III: III: 1, vol. 3, sect. 3, subsection 1). Munich, 1957.

CCIII. — *Madduwattaš* (= *MVAÄG*, 32, 1927, No. 1). Leipzig, 1928.

CCIV. — "An Old Babylonian Itinerary." *JCS*, VII (1953), 51-72.

CCV. Victor Roland GOLD, "The Gnostic Library of Chenoboskion." *Ap. The Biblical Archaeologist Reader*, edit. by D. N. FREEDMAN and G. E. WRIGHT, New York, 1961, 299-329.

CCVI. Ignaz GOLDZIHER, *Mythology Among the Hebrews and its Historical Development*. Transl. by Russel MARTINEAU. London, 1877.

CCVII. Cyrus H. GORDON, "Akkadian Tablets in Minoan Dress." *Antiquity*, XXXI (1957), 237-240.

CCVIII. — "The Aramaic Incantation in Cuneiform." *AfO*, XII (1938), 105-117.

CCIX. — "Azitawadd's Phoenician Inscription." *JNES*, VIII (1949), 108-115.

CCX. — *Before the Bible: The Common Background of Greek and Hebrew Civilisations*. New York, 1962.

CCXI. — "Canaanite Mythology." *Ap*. CCXCIV, 181-218.

CCXII. — "The Cuneiform Aramaic Incantation." *Orientalia*, IX (1940), 29-38.

CCXIII. — "The Dreros Bilingual." *JSS*, VIII (1963), 76-79.

CCXIV. — "Eteocrtan." *JNES*, XXI (1962), 211-214.

CCXV. — "Homer and Bible: The Origin and Character of East Mediterranean Literature." *HUCA*, XXVI (1955), 43-108.

CCXVI. — "The Language of the Hagia Triada Tablets." *Klio*, XXXVIII (1960), 63-68.

CCXVII. — "Minoan Linear A." *JNES*, XVII (1958), 245-255.

CCXVIII. — "Minoica." *JNES*, XXI (1962), 207-210.

CCXIX. — "Notes on Minoan Linear A." *Antiquity*, XXXI (1957), 124-130.

CCXX. — "Observations on the Akkadian Tablets from Ugarit." *RA*, L (1956), 127-133.

CCXXI. — Review of *Ancient Near Eastern Texts*. *AJA*, LVI (1952), 93-94.

CCXXII. — "Ugaritic *ḫrt*/*ḫirîtu* 'Cemetery'." *Syria*, XXXIII (1956), 102-103.

CCXXIII. — *Ugaritic Literature. A Comprehensive Translation of the Poetic and Prose Texts*. Rome, 1949.

CCXXIV. — *Ugaritic Manual: Newly Revised Grammar — Texts in Transliteration — Cuneiform Selections — Paradigms — Glossary — Indices* (= *AnOr*, 35). Rome, 1953.

CCXXV. — *The World of the Old Testament*. New York, 1958.

CCXXVI. Felix GÖSSMANN, *Planetarium Babylonicum, oder die Sumerisch-Babylonischen Stern-Namen* (= CXII, vol. IV, 2). Rome, 1950.

CCXXVII. Robert GRAVES, *The Greek Myths*. Two volumes. Harmondsworth, 1955.

CCXXVIII. John GRAY, "The Hunting of Baʿal: Fratricide and Atonement in the Mythology of Ras Shamra." *JNES*, X (1951), 146-155.

CCXXIX. — *The Krt Text in the Literature of Ras Shamra. A Social Myth of Ancient Canaan* (= *DMOA*, V). Leiden, 1955.

CCXXX. — *The Legacy of Canaan. The Ras Shamra Texts and their Relevance to the Old Testament* (= *Supplements to VT*, V). Leiden, 1957.

CCXXXI. Henri GRÉGOIRE, "Azitawadda-Estwed." *Nouvelle Clio*, II (1950), No. 3, 122-127.

CCXXXII. P. GRELOT, "Isaïe XIV 12-15 et son arrière-plan mythologique." *RHR*, CXLIX (1956), 18-48.

CCXXXIII. Hugo GRESSMANN, Hermann RANKE, Erich EBELING, Nikolaus RHODOKANAKIS, *Altorientalische Texte zum Alten Testament*. Second edition. Berlin, 1926.

CCXXXIV. J. Gwyn GRIFFITHS, "The Egyptian Derivation of the Name Moses." *JNES*, XII (1953), 225-231.

CCXXXV. Otto GRUPPE, *Griechische Mythologie und Religionsgeschichte* (= *Hbuch der Klass. Altertumswiss.*, V. Band, 2. Abteil.). Two volumes. Munich, 1906.

CCXXXVI. — *Die Griechischen Culte und Mythen in ihren Beziehungen zu den Orientalischen Religionen. Erster Band: Einleitung*. Leipzig, 1887.

CCXXXVII. O. R. GURNEY, *The Hittites*. Harmondsworth, 1952.

CCXXXVIII. Hans Gustav GÜTERBOCK, "Hittite Mythology." *Ap.* CCXCIV, 139-179.

CCXXXIX. — "The Hittite Version of the Hurrian Kumarbi Myths: Oriental Forerunners of Hesiod." *AJA*, LII (1948), 123-134.

CCXL. — *Kumarbi, Mythen vom churritischen Kronos*. Zürich and New York, 1946.

CCXLI. W. K. C. GUTHRIE, *The Greeks and their Gods*. Boston, 1956.

CCXLII. — *Orpheus and Greek Religion*. Second edition. London, 1952.

CCXLIII. H. R. HALL, "The Discoveries in Crete and their Relation to the History of Egypt and Palestine." *PSBA*, XXXI (1909), 135-148, 221-238, 280-285, 311-318.

CCXLIV. — "The Keftians, Philistines, and Other Peoples of the Levant." *Ap.* LXXXVI, II, 275-295.

CCXLV. George M. A. HANFMANN, "Archaeology in Homeric Asia Minor." *AJA*, LII (1948), 135-155.

CCXLVI. Zellig S. HARRIS, *A Grammar of the Phoenician Language*. Philadelphia, 1936.

CCXLVII. Jane Ellen HARRISON, *Prolegomena to the Study of Greek Religion* (Offset reprint of the third edition, 1921). New York, 1957.

CCXLVIII. — *Themis. A Study of the Social Origins of Greek Religion.* (Offset reprint of the second edition, 1927). New York, 1962.

CCXLIX. W. C. HAYES, "Egypt." Ap. *CAH*², fasc. 4, Cambridge, 1962, 1-22.

CCL. Wolfgang HELCK, *Die Beziehungen Ägyptens zu Vorderasien im 3. und 2. Jahrtausend v. Chr.* Wiesbaden, 1962.

CCLI. Andrée HERDNER, "Dédicace araméenne au dieu Melqart." *Syria*, XXV (1946-48), 229-230.

CCLII. — "La légende canaanéenne d'Aqhat d'après les travaux récents." *Syria*, XXVI (1949), 1-16.

CCLIII. — Review of J. FRIEDRICH, "Churritisch-Ugaritisches und Churritisch-Luwisches." *Syria*, XXV (1946-48), p. 161.

CCLIV. George HILL, *A History of Cyprus*, vol. I. Cambridge, 1949 (reprint of 1940).

CCLV. A. S. HIRAM, "A Votive Altar From Upper Galilee." *BASOR* No. 167 (Oct., 1962), 18-23.

CCLVI. Leicester B. HOLLAND, "The Danaoi." *HSCP*, XXXIX (1928), 59-92.

CCLVII. Gustav HÖLSCHER, *Die Profeten. Untersuchungen zur Religionsgeschichte Israels*. Leipzig, 1914.

CCLVIII. A. M. HONEYMAN, "Epigraphic Discoveries at Karatepe." *PEQ*, 1949, 21-39.

CCLIX. — "Phoenician Inscriptions from Karatepe." *Le Muséon*, LXI (1948), 43-57.

CCLX. — "The Tributaries of Ugarit, a Toponymic Study." *JKF*, II (1952-53), 74-87.

CCLXI. S. H. HOOKE (editor), *Myth and Ritual. Essays on the Myth and Ritual of the Hebrews in Relation to the Cultural Pattern of the Ancient East*. Oxford, 1933.

CCLXII. — (editor), *Myth, Ritual, and Kingship. Essays on the Theory and Practice of Kingship in the Ancient Near East and in Israel*. Oxford, 1958.

CCLXIII. Ph. H. J. HOUWINK TEN CATE, *The Luwian Population Groups of Lycia and Cilicia Aspera During the Hellenistic Period* (= *DMOA*, X). Leiden, 1961.

CCLXIV. Bedřich HROZNÝ, *Histoire de l'Asie Antérieure, de l'Inde et de la Crète, depuis les origines jusqu'au début du second millénaire*. Trad. franç. par Madeleine DAVID. Paris, 1947.

CCLXV. — "L'inscription 'hittite'-hiéroglyphique d'Apamée." *Syria*, XX (1939), 134-135.

CCLXVI. — "Les Ioniens à Ras Shamra." *ArOr*, IV (1932), 169-178.

CCLXVII. R. W. HUTCHINSON, *Prehistoric Crete*. Baltimore, 1962.

CCLXVIIa. — "Two Mesopotamian Daggers and their Relatives." *Iraq*, I (1934), 163-170.

CCLXVIII. Sara A. IMMERWAHR, "Mycenaean Trade and Colonization." *Archaeology*, XIII (1960), No. 1, 3-13.

CCLXIX. William A. IRWIN, "The Mythological Background of Habakkuk, Chapter 3." *JNES*, XV (1956), 47-50.

CCLXX. Thorkild JACOBSEN, "Mesopotamia." *Ap.* CLXXIII, 135-234.

CCLXXI. — "Sumerian Mythology: a Review Article." *JNES*, V (1946), 128-152.

CCLXXII. Felix JACOBY, *Die Fragmente der griechischen Historiker*. Fourteen volumes. Berlin, 1926—Leiden, 1958.

CCLXXIII. A. JAMME, "Le panthéon sud-arabe préislamique d'après les sources épigraphiques." *Le Muséon*, LX (1947), 57-147.

CCLXXIV. Marcus JASTROW, *A Dictionary of the Targumim, the Talmud Babli and Yerushalmi, and the Midrashic Literature*. Two volumes. New York, 1903.

CCLXXV. Morris JASTROW, JR., *Die Religion Babyloniens und Assyriens*. Two volumes (three books). Giessen, I, 1905; II, 1912.

CCLXXVI. Charles-F. JEAN, "Pharmacopée et parfumerie dans quelques lettres de Mari." *ArOr*, XVII (1949), I, 320-329.

CCLXXVII. — "Quelques divinités du panthéon suméro-akkadien sous les dynasties d'Isin-Larsa 2186-1925." *Babyloniaca*, XVI (1936), 155-168.

CCLXXVIII. — *La religion sumérienne*. Paris, 1934.

CCLXXIX. Peter JENSEN, "Alttestamentlich-Keilinschriftliches." *ZA*, NF VIII (1934), 232-237.

CCLXXX. Alfred JEREMIAS, *Der Schleier von Sumer bis Heute* (= *AO*, 31, 1/2). Leipzig, 1931.

CCLXXXI. Raymond JESTIN, "Un rite sumérien de fécondité: le mariage du dieu Nin-G̃ir-Su et de la déesse Ba-ba." *ArOr*, XVII (1949), I, 333-339.

CCLXXXII. — "Textes religieux sumériens." *RA*, XLI (1947), 55-66.

CCLXXXIII. Anton JIRKU, *Die ägyptischen Listen palästinensischer und syrischen Ortsnamen. In Umschrift und mit historisch-archäologischem Kommentar* (= *Klio*, Beiheft XXXVIII, N.F. Heft 25). Leipzig, 1937.

CCLXXXIV. Helene J. KANTOR, *The Aegean and the Orient in the Second Millennium B.C.* (= *The Arch. Inst. of America*, Monograph No. 1). Menasha, Wisc., 1947.

CCLXXXV. Jacqueline V. KARAGEORGHIS, "Quelques observations sur l'origine du syllabaire chypro-minoén." *RAr*, 1958, Tome II, 1-19.

CCLXXXVI. C. KERÉNYI, *The Heroes of the Greeks*. Transl. by H. J. ROSE. London, 1959.

CCLXXXVII. Otto KERN, *Die Religion der Griechen*. Three volumes. Berlin, 1926-1938.

CCLXXXVIIa. K. A. KITCHEN, *Suppiluliuma and the Amarna Pharaohs. A Study in Relative Chronology*. Liverpool, 1962.

CCLXXXVIII. A. KLEVETA, "Le jugement infernal dans les croyances babyloniennes." *ArOr*, XVII (1949), I, 374-385.

CCLXXXIX. Ludwig KOEHLER — Walter BAUMGARTNER, *Lexicon in Veteris Testamenti Libris*. Leiden, 1958, *Supplementum*, ibid. 1958.

CCXC. K. M. KOLOBOVA, *Iz istorii rannegrečeskogo obščestva (O. Rodos IX-VII vv. do n.è.)*. Leningrad, 1951.

CCXCI. Emil G. KRAELING, "A Unique Babylonian Relief." *BASOR* No. 67 (Oct., 1937), 16-18.

CCXCII. Samuel Noah KRAMER, "The Death of Gilgamesh." *BASOR* No. 94 (Apr., 1944), 2-12.

CCXCIII. — " 'Inanna's Descent to the Nether World' Continued and Revised." *JCS*, V (1951), 1-17.

CCXCIV. — *Mythologies of the Ancient World. Edited and with Introduction by* . . . Garden City, N.Y., 1961.

CCXCV. — "Mythology of Sumer and Akkad." *Ap.* CCXCIV, 93-137.

CCXCVI. — *Sumerian Mythology* (= *MAPS*, XXI). Philadelphia, 1944.

CCXCVII. — "Sumerian Myths and Epic Tales." *Ap.* XXXII, 37-59.

CCXCVIII. Paul KRETSCHMER, *Aus der Anomia*. Göttingen, 1892.

CCXCIX. — *Einleitung in die Geschichte der griechischen Sprache*. Göttingen, 1896.

CCC. — "Die Hypachäer." *Glotta*, XXI (1932), 213-257.

CCCI. — "Nochmals die Hypachäer und Alaksandus." *Glotta*, XXIV (1936), 203-251.

CCCII. — "Zum Balkan-Skythischen." *Glotta*, XXIV (1936), 1-56.

CCCIII. — "Zur ältesten Sprachgeschichte Kleinasiens." *Glotta*, XXI (1932), 76-100.

CCCIV. Franz Xaver KUGLER, *Sternkunde und Sterndienst in Babel. Assyriologische, astronomische und astralmythologische Untersuchungen*. Münster, Vol. I, 1907; vol. II, 1909-1924; supplementary vol., 1913-1935, in three parts (Part 3 by Johann SCHAUMBURGER).

CCCV. Jean-Robert KUPPER, *Les nomades en Mésopotamie au temps des rois de Mari* (= *Bibl. de la Fac. de Philos. et Lettres de l'Univ. de Liège*, fasc. CXLII). Paris, 1957.

CCCVI. — *Northern Mesopotamia and Syria* (= *CAH*², fasc. 14). Cambridge, 1963.

CCCVII. René LABAT, *Manuel d'épigraphie akkadienne* (*Signes, Syllabaire, Idéogrammes*). Third edition. Paris, 1959.

CCCVIII. Marie-Joseph LAGRANGE, *Études sur les religions sémitiques*. Paris, 1903.

CCCIX. Maurice LAMBERT, "En marge du problème de la Siqqurat. Les Pontifes du Temple d'En-Haut." *Sumer*, VII (1951), 58-65.

CCCX. — "Notes d'archéologie et d'épigraphie sumeriennes." *RA*, XLII (1948), 189-210.

CCCXI. Oscar LANDAU, *Mykenisch-Griechische Personennamen* (= *Studia Graeca et Latina Gotheburgensia*, 7). Göteborg, 1958.

CCCXII. Benno LANDSBERGER, *Sam'al. Studien zur Entdeckung der Ruinenstaette Karatepe*. Erste Lieferung (= *Veröffentl. der Türk. Hist. Ges.*, VII. Serie, No. 16). Ankara, 1948.

CCCXIII. Stephen LANGDON, *The Babylonian Epic of Creation, Restored from the Recently Recovered Tablets from Aššur. Transcription and commentary*. Oxford, 1923.

CCCXIV. — *Oxford Edition of Cuneiform Texts, vol. II. The Weld-Blundell Collection, vol. II. Historical Inscriptions, Containing Principally the Chronological Prism, W.-B.* 444. Oxford, 1923.

CCCXV. — *Le poème sumérien du paradis, du déluge et de la chute d'homme.* Traduit de l'anglais par Ch. VIROLLEAUD. Paris, 1919.

CCCXVI. — *Semitic (The Mythology of All Races, in* 13 volumes, vol. V). Boston, 1931.

CCCXVII. — *Sumerian and Babylonian Psalms.* Paris, 1909.

CCCXVIII. Emmanuel LAROCHE, "Documents hiéroglyphiques provenant du palais d'Ugarit." *Ap.* CDLIII, 97-160.

CCCXIX. — "Études sur les hiéroglyphes hittites." *Syria,* XXXI (1954), 99-117.

CCCXX. — "Études sur les hiéroglyphes hittites: 5. Adana et les Danouniens." *Syria,* XXXV (1958), 252-283.

CCCXXI. — *Les hiéroglyphes hittites. Première partie. L'écriture.* Paris, 1960.

CCCXXII. — *Recueil d'onomastique hittite.* Paris, 1951.

CCCXXIIa. — "Teššub, Ḫebat et leur cour." *JCS,* II (1948), 113-134.

CCCXXIII. Gustave LEFEBVRE, *Romans et contes égyptiens de l'èpoque pharaonique. Traduction avec introduction, notices et commentaires.* Paris, 1949.

CCCXXIV. François LENORMANT, *Les origines de l'histoire d'après la Bible et les traditions des peuples orientaux.* Paris, tome I; 1880; tome II, 1, 1882; tome II, 2, 1884.

CCCXXV. — *Les premières civilisations.* Two volumes. Paris, 1874.

CCCXXVI. G. LEVI DELLA VIDA, "The Phoenician God Satrapes." *BASOR* No. 87 (Oct., 1942), 29-32.

CCCXXVII. — "Some Notes on the Stele of Ben-Hadad." *BASOR* No. 90 (Apr., 1943), 30-32.

CCCXXVIII. Isidore LÉVI, "Les inscriptions de Karatepe." *Nouvelle Clio,* II (1950), No. 3, 105-121.

CCCXXIX. Naphthali LEWIS, *Samothrace: The Ancient Literary Sources (= Samothrace. Excav. Conducted by the Inst. of Fine Art of New York Univ.* Karl LEHMANN, editor. Vol. I = *Bollingen Series* LX). New York, 1958.

CCCXXX. Heinrich LEWY, *Die semitischen Fremdwörter im Griechischen.* Berlin, 1895.

CCCXXXI. Julius LEWY, "Ḫatta, Ḫattu, Ḫatti, Ḫattuša and 'Old Assyrian' ḫattum." *ArOr,* XVIII, 3 (1950), 366-441.

CCCXXXII. — Origin and Signification of the Biblical Term 'Hebrew'." *HUCA,* XXVIII (1957), 1-13.

CCCXXXIII. — "Studies in the Historic Geography of the Ancient Near East." *Orientalia,* NS XXI (1952), 1-12, 265-292, 393-425.

CCCXXXIV. — "Les textes paléo-assyriens et l'Ancien Testament." *RHR,* CX (1934), 29-65.

CCCXXXV. Mark LIDZBARSKI, *Ephemeris für semitische Epigraphik.* Three volumes. Giessen, 1900-1919.

CCCXXXVI. — *Handbuch der nordsemitischen Epigraphik.* Weimar, 1898.

CCCXXXVII. Joh. LINDBLOM, "Zur Frage des Kanaanäischen Ursprungs des altisraelitischen Prophetismus." *Ap.* DXXXV, 58-104.

CCCXXXVIII. Mario LIVERANI, *Storia di Ugarit nell'etá degli archivi politichi (= Universitá di Roma, Centro di Studi Semitichi. Studi Semitichi,* 6). Rome, 1962.

CCCXXXIX. Seton LLOYD, *Early Anatolia.* Harmondsworth, 1956.

CCCXL. Adolphe LODS, *Histoire de la littérature hébraique et juive depuis les origines jusqu'à la ruine de l'Etat juif (135 après J.-C.).* Préface d'André PARROT. Paris, 1950.

CCCXLI. — *Israël, des origines au milieu du VIIIe siècle.* Paris, 1932.

CCCXLII. — "Une tablette inédite de Mari, intéressante pour l'histoire ancienne du prophétisme sémitique." *Ap. Studies in OT Prophecy, presented to Th. H. Robinson ... Edited by* H. H. ROWLEY, New York, 1950, 103-110.

CCCXLIII. A. F. LOSEV, *Antičnaja mifologija v eë istoričeskom razvitii.* Moscow, 1957.

CCCXLIV. Friedrich LÜBKERS *Reallexikon des klassischen Altertums.* Russian translation of the sixth German edition. St. Petersburg-Moscow, 1888.

CCCXLV. Daniel David LUCKENBILL, *Ancient Records of Assyria and Babylonia.* Two volumes. Chicago, 1926-1927.

CCCXLVI. Salomo LURIA (S. Ja. LUR'E), "Die ägyptische Bibel (Joseph- und Mosesagen)." *ZAW,* NF III (1926), 94-135.

CCCXLVII. — *Gerodot.* Moscow-Leningrad, 1947.

CCCXLVIII. — *Jazyk i kul'tura mikenskoj Grecii.* Moscow-Leningrad, 1957.

CCCXLIX. — *Mikenskie nadpisi i Drevnij Vostok. Doklad, pročitannyj v 1958 g. na obščesojuznoj konferencii vostokovedov.* Lvov, 1958 (typewritten).

CCCL. Ernst MAAS, *Griechen und Semiten auf dem Isthmus von Korinth. Religionsgeschichtliche Untersuchungen.* Berlin, 1903.

CCCLI. B. MAISLER, "Canaan and the Canaanites." *BASOR* No. 102 (Apr., 1946), 7-12.

CCCLII. M. I. MAKSIMOVA (translator and editor), KSENOFONT, *Anabasis.* Moscow-Leningrad, 1951.

CCCLIII. Ralph MARCUS and I. J. GELB, "The Phoenician Stele Inscription from Cilicia." *JNES,* VIII (1949), 116-120.

CCCLIV. — "A Preliminary Study of the New Phoenician Inscription from Cilicia." *JNES,* VII (1948), 194-198.

CCCLV. Spyridon MARINATOS, "Grammaton didaskalia." Ap. CCCLXVIII, 226-231.

CCCLVI. Gaston MASPERO, *History of Egypt, Chaldea, Syria, Babylonia, and Assyria.* Edited by A. H. SAYCE. Transl. by M. L. McCLURE. Nine volumes. London, 1903 and following years.

CCCLVII. B. MAZAR, "Gᵉšûr u-Maʿakā." *Zion,* XXIII-XXIV (5718-19), fasc. 3-4, 115-123.

CCCLVIII. Bruno MEISSNER, *Babylonien und Assyrien.* Two volumes. Heidelberg, 1920 and 1925.

CCCLIX. *Mélanges syriens, offerts à M. René Dussaud ... par ses amis et ses élèves.* Two volumes. Paris, 1939.

CCCLX. Samuel A. B. MERCER, *The Tell el-Amarna Tablets. With the Assistance of* Frank Hudson HALLOCK. Two volumes. Toronto, 1939.

CCCLXI. Eduard MEYER, *Forschungen zur alten Geschichte.* Band I. *Zur ältesten griechischen Geschichte.* Halle a. S., 1892.

CCCLXII. — *Geschichte des Altertums. Zweite Auflage.* I. Band, 2. Hälfte. Stuttgart-Berlin, 1909.

CCCLXIII. — *Geschichte des Altertums.* Third-seventh edition. Five volumes, eight books. Reprint. Basel and Darmstadt, 1953-58.

CCCLXIV. — *Die Israeliten und ihre Nachbarstämme. Alttestamentliche Untersuchungen. Mit Beitragen von* Bernhard LUTHER. Halle a. S., 1906.

CCCLXV. — *Ursprung und Anfänge des Christentums.* Band II. *Die Entwicklung des Judentums und Jesus von Nazaret.* Stuttgart-Berlin, 1921.

CCCLXVI. Ernst MICHEL, "Die Assur-Texte Salmanassars III (858-824)." *WO,* Fasc. 1 (May-June, 1947), 5-20; Fasc. 2 (Dec., 1947), 57-71; Fasc. 3 (Aug., 1948), 205-220.

CCCLXVII. J. T. MILIK and Frank M. CROSS, Jr., "Inscribed Javelin-Heads from the Period of the Judges: a Recent Discovery in Palestine." *BASOR* No. 134 (Apr., 1954), 5-15.

CCCLXVIII. *Minoica. Festschrift zum* 80. *Geburtstag von Johannes Sundwall. Hrsg. von* Ernst GRUMACH. Berlin, 1958.

CCCLXIX. Pierre MONTET, "Avaris, Pi-Ramsès, Tanis." *Syria,* XVII (1936), 200-202.

CCCLXX. — *Le drame d'Avaris.* Paris, 1941.

CCCLXXI. — "Écrit à Tanis au printemps de 1956." *RAr,* 1958, tome I, 1-20.

CCCLXXII. Anton MOORTGAT, *Geschichte Vorderasiens bis zum Hellenismus.* Ap. CDLIV, 193-535.

CCCLXXIII. Sabatino MOSCATI, "Sulla storia del nome Canaan." *Studia Biblica et Orientalia,* III (= *Analecta Biblica,* 12), Rome, 1959, 266-269.

CCCLXXIV. F. C. MOVERS, *Die Phönizier.* Vol. I, Bonn, 1841; vol. II, 1, Berlin, 1849; vol. II, 2, Berlin, 1850.

CCCLXXV. W. Max MÜLLER, *Egyptian* (*The Mythology of All Races,* in 13 volumes, vol. XII, first part). Boston, 1918.

CCCLXXVI. W. MUSS-ARNOLT, *Assyrisch-Englisch-Deutsches Handwörterbuch.* Two volumes. Berlin, 1905.

CCCLXXVII. David W. MYHRMAN, *Babylonian Hymns and Prayers.* Philadelphia, 1911.

CCCLXXVIII. John Linton MYRES, *Who Were the Greeks?* Berkeley, Cal., 1930.

CCCLXXIX. Paul NASTER, *L'Asie Mineure et l'Assyrie aux VIIIe et VIIe siècles d'après les Annales des Rois Assyriens.* (= *Bibl. du Muséon,* 8). Louvain, 1938.

CCCLXXX. Martin P. NILSSON, *Geschichte der griechischen Religion* (= *HBAW,* V: II: 1-2). Munich, vol. I, second edition, 1955; vol. II, 1950.

CCCLXXXI. — *The Minoan-Mycenaean Religion and its Survival in Greek Religion.* Second, revised edition. Lund, 1950.

CCCLXXXII. — *The Mycenaean Origin of Greek Mythology.* Berkeley, Cal., 1932.

CCCLXXXIII. Theodor NÖLDEKE, Review of W. ROBERTSON SMITH, *Kinship and Marriage in Early Arabia. ZDMG,* XL (1886), 148-187.

CCCLXXXIV. F. NORK, *Etymologisch-symbolisch-mythologisches Real-Wörterbuch zur Handgebrauche für Bibelforscher, Archäologen und Bildende Künstler.* Four volumes. Stuttgart, 1845.

CCCLXXXV. Martin NOTH, *Die israelitischen Personennamen im Rahmen der gemeinsemitischen Namenbildung.* Stuttgart, 1928.

CCCLXXXVI. — *Das System der zwölf Stämme Israels*. Stuttgart, 1930.
CCCLXXXVII. Jean NOUGAYROL, "Documents du Habur." *Syria*, XXXVII (1960), 205-214.
CCCLXXXVIIa. — "Nouveaux textes accadiens de Ras Shamra." *CRAI*, 1960, 163-171.
CCCLXXXVIII. — "Nouveaux textes accadiens du palais d'Ugarit (campagne 1954)." *CRAI*, 1955, 141-146.
CCCLXXXIX. — "Les nouveaux textes babyloniens de Ras-Shamra (campagne 1955)." *CRAI*, 1956, 126-135.
CCCLXXXIXa. — "Nouveaux textes d'Ugarit en cunéiformes babyloniens." *CRAI*, 1957, 77-86.
CCCXC. — *Le palais royal d'Ugarit, III. Textes accadiens et hourrites des archives est, ouest et centrales, avec les études de* G. BOYER *et* E. LAROCHE. With a supplementary volume of plates. Paris, 1955.
CCCXCI. — *Le palais royal d'Ugarit, IV. Textes accadiens des archives sud* (*Archives internationales*). With a supplementary volume of plates. Paris, 1956.
CCCXCII. — "Les rapports des haruspicines étrusque et assyro-babylonienne, et le foie d'argile de Falerii Veteres (Villa Giulia 3786." *CRAI*, 1955, 509-518.
CCCXCIII. Roger T. O'CALLAGHAN, *Aram Naharaim. A Contribution to the History of Upper Mesopotamia in the Second Millennium B.C. With an Appendix on Indo-Aryan Names by* P.-E. DUMONT (= *AnOr*, 26). Rome, 1948.
CCCXCIV. W. O. E. OESTERLEY, "Early Hebrew Festival Rituals." *Ap*. CCLXI, 111-146.
CCCXCV. H. OLDENBERG, *La religion du Véda. Traduit de l'allemand par* Victor HENRY, *avec préface du traducteur*. Paris, 1903.
CCCXCVI. A. T. OLMSTEAD, *History of Assyria*. New York and London, 1923.
CCCXCVII. — "Near-East Problems in the Second Pre-Christian Millennium." *JEA*, VIII (1922), 223-234.
CCCXCVIII. Dietrich OPITZ, "Die vogelfüssige Göttin auf den Löwen." *AfO*, XI (1936-37), 350-353.
CCCXCIX. A. Leo OPPENHEIM, "Babylonian and Assyrian Historical Texts." Ap. XXXII, 265-317.
CD. Heinrich OTTEN, "Ein kanaanäischer Mythus aus Boğazköy." *MIO*, I (1953), 125-150.
CDI. Walter OTTO, *Dionysos*: *Mythos und Kultus* (= *Frankfurter Studien zur Religion und Kultur der Antike*, IV). Frankfurt am Main, 1933.
CDII. Leonard R. PALMER, *Mycenaeans and Minoans. Aegean Prehistory in the Light of the Linear B Tablets*. London, 1961.
CDIII. Wilhelm PAPE, *Wörterbuch der griechischen Eigennamen*. 3. *Aufl., neu bearbeitet von* Gustav Eduard BENSELER. Two volumes. Braunschweig, 1875.
CDIV. André PARROT, *Archéologie mésopotamienne*. II. *Technique et problèmes*. Paris, 1953.
CDV. — *The Arts of Assyria*. Transl. by Stuart GILBERT and James EMMONS. New York, 1961.
CDVI. — "Les fouilles de Mari. Cinquième campagne (automne 1937)." *Syria*, XX (1939), 1-22.

CDVII. — "Mari et l'Ancien Testament". *Ap. La Bible et l'Orient, travaux du 1er congrès d'archéologie et d'orientalisme bibliques* (= *Cahiers de la RHPR*, 34), Paris, 1955, 117-120.

CDVIII. — Review of Ekrem AKURGAL, *Späthethitische Bildkunst. Syria*, XXVII (1950), 350-351.

CDIX. — and Jean NOUGAYROL, "Un document de fondation hurrite." *RA*, XLII (1948), 1-20.

CDX. Lewis Bayles PATON, "Sanchuniathon." *Ap.* HASTINGS, *Encycl. of Religion and Ethics*, XI, 177-181.

CDXI. *Paulys Realencyclopädie der classischen Altertumswissenschaft. Neue Bearbeitung* . . . hrsg. von Georg WISSOWA (continued by KROLL *et al.*). Thirty-three double volumes, nine double volumes of second series, eight volumes of supplements. Stuttgart, since 1894.

CDXII. T. E. PEET, "The Egyptian Writing-Board B. M. 5647, Bearing Keftiu Names." *Ap. Essays in Aegean Archaeology, Presented to Sir Arthur Evans . . . edited by* S. CASSON. Oxford, 1927, 90-99.

CDXIII. J. D. S. PENDLEBURY, *The Archaeology of Crete, an Introduction*. London, 1939.

CDXIV. Emilio PERUZZI, "L'iscrizione HT 13." *Minos*, V (1957), 35-40.

CDXIVa. — "Note minoiche." *Minos*, VI, 1 (1958), 9-15.

CDXV. Charles PICARD, *Éphèse et Claros. Recherches sur les sanctuaires et les cultes de l'Ionie du Nord*. Paris, 1922.

CDXVI. Stuart PIGGOTT (editor), *The Dawn of Civilisation. The First World Survey of Human Cultures in Early Times*. London, 1961.

CDXVII. Vladislav POPOVITCH, "Observations sur l'origine de la spirale en Égée." *RAr*, 1958, I, 129-136.

CDXVIII. A. PREOBRAŽENSKIJ, *Ètimologičeskij slovar' russkago jazyka*. Vol. I, Moscow, 1910-14; vol. II (n.d.); final fasc., Moscow-Leningrad, 1949 (offset reprint, New York, 1951).

CDXIX. Ira Maurice PRICE, *The Great Cylinder Inscriptions A and B of Gudea*. Leipzig, part I, 1899; part II, 1927.

CDXX. James B. PRITCHARD, *The Ancient Near East in Pictures, Relating to the Old Testament*. Princeton, 1954.

CDXXI. — *Gibeon, Where the Sun Stood Still. The Discovery of the Biblical City*. Princeton, 1962.

CDXXII. Isaac RABINOWITZ, "Another Aramaic Record of the North-Arabian Goddess Han-ʾIlat." *JNES*, XVIII (1959), 154-155.

CDXXIII. — "Aramaic Inscriptions of the Fifth Century B.C.E. From a North-Arab Shrine in Egypt." *JNES*, XV (1956), 1-9.

CDXXIV. Hermann RANKE, *Die ägyptischen Personennamen*. Vol. I, Glückstadt, 1935; vol. II, n.d., Glückstadt-Locust Valley, N.Y.

CDXXV. A. B. RANOVIČ, "Iz literatury o tekstax Ras-Šamry." *VDI*, 1938, No. 2, 150-158.

CDXXVI. *Reallexikon der Assyriologie*. Erich EBELING and Bruno MEISSNER, editors. Volumes I and II, Berlin and Leipzig, 1932 and 1938; vol. III (prepared by Ernst WEIDNER), 1957.

CDXXVII. Alexander ROBERTS and James DONALDSON (editors). *The Ante-Nicene Fathers. Translations of the Writings of the Fathers Down to A.D. 325*. Ten volumes. Offset reprint, Grand Rapids, Mich., 1951.

CDXXVIII. William ROBERTSON SMITH, *The Religion of the Semites. The Fundamental Institutions.* (Offset reprint of second edition, 1894). New York, 1959.

CDXXIX. Günther ROEDER, *Altägyptische Erzählungen und Märchen. Ausgewählt und übersetzt.* Jena, 1927.

CDXXX. Anne ROES, "The Origin of the Chimaera." *Ap. Studies Presented to David M. Robinson,* vol. II. St. Louis, Mo., 1953, 1155-1163.

CDXXXI. — "The Representation of the Chimaera." *JHS,* LIV (1934), 21-25.

CDXXXII. Erwin ROHDE, *Psyche. The Cult of Souls and Belief in Immortality among the Greeks.* Transl. from the 8th edition by W. H. HILLIS. New York-London, 1925.

CDXXXIII. Wilhelm H. ROSCHER (editor), *Ausführliches Lexikon der griechischen und römischen Mythologie.* Five volumes. Leipzig, 1884-1890.

CDXXXIV. Franz ROSENTHAL, "Canaanite and Aramaic Inscriptions." *Ap.* XXXII, 499-505.

CDXXXV. M. B. ROWTON, "Comparative Chronology at the Time of Dynasty XIX." *JNES,* XIX (1960), 15-22.

CDXXXVI. — "Manetho's Date for Ramesses II (with an Appendix by Professor H. KEES)." *JEA,* XXXIV (1948), 57-74.

CDXXXVII. Abraham SACHS, "Akkadian Rituals." Ap. XXXII, 331-345.

CDXXXVIII. Fuad SAFAR, "A Further Text of Shalmaneser III from Assur." *Sumer,* VII (1951), 3-21.

CDXXXIX. N. K. SANDARS, "The First Aegean Swords and their Ancestry." *AJA,* LXV (1961), 17-29, pl. 15-20.

CDXL. Fritz SCHACHERMEYR, "Welche historische Ereignisse führten zu der Entstehung der Mykenischen Kultur?" *ArOr,* XVII (1949), II, 331-350.

CDXLI. — "Zur Frage der Lokalisierung von Achiawa." *Ap.* CCCLXVIII, 365-380.

CDXLII. Claude F.-A. SCHAEFFER, "La XVIIIe campagne de fouilles à Ras Shamra-Ugarit." *CRAI,* 1955, 249-263.

CDXLIII. — *Enkomi-Alasia. Nouvelles missions en Chypre* 1946-1950. *Avec une note préliminaire de* René DUSSAUD *et des contributions de* H. J. PLENDERLEITH et O. MASSON. Paris, 1952.

CDXLIV. — "Les fouilles de Ras Shamra-Ugarit. Neuvième campagne (printemps 1937). Rapport sommaire." *Syria,* XIX (1938), 193-255.

CDXLV. — "Les fouilles de Ras-Shamra-Ugarit. Dixième et onzième campagnes (automne et hiver 1938-39). Rapport sommaire." *Syria,* XX (1939), 277-292.

CDXLVI. — *Missions en Chypre 1932-1935.* Paris, 1936.

CDXLVII. — "Note sur la chronologie de la période de transition du bronze moyen au bronze récent (1700-1500 av. notre ère)." *Syria,* XXV (1946-48), 185-198.

CDXLVIII. — "Reprise de recherches archéologiques à Ras Shamra-Ugarit. Sondages de 1948 et 1949 et campagne de 1950." *Syria,* XXVIII (1951), 1-21.

CDXLIX. — "Reprise des fouilles à Atchana-Alalakh en 1946." *Syria,* XXV (1946-48), 323-329.

CDL. — *Stratigraphie comparée et chronologie de l'Asie Occidentale (III et II millénaires). Syrie, Palestine, Asie Mineure, Chypre, Perse et Caucase.* London, 1948.

CDLI. — *Ugaritica. Études relatives aux découvertes de Ras Shamra.* Première série. Paris, 1939.

CDLII. — *Ugaritica II. Nouvelles études relatives aux découvertes de Ras Shamra.* Paris, 1949.

CDLIII. — *Ugaritica III. Sceaux et cylindres hittites, épée gravée du cartouche de Mineptah, tablettes chypro-minoénnes et autres découvertes nouvelles de Ras Shamra. Avec des contributions de* Chr. DESCROCHES-NOBLECOURT, H. G. GÜTERBOCK, P. KRIEGER, E. LAROCHE, O. MASSON, J. VENDIER. Paris, 1956.

CDLIV. Alexander SCHARFF und Anton MOORTGAT, *Ägypten und Vorderasien im Altertum.* Containing: Alexander SCHARFF, *Geschichte Ägyptens von der Vorzeit bis zur Gründung Alexandrias*; Anton MOORTGAT, see CCCLXXII. Munich, 1950 (second print, 1959).

CDLV. V. SCHEIL, *Textes élamites-sémitiques* (= *Délégation en Perse, tome II*). Paris, 1900.

CDLVI. Sina SCHIFFER JUN., *Die Aramäer. Historisch-geographische Untersuchungen.* Leipzig, 1911.

CDLVII. Hermann SCHNEIDER, *Kultur und Denken der Babylonier und Juden.* Leipzig, 1910.

CDLVIII. Otto SCHRÖDER, *Keilinschrifttexte aus Assur verschiedenen Inhalts.* Leipzig, 1920.

CDLIX. Paul SCHRÖDER, *Die phönizische Sprache.* Halle, 1869.

CDLX. Martin SCHULTZE, *Handbuch der ebräischen Mythologie. Sage und Glaube der alten Ebräer in ihrem Zusammenhang mit den religiösen Anschauungen anderer Semiten, sowie der Indogermanen und Aegypter.* Nordhausen, 1876.

CDLXI. Henry SEYRIG, "Antiquités syriennes." *Syria,* XV (1934), 155-186.

CDLXII. — "Antiquités syriennes." *Syria,* XXXII (1955), 29-48.

CDLXIII. J. SIMONS, *Handbook for the Study of Egyptian Topographical Lists Relating to Western Asia.* Leiden, 1937.

CDLXIV. W. K. SIMPSON, "New Light on the God Reshef." *JAOS,* LXXIII (1953), 86-89.

CDLXV. Sidney SMITH, "Ḳizzuwadna." *JEA,* X (1924), 104-115.

CDLXVI. — "Ḳizzuwadna and Ḳode." *JEA,* VIII (1922), 45-47.

CDLXVII. — "Sennacherib and Esarhaddon." *Ap.* LXXXVI, III, 61-88.

CDLXVIII. — *The Statue of Idri-mi. With an Introduction by Sir* Leonard WOOLLEY (= *Occasional Public. of the British Inst. of Arch. in Ankara,* No. 1). London, 1949.

CDLXIX. Ferdinand SOMMER, *Die Aḫḫijavā-Urkunden* (= *Abhandl. d. Bayer. Akad. d. Wiss., Phil.-Hist. Abt.,* NF 6). Munich, 1932.

CDLXX. E. A. SPEISER, "Akkadian Documents from Ras Shamra." *JAOS,* LXXV (1955), 154-165.

CDLXXI. — "Akkadian Myths and Epics." *Ap.* XXXII, 60-119, 514-516.

CDLXXII. — " 'Hurrians and Subarians'." *JAOS,* LXVIII (1948), 1-13.

CDLXXIII. — *Introduction to Hurrian* (= *AASOR,* XX, 1940-41). New Haven, 1941.

CDLXXIV. — "The Name *Phoinikes*." *Language*, XII (1936), 121-126.

CDLXXV. Shalom SPIEGEL, "Noah, Danel, and Job, Touching on Canaanite Relics in the Legends of the Jews." *Ap. Louis Ginzberg Jubilee Volume*, New York, 1945, 305-355.

CDLXXVI. Agnès SPYCKET, "La déesse Lama." *RA*, LIV (1960), 73-81.

CDLXXVII. W. E. STAPLES, "Cultic Motives in Hebrew Thought." *AJSL*, LV (1938), 44-55.

CDLXXVIII. Jean STARCKY, "Autour d'une dédicace palmyrénienne à Šadrafa et à Du ʿAnat." *Syria*, XXVI (1949), 43-85.

CDLXXVIIIa. Chester G. STARR, *The Origins of Greek Civilization*, 1100-650 *B.C.*" New York, 1961.

CDLXXIX. Georg STEINDORFF, *Die Blütezeit des Pharaonenreiches*. Second edition (= *Monographien zur Weltgeschichte*, 10). Bielefeld and Leipzig, 1926.

CDLXXX. Henricus STEPHANUS, *Thesaurus Graecae Linguae, ab Henrico Stephano constructus . . . tertio ediderunt* Carolus Benedictus HASE *et al.* Paris, 1831-1865. 9 vol. (reprint, Graz, 1954).

CDLXXXI. Ferris J. STEPHENS, "Sumero-Akkadian Hymns and Prayers." *Ap.* XXXII, 383-392.

CDLXXXIa. Hanns STOCK, *Studien zur Geschichte und Archäologie der 13. bis 17. Dynastie Ägyptens, unter besonderer Berücksichtigung der Skarabäer dieser Zwischenzeit*. Glückstadt and New York, 1951.

CDLXXXII. V. V. STRUVE, Preface to Russian transl. of CDXIII, Moscow, 1950, 5-20.

CDLXXXIII. Frank H. STUBBINGS, "The Aegean Bronze Age." Ap. *CAH*², fasc. 4, Cambridge, 1962.

CDLXXXIV. *Studia Mariana, publiées sous la direction de* André PARROT (= *DMOA*, IV). Leiden, 1950.

CDLXXXV. Knut TALLQVIST, *Sumer. kur.gi = fi. kurki "Kranich"?* (= *StOr*, XIII, 10). Helsinki, 1947.

CDLXXXVI. Hermann THIERSCH, *Ependytes und Ephod*. Stuttgart-Berlin, 1936.

CDLXXXVII. François THUREAU-DANGIN, "Bir-ia-wa-za. "*RA*, XXXVII (1940), 171.

CDLXXXVIII. — "Un comptoire de laine pourpre à Ugarit, d'après une tablette de Ras Shamra." *Syria*, XV (1934), 137-146.

CDLXXXIX. — *Rituels accadiens*. Paris, 1921.

CDXC. — "Une tablette bilingue de Ras Shamra." *RA*, XXXVII (1940), 97-118.

CDXCI. — "Trois contrats de Ras-Shamra." *Syria*, XVIII (1937), 245-255.

CDXCII. A. I. TJUMENEV, "K voprosu ob ètnogeneze grečeskogo naroda." *VDI*, 1953, No. 4, 19-46.

CDXCIII. Harry TORCZYNER, "A Hebrew Incantation Against Night-Demons from Biblical Times." *JNES*, VI (1947), 18-29.

CDXCIV. Matitiahu TSEVAT, "The Canaanite God Šälaḥ." *VT*, IV (1954), 41-49.

CDXCV. — "The Ugaritic Goddess Nikkal-wīb." *JNES*, XII (1953), 61-62.

CDXCVI. B. A. TURAEV, *Istorija drevnego Vostoka. Pod redakciej* V. V. STRUVE *i* I. L. SNEGIREVA. Third reprint. Two volumes. Leningrad, 1936 and 1937.

CDXCVII. Arthur UNGNAD, *Hebräische Grammatik*. Tübingen, 1912.

CDXCVIII. — *Die Religion der Babylonier und Assyrier. Übergetragen und eingeleitet von* . . . (= *Religiöse Stimmen der Völker*, III). Jena, 1921.

CDXCIX. Roy Yasunori UYECHI, *A Study in Ugaritic Alphabetic Names. A Dissertation Presented to the Faculty of the Graduate School, Brandeis University, Mediterranean Studies* . . . Waltham, Mass., 1961 (typewritten).

D. E. Douglas VAN BUREN, "Entwined Serpents." *AfO*, X (1935-36), 53-65, pl. 1-12.

DI. — "The God Ningizzida." *Iraq*, I (1934), 60-89, pl. IX-XI.

DII. — "The Scorpion in Mesopotamian Art and Religion." *AfO*, XII (1937-39), 1-28.

DIII. — *Symbols of the Gods in Mesopotamian Art* (= *AnOr*, 23). Rome, 1945.

DIV. P. VAN DER MEER, *The Chronology of Ancient Western Asia and Egypt*. Second, revised edition (= *DMOA*, II). Leiden, 1955.

DV. Michael VENTRIS and John CHADWICK, *Documents in Mycenaean Greek. Three Hundred Selected Tablets from Knossos, Pylos and Mycenae. With Commentary and Vocabulary. With a Foreword by* Alan J. B. WACE. Cambridge, 1956.

DVI. Jean VERCOUTTER, *L'Égypte et le monde égéen pré-hellénique. Étude critique des sources égyptiennes* (*Du début de la XVIII à la fin de la XIX*[e] *Dynastie*) (= *Inst. Franç. d'arch. orient. Bibl. d'étude*, XXII). Cairo, 1956.

DVII. Emily Townsend VERMEULE, "The Fall of the Mycenaean Empire." *Archaeology*, XIII (1960), No. 1, 66-75.

DVIII. I. N. VINNIKOV, "Novye finikijskie nadpisi iz Kilikii." *VDI*, 1950, No. 3, 86-97.

DIX. R. Ju. VIPPER, *Istorija Grecii v klassičeskuju èpoxu, IX-IV vv. do R.X.* Moscow, 1916.

DX. Charles VIROLLEAUD, "ʿAnat et la génisse. Poème de Ras Shamra (IV AB)." *Syria*, XVII (1936), 150-173.

DXI. — "A propos du nom de *Nqmd* > *Nqm-(H)d*." *Syria*, XXI (1940), 110-112.

DXII. — *L'astrologie chaldéenne. Le livre intitulé "Enuma (anu) ilu Bel", publié, transcrit et traduit par* . . . Fourteen fascicles. Paris, 1905-1912.

DXIII. — "Les chasses de Baal. Poème de Ras-Shamra." *Syria*, XVI (1935), 247-266.

DXIV. — *La déesse ʿAnat. Poème de Ras Shamra, publié, traduit et commenté par* . . . Paris, 1938.

DXV. — "Fragment nouveau du poème de Môt et Aleyn-Baal (I AB)." *Syria*, XV (1934), 226-243.

DXVI. — "Les inscriptions cunéiformes de Ras Shamra." *Syria*, X (1929), 304-310, pl. LXI-LXXX.

DXVII. — *La légende de Keret, roi des Sidoniens, publiée d'après une tablette de Ras-Shamra*. Paris, 1936.

DXVIII. — *La légende phénicienne de Danel. Texte cunéiforme alphabétique avec transcription et commentaire, précédé d'une introduction à l'étude de la civilisation d'Ugarit*. Paris, 1936.

DXVIIIa. — "Lettres et documents administratifs provenant des archives d'Ugarit." *Syria*, XXI (1940), 247-276.

DXIX. — "La mort de Baal. Poème de Ras Shamra (I* AB)." *Syria*, XV (1934), 305-336.

DXX. — "Un nouvel épisode du mythe ugaritique de Baal." *CRAI*, 1960 (appeared Dec., 1961), 180-186.

DXXI. — "Les nouvelles tablettes alphabétiques de Ras-Shamra (XIX campagne, 1955)." *CRAI*, 1956, 60-67.

DXXII. — "Les nouvelles tablettes de Ras-Shamra (1948-1949)." *Syria*, XXVIII (1951), 22-47.

DXXIII. — "Nouveaux textes administratifs de Ras-Shamra." *RA*, XXXVII (1940), 130-153.

DXXIV. — *Le palais royal d'Ugarit, II. Textes en cunéiformes alphabétiques des archives est, ouest et centrales.* Paris, 1957.

DXXV. — "Le roi Kerét et son fils (II K). Poème de Ras-Shamra." *Syria*, XXII (1941), 107-136, 197-217; XXIII (1942-43), 1-20.

DXXVI. — "Six textes des Ras Shamra, provenant de la XIVe campagne (1950)." *Syria*, XXVIII (1951), 163-169.

DXXVII. — "Les tablettes cunéiformes de Mishrifé-Kaṭna." *Syria*, IX (1928), 90-96.

DXXVIII. — "Textes administratifs de Ras-Shamra en cunéiforme alphabétique." *RA*, XXXVII (1940), 11-44.

DXXIX. — "Les villes et les corporations du royaume d'Ugarit." *Syria*, XXI (1940), 123-151.

DXXX. Daniel Völter, *Die Patriarchen Israels im Licht der ägyptischen Mythologie. Zweite, völlig neu bearbeitete Auflage.* Leipzig, 1921.

DXXXI. Wolfram von Soden, *Grundriss der akkadischen Grammatik* (= *AnOr*, 33). Rome, 1952.

DXXXII. — "Kleine Beiträge zur Verständniss der Gesetze Hammurabis und Bilalamas." *ArOr*, XVII (1949), II, 359-373.

DXXXIII. — "Verkündung des Gotteswillens durch prophetisches Wort in den altbabylonischen Briefen aus Mâri." *WO*, I (1950), 397-403.

DXXXIV. — "Zu einigen altbabylonischen Dichtungen." *Orientalia*, NS XXVI (1957), 306-320.

DXXXV. *Von Ugarit nach Qumran. Beiträge zur alttestamentlichen und altorientalischen Forschung, Otto Eissfeldt . . . dargebracht . . . hrsg . . . von* Johannes Hempel und Leonard Rost (= *Beihefte zur ZAW*, 77). Berlin, 1958.

DXXXVa. G. A. Wainwright, "Early Tin in the Aegean." *Antiquity*, XVIII (1944), 57-64.

DXXXVI. Otto Weber, *Die Literatur der Babylonier und Assyrier.* Leipzig, 1907.

DXXXVII. T. B. L. Webster, *From Mycenae to Homer.* London, 1958.

DXXXVIII. — "Homer and the Mycenaean Tablets." *Antiquity*, XXIX (1955), 10-14.

DXXXIX. Ernst F. Weidner, "Die Feldzüge Šamši-Adads V. gegen Babylonien." *AfO*, IX (1934), 89-104.

DLX. — "Hof- und Harem-Erlasse assyrischen Könige aus dem 2. Jahrtausend v. Chr." *AfO*, XVII (1954-56), 257-293.

DXLI. — "The Inscription from Kythera." *JHS*, LIX (1939), 137-138.

DXLII. — "Neue Endeckungen in Ugarit." *AfO*, XVIII (1957-58), 167-170.

DXLIII. Raymond WEILL, *La fin du Moyen Empire égyptien. Étude sur les monuments et l'histoire de la période comprise entre la XIIe et la XVIIIe dynastie*. Two volumes. Paris, 1918.

DXLIV. — "L'installation des Israélites en Palestine et la légende patriarcale." *RHR*, LXXXVII (1923), 69-120; LXXXVIII (1923), 1-44.

DXLV. Julius WELLHAUSEN, *Prolegomena to the History of Ancient Israel . . . Preface by* W. ROBERTSON SMITH. Offset reprint, New York, 1958.

DXLVI. — *Reste arabischen Heidentums, gesammelt und erläutert von* . . . Second edition, Berlin, 1897.

DXLVII. Geo WIDENGREN, "Early Hebrew Myths and their Interpretation." *Ap.* CCLXII, 149-203.

DXLVIII. Ulrich von WILAMOWITZ-MOELLENDORFF, *Der Glaube der Hellenen*. Two volumes. Basel, 1956.

DXLIX. John A. WILSON, "Egyptian Texts." *Ap.* XXXII, *passim*.

DL. Hugo WINCKLER, *Altorientalische Forschungen*. Three volumes. Leipzig, I, 1897; II, 1901; III, 1902-1905.

DLI. — *Geschichte Israels in Einzeldarstellungen*. Leipzig, I, 1895; II, 1900.

DLII. D. J. WISEMAN, *The Alalakh Tablets* (= *Occasional Public. of the British Inst. of Arch. in Ankara*, No. 2). London, 1953.

DLIII. — *Chronicles of Chaldaean Kings* (626-556 *B.C.*) *in the British Museum*. London, 1956.

DLIV. Maurus WITZEL, "Die Überlistung des Zû (und die Totenklage der Frau Zû)." *Orientalia*, NS II (1933), 26-44.

DLV. Leonard WOOLLEY, *A Forgotten Kingdom. Being a Record of the Results Obtained from the Excavation of Two Mounds Atchana and al Mina, in the Turkish Hatay*. Baltimore, 1953.

DLVI. S. YEIVIN, "Ya'qob'el." *JEA*, XLV (1959), 16-18.

DLVII. Thaddaeus ZIELIŃSKI, *Tragodumenon libri tres*. Cracow, 1925.

DLVIII. H. ZIMMERN und H. WINCKLER, *Die Keilinschriften und das Alte Testament von* Eberhard SCHRADER. *Dritte Auflage . . . neu bearbeitet von* . . . Containing: Hugo WINCKLER, *Geschichte und Geographie*, 1-342; Heinrich ZIMMERN, *Religion und Sprache*, 343-654. Berlin, 1903.

ADDITIONS AND CORRECTIONS

P. 27. Instead of [*Kikk*]*ipra*, GOETZE, CXCIX, 19, nn. 19 and 22, now reads *El-li-ib-ra*, on the basis of KBo IX 123, and identifies it with the Cilician *El-li-bir* (Sargon II) or *Il-lu-ub-ri* (Sennacherib), which FORRER, CLXVII, 79, located at the Byzantine Lampron, mod. Nemrun, north of Mersin.

P. 40. S. SMITH transliterated *Ḫu-laḫ-ḫa-an*, but the second sign, according to the authography, is the sign No. 321: *luḫ*/*làḫ*/*liḫ*, with the basic value *luḫ* in the second millennium. The mineral *ḫuluḫḫu* is defined as *an-zaḫ*-UD "light-colored heated (fused) lead" (LXXXV, VI, 232). *Ḫuluḫḫu* is the Akkadianized form of Sumerian *ḫu-luḫ-ḫa*. In Semitic (Akk. or W-S), "fused lead" would be *anâk*(*u*) *ṣarpu*. This immediately recalls Anazarbus —the Cilician city of classical period, the location of which closely corresponds to that of *Ḫuluḫḫân* according to our reconstruction of Idri-mi's itinerary (cf. p. 40, n. 2). Taking into account the exceptionally advantageous strategic location of Anazarbus, one is allowed to presume that its site was already inhabited in the Bronze Age, and its topographic and toponymic identity with *Ḫuluḫḫân* becomes very plausible. For the toponymic ending *-ân*, cf. *Amakwân* (Alal. texts), *Appân*, *Ḫimarân*, *Mišlân*, *Qattunân*, *Zaluḫân*, *Zurubbân* (Mari texts).

P. 41. Our location of Ṣaruna is confirmed by the *Res Gesta* of Ḫattušiliš I (see p. 43, n. 5 above), in which it appears as *Ṣaruna* (Hittite version) or *Ṣarunti* (Akkadian version). After having captured this city, the Hittite king defeated the armies of Haššu and Aleppo near Mount Atalur which (according to the Annals of Shalmaneser III) must be identified with the southern part of Mount Amanus (cf. CDXXVI, I, 310; CCCXLV, I, § 600).

P. 57. Another Anatolian toponym of this kind is that of a Cappadocian city (located probably near the Halys, northwest of Caesarea-Kayseri) named *Môkêsos*, *Môkissos*, *Môkysos*, or *Mukissos* in Greek, *Mucissos* in Latin (CDXI, XV, 2, 2514 s.).

P. 146, n. 1. The questions sketched here and p. 147, n. 1, are substantiated in more detail in this author's paper "The Origin of the Terms 'Canaan,' 'Phoenicia,' and 'Purple,'" read at the 174th Annual Meeting of the American Oriental Society, New York City, April 9, 1964 (to be published in *JNES*, 1965).

P. 149. Part of the Mycenaean age royal palace in Theban Cadmeia was excavated from fall 1963 to spring 1964 (chief director N. PLATON). A treasury chamber of 1300 or slightly later yielded a find which those writing about it characterize as "sensational," "spectacular," "unique," "remarkable" etc. It consists of 37 cylinder seals, of which only 3 are Mycenaean, the remainder being Babylonian and Syrian. Most of the Oriental cylinders are made of lapis-lazuli, some have long cuneiform inscriptions. They date from the Ancient Akkadian to the Cassite period; one of the latter seals is inscribed with the name of Kidin-Marduk, son of Ša-ilimma-damqa, a high official of the Babylonian Cassite king Burraburiyaš (Burnaburiaš III, first half of the XIVth century); another seal of the same man was found, many years ago, in Babylonia. Until now, only 11 seals from Western Asia have been found in the entire Aegean area. About ten tablets inscribed in Linear B were found on the same spot. Pending the publication of the discovered materials, the full evaluation and explanation of the find is not yet possible; however, some authors are startled by the coincidence that this unprecendented discovery was made precisely in Thebes, the foundation of which was ascribed to the Phoenician Cadmos, and are seriously considering the possibility that the Greek legend may have contained some historical nucleus. In any case, the Cadmeian hoard proves that Thebes, though not a port, had connections with Syria and Mesopotamia, that its rulers were interested in importing masterpieces of Oriental glyptic art, and that local artists (judging from the presence of uncut or unfinished cylinders) tried to imitate them. Preliminary information was given in the following articles: M. Paraskeuaidês, "Hoi mystêriodeis sphragidokylindroi tôn anaktorôn tês Kadmeias akropoleôs," *Kathêmerinê*, April 19, 1964; same author, "To mystikon tês katagôgês tu Kadmu," *ibid.*, August 6, 1964; Eugene Vanderpool, "News Letter from Greece," *AJA*, LXVIII (1964), p. 293; Mogens Trolle Larsen, "A datable Kassite seal from Thebes," *Nestor*, 1964, pp. 335 s.; Hugo Mühlenstein, "Historischer Kern der Kadmos-Sage bestätigt," *Basler Nachrichten*, July 11/12, 1964; L. R. Palmer and O. R. Gurney, "New Light Thrown on Ancient Crete," *Times*, July 17, 1964; Athêna G. Kalogeropulu, "Hoi sphragidokylindroi kai ta mystika tus," *Eleutheria*, September 13, 1964.

P. 345, n. 3. Several Hurrian texts in Ugaritic alphabetic script, found at Ras Shamra during recent excavation campaigns, are to be published and commented upon by E. Laroche in the forthcoming *Ugaritica V*.

ERRATUM. P. 24, line 24, read *Gal-mi-ia-aš*.

INDEX OF CLASSICAL PASSAGES

Names of authors and titles of works appear in this Index in their Latin forms.

INDEX OF PROPER NAMES

This index includes all proper names (personal, divine, mythical, geographical, ethnic, and those of religious sects) mentioned in the book, except:

1. names of modern authors;
2. names quoted only as linguistic parallels to those discussed;
3. presumable and reconstructed names;
4. Mycenaean names from Linear B tablets that are listed in alphabetic order on pp. 340-344.

If a name is quoted both in syllabic transliteration and in normalized form, only the latter appears in the index. Anglicized and Latinized forms have precedence over original forms. Insignificant spelling variants are disregarded.

Italic figures refer to pages where the etymology of the name is discussed.

's.' after page-number indicates the following page, 'ss.' two following pages.

A. Vocalized Names

The order of the letters, based on the sequence of the English alphabet, is as follows:

a, b, c, d, ḏ, ḍ, e, f, g, ǧ, ğ, ġ, h, ḥ, ḫ, ẖ, i, j, k, l, m, n, o, p, q, r, s, ṣ, ś, š, ṣ̌, t, ṯ, ṭ, u, v, x, y, z, ž, ẓ.

ʾ, ʿ and accents are not taken into account.

B. Unvocalized Names

The order of the letters, based on the sequence of the West Semitic alphabet, is as follows:

ʾ, 3, ỉ, a, i, u, b, g, d, ḏ, h, w, z, ž, ḥ, ḫ, ṭ, y, k, l, m, n, s, ṡ, ʿ, ġ, p, ṣ, ḍ, ẓ, q, r, ś, š, ŝ, t, ṯ